Child development
and personality

SIXTH EDITION
Child Development and Personality

PAUL HENRY MUSSEN
University of California, Berkeley

JOHN JANEWAY CONGER
University of Colorado School of Medicine

JEROME KAGAN
Harvard University

ALETHA CAROL HUSTON
University of Kansas

HARPER & ROW, PUBLISHERS, New York

Cambridge, Philadelphia, San Francisco,
London, Mexico City, São Paulo, Sydney

Sponsoring Editor: Susan Mackey
Project Editor: Holly Detgen
Designer: Gayle Jaeger
Production Assistant: Debi Forrest-Bochner
Photo Researcher: Inge King
Compositor: Ruttle, Shaw & Wetherill, Inc.
Printer and Binder: R. R. Donnelley & Sons Company
Art Studio: J & R Art Services, Inc.
Cover Photo: Bill Longcore

CHILD DEVELOPMENT AND PERSONALITY, Sixth edition

Library of Congress Cataloging in Publication Data
Main entry under title:

Child development and personality.

   Rev. ed. of: Child development and personality /
Paul Henry Mussen. 5th ed. cl979.
   Includes indexes.
   1. Child psychology. 2. Personality. I. Mussen,
Paul Henry. II. Mussen, Paul Henry. Child development
and personality. [DNLM: 1. Child development. WS 105
C5333]
BF721.C5143 1984   155.4   83-22707
ISBN 0-06-044694-3

Harper International Edition
ISBN 0-06-350534-7

Contents in brief

Contents in detail

Preface

One of the most significant, recurrent problems in communicating psychology to students is showing them how scientific knowledge can be applied to real problems and to the practical concerns of parents, teachers, and others who work with children. Another is showing how progress is made in the field—conveying the understanding that theoretical controversy, evidence, and counter-evidence all contribute to cumulative gains in knowledge, and are not just reflections of the trendy concerns of scholars in the fickle spotlight of the moment. In the sixth edition of this book, many of the changes are stimulated by, or addressed to, one of these problems in teaching psychology.

In the five years since the fifth edition was published, scholars in the field of child development have continued to make conceptual advances and generate new data that permit a more refined understanding of the processes of development. Cognitive and social development have become increasingly integrated as the cognitive bases for social and emotional reactions have been recognized. We have moved beyond the platitude that both heredity and environment contribute to development and have invented concepts and implemented empirical studies that shed light on *how* the child's biological qualities interact with experience. The issues of continuity versus discontinuity in growth, and of stability of individual differences over time remain important, but these questions are addressed with more sophisticated concepts. Many psychologists have ventured to investigate complex, but important, constructs, such as self and identity. While the thinking of most developmental psychologists continues to be guided by developmental theory, important ideas are also drawn from other areas of psychology, including adult cognition, psycholinguistics, and social psychology. As a result, the field sometimes seems fragmented, but the richness of new ideas makes the effort at integrating those fragments exciting and fruitful.

In the preface to the fifth edition, we listed many social concerns about the welfare of children, such as: child abuse; increases in adolescent pregnancy; single-parent families; the high rate of divorce in families with children; the effects of television violence; the need for adequate day care; the lack of educational opportunities for many children whose families are poor; racial discrimination; changing sexual mores; drug abuse among young people; and problems faced by physically and mentally handicapped children. Unfortunately, little progress has been made toward dealing with many of these problems in the last five years. In fact, reduced government services for children and the economic recession in the early 1980s led to exacerbation of many of them. High unemployment and reduced services strike disproportionately at poor families, especially those headed by women. As a result, children have a higher probability than adults of living in poverty in America today.

Partly in response to these social changes, child psychologists have become increasingly involved in efforts to influence social policies that affect children and families, and to contribute their expertise to the solution of social problems. They have directed more of their research efforts to studies of applied problems and to evaluation of intervention programs designed to ameliorate such problems.

The sixth edition reflects some of these changes in the field. It contains more discussion of social issues and applied research than earlier editions, but we have attempted to integrate this information with theory and basic research. This edition retains a chronological organization in four age periods: the prenatal period, infancy, childhood, and adolescence. Within age periods, the organization is topical. The three major theories of development—psychoanalytic, learning, and cognitive-developmental—are applied to the topics in each chapter rather than being described in the introductory chapter. This change is designed to help the student understand how each theory is related to empirically based knowledge for different age levels and different topic areas. Separated from the contexts in which they can be applied, brief descriptions of the theories may have little meaning for the student approaching the field for the first time. We have retained in the introductory chapter, however, a discussion of major issues in the study of development, in order to provide a broad framework for the subsequent chapters.

There are two new chapters that reflect recent developments in the field. One of these is "The Transition to Childhood: The Second and Third Years." Recent research on this previously neglected age period has generated a number of exciting insights about the transition from infancy to childhood. Another new chapter is "The Development of Social Cognition," which contains some of the recently garnered knowledge about children's understanding of their social worlds. The previous chapter on "Socialization in the Family" has been divided into two chapters. Topics such as sex typing, self-esteem, moral behavior, prosocial behavior, and aggression are covered in a chapter titled "Identity and Social Development." Child rearing, sibling influences, and family structure are considered in the chapter on "Socialization in the Family." Hence, each chapter title reflects its contents more accurately than in the earlier edition. The principal description of Piaget's theory now appears in the chapter "Cognitive Development in Childhood" rather than in the chapter "Intelligence and Achievement." The "Intelligence and Achievement" chapter, in turn, contains more discussion of motivation and school achievement than it did in earlier editions.

But, the basic orientation of the book has been retained. We have attempted to present a balanced picture of the field with samples of different theoretical views on the topics covered. Inevitably, the selections were guided by our judgments about what is most interesting, creative, exciting, or illuminating among the vast array of information available. As in previous editions we maintain a scholarly and research-oriented focus, but in a style that is intended to communicate the excitement of research and theory to the student without being ponderous. We have continued earlier efforts to place the field in cultural and historical perspective with frequent references to cross-cultural research and occasional discussions of historical information. Finally, we have tried to present controversies in the field in a way that includes different viewpoints, but does not leave the student feeling as though no lasting answers are possible.

Writing a book, or even revising one, requires the help and support of many other people. We thank Carrie Freeseman, Patricia Parker, Jane Rateaver, Dorothy Townsend, and Whitney Walton for typing and retyping large portions of the manuscript and making useful suggestions. Catherine Brown did valuable editing, which helped to make the manuscript clearer and more readable. We have also been fortunate to have had the help of a group of excellent reviewers: Ray H. Bixler, University of Louisville; Joseph J. Campos, University of Denver; Frank Curcio, Boston University; Jill deVillers, Smith College; Ira Gross, University of Rhode Island; John Hagen, University of Michigan; Willard W. Hartup, University of Minnesota; Martin L. Hoffman, University of Michigan; Spencer Kagan, University of California, Riverside; Lorraine A. Low, Framingham State College; Ellen M. Markman, Stanford University; Gerald E. McClearn, Pennsylvania State University; Martin J. Meade, Rockhurst College; Patricia P. Minuchin, Temple University; Nora Newcombe, Temple University; Anne C. Petersen, University of Chicago; Alvin H. Price, Brigham Young University; Marian Radke-Yarrow, National Institute of Mental Health; Freda Rebelsky, Boston University; Thomas R. Sommerkamp, Central Missouri State University; Ross Vasta, SUNY College at Brockport; Marian M. Wilton, Framingham State College. Most important, we are grateful to our families for their support, understanding, and forebearance.

P.H.M.
J.J.C.
J.K.
A.C.H.

Child development and personality

Introduction

*S*ome letters a child psychologist might receive will serve to introduce the subject of development.

Dear Professor Smith:

I am a judge in California, and I handle many divorce cases in which decisions about the custody of young children must be made. What information can you provide that will be useful in deciding what is the best environment for a child when both the mother and father want primary custody? Is there any way to determine which parent the child is more attached to? Is it more important for a young child to be with the mother than the father, or can fathers provide a child with just as much love and care as mothers? How can I evaluate how good a parent someone is?

What are the effects of joint custody, in which the children spend half their time with each parent, often going back and forth between the parents' homes every few days? Is it confusing to children? Are there some ages when it is better than others? Is it better for a child to have a lot of contact with both parents or to have a consistent home life with one parent? I would like your considered judgment about these issues, even though the information available may be incomplete, because the decisions must be made.

Sincerely,

Dear Professor:

I am a pediatrician in a small Midwestern city. Although my medical training prepared me well to diagnose and treat physical illnesses of children, it did not prepare me to deal with questions about the psychological and behavioral development of children. Parents often ask me for advice about how to handle such problems as bed wetting, nail biting, sleeplessness, and fighting. They also ask me for information about what behavior is normal at different ages. Answers to these questions do not come from medicine but from psychology and child development. I would appreciate your suggestions for any good books that I can read or recommend to parents.

Sincerely,

Dear Dr. Jones:

I am a mother of a 5-year-old boy and a 7-year-old girl. I am concerned about raising my children in a way that will avoid sex-stereotyped roles. In my opinion, traditional masculine and feminine roles are harmful to children and lead to many kinds of problems when the child grows up. I have spent the last 10 years of my life trying to overcome my early training to be a passive female, and my husband has worked to overcome the ''macho'' image of masculinity with which he was raised.

How can I raise my children to avoid traditional roles? I try to encourage them both to play with many kinds of toys, such as trucks or dolls, and to be kind and sensitive, while also standing up for themselves when they need to. But these efforts are contradicted by the messages my children get from television, from their grandparents, from their preschool, and from other children. In fact, I was shocked when my daughter at age 3 told me that women could not be doctors.

I am also concerned about whether my children will be maladjusted or suffer social rejection if they do not conform to social expectations about males and females. Will my son be teased by other children if he plays with a doll? Will my daughter be unhappy if she is too independent? Is there any way to avoid the old evils without encountering new ones to take their place?

Sincerely,

NOTE: Parents get advice about their children from physicians more often than from any other professional source.

Dear Dr. Jones:

My child's first-grade teacher says that he is hyperactive and cannot concentrate on learning to read. The teacher wants him sent back to kindergarten, although there is nothing to indicate that his intelligence is below normal. Do you think this would be a good idea? How shall I explain it to my son?

Sincerely,

Dear Dr. Miller:

I am a child welfare official in a large city agency that deals with cases of child abuse. We see a disturbingly high number of children who have been seriously beaten and injured by their parents. In some cases, harder to detect, children have been sexually molested by members of their families. Once we identify a case, we try to work with the family, help them to get counseling, and do whatever we can to change the situation. Sometimes we remove a child from the home, but we do not have enough good foster homes to offer quality substitute care to all children.

What factors should we consider in deciding when the child should be removed from the home or when the family has a good chance to profit from counseling? Is it worse for the child to be separated from the family than to be abused? How should the age of the child affect these decisions? When we must remove children from their homes, what suggestions can you make about ways to provide good foster care?

Sincerely,

Dear Professor,

I am a staff member in the office of a Congressional representative who serves on the committee making recommendations about funding for Head Start, Follow Through, and other educational programs designed to help poor children who have problems in school. The committee recently heard testimony from psychologists suggesting that intelligence is primarily influenced by heredity and that intervention programs cannot do very much to change it. They told us we were probably wasting taxpayers' money by sponsoring massive intervention programs designed to raise children's IQs. Other psychologists have testified that children's intellectual performance is strongly affected by their environment and that early intervention programs like Head Start have long-term benefits.

What does the research evidence say about the importance of heredity and environment as influences on children's IQs? How important are IQ tests as predictors of children's school achievement? Should we be focusing only on IQ, or are there better indexes of children's capacity to learn in school?

Sincerely,

News Item:
In 1974, the movie Born Innocent *was broadcast early in the evening on a major network television channel in San Francisco, immediately following "The Wonderful World of Disney."* Born Innocent *contained a scene in a reformatory for adolescent girls in which a girl was brutally raped with a broom handle by four other girls. Viewer complaints were so numerous that the scene was omitted from later television broadcasts of the film. A few days after this broadcast, two 7-year-old girls were raped in a similar fashion by three girls and a boy ranging in age from 11 to 15. When the children were caught, they said they got the idea from seeing a similar scene on television (Daltry, 1978).*

The mother of one of the 7-year-olds sued the network on the grounds that the film had contributed to the crime committed against her daughter. Psychologists and other experts were called to testify on the question of whether exposure to this kind of film violence could cause young people to engage in violent behavior. Similar testimony was given in a Florida trial in which a teenage boy claimed that he was not responsible for committing a murder because he had been stimulated by violent television. Although psychologists supported the claim that television violence could contribute to aggressive actions, they could not state with certainty that television inspired these particular crimes. Both trials ended without a decision that television had definitely contributed to the particular crimes committed, but the evidence for the effects of television violence is sufficiently strong that many citizens continue to exert pressure for change in commercial programming.

Dear Professor:
My wife and I are about to have our first child. Both of us have careers that we enjoy, and we need two incomes to maintain our standard of living. If we both continue to have full-time jobs, will the baby suffer because someone else takes care of her for 40 hours a week? Will she love us if we are away that much, or will she think the baby sitter is her parent? Are there any benefits for the baby if we continue our jobs, such as the opportunity to be with other children in a day-care situation?

Assuming we do have some outside care, is it better to have a sitter who comes to our house, to take the baby to a day-care center, or to take her to a sitter who has other children in her home? What qualities should we look for in a child-care setting, whether it is a center or a home?

Sincerely,

CHILD DEVELOPMENT AS A CROSSROAD OF BASIC AND APPLIED RESEARCH

Though all of these letters except the news item are fictional, they illustrate important social questions that knowledge in the field of child development can help to answer. Information about children's development is important in forming educational policies, providing advice to parents, offering therapy and counseling when children have problems, and making legal decisions affecting children and families. To answer some of the questions raised in these letters, the psychologist would need to know about age changes, intellectual skills, and social behavior, the role of hereditary and environmental influences on intelligence, what kinds of stimulation and caregiving are important for cognitive and social development in infancy, how sex-typed learning comes about, how children learn from observing others in their own environment and on television, and what types of parenting affect children in what ways, to name just a few topics.

These and similar questions are the core of developmental psychology. Although there are important applied reasons for studying them, an equally important motive for many psychologists is the desire to gain basic knowledge about the most complex organism that exists — the human being. In many cases, investigators explore an aspect of development because they consider it interesting or important to understand in its own right, not just because there is an immediate social need for the knowledge. Of course, the knowledge generated is often used later in ways that were not originally anticipated.

These two approaches to the field of child development — concern with social issues and interest in fundamental processes of development — are often described as *applied* and *basic.* In the field of child development, both are important, and each contributes to the other. We turn now to consider some of the issues that stimulate basic research in the field: then we will discuss how both basic and applied issues contribute to the kinds of questions that developmental psychologists choose to study.

Basic questions about development

Developmental psychologists are interested in how and why the human organism grows and changes from its initial form in utero to an adult being. *Development* can be defined as changes in a person's physical and neurological structures, behavior, and traits that emerge in orderly ways and are reasonably enduring. In the first 20 years of life, these changes usually result in new, improved ways of reacting — that is, in behavior that is healthier, more organized, more complex, more stable, more competent, or more efficient. We speak of the advances from creeping to walking, from babbling to talking, from concrete to abstract thinking as development. In each instance, we judge the later-appearing state to be a more adequate way of functioning than the earlier one.

One goal of developmental psychology is to understand the changes with increasing age that appear to be *universal* — changes that occur in all children regardless of the culture in which they grow up or the experiences they have. For example, children all over the world smile at human faces during the second or third month of life, utter their first word around age 12 months, and walk alone around 13 months. Psychologists try first to describe these changes. Then they attempt to explain why they occur and to understand what neurological patterns and experiences influence them. The knowledge they generate can be used to answer questions such as those raised in the letters about what behaviors are normal for different ages or whether separation from the parents has different effects at different ages.

A second focus in developmental psychology is to explain *individual differences* in behavior. Some infants react by crying loudly when their mothers leave the room; others play happily. Some children learn mathematical concepts quickly; others find math more difficult. Information about individual differences can help to answer the question raised earlier about the possible effects of Head Start or about what characteristics of individual children should be considered in making decisions about day care, custody, or placement outside the home.

Third, much of children's behavior depends on the *context,* or situation, in which they find themselves. If a child sees a play companion hitting others frequently, she may imitate that aggressive behavior. The same child with a nonaggressive peer may show nonaggressive behavior. Research investigating situational influences helps to determine what experiences affect children's development in important ways. That information might be used to answer a question about what qualities are important for good infant day-care centers or for adequate parenting.

These three ways of examining children's behavior—searching for universal patterns, individual differences, and situational or contextual influences—are all necessary for a full understanding of development. The emphasis placed on any one of the three depends on the theoretical orientation of the investigator and on the type of question being studied.

Choosing questions for research

Both applied social issues like those suggested in the letters at the beginning of the chapter and interest in basic knowledge about how children develop generate questions for research. Answers to these questions cannot be drawn solely from folk wisdom or from informal experiences with children. They require systematic and painstaking collection and evaluation of information. Therefore, research is one of the major tasks of the developmental psychologist, and the results of that research provide most of what you will read in this book. The first step in research is to identify a question. Because that process is extremely important, we turn now to consider in more depth how developmental psychologists decide what to study. How do they choose their questions?

"Just when I knew all of life's answers, they changed all the questions" (Springbok poster, Hallmark). This saying illustrates a profound truth about science: The answers and knowledge we gain are only as good as the questions we ask.

Questions sometimes arise from the need for basic descriptive information about what children do at what ages or under particular circumstances. Questions can also originate in theories or hypotheses about what conditions and processes are important in children's development. For example, much of the research on child-rearing practices conducted during the 1950s and 1960s was based directly or indirectly on Freud's psychoanalytic theory, which emphasizes early feeding and toilet-training experiences. Psychologists testing the theory studied feeding practices and toilet training; they could just as easily have studied the development of play patterns or interests, but the theory did not lead to hypotheses or questions about those domains of children's behavior.

Social issues and practical dilemmas are a third source of questions, as was amply demonstrated by the letters at the beginning of this chapter. If a social issue becomes nationally prominent, it often receives research attention because government funds are made available to study it. For example, during the 1960s and 1970s, there was considerable social concern about the effects of poverty on children's intellectual development (as suggested in the letter concerning Head Start). As a result, government funds were appropriated to establish early childhood education programs and to carry out research evaluating them. A large body of information about environmental influences on young children's cognitive development was generated from these funded research programs.

Whatever the initial source of a research question, the process by which knowledge is generated is continuous. The diagram in Figure 1.1 illustrates how issues from basic theory or from social concerns may be an initial impetus for a research question, but, as answers are provided, they feed back to stimulate further questions. Indeed, very often, an applied social issue will lead to new theories and basic questions, or the results of basic research will suggest new ways of fostering children's development in the real world. For example, early concerns about the severe intellectual and emotional problems of infants in institutions led to careful basic research on the conditions that are important for visual perception, cognition, and emotional health in infancy. That research, in turn, was used to change institutional and hospital settings for infants so that there were mobiles and varied visual stimuli, opportunities to play with toys, and social interactions with adults.

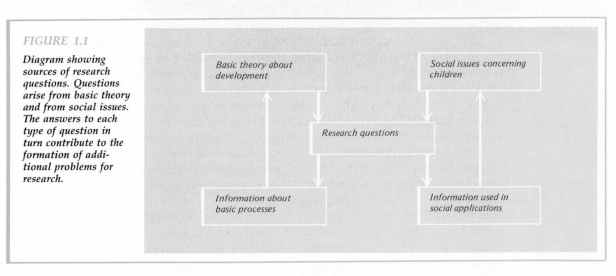

FIGURE 1.1

Diagram showing sources of research questions. Questions arise from basic theory and from social issues. The answers to each type of question in turn contribute to the formation of additional problems for research.

Basic theory about development

Social issues concerning children

Research questions

Information about basic processes

Information used in social applications

Questions selected for study are inevitably affected by contemporary social and cultural values. For example, because psychologists and others in the United States assume that infants should be cared for primarily by their mothers, investigations of day care for infants are almost always focused on possible harmful effects. Investigators have rarely asked, as the father in one of our letters did, what benefits might accrue from day care. In China, all men and women are expected to be employed, and many children are in day-care centers for 12 hours a day, 6 days a week. A researcher in that culture might be more likely to study the beneficial effects of day care for teaching children the cooperative values of the society.

The effects of social values on research questions are especially apparent when those values change. In the 1950s and 1960s, many psychologists investigated the child-rearing practices and other experiences that contributed to sex-role development. They assumed that the emotionally healthy boy should acquire "masculine" behavior and the healthy girl should become "feminine." In the 1970s, when the women's movement became prominent, many people, like the mother writing one of our hypothetical letters, argued that children would be better off to avoid traditionally defined sex roles and to develop a broad range of interests and behavior. These researchers began to explore what socialization experiences led children to nontraditional patterns of sex-role adoption.

THEORETICAL
ISSUES

Anyone who studies children, whether as a scientist or a practitioner, confronts certain fundamental issues. Some of these questions have been discussed for many centuries by philosophers, theologians, and educators, as you can see from the discussion in Box 1.1. There is no one "right" answer to most of them; instead, different points of view represent different assumptions about human nature and lead to different theories of development. These varying points of view represent honest differences among scientists about how to interpret existing information and about what are the most promising approaches for advancing knowledge about human development.

This issue is the well-known nature-versus-nurture controversy. Some scientists believe that much of human behavior is guided by genetic makeup, physiological maturation, and neurological functioning. According to their view, the universals of development, such as the emergence of walking, speaking, and responding to people, can be best explained as resulting from inborn, biological factors. They also believe that individual differences are largely a result of genetic and physiological differences. Such a scientist might argue, for instance, that poor performance of lower-class children on intelligence tests is largely due to genetic factors and to poor prenatal nutrition and health care in lower-class mothers. Accordingly, this scientist might recommend a government program that assured pregnant lower-class women of a good diet but would be less enthused about preschool programs for their children.

Environmental versus biological determinants of behavior

At the other end of the continuum, environmentalists emphasize the influence of the physical and social environment on patterns of development. They believe that children respond to the people and objects around them and that developmental changes result largely from experience. Individual differences in intelligence-test performance, according to this view, are due primarily to differences in cognitive stimulation and opportunities to learn about the world. Therefore, preschool education programs that provide good learning experiences should lead to improvements in performance.

Both extremes on the nature-nurture argument have obvious weaknesses. Most psychologists agree that both biological and environmental variables play a role in development. It appears that biological factors are more important for some aspects of development (such as learning to walk), while environmental variables are more important for others (such as learning to read). The beginnings of speech depend heavily on biological maturation (though they do

BOX 1.1

*Some
contrasting
early views
of education*

Almost all major philosophers of the seventeenth and eighteenth centuries formed theories about the nature of childhood, the child's mind and development, and education. Each philosopher also offered advice to parents and teachers. John Locke, writing at the end of the seventeenth century, believed that children should be trained through rewards and punishment from the very earliest months onward; he was, in effect, a learning theorist. In contrast, Rousseau, writing in the middle of the eighteenth century, believed that the child was by nature an active explorer who had enormous potentialities that would be actualized if adults did not interfere too much.

The contrasting points of view of these philosophers are evident in the following quotations from their major works. Here is what Locke believed:

> Rewards . . . *and* Punishments *must be proposed to Children, if we intend to work upon them. The Mistake . . . is, that those that are generally made use of, are* ill chosen. . . . Esteem *and* Disgrace *are, of all others, the most powerful incentives to the Mind. . . . If you can once get into Children a love of Credit, and an apprehension of Shame and Disgrace, you have put into them the true Principle, which will constantly work, and incline them to the right. . . . If therefore the Father* caress *and* commend *them, when they do well; shew a cold and neglectful Countenance to them upon doing ill; And this accompanied by a like Carriage of the Mother, and all others that are about them, it will in a little Time make them sensible of the Difference; and this if constantly observed, I doubt not but will of itself work more than Threats or blows.*[1]

Rousseau, on the other hand, held a different view:

> *Leave childhood to ripen in your children. . . . It is the child's individual bent, which must be thoroughly known before we can choose the fittest moral training. Every mind has its own form, in accordance with which it must be controlled; and the success of the pains taken depends largely on the fact that he is controlled in this way and no other. Oh, wise man, take time to observe nature; watch your scholar well before you say a word to him; first leave the germ of his character free to show itself, do not constrain him in anything, the better to see him as he really is.*[2]

[1] From John Locke's *Some thoughts concerning education* (4th ed., enlarged). London: Churchill, pp. 54–66, 101–108, 118–121. The first edition was published in 1693.
[2] From Jean Jacques Rousseau, *Emile, or on education* (translated by Barbara Foxley). London: Dent, 1911. The first French edition was published in 1762; the first English edition in 1763.

not occur in the absence of relevant experience). On the other hand, individual differences in altruism or generosity appear to depend primarily on children's experiences.

Finally, many scientists contend that there is no way to separate or assign weights to biological and environmental variables because the two interact from the moment of birth (and probably before). A child who is highly aggressive may have begun life with a biologically based tendency to be active or assertive; he may then have experienced success when he hit or pushed other children out of the way, so that his tendency to be aggressive increased over time. A child with a different biological predisposition *or* a different set of experiences might not show the same aggressive pattern.

Active versus passive nature of the child

A philosophical issue of considerable importance to theorists asks whether the child is a passive receiver of experience or an active seeker and creator of it. A theorist who assumes that children are passive does not mean they are unresponsive but that they enter the world ready to absorb whatever knowledge is provided by the environment. According to this view, children are molded by external rewards and punishments in the environment and are driven by internal needs over which they have little control. Theorists and educators who view the child as essentially passive often favor direct and carefully structured teaching methods. For example, some methods for teaching children to play the piano contain a series of specific steps, chords, and tunes to be learned in a prescribed order. The child must master each step before proceeding to the next.

Contrast this approach with that of an educator who believes that children learn best when they explore and select their own learning materials and tasks. When teaching piano, such an instructor might encourage the child to make up tunes or to select among different exercises. This approach awards children a more active part in their own development. A tendency to be curious, to explore the environment, and to organize the resulting experience in their own mental frameworks is assumed to be inborn in the human species. Efforts to program learning too closely, according to this view, are likely to fail because they do not correspond to the child's interests or patterns of learning. Instead, a relatively unstructured situation that offers opportunities for varied stimulation and exploration is optimal. What the child does and learns, then, depends mainly on internally generated interests and levels of understanding.

Continuity versus discontinuity in development

Do developmental changes occur in small, gradual steps (continuously) or in jumps that produce qualitatively new patterns of behavior (discontinuously)? Most theorists who assume that children are passive and emphasize environmental influences also see developmental change as continuous and gradual. The curve of behavioral development, according to this approach, might look like this:

An alternative view is that development is segmented or divided into *stages* and that the child's abilities and behavior are qualitatively different at each stage. When a child enters a new stage, abrupt changes occur that lead to major differences in a wide range of behaviors. A stage theorist's curve of development might look like this:

Take an example from motor development. Babies typically begin to crawl sometime during the second 6 months of life. At first they creep on the stomach, then rock on hands and knees, then finally lurch forward and start to crawl. Over time, they become better coordinated, faster, and more skilled at crawling. These changes are continuous—that is, they show a gradual improvement in skill. To stand on two feet and walk across the room, however, requires a completely different set of movements. The change from crawling to walking is not just a simple extension of crawling skills; it represents a qualitatively different behavior pattern. It is a discontinuous change.

The change from crawling to walking demonstrates another important point about developmental stages: When a more advanced stage is reached, children still retain the functions or skills of the earlier stage. When walking first begins, children do it with some difficulty; they revert to crawling when they want to move fast or they are tired. As they become more skilled at walking, they are less likely to crawl, but even adults have not forgotten how to crawl if they need to.

Many theorists believe that children's intellectual and social development goes through stages that are discontinuous, just as walking is qualitatively different from crawling. At certain points, the child acquires a whole new way of thinking that gradually replaces the earlier way.

Stability over time　　Is an aggressive 2-year-old likely to be an aggressive adult? Does an experience of early separation from the family leave long-term feelings of anxiety about separation? Does early education produce lasting changes in intelligence? Affirmative answers to these questions would mean that children's behavior is reasonably stable over time—that is, that early formed behaviors and personal characteristics predict later behavior. A considerable amount of research has been devoted to studying the stability of children's behavior. Nevertheless, that evidence is open to different interpretations, depending on which findings are given the greatest emphasis. Some people stress the changes and malleability of the human organism; others focus on the stability or sameness over time.

One reason for differing interpretations is that the answer to a question of stability is more complicated than a simple yes or no. In general, children's behavior is more stable as they get older. For example, IQ scores in the first few years of life are not good predictors of later IQ, but IQ measured at age 7 is a reasonably good predictor of IQ in adolescence and adulthood. Second, some kinds of behavior are more stable than others. For example, aggression is a reasonably stable behavior pattern; children who are aggressive in early and middle childhood are likely to be aggressive in adolescence and adulthood. Altruism and helpfulness are less stable from one time period to another (Mischel, 1968).

The question of stability over time is complicated by the fact that the same characteristics may be expressed in different ways at different ages. An aggressive nursery school child hits others; at age 12, insults and subtle hostility are more likely. A dependent nursery school child clings to an adult; at 10, this child may show the same characteristic by asking for help with many decisions and problems. Because all children's behavior changes with age, psychologists examine the question of stability by comparing the rank order of children at one age with their rank order at a later age. If a child who has a high rate of clinging to adults in nursery school, compared to other children, is also relatively high on a test of seeking help at age 10, then we infer that a trait such as dependency is stable over time.

Consistency across situations

Is a child who is highly aggressive at home also aggressive in school? Is the child who is shy with peers also shy with adults? Is children's behavior specific to particular situations, or do children have "traits" that they manifest in a wide range of settings? Again, research on this question has produced evidence that shows that both individual traits and situational variables influence behavior. Some theorists emphasize consistency across situations; others stress situational influences. In line with their general emphasis on external influences, strong environmentalists stress situational determinants of behavior. Therefore, they expect children to show little consistency across situations or stability over time unless the environment remains reasonably constant. People who focus on biological bases for development and internal characteristics of the child tend to expect consistency across situations and stability over time.

These five issues—biological versus environmental bases of behavior, the passive versus active nature of the child, continuity versus discontinuity of development, stability over time, and consistency across situations—have affected the thinking and research of developmentalists for many years. Their influence can be demonstrated through a brief overview of the history of the field of child development during the twentieth century.

HISTORICAL PERSPECTIVES ON DEVELOPMENTAL PSYCHOLOGY

The systematic study of child psychology began early in the present century. Around the turn of the century, many reformers became concerned with children's welfare. Child labor laws, compulsory education legislation, juvenile courts, and child welfare services were introduced. As professionals began to try to help children, they also began to recognize the need for knowledge about children so that they could assess developmental patterns and normal behavior. In the United States, the scientific study of development was given a major boost by the establishment of research institutes for the study of child welfare on several university campuses using funds from one of the first private foundations (Sears, 1975).

Research in the early twentieth century

The approach that typified research during this early period began with G. Stanley Hall, a pioneer in the scientific study of children. He tried to investi-

gate "the contents of children's minds" (Hall, 1891) using a new research technique, the questionnaire. Children were asked about their activities and interests. Hall's goal was to describe the sequence and timing of development, and he was one of the first to apply objective measures to large numbers of children.

Many psychologists during this period assumed that developmental changes were largely a result of maturation. They assumed that the age differences they observed represented innate universal patterns of development for all children. This approach led to descriptions of "normal" behavior for different ages, illustrated in the following discussion by two psychologists at the Gesell Institute of Child Development:

> First of all, we have observed that 2 years of age, 5 years and 10 years all constitute focal points at which behavior seems to be in good equilibrium, the child having relatively little difficulty within himself or with the world about him. Each of these relatively smooth and untroubled ages is followed by a brief period when behavior appears to be very much broken up, disturbed and troubled, and when the child shows himself to be in marked disequilibrium. Thus, the smoothness of 2-year-old behavior characteristically breaks up at $2\frac{1}{2}$; 5-year-old behavior breaks up at $5\frac{1}{2}$ to 6; and 10 breaks up at 11, the 11-year-old child characteristically showing himself to be at definite odds with his environment and with himself. . . .
>
> All three of these ages are followed by periods of extreme expansiveness. Four, eight and fourteen are all times at which the child's behavior is

markedly outgoing in most major respects. He is even in danger of expanding too much. He wanders from home and gets lost at 4, he demands to ride his bicycle in the street at 8 and may get hit, and he gets all tangled in his multiple and conflicting social plans at 14 (Ilg & Ames, 1955, pp. 10–11).

One major goal of research in the early part of the century was to collect descriptive information about normal development. For example, on the basis of extensive observations of children's language, information was published showing the average number of words that a child of one year could say, the average age when children use two-word combinations, and many other such "statistics" (McCarthy, 1946). Age changes in children's peer interactions from parallel play (one toddler builds a tower of blocks while another takes a doll for a ride in a wagon) to cooperative play (two children play house or build a road of blocks together) were described (Parten, 1932). And intelligence tests were designed on the basis of the average level of intellectual performance for each age level. Such descriptive research was intended to provide behavioral norms similar to the physical norms for height and weight that physicians use to determine when children's physical growth is normal.

Social practices with children also were based on the assumption that developmental changes depend largely on maturation and heredity. For example, when babies became eligible for adoption during the early part of the century, they were placed in orphanages until they were 6 months old in order to determine whether they had normal intelligence. Most orphanages provided little intellectual stimulation. Children who showed delayed development in these circumstances were diagnosed as mentally retarded and transferred to institutions for the retarded. The people making these decisions were not aware that the environment of the orphanage might have a significant influence on the intellectual development of young infants.

Three other movements in American and European psychology during this period had a strong influence on later developmental psychology. First, Freud's psychoanalytic theory was becoming known, and his hypotheses about the importance of early experience began to permeate many people's thinking.

Second, John Watson founded the behaviorist movement and conducted some pioneering experiments using learning theory. He was not only a "radical environmentalist" but also a vivid writer who did not hesitate to state his position strongly.

Give me a dozen healthy infants, well-formed, and my own specified world to bring them up in and I'll guarantee to take any one at random and train him to become any type of specialist I might select—doctor, lawyer, merchant, chief, and yes, even beggar-man and thief, regardless of his talents, penchants, abilities, vocations, and the race of his ancestors (Watson, 1930/1967).

Third, Piaget began his investigations of children's intellectual development in Switzerland. These three theoretical movements eventually formed the backbone of modern child psychology.

Post–World War II to the mid-1960s

After World War II, a new brand of child psychologist emerged who approached the study of children as a branch of experimental psychology. Instead of describing developmental changes, these psychologists wanted to formulate and test theoretical explanations of children's behavior. They turned to both psychoanalytic theory and learning theory to generate hypotheses about what processes and variables influence the behavior of children. They were concerned with such questions as: What effects does early feeding experience have on dependency? How do different types of reward and punishment affect learning? What child-rearing practices are associated with the development of conscience?

These psychologists were interested not just in describing behavior but also in predicting and explaining the reasons for children's actions. They emphasized overt behavior in their studies of children rather than unobservable mental events. The dominant view during this period was strongly environmentalist, and researchers were reluctant to assume that children's behavior was biologically determined. They became less interested than earlier psychologists in age changes or developmental stages and correspondingly more concerned with situational, environmental influences.

Researchers in this period preferred laboratory experiments in which they could control all aspects of a situation to naturalistic observation. They argued that there were too many uncontrolled influences in natural situations to draw any conclusions about which of these influences were important. For example, Albert Bandura (1969) conducted a classic set of experiments investigating children's imitative behavior. In one study, he tested the theoretical hypothesis that children would imitate a warm, friendly adult more than a cool, distant one. He set up experimental situations in which some children had warm, friendly interactions with an adult and others experienced a cool, detached adult. Then the children watched the adult model perform a series of actions, such as hitting a rubber doll, and subsequently had an opportunity to play in the same setting themselves. When they imitated the warm, friendly adult more than the cool adult, Bandura concluded that the hypothesis had been supported (Bandura & Huston, 1961).

Mid-1960s to the present

In the early 1960s, American psychology rediscovered Piaget's theory of cognitive development, and his ideas influenced basic views about the child. Piaget was interested in the universals in children's development (rather than in individual differences), and he believed development resulted from the interaction between maturational changes and experience. Intensive observations of his own three children convinced him that children were active organisms who seek stimulation and organize their own experience without any direct instruction or programming from the environment. He proposed four major stages of cognitive development that all children go through. (These are discussed in later chapters.)

Partly as a result of Piaget's approach, there has been increased interest during the past 20 years in biological, genetic, and maturational influences on behavior. The field has not, however, simply returned to the assumptions of the early part of the century. Present-day investigations are typically guided by a theory that helps establish which behavior is important and generates predictions. The purpose of most current research is to identify the processes involved in development, not merely to describe it. For example, Mary Ainsworth and her associates (Ainsworth, Blehar, Waters, & Wall, 1978) have studied the development of infants' emotional relationships with their parents. The theory guiding this research (described more fully in Chapter 4) assumes that human infants are biologically predisposed to respond to people and to become attached to the people who care for them. Ainsworth and her colleagues have studied how different patterns of parental behavior interact with this biological predisposition, producing different types of parent-child relationships.

Another trend in recent years is the attempt to relate children's social behavior to their cognitive development. In earlier periods, researchers tended to study cognitive changes as they affect learning, school performance, and the like. Social and emotional behavior (such as aggression, dependency, and morality) were treated as a separate subject. Today it has become apparent that children's *social cognitions,* or ways of thinking about social situations and moral issues, help to determine social behavior (see Chapter 9). For example, whether a child retaliates when hurt by another child depends partly on whether the victim believes the aggressor inflicted the hurt intentionally or by accident—a social cognition.

Finally, the field has returned to a concern with social applications of the knowledge gained about children. During the 1950s and early 1960s, many developmental psychologists avoided applied questions; they felt they did not know enough to give advice to parents and others who deal with children. While we still lack knowledge in many areas, children growing up today cannot wait for science to progress. As the writer of the letter that starts this chapter observed, decisions must be made even though the information available is incomplete. Developmental psychologists are in a better position than most others to offer some wisdom that can contribute to the welfare of children.

METHODS FOR
STUDYING
CHILDREN

Many of us observe children every day. Teachers and parents know a great deal about children from these frequent contacts. What is different about the way a developmental psychologist observes children? What is required for the scientific study of their behavior? The different methods described here are alike in one way: all of them call for the *controlled, systematic* observation of behavior. In some investigations, behavior is observed as it occurs in real-life settings, such as home or school. In others, specific tasks or situations are created, often in laboratories, so that the reactions of different children can be observed in comparable circumstances. Sometimes children are interviewed; sometimes, they are given tests; and sometimes observers use a prearranged set of categories and count the number of times each child displays behaviors in each category. In each case, however, the investigator tries to carry out similar procedures with all children and tries to control or evaluate the situational variables that may affect the child's responses.

Objectivity is another fundamental feature of scientific research. No matter how a study is designed, its measuring techniques must be as free of subjective bias as possible. For example, in studying aggressive behavior, a researcher has to specify exactly and objectively what behaviors are to be called "aggressive." Using such precise definitions, different observers can

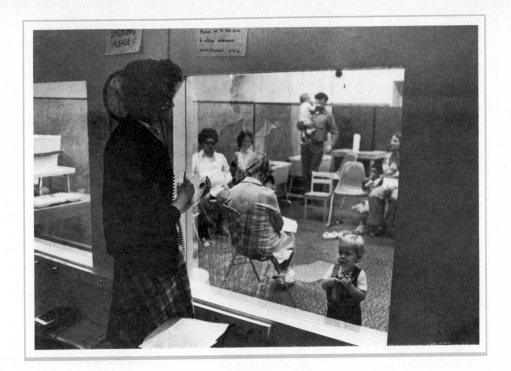

code the behavior of the same children. If these independent observers score a child's behavior similarly, the coding system is assumed to be objective. Objective measures are usually quantifiable—that is, they yield a set of numbers rather than just a verbal description of children's behavior. For example, the number of times a child hits other children might be counted and perhaps then compared with the number of times other children hit the child being observed.

We will examine different methods of research in the context of a particular research problem: What is the effect of television violence on aggressive behavior? As the discussion will show, each of several methods can provide important information about a question, but no one method yields a definitive answer. In general, we feel most confident in drawing conclusions when they are based on several different methods.

Correlational or field studies

In a *correlational* study, an investigator measures two variables for a group of people and determines whether people who score high on one measure also score high on the other. For example, information was obtained for a large sample of elementary school children about how much violent television they watched and how much aggressive behavior they displayed at school (according to other children's reports). The investigators then examined the data to determine whether children who watched more violent television were more aggressive—that is, whether viewing violence was positively correlated with aggression. Their findings demonstrated a correlation between watching violent television and aggressive behavior in school (Huesmann, 1982).

The correlational approach is often used in *field studies,* studies conducted in real-life settings. One advantage of this approach is that the investigator measures the variables of interest as they exist in the real world, without tampering or intervening. The study just described measured real aggression as it happens naturally in school and real television viewing as it happens naturally at home.

Correlational data help to determine whether or not a relationship exists between viewing violence and aggressive behavior, but such data do not permit conclusions about *causes* in that relationship. The correlation between watching violent television and behaving aggressively at school, for instance, could be accounted for in at least three ways. First, watching violent television may instigate aggression. Second, highly aggressive children may prefer to watch violence (that is, the child's aggression may "cause" the television viewing). Third, children's aggression and their preference for watching violent television may arise from some other cause, such as having an aggressive parent who turns on violent television programs often and whose aggression the child imitates.

Correlational studies sample the richness of real-world events, but that very richness can be a drawback. So many factors contribute to naturally occurring events that it is difficult to know which of them are most important. For these reasons, correlational studies are often complemented by experimental investigations.

Experiments   The essence of the experimental method is that the investigator systematically changes one variable (the *independent variable*) and collects objective measurements on another variable (the *dependent variable*). Meanwhile, all other factors that might affect the dependent variable are held constant. For example, one experiment to test the effects of violent television on aggressive behavior was conducted by bringing individual children to a laboratory where they watched either a violent television program or a nonviolent travelog. Exposure to television violence was the independent variable. After viewing, children were placed in situations where they could behave aggressively—they could play with aggressive toys (such as bobo dolls and toy guns) or interfere with another child's efforts to complete a task. These aggressive behaviors were the dependent variable (Liebert & Baron, 1972).

Children were randomly assigned to the violent-TV or travelog group; that is, they were placed in the experimental or control group by chance (for instance, by flipping a coin). Random assignment is a critical feature of experiments because it is the means of controlling individual differences among children. With a sufficiently large number of children in each group, we can assume that children who differed initially in their levels of aggression are evenly distributed in the violent and nonviolent viewing groups. Therefore, differences between the two groups are not due to predispositions or personality differences among children.

The experimental method does not always permit the conclusion that "X causes Y," but it does permit inferences about the causal direction of effects. Because viewing violent television was varied systematically and other variables were controlled, we can conclude that the television viewing influenced the aggressive behavior. Because the control group also watched television, we

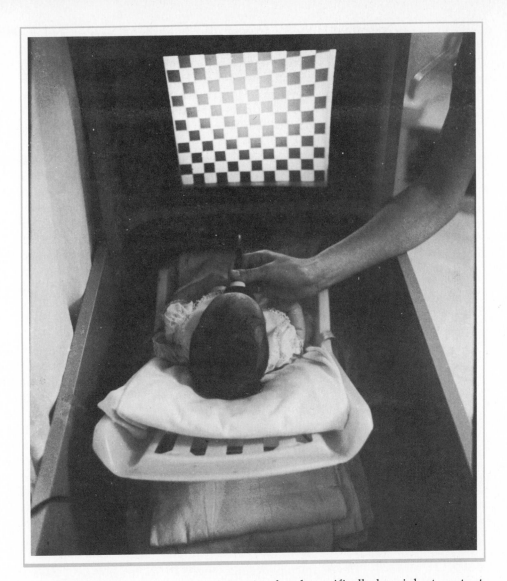

can also conclude that aggression is stimulated specifically by violent content and not simply by viewing television for a period of time. Thus, the experimental method enables the scientist to separate possibly important variables and to test hypotheses about the processes that account for the behavior of interest—in this case, aggression.

The experimental method alone also leaves unanswered questions. Most experiments are necessarily short-term. For example, in the study described above, the total time that the children watched television in the laboratory was about 10 minutes. We cannot be sure whether the many hours children spend watching television in the real world would have the same effect. Another problem with experiments is that one cannot be sure how well laboratory findings will generalize to natural settings. For example, the aggressive behavior measured in the study described here was not very violent, for ethical reasons. Children in a laboratory cannot be allowed to hit, kick, or bite each other. Naturally occurring aggression, such as interactions between siblings in the home living room, may be more hurtful. Further, the children did not choose the program they viewed, and this may have affected the results. The laboratory experiment provides precise and unique information about human development, but it must be considered in combination with observations of naturally occurring events.

Field experiments

A field experiment is an attempt to combine the advantages of the field-correlational and experimental approaches. In a field experiment, children are randomly assigned to groups that undergo different experiences as in an experiment. As in a field study, however, the groups are observed in naturally occurring situations and for a relatively long period of time. For example, adolescent males living in residential treatment facilities were randomly assigned to see violent or nonviolent movies every evening for a week. Trained observers rated their aggressive behavior in their residences before, during, and after the week of movies. The boys who had seen violent movies behaved more aggressively than those who were shown nonviolent movies (Parke, Berkowitz, Leyens, West, & Sebastian, 1977).

The field experiment shows causal direction—the preceding one showed that violent movies affected aggressive behavior—and at the same time preserves the "real life" quality of measurement in field settings. However, there is still the problem that the experimenter has assigned people to treatments; the effects of viewing something that someone has prescribed could be different from the effects of viewing one's own choices.

Some problems in developmental psychology cannot be studied by experimental methods, either in the laboratory or in the field. Ethical considerations prevent us from manipulating variables in a way that might produce permanent harm to a child. For example, an experimental study of prenatal nutrition could not include a treatment in which mothers were experimentally assigned to an inadequate diet during pregnancy. Similarly, in the case of television violence, we would not assign children to watch violence over long periods of time if there was a reasonable possibility that they would become seriously aggressive as a result.

Developmental changes over time, and the processes that account for them, cannot be manipulated experimentally. Children grow older, and there is no way to make them grow younger, even if we should want to. Because much of developmental psychology is concerned with stability and change over time and with the impact of early experiences or characteristics on later behavior, methods for studying children at different ages are important tools.

Cross-sectional and longitudinal studies

Researchers usually begin investigating developmental changes with *cross-sectional* investigations in which children of different ages are compared at one point in time. For example, if we compared groups of children ages 4, 8, 12, and 16, we might find that the amount of hitting and physical aggression is greater for younger children and the amount of verbal insulting aggression is greater for older children. Such cross-sectional studies provide information about age differences, but to find out whether individual children undergo a transition from physical to verbal aggression, we would need to follow the same children over time. Differences between children of various ages at one point in time could be a result of differences in experience associated with particular historical time periods. For example, suppose that large amounts of television violence had been introduced within the two years preceding the study. The 4-year-olds might be responding to the television violence; their behavior might be quite different from that of 4-year-old children 10 years earlier.

In a *longitudinal* study, the same children are observed or tested at regular intervals over an extended period of time, sometimes a decade or longer. This approach is especially valuable when an investigator wants to study stability and change in such characteristics as intelligence and aggression. It can also be used to determine whether an experience at one time period has an impact later. A longitudinal study of television violence, for example, assessed the same children at age 8 and again at age 18. Children who liked to watch television violence at age 8 were more aggressive at age 18 than their peers whose childhood television preferences were nonviolent (Eron, Lefkowitz, Huesmann, & Walder, 1972). Longitudinal studies are also useful for investigating patterns of developmental change or transitions across stages.

Cross-cultural studies

It is tempting to make generalizations about trends in development after studying children who share a common cultural background, such as middle-class Americans. Comparative studies in other cultures can serve as an antidote to overgeneralization. For example, observers in Western societies, particularly

the United States, have often described adolescence as a period of "storm and stress," characterized by mood swings, rebellion, and conflict with parental authority. However, in many cultures, adolescents become fully integrated, adult members of their societies, doing adult work and beginning families.

Sometimes information from different cultures extends the range of variables that can be observed. For example, investigators of television violence in the United States are hampered by the fact that virtually every American child is exposed to television from birth onward, and television in every part of the country contains a great deal of violence. Therefore, the range of exposure to violent television in the United States is limited; there are almost no children who have grown up without it. Television programming in some other countries, such as Sweden, is quite different. Cross-cultural studies permit comparisons of children who are accustomed to television violence and those who experience it less often.

"Universals" of development can be evaluated in cross-cultural studies. The first primitive sentences of English-speaking babies contain names of concrete objects ("my doll") and action words ("hit ball"). Is this due to characteristics of the English language and the language environments provided by English-speaking parents, or do infants learning to speak other languages also name concrete objects first? This question can be answered by cross-cultural investigations of children's early speech in many languages. In fact, such investigations have shown many common speech patterns in children in different cultures (see Chapter 6).

Cross-species studies

Developmental questions are sometimes studied using animals instead of human beings. One major reason is that animals can be treated in ways that would be dangerous or unethical for humans. For example, Harry Harlow carried out a classic set of studies with monkeys investigating early deprivation of maternal care. Newborn monkeys were raised in isolation or with artificial mothers of different sorts, and the effects of the deprivation on their later behavior was measured (Harlow & Suomi, 1970). Human children cannot be deprived of mothering, nor can they be kept in a laboratory for lifetime observation as the monkeys were.

Although we must exercise caution in generalizing from other species to humans, cross-species studies can provide valuable information about developmental processes that are comparable to those that occur in human beings. For instance, the infant monkeys in Harlow's studies seemed to prefer a soft, terry-cloth "mother" that gave no food to a wire-mesh "mother" that dispensed food. This led Harlow to suggest that feeding was not the critical reason why human babies become emotionally attached to their mothers—an important developmental issue that is more fully explored in Chapter 4.

Summary of research methods

Each of the many methods used to study human development has strengths and weaknesses. Together, they complement and compensate for one another. We can feel more confident of conclusions from studies using a variety of methods than of those from only one type. In the case of television violence, the fact that correlational studies, laboratory experiments, field experiments, and longitudinal studies yield similar findings provides strong support for the conclusion that television violence contributes to aggressive behavior. Similarly, when longitudinal studies in the United States, cross-cultural studies, and cross-species studies all show that infants develop certain fears in a particular order, we feel confident that a universal developmental sequence has been identified (see Chapter 3).

Research in child development raises complex ethical dilemmas. The occasional horror story from medical research, such as prisoners being injected with cancer-producing drugs without their knowledge, has made researchers particularly aware of the need to establish ethical guidelines and to monitor research procedures. Gross violations of children's rights, such as deliberately depriving them of stimulation in early life, are recognized by everyone as unethical.

More subtle ethical problems also require careful consideration. If investigators ask children questions about their parents' child-rearing practices, are they invading the children's or the parents' right to privacy? Might the questions themselves lead to problems in parent-child relationships? Is it ever morally justified to deceive a child (for instance, by misleading him about his performance on a test or telling him that he will be alone in a room when he is being observed through a one-way mirror)? Is it ethical to subject a child to mild frustration or stress for experimental purposes? Is it permissible to observe people in public settings without their consent? These are difficult questions that have no absolute answers.

Both the American Psychological Association (1972) and the Society for Research in Child Development (1973) have formulated written guidelines and principles for research, particularly research with children. Some of the principles taken from the report of the Committee on Ethics in Research with Children (Society for Research in Child Development) are summarized in Box 1.2.

Of course, ethical problems in research with children cannot be solved simply by applying a set of rules. Investigators must continually weigh the advantages and disadvantages of conducting a particular study. Can the investigator's judgment about possible harm to children or about potential benefits of the research be trusted? Often it can be, but many feel that any individual's decisions about ethical problems need to be evaluated or monitored by some sort of jury. Therefore, many universities and other research facilities— as well as the U.S. Public Health Service, which supports a great deal of research in child development—require that an ethics advisory committee, consisting of other researchers representing several disciplines, review every research proposal that involves human subjects and attempt to ensure that the investigators act in accordance with the highest ethical standards. This committee serves as a panel of judges, considers the objectives and potential benefits of the study, weighs these against the possible harmful effects on the children, and most important, guarantees that all possible steps are taken to safeguard the welfare and integrity of all participants.

In the final analysis, neither codes nor committees can substitute for the investigator's moral integrity, maturity, honesty, sensitivity, and respect for the rights of others. Ultimately, the investigator is responsible for the conduct of the study and for applying the highest ethical standards in research.

BOX 1.2

*Ethical issues
in research*

Developmental psychologists do research with human beings, and this entails many ethical issues and responsibilities. The researcher's primary obligation is to safeguard the welfare, dignity, and rights of all participants in research, children and adults alike. Some of the ethical dilemmas encountered in developmental research are easy to solve, but others are more subtle.

To help psychologists in making ethical decisions, professional organizations such as the American Psychological Association and the Society for Research in Child Development have formulated some broad ethical principles for conducting research with children. Of course, ethical problems cannot be solved simply by applying a set of rules; investigators must continually weigh the advantages and potential contributions of research against the disadvantages that may be involved in conducting it.

The following is a sample of principles formulated by a committee of the Society for Research in Child Development.

1. No matter how young the child, he has rights that supersede the rights of the investigator. The investigator should measure each operation he proposes in terms of the child's rights, and before proceeding he should obtain the approval of a committee of [the investigator's] peers. . . .

5. The investigator should respect the child's freedom to choose to participate in research or not, as well as to discontinue participation at any time. . . .

6. The informed consent of parents or of those who act *in loco parentis* (e.g., teachers, superintendents of institutions) similarly should be obtained, preferably in writing. Informed consent requires that the parent or other responsible adult be told all features of the research that may affect his willingness to allow the child to participate. . . . Not only should the right of the responsible adult to refuse consent be respected, but he should be given the opportunity to refuse without penalty. . . .

9. The investigator uses no research operation that may harm the child either physically or psychologically. Psychological harm, to be sure, is difficult to define; nevertheless, its definition remains the responsibility of the investigator. When the investigator is in doubt about the possible harmful effects of the research operations, he seeks consultation from others. When harm seems possible, he is obligated to find other means of obtaining the information or to abandon the research.

Four age periods define the four sections of this book: prenatal development (before birth), infancy (birth to around 2 years), early and middle childhood (around 2 to 12 years), and adolescence (around 12 to 20). Of course, the content discussed for different ages overlaps because most features of human development are not perfectly correlated with age.

Within each section, development in the domains of physical and biological growth, cognitive functioning, and social-emotional behavior are discussed. The universals of human development, as well as the bases for individual differences, are considered. Central influences—the family, school, peer group, and mass media—are considered as they apply to different age periods. Major theories and applied social issues are both addressed whenever they apply.

When you have read some or all of the following chapters, it may be advisable to return to the introduction. Many of the general points will take on added meaning as you apply them to the specific knowledge presented in later chapters.

The field of child development is important in finding solutions to many questions and problems concerning the welfare of children. A sample of such questions included: What factors should be considered in making legal decisions about custody in divorce cases or about removing children from abusing families? What experiences are important in the development of sex-typed behavior? What qualities are important for infant day care? Can children's intellectual development be significantly affected by early childhood educational programs? How may children with behavior or emotional problems be helped?

Developmental psychology is also guided by the desire to gain basic knowledge about processes of children's development. Such knowledge may be about universal patterns of developmental change, about individual differences, or about situational influences on children's behavior. Both basic knowledge and applied social issues contribute to the research questions that are the core of the field of child development.

Five theoretical issues underlie many differences of approach and emphasis by different scientists and practitioners in the field: the role of heredity versus environmental influences, the passive or active nature of the child, continuity or discontinuity of developmental change, stability of behavior over time, and consistency across situations. Different assumptions about these issues lead to different theoretical hypotheses and to different conclusions about appropriate interventions in children's development.

Approaches toward child development changed during the twentieth century. Before World War II, the major thrust was to describe age differences in behavior, and many psychologists assumed that these changes were maturational or biologically based. Between about 1945 and the early 1960s, child psychologists attempted to test theories about processes of development, and they had a strong bias toward environmental rather than biological explanations for behavior. Since the early 1960s, the interactions of maturation with experience have been stressed, and cognitive developmental changes have been emphasized.

Scientific methods for studying children have in common the requirement that they be objective and that observations be collected in a systematic, controlled fashion. Five methods are frequently used. Correlational methods entail collecting information about two qualities of a group of children and determining whether children who score high (or low) on one quality also score high (or low) on the other. In experiments, one variable is manipulated by the investigator, and children's responses are observed. Field experiments also involve manipulation of an important variable by the investigator, but responses are observed in real-life settings rather than in a laboratory. Age changes can be investigated by cross-sectional comparisons of children of different ages and by longitudinal studies following the same children over time. Cross-cultural and cross-species comparisons are often used to evaluate conclusions or hypotheses that cannot be tested in one society or solely using human subjects. Each method has strengths and weaknesses. Conclusions are more solid when they are derived from studies using several different methods than when they are based on only one method.

Ethical standards for research with children have been spelled out by the American Psychological Association and by the Society for Research in Child Development. Children must freely consent to participate in research; they must not be subjected to procedures that could be physically or psychologically harmful; and information collected must be kept in confidence.

REFERENCES

Ainsworth, M. D. S., Blehar, M. C., Waters, E., & Wall, S. *Patterns of attachment: A psychological study of the strange situation.* Hillsdale, N.J.: Erlbaum, 1978.

American Psychological Association, Committee on Ethical Standards in Psychological Research. Ethical standards for research with human subjects. *APA Monitor*, 1972 (May), I–XIX.

Bandura, A. *Principles of behavior modification.* New York: Holt, Rinehart and Winston, 1969.

Bandura, A., & Huston, A. C. Identification as a process of incidental learning. *Journal of Abnormal and Social Psychology*, 1961, *63*, 311–318.

Daltry, L. Television on trial: The tube made me do it. *New West*, March 13, 1978, p. 69.

Eron, L. D., Lefkowitz, M. M., Huesmann, L. R., & Walder, L. O. Does television violence cause aggression? *American Psychologist*, 1972, *27*, 253–263.

Hall, G. S. The content of children's minds on entering school. *Pedagogical Seminary*, 1891, *1*, 139–173.

Harlow, H. F. & Suomi, S. J. The nature of love — simplified. *American Psychologist*, 1970, *25*, 161–168.

Huesmann, L. R. Television violence and aggressive behavior. In D. Pearl, L. Bouthilet, & J. Lazar (Eds.), *Television and behavior: Ten years of scientific progress and implications for the eighties.* Washington, D.C.: U.S. Government Printing Office, 1982.

Ilg, F. L. & Ames, L. B. *Child behavior.* New York: Harper & Row, 1955.

Liebert, R. M., & Baron, R. A. Some immediate effects of televised violence on children's behavior. *Developmental Psychology*, 1972, *6*, 469–475.

McCarthy, D. Language. In L. Carmichael (Ed.), *Manual of child psychology.* New York: Wiley, 1946.

Mischel, W. *Personality and assessment.* New York: Wiley, 1968.

Parke, R. D., Berkowitz, L., Leyens, J. P., West, S., & Sebastian, R. J. Some effects of violent and nonviolent movies on the behavior of juvenile delinquents. In L. Berkowitz (Ed.), *Advances in experimental social psychology* (Vol. 10). New York: Academic Press, 1977.

Parten, M. B. Social participation among preschool children. *Journal of Abnormal and Social Psychology*, 1932, *27*, 243–269.

Sears, R. R. Your ancients revisited: A history of child development. In E. M. Hetherington (Ed.), *Review of child development research* (Vol. 5). Chicago: University of Chicago Press, 1975.

Society for Research in Child Development. Ethical standards for research with children. *SRCD Newsletter*, 1973 (Winter), 3–4.

Watson, J. B. *Behaviorism* (Rev. ed.). Chicago: University of Chicago Press, 1967. (Originally published, 1930.)

part O*ne*

THE PRENATAL PERIOD

CHAPTER 2

Genetic and prenatal factors in development

*I*n attempting to understand the behavior of the developing child, many factors must be considered. Even the simplest behavior is often the result of many different influences. Basically, these influences fall into five categories: (a) genetically determined biological variables, (b) nongenetic biological variables (for example, lack of oxygen during the birth process, malnutrition), (c) the child's past learning, (d) the immediate sociopsychological environment (parents, siblings, peers, teachers), and (e) the general social and cultural milieu in which the child develops. As we noted at the beginning of this book, the child's behavior and personality are, at any one time, a product of the continuing and continual interaction of nature and nurture.

Although we normally consider biological and environmental influences separately for ease of exposition, it is important to realize that they always act in unison. This is as true of the individual cell as it is of the whole person. Thus, the chemical action of the genetic material in a particular cell can be affected by the material outside the nucleus of the cell. Indeed, the effect of a single gene will depend on the constellation of other genes in that cell. Scientists try to discover the specific genetic and environmental forces that are controlling a specific behavior. They do not ask which influence is the cause, just as they would not ask about the relative importance of moisture or cold in producing a snowfall: Both are important.

This realization of the intimate interaction of genes and environment is relatively recent. As discussed in Chapter 1, even in the twentieth century, many scientists still took dogmatic, one-sided views of the nature-nurture issue, attributing virtually all human behavior either to heredity or to environment. Consider, for example, this statement by J. B. Watson, the father of early behaviorism: "There is no such thing as an inheritance of capacity, talent, temperament, mental constitution, and characteristics" (Allport, 1937, pp. 102–103).

In the light of recent advances in biology and psychology, both extreme environmentalism and extreme genetic determinism are naive. Scientists must search for the ways in which the combined action of our inherited potentialities and the events we experience make us the way we are. The sciences of genetics and embryology have shown dramatic progress during the last 25 years. This chapter will deal with our current knowledge of human genetics (particularly as it affects behavior) and with prenatal factors affecting the course of develop-ment.

BEGINNINGS
OF LIFE

The development of each individual begins when a sperm cell from the father penetrates the wall of an ovum, or egg, from the mother. As we shall see in some detail later, the fertilization of an ovum by a sperm sets in motion an intricate process called *mitosis*. In this process the original fertilized ovum divides and subdivides until thousands of cells have been produced. Gradually, as the process continues, groups of cells begin to assume special functions as parts of the nervous, skeletal, muscular, and circulatory systems. The embryo, which at first resembles a gradually expanding ball, begins to take shape, and the be-ginnings of head, eyes, trunk, arms, and legs appear. Approximately 9 months after fertilization, the fetus is ready for birth.

HEREDITARY
TRANSMISSION

Development begins at conception. But what are the forces that, throughout the individual's existence, will influence that process? When do they begin? The answer, again, is at conception. At the moment that the tiny, tadpole-shaped sperm penetrates the wall of the ovum, it releases 23 minute particles called *chromosomes*. At approximately the same time, the nucleus, the inner core of the ovum, breaks up, releasing 23 chromosomes of its own, so that the new individual begins life with 46 chromosomes.

This process is of great interest to us because it has been established through painstaking research that these chromosomes, which are further sub-divided into even smaller particles called *genes*, are the carriers of the child's heredity. (There are about 1 million genes in a human cell or, on the average, about 20,000 genes per chromosome.) All the child's biological heritage from the father and mother is contained in these 23 pairs of chromosomes. Of these pairs, 22 are *autosomes*, possessed equally by males and females. The twenty-third pair, the *sex chromosomes*, differ in males and females. It is these chromo-somes that determine a child's sex. Normal females have two X chromosomes (XX), while normal males have an X and a Y (XY) (see Figure 2.1).

What is
transmitted?

Long before the geneticists established the existence of chromosomes and genes, scientists were convinced that many characteristics of a child's parents were transmitted to the child at conception. They often differed, how-ever, about just what was transmitted and how. For example, one school of thought, dating back to Lamarck, a French zoologist who published a book called *Philosophie zoologique* in 1773, maintained that acquired characteristics could be inherited. Lamarck felt that individuals improved or weakened their own physical capacities through experience or training and that the effects of such changes could be transmitted to their offspring. For example, by devel-oping a diseased lung or poor digestion, a prospective father was thought to be hurting his child's chances of being healthy. People began to postulate such notions as that of the giraffe acquiring a long neck because its ancestors had spent a great deal of time reaching into trees for food or that of snakes losing their legs as a result of their forebears' propensity for creeping through crevices (McGraw, 1946). Nor were such speculations confined only to obvious physical characteristics. Many people believed that a mother could influence her child's

FIGURE 2.1

Idiogram of the human male chromosomes. (Courtesy of Dr. Theodore Puck.)

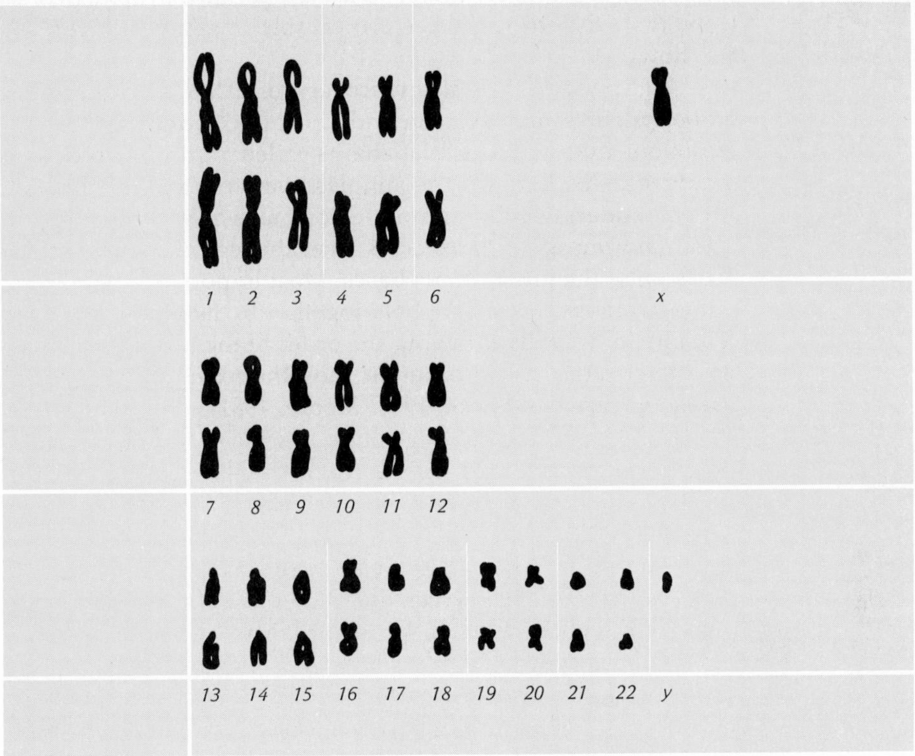

chances of being born with a talent for singing if she had, in her youth, carefully cultivated her own voice or that if a father had previously developed an interest in mathematics, this interest was likely to be inherited by his son.

We now know that such fascinating prospects are without basis in fact. Although chromosomes and their component genes may sometimes change or be inactivated by radiation, viruses, and certain chemicals or drugs, genes are not subject to the usual influences that build up our bodies or improve our minds. Hence there is—fortunately or unfortunately—no reason for believing that we can affect our children's genetic constitutions by engaging in self-improvement.

Genes and DNA For many years, geneticists agreed that genes were the basic units of hereditary transmission, but the nature of the chemical substances responsible for their action was in doubt. Many considered that complex proteins played this role. Few scientists suspected the critical importance of another component of the genes, deoxyribonucleic acid, or DNA. The DNA molecule is composed of long chains of smaller molecules called *nucleotides*. These nucleotides are composed of a sugar molecule (deoxyribose), a phosphate molecule, and four nitrogenous *bases* (called *adenine, thymine, cytosine,* and *guanine*). One reason that DNAs importance was overlooked was that its chemical structure appeared too simple to account for the many complex tasks it would have to perform. However, in the 1940s, Oswald Avery, a research physician at the Rockefeller Institute, produced evidence, overlooked at the time, that DNA did play the critical role in genetic transmission (Borek, 1973). But how?

Eight years after the discovery of DNA as the basic genetic material, Nobel prizewinners Watson and Crick (1953) deduced that DNA is composed of not one but two molecular chains coiled around each other to form a double-stranded helix. Perhaps the simplest way to visualize this is to imagine a long rubber ladder, twisted around its long axis as shown in Figure 2.2. Alternating sugar and phosphate molecules form the legs of the ladder. The cross steps are made up of the nitrogenous bases. Most important, the nitrogenous bases from the two strands, which are held together by hydrogen bonds, are always paired in a special way. By knowing the order of the nitrogenous bases in one strand, we can determine the order in the other. Only the permutations of the four bases are variable (Borek, 1973; Moore, 1982).

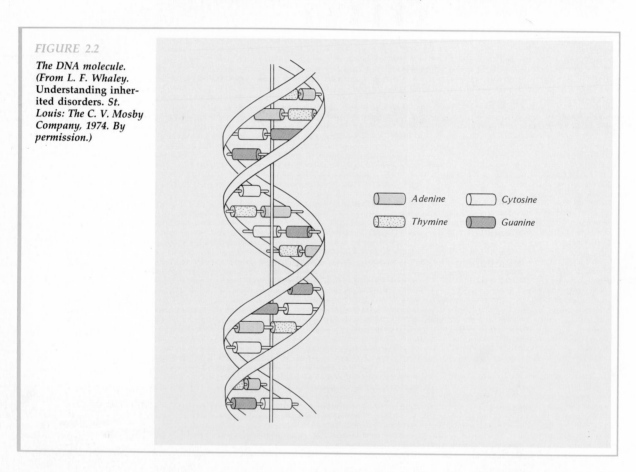

FIGURE 2.2

The DNA molecule. (From L. F. Whaley. Understanding inherited disorders. St. Louis: The C. V. Mosby Company, 1974. By permission.)

Adenine   Cytosine

Thymine   Guanine

Replication of DNA   When DNA reproduces itself, the original strands first separate at the hydrogen bonds to form two separate single strands, much in the manner of a zipper. Bases from a pool of free nucleotides in the cell nucleus attach themselves to the appropriate bases in the chain to form a complementary chain. "The result is that two new chains are constructed along the original chains to form two new helixes, each chemically identical to the helix from which it was derived. [See Figure 2.3.] When cells divide in this way the genetic information is preserved and transmitted unchanged to the daughter cells" (Whaley, 1974, p. 18). DNA in each of us today is "a direct, continuing descendant of DNAs which existed millions of years ago" (Borek, 1973, p. 23).

FIGURE 2.3

DNA replication: (a) Portion of one DNA molecule. (b) The two strands separate at the hydrogen bonds, and free bases attach to the appropriate base in the original strand. (c) Two new DNA molecules, each identical to the original molecule. (From L. F. Whaley. Understanding inherited disorders. St. Louis: The C. V. Mosby Company, 1974. By permission.)

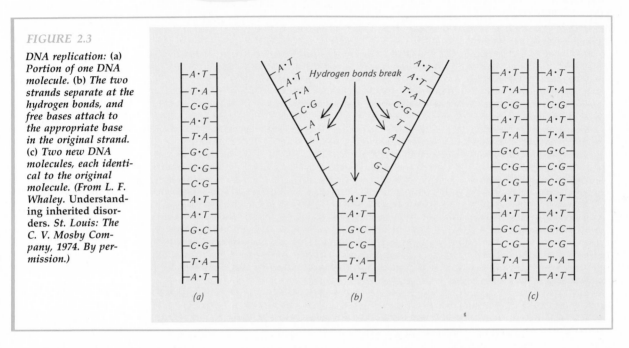

The mechanisms of hereditary transmission

One of the things that must have puzzled parents in prescientific days was why two children of the same parents are often so different physically. The answer lies in the mechanics of hereditary transmission.

If each child received all of both parents' genes, we could not explain individual genetic differences between siblings, as all brothers and sisters would then have identical heredities. The fact, however, is that each child inherits only half of each parent's genes. Moreover, different children in a family inherit different combinations of their mother's and father's genes. Thus, individual differences between them are not only possible but inevitable.

The way in which this happens will become clear as we proceed. Recall that the original fertilized ovum contains 46 chromosomes. As this cell divides to form two new cells through a process known as *mitosis*, each of its 46 chromosomes first doubles. Then each doubled chromosome divides in half by separating lengthwise down its center (see Figure 2.4). The chromosomes go to opposite sides of the cell. Thus, when the cell itself divides down the center, the new cells will each contain 46 chromosomes, as did the original cell.

Germ cells But if this is true, why don't the sperm and ovum that combine to make up a new individual also contain 46 chromosomes each, because cer-

FIGURE 2.4

Mitosis: How a fertilized ovum multiplies. (Adapted from R. Rugh & L. B. Shettles. From conception to birth: The drama of life's beginnings. *New York: Harper & Row, 1971. By permission.)*

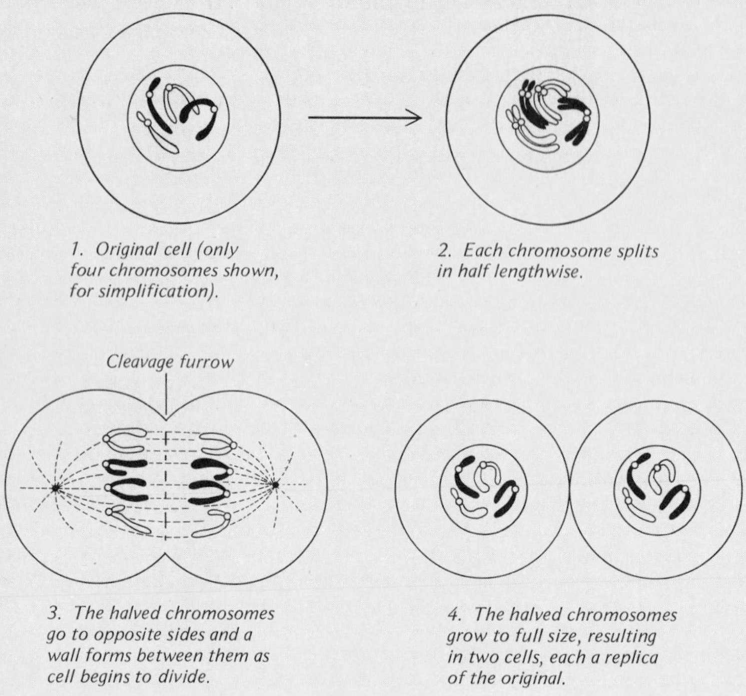

1. Original cell (only four chromosomes shown, for simplification).

2. Each chromosome splits in half lengthwise.

Cleavage furrow

3. The halved chromosomes go to opposite sides and a wall forms between them as cell begins to divide.

4. The halved chromosomes grow to full size, resulting in two cells, each a replica of the original.

tainly they too are cells? Recall that the new individual receives only 23 chromosomes from each parent.

The answer, stripped of genetic complexities, is actually simple. The adult organism contains not one but two kinds of cells: body cells, which make up bones, nerves, muscles, and organs, and germ cells, from which the sperm and ova are derived. While the process of chromosome and cell division described earlier applies to the *somatoplasm* (the body cells), it does not apply completely to the germ cells. Throughout most of their history, the latter develop just as the body cells do. But prior to their division into recognizable sperm or ova, the pattern changes. At this point, a two-step process called *meiosis* (from the Greek word meaning "to make smaller") results in cells whose nuclei each contain only half the number of chromosomes (23) in the parent cell (Moore, 1982; Whaley, 1974) (see Figure 2.5). In the male, during each division, the essential living matter of the cell that surrounds the nucleus (*cytoplasm*) itself divides equally, permitting the new cells to remain viable, so that ultimately four active sperm result from each original parent cell. Of course, in the male such cells are constantly being mass-produced, resulting in the release of millions of sperm in each mating. In fact, a number of sperm equal to the present population of the earth could be produced from six or seven ejaculations.

In the female, in contrast to the male, during meiosis there is unequal division of the cytoplasm. The result is that each division results in only one

FIGURE 2.5

How male and female germ cells are produced. (a) Spermatogenesis results in four spermatozoa (sperm). (b) Oogenesis results in only one ovum. (From L. F. Whaley. **Understanding inherited disorders.** St. Louis: The C. V. Mosby Company, 1974. By permission.)

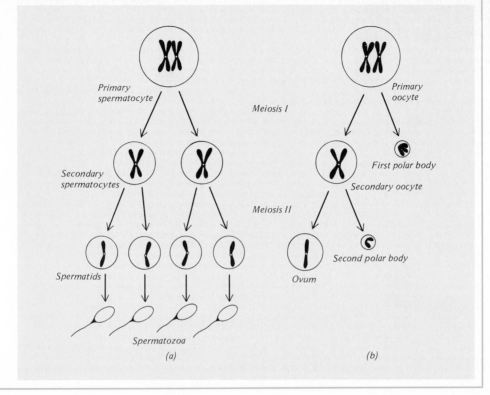

viable cell; the other, undernourished cell (called the *polar body*) quickly disintegrates. Consequently, the end product of meiosis is only one viable ovum or egg. Although a million or two primordial egg cells are already formed in the female's ovaries at the time of birth, normally only one ovum is produced and released each month.

Because each final sperm or ovum contains only half the chromosomes of the original parent cell, we can see why children of the same parents do not all have to be alike. As may be seen from Figure 2.6, if sperm A unites with ovum D, the new individual will possess a different set of chromosomes than if sperm B unites with it. (Ovum C is indicated in dotted lines because, as we have noted, ordinarily at any one conception only one ovum from the mother is ready for fertilization).

Is identity possible? We have seen how it is possible for individuals in the same family to be different in their genetic makeup. But is identity between siblings possible? The answer is no, except in the case of identical twins, who develop from a single fertilized ovum. If the 46 chromosomes in the germ cells divided the same way, with one combination going to one sperm or ovum and the rest to the other, identity would be possible; in fact, it could be anticipated frequently. But these 46 chromosomes do not divide in this way. Except for the fact that one half of each of the 23 pairs goes to one sperm or ovum and the other half to the other, the pattern is pretty much random. In other words, the way

FIGURE 2.6

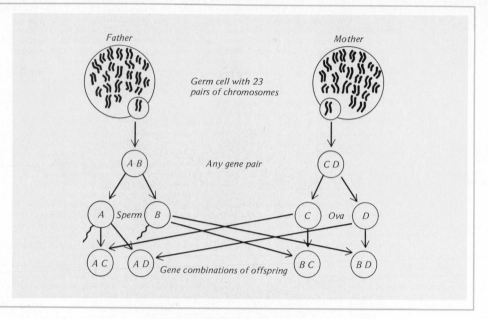

one pair of chromosomes separates does not influence the way another pair will split.

Moreover, in the formation of the germ cells (the sperm or ova) there is a process called *crossing-over* that further increases the likelihood that each sperm or ovum will be unique and, therefore, that each individual will be unique (Scarr & Kidd, 1983). When the 23 pairs of chromosomes line up in pairs during meiosis (one set from the father and one from the mother), they can exchange blocks of corresponding genetic material much as if human beings facing each other were to exchange parts of their fingers. One part of one half of the pair exchanges some DNA with the other. The likelihood that two genes will be exchanged together depends on how close to each other the gene sites are along the length of a chromosome. Those that are close to each other will usually be inherited together, while those at opposite ends of one of the larger chromo-somes are likely to be inherited independently (Scarr & Kidd, 1983).

If crossing-over did not occur, the total number of different combinations of sperm and ovum from one mother and father would be estimated at 64 bil-lion. Thus, one pair of parents could produce many more different kinds of children than the total number of people on the earth today. But with crossing-over, the number of possible different offspring is many, many times that number. Except for identical twins, then, each human being is genetically unique and biologically different from every other person on earth.

Sex determination   As we saw in Figure 2.1, one of the 23 pairs of chromosomes is called the *sex chromosomes* and determines the sex of the child. In the normal female, both members of this pair are large in size and are called the *X chromo-somes*. In the normal male, one member of the pair is an X chromosome; the second member is smaller in size and is called the *Y chromosome*. Thus, the body cells of males (except for sperm cells) contain one X and one Y chromosome.

One-half of the sperm cells of the male contain an X chromosome; the remaining half contain a Y chromosome. When a female ovum containing an X chromosome unites with a sperm containing a Y chromosome at conception, a male child is produced. When an ovum unites with a sperm carrying an X chromosome, a female child develops. Since one-half of the sperm cells contain X and one-half Y chromosomes, theoretically the odds are 50:50 that a boy or girl will be conceived. There is actually a slight excess of male over female births (106 boys to 100 girls among whites in the United States), and this may mean that Y sperm are more likely than X sperm to penetrate the ovum (Falkner & Tanner, 1978a; Moore, 1982).

DETERMINING THE EXTENT OF GENETIC INFLUENCES

Some of the ways in which genetic influences affect development are relatively simple and well understood, even though at times the effects may be profound. If a brown-eyed man and a blue-eyed woman have children, the likelihood is that at least half their children will have brown eyes. This is because the gene for brown eye color is more effective than the gene for blue eye color. When the two are paired, it will be *dominant,* while the gene for blue eye color will be *recessive*—that is, its effects will be masked. If the father happens to have two brown-eyed genes rather than one for brown eyes and one for blue, then all the couple's children will receive one brown-eyed gene and all will have brown eyes. If, however, the father has one blue eye-color gene, then half the children will probably have blue eyes. Huntington's chorea—a degenerative disease of the central nervous system that usually has its onset around age 35—is similarly dependent on the action of a single dominant gene. Consequently, the child of a parent with this disease will have a 50 percent chance of inheriting it.

Phenylketonuria (PKU) is a disorder caused by the presence of a particular pair of recessive genes. It provides a good example of the kind of knowledge that we need, but frequently lack, about the relation between genetic inheritance and behavioral characteristics. Many of the foods we eat contain a chemical called *phenylalanine.* Most people possess an enzyme that converts phenylalanine to a harmless by-product. However, a small number of children are born without the enzyme that converts the phenylalanine; they lack a gene that produces this critical enzyme. As a result, the concentration of phenylalanine rises above that which is normal, and the chemical is converted to phenylpyruvic acid. The nerve cells of the central nervous system become damaged, and mental retardation results. Once scientists learned the nature of the specific metabolic disorder in PKU, they began to think about ways of helping these children. They devised a diet that was nutritious but contained very low levels of phenylalanine. When children with PKU followed this diet, the toxic acid did not accumulate and their mental development was almost normal. Knowledge of the exact biological mechanism that mediates a genetic defect can occasionally lead to effective cures.

In other instances, clearly identifiable deviations from the usual number of chromosomes may affect development. For example, in some conditions, a male may have several X chromosomes (e.g., XXY, XXXXY) or several Y chromosomes (e.g., XYY) rather than the normal XY pattern. Extra autosomal chromosomes can also occur, typically with adverse effects on development.

Such relatively simple genetic models are, however, more the exception than the rule in human behavioral genetics. Most behavioral traits are multifactorial—that is, they depend on more than one genetic or environmental factor (Scarr & Kidd, 1983). At the genetic level, a particular characteristic may require the presence of a number of genes *(polygenetic inheritance)*. While progress is currently being made in identifying the genes (and their chromosomal locations) that affect polygenic, multifactorial characteristics, this often is not possible. For estimates of the role of genetic factors, we must still rely largely on incidence patterns among individuals who are genetically related to one another to varying degrees and who have been exposed to similar or different environmental influences. As we shall see in subsequent sections, a variety of techniques have been employed, including "pedigree" studies of incidence within individual families, adoption studies, and studies comparing *monozygotic* ("identical") twins and *dyzygotic* (nonidentical or "fraternal") twins.

Physical features

Our physical features depend heavily on heredity. The color of our eyes, the pigmentation of our skin, and the color and curliness of our hair are typically a function of the genes we inherit. Some features, such as eye color, depend upon fairly simple combinations of genes. Others, such as skin color, are more complex and involve many sets of genes acting together.

For the most part, variations in physical features within the American population bear little relation to an individual's biological ability to adapt to the demands of living. A person with brown eyes can see as well as one with blue. One with fair skin may have greater difficulty with sunburn than one whose skin has more pigment to protect it, but the difference is of minimal importance in terms of physical survival. The principal effects of variation in physical features upon the individual's adjustment are not biological in the sense of affecting physical adaptation to the environment. Instead, they are social and psychological. People do not always treat a person with black or brown skin the way they treat one with white skin. Similarly, children and adolescents whose appearance conforms to current social stereotypes of physical attractiveness are likely to be favored by their peers.

Intelligence

To what extent are the kinds of abilities measured by intelligence tests influenced by heredity? The topic is a controversial one, and discussions of it are frequently characterized by a good deal more heat than light. Some authorities assert that genetic influences play a dominant role in determining intellectual abilities; others claim that evidence for such an assertion is at most slight. How can these conflicting views be resolved?

If genetic factors do play a significant role in determining an individual's intellectual abilities, we would expect to find that a child's or adolescent's IQ is more highly correlated with the IQs of parents and other immediate relatives than with those of randomly selected nonrelatives. This is indeed the case. Unfortunately for investigators, however, the matter is not so simple. Parents who may have provided their children with a superior genetic endowment may be providing them with other advantages that are also related to intellectual ability, such as good health, a stimulating home environment, and superior educational opportunities. Thus, if we are to isolate the potential contributions of heredity, we must find a way to control the potential effects of other variables.

Twin studies Investigation of the effects of heredity on intellectual ability is greatly aided by comparing *monozygotic* (identical) twins with ordinary brothers and sisters and with *dizygotic* (nonidentical, or fraternal) twins. The latter are no more alike genetically than ordinary siblings, although they are more likely to have been subjected to similar experiences, having been conceived and born at the same time. They need not be of the same sex, nor do they necessarily resemble each other. If genetic influences play an important role in the determination of intellectual ability, we would expect the IQs of monozygotic twins to be more highly correlated or more similar to one another than those of dizygotic twins or nontwin siblings.

This turns out to be true (Scarr & Kidd, 1983). In a recent review of more than 200 studies comparing the intelligence and abilities of monozygotic (MZ) and dizygotic (DZ) twins of the same sex, Robert Nichols (1978) found an average correlation of .82 for monozygotic twins and .59 for dyzygotic twins. The correlation for dizygotic twins is approximately the same as that for nontwin siblings reared in the same family. Both of these, in turn, are substantially higher than the correlation for unrelated individuals reared in the same family (Scarr & Kidd, 1983; Wilson, 1977, 1983).

One fascinating investigation has found that even the patterns of developmental change at early ages may have a genetic component (Wilson, 1972, 1983; Wilson & Harpring, 1972). Repeated measurements of mental and motor development were conducted during the first two years of life using techniques described more fully in Chapter 3. When the scores of 261 monozygotic (MZ) and dizygotic (DZ) twins were analyzed, the profiles of the developmental

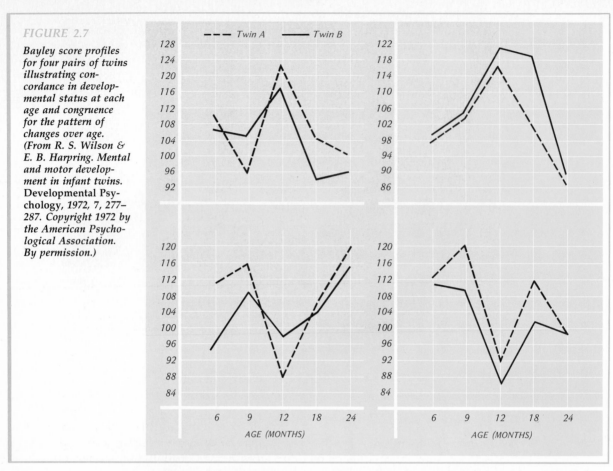

FIGURE 2.7

Bayley score profiles for four pairs of twins illustrating concordance in developmental status at each age and congruence for the pattern of changes over age. **(From R. S. Wilson & E. B. Harpring. Mental and motor development in infant twins. Developmental Psychology, 1972, 7, 277–287. Copyright 1972 by the American Psychological Association. By permission.)**

spurts and lags were very similar, especially for MZ twins (see Figure 2.7). Apparently, "the developmental sequence is an expression of timed gene action which may produce spurts or lags between ages" (Wilson & Harpring, 1972, p. 280). In a follow-up study of these same subjects during the preschool and school years, similar results were found; indeed, the mental developmental correlations between MZ twins rose slightly with increasing age, while those for DZ twins showed a significant decrease (Wilson, 1974, 1975, 1983).

While twin studies comparing monozygotic and dizygotic twins can be extremely valuable in the search for genetic influences, some qualifications are appropriate. For one thing, it is frequently assumed that monozygotic twins, because they have the same genetic makeup, are biologically identical at birth. This is not necessarily so. For example, one twin usually weighs slightly more than the other, perhaps because the two fetuses shared disproportionately in intrauterine blood circulation. It has been shown that even small differences between identical twins at birth can interact with the environment to produce larger differences in behavior (Smith, 1976). For example, if one identical twin is born slightly smaller and weaker than the other, this twin may be treated more protectively by the parents. Perhaps the child responds with dependence, setting off an escalating series of reciprocal interactions. To the extent this occurs, it should reduce rather than magnify differences between monozygotic and dizygotic twins.

Another inaccurate assumption is that the environmental influences to which DZ twins are exposed are as similar as those for MZ twins. It is true that both DZ and MZ twins grow up in the same family and share many common experiences. However, several studies have found that identical twins spend more time together, enjoy more similar reputations, and are more likely to be in the same classrooms, have more similar health records, and in many other respects share a more nearly identical physical and social environment than that ordinarily experienced by fraternal twins (Jones, 1946). MZ twins may also be treated more alike by parents and others than DZ twins, partly because they look alike and partly because their behavior is more alike to begin with (Lytton, 1977; Plomin, Willerman, & Loehlin, 1976; Scarr & Carter-Saltzman, 1979). Even in twin studies, then, the effects of environment cannot be fully controlled.

In a few studies an attempt has been made to avoid this problem by comparing identical twins reared apart with identical twins, fraternal twins, or other siblings reared together (Erlenmeyer-Kimling & Jarnik, 1963; Scarr & Kidd, 1983). In these instances, MZ twins are still found to be far more alike in IQ than DZ twins or siblings reared together. Not surprisingly, the correlation between MZ twins reared apart is somewhat smaller than it is for MZ twins reared together.

Adoption studies   Another useful way to investigate genetic influences on intelligence is to study children and adolescents raised from a very early age by adoptive parents and to compare their IQs with those of their biological and adoptive parents (DeFries & Plomin, 1978; Scarr & Kidd, 1983). Because these children have had little or no contact with their biological parents, any similarity to the biological parents is assumed to reflect genetic influences. The correlation between the IQs of children and adopted parents is assumed to indicate environmental influences. In a comprehensive analysis in 1975 of the best controlled investigations then available, it was found that when all subjects from these studies were combined, a correlation of .19 was obtained between adoptive parents' intelligence test scores (obtained by averaging mother's and father's scores) and those of their adopted children (Munsinger, 1975). In contrast, the correlation between these children's scores and those of their biological parents was .48. Adopted children are also sometimes compared to children raised by their own biological parents; parent-child similarities in the latter group represent both genetic and environmental contributions. The correlation between parents' and children's scores for children raised by their biological parents was .58, suggesting that both heredity *and* environment were important contributors (Munsinger, 1975). More recent adoption studies generally support these conclusions (Horn, 1983; Scarr & Weinberg, 1976, 1978, 1983; Scarr & Yee, 1980).

In summary, similarities in IQ are highest between persons most closely related genetically (i.e., monozygotic twins) and lowest between those who are unrelated. It seems clear that an individual's genetic inheritance is one important determinant of IQ. However, there are also similarities between adoptive parents and their adopted children. Although some of these similarities could be due to selective placement by adoption agencies of children whose biological parents are bright or well educated with bright adoptive parents, they also reflect the importance of the home environment (Scarr & Kidd, 1983; Munsinger, 1975; Willerman, 1979). Environmental as well as genetic factors are important in raising or lowering a child's level of intellectual performance, as we shall see in Chapter 8. Of course, environmental forces are effective only within the ultimate limits set by heredity.

Mental retardation

There are more than 150 known gene defects that may result in mental retardation, although fortunately most occur rarely (Scarr & Kidd, 1983). In some instances, as in the case of PKU, genes fail to give directions to produce enzymes needed for normal development, or they may code for incorrect enzymes. In other instances, abnormalities in the structure of the chromosomes may be responsible for mental retardation. These abnormalities may occur in either the *autosomes* or the *sex chromosomes*. A good example of the former is *Down's syndrome* (mongolism), a form of mental retardation that results from the presence of an extra chromosome at the twenty-first pair of autosomes (a normal pair is shown in Figure 2.1). Children with this disorder are born with an Oriental cast to their facial appearance and may have eye, heart, and other developmental defects. Most have IQs in the 25 to 45 range, though a few have IQs as high as 70, and about 4 percent can read. Generally, they are cheerful, have a faculty for mimicry, and enjoy music (Kopp & Parmelee, 1979; Reed, 1975; Scarr & Kidd, 1983).

Aberrant numbers of sex chromosomes are *sometimes* associated with behavioral problems and retarded intellectual development. For example, in *Klinefelter's syndrome,* which results from an excessive number of X chromosomes in males (e.g., XXY or XXXXY, rather than the normal XY), secondary masculine characteristics fail to develop at puberty, and there may be breast enlargement. Administration of androgen (male hormone) promotes development of male secondary sex characteristics, but the boy remains sterile. Boys with Klinefelter's syndrome are more likely than their peers to have behavioral problems and retarded intellectual development (Reed, 1975; Scarr & Kidd, 1983).

It should be kept in mind that there are many nongenetic causes of mental retardation, including radiation, drugs, disease, injury, and environmental deprivation. Furthermore, in many instances of retardation no specific genetic defects can be identified even though family histories suggest that hereditary influences are likely.

Mental disorders

The role of genetic factors in the development of mental disorders has been a source of considerable controversy. It has been established that certain disorders, such as general paresis (advanced syphilis, which damages the central nervous system) are caused by infection. Others, such as toxic psychosis, may be caused by the ingestion of various drugs or poisons. The agents responsible for these disorders come from outside the person; they are physiological but not genetic. Some other rather rare forms of mental disorder (such as Huntington's chorea) are known to result from specific, clearly identifiable genetic defects.

There has been considerably less agreement—especially until recently—regarding the role of genetic influences in schizophrenia and the affective (depressive) disorders. One reason is that unless we are able to isolate the specific genetic mechanisms by which a disorder (or vulnerability to a disorder) is transmitted or identify the biochemical processes involved, we must rely primarily on statistical studies of familial incidence. And despite substantial recent progress, neither the genetic mechanisms nor the biochemical processes that may be involved in schizophrenia or the affective disorders have been definitively established. In studies of familial incidence, it is necessary to devise methodological and statistical techniques for separating potential environmental influences from genetic influences. Simple studies, such as those showing that schizophrenic parents have more schizophrenic children than do normal parents, are not conclusive. Recently, however, more sophisticated studies have been conducted.

Schizophrenia   Schizophrenia, the most common form of major mental disorder, is characterized by severe defects in logical thinking and emotional responsiveness. Some schizophrenics suffer from delusions, and many display so-called inappropriate affect (laughing or crying when the circumstances do not call for it, for example). Schizophrenic behavior probably comes closest to the average person's idea of what it means to be "crazy." Several generations ago, informed opinion held that traumatic experiences in childhood were the major determinant of schizophrenia. However, recent research suggests that biological and hereditary factors frequently play a significant role (Kessler, 1975, 1980; O'Rourke, Gottesman, Suarez, Rice, & Reich, 1981; Scarr & Kidd, 1983).

In a number of studies, the incidence of this disorder (or, perhaps, set of disorders with similar symptoms) among the relatives of schizophrenics has been shown to vary with how closely they are related biologically (Gottesman & Shields, 1966; Kessler, 1980; Rosenthal, Wender, Schulsinger, & Jacobsen, 1975). For example, schizophrenia occurs more frequently in the children of schizophrenics than in their nieces and nephews. More critically, from the point of view of separating genetic form from environmental influences, several well-controlled investigations have found that if one identical twin has schizophrenia, the chances are about 1 in 2 that the other twin will also develop it (O'Rourke et al., 1981). But if one nonidentical (dizygotic) twin has schizophrenia, the chances of the other twin also developing it are less than 1 in 10 (Kessler, 1975, 1980; Rosenthal, 1970). Studies of identical twins reared apart also suggest that genetic factors play a role in at least a significant percentage of cases of schizophrenia, although the number of cases to date is too small to be conclusive (DeFries & Plomin, 1978; Scarr & Kidd, 1983).

Even more compelling evidence of a genetic contribution to schizophrenia comes from studies of adopted children (Kessler, 1980; Kety et al., 1975). In an extensive study in Denmark, two groups of children who had been adopted early in life were studied after they had reached adulthood. One group consisted of individuals who had become schizophrenic in the course of their development. The other was a control group matched for age, sex, age at adoption, and socioeconomic status of the adopting family. The incidence of schizophrenia was then examined among both the biological and adoptive relatives (parents, siblings, and half-sibs) of each group. There was no significant difference in the prevalence of schizophrenic disorders among the adoptive relatives of the two groups. However, schizophrenia occurred at a rate almost six times higher among the biological relatives (11 percent) of schizophrenics than among their adoptive relatives (about 2 percent). In the control group there was no significant difference in the incidence of schizophrenia between biological and adoptive relatives.

Note that having close biological relatives with schizophrenia does not mean that one is likely to develop this disorder; indeed, as the above figures indicate, it is *unlikely*. There may be a variety of reasons for this. In the first place, except in the case of identical twins, relatives do not share all of the same genes. Second, the disorder called schizophrenia may in fact be a number of different disorders with similar symptoms (Matthysse, 1978; Scarr & Kidd, 1983). In recent reanalyses of the Danish study just described, Seymour Kety and his colleagues reclassified the schizophrenic subjects into three groups: chronic schizophrenics, "latent" schizophrenics (those without full-blown symptoms), and "acute" schizophrenics (those who have schizophrenic episodes, usually of fairly brief duration, preceded and followed by adequate functioning). They are finding that few, if any, of the biological relatives of the acute group were schizophrenic; in contrast, the chronic schizophrenic subjects show the highest rate of schizophrenic relatives. Those classified as latent occupy an intermediate position (Kety et al., 1975; Kety, Rosenthal, Wender, Schulsinger, & Jacobsen, 1978).

Third, unlike, for example, Huntington's chorea (which is produced by a single dominant gene), an adequate genetic model for schizophrenia does not exist. Neither a single gene nor a "polygenic" model (representing a complex combination of interacting genes) currently appears adequate to predict the occurrence of schizophrenia (Scarr & Kidd, 1983).

All in all, it may be more correct to speak of inheriting an increased *vulnerability to schizophrenia* than of inheriting schizophrenia per se. In that case, whether or not the disorder is precipitated would depend on two factors: how vulnerable a particular individual is and how much or what kind of stress the person is subjected to. Lung cancer might serve as an appropriate analogy. One person may have a greater likelihood than another of developing this disease because of a greater genetic susceptibility to cancer. But if this person smokes cigarettes, the chances of developing lung cancer are greatly increased. Similarly, certain life experiences may increase the chances that a person with a genetic susceptibility to schizophrenia will actually develop it.

Depression   As commonly employed, the term *depression* is primarily descriptive and refers to a wide variety of conditions in which a *depressed mood* is present. Such conditions may range from occasional minor bouts of "the blues" through acute grief reactions following the death of a child or marriage partner to severe disturbances in psychological functioning, as in the case of a depressive psychosis. In many forms of depression, particularly those that are relatively minor and transient, psychological and social factors obviously play the principal etiological (causative) role. In such conditions, the depressed feelings may be expected to recede when the problems that have brought them about—school failure, loss of a job, disappointment in love, death of a friend—are somehow resolved or worked through. In the case of severe depressive (affective) disorders, however, genetic factors, mediated by biochemical processes (which often respond favorably to antidepressant drugs) appear to play a significant role (Davis, 1978; Klerman, 1978; Scarr & Kidd, 1983).

Severe affective illnesses are not all alike, and genetic factors play different roles from one to another. The strongest evidence to date for this view comes from comparative studies of patients who suffer periods of both manic excitement and depression (*bipolar disorder*) and those who suffer from serious depression only (*unipolar depression*).

Of the major mental disorders, bipolar disorder appears to have the strongest genetic component. If one identical twin has bipolar disorder, the chances are 3 out of 4 (74 percent) that the other twin will also suffer from this disorder (Kessler, 1975; Klerman, 1978). In the case of nonidentical twins, the chances of the other twin also developing bipolar disorder are less than 1 in 4 (23 percent). While sample sizes are still inadequate, studies of identical twins reared apart show a relatively high incidence of bipolar disorder in the twins of individuals who have developed it. The incidence is not as high as for identical-twin siblings reared with the patient, however. Genetic factors also appear to play a role, though not as strong a one, in unipolar depression. This disorder is far more common, but less well defined, than manic-depressive illness (bipolar disorder). In one study of monozygotic (identical) twins reared apart, it was found that if one twin had unipolar depression, the chances were greater than 2 in 5 that the other member of the twin pair also suffered from the disorder. Among dizygotic (nonidentical) twins, the comparable figure was 29 percent (Winokur, 1975).

As with schizophrenia, even the identical twin of a person with bipolar disorder does not necessarily develop the disorder. Despite an apparently strong genetic influence, then, psychological stress or its absence may play an important role. There are also individuals who develop depressive disorders in the apparent absence of family histories of disturbance. It may be relevant that stress itself has been found to produce measurable changes in the levels of certain chemicals in the brain (such as norepinephrine) similar to those found in patients with depressive illness (Bunney & Davis, 1965; Davis, 1978; Fawcett, 1975).

Personality characteristics

Investigating the role of genetic factors in determining personality characteristics presents special problems. Unlike some kinds of physical traits, mental disorders, or retardation, in which the characteristics to be studied are specific and clearly defined, personality characteristics can be somewhat difficult to define and measure. Unlike biological factors, such as the absence of a specific enzyme in phenylketonuria, personality characteristics are rarely all-or-nothing phenomena. Friendliness, impulsiveness, apathy, aggressiveness, shyness are present in different individuals in different degrees and blends. Nevertheless, progress is being made, most clearly through studies of monozygotic and dizygotic twins (Scarr & Kidd, 1983).

In general, it appears that genetic influences are strongest on basic temperamental characteristics (e.g., active-passive, impulsive-reflective) that tend to be relatively stable during development and weakest on characteristics highly dependent on learning and social experience (e.g., ethical and social values, objectivity).

Studies of infants reveal that MZ (identical) twins are more alike than DZ (fraternal) twins in their responses to strangers, including smiling, playing, cuddling, and expressions of fear (Freedman, 1965; Plomin, 1983; Scarr & Kidd, 1983). Identical twin babies also appear more alike in frequency of displays of temper, demands for attention, and amount of crying (Wilson & Harpring, 1972).

At any one time, from infancy to adolescence, MZ twins resemble each other significantly more than DZ twins on many temperamental traits, including activity, attention, task persistence, irritability, emotionality, sociability, and impulsiveness (Goldsmith, 1983; Matheny, 1983; Torgeson & Kringlen, 1978). Significant differences between MZ and DZ twins have also been found on such personality characteristics as introversion-extraversion and neuroticism (Floderus-Myrhed, Pederson, & Rasmuson, 1980; Matheny, 1983; Scarr & Kidd, 1983).

Although these studies do suggest that temperament is to some extent a genetic matter, it should be kept in mind that virtually all personality characteristics are influenced by both genetics and environment. Further, genetic predispositions can frequently be "overridden" by environmental influences. Naturally shy persons can often be helped to become more assertive, and punitive experiences can lead exuberant extraverts (both human and animal) to become hesitant or withdrawn.

*PRENATAL
DEVELOPMENT*

*Conception
and earliest
development*

It is a rather curious fact that while we recognize that development begins at conception, we reckon a person's age from the moment of birth. It almost seems that we regard the events prior to birth as unimportant. Yet the environment in which the unborn child grows has a tremendous influence on later development, both physical and psychological.

Conception occurs when a sperm from the male penetrates the cell wall of an ovum, or egg, from the female. The occasions on which this is possible are strictly limited physiologically and are quite independent of the vagaries of human impulse. Figure 2.8 shows a schematic diagram of the female reproductive system. Once every 28 days (usually around the middle of the menstrual cycle) an ovum ripens in one of the two ovaries, is discharged into the corresponding fallopian tube, or oviduct, and begins its slow journey toward the uterus, propelled by small, hairlike cilia that line the tube. In most cases, it takes from 3 to 7 days for the ovum to reach the uterus. If the ovum has not been fertilized in the course of this journey, it disintegrates in the uterus after a few days, and its remains, which are smaller than a grain of dust, disperse unnoticed.

If, on the other hand, a mating has taken place, one of the many millions of tiny sperm released by the male may find its way up into the oviduct during the time the ovum is making its descent. There, if it unites with the ovum, a new individual is conceived.

FIGURE 2.8

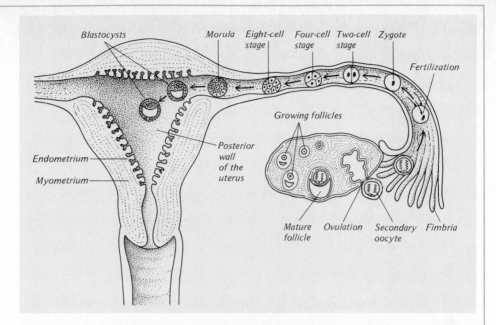

Diagrammatic summary of the ovarian cycle, fertilization, and human development during the first week. Developmental stage 1 begins with the zygote forms. Stage 2 (days 2 to 3) comprises the early stages of cleavage (from 2 to about 16 cells, or the morula). Stage 3 (days 4 to 5) consists of the free, unattached blastocyst. In stage 4 (days 5 to 6), the blastocyst attaches to the center of the posterior wall of the uterus, the usual site of implantation. (From K. L. Moore. **The developing human: Clinically oriented embryology** [3rd ed.]. *Philadelphia: W. B. Saunders, 1982. By permission.*)

As indicated earlier, each sperm is a tadpolelike cell. The oval head of the sperm is packed with the 23 chromosomes. Behind the head are special structures that supply the energy the sperm cell needs to travel the distance to reach the ovum. It is estimated that the sperm travels at a velocity of about $\frac{1}{10}$ inch per minute.

At the moment of conception, the ovum, the largest cell in the human body, is still very small, only about $\frac{1}{175}$ inch in diameter. When the sperm enters the ovum, a process is initiated that results in the fusing of the nucleus of the sperm with the nucleus of the ovum. Consequently, the fertilized ovum, called a *zygote*, contains 23 pairs of chromosomes. As explained earlier, these 46 chromosomes contain all the new individual's heredity. The zygote immediately begins to grow and subdivide through the process of mitosis, and development has begun. The time from the sperm's penetration of the ovum to the development of the first two cells usually is between 24 and 36 hours.

The time from conception to birth is usually divided into three phases. The first phase, called the *period of the ovum*, lasts from fertilization until implantation, the time when the many-celled zygote, now called a *blastocyst*, becomes firmly attached to the wall of the uterus. This period is about 10 to 14 days long.

FIGURE 2.9

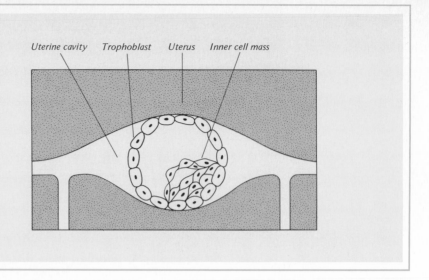

Uterine cavity   Trophoblast   Uterus   Inner cell mass

The second phase, from 2 to 8 weeks, is called the *period of the embryo.* This period is characterized by cell differentiation as all the major organs begin to develop. The last phase, from 8 weeks until delivery (normally at around 40 weeks), is called the *period of the fetus* and is characterized mainly by growth rather than by the formation of new organs.

The period of the ovum

The fertilized ovum continues to double its cells during its journey from the oviduct, where it was fertilized, to the uterus, where it will become implanted. By the time the fertilized ovum reaches the uterus, it is about the size of a pinhead and has several dozen cells. A small cavity is formed within the mass of cells, resulting in an outer and a separated inner cluster of cells (see Figure 2.9). The outer layer, called the *trophoblast*, will ultimately develop into accessory tissues that protect and nourish the embryo. The inner cluster of cells will become the embryo itself.

While these developments are taking place, small burrlike tendrils have begun to grow around the outside of the trophoblast. In a few more days, these tendrils will attach the ovum to the uterine wall.

In the meantime, the uterus itself has begun to undergo changes in preparation for receiving the fertilized ovum. At the time of implantation, extensions of the tendrils from the trophoblast reach into blood spaces that have formed within the maternal tissue. At this time, the period of the ovum comes to an end, and the second phase of prenatal development, the period of the embryo, begins. The new individual has ceased to be an independent, free-floating organism and has established a dependent relationship with the mother.

The period of the embryo

Once the growing egg has been successfully lodged in its new home, development is rapid. Its inner cell mass, which will become a recognizable embryo, begins to differentiate itself into three distinct layers: (a) the *ectoderm* (outer layer), from which will develop the epidermis (outer layer of the skin), the hair, the nails, parts of the teeth, skin glands, sensory cells, and the nervous system; (b) the *mesoderm* (middle layer), from which will develop the dermis (inner skin layer), the muscles, the skeleton, and the circulatory and excretory organs; and (c) the *endoderm* (inner layer), from which will develop the lining of the entire gastrointestinal tract, the eustachian tubes, trachea, bronchia, lungs, liver, pancreas, salivary glands, thyroid glands, and thymus (Falkner & Tanner, 1978a; Nilsson, Furuhjelm, Ingelman-Sundberg, & Wirsen, 1981; Rugh & Shettles, 1971).

While the inner cell mass is being differentiated into a recognizable embryo, the outer layers of cells are giving rise to two fetal membranes, the *chorion* and the *amnion*. These, together with a third membrane derived from the uterine wall of the mother, extend from the wall of the uterus and enclose the developing embryo (see Figure 2.10). They form a sac filled with a watery fluid (amniotic fluid) that acts as a buffer to protect the embryo from shocks experienced by the mother. It also helps to provide an even temperature for the embryo and serves to prevent adhesions between the embryo and the amniotic membrane.

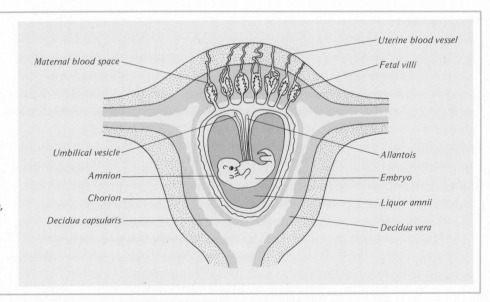

FIGURE 2.10

Diagram representing the relationship between the uterus, the membrane, and the embryo during early pregnancy. (From L. Carmichael. Origins and prenatal growth of behavior. In C. Murchinson [Ed.], A handbook of child psychology [2nd ed.]. Worcester, Mass.: Clark University Press, 1983, p. 50. By permission.)

Uterine blood vessel
Fetal villi
Maternal blood space
Umbilical vesicle
Amnion
Chorion
Decidua capsularis
Allantois
Embryo
Liquor amnii
Decidua vera

Simultaneously, other fetal sacs are formed, the most important of which becomes the umbilical cord. It extends from the embryo to the section of the uterine wall where the uterus and the chorion are joined. This area is called the *placenta.*

The umbilical cord is the lifeline of the embryo. Through it, two arteries carry blood from the embryo to the placenta, and a vein carries blood to the infant from the placenta. However, the relationship between the child's bloodstream and the mother's is not a direct one. Both the child's and the mother's bloodstreams open into the placenta. But the two systems are always separated by cell walls within the placenta. These cell walls consist of semipermeable membranes that function as extremely fine-mesh screens, large enough to permit the passage of gases, salts, and other substances of small molecular size but too small to allow blood cells to get through.

Although a precise knowledge of all the substances that pass through a normal placenta is lacking, it is known that various nutrient substances from the mother's blood—sugars, fats, and some protein elements—permeate it. Waste products from the infant, primarily carbon dioxide and other metabolites, can also pass through the placenta. In addition, some vitamins, drugs (including nicotine and alcohol), vaccines, and some disease germs (notably those of diphtheria, typhoid, influenza, and rubella) may also get through and affect the embryo's development. Hence, the health of the mother can directly affect the health of the fetus.

There are no direct neural connections between the maternal and embryonic nervous systems; only chemicals can cross the placental barrier. Nevertheless, a mother's emotional state may indirectly influence the physiological functioning of her child. When the mother is emotionally aroused, a variety of physiological reactions occur, and specific hormones such as adrenaline, are released into the mother's bloodstream. Some of these substances may pass through the placenta and affect the ongoing physiological processes in the unborn child (Apgar & Beck, 1974; Lubchenco, 1976).

Much of our knowledge of prenatal development has been derived from the intensive study of embryos and fetuses that for medical reasons had to be surgically removed from the uterus. Such studies show extremely rapid development during the period of the embryo. By the eighteenth day, the embryo has already begun to take some shape. It has established a longitudinal axis; its front, back, left and right sides, head, and tail are discernible. By the end of the third week, a primitive heart has developed and has begun to beat.

By 4 weeks, the embryo is about $\frac{1}{5}$ inch long. It has the beginnings of a mouth region, a gastrointestinal tract, and a liver. The heart is becoming well developed, and the head and brain regions are becoming more clearly differentiated. At this stage the embryo is still a very primitive organism. It has no arms or legs, no developed features, and only the most elementary of body systems.

By 8 to 9 weeks, the picture has changed markedly (see Figure 2.11). The embryo is now about 1 inch long. Face, mouth, eyes, and ears are fairly well defined. Arms and legs, hands and feet, even stubby fingers and toes have appeared. At this stage the sex organs are just beginning to form. The development of muscle and cartilage also begins, but well-defined neuromotor activity (activation of the muscles by impulses from the nerves) is still absent (Nilsson et al., 1981; Rugh & Shettles, 1971). The internal organs—intestines, liver, pancreas, lungs, kidneys—take on a definite shape and assume some degree of function. The liver, for example, begins to manufacture red blood cells.

The period of the embryo is characterized by an extremely rapid development of the nervous system. During this period the head is large in relation to other body areas. This suggests that the first 8 weeks constitute a sensitive period with respect to the integrity of the nervous system. Mechanical or chemical interference with development at this time (such as the mother falling down

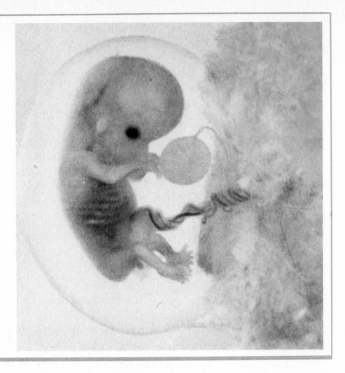

FIGURE 2.11

The human embryo at 8 weeks. The eye is seen as a dark-rimmed circle. (From R. Rugh & L. B. Shettles. **From conception to birth: The drama of life's beginnings.** *New York: Harper & Row, 1971. By permission.)*

stairs or taking an overdose of drugs) is more likely to cause permanent nervous-system damage than would a similar disruption at a later date. For example, if the mother should contract rubella (German measles) during this period, the child is more likely to be mentally deficient than if she were to have this illness during the last 8 weeks of pregnancy (Lubchenco, 1976).

The period of the fetus

The third period of prenatal development, the period of the fetus, extends from the end of the second month until birth. During this time, the various body systems, which have been laid down in rudimentary form earlier, become quite well developed and begin to function. Up until about $8\frac{1}{2}$ weeks, the fetus has led a relatively passive existence, floating quiescently in the amniotic fluid. At this time, however, it becomes capable of responding to tactile (touch) stimulation. The trunk flexes and the head extends. From this point on, motor functions become increasingly more differentiated and complex (Figure 2.12).

Toward the end of the eighth week, the reproductive system begins to develop. The gonads (the ovaries and the testes) initially appear as a pair of blocks of tissue in both sexes. Moreover, it appears that the hormones manufactured by the male's testes are necessary to stimulate the development of a male reproductive system. If the testes are removed or fail to perform properly, the baby that is born possesses a primarily female reproductive system. Evidence from rabbits indicates that if the tiny ovary is removed immediately after its formation, the female fetus develops normally. It appears, therefore, that the anatomy of the female reproductive system is basic; it is the form that will develop if either testes or ovaries are removed or do not function.

BOX 2.1

*Steps in
prenatal
development*

1 week	Fertilized ovum descends through fallopian tube toward uterus.
2 weeks	Embryo has attached itself to uterine lining and is developing rapidly.
3 weeks	Embryo has begun to take some shape; head and tail regions discernible. Primitive heart begins to beat.
4 weeks	Beginnings of mouth region, gastrointestinal tract, and liver. Heart is developing rapidly, and head and brain regions are becoming more clearly differentiated.
6 weeks	Hands and feet begin developing, but arms are still too short and stubby to meet. Liver is now producing blood cells.
8 weeks	Embryo is now about 1 inch long. Face, mouth, eyes, and ears have begun taking on fairly defined form. Development of muscle and cartilage has begun.
12 weeks	Fetus is about 3 inches long. It has begun to resemble a human being, though the head is disproportionately large. Face now has babylike profile. Eyelids and nails have begun to form, and sex can be distinguished easily. Nervous system still very primitive.
16 weeks	Fetus is about $4\frac{1}{2}$ inches long. The mother may be able to feel the fetus's movements. Extremities, head, and internal organs are developing rapidly. Body proportions are becoming more babylike.
5 months	Pregnancy half completed. Fetus is now about 6 inches long and is able to hear and move about quite freely. Hands and feet are already complete.
6 months	Fetus is about 10 inches long. Eyes are now completely formed, and taste buds appear on tongue. Fetus is now capable of inhaling and exhaling and of making a thin crying noise, should birth occur prematurely.
7 months	An important age. The fetus has now reached the "zone of viability" (having a chance to live if born prematurely). Fetus is physiologically capable of distinguishing basic tastes and odors. Pain sensitivity appears to be relatively absent. Breathing ability is still shallow and irregular, and sucking and swallowing ability are weak.
7 months to birth	Fetus becomes increasingly ready for independent life outside the womb. Muscle tone increases; movement becomes sustained and positive; breathing, swallowing, sucking, and hunger cry all become strong. Visual and auditory reactions are firmly established.

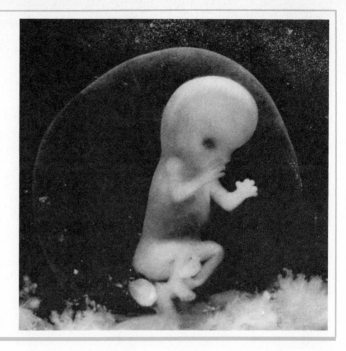

FIGURE 2.12

The human embryo at 10 weeks. Hands and fingers are now clear. (From R. Rugh & L. B. Shettles. From conception to birth: The drama of life's beginnings. *New York: Harper & Row, 1971. By permission.)*

By the end of 12 weeks, the fetus is about 3 inches long and weighs about $\frac{3}{4}$ ounce. It has definitely begun to resemble a human being, though the head is disproportionately large. Muscles are becoming well developed, and spontaneous movements of the arms and legs may be observed. Eyelids and nails have begun to form, and the fetus's sex can now be distinguished easily. The nervous system is still very incomplete, however. During the next 4 weeks, motor behavior becomes more complex.

By the end of 16 weeks, the mother can feel the fetus's movements (known popularly as "the quickening"). At this point the fetus is about $4\frac{1}{2}$ inches in length. In the period from 16 to 20 weeks, the fetus increases to about 10 inches in length and 8 or 9 ounces in weight (see Figure 2.13). It becomes more human-looking, and hair appears on the head and body. The mouth becomes capable of protrusion, as well as opening and closing, a precursor of later sucking movements. Blinking of the eyes occurs, although the lids are still tightly fused. The hands become capable of gripping in addition to closing.

After 20 weeks, the skin begins to assume adult form, hair and nails appear, and sweat glands are developed. By 24 weeks of age, the eyes are completely formed and taste buds appear on the tongue. The fetus is now capable of "true inspiration and expiration, and of a thin crying noise" if born prematurely (Gessell, 1945, p. 71).

The fetal age of 28 weeks is an important time. It demarcates the zone between viability (the ability to live if born) and nonviability. By this age, the child's nervous, circulatory, and other bodily systems have become sufficiently mature to stand a chance of functioning adequately in the extrauterine environment, although, of course, special care is required. At this point, reactions to

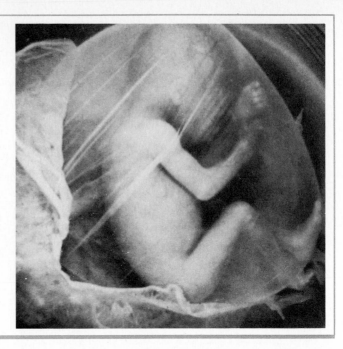

FIGURE 2.13

Human fetus at 16 weeks. *(From R. Rugh & L. B. Shettles. From conception to birth: The drama of life's beginnings. New York: Harper & Row, 1971. By permission.)*

changes in temperature approximate those of the full-term infant. Experimental studies of infants born at this age indicate that basic tastes such as sweet, salt, sour, and bitter can be differentiated by the fetus. So can basic odors. Visual and auditory reactions occur, though not as clearly as in the full-term infant. On the other hand, sensitivity to pain seems to be slight or absent in the premature infant.

The last 3 months   The period from 28 weeks to birth at full term (38 to 42 weeks) is marked by further development of the basic body structures and functions. Gains in body weight and height continue to be rapid. By 7 months, the average unborn baby weighs about 4 pounds and is 16 inches long. During the eighth month another $1\frac{1}{3}$ pounds and 2 inches will be added. "Much of the weight gain during these last three months comes from a padding of fat beneath the skin which will help to insulate the newborn baby from changes in temperature after his birth" (Apgar & Beck, 1974, p. 58).

Each additional week that the fetus remains within the mother's uterus increases the likelihood of survival and normal development. As muscle tone improves, a good hunger cry and a strong sucking reflex develop, and mental alertness and perceptual and motor development increase. By the time the unborn infant weighs $3\frac{1}{2}$ pounds, the chances of successful postnatal development are markedly improved; a baby born weighing at least 5 pounds will probably not need to be placed in an incubator (Apgar & Beck, 1974; Lubchenco, 1976).

By the beginning of the ninth month, the unborn baby, who once floated in weightless ease in the fluid of the amniotic sac, has grown so large that movement inside the uterus is quite constricted. Usually the fetus settles into a head-down position, because this provides the most room in the uterus, which is shaped like an inverted pear. Consequently, most babies are born head first, the easiest and safest way. However, about 10 percent of babies assume a feet-first position, requiring breech delivery. A few seem stubbornly to insist on maintaining a crosswise position and may require delivery by a cesarean section (Apgar & Beck, 1974). The average full-term baby is 20 to 21 inches long and weighs $7\frac{1}{2}$ pounds, but a wide range of heights and weights are "normal."

The "normal" or typical pattern of prenatal development just described can occur only when the organism and its environment fall within what might be thought of as normal limits. There are many variations in prenatal environment, and the pressures to which one fetus is subjected may differ greatly from those exerted on another. Recent research suggests that the mother's physical and emotional status and consequently the prenatal environment she provides have important influences on the course of fetal development and the subsequent health and adjustment of the child. Some of the more important prenatal environmental factors that have been investigated will be discussed in the following sections.

Age of the mother

With increasing numbers of adolescents becoming pregnant and of women in their thirties who want to begin having children, there has been a growing interest in the effects of age on fertility and on the health of infant and mother. To place the issue in proper perspective, it should be noted that the morbidity (disease or illness) and mortality risks at all ages have declined markedly in recent years. For example, in the United States, infant mortality has declined from 140 per 1000 live births at the turn of the century to 12.5 per 1000 today (Richmond, 1982). Approximately 14 countries in the world have better records than the United States, due to greater availability of proper health care and nutritional assistance for all infants and their mothers—this despite our wealth as a nation. With good medical care, proper health practices, and adequate nutrition, most women of all ages will have healthy babies and will remain healthy themselves.

Nevertheless, the years between 20 and 35 remain the most favorable for childbearing. As we shall see, pregnancies of adolescents are more likely than those of women in their twenties to endanger the physical health of both mother

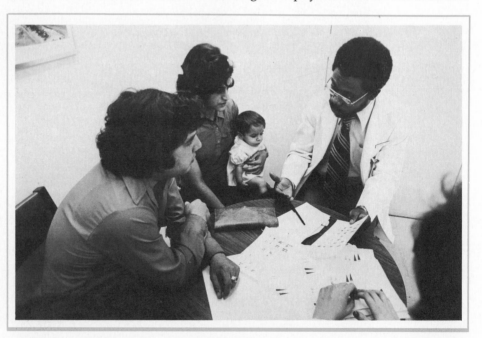

and child, although the risks are substantially reduced by adequate prenatal and postnatal care and good nutrition. Currently, babies of teenage mothers are more likely to have low birth weights, a major cause of infant mortality, as well as neurological defects and childhood illnesses. The mothers themselves are more likely to have complications of pregnancy such as toxemia and anemia. Among very young teenagers, pregnancy tends to deplete nutritional requirements needed for their own growth (Gunter & LaBarba, 1980; Planned Parenthood, 1976, 1981).

Women over 35 have a lower fertility rate than those in their twenties, and fertility continues to decline with age. They are also more likely than younger women to experience illnesses during pregnancy and longer and more difficult labor. Mothers over 40 run a greater risk of having a child with a chromosomal abnormality, particularly Down's syndrome. The average incidence of this disorder increases from 1.66 per 1000 at ages 30–34 to 3.22 at ages 35–39, 12.52 at 40–44, and 29.74 over age 45 (Hansen, 1978). Women over 35 are also more likely to have miscarriages and underweight or stillborn babies (Kopp & Parmelee, 1979; Lubchenco, 1976; Rubin, 1980). The older the woman, the greater the likelihood that these problems will arise, but the absolute incidence of serious complications is nevertheless relatively small, especially for those with good health practices and good medical care. In instances where there is reason to suspect the possibility of chromosomal or other abnormality, *amniocentesis* may be recommended (see Box 2.2).

Maternal nutrition

The expectant mother should have an adequate diet if she is going to maintain her own good health during pregnancy and deliver a healthy infant. This appears entirely reasonable when we remember that the growing fetus's food supply comes ultimately from the mother's bloodstream, via the semipermeable membranes of the placenta and the umbilical cord.

Women with nutritionally sound diets remain in better general health throughout pregnancy than those with inadequate diets. They also encounter fewer complications such as anemia, toxemia, threatened and actual miscarriages, premature births, prolonged labor, and stillbirths (Knoblock & Pasamanick, 1966; Kopp & Parmelee, 1979; Metcoff, 1978). Babies born to mothers with nutritionally deficient diets are more likely to have low birth weights, to suffer from impaired brain development with abnormal brain waves, to be less resistant to illnesses (such as pneumonia and bronchitis), and to have a higher mortality rate in the first year of life (Dobbing, 1974, Katz, Keusch, & Mata, 1975; Metcoff, 1978).

In one well-controlled study in Guatemala, the residents of two villages received nourishing supplemental diets for several years, while the residents of two similar (control) villages received soda pop supplements instead. Not only did infant mortality and morbidity go down and birth weight up in the nourished villages, but children from these villages scored somewhat better on mental tests, especially vocabulary scores, at the end of 7 years. Severe maternal malnutrition may impair the child's intellectual development, in addition to having adverse effects on physical development (Cravioto & DeLicardie, 1978; Katz et al., 1975; Lechtig, Habicht, Delgado, Klein, Yarbrough, & Martorell, 1975; Metcoff, 1978).

In amniocentesis, a fine, hollow needle is inserted through the lower part of the abdominal wall into the amniotic sac that surrounds and protects the fetus, and a small amount of amniotic fluid (about two-thirds of an ounce) is removed (see Figure B2.2). The procedure is usually done between 16 and 18 weeks after pregnancy has begun. Amniotic fluid contains fetal cells that have been sloughed off in the normal course of events, just as we shed cells when we peel after a sunburn. These cells are cultured in a cytogenetics laboratory, and a chromosome analysis is then done. Because each cell in the body contains a replication of all the 46 chromosomes that constitute our genetic inheritance, these cells can be examined for the presence of a number of chromosomal and metabolic disorders.

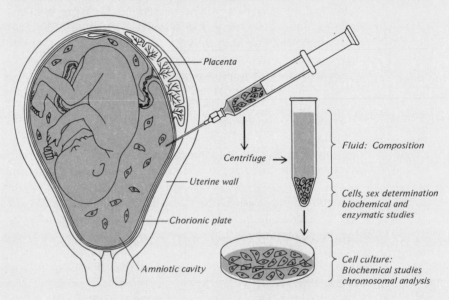

To date, over 75 different genetic diseases—many of them extremely rare—can be detected by amniocentesis, and the number is growing. Included are abnormalities in the *autosomal chromosomes*, as in Down's syndrome, and *sex-chromosome* abnormalities, where there is an excess number of X or Y chromosomes. Amniocentesis can also detect a number of *metabolic diseases* (inborn errors of body chemistry that result in faulty production of enzymes) through excretions that appear in the amniotic fluid. Some of these metabolic diseases, such as Tay-Sachs disease (which leads to mental retardation and early death at age 2 or 3), are concentrated in particular races, religions, or geographical areas because of selective mating over long periods of time.

A number of genetic disorders are sex-linked—that is, their genes are carried on a sex chromosome. For example, *hemophilia*, a defect in the ability of the blood to clot properly, is carried on the X chromosome.

The daughter of a woman who is a carrier of this disease will almost never have the disease, because it will be masked by the presence of a second, normal gene on her other X chromosome. Any sons, however, will have a 50 percent chance of developing the disease because they do not have a second X chromosome that can carry a normal gene to protect them. Because amniocentesis reveals the sex of the fetus, a mother who may be a carrier for hemophilia or other X-linked disorder can normally feel reassured if her unborn baby is a girl.

The risk from amniocentesis to mother and fetus is minimal. Harmless ultrasonic pictures (sonographs) are used to show the exact location of the baby and the placenta in the uterus. Nevertheless, the test is *not* indicated for every pregnant woman. It should be done only where there is a good medical reason for such prenatal diagnosis—not, for example, merely to determine the sex of the baby out of curiosity.

In general, amniocentesis is recommended when the family history of either the mother or father indicates that the fetus might have a genetic disease that can be detected—or ruled out—by this procedure. It is also useful for older women, particularly after age 40, largely because of the increased risk of Down's syndrome (from Moore, 1982; Rubin, 1980; Rugh & Shettles, 1971).

In view of the importance of adequate nutrition for pregnant women and young infants, the severe cutbacks sometimes proposed in federal programs that provide special food supplements to needy, high-risk pregnant women, mothers, and children may seem unwise. In a controlled study in Massachusetts of the effectiveness of one such program, it was found that participation by pregnant women for at least 4 months resulted in significantly higher birth weight, less prematurity, and decreased neonatal mortality (Kotelchuck, Schwartz, Anderka, & Finison, 1983). Furthermore, the longer the participation in the program, the more impressive were the results (see Figure 2.14). Even from a purely financial perspective, the relatively small cost of these nutritional programs is a good investment; it saves later medical and educational costs that are required for children who may have birth defects, mental retardation, or other problems as a result of poor prenatal nutrition.

Drugs

During the past decade or so, physicians and parents have become increasingly concerned about the potentially harmful effects of drugs on the developing embryo and fetus. One of the most dramatic reasons for this concern was the discovery that the gross anatomical defects of the limbs of a certain group of babies had been caused by the mothers' taking a drug called thalidomide during pregnancy. Many other drugs are now suspected of producing birth defects when taken during pregnancy; these include some antibiotics, hormones, steroids, anticoagulants, narcotics, tranquilizers, and possibly some hallucinogenic drugs, such as LSD and PCP ("angel dust") (Apgar & Beck, 1974; Catz & Yaffe, 1978; Moore, 1982). Also suspect are excessive doses of some

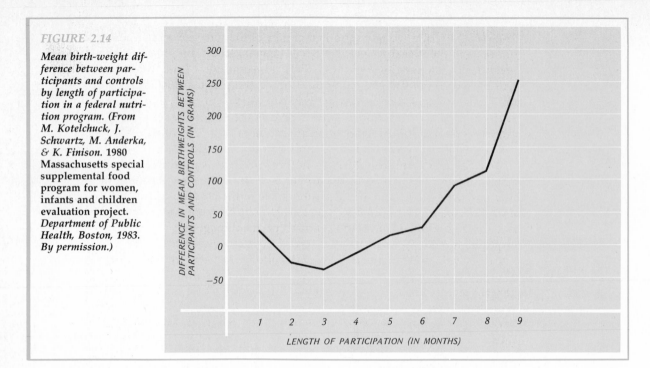

FIGURE 2.14

Mean birth-weight difference between participants and controls by length of participation in a federal nutrition program. (From M. Kotelchuck, J. Schwartz, M. Anderka, & K. Finison. 1980 Massachusetts special supplemental food program for women, infants and children evaluation project. Department of Public Health, Boston, 1983. By permission.)

vitamins, such as vitamins A and K. Adequate studies of possible effects of marijuana on the reproductive system of the mother or on the fetus are still lacking. However, it is known that marijuana has a modest suppressive effect on sperm production, that it can interfere with ovulation (at least in monkeys), that it may affect chromosome segregation during cell division, and that its chemicals do cross the placental barrier (*Committee*, 1982, Conger & Petersen, 1984).

Recent lawsuits have called attention to the fact that many women who took the drug stilbestrol (an estrogenic compound) during pregnancy to prevent miscarriages had daughters who developed cancer of the vagina during adolescence (Moore, 1982). Industrial pollutants may also pose serious hazards. Pregnant women in Japan and Iraq who ate fish containing high levels of mercury gave birth to brain-damaged infants (Amin-Zaki, Elhassain, Majeed, Clarkson, Doheaty, & Greenwood, 1974; Moore, 1982). Even commonly used substances may adversely affect fetal development, particularly in the early months of pregnancy. For example, there is some evidence that aspirin in large doses may be harmful to the embryo or fetus (Catz & Yaffe, 1978; Corby, 1978; Moore, 1982).

Fetal alcohol syndrome   Heavy drinking by a pregnant woman can produce what is known as *fetal alcohol syndrome* (DeLuca, 1981; Kliegman & King, 1983; Mulvihill & Yeager, 1976; Moore, 1982). Recent research suggests that the syndrome may result from maternal consumption of 3 ounces of absolute alcohol per day (about four or five drinks). The symptoms include retarded prenatal and postnatal growth, premature birth, mental retardation, physical malfor-

mations, sleep disturbances, and congenital heart disease. "Binge drinking" (heavy consumption of alcohol for 1 to 3 days) during early pregnancy is especially likely to harm the fetus. Smaller doses of alcohol (1 ounce or more a day) increase the likelihood of low birth weight, developmental delays, physical difficulties (e.g., breathing and sucking difficulties), and spontaneous abortion (DeLuca, 1981; Moore, 1982). It is estimated that each year at least 6000 infants born in the United States are victims of fetal alcohol syndrome (DeLuca, 1981).

Nicotine and caffeine It has now been clearly established that smoking by pregnant women retards physical growth and lowers the newborn's birth weight and resistance to illness (Moore, 1982; Page, Villee, & Villee, 1981). It also increases the chances of spontaneous abortion and premature birth and may possibly affect long-term physical and intellectual development as a consequence of reduced capacity of the smoking mother's blood to transport oxygen to the fetus (Moore, 1982; Page et al., 1981; *Smoking and health*, 1979).

Although there is as yet no clear evidence regarding adverse effects of caffeine on the fetus, there are some suggestions that high levels of coffee consumption by the mother may increase the likelihood of miscarriage (Annis, 1978). Consequently, it would seem a wise precaution to avoid *excessive* drinking of coffee, tea, and cola during pregnancy, in addition to eliminating smoking (Moore, 1982).

Drugs during labor and delivery   Drugs taken just prior to delivery of a baby to ease a mother's distress or pain, such as pentobarbital or meperidine (Demerol), may make the infant less attentive, at least temporarily (Bowes, 1970; Stechler, 1964). One study of the effects of anesthetic drugs on sensorimotor functions in the newborn found lags in muscular, visual, and neural functioning (Brackbill, 1979; Conway & Brackbill, 1970). Although most such effects were greatest in the first few days of life, longer-term effects on cognitive functioning and gross motor abilities, particularly of heavy drug dosages, have been found at 1 year of age (Brackbill, 1976, 1979; Goldstein, Caputo, & Taub, 1976; Standley, 1979). Where feasible, it would appear desirable to limit the use of obstetrical drugs to mild sedation (Annis, 1978).

Other drugs   The rise in drug addiction among some groups of young people has led to an increased number of addicted fetuses and newborns (Brackbill, 1979). Babies born to chronic users of heroin and methadone characteristically weigh less, have higher rates of illness, and often show symptoms of drug withdrawal, such as restlessness, irritability, tremors, high-pitched excessive crying, respiratory distress, fever, and, in some cases, convulsions (Brackbill, 1979; Kopp & Parmelee, 1979; Kron, Kaplan, Phoenix, & Finnegan, 1977; Kron, Litt, & Finnegan, 1975; *Proceedings,* 1971). Whether all of these symptoms can be attributed to maternal narcotic use is not clear, partly because so many young addicted mothers are also likely to suffer from malnutrition, anemia, and infectious disease. They are also likely to be heavy users of alcohol, tobacco, and other drugs, all of which may themselves affect development. What is clear, however, is that every effort should be made to discourage the use of narcotics during pregnancy.

In view of the fact that the ultimate effects of many drugs, including some of the most common, are still unknown, "a woman who is pregnant, or thinks she could possibly be pregnant, should not take any drugs whatsoever unless absolutely essential—and then only when prescribed by a physician who is aware of the pregnancy" (Apgar & Beck, 1974, p. 485).

Radiation   Another potential source of birth defects is radiation (x-ray) of the mother during pregnancy, whether for treatment of pelvic cancer, for diagnostic, or from atomic energy sources, occupational hazards, or fallout (Brent & Harris, 1976; Kliegman & King, 1983). Although the hazards are not fully understood, it is clear that radiation can cause a full range of damage to unborn children, including death, malformation, brain damage, increased susceptibility to certain forms of cancer, shortened life span, and "mutations in genes whose effects may not be felt for generations" (Apgar & Beck, 1974, p. 107). Radiation between fertilization and the time the ovum implants in the uterus is now thought to destroy the fertilized ovum in almost every case. The greatest danger of malformations comes between the second and sixth week after conception.

Although the effects of x-ray may be less dramatic later in pregnancy, there are still risks of damage, particularly to the brain and other body systems.

In general, x-ray examinations or radiation treatment should not be given to anyone who thinks she could possibly be pregnant or who is pregnant, particularly during the first 3 months of pregnancy. Physicians using x-rays of the abdomen or pelvis on any adolescent or adult woman of childbearing age should do so only during the first two weeks following a normal menstrual period, so there is no possibility she could be pregnant without realizing it.

Maternal diseases and disorders during pregnancy

In early pregnancy the placenta acts as a barrier against some harmful agents (e.g., larger organisms, such as syphilitic spirochetes and some bacteria). But even at this stage it allows many substances to reach the unborn child, and more can permeate it later. Some of these substances are positive in their effects. Antibodies produced by the mother to combat infectious diseases are transmitted to the fetus, usually producing immunity at birth and for some months thereafter. Other substances, including viruses, microorganisms, and various chemicals, may be extremely negative.

Viral diseases in the mother—such as cytomegalovirus disease (which affects 5 to 6 percent of pregnant women), rubella (German measles), chicken pox, and hepatitis—are particularly dangerous during the embryonic and early fetal periods. One of the most serious viral diseases during the first 3 months is rubella, which may produce heart malformations, deafness, blindness, or mental retardation. About 50 percent of babies whose mothers have had German measles in the first month of pregnancy suffer birth defects, 22 percent of those infected in the second month, 6 percent in the third month, and only a small number thereafter (Babson, Pernoll, & Benda, 1980; Lubchenco, 1976; Moore, 1982). Virginia Apgar, a pediatrician and expert on prenatal development, has warned: "No woman should become pregnant unless she is sure she has had rubella or has been effectively immunized against it" (Apgar & Beck, 1974, p. 481). A pregnant woman can be tested to see whether she has already had rubella, but if she has not she cannot be given the vaccine for rubella. The vaccine contains live German measles viruses and should not be given to any woman who might be pregnant or become so within 2 or 3 months.

Currently, the rapid spread of the genital herpes virus among young adults poses another danger. Infection of the fetus with this virus usually occurs late in pregnancy—probably most often during delivery—and can result in severe neurological damage; when infection occurs several weeks prior to birth, a variety of congenital anomalies can result. Prompt medical intervention is required if the presence of herpes during pregnancy is suspected (Dudgeon, 1976; Moore, 1982).

Infection of the fetus with spirochetes from a syphilitic mother is not infrequent, though, fortunately, the placenta barrier does not permit passage of the spirochetes until after the fourth or fifth month of pregnancy. Consequently, transmission of the spirochetes (which otherwise would take place in about 24 percent of cases) may be prevented if treatment of a syphilitic mother begins early in pregnancy. Otherwise, these spirochetes may produce miscarriage or a weak, deformed, or mentally deficient newborn. In some cases, the child may not manifest syphilitic symptoms until several years later.

There are also some general disturbances of the mother during pregnancy that may affect the fetus. One of the most common is called *toxemia of pregnancy*, a disorder of unknown cause that affects about 5 percent of pregnant women in the United States. In its mildest form, toxemia is characterized by high blood pressure, rapid and excessive weight gain, and retention of fluid in the tissues. Fortunately, prompt treatment usually ends the danger. However, if the disorder continues to progress, it can lead to convulsions and coma, resulting in death in about 13 percent of mothers and about 50 percent of their unborn infants. Children whose mothers had significant toxemia during pregnancy run an increased risk of lowered intelligence (Lubchenco, 1976).

The Rh factor

Until recently, probably no cause of birth defects aroused more parental concern than Rh problems. The term *Rh factor* stands for a chemical factor present in the blood of approximately 85 percent of people, although there are racial and ethnic variations. In itself, the presence or absence of this chemical factor makes no difference in a person's health. But when an Rh-positive man is married to an Rh-negative woman (about 1 chance in 9), there can sometimes be adverse consequences for their offspring. If their baby has Rh-positive blood, the mother's blood may form antibodies against the "foreign" positive Rh factor. During the next pregnancy, the antibodies in the mother's blood may attack the Rh-positive blood of the unborn infant. Such destruction can be limited, resulting only in mild anemia, or extensive, resulting in cerebral palsy, deafness, mental retardation, or even death.

Fortunately, a preventive control for the Rh problem has been developed. The blood of the newborn infant is tested immediately after birth (by a blood sample from the umbilical cord). If an Rh-positive child has been born to an Rh-negative mother, the mother is given a vaccine to seek out and destroy the baby's Rh-positive blood cells before the mother's body begins producing antibodies. The red cells of later children will not be attacked because the blood of the mother was never allowed to develop the antibodies (Apgar & Beck, 1974; Lubchenco, 1976).

Maternal emotional states and stress

Despite the fact that there are no direct connections between the maternal and fetal nervous systems, the mother's emotional state can influence fetal reactions and development. This is true because emotions such as rage, fear, and anxiety bring the mother's autonomic nervous system into action, liberating certain chemicals (such as acetylcholine and epinephrine) into the bloodstream. Furthermore, under such conditions the endocrine glands, particularly the adrenals, secrete different kinds and amounts of hormones. Cell metabolism is also modified. As the composition of the blood changes, new chemical substances are transmitted through the placenta, producing changes in the fetus's circulatory system.

These changes may be irritating to the fetus. One study noted that bodily movements of fetuses increased several hundred percent while their mothers were undergoing emotional stress (Sontag, 1941, 1944). If the mother's emotional upset lasted several weeks, fetal activity continued at an exaggerated level throughout the entire period. When these upsets were brief, heightened irritability usually lasted several hours. Prolonged maternal emotional stress during pregnancy—whether from marital difficulties, negative attitudes toward having a child, or catastrophic life events—may have enduring consequences for the child. Infants born to upset, unhappy mothers are more likely to be premature or have low birth weights; to be hyperactive, irritable, squirming; and to manifest difficulties such as irregular eating, excessive bowel movements, gas pains, sleep disturbances, excessive crying, and unusual needs to be held (David, DeVault, & Talmadge, 1961; Joffe, 1969; Sameroff & Zax, 1973; Sontag, 1941, 1944).

It may seem that we have overemphasized potentially adverse influences on prenatal development, including some maternal behaviors. If so, this is not our intent. As we have already noted, the great majority of babies are born healthy, including those of mothers who may have smoked, drunk liquor in moderation, eaten a less than perfect diet, or received medication during delivery. Furthermore, infants and young children have a great capacity for recovering from all but severe prenatal and perinatal stress (see Box 2.3). However, it still seems important for future mothers and fathers to do everything they reasonably can to foster their baby's optimal development.

THE BIRTH PROCESS AND ITS CONSEQUENCES

Anoxia and other complications

The ease or difficulty with which a baby is born and how quickly the newborn begins to breathe can affect the infant's well-being. One major danger associated with birth is *hemorrhaging,* caused when very strong pressure on the head of the fetus breaks blood vessels in the brain. Another is failure to begin to breathe soon after being separated from the maternal source of oxygen. Both hemorrhaging and failure to breathe affect the supply of oxygen to the nerve cells of the brain and produce a state called *anoxia* (lack of oxygen). The neurons of the central nervous system require oxygen; if they are deprived of oxygen,

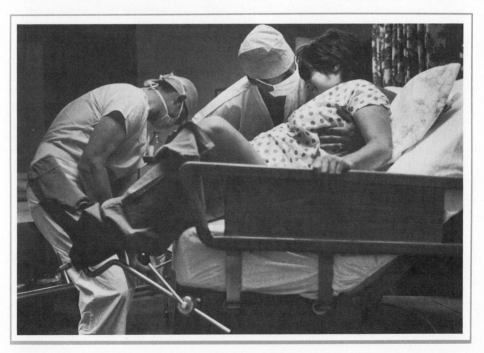

BOX 2.3

*The children
of Kauai*

A massive longitudinal study of all pregnancies and births on the Hawaiian island of Kauai over more than a decade focused on later consequences of *perinatal stress* (problems around the time of birth). With increasing severity of stress, there was a corresponding increase in the percentage of children who by age 2 were rated below normal in physical and intellectual status. However, by age 10, differences between children who had encountered varying degrees of perinatal complications were less than at age 2. Most of the negative outcomes occurred in a small group of survivors of severe perinatal stress. The strongest relationships were with physical handicaps related to central nervous system impairment and with mental retardation or learning difficulties.

By age 18, the greatest number of physical, mental, social, and emotional problems were still concentrated in survivors of severe perinatal stress. Among the survivors of moderate perinatal stress, the rate of serious mental health problems, mental retardation, and teenage pregnancies was considerably higher than in 18-year-olds born without stress, but in both groups only a small minority were involved. In brief, the long-term consequences of mild or moderate perinatal stress appear to be modest. Even among those with severe stress, a clear majority are functioning adequately.

Furthermore, at both ages 10 and 18, ten times more children had problems attributable to a poor childrearing environment than to the effects of severe perinatal stress (from Werner, Bierman, & French, 1971; Werner & Smith, 1982). Overall, the investigators found that

> *Perinatal complications were consistently related to later impaired physical and psychological development* only *when combined with persistently poor environmental circumstances (e.g., chronic poverty, family instability, or maternal health problem). Children who were raised in more affluent homes, with an intact family and a well-educated mother, showed few, if any, negative effects from reproductive stress, unless there was severe central nervous system impairment.* (Werner & Smith, 1982, p. 31)

some cells may die, which can cause later physical and psychological defects. If too many neurons die, the infant may suffer serious brain damage or, in extreme cases, death.

Anoxia in a newborn is more likely to damage the cells of the brain stem than those of the cortex. When the cells of the brain stem are damaged, motor defects are likely to occur. The child may show a paralysis of the legs or arms, a tremor of the face or fingers, or an inability to use the vocal muscles. In this last case, the child may have difficulty in learning to speak. The general term *cerebral palsy* describes a variety of motor defects associated with damage to the brain cells, possibly as a result of lack of oxygen during the birth process. It is estimated that about 30 percent of cases of cerebral palsy involve problems that occurred during birth or immediately afterward (Apgar & Beck, 1974; Kopp & Parmelee, 1979; Lubchenco, 1976).

It is more difficult to determine whether children who suffer a mild oxygen deficit at birth but do not show obvious motor paralysis or tremors suffer any brain damage that might influence their future psychological development. One way to study this issue is to find a group of infants who experienced mild anoxia during the delivery process and compare them with a group of infants from the same social class and ordinal position who did not experience anoxia.

Anoxic infants appear more irritable and show more muscular tension and rigidity than do normal infants during the first week (Graham, Matarazzo, & Caldwell, 1956). Infants with mild anoxia score lower on tests of motor development and attention during the first year and are more distractible (Corah, Anthony, Painter, Stern, & Thurston, 1965; Ernhart, Graham, & Thurston, 1960; Lubchenco, 1976). At age 3, they perform less well on tests of conceptualization. By age 7 or 8, behavioral differences between normal and mildly anoxic children are generally small, and their IQ scores are equal. In brief, the differences between mildly anoxic and normal children become smaller with age, and there is presently no firm evidence of serious and permanent intellectual damage. As indicated in Box 2.3, the same is true for children who suffer other stresses at the time of birth.

Prematurity   Infants born earlier than the thirty-eighth week of gestation and weighing less than about 5 pounds are called premature. Prematurity is more frequent among economically disadvantaged mothers than among the affluent. We have already noted that smoking, alcohol, and various drugs increase the likelihood that a baby will be premature. Children in multiple births (twins, triplets, and the like) also tend to be premature. In addition, premature births often occur for unknown reasons.

The long-term effects of prematurity on development depend on how early the infant is born (gestational age), birth weight, the type of postnatal care provided, and the quality of the child's environment during early and middle childhood. Infants with gestation periods of less than 28 weeks ("extreme prematurity") or weights of less than 3.3 pounds have a reduced chance of survival. In contrast, those who are only slightly premature (34–38 weeks) and who are of appropriate weight for their gestational age resemble full-term babies in many ways. They are generally healthy, though they are less mature, are more vulnerable to illness, gain weight more slowly, and must be monitored carefully (Hack, 1983; Kopp & Parmelee, 1979; Lubchenco, 1976).

Neonatal (newborn) risk of mortality or some type of handicap is a function of both gestational age and birth weight (although, of course, the two factors generally tend to go together). An infant who is significantly premature and low in birth weight even for his or her gestational age faces a more serious risk than an infant of the same gestational age whose birth weight is age-appropriate. In general, risks appear highest for the small minority of prematures weighing less than 1500 grams (3.3 pounds) at birth (Battaglia & Simmons, 1978; Kopp & Parmelee, 1983; Lubchenco, 1976). Current findings suggest, however, that even for many of these babies, intensive, expert care can reduce the incidence of handicaps substantially. Several recent studies conducted at "premature centers" providing skilled, specialized care have found that 90 percent or more of these infants develop normally when they survive (Battaglia & Simmons, 1978).

Considerable progress has also been made in caring for "intermediate-term" infants falling in the middle range of prematurity—babies whose gestational ages range between 30 and 33 weeks and who are of at least average weight for their age—around 1500 grams (3.3 pounds) or more at 30 weeks and 2000 grams (4.4 pounds) or more at 33 weeks. By instituting intensive, highly specialized care in technologically sophisticated premature nurseries in university medical centers and major community hospitals, many more premature babies have not only survived, but have gone on to develop normally (Battaglia & Simmons, 1978; Brandt, 1978).

One feature of many treatment programs for premature infants is to provide the baby with sensory and tactile stimulation and to encourage parents to participate in the child's care during the time the child is hospitalized after birth. Some investigators have thought that children would benefit from rocking and gentle tactile stimulation that simulates the conditions in the uterus. Others have provided visual, tactile, and auditory stimuli (such as mobiles and sounds) that are thought to facilitate development in newborn infants. Such programs appear to produce at least short-term benefits for premature children, but the differences attributable to them decrease with the child's age. One major reason for encouraging parents to visit their infants regularly and to touch and care for them as much as possible is the belief that such contacts promote attachment to infants. There is considerable controversy, however, about the effectiveness of such programs and about how critical these early parent-infant contacts are for the long-term parent-child relationship. These are discussed more fully in Chapter 4.

Many of the neurological problems that can occur in low-birth-weight children may not be apparent in the first months of life. Some disabilities, such as cerebral palsy, major defects in vision or hearing, or significant mental retardation, may be discerned in the first year, but others, including below-average IQ, perceptual disorders, learning problems, and behavioral symptoms (such as restlessness and hyperactivity), may not become apparent until after school entrance (Hack, 1983; Kopp & Parmelee, 1979; Lubchenco, 1976).

Like children who experience anoxia or complications during birth, premature children are particularly vulnerable to the effects of their environment. In homes with poor parental care and living conditions, premature babies are far more likely than full-term children to have difficulties, both physical and psychological. Unfair as it may be, prematurity and perinatal complications, are more frequent among economically disadvantaged families than among middle-class families, thus heightening the chances that a poor child will have to deal with both impairment at birth *and* a less favorable rearing environment (Lubchenco, 1976; Richmond, 1982).

Premature children who are born into loving, nurturing homes where they receive competent physical and psychological care usually show little long-range handicap, unless they were very premature or did not receive appropriate neonatal or postnatal hospital care (Apgar & Beck, 1974; Battaglia & Simmons, 1978; Werner & Smith, 1982).

The developing child's behavior results from many different influences—genetic, biological, psychological, and social. Although we usually discuss genetic and environmental influences separately, in reality these forces interact, and it is often difficult to determine the relative contribution of each to a particular behavior.

Development begins when a sperm cell from the father penetrates the wall of an ovum, or egg, from the mother. At this moment, 23 *chromosomes* from each parent combine; all the child's biological heritage is contained in these 46 chromosomes. Each chromosome, in turn, is made up of about 20,000 smaller particles called *genes*. The genes contain a complex chemical substance, deoxyribonucleic acid, or DNA, which is responsible for the action of the genes. DNA is composed of two molecular chains coiled around each other to form a double-stranded helix, which looks much like a twisted ladder. When DNA replicates itself, this ladder divides down the middle, and each side reconstitutes itself into a new ladder.

The adult organism contains two kinds of cells, body cells and germ cells. While all body cells—like the original fertilized ovum—contain 46 chromosomes, germ cells, through a process called *meiosis*, ultimately divide into four cells, each of which contains only 23 chromosomes. It is from these cells that sperm and ova are formed, and because each contains only half the chromosomes of the original parent cell, children of the same parents do not all have to be alike. In fact, identity is possible only in the case of identical twins, who come from the same original fertilized ovum, which only later divides to form separate individuals.

Of the 23 pairs of chromosomes in each individual, 22 pairs are called *autosomes*. The twenty-third pair is called the *sex chromosomes*. In the normal female, both members of this pair are large in size and are called *X chromosomes*; in the male, one member of the pair is an X chromosome, while the second member is smaller and is called the *Y chromosome*.

Some genetic influences on development involve the action of only a single pair of genes, one of which may be *dominant* (i.e., more effective) and mask the effects of the other *(recessive)* gene. Huntington's chorea, a degenerative disease of the nervous system, results from the action of a single dominant gene; phenylketonuria (PKU), which may lead to mental retardation if untreated, is caused by a pair of recessive genes. However, most behavioral characteristics are multifactorial; that is, they depend on a number of genes *(polygenetic inheritance)* interacting with environmental influences.

Sometimes, the specific genes involved can be determined; more often, however, studies of incidence patterns among genetically related individuals must be relied on. Frequently, identical *(monozygotic)* twins, who share the same heredity, are compared with nonidentical or "fraternal" *(dizygotic)* twins, whose heredity is less similar. The assumption is that if identical twins are more similar in a particular characteristic (e.g., intelligence, extraversion) than nonidentical twins, genetic factors play a role in determining the characteristic. Such studies assume that nonidentical twins share as nearly similar an environment as identical twins, which may be open to some question. In order to achieve still tighter controls, identical twins who are reared apart are sometimes compared to fraternal twins or other siblings who are reared together. Another useful approach is to compare adopted children with both their adoptive parents and their biological parents. Using such methods, it has been determined that genetic factors play a significant role in intelligence, though environmental factors are also important.

A number of genetically determined disorders leading to mental retardation have been identified, including PKU, which results from a specific enzyme deficiency. Some other disorders result from abnormalities in the *autosomes* (chromosomes other than the X or Y sex chromosomes). A good example is *Down's syndrome.* Disorders can also involve the sex chromosomes.

Genetic factors have also been shown to play a part in the development of a number of serious mental disorders, including at least some types of *schizophrenia.* For example, if one identical twin has schizophrenia, the chances are almost 1 in 2 that the other twin will also develop this disorder. But in the case of nonidentical twins, the chances of the other twin's also developing schizophrenia are less than 1 in 10. Some types of severe depression are also influenced by genetic factors. In both schizophrenia and depression, however, a majority of even close relatives of these patients do not develop the disorder. Genetic factors may make a person susceptible to developing these disorders if certain environmental stresses or experiences occur.

The role of genetic influences in the development of personality characteristics is more difficult to investigate, at least partly because personality characteristics are harder to define. Nevertheless, it appears that genetic factors may play some part in the development of such basic "temperamental" characteristics as activity versus passivity, inhibition versus spontaneity, introversion versus extraversion, and personality characteristics such as neuroticism.

In the course of prenatal development, the individual goes through three successive phases. First is the *period of the ovum*, lasting 10 to 14 days from fertilization until the fertilized ovum (called the *zygote*) is firmly implanted in the wall of the uterus. The second phase, from 2 to 8 weeks, is called the *period of the embryo.* By the end of this period, the embryo is about 1 inch in length; face, mouth, eyes, and ears have begun to take on fairly well defined forms, and internal organs and the nervous system have begun to take shape. The organism is particularly vulnerable at this stage to the effects of disease, drugs, and malnutrition.

The third phase, *the period of the fetus,* extends from the end of the second month until birth. By the end of 12 weeks, the fetus is about 3 inches long and has definitely begun to resemble a human being, though the head is disproportionately large. By the end of 16 weeks, the mother can feel the fetus's movements. The fetal age of 28 weeks is an especially important one; it demarcates the zone between viability (the ability to live if born) and nonviability. By this age, the fetus's nervous, circulatory, and other bodily systems are sufficiently well developed to stand the chance of functioning adequately in the extra-uterine environment.

Prenatal environmental influences can significantly affect the individual's development. These influences include the age of the mother (the years between 20 and 35 appear most favorable); maternal nutrition; drugs, including alcohol, nicotine, certain antibiotics, hormones, steroids, and narcotics—all of which can adversely affect fetal development; x-rays; maternal diseases and disorders, such as rubella, chicken pox, hepatitis, cytomegalic inclusion disease, syphilis, genital herpes, toxemia of pregnancy, and a negative Rh factor in the blood. The mother's emotional state also affects the fetus.

Anoxia (lack of oxygen), excessive use of drugs and anesthetics during delivery, and physical injury during the birth process may also affect the baby's development adversely, either temporarily or over a prolonged period, depending largely on the degree of disruption caused. Mild to moderate *perinatal stress* can often be significantly compensated for by a favorable rearing environment.

Prematurity may also affect physical and psychological development. The more premature or underweight the infant is, the greater is the likelihood of physical or mental impairment. Babies with gestation periods of less than 28 weeks and weighing less than 3.3 pounds have little chance of survival. Premature children are particularly influenced by their environment. Those receiving superior care usually show little long-range handicap, while those with poor care are much more likely than full-term children to have difficulties.

Fortunately, the vast majority of all babies born in this country do not experience any of the problems discussed in this chapter. Most infants begin life well within the normal range. In addition, infants are surprisingly malleable, and many children apparently recover from early deficits, whether due to prematurity, anoxia, or other mild to moderate developmental problems.

REFERENCES

Allport, G. *Personality: A psychological interpretation.* New York: Holt, Rinehart and Winston, 1937.

Amin-Zaki, L., Elhassain, S., Majeed, M. A., Clarkson, T. W., Doheaty, R. A., & Greenwood, M. Intrauterine methylmercury poisoning in Iraq. *Pediatrics,* 1974, *54,* 587–595.

Annis, L. *The child before birth.* Ithaca, N.Y.: Cornell University Press, 1978.

Apgar, V., & Beck, J. *Is my baby all right?* New York: Pocket Books, 1974.

Babson, S. G., Pernoll, M. L., & Benda, G. I. *Diagnosis and management of the fetus and neonate at risk.* St. Louis: Mosby, 1980.

Battaglia, F. C., & Simmons, M. A. The low-birth-weight infant. In F. Falkner & J. Tanner (Eds.), *Human growth* (Vol 2): *Postnatal growth.* New York: Plenum, 1978, pp. 507–556.

Blau, A., Staff, B., Easton, E., Walkowitz, J., & Cohen, J. The psychogenic etiology of premature births: A preliminary report. *Psychosomatic Medicine,* 1963, *25,* 201–211.

Borek, E. *The sculpture of life.* New York: Columbia University Press, 1973.

Bowes, W. A. I. Obstetrical medication and infant outcome: A review of the literature. In W. A. Bowes, Y. Brackbill, E. Conway, & A. Steinschneider (Eds.), The effects of obstetrical medication on fetus and infant. *Monographs of the Society for Research in Child Development,* 1970, *35*(4), 3–23.

Brackbill, Y. Long-term effects of obstetrical anesthesia on infant autonomic function. *Developmental Psychobiology,* 1976, *9,* 353–358.

Brackbill, Y. Obstetrical medication and infant behavior. In J. Osofsky (Ed.), *Handbook of infant development.* New York: Wiley, 1979, pp. 76–125.

Brandt, I. Growth dynamics of low-birth-weight infants with emphasis on the perinatal period. In F. Falkner & J. Tanner (Eds.), *Human growth* (Vol. 2): *Postnatal growth.* New York: Plenum, 1978.

Brent, R. L., & Harris, M. I. *Prevention of embryonic, fetal, and perinatal disease.* Fogarty International Center Series on Preventive Medicine (Vol. 3), 1976.

Bunney, W. E., Jr., & Davis, J. M. Norepinephrine in depressive disorders. *Archives of General Psychiatry*, 1965, *13*, 483–494.

Catz, C., & Yaffe, S. J. Developmental pharmacology. In F. Falkner & J. M. Tanner (Eds.), *Human growth* (Vol. 1): *Principles and prenatal growth*. New York: Plenum, 1978.

Committee to Study the Health-Related Effects of Cannabis and Its Deviations. National Academy of Sciences, Institute of Medicine. *Marihuana and health.* Washington, D.C.: National Academy Press, 1982.

Conger, J. J., & Petersen, A. C. *Adolescence and youth: Psychological development in a changing world* (3rd ed.). New York: Harper & Row, 1984.

Conway, E., & Brackbill, Y. Delivery medication and infant outcomes: An empirical study. In W. A. Bowes, Y. Brackbill, E. Conway, & A. Steinschneider (Eds.), The effects of obstetrical medication on fetus and infant. *Monographs of the Society for Research in Child Development*, 1970, *35*(4), 24–34.

Corah, N. L., Anthony, E. J., Painter, P., Stern, J. A., & Thurston, D. Effects of perinatal anoxia after 7 years. *Psychological Monographs*, 1965, *79*, 1–34.

Corby, D. G. Aspirin in pregnancy: Maternal and fetal effects. *Pediatrics*, 1978, *62*, 930–937.

Cravioto, J., & DeLicardie, E. R. Nutrition, mental development, and learning. In F. Falkner & J. M. Tanner (eds.), *Human growth* (Vol. 3): *Neurobiology and nutrition.* New York: Plenum, 1978.

David, A., DeVault, S., & Talmadge, M. Anxiety, pregnancy, and childbirth abnormalities. *Journal of Consulting Psychology*, 1961, *25*, 74–77.

Davis, J. M. Antidepressant drugs. In H. I. Kaplan, A. M. Freedman, & B. J. Sadock (Eds.), *Comprehensive textbook of psychiatry* (Vol. 2) (3rd ed.). Palo Alto, Calif.: Annual Reviews, Inc., 1978.

DeFries, J. C., & Plomin, R. Behavioral genetics. *Annual Review of Psychology*, 1978, *29*, 473–515.

DeLuca, J. R. (Ed.). Alcohol and health: Fourth special report to the U.S. Congress. Rockville, Md.: National Institute of Alcohol and Alcohol Abuse, 1981.

Dobbing, J. The later development of central nervous system and its vulnerability. In A. V. Davison & J. Dobbing (Eds.), *Scientific foundations of pediatrics.* London: Heinemann, 1974.

Dudgeon, J. A. Infective causes of human malformations. *British Medical Bulletin*, 1976, *32*, 77–83.

Epstein, C. J., & Golbus, M. S. Prenatal diagnosis of genetic diseases. *American Scientist*, 1977, *65*, 703–711.

Erlenmeyer-Kimling, L., & Jarvik, L. F. Genetics and intelligence: A review. *Science*, 1963, *142*, 1477–1479.

Ernhart, C. B., Graham, F. K., & Thurston, D. Relationship of neonatal apnea to development at three years. *Archives of Neurology*, 1960, *2*, 504–510.

Falkner, F. Implications for growth in human twins. In F. Falkner, & J. M. Tanner (Eds.), *Human growth* (Vol. 1): *Principles and prenatal growth*. New York: Plenum, 1978.

Falkner, F., & Tanner, J. M. (Eds.). *Human growth* (Vol. 1): *Principles and prenatal growth.* New York: Plenum, 1978(a).

Falkner, F., & Tanner, J. M. (Eds.). *Human growth* (Vol. 2): *Postnatal growth.* New York: Plenum, 1978(b).

Falkner, F., & Tanner, J. M. (Eds.), *Human growth* (Vol. 3): *Neurobiology and nutrition.* New York: Plenum, 1978(c).

Fawcett, J. Biochemical and neuropharmacological research in the affective disorders. In E. J. Anthony & T. Benedek (Eds.), *Depression and human existence.* Boston: Little, Brown, 1975.

Ferreira, A. *Prenatal environment.* Springfield, Ill.: Thomas, 1969.

Field, T. M., Widmayer, S. M, Stringer, S., and Ignatoff, E. Teenage, lower-class, black mothers and their preterm infants: An intervention and developmental follow-up. *Child Development*, 1980, *51*, 426–436.

Floderus-Myrhed, B., Pederson, N., & Rasmuson, I. Assessment of heritability for personality based on a short form of the Eysenck Personality Inventory: A study of 12,898 twin pairs. *Behavior Genetics*, 1980, *10*, 153–162.

Freedman, D. An ethological approach to the genetic study of human behavior. In S. G. Vandenberg (Ed.), *Methods and goals in human behavior genetics.* New York: Academic Press, 1965.

Fuchs, F. Genetic amniocentesis. *Scientific American*, 1980, *242*, 47–53.

Gesell, A. *The embryology of behavior.* New York: Harper & Row, 1945.

Golbus, M. S. Teratology for the obstetrician: Current status. *Obstetrics and Gynecology*, 1980, *55*, 269–277

Goldsmith, H. H. Genetic influences on personality from infancy to adulthood. *Child Development*, 1983, *54*, 331–355.

Goldsmith, H. H., & Gottesman, I. I. Origins of variation in behavioral style: A longitudinal study of temperament in young twins. *Child Development*, 1981, *52*, 91–103.

Goldstein, K. M., Caputo, D. V., & Taub, H. B. The effects of perinatal complications on development at one year of age. *Child Development*, 1976, *47*, 613–621.

Gottesman, I. I., & Shields, J. Contributions of twin studies to perspectives on schizophrenia. In B. A. Maher (Ed.), *Progress in experimental personality research*. New York: Academic Press, 1966.

Gottesman, I. I., & Shields, J. A polygenic theory of schizophrenia. *Proceedings of the National Academy of Science, U.S.A.*, 1967, *58*, 199–205.

Graham, F. K., Matarazzo, R. G., & Caldwell, B. M. Behavioral differences between normal and traumatized newborns. *Psychological Monographs*, 1956, *70*(5).

Gunter, N. C., & LaBarba, R. C. The consequences of adolescent childbearing on postnatal development. *International Journal of Behavioral Development*, 1980, *3*, 191–214.

Hack, M. The sensorimotor development of the preterm infant. In A. A. Fanaroff, R. J. Martin, & J. R. Merkatz (Eds.), *Behrman's neonatal-perinatal medicine*. St. Louis: Mosby, 1983.

Hansen, H. Decline of Down's syndrome after abortion reform in New York State. *American Journal of Mental Deficiency*, 1978, *83*, 185–188.

Horn, J. M. The Texas Adoption Project: Adopted children and their intellectual resemblance to biological and adoptive parents. *Child Development*, 1983, *54*, 268–275.

Javert, C. T. Further follow-up on habitual abortion patients. *American Journal of Obstetrics and Gynecology*, 1962, *84*, 1149–1159.

Joffe, J. M. *Prenatal determinants of behavior*. Oxford: Pergamon, 1969.

Jones, H. E. Environmental influence on mental development. In L. Carmichael (Ed.), *Manual of child psychology*. New York: Wiley, 1946.

Katz, M., Keusch, G. T., & Mata, L. (Eds.). Malnutrition and infection during pregnancy: Determinants of growth and development of the child. *American Journal of Diseases of Children*, 1975, *29*, 419–463.

Kessler, S. Psychiatric genetics. In D. A. Hamburg & K. Brodie (Eds.), *American handbook of psychiatry* (Vol. VI): *New psychiatric frontiers*. New York: Basic Books, 1975.

Kessler, S. The genetics of schizophrenia: A review. *Schizophrenia Bulletin*, 1980, *6*, 404–416.

Kety, S. S., Rosenthal, D., Wender, P. H., Schulsinger, F., & Jacobsen, B. Mental illness in the biological and adoptive families of adoptive individuals who have become schizophrenic: A preliminary report based on psychiatric interviews. In R. Fieve, D. Rosenthal, & H. Brill (Eds.), *Genetic research in psychiatry*. Baltimore: Johns Hopkins University Press, 1975.

Kety, S. S., Rosenthal, D., Wender, P. H., Schulsinger, F., & Jacobsen, B. The biologic and adoptive families of adopted individuals who became schizophrenic: Prevalence of mental illness and other characteristics. In L. C. Wynne, R. L. Cromwell, & S. Matthysse (Eds.), *The nature of schizophrenia: New approaches to research and treatment*. New York: Wiley, 1978.

Klerman, G. L. Affective disorders. In A. M. Nicholi, Jr. (Eds.), *The Harvard guide to modern psychiatry*. Cambridge, Mass.: Harvard University Press, 1978.

Kliegman, R. M., & King, K. C. Intrauterine growth retardation: Determinants of aberrant fetal growth. In A. A. Fanaroff, R. J. Martin, & J. R. Merkatz (Eds.), *Berhman's neonatal-perinatal medicine*. St. Louis: Mosby, 1983.

Knoblock, H., & Pasamanick, B. Prospective studies on the epidemiology of reproductive casualty: Methods, findings, and some implications. *Merrill-Palmer Quarterly of Behavior and Development*, 1966, *12*, 27–43.

Kopp, C. B., & Parmelee, A. H. Prenatal and perinatal influences on infant behavior. In J. Osofsky (Ed.), *Handbook of infant development*. New York: Wiley, 1979.

Kotelchuck, M., Schwartz, J., Anderka, M., & Finison, K. 1980 Massachusetts Special Supplemental Food Program for Women, Infants, and Children (WIC) evaluation project. Prepublication manuscript, 1983.

Kron, R. E., Kaplan, S. L., Phoenix, M. D., & Finnegan, L. P. Behavior of infants born to narcotic-dependent mothers: Effects of prenatal and postnatal drugs. In J. L. Renentaria (Ed.), *Drug abuse in pregnancy and neonatal effects.* New York: Wiley, 1977.

Kron, R. E., Litt, M., & Finnegan, L. P. Narcotic addiction in the newborn: Differences in behavior generated by methadone and heroin. *International Journal of Clinical Pharmacology and Biopharmacy,* 1975, *12,* 63–69.

Lechtig, A., Habicht, J.-P., Delgado, H., Klein, R. E., Yarbrough, C., & Martorell, R. Effects of food supplementation during pregnancy on birth-weight. *Pediatrics,* 1975, *56,* 508–520.

Lenke, R. R., & Levy, H. L. Maternal phenylketonuria and hyperphenylalaninemia: An international survey of the outcome of untreated and treated pregnancies. *New England Journal of Medicine,* 1980, *303,* 1202–1203.

Lubchenco, L. O. *The high risk of infant.* Philadelphia: Saunders, 1976.

Lubchenco, L. O., Searls, D. T., & Brazie, J. V. Neonatal mortality rate: Relationship to birth weight and gestational age. *Journal of Pediatrics,* 1972, *81,* 814–822.

Lytton, H. Do parents create, or respond to, differences in twins? *Developmental Psychology,* 1977, *13,* 456–459.

Matheny, A. P. A longitudinal twin study of stability of components from Bayley's Infant Behavior Record. *Child Development,* 1983, *54,* 356–360.

Matthysse, S. Etiological diversity in the psychoses. In N. E. Morton & C. S. Chung (Eds.), *Genetic epidemiology.* New York: Academic Press, 1978, pp. 311–363.

McDonald, R. I. The role of emotional factors in obstetric complications: A review. *Psychosomatic Medicine,* 1968, *30,* 322–327.

McGraw, M. B. Motivation of behavior. In L. Carmichael (Ed.), *Manual of child psychology.* New York: Wiley, 1946.

Metcoff, J. Association of fetal growth with maternal nutrition. In F. Falkner, & J. M. Tanner (Eds.), *Human growth* (Vol. 1): *Principles and prenatal growth.* New York: Plenum, 1978.

Moore, K. L. *The developing human: Clinically oriented embryology* (3rd ed.). Philadelphia: Saunders, 1982.

Mulvihill, J. J., & Yeager, A. M. Fetal alcohol syndrome. *Teratology,* 1976, *13,* 345–348.

Munsinger, H. Children's resemblance to their biological and adopting parents in two ethnic groups. *Behavior Genetics,* 1975, *5,* 239–254.

Nichols, R. C. Heredity and environment: Major findings from twin studies of ability, personality, and interests. *Homo,* 1978, *29,* 158–173.

Nilsson, L., Furuhjelm, M., Ingelman-Sundberg, A., & Wirsen, C. *A child is born.* New York: Dell (Delacorte Press), 1981.

O'Rourke, D. H., Gottesman, I. I., Suarez, B. K., Rice, J., & Reich, T. Refutation of the general single locus model for the etiology of schizophrenia. Unpublished manuscript, 1981.

Page, E. W., Villee, C. A., & Villee, D. B. *Human reproduction: Essentials of reproductive and perinatal medicine* (3rd ed.). Philadelphia: Saunders, 1981.

Planned Parenthood Federation of America. *11 million teenagers: What can be done about the epidemic of adolescent pregnancies in the United States.* New York: Alan Guttmacher Institute, Planned Parenthood Federation of America, 1977.

Planned Parenthood Federation of America. *Teenage pregnancy: The problem that hasn't gone away.* New York: Alan Guttmacher Institute, Planned Parenthood Federation of America, 1981.

Plomin, R., cited in S. Scarr & K. K. Kidd, Developmental behavior genetics. In M. Haith and J. Campos (Eds.), *Mussen handbook of child psychology.* New York: Wiley, 1983.

Plomin, R., DeFries, J. C., & McClearn, G. E. *Behavioral genetics: A primer.* San Francisco: Freeman, 1980.

Plomin, R., Willerman, L., & Loehlin, J. C. Resemblance in appearance and the equal environments assumption in twin studies of personality. *Behavior Genetics,* 1976, *6,* 43–52.

Proceedings, third national conference on methadone treatment (U.S. Public Health Service Publication No. 2172). Washington, D.C.: U.S. Government Printing Office, 1971.

Reed, E. W. Genetic anomalies in development. In F. D. Horowitz (Ed.), *Review of child development research* (Vol. 4). Chicago: University of Chicago Press, 1975.

Richmond, J. B. Health needs of young children. Paper presented at the John D. and Catherine MacArthur Foundation conference on child care: Growth-fostering environments for young children. Chicago, November 29, 1982.

Rosenthal, D. *Genetic theory and abnormal behavior.* New York: McGraw-Hill, 1970.

Rubin, S. *It's not too late for a baby: For women and men over 35.* Englewood Cliffs, N.J.: Prentice-Hall, 1980.

Rugh, R., & Shettles, L. B. *From conception to birth: The drama of life's beginnings.* New York: Harper & Row, 1971.

Sameroff, A. M., & Zax, M. Perinatal characteristics of the offspring of schizophrenic women. *Journal of Nervous and Mental Diseases,* 1973, *157,* 191–199.

Scarr, S. Environmental bias in twin studies. *Eugenics Quarterly,* 1968, *15,* 34–40.

Scarr, S., & Carter-Saltzman, L. Twin method: Defense of a critical assumption. *Behavior Genetics,* 1979, *9,* 527–542.

Scarr, S., & Kidd, K. K. Developmental behavior genetics. In M. Haith & J. Campos (Eds.), *Mussen handbook of child psychology.* New York: Wiley, 1983.

Scarr, S., & Weinberg, R. A. IQ test performance of black children adopted by white families. *American Psychologist,* 1976, *31,* 726–739.

Scarr, S., & Weinberg, R. A. Intellectual similarities within families of both adopted and biological children. *Intelligence,* 1977, *1,* 170–191.

Scarr, S., & Weinberg, R. A. The influence of "family background" on intellectual attainment. *American Sociological Review,* 1978, *43,* 674–692.

Scarr, S., & Weinberg, R. A. The Minnesota adoption studies: Genetic differences and malleability. *Child Development,* 1983, *54,* 260–267.

Scarr, S., & Yee, D. Heritability and educational policy: Genetic and environmental effects on IQ, aptitude, and achievement. *Educational Psychologist,* 1980, *15,* 1–22.

Smith, N. W. Twin studies and heritability. *Human Development,* 1976, *19,* 65–68.

Smoking and health: A report of the Surgeon General. (DHEW Publication No. (PHS) 79-50066, U.S. Department of Health, Education and Welfare.) Washington, D.C.: U.S. Government Printing Office, 1979.

Sontag, L. W. The significance of fetal environmental differences. *American Journal of Obstetrics and Gynecology,* 1941, *42,* 996–1003.

Sontag, L. W. War and fetal maternal relationship. *Marriage and Family Living,* 1944, *6,* 1–5.

Standley, K. Personal communication. Cited in Y. Brackbill, Obstetrical medication and infant behavior. In J. Osofsky (Ed.), *Handbook of infant development.* New York: Wiley: 1979.

Stechler, G. Newborn attention as affected by medication during labor. *Science,* 1964, *38,* 338–346.

Torgeson, A. M., & Kringlen, E. Genetic aspects of temperamental differences in infants: A study of same-sexed twins. *Journal of American Academy of Child Psychiatry,* 1978, *17,* 433–444.

Wagner, M. G., & Arndt, R. Postmaturity as an etiological factor in 124 cases of neurologically handicapped children. *Clinics in Developmental Medicine,* 1968, *27,* 89.

Watson, J. D., & Crick, F. H. C. Molecular structure of nucleic acids: A structure for deoxyribose nucleic acid. *Nature,* 1953, *171,* 737–738.

Werner, E. E., Bierman, J. M., & French, F. E. *The children of Kauai: A longitudinal study from the prenatal period to age ten.* Honolulu: University of Hawaii Press, 1971.

Werner, E. E., & Smith, R. S. *Vulnerable but invincible.* New York: McGraw-Hill, 1982.

Whaley, L. F. *Understanding inherited disorders.* St. Louis: Mosby, 1974.

Willerman, L. Effects of families on intellectual development. *American Psychologist,* 1979, *34,* 923–929.

Wilson, R. S. Twins: Early mental development. *Science,* 1972, *175,* 914–917.

Wilson, R. S. Twins: Mental development in the preschool years. *Developmental Psychology,* 1974, *10,* 580–588.

Wilson, R. S. Twins: Patterns of cognitive development as measured on the Wechsler Preschool and Primary Scale of Intelligence. *Developmental Psychology,* 1975, *11,* 126–134.

Wilson, R. S. Twins and siblings: Concordance for school-age mental development. *Child Development,* 1977, *48,* 211–216.

Wilson, R. S. The Louisville twin study: Developmental synchronies in behavior. *Child Development,* 1983, *54,* 298–316.

Wilson, R. S., & Harpring, E. B. Mental and motor development in infant twins. *Developmental Psychology,* 1972, *7,* 277–287.

part *T*wo

THE FIRST 2 YEARS

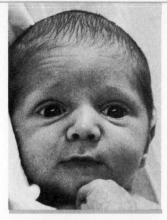

CHAPTER 3

Physical and cognitive growth in infancy

*T*he period of infancy is recognized by all societies as a special time and given a special name to distinguish it from the later life stages. Because the behaviors and abilities of the infant are so different from those of older children, the child under 2 years is often defined in terms of the absence of qualities that characterize the school-age child, such as the ability to speak, to act with intention, to reason, to be self-conscious, and to experience the emotions of guilt, empathy, and pride. But scientists face a serious problem of selection when they try to describe the qualities that infants *do* possess. Infants display a variety of behaviors: They eat, cry, move, babble, play, kick, and smile, among other things. Unfortunately, it is by no means obvious which of these reactions should be awarded special status in objective descriptions and abstract inferences.

THEORIES AND
ASSUMPTIONS
_____

The terms psychologists use to describe infants are sometimes influenced by deep, often unconscious, beliefs. These beliefs, which are usually shared by the larger society, change with history. For example, nineteenth-century observers compared the human infant with infant calves and foals, which are born in a more mature state and, therefore, can walk immediately after birth. Because the human infant appeared so helpless compared with most other newborn mammals, these observers called the human infant incompetent. Now that recent research has demonstrated some impressive though less obvious psychological capacities of the human newborn, contemporary psychologists call the infant competent. They do so in part because their frame of reference is the opinion of the nineteenth-century scholar. Infants have not changed over the last century; only our evaluation of them has.

Each scholar comes to the infant armed with a set of biases about what qualities are important, puts his or her observation "lens" closest to those phenomena, and chooses words to describe them. Consider, as an analogy, two people visiting Los Angeles for the first time. One comes from a rural village in Indonesia, the second from London. To the Indonesian, the crowds of people, traffic, and tall buildings are the most unusual aspects. After returning home, this traveler describes Los Angeles as a place with many people, cars, and buildings. But because those qualities are not unusual to the visitor from London, she ignores them and concentrates on the lack of public transportation and the high rate of street crime, both of which distinguish Los Angeles from London. Each visitor conceptualizes Los Angeles in a different way because each came with different ideas of what cities are like.

The influence of a theorist's suppositions on the selection of descriptive terms is nicely illustrated by comparing three important theorists: Sigmund Freud, Erik Erikson, and Jean Piaget. Each man highlighted a different aspect of the infant because each was loyal to assumptions that were part of the larger cultural context in which he lived.

When Freud was thinking and writing about the human infant, soon after the turn of the century, Darwinian evolutionary theory and the physical concept of energy were major sources of metaphors for human development. Scholars promoting Darwinian theory believed that the human infant was a link between apes and human adults; hence, infants should have the same basic biological drives as animals. Because hunger and sexuality were regarded as the two most important drives of animals, Freud assumed they were also central to human psychological development. In a brilliant set of essays he suggested that each child was born with a fixed amount of energy—he called this energy *libido*—which, in time, would become the basis for adult sexual motives. During the period of infancy, the libido's energy was bound up with the mouth, tongue, lips, and the activities of nursing. For this reason, Freud called this first period of development the *oral stage*. Although that bold hypothesis (which is discussed more fully in Chapter 4) may sound a little odd today, it was much more credible at the turn of the century because it was closely related to major ideas in the respected disciplines of evolutionary biology, physiology, and physics.

A half century later, many American social scientists had come to believe that social experience, not biology, was responsible for the emergence of significant human qualities and for the obvious variations in adult talent, economic success, and character. Hence, theorists looking at the infant during the period between the two World Wars focused on social interaction between mother and infant. In their view, Freud's hungry, nursing baby became a social being who was cared for by an adult. Hence, Erik Erikson (1963) regarded the first phase of development as one in which the baby learned whether adults could be relied on for care, love, and emotional security. Erikson called this first period the *stage of trust*. This idea had the same ring of validity in the 1950s that Freud's concept of the oral stage did a half century earlier.

Although Piaget was also influenced by evolutionary theory, he differed from Freud in that he focused on changes in thought that permitted successful adaptation rather than on neurotic symptoms of maladaptation. Piaget believed that the first structures of an infant's mind were created through the active manipulation of objects rather than through repeated cycles of frustration and gratification of the hunger drive. Thus, when Piaget looked at the infant he saw a baby playing with the mother's face, hair, and fingers.

Nursing, receiving love and nurture, and exploring the caregiver's fingers and face are all characteristics of the human infant. It is not obvious that one of these functions is more central than the other; only theory awards one class of events greater status than another. In our view, the infant's cognitive development provides the most comprehensive framework for the changes seen during this period; our approach to infancy therefore emphasizes cognitive functions. Although these concepts reflect the current views of a large segment of modern psychology, at another time the words chosen to describe the human infant might be different.

PHYSICAL GROWTH

The first year of life is characterized by rapid physical growth. Between birth and 1 year of age, healthy, well-fed children undergo a 50 percent increase in length and an almost 200 percent increase in weight. Rate of growth is faster during the first 6 months of life than it will ever be again. But not all parts of the body grow at the same rate, and there is no necessary relation between growth in the size of the head and growth of the muscles (Johnston, 1978).

Most scholars believe that during the first 6 months, infants from a range of cultural and social-class groups grow rather uniformly in length and weight. But after 6 months, infants from affluent homes grow more rapidly because of better nutrition and higher standards of health. After the first birthday there is a slowing of the growth rate, followed by a steady, almost linear increase in height and weight until adolescence (Figure 3.1).

FIGURE 3.1

Changes in form and proportion of the human body during fetal and postnatal life. (From C. M. Jackson. Some aspects of form and growth. In W. J. Robbins, S. Brody, A. F. Hogan, C. M. Jackson, & C. W. Green [Eds.], Growth. New Haven, Conn.: Yale University Press, 1929, p. 118. By permission.)

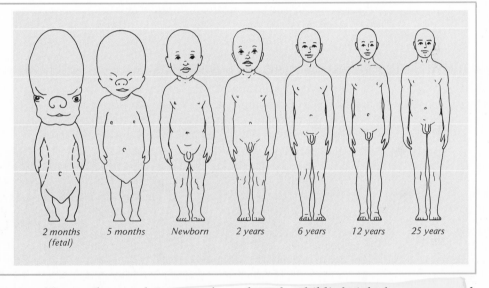

2 months (fetal)   5 months   Newborn   2 years   6 years   12 years   25 years

Not until around 3 years of age does the child's height become a good predictor of height at maturity. The correlation between a child's stature at that age and stature at maturity is about 0.7. As a child grows, the legs become longer relative to the trunk, while the trunk lengthens relative to the child's breadth. Thus, the chunky, round physique of the newborn gradually becomes the more elongated physical form of the older child.

The concept of maturation

To understand some of the major changes that occur during the first 24 months of life, it is necessary to introduce the concept of *maturation*. Maturation refers to a universal sequence of biological events in the central nervous system that permits a psychological function to appear, assuming that the child is physically healthy and lives in an environment containing people and objects. The emergence of speech between 1 and 3 years of age in almost all children exposed to adult language is one of the best illustrations of the maturation of psychological function. The brain of the 3-month-old is not sufficiently developed to permit the infant to understand or to speak language. But the 2-year-old, whose brain has become sufficiently mature, will not speak unless first exposed to the language of other people. *Maturation cannot cause a psychological function to occur; it only sets the limits on the earliest time of its appearance.* Consider an analogy to a biological event. The beginning of reproductive fertility, which occurs between 12 and 15 years of age in most American youth, is a maturational event, dependent on the release of certain hormones from the pituitary gland located at the base of the brain. But environmental factors, such as the quality of nutrition during childhood, can accelerate or retard the emergence of puberty by several years.

We do not possess a detailed understanding of the biological changes that permit new capabilities to emerge, but we can describe some of the psychological milestones of the first year that seem to be correlated with changes in the central nervous system.

Motor development during infancy

The newborn can display a variety of complex motor reflexes, some of which are necessary for survival. Infants will follow a moving light with their eyes, suck on a nipple inserted into the mouth, turn toward a touch on the corner of the mouth, and grasp an object placed in the palm. Table 3.1 lists some of the major reflexes of the newborn and the classes of stimuli that release them. They are illustrated in Figures 3.2 through 3.5.

The child's abilities to sit, stand, and walk exemplify the influence of maturation on development. Each competence occurs in sequence during the first 2 to 3 years of life as a consequence of children's use of their limbs in coordination with the maturation of specific neural tissues and the growth of bones and muscles.

TABLE 3.1	*Effective stimulus*	*Reflex*
Reflexes of the newborn	Tap upper lip sharply	Lips protrude
	Tap bridge of nose	Eyes close tightly
	Bright light suddenly shown to eyes	Eyes close
	Clap hands about 18 inches from infant's head	Eyes close
	Touch cornea with light piece of cotton	Eyes close
	With baby held on back, turn face slowly to right side	Jaw and right arm on side of face extend out; left arm flexes
	Extend forearms at elbow	Arms flex briskly
	Put fingers into infant's hand and press the palm	Infant's fingers flex and enclose finger
	Press thumb against the ball of infant's foot	Toes flex
	Scratch sole of foot from toes toward the heel	Big toe bends upward and small toes spread
	Prick sole of foot with pin	Infant's knee and foot flex
	Tickle area at corner of mouth	Head turns toward side of stimulation
	Put index finger into mouth	Infant sucks
	Hold infant in air, stomach down	Infant attempts to lift head and extends legs

FIGURE 3.2

The withdrawal reflex:
(a) Stimulation. The
examiner pricks the in-
fant's sole with a pin.
(b) Response. The
infant withdraws his
foot. (From H. Prechtl
& D. Beintema. The
neurological examina-
tion of the full-term
new-born infant.
**Little Club Clinics in
Developmental
Medicine,** 1964, **12,** 40.
London: Spastics
Society Medical Infor-
mation Unit and
William Heinemann
Medical Books, Ltd.
By permission.)

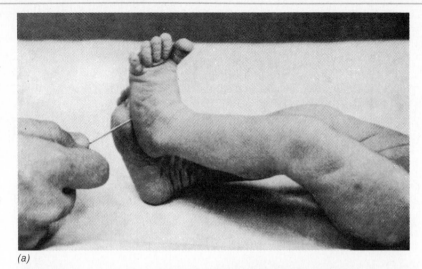

(a)

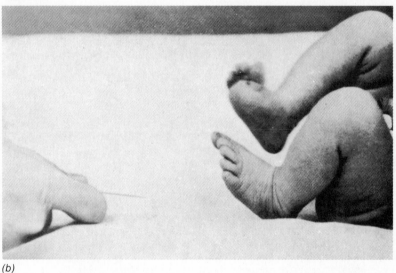

(b)

Sitting   Although the newborn cannot sit without support, this ability develops early (Gesell & Amatruda, 1941). Babies of 4 months are able to sit with
support for a minute, and by 9 months most can sit without support for 10 or
more minutes.

Crawling and creeping   Although there are individual differences in the age at
which infants begin to crawl and creep, all who are allowed to locomote on the
ground tend to go through the same sequence (Ames, 1937). The average age
for crawling (moving with the abdomen in contact with the floor) is about 9
months; creeping on hands and knees is seen at about 10 months. An infant
may skip one or two stages in development, but most children progress
through most of the stages (Ames, 1937).

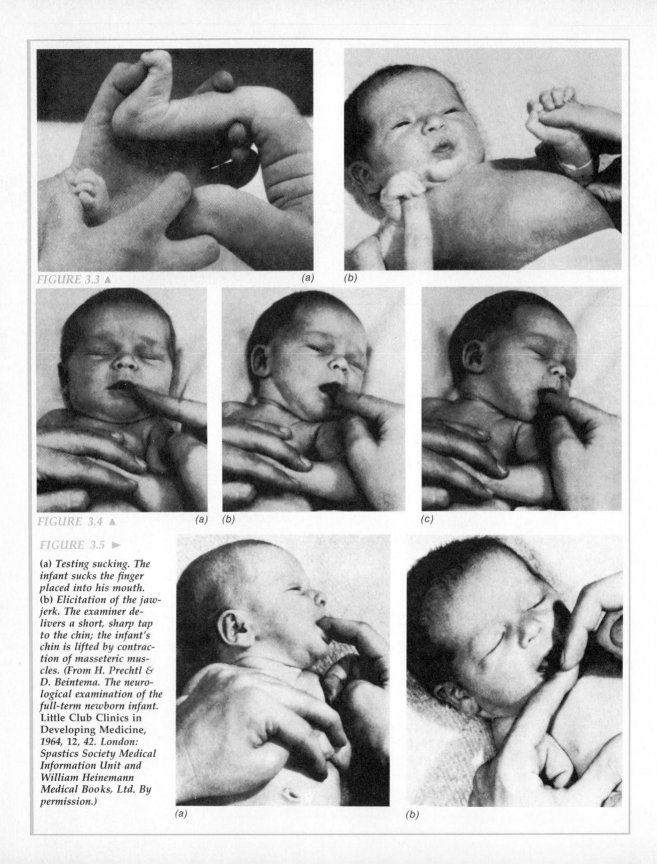

FIGURE 3.3 ▲

(a)   (b)

FIGURE 3.4 ▲

(a)   (b)   (c)

FIGURE 3.5 ▶

(a) *Testing sucking. The infant sucks the finger placed into his mouth.*
(b) *Elicitation of the jaw-jerk. The examiner delivers a short, sharp tap to the chin; the infant's chin is lifted by contraction of masseteric muscles. (From H. Prechtl & D. Beintema. The neurological examination of the full-term newborn infant.* Little Club Clinics in Developing Medicine, *1964, 12, 42. London: Spastics Society Medical Information Unit and William Heinemann Medical Books, Ltd. By permission.)*

(a)   (b)

Standing and walking   The ability to walk is built on a series of earlier achievements. As in other aspects of development, the ages at which these achievements occur cover a wide range. The median age for pulling up to a standing position and standing while holding on to furniture is between 9 and 10 months. The average child stands alone at about 11 months, walks when led by one hand at 1 year, and can walk alone, although awkwardly, at about 13 months. By 18 months, the child can get up and down stairs without help (and usually without falling) and can pull a toy along the ground. By the second birthday, the child can pick up an object from the floor without falling down and can run and walk backward (Gesell & Amatruda, 1941; Gesell, Halverson, Thompson, Ilg, Costner, Ames, & Amatruda, 1940). The progress in motor development through the first year is illustrated in Figure 3.6.

FIGURE 3.6 ►

The development of posture and locomotion in the infant.

Exactly when a child sits, stands, or walks depends on both maturation of the neural and muscular systems and the opportunity to practice emerging motor skills. Dennis (1941) prevented a pair of female twins from practicing sitting or standing by keeping them on their backs until they were 9 months old. When the children were given their first opportunity to sit alone at about 9 months, they were unable to do so. But after only a few weeks without any restriction, the children were able to sit up. Thus, although these maturational abilities develop without any special teaching, restriction of the opportunity for practice can retard their appearance. Specific training does seem to facilitate somewhat earlier appearance of motor skills (Super, 1976; Zelazo, Zelazo, & Kolb, 1972). African babies are often ahead of Caucasians in age of sitting, standing, and walking, perhaps because these are precisely the motor acts that African mothers encourage in their infants. There are no differences between African and Caucasian infants in the time of appearance of responses that are not taught, such as rolling over or crawling (Super, 1976).

It would be a mistake to suppose that a child who walks early is also unusually intelligent or advanced in other ways. Among normal children there is no predictive relation between age of walking—or between rate of physical development in general during the first 2 years—and measures of intelligence during the school years.

Infants not only acquire motor skills during the first year; they also develop many elements of the ability to think and to understand the world around them. Psychologists' efforts to study infant cognition have followed two divergent paths. One path is represented by efforts to devise infant intelligence tests. The nature of these tests and the limitations on their usefulness are described in Box 3.1.

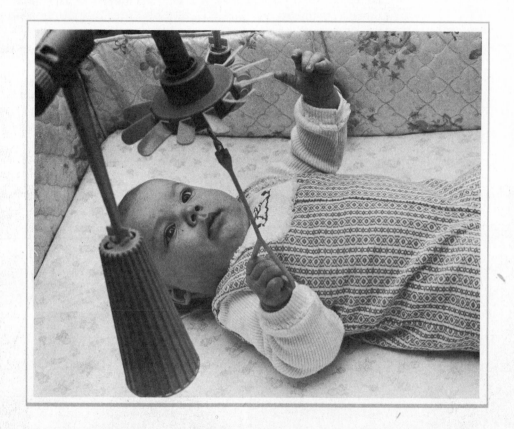

The second path consists of attempts to describe and explain some of the universal changes in infant cognitive processes and capabilities. Although many changes in cognitive functioning occur during the first year of life, four are especially prominent. First, infants acquire a major set of representations of sensory experiences from sights, sounds, tastes, and smells. These capacities are described as *perception*. Second, they make increasingly fine discriminations among physically similar events. They learn to *recognize* information and relate it to their existing knowledge. Third, they use similarities among groups of objects and events to form *categories* for events that share certain qualities. Fourth, they *remember* past experiences over increasingly longer delays.

Perception in the young infant

Infants are remarkably competent organisms, even on the first day of life. Newborns are ready to experience most, if not all, of the basic sensations of our species. They can see, hear, and smell, and they are sensitive to pain, touch, and changes in bodily position.

BOX 3.1
Assessing infant intelligence

Until recently, many psychologists believed that it was useful to regard infants, as well as older children, as possessing varying degrees of intelligence. They also believed it should be possible to predict the intelligence of the school-age child from the behaviors of the infant. Some scientists created scales to measure infant intelligence. In practice, these tests turned out to consist of procedures that determined if an infant had passed various developmental milestones at the same time as most children or earlier or later. For example, most infants can sit up without support at about 6 months of age. A 6-month-old who is not capable of sitting would be scored as being behind other infants; one who could sit up at 5 months would be scored as being ahead. By adding up a child's scores on many such maturational behaviors, such as vocalizing, making a stack of blocks, and imitating an adult, the psychologist arrives at an overall score for the infant.

When infant scales were created initially, it was hoped that they would measure infants' intelligence. Many studies over the last 20 years have shown, however, that, for most children, scores on infant intelligence scales do not predict later IQ scores, grades in school, or any other index of intellectual ability. Infant scales do make good predictors of later IQ for a very small group of children—about 5 percent—whose development is seriously delayed, often because of motor paralysis or mental retardation. But in these cases it is not necessary to use infant scales because the retardation is obvious in their behaviors.

Because infant scales do not predict later IQ, psychologists who use such scales now claim only to be assessing infants' current developmental status, not their future intelligence. Current scales are also based on the assumption that development may proceed at different rates in different domains. A child who is advanced in motor development may not be advanced in language development. For example, one of the most widely used and well standardized tests is the Bayley Scale of Infant Development. It contains separate scales to measure mental and motor development. The mental scales include imitating the actions of an adult and vocalizing; the motor scales include standing without support and grasping objects.

Because tests of infant development take a considerable amount of time and examiner skill, they are usually administered only if there is some question about the baby's developmental status. Some briefer screening instruments have been created for use by nurses and others who work with babies. One such test is the Denver Developmental Screening Test, which has items designed to measure development in four domains: personal-social (e.g., playing peek-a-boo), fine motor (e.g., bangs two cubes held in hands), language (e.g., says "dada" or "mama"), and gross motor (e.g., stands while holding on). This instrument may be used to identify children with developmental delays who need more thorough attention.

Users of infant developmental tests suggest that such scales may help to identify delays in development, which in some cases may need medical attention. For example, an infant who is behind in the language (or vocalization) items may have an undetected hearing problem. Users of these tests do not claim to be measuring the baby's intelligence.

Newborns search actively for information rather than passively waiting for people or events to prod them into action and mental work. Change in the physical characteristics of events is a central quality governing the alerting and maintenance of newborns' attention. Hence, the movement of objects, the presence of black-white contrast, and sounds that vary in loudness, rhythm, and pitch are most likely to attract and hold an infant's attention. Motion picture recordings reveal that when a newborn is placed in a dark room, he opens his eyes and looks around for subtle shadows or edges (Haith, 1980). For example, if an alert infant is shown a thick black bar on a white background, such as those in Figure 3.7, his eyes dart to the black contour and hover near it, rather than wander randomly across the entire visual field. One psychologist has suggested that newborns' attention seems to be guided by the following set of rules:

Rule 1: If awake and alert, open your eyes.

Rule 2: If you find darkness, search the environment.

Rule 3: If you find light but no edges, engage in a broad uncontrolled search of the environment.

Rule 4: If you find an edge, look near the edge and try to cross it.

Rule 5: Stay near areas that have lots of contour; scan broadly near areas of low contour and narrowly near areas of high contour (Haith, 1980).

FIGURE 3.7

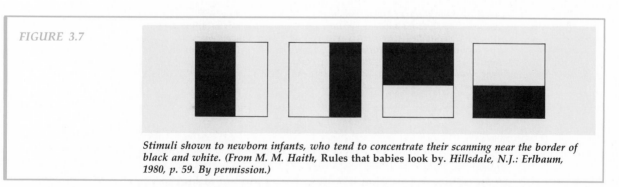

Stimuli shown to newborn infants, who tend to concentrate their scanning near the border of black and white. (From M. M. Haith, Rules that babies look by. *Hillsdale, N.J.: Erlbaum, 1980, p. 59. By permission.)*

Infants' attention to contrast is used to test visual acuity. In one procedure a baby is presented simultaneously with two stimuli alongside each other. One stimulus is a set of vertical black lines separated from each other by only a few centimeters, while the other stimulus is a blank field of equal brightness. Infants who can discriminate the stimulus with closely spaced lines from the stimulus without lines will look longer at the former because they prefer to look at the contrast created by the dark lines. Infants who cannot detect the lines as separate will look equally long at both stimuli. Using this procedure, psychologists have found that young infants can detect the difference between a pattern composed of stripes only $\frac{1}{8}$ inch wide and a patch that is completely gray.

Particular visual patterns have a special power to recruit and hold young infants' attention. Infants under 1 year look longer at concentric than at nonconcentric forms (see Figure 3.8), devote more attention to patterns composed of curved than of linear segments, and become more excited by a change from a linear to a curved line than by the reverse change.

FIGURE 3.8

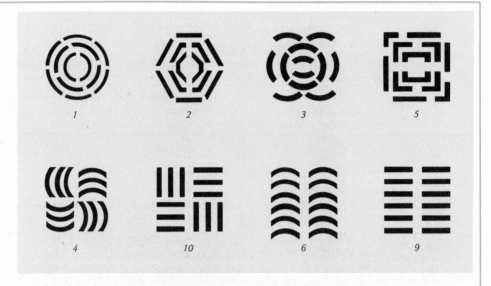

When 13-week-old infants were shown pairs of patterns composed of curves and straight-line segments, they were found to prefer forms constructed of arcs to forms constructed of straight lines, and they studied concentric patterns longer than nonconcentric ones. The number below each pattern refers to the relative power of that stimulus to maintain the infant's attention; stimulus 1 elicited the most attention, stimulus 10 the least. (From H. A. Ruff & H. G. Birch. Infant visual fixation. Journal of Experimental Child Psychology, 1974, 17, 460–473. By permission.)

Infants appear to be especially interested by a change in the size and spatial orientation of elements that are part of a larger pattern. Infants first saw a pair of identical stimuli like design 1 at the top of Figure 3.9. They then saw one of the 12 different figures shown in the two columns in Figure 3.9, along with one of the original stimuli. Only the larger circles (design 2) and the vertically arranged circles (design 3) produced prolonged attention in comparison to the original stimulus. It would be adaptive if infants were alerted by an increase in the size of objects because, in the real world, an enlarging stimulus is a clue to an approaching object. It is more puzzling why the change from hori-

FIGURE 3.9

Five- and 10-month-old infants were shown a pair of stimuli identical to stimulus 1. Then the pair of stimuli was removed, and the child saw stimulus 1 paired with one of the stimuli labeled 2 through 13. The infants showed an increase in attention to the changed stimulus 2 or 3 but did not show increased attention to the remaining stimuli. (From S. Linn, J. S. Reznick, J. Kagan, & S. Hans. Salience of visual patterns in the human infant. Developmental Psychology, 1982, 18, 651–657. By permission.)

zontal to vertical circles should be so attractive and why there was so little reaction to some of the other variations (Linn, Reznick, Kagan, & Hans, 1982).

Infants also perceive colors as belonging to discrete categories, just as adults do. The visible color spectrum from red to purple rests on continuous differences in the wavelength of light, but we perceive the colors as if they belonged to separate categories. The wavelength of a stimulus is measured in millionths of a millimeter. Even though the differences in wavelength between two shades of blue, on the one hand, and a blue and a green, on the other, are equal, infants show a greater increase in attention to a change from blue to green than to a change from one shade of blue to the other (Bornstein, Kessen, & Weisskopf, 1975). This phenomenon is called *categorical perception*. One reason that psychologists have learned so much about infants' perceptual and cognitive capacities in recent years is their invention of ingenious methods of measurement. Some techniques for measuring infant perception are described in Box 3.2.

In sum, young infants are prepared to orient to particular dimensions in the external world. Contrast, movement, curvilinearity, color, and many other qualities attract and hold infants' attention, especially when they indicate a change in the immediate perceptual field. These preferences, like a honeybee's attraction to certain colored blossoms, appear to be inborn.

The recognition of information: The schema

Psychologists have hypothesized that infants create representations of their experiences from the first days of life. Most psychologists call these representations *schemata* (plural of *schema*). A schema is an abstract representation of the original elements in an event and their relation to one another. The infant's schema for a face, for example, is likely to emphasize an oval frame containing two horizontally placed circular shapes (the eyes). Once a schema for an event is established, the child's attention tends to be prolonged when events are a little different from, but not totally unrelated to, the ones that created the original schema. Four-month-old infants, who have schemata for their parents' faces, will look a long time at a picture or a sculpture of a human face in which the eyes are placed where the mouth normally is, but they will not look very long at a face with no eyes at all. This finding illustrates their preference for moderate rather than extreme novelty.

The source of schemata in the child's experience continues to be a focus of debate. It is likely that a schema is not an exact copy of any particular object or event. First, the mind cannot register every feature of an event, even one as meaningful as the mother's face. Second, succeeding exposures to the same object or type of event are never truly identical. Because it is likely that the infant relates the second experience to the first while simultaneously recognizing some differences between the two, it is assumed that the child creates a composite of similar experiences. The composite is called a *schematic prototype*.

There is some evidence that infants can detect a similarity between two events when the events originate in different sense modalities, like vision and hearing or vision and touch. If a 6-month-old baby is first given a smooth or nubby nipple to suck on (see Figure 3.10) without being able to see the object, and later is shown a smooth and a nubby nipple, the infant looks longer at the nipple she explored with her tongue. This surprising fact suggests that the infant may have created a schema for "nubbiness" through sucking the nipple and used that schema in her visual search (Meltzoff & Borton, 1979).

In a related experiment, babies first heard either a pulsing or a continuous tone and subsequently were shown a series of short, discontinuous line segments and a continuous line. The infants looked longer at the broken line after they had heard the intermittent tone, but looked longer at the continuous line after they had heard the continuous tone (Wagner, Winner, Cicchetti, & Gardner, 1981). These findings suggest that the infants were able to extract the dimension of "discontinuity" in both the auditory and the visual modes.

Categorization ability

The ability to create a schema for a dimension that is common to varied experiences—like the dimension of continuity or discontinuity—implies that

0   2   4
cm

FIGURE 3.10

Stimuli shown in demonstrating that infants can recognize similarities between objects across sensory modalities. Infants looked at the jagged form longer than the smooth one after they had sucked the jagged form, but looked at the smooth form longer after they had sucked that one, implying that they recognized that the object they were seeing was similar to the one they had sucked (but had not seen). (From A. M. Meltzoff & R. W. Borton. Intermodal matching by human neonates. Nature, 1979, 282, 403–404. Copyright © 1979 Macmillan Journals Limited. By permission.)

infants can create categories. A *category* is usually defined as a mental representation of the dimensions that are shared by a set of similar but not identical events. The shared dimensions can be physical features, such as size and color, or actions, such as eating and throwing. Later in development the shared dimensions can be words and ideas. When a 1-year-old child playing with 20 different toys belonging to different categories confidently picks up an oblong yellow banana and then a cluster of purple grapes, we wonder why those two toys were selected from the larger array. One hypothesis is that these two objects share the quality of being edible foods. Many 1-year-olds possess categories for household furniture and animals as well as edible foods. One-year-olds will even treat pictures of objects as belonging to appropriate categories. For example, after watching a series of slides depicting different women, infants responded with prolonged attention and excited facial expressions to a picture of a dog (Reznick, 1982). The fact that dishabituation occurred (see Box 3.2) suggests that the dog represented a different category from the women.

Infants are innately prepared to detect qualities that are shared by different events. Although we say that infants breathe in order to get oxygen, it is less clear why they spontaneously form categories. Even if we posited an innate tendency to recognize dimensions of similarity among events, it is not obvious why children should go to the trouble of putting the similar objects together. One-year-olds are not trying to communicate any information to another person, and the act of grouping the objects expends energy, gains no external prize, and is not accompanied by any obvious signs of sensory pleasure. Perhaps the act of grouping together similar objects is a human example of what Konrad Lorenz calls a *fixed action pattern:* a stereotyped behavior pattern that is triggered by a certain environmental event, in this case a set of objects with similarities that can be perceptually recognized. According to this line of reasoning, the act of grouping occurs because the human infant is capable of performing that act. In the same way, a well-fed seagull will swoop down over a sandy spit just because the spit is there and gulls are capable of swooping.

The discrepancy hypothesis   By 2 to 3 months of age, infants are most likely to display prolonged attention to events that are somewhat different from those encountered in the past and to attend somewhat less to very familiar or very novel events. These "somewhat different" stimuli are called *discrepant events.* The increase in vocal excitement and attentiveness to discrepant events is part of a larger set of changes that occurs at 2 to 3 months of age. At this time the amount of spontaneous crying decreases, babbling and cooing increase, and new wave forms are seen in recordings from the infant's brain. The fact that these and other changes occur at the same time implies, but does not prove, the presence of a new stage of psychological organization resulting from maturational changes in the brain. These changes permit infants to relate an event in the perceptual field to their stored knowledge.

In order to understand the relation between the schemata the child has acquired and the degree of interest the infant will show to a discrepant event, it is necessary to realize that the various dimensions of any particular schema are not of equal importance. They differ in what psychologists call *salience.* For most 1-year-olds, the head of a person is a psychologically more salient dimen-

BOX 3.2

*How do we
know what
the baby
perceives?*

When psychologists want to determine what infants hear, see, smell, or feel, their usual strategy is the method of *habituation-dishabituation*, a procedure based on the following reasonable assumptions. When infants become bored with a particular event, because of repeated presentation or prolonged exposure, they will look at it for shorter and shorter intervals before looking away. When a changed stimulus appears, they will show increased attention (longer looks) if they detect the change. The decreased interest or boredom that accompanies the repeated presentation is called *habituation;* the recovery of interest in response to the new event is called *dishabituation*.

To cognitive psychologists, the increase in attention is important because it implies that the infant recognizes the new event as different from the original. For instance, if infants are shown a card picturing two identical red spheres until they look away out of boredom and are then shown one of the red spheres alongside a red cube, most will show longer looks at the cube, implying that they detect the difference in the shapes of the two objects.

But we must be cautious in concluding that infants do *not* detect a difference between an old and a new event simply because they do not look longer at the new stimulus. For example, when infants were shown the stimuli in Figure 3.9, those who had become habituated on stimulus 1 did not look longer at stimulus 11, the one with two circles outside the frame, even though they should have been capable of perceiving the differences between those two stimuli (Linn et al., 1982). These observations reveal a common problem in inferring mental states in others. If the child looks longer at a new stimulus, we can conclude she discriminated it from an older one. But if she does not look longer, we cannot conclude that she was unable to make the discrimination.

Because children do not always reveal their discrimination of a new stimulus by increased looking, it has proved valuable to record other behaviors besides fixation time when a dishabituation stimulus is presented. Changes in facial expression, increases or decreases in vocalization, or motor movements often occur. Some infants show a decrease in heart rate when they examine a new stimulus, suggesting that they are surprised by it.

Psychologists who are interested in discrimination of auditory stimuli cannot use visual fixation time. If the baby is young, they record high-amplitude sucking. A rubber nipple is placed in the baby's mouth, and every time the infant sucks with a specific pressure he hears a particular syllable—for instance, the syllable *pa*. When the baby becomes bored, as indicated by less frequent and less intense sucking pressure, the stimulus is changed—say, to *ba*. If the infant increases the rate and pressure of sucking, the psychologist concludes that the child detected a difference between the syllables *pa* and *ba*. Each of these changes in behavior—looking time, vocalization, sucking, heart rate—is a valid indicator that the child has detected a new stimulus.

sion than the arms and legs, because of the frequent face-to-face interaction between infant and adult. However, when a 1-year-old looks at a dog, which is typically seen at a distance and has four rather than two legs, the limbs are likely to be more salient than the head. One-year-old children were shown, one at a time, pictures of different adult women and of different dogs. After they were habituated on these pictures (that is, once they showed a pattern of decreasing interest), each child saw three different transformations of either the woman or the dog—a woman or dog without a head, a woman or dog without limbs, and a woman or dog without a body. After seeing the pictures of women, the infants showed their greatest recovery of interest to the picture of a women without a head. But after seeing a series of dogs, they showed their greatest recovery of attention to the picture of a dog without limbs. This pattern of attention suggests that the head was the more salient dimension for the schema of a person, while the limbs were more salient for the schema of a dog.

We now state a hypothetical principle, called the *discrepancy principle,* which relates an infant's interest in an event to the extent to which the event differs from the schema the child has formed. For infants under 18 months, the principle states, events that contain transformations of noncentral dimensions (like the ears of a human face or the whiskers of a cat), as well as events that transform all the central elements, usually elicit less sustained attention than events that transform one or two of the salient dimensions of a schema (like the head of a person). Stated more plainly, very slight or very extreme transformations in a schema provoke less sustained attention than moderate transformations.

In a demonstration of this principle with geometric figures, $7\frac{1}{2}$-month-old infants were shown design a or d (shown in Figure 3.11) until they became bored. Each child sat on the mother's lap in front of a viewing box. When the infant pressed a bar in front of the box, a light went on, illuminating one of the objects. When the child became bored with that object, pressing the bar would produce a different one. Infants who became bored with object a were shown either object b, c, d, or e, while those originally shown object d were shown objects a, b, c, or e. Object e can be regarded as novel for all the children. Very few infants showed their greatest interest and excitement in reaction to this object. Instead, the greatest increase in interest and excitement occurred in response to stimuli that differed slightly less than e from the original—that is, to the stimulus three steps removed in similarity from one the infant saw first. Thus, infants who had initially studied the sphere (object a) looked longest at the cylinder (object d). Those who originally saw the cylinder looked longest at the sphere (Hopkins, Zelazo, Jacobson, & Kagan, 1976).

Most of the time a discrepant event elicits attention, excitement, and even smiling because the infant is able to relate the experience to existing schemata. But sometimes a discrepancy can elicit distress. Three groups of infants were trained over a prolonged period to kick a mobile constructed of either 2, 6, or 10 units. After learning to make a kicking movement to make a mobile move, all infants were given a mobile containing only 2 units. The children who originally played with the 2-unit mobile showed no change in their behavior. But those who experienced the change from a 10- or 6-unit mobile to one made

FIGURE 3.11

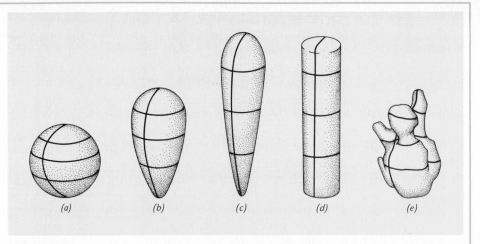

Infants were shown either stimulus A or D until they became bored with it. Infants who had seen A showed the greatest interest in D, and those who had seen D showed the greatest interest in A out of the remaining stimuli. In each case, they were more attentive to the stimuli that were moderately discrepant from the one they saw initially than to stimulus E, which was very different. (From J. R. Hopkins, P. R. Zelazo, S. W. Jacobson, & J. Kagan. Infant reactivity to stimulus schema discrepancy. **Genetic Psychology Monographs,** *1976, 93, 27–62. By permission.)*

of only 2 units fretted and cried. Their distress can be viewed as a reaction to a comparison of the amount of movement produced by a 2-unit mobile in front of them with their schema of the previous day's more exciting experience with the larger, more interesting mobile. The fact that the infants' kicking produced less variety of stimulation than it did formerly may also have contributed to their distressed state (Mast, Fagen, Rovee-Collier, & Sullivan, 1980).

The discrepancy principle has several implications worth noting. Infants are most likely to become alerted by events that are a little different from their knowledge. But, because each infant has a different set of schemata, the events that will be most alerting will not be the same for all children. At any one time an infant is maximally sensitive to a narrow band of events. As that set of experiences is understood and new schemata created or old ones modified, the child becomes receptive to a new envelope of events. Through this successive understanding of discrepant experience, cognitive abilities grow.

Because variations in what is known are most likely to provoke an attempt at understanding and therefore to promote cognitive development, the intellectual growth of infants living in environments with little variety should be a little slower than that of infants living in environments that contain considerable change. Cross-cultural data gathered on children living in isolated rural villages, as well as information on children growing up in institutions with high ratios of infants to caregivers, confirm this prediction. These children experience less variety each day and show a slower rate of attainment of the cognitive milestones of the first year (Kagan, Kearsley, & Zelazo, 1978).

Very young infants can recognize that an event in their present experience is related to their schemata. This ability is called *recognition memory*. For example, an infant who is given a new doll one day will recognize it the next day. One way infants announce their recognition of an event is by looking back and forth between a new and a familiar object as though they were comparing the two. Infants tested monthly from 6 to 11 months of age were first shown a card containing three identical toys (toy ducks or dolls). After either a 1- or a 7-second delay, the first card was replaced by a second card which was sometimes identical to the first and sometimes had one or more of the three toys replaced by a different toy. After a 1-second delay, the 8-month-olds moved their eyes back and forth between the new and the old toys more often than the 6-month-olds, suggesting that the older infants recognized the items on the first card. However, recognition memory decayed quickly in the 8-month-olds, for if they had to wait 7 seconds, they showed fewer alternating glances. Eleven-month-olds looked back and forth after a 7-second delay as well as after a 1-second delay, implying that they had not forgotten the toys they had seen on the original card (Kagan & Hamburg, 1981).

Soon after the middle of the first year, two additional aspects of memory emerge. The first is the ability to retrieve or recall a schema even if there is no relevant stimulus in the immediate field—often described as *recall memory*. Four-month-olds can recognize that a face in front of them is or is not similar to one they have seen before, but they are far less able to retrieve the schema for their father if their father is not in the room to prod their memory. This distinction between recognizing the father when he is present and retrieving the schema for the father when he is not present is similar to the difference between recognition and recall memory applied to older children and adults. In recognition, the person remembers that a present stimulus was experienced in the past. In recall, no relevant stimulus is present, and the person must retrieve the schema or knowledge. True-false questions on an examination require recognition, whereas essays require recall memory. It appears that the capacity for recall—the ability to retrieve schemata without relevant stimuli in the perceptual field—is enhanced after 8 months of age.

A related ability that emerges at the same time might be called *working memory*. When older children and adults read a sentence or listen to a conversation, they are able to hold the incoming information and integrate it with their knowledge, even if some of the incoming information occurred 30 to 60 seconds earlier. Most adults who read or hear the sentence "The Senegalese woman whose father had fought against the French decided before the end of colonialism to live in Nigeria" would understand and mentally rephrase it, despite its length. They are able to hold all the information in the sentence in active memory while retrieving their stored knowledge of Senegal, French rule, and the location of Nigeria. Children seem to develop a working memory around 8 months of age, permitting them to compare and relate incoming information with past knowledge, though, of course, much less effectively than older children and adults.

A convenient and reasonable way to evaluate retrieval memory requires infants to remember over a short period where an attractive toy, such as a rattle, has been hidden. In one experiment the infants had to find a toy that was hidden under one of two identical cloths in front of them. On each of the trials there was a delay of either 1, 3, or 7 seconds before the child was permitted to reach for the toy; a screen separated the child from the toy during the brief delay. Infants improved steadily in their ability to remember the location of the toy across the last half of the first year. Very few 8-month-olds could remember the toy's location after a 1-second delay, but by 1 year, all infants could find the toy after a 3-second delay, and a majority could solve the problem when the delay was as long as 7 seconds. By 18 months, infants rarely made an error, even after a delay as long as 10 seconds.

Uncertainty and infants' fears

During the period from about 8 to 12 months, infants develop certain new fears, possibly because of the improvement in active memory and other cognitive processes. Although a moderately unfamiliar event usually produces increased interest and, occasionally, excited babbling and smiling, it can also produce a state psychologists call *uncertainty* if the infant's efforts to relate the event to one of his schemata are not successful. For example, an infant may cry if his mother is wearing an unusual hat that makes her look different or if the child hears for the first time a human voice coming from the speaker in a tape recorder. If, in addition, the infant has no behavior he can issue to divert his attention from the state of uncertainty (such as playing with a toy or reaching for his mother), a more serious state is likely to arise. This state is often called *fear* or *anxiety*. If a 1-year-old can control the appearance of a jack-in-the-box by hitting a panel, he will show less fear than an infant who has no control over when the toy will pop up (Gunnar, 1980). Although the state of uncertainty produced by the inability to understand a discrepant event is not synonymous with the emotions of fear or anxiety, it often precedes them.

Fear of strangers One of the most common fears of the last part of the first year is usually called *stranger anxiety*. A child of 8 months is showing stranger anxiety when she wrinkles her face as a stranger approaches, looks back and forth between the stranger and the mother, and after a few seconds begins to cry. Children do not always react to a stranger with fear. The fear is least likely to occur if the stranger approaches slowly, talks gently, and initiates play with the child; it is most likely if the stranger walks toward the child quickly, is quiet or very loud, and attempts to pick up the child. Although some children are more fearful than others, almost all infants show a fear reaction to a stranger on some occasion between 7 and 12 months of age.

One explanation of this fear is based on the assumption that infants compare the schemata for the faces of familiar people with their perception of the stranger and try to relate the two. If they are unable to understand the discrepancy, they become distressed. Although this distress resembles the upset shown by the 3-month-olds who saw the 2-unit mobile following exposure to the 10-unit toy, two important elements have been added to the competence of the 8-month-old. First, recognition of the discrepancy occurs much more quickly. The older child cries within the first 20 seconds of seeing the unfamiliar adult. More important, the older child does not have to be looking at the familiar person in order to become uncertain. The 8-month-old compares the stranger with her retrieved schema of the familiar person; because she cannot assimilate it, she becomes uncertain and may cry.

Separation fear   The fear of temporary separation from a familiar caregiver shows up most clearly when the infant is left in an unfamiliar room or in the presence of an unfamiliar person. It is less likely to occur if the child is left at home or with a familiar relative or baby sitter. The mother tells her 1-year-old, who is playing happily, that she is leaving but will return shortly, and then departs. The child will gaze at the door where the mother was last seen and a few seconds later begin to cry. Blind 1-year-olds who cannot see the mother are not protected against this distress, for they cry when they *hear* the mother leave the room (Fraiberg, 1975). Separation fear usually appears between 7 and 12 months of age, peaks between 15 and 18 months, then gradually declines.

An explanation of separation distress similar to the one applied to stranger

anxiety seems appropriate. Following the mother's departure, the infant generates from memory the schema of the mother's former presence and compares that knowledge with the present situation. If the child cannot resolve the discrepancy inherent in the comparison of the schemata for the present and past, she becomes uncertain and may cry. However, some children begin to cry as soon as their mother goes toward the door. Why?

One possibility is that the enhanced retrieval and comparison capacities of the maturing infant are accompanied by the ability to generate anticipations of the future—mental representations of possible events. The child may think something like, "What will happen now? Will the parent return? What can I do?" If the child cannot answer such questions (and thus anticipate the mother's return) or make an instrumental response that might resolve the uncertainty, she becomes vulnerable to distress and may cry. If, however, the child can anticipate what might happen (say, that the parent will return soon with a treat for the child), she may laugh. Laughter in anticipation of a novel event increases after 8 months of age.

This interpretation of separation distress differs from an earlier, more traditional one. The earlier explanation assumed that children cried after maternal departure because they anticipated pain or danger as a consequence of the mother's absence, that is, because of what psychologists call a conditioned fear reaction. Although this explanation seems reasonable, it does not explain why infants all over the world suddenly develop, between 8 and 12 months of age, an expectation that an unpleasant event will occur when the mother leaves (see Figure 3.12). Moreover, children whose mothers leave them

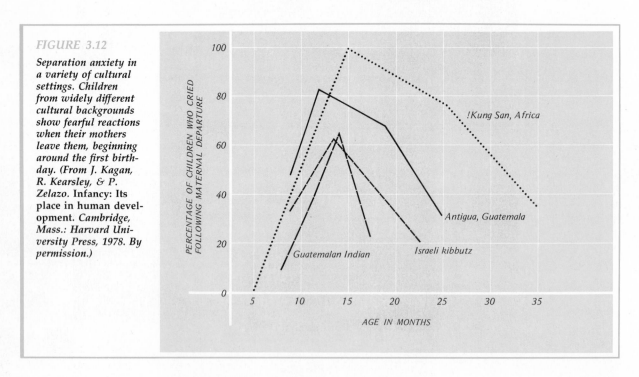

FIGURE 3.12

Separation anxiety in a variety of cultural settings. Children from widely different cultural backgrounds show fearful reactions when their mothers leave them, beginning around the first birthday. (From J. Kagan, R. Kearsley, & P. Zelazo. Infancy: Its place in human development. *Cambridge, Mass.: Harvard University Press, 1978. By permission.)*

each morning in a day-care center do not show separation distress earlier or with less intensity than those who are cared for by their mothers continually (Kagan, et al., 1978). The age of emergence of separation distress during the first 2 years of life is very similar for children being raised in nuclear families, kibbutzim in Israel, barrios in Guatemala, Indian villages in Central America, and American day-care centers. Although these settings provide for different degrees and types of contact with the mother, separation anxiety appears at remarkably similar times.

The intensity of distress over temporary separation may depend in part on the quality of the emotional relationship with the caregiver, a topic discussed in Chapter 4. The first appearance of separation anxiety, however, seems to be related to the emergence of three important cognitive competences: the abilities to retrieve the past, to compare past and present, and to generate (anticipate) possible events that might occur in the immediate future. Retrieval of knowledge, relation of present to past, and inference about the future —three stalwarts of cognitive functioning in the older child—seem to be present, albeit in rudimentary form, by the end of the first year.

We are left with one final puzzle. The presence of a familiar person, such as a grandparent, or a familiar setting, such as home, decreases the likelihood of crying in response to maternal departures, to strangers, and to unfamiliar toys. Why is this so? The presence of a familiar person or setting may make it easier for the child to make some response other than crying when the state of uncertainty is generated. Action often dispels anxiety in infants as it does in adults. When the mother leaves but the grandparent remains in the room, the grandparent's presence provides the infant with a potential target for particular behaviors. The child can approach if he wishes, vocalize, or simply turn to the grandparent. That knowledge seems to keep uncertainty under control.

Separation distress recedes after 2 years of age because the older child is able to understand the event or predict the return of the mother. The child's experiences during the second year have created knowledge that permits solution of the problem that engendered the anxiety in the first place.

Other fears Similar cognitive changes may help account for other fears during the period of infancy. One such fear is called avoidance of the visual cliff. An infant is placed on a narrow runway that rests on a large sheet of glass (Figure 3.13). On one side of the runway is a checkerboard pattern placed directly under the glass; on the other, the checkerboard pattern is placed 1 to 2 feet below the glass, giving the appearance of depth to that side—hence the term *visual cliff*. Prior to 7 months, most infants do not avoid the deep side of the glass. If their mother calls them from the deep side, they will cross to her. But after 8 months, most infants avoid the side that has the appearance of a cliff and will cry if they are placed on the deep side. Why do these signs of fear appear at this time? They are not due to a new ability to perceive depth, for younger infants can perceive the difference between the deep and shallow sides, as evidenced by the fact that they show a distinct cardiac reaction when lowered face down on the deep side (Campos, Langer, & Krawitz, 1970).

One possibility is that the older child is mature enough to compare the visual information implying depth and the retrieved memory of unpleasant

FIGURE 3.13

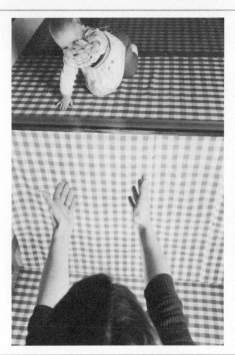

The "visual cliff." On one side of the glass-covered table, the checkerboard is immediately under the glass; on the other, it is lowered. Infants show that they can perceive depth when they hesitate to cross the deep side. (Enrico Feroeili, Wheeler Pictures.)

experiences, perhaps associated with a fall or a warning from the mother, with the secure feeling of solidity provided by the glass. If the child cannot resolve the uncertainty generated by these conflicting sources of information—it looks dangerous but feels safe—he may cry and show signs of fear.

The cognitive changes that seem to account for the appearance of new fears during the last part of the infant's first year are probably based on maturational changes in the central nervous system. This notion receives support from developmental changes in the fear reaction of monkeys when they are put in an unfamiliar place. Each of six rhesus monkeys was raised alone with an inanimate toy (a hobbyhorse) in a restricted, confining environment. Each monkey was regularly placed in a novel environment, and the investigators noted two indexes of fear: a rise in heart rate and the occurrence of distress vocalizations. The highest heart rates and most distress calls occurred when the monkeys were about 4 months old, and there was a dramatic increase in these two signs of fear between 2 and 4 months of age. The growth rate for brain and body in the monkey is about three to four times the rate observed in the human infant. Hence, the comparable period in the human child would be the interval between 7 and 15 months. This is precisely the time when fear reactions to unfamiliar persons, to temporary separation, and to the visual cliff appear in human infants. Because the monkeys raised with the inanimate object had no opportunity to develop learned fears through interaction with other living creatures, it seems likely that their increased uncertainty and apprehension in response to discrepant events at 2 to 4 months were due in part to maturational changes in the central nervous system (Mason, 1978).

The changes in the motor and cognitive capabilities of the infant that have been discussed so far are summarized in Table 3.2. Many of them undoubtedly have a maturational basis—they depend at least partly on changes in the neurological system and on other aspects of physical maturation. As we have already noted, however, complex human behavior is almost always influenced both by the biological attributes of the individual and by experience. One framework used by psychologists to study the changes produced by experience is learning theory, particularly the basic concept of conditioning. We will discuss conditioning in this section as it applies to infants, but the concepts presented apply more generally to learning by humans at all ages and by many animals as well.

TABLE 3.2
Developmental milestones during the first year

| Area | AGE IN MONTHS | | | | | |
	0–2	3–4	5–6	7–8	9–10	11–12
Motor	Turns head; lifts chin when lying on stomach	Lifts chest; holds head erect; reaches for an object	Holds head steady; transfers an object from one hand to another	Sits with support	Stands with help; crawls	Pulls self to standing position; walks with support
Cognitive		Recognition of the past; controlled scanning of stimuli	Selected imitation	Retrieval memory; object permanence	Comprehension of language	Symbolic play; first meaningful words
Emotion		Distress to discrepancy; smile to assimilation		Stranger and separation anxiety begin; facial signs of anger to frustration		Sadness to loss of an attachment figure

Infants learn new habits and emotional reactions through two types of conditioning, classical and instrumental. *Conditioning* refers to the creation of a new association between a feeling, physiological state, or action on the one hand and a stimulus event on the other.

Classical conditioning

The most famous example of classical conditioning (sometimes called respondent conditioning) is Pavlov's pioneering set of experiments with the salivation response in dogs. Pavlov showed that a dog could be conditioned to salivate to the stimulus of a buzzer. This was accomplished by pairing the presentation of the sound of the buzzer (called the *conditioned stimulus*) with the presentation of food (called the *unconditioned stimulus*). Food in an animal's mouth innately elicits the salivation response, while salivation does not ordinarily occur to the sound of a buzzer. As a result of repeated pairing of the buzzer and the food, the buzzer alone came to elicit the salivation response. The dog had learned a new association between the buzzer and salivation.

An *unconditioned stimulus* is an event that produces a certain response (the *unconditioned response*) automatically, that is, without learning. The *unconditioned response* to food is the production of saliva; to thunder it is an increase in heart rate. If the unconditioned stimulus is repeatedly associated in time or space with a neutral stimulus that does not ordinarily produce the response, a link is formed between the neutral stimulus and the response. Soon the neutral stimulus alone (now called the *conditioned stimulus*) will elicit the response (now called the *conditioned response*).

A child looking out a window at a passing bus hears an unexpected clap of thunder and cries. The next time he sees a bus pass the house, he may experience the feeling of fear. The association of the sight of the bus (the conditioned stimulus) and the fear reaction to the thunder (the unconditioned stimulus) changes the child. The sight of the bus now has the capacity to elicit the conditioned response. It is likely that many feeling states are classically conditioned in children. Fear of lightning and fear of dogs are two obvious candidates.

Despite almost three-quarters of a century of research, we still do not know how classically conditioned associations are established. Psychologists assume that infants (and older people as well) are prepared, by their biology, to associate certain events with certain internal reactions or overt responses. Not all stimuli are capable of becoming conditioned stimuli for a particular response, and conditioned associations do not occur every time two events occur close together in time. A nursing baby, for example, is prepared to associate the fragrance of the mother's perfume with the feeling state that accompanies feeding but is less prepared to associate the temperature of the room or color of the walls with that feeling state.

Instrumental conditioning

There is another form of conditioning, called instrumental or operant conditioning, which differs from classical conditioning in many respects. A 1-year-old cries when his mother tucks him into bed, turns out the light, and begins to leave the room. The child's cry provokes the mother to reenter the room, turn on the light, and return to the infant's side. That sequence increases the probability that the child will cry when put to bed the next day, because the mother's return is a reinforcing event. Another 1-year-old picks up her glass of milk by the top, causing it to spill. When she picks up the second glass and holds it by the side, it does not spill, and she drinks the contents. The successful outcome is called the reinforcing event. Because the reinforcement—the return of the mother or being able to drink the milk—was attained by crying or holding the glass on the side, those responses have a higher probability of occurring again in response to those specific conditions.

The exact form of a young infant's sucking response can be modified by presenting or withholding milk, and babies can be instrumentally conditioned to turn their heads to certain sounds. They learn to *discriminate* cues in the environment that signal when they will be reinforced or which of several behaviors will be reinforced. One scientist (Papousek, 1967), presented 6-week-old infants with either a bell or a buzzer. When the bell sounded, the baby would receive milk only from the nipple on the left, not from the one on the right. When the buzzer sounded, milk was available only on the right and not on the left. After about 30 days of such experiences, the infants learned to turn to the left when they heard the bell and to the right when they heard the buzzer. Papousek was even able to condition 4-month-old infants to make two consecutive turns to one side or to alternate turns to the left with turns to the right.

Reinforcement increases the probability of the recurrence of the instrumentally conditioned response in a particular context. When the reinforcing event reduces a biological drive like hunger or thirst, it is called a *primary reinforcer*. Any objects or people who were present when the biological drive was reduced may acquire reinforcing value and are called *secondary reinforcers*.

In the past, it seemed that the important thing about a reinforcement was its ability to provide pleasure. But this definition is too simple. We do not feel pleasure every time we engage in instrumental behavior—that is, in actions that attain a goal. Getting in a car to commute to school or work, for instance, is an instrumental behavior that may be performed daily even though it produces little if any pleasure.

Some psychologists argue, therefore, that any change in experience can be reinforcing if it increases the probability that a response will recur. But changes in experience do not always increase the likelihood of a response. In addition, with repetition, an event that is initially reinforcing seems to lose its reinforcing qualities. Consider an example of a baby who strikes a balloon full of plastic beads, causing it to move and make a noise. The baby laughs and repeats the action, and the baby smiles. The movement and interesting noise appear to be reinforcing. This sequence seems to be a nice example of the principle of instrumental conditioning, implying that the baby should repeat the act again and again. But after only a few minutes the baby stops, as if bored. This remarkably common phenomenon—boredom following attainment of what appears to be a desirable goal—suggests that the child's state changes after he experiences reinforcements, and as a result the child's motivation for the reinforcing event is altered. This process is described in learning theory as *satiation*.

Instrumental conditioning has proved to be extremely useful in changing human behavior. For example, it has been used to help retarded children learn basic skills, such as how to tie their shoes or eat with silverware. Both primary reinforcers like cake and candy, and secondary reinforcers, like money, tokens, and gold stars have been used effectively.

<table>
<tr><td>

PIAGET'S CONCEPTION OF INFANCY

</td><td>

A second approach to understanding how the infant's experience combines with maturational changes is the cognitive developmental theory of Jean Piaget. Our description of growth over the first year has awarded special emphasis to perceptual schemata and enhancement of recognition, retrieval, and active memory. Each of these cognitive functions develops through attention to new experiences and maturation of the central nervous system. Jean Piaget also emphasized the cognitive functions of the infant, but he awarded greater importance to infants' actions with objects than to attention, discrepancy, retrieval memory, and the creation of perceptual representations that are not linked to action.

</td></tr>
<tr><td>

Sensorimotor schemes

</td><td>

The central unit of knowledge in Piaget's view of infancy is the *sensorimotor scheme*, best defined as a representation of a class of motor actions that is used to obtain a goal. Piaget's use of the term *scheme* is similar to the term *schema* used earlier in the chapter in that it is the child's representation of the elements in several events, but Piaget emphasized the child's *actions* as the

</td></tr>
</table>

content of these early schemes. Some important sensorimotor schemes include grasping, throwing, sucking, banging, and kicking. Additionally, when a 1-year-old wants a distant toy resting on a blanket, the infant pulls the blanket closer in order to obtain the object. Pulling the blanket is a sensorimotor action scheme, a generalized response that can be used to solve a variety of problems. Bouncing in the crib in order to make toys attached to the crib shake or move is another example of a sensorimotor scheme.

Piaget claimed that children acquire knowledge about objects through their actions with them. For example, children learn about their fingers by clasping and sucking them, and they learn about mobiles by tracking and kicking them. These sensorimotor schemes change as a function of two important processes that Piaget calls *assimilation* and *accommodation.* In assimilation, the child interprets the meaning of an object in relation to an existing motor scheme. For example, a child of 8 or 9 months who sees a small wooden ball will probably try to put it into her mouth. In Piagetian language we say the child is assimilating the ball to her sucking scheme. In the complementary process of accommodation, the child changes her sensorimotor scheme so that her response is better tailored to the object. Once the child learns that a ball is something to be thrown, she will accommodate to that new function, and the next time she sees a ball she may try to throw it instead of mouthing it. Piaget believes that assimilation and accommodation are involved in all cognitive functioning. There is always a tension between assimilation and accommodation when a child encounters a new event. Understanding occurs, Piaget says, when the two processes are in balance or in *equilibrium.*

Stages of the sensorimotor period

Piaget believed that intellectual development passes through a series of connected stages during which children's knowledge of the world takes different forms. During the first 18 to 24 months, when the infant is in the *sensorimotor period* of development, intelligence is manifested in action. Piaget proposed that the sensorimotor period is differentiated into six developmental stages (Piaget, 1954). Major changes occur across these six stages, with the infant gradually progressing from a newborn who executes a set of automatic reflexes to a 2-year-old who invents new ways to solve problems.

The first stage of the sensorimotor period is seen in the automatic inborn reflexes of infants, including their ability to suck, cry, move their arms and legs, track a moving object, and orient to a sound. In the second stage, which Piaget calls primary circular reactions, the coordination of these reflexes improves. A hungry infant who flails about may accidentally brush his finger against his lips and subsequently repeat that action, which is not an inborn reflex.

In the third stage of the sensorimotor period, which typically occurs by 6 months of age, infants try to preserve or maintain interesting experiences and seem to be oriented toward an external goal. A child will kick the crib in order to hear the bells on a crib toy ring, for example. In the fourth stage, children seem to coordinate their sensorimotor schemes to attain an external goal. For example, toward the end of the first year, a child will pick up a cover in order to retrieve a toy he saw his father place there earlier.

After the first birthday, when children have entered the fifth stage, they invent new sensorimotor schemes. A 15-month-old who sees an attractive toy roll under a couch will try to retrieve it. Realizing that his arm is not long enough, he may try to push the toy with a stick—an invention of a new sensorimotor scheme to attain a desired goal.

In the last stage, children invent new schemes through a kind of mental exploration in which they imagine certain events and outcomes. An 18-month-old who wants to reach a light switch that is too high will look back and forth between the light switch and a chair, then suddenly pull the chair over to the light switch, stand on it, and turn on the light. This behavior, which occurs later during the second year, represents the final stage of the sensorimotor period. For Piaget, the most significant feature of the sixth stage is the development of a form of imagery that can be used to solve a problem or attain a goal for which the child has no habitual, available action. At this stage infants do not solve problems by trial-and-error explorations, as in the fifth stage, but by "internal experimentation, an inner exploration of ways and means" (from Flavell, 1963). Piaget gives a vivid illustration:

> At one year, six months, for the first time Lucienne plays with a doll carriage whose handle comes to the height of her face. She rolls it over the carpet by pushing it. When she comes against a wall, she pulls, walking backward. But as this position is not convenient for her, she pauses and without hesitation goes to the other side to push the carriage again. She therefore found the procedure in one attempt, apparently through analogy to other situations but without training, apprenticeship, or chance.
> (quoted in Flavell, 1963)

Object concept

Piaget made some ingenious observations on the development of what he calls the *permanence of the object*—the belief that objects continue to exist even when they are out of sight. During the first 2 or 3 months of life, children will follow an object visually until it passes out of their line of sight and then abandon their search for it. From 3 to 6 months, vision and movement of arms and hands become coordinated. Infants now grab for objects they can see but do not reach for objects outside their immediate visual field. Piaget interprets the failure to search for hidden objects as indicating that children do not realize that the hidden objects still exist.

During the last 3 months of the first year, children advance one step further. They reach for an object that is hidden from view if they have watched it being hidden. Thus, a child who sees the mother place a toy under a blanket will search for the toy there. Ten-month-old infants show surprise if they first see an object being covered by a person's hand and discover later when the hand is removed that the object is missing. Their surprise suggests that they expected the object to be there; in other words, they believe in the permanence of the object (Charlesworth, 1966).

Piaget interprets the growth of the concept of object permanence as a result of the child's prior interactions with objects. Piaget believes that a 9-month-old's knowledge of the location of an object is contained in the actions necessary to retrieve it. A child is shown two covers—let us call them A and B—and the examiner hides an object under cover A, allowing the child to re-

trieve it successfully on two occasions. According to Piaget, the child's knowledge of the location of the object is contained in the sensorimotor schemes that were used in reaching for it at location A. Hence, if the examiner now hides the toy under cover B while the child watches, the child will still search under cover A. However, this error is most likely to occur if there is a delay of 5 or 6 seconds between hiding the toy at location B and permitting the child to reach for it. If the delay is very short—say, only 1 second—the child does not make this error. This suggests that memory must be an important component in the child's ability to search for hidden objects.

How different is this interpretation of the child's behavior from Piaget's? At one level it must be true that the 12-month-old believes in the permanence of the hidden object: Otherwise the child would not search for the toy. But perhaps this competence can only occur after retrieval memory has matured. Should we view the 8-month-old's reaching for a covered rattle as reflecting an improvement in retrieval memory, the development of the concept of the permanent object, or both? Either explanation is possible.

Piaget's assumptions about development

Because Piaget's theory was so rich in hypotheses about children's development, it stimulated much of the research investigating infant cognition over recent years. But, as the preceding discussion of object permanence demonstrates, many psychologists have come to question certain aspects of the theory. Some of these questions concern Piaget's basic assumptions about the nature of development during the first 2 years of life.

Piaget's theory of the sensorimotor period of intellectual development contains four major assumptions. The first, with which most psychologists agree, states that interaction with the environment is an essential facilitator of development, though maturational changes affect *how* the child will use that experience to construct new knowledge. For Piaget, the central force for growth is the child's action on objects. Throwing, pushing, pulling, sucking of balls, fingers, and cups change the sensorimotor schemes and create more sophisticated ways of dealing with them.

Second, within infancy, psychological growth is viewed by Piaget as gradual or continuous rather than discontinuous (see Chapter 1). For instance, the child's ability to know that objects are permanent grows slowly from the first days of life. Piaget proposed more qualitative or discontinuous changes between other major stages. However, some psychologists assert that there are qualitative changes during infancy, for example, when working memory emerges.

A third assumption is that there is a connection between successive periods of development. Connectivity means that each new advance in cognitive functioning is dependent on the preceding phase and includes some of the prior competences. Mastering the piano is a nice example, for the growth of that skill is gradual and cumulative, each new improvement being built on earlier achievements. Most developmental theorists have assumed that the growth of mental structures during the early years is like learning to play the piano. This description is likely to be valid for many aspects of development, but perhaps not for all. For example, the onset of separation fear may not have obvious roots in developments during the first 3 months of life.

A fourth assumption in Piaget's theory of infancy is that increased intentionality is one of the major competences to develop during the first 2 years of life. Children of 2 can make a plan, select the objects the plan requires, and implement the plan with a resistance to distraction not possible in the opening weeks or months of life. Piaget believed that intentionality gradually emerges from the repetition of actions that produce change in the world, but some psychologists argue that intentionality might appear in the repertoire late in the first year partly as a result of the maturation of parts of the brain.

SUMMARY

Present-day psychologists speak of the "competent infant" because they have recognized the many capabilities with which human infants enter the world. Scholars in different periods of history have focused on various features of infants, such as their emotional needs or physical growth. In recent years, infants' cognitive skills have been the subject of a great deal of research attention, with the result that we know considerably more about what infants can perceive and understand than we did 20 years ago.

One obvious and dramatic change during the first year of life occurs in the physical growth of the child. On the average, infants increase by 50 percent in length and by about 200 percent in weight during the first 12 months. Also, the body proportions change.

Many changes during infancy are at least partly due to maturation. Maturation refers to a universal sequence of biological events in the central nervous system that permits a psychological function to appear. Maturation alone cannot cause a psychological attribute to emerge; it only sets the limits on the earliest time of appearance.

Motor developments during infancy are good examples of functions that depend on maturation. During the first year, children acquire the ability to sit unsupported, then to crawl, and finally to walk. Even though these abilities depend on maturation, they also depend on the opportunity to practice motor skills—that is, on the child's experience. In general, the time at which motor functions, such as walking, appear is not related to intelligence or even to later physical development.

Cognitive developments during the first year occur in many domains, but four are especially prominent. The first is in perception. The young infant is capable of perceiving objects and qualities, like color, rigidity, depth, and shape. Young infants are particularly likely to look at movement, contrast, and change in size or spatial orientation of elements.

The second cognitive capacity is recognition of information. Infants can recognize stimuli that are similar but not identical, such as repeated views of a face from slightly different angles. Many psychologists propose that infants create mental representations of their experiences, called schemata. The schema is probably not an exact copy of any object or event, but it contains many of its crucial elements. Infants use these schemata to recognize when an object is similar or identical to one they have encountered before. They can even recognize objects they have experienced in one sensory modality (such as touching) when they encounter them in another modality (such as looking).

The third cognitive capacity is the ability to categorize—to group objects or events on the basis of some common characteristics. By age 1, for instance, children may group objects by color, or they may group foods together, separating them from inedible objects.

The discrepancy hypothesis is one attempt to explain the child's attention to cognitive processing of events. According to this hypothesis, children are most likely to display prolonged attention and interest in response to events that are somewhat discrepant from those encountered previously, but are not completely unfamiliar. The underlying process proposed is that infants compare an event to their existing schemata and are most interested in events that are slightly, but not completely, different from a schema they already know.

The fourth cognitive achievement in the first year is the enhancement of memory. Very young infants can recognize a stimulus they have seen before, but as they grow older, they can recognize things over an increasingly longer time delay. Soon after the middle of the first year, they appear to develop the ability to recall events that are not present and to retrieve information about something they have previously experienced.

During the second 6 months, infants also develop particular fears. They often become wary or fearful of strange people, and they react with distress when a familiar caregiver leaves them (separation fear). The onset of these fears occurs at a similar time (between 6 and 12 months) in infants from different cultures, in blind as well as sighted babies, and in infants with different patterns of experience with day care. It is likely that maturation and the resulting development of cognitive capacities contribute to the onset of various fears.

Two major theories have stimulated much of the research in infant cognitive development—learning theory and the cognitive developmental theory of Jean Piaget. Conditioning is the major concept from learning theory that is used to understand infants. Classical or respondent conditioning occurs when an initially neutral stimulus, such as a bell ringing, occurs at the same time as an unconditioned stimulus, such as milk flowing through a nipple into a child's mouth. The unconditioned response to the nipple is sucking. When the bell is repeatedly associated with the experience of milk in the nipple, the baby will begin to suck upon hearing the bell.

Instrumental conditioning occurs when the child makes a response, a reinforcing event follows the response, and as a result the probability that the child will repeat the response increases. If a baby smiles, father coos and tickles the baby's belly, and baby smiles again, instrumental conditioning may be under way. Instrumental or operant conditioning can be used effectively to teach children skills or to modify their behavior.

Piaget's cognitive developmental theory defines the first 2 years of life as the sensorimotor period of development. During this period, according to the theory, much of the infant's cognitive development occurs as a result of *actions* on objects, such as grasping, throwing, and manipulating objects.

Piaget believed that intellectual development passes through a series of six connected stages within the sensorimotor period. In these stages, the child gradually progresses from reflexive responses to an increasingly flexible, deliberate, and varied way of interacting with things in the environment. One major achievement during this period is understanding that objects that are out of sight still exist—called the concept of the permanent object.

Piaget assumed that all development is a product of both maturation and experience with the environment, but he emphasized the latter. He viewed the transitions during infancy as gradual and continuous, each building on the knowledge accumulated in earlier stages. One major achievement is the development of the ability to make a plan and carry it out over a short period of time.

REFERENCES

Ames, L. B. The sequential patterning of prone progression in the human infant. *Genetic Psychology Monographs*, 1937, *19*, 409–460.

Bornstein, M. H., Kessen, W., & Weiskopf, S. The categories of hue in infancy. *Science*, 1975, *191*, 201–202.

Campos, J. J., Langer, A., & Krawitz, A. Cardiac responses on the visual cliff in prelocomotor human infants. *Science*, 1970, *170*, 196–197.

Charlesworth, W. Development of the object concept. Paper presented at a meeting of the American Psychological Association, New York, 1966.

Dennis, W. Infant development under conditions of restricted practice and of minimum social stimulation. *Genetic Psychology Monographs*, 1941, *23*, 143–191.

Erikson, E. H. *Childhood and society*. New York: Norton, 1963.

Flavell, J. H. *The developmental psychology of Jean Piaget*. New York: Van Nostrand Reinhold, 1963.

Fraiberg, S. The development of human attachments in infants blind from birth. *Merrill-Palmer Quarterly*, 1975, *21*, 315–334.

Gesell, A., & Amatruda, C. S. *Developmental diagnosis: Normal and abnormal child development.* New York: Hoeber, 1941.

Gesell, A., Halverson, H. M., Thompson, H., Ilg, F. L., Costner, B. M., Ames, L. B., & Amatruda, C. S. *The first five years of life: A guide to the study of the preschool child.* New York: Harper & Row, 1940.

Gunnar, M. R. Control, warning signals, and distress in infancy. *Developmental Psychology*, 1980, *16*, 281–289.

Haith, M. M. *Rules that babies look by.* Hillsdale, N. J.: Erlbaum, 1980.

Hopkins, J. R., Zelazo, P. R., Jacobson, S. W., & Kagan, J. Infant reactivity to stimulus schema discrepancy. *Genetic Psychology Monographs*, 1976, *93*, 27–62.

Johnston, F. E. Somatic growth of the infant and preschool child. In F. Falkner & J. M. Tanner (Eds.), *Human growth* (Vol. 2): *Postnatal growth.* New York: Plenum, 1978.

Kagan, J., & Hamburg, M. The enhancement of memory in the first year. *Journal of Genetic Psychology*, 1981, *138*, 3–14.

Kagan, J., Kearsley, R., & Zelazo, P. *Infancy: Its place in human development.* Cambridge, Mass.: Harvard University Press, 1978.

Linn, S., Reznick, J. S., Kagan, J., and Hans, S. Salience of visual patterns in the human infant. *Developmental Psychology*, 1982, *18*, 651–657.

Mason, W. A. Social experience and primate cognitive development. In G. M. Burghardt and M. Bekoff (Eds.), *The development of behavior.* New York: Garland Press, 1978.

Mast, V. K., Fagen, J. W., Rovee-Collier, C. K., & Sullivan, M. W. Immediate and long-term memory for reinforcement context: The development of learned expectancies in early infancy. *Child Development*, 1980, *51*, 700–707.

Meltzoff, A. N., & Borton, R. W. Intermodal matching by human neonates. *Nature*, 1979, *282*, 403–404.

Papousek, H. Experimental studies of appetitional behavior in human newborns and infants. In H. W. Stevenson, E. H. Hess, & H. L. Reingold (Eds.), *Early behavior.* New York: Wiley, 1967.

Piaget, J. *The construction of reality in the child.* New York: Basic Books, 1954.

Reznick, J. S. The development of perceptual and lexical categories in the human infant. Unpublished doctoral dissertation, University of Colorado, 1982.

Ross, G. Concept categorization in 1- to 2-year-olds. *Developmental Psychology*, 1980, *16*, 391–396.

Super, C. M. Environmental effects on motor development: The case of African infant precocity. *Developmental Medicine and Child Neurology*, 1976, *18*, 561–567.

Wagner, S., Winner, E., Cicchetti, D., & Gardner, H. Metaphorical mapping in human infants. *Child Development*, 1981, *52*, 728–731.

Zelazo, N. A., Zelazo, P. R., & Kolb, S. Walking in the newborn. *Science*, 1972, *176*, 314–315.

Social and emotional development in infancy

From the beginning of life, infants are social beings. Children's social relationships and emotions are central aspects of early development. Although we separate the domains of cognitive, social, and emotional development in order to study and write about them, the student should appreciate that they are interdependent. An infant's attachment to another person and the emotional experience of anxiety about possible loss of that attachment cannot be completely understood without considering the child's cognitive capacities. Equally often, cognition is influenced by the child's feeling states and interactions with others.

THEORIES OF EARLY SOCIAL AND EMOTIONAL DEVELOPMENT

During most of this century, psychologists have emphasized children's relationships with people who care for them and regarded these interactions as the major bases for emotional and cognitive development (Bowlby, 1969; Freud, 1964; Watson, 1928). Until recently, these theorists focused almost entirely on the mother as the person whose love, care, and attention were paramount in the baby's feelings of security and insecurity. Only during the last decade have scientists studied the influence of fathers, siblings, and other caregivers, as well as that of the infant's own temperament, on development. Additionally, most theorists have emphasized the significance of pleasure and pain in the development of behavior. They assumed that human beings were motivated by the desire to obtain pleasure and to avoid pain. As a result, they awarded the greatest significance to the actions of caregivers who provided pleasure. Infants were thought to develop positive feelings and close attachments to the people who were frequent sources of pleasure, either because these people soothed and played with them or because they reduced the discomfort of pain, cold, hunger, or psychological distress.

Psychoanalytic theory

Sigmund Freud's conception of infants' relations to their parents was based on this assumption. Freud assumed that infants were born with biological instincts that demanded satisfaction. A child's need for food, for warmth, and for reduction of pain represented a "striving for sensory pleasure." As explained in Chapter 3, Freud described the biological basis for this striving as a kind of physical energy, called *libido*.

As Freud saw it, the activities, people, and objects in which children invest libidinal energy change in predictable ways as the child grows older.

During infancy, Freud argued, the events surrounding feeding are the most important sources of gratification. When children are being fed and cared for, their attention, derived from the energy of the libido, becomes focused on the person providing the gratification. Freud called this process *cathexis*. He envisioned infants as continually investing libidinal energy in the people who cared for them and also in the surfaces of the mouth, tongue, and lips because these surfaces are important in feeding. For this reason, Freud named the period of infancy the *oral stage*. Freud suggested that too much or too little gratification of a child's oral needs could slow the child's progress into the next developmental stage; that is, a *fixation* or internal resistance to transferring the libidinal energy to a new set of objects and activities might occur. Freud proposed the bold hypothesis that a fixation at the oral stage, caused by excessive or insufficient gratification, could predispose an adult toward specific psychological symptoms. For example, infants who were undergratified might develop serious depression or schizophrenia, and those who were overly gratified might be excessively dependent on others.

Freud suggested that the anal area and the activities surrounding defecation became important sources of libidinal gratification during the second year of life. Hence, interactions with the parents over the socialization of toileting assumed special significance. Freud called this second stage of development the *anal stage*. Despite little firm scientific support, Freud's ideas about early development spread quickly in this country to textbooks on child development and eventually into the popular media through magazines, books, plays, and movies.

More recent theories derived from Freud's have retained the basic assumption that early mother-child interactions have a special quality that is necessary for the infant's development (Ainsworth, Blehar, Waters, & Wall, 1978; Bowlby, 1969; Erikson, 1963). But these theorists emphasize the psychological consequences of being cared for in an affectionate, consistent, reliable, and gentle manner, rather than the biological functions of feeding and toileting. Erik Erikson, for example, proposed that the critical developmental event during infancy is the establishment of a sense of trust in another person. Infants who have consistently satisfying experiences of nurturance traverse this first developmental stage successfully. Those who do not will lack a basic sense of trust in others.

In the second year, Erikson suggested, children attempt to establish a sense of autonomy and independence from their parents. Children who fail to gain a sense of autonomy may be vulnerable to feelings of shame and doubt about their ability to function independently. In discussing these and later stages in the life cycle, Erikson retained the essence of the Freudian idea of fixation: He believed that failure to progress through one stage satisfactorily would interfere with easy progression through subsequent stages. His theory differed from Freud's because it emphasized *psychosocial* stages in contrast to Freud's *psychosexual* stages.

Social learning theory

A parallel theoretical movement appeared in the writings of behaviorists. These scientists also assumed that hunger, thirst, and pain were basic drive states that propelled infants to action. But the behaviorists rejected the Freudian concept of libido because it could not be measured. The impetus for psychological change, they believed, was not invisible feelings and cathexes but biological drives and other measurable responses. An event that satisfied a child's biological needs (that is, reduced a drive) was called a *primary reinforcer*. For example, for a hungry infant, food is a primary reinforcer. People or objects present when a drive is reduced become *secondary reinforcers,* this line of reasoning continues, through their association with the primary reinforcer. As a frequent source of food and comfort, an infant's mother is an important secondary reinforcer. The child therefore approaches her not only when hungry or in pain but on a variety of other occasions, displaying a generalized dependency toward her. Social learning theorists assumed that the strength of the child's dependency was determined by how rewarding the mother was, that is, by how often she had been associated with pleasure and the reduction of pain and discomfort (Sears, Maccoby, & Levin, 1957).

The idea that infants' emotional ties to the mother and approach behaviors to her were based on the reduction of biological drives dominated American theories of infancy from World War I until the early 1960s, as observed in Chapter 3. Because the feeding situation was considered so important, child development experts and parents devoted a great deal of attention to whether a child was breast-fed or bottle-fed, whether fed on schedule or on demand, and when and how the child should be weaned from breast to bottle or from bottle to cup. Although these important questions were investigated extensively by scientists, no consistent relations between feeding patterns and the child's subsequent social and emotional development were discovered. The results of this research cast some doubt on the utility of the concept of the oral stage. More recent evidence also indicates that the strength of a child's attachment to either parent is not related in any simple way to the frequency with which that parent feeds, changes, or cares for the physical needs of the child (Ainsworth et al., 1978).

But a more fatal blow to theories emphasizing biological drive reduction was dealt by Harry Harlow and his colleagues in a series of experiments with infant monkeys that identified a new source of the mother-infant bond: *contact comfort.* In some of these studies, young monkeys were raised in a cage with two different kinds of inanimate "mothers" (Harlow & Harlow, 1966). One mother was made of wire, and the infant could nurse from a nipple that was mounted on this mother's chest (see Figure 4.1). The other mother was covered with soft terry cloth but did not provide the infant with any food. Contrary to predictions from both psychoanalytic and behavioral theories, the infant monkeys spent most of their time resting on the terry-cloth mother. They went to the wire mother only when they were hungry. When an infant monkey was frightened by an unfamiliar object, such as a large wooden spider, it ran to the cloth mother and clung to it, as though it felt more secure there than clinging to the wire mother (see Figure 4.2). At least for these primates, the pleasure associated with feeding seemed not to be the foundation for the attachment bond between parent and infant.

Ethology   At about the time Harlow began his experiments with monkeys, the field of ethology was being created by a group of European naturalists, notably

Konrad Lorenz (1981) and Nikko Tinbergen (1951). These scientists emphasized the need to study animals in their natural environments. In part, they were rebelling against the behaviorists' stress on conditioning and on research under strictly controlled laboratory conditions.

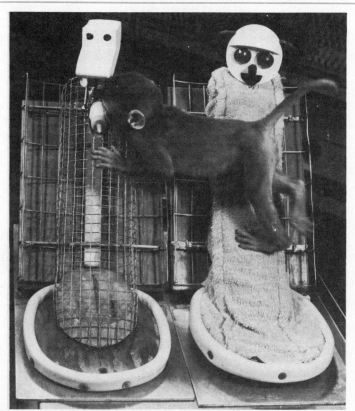

FIGURE 4.1

Wire and cloth mother surrogates used in studies investigating the effects of different types of mothering on infant monkeys. Wire mother had a nipple on her chest to feed the baby, but the cloth mother was padded and soft. Infants spent more time on the cloth mother and ran to her when frightened, suggesting that contact comfort rather than food was important for the infant's attachment to its "mother." (From H. F. Harlow & R. R. Zimmerman. Affectional responses in the infant monkey. Science, 1959, 130, 422. By permission.)

FIGURE 4.2

When a frightening object was introduced into a large open space (the open-field test), infant monkeys ran to the cloth mother and clung to her. This reaction was one indication that they were attached to the cloth mother rather than the wire mother. (From H. F. Harlow & R. R. Zimmerman. Affectional responses in the infant monkey. Science, 1959, 130, 430. By permission.)

According to the ethologists, each species of animal is born with a set of *fixed action patterns*. A fixed action pattern is a stereotyped behavioral sequence that is set in motion when the proper environmental stimulus, called a releaser, occurs. Some fixed action patterns can be triggered only during a limited time span during the animal's development, called a *critical* or *sensitive period*. Releasers occurring before or after the critical period have little or no effect on the animal's behavior.

Imprinting is a fixed-action pattern that takes place shortly after birth in ducks, geese, chickens, and some other species. A newly hatched duckling is innately prepared to follow the first moving object it sees. If that object is its biological mother, the duckling learns to follow the mother and to approach the mother when in distress. But if the moving object that the duckling sees during the critical period for imprinting is something else, such as a human being or an electric train, the young bird will follow that object instead of the mother duck.

The idea that human infants might be born into the world prepared to issue certain behaviors that are neither the result of prior learning nor based on the experience of drive reduction was attractive to a young British psychiatrist named John Bowlby, who was trained in psychoanalytic theory but receptive to the new ethological findings. Bowlby proposed that human infants are programmed to emit certain behaviors that will elicit caregiving from those around them and will keep adults nearby. These behaviors include crying, smiling, cooing, and crawling toward someone. From an evolutionary standpoint, these patterns have adaptive value, because they help to assure that infants will receive the care necessary for their survival (Bowlby, 1969).

A major result of mother-infant interactions, according to Bowlby, is the development of an emotional *attachment* to the mother. This concept of attachment, as expanded and investigated by Ainsworth and her associates (1978), was defined as an emotionally toned relationship or tie to the mother that led the infant to seek the mother's presence and comfort, particularly when the infant was frightened or uncertain. These theorists proposed that all normal infants form attachments and that a strong attachment provides the basis for healthy emotional and social development during later childhood. Children with strong attachments were expected, for example, to become socially outgoing and curious about their environments, to be willing to explore, and to develop the ability to cope with stress. Serious disruptions in the attachment process were thought to produce problems in the child's later social development.

Common themes in theories of infant social development

All three theories emphasize the child's relationship to the mother and other primary caregivers as a central part of early social and emotional development. One reason for this emphasis is the assumption that attachment to the mother has long-term consequences by providing a foundation of emotional security for the child and by forming the basis for the parent's later influence on the child. As children grow, they will be reluctant to break the emotional bond with a parent to whom they are attached and, as a result, will be receptive to adopting the behaviors that fit the parent's values. Because, in most instances, parents encourage behaviors that are adaptive—that is, behaviors that help children to get along well in the larger society—attachments usually serve children well. If, however, parents encourage behavior that is maladaptive, the strongly attached child's efforts to conform to parents' wishes may not be beneficial. For example, if a contemporary American mother taught her daughter to be passive, quiet, and uninterested in intellectual achievement, and if the daughter adopted those attitudes and behaviors because of her attachment to her mother, she might experience problems in adjustment during adolescence and adulthood (see Chapter 11 for further discussion). Hence, although attachment to parents is generally thought to produce benefits for the child, there are occasional exceptions to that generalization.

Cultural ideals and child rearing

All theories about infants' social development and the child-rearing practices associated with healthy development must be considered in cultural perspective. Cultures hold different conceptions of the ideal child, and these beliefs determine how parents will rear their children. Puritan parents in colonial New England believed infants were willful and had to be tamed. They punished their young children severely, and the children were generally conforming. Contemporary parents in Calcutta believe children are fundamentally uncontrollable. They are more tolerant of tantrums in 2-year-olds, and their children are less obedient than were Puritan children in colonial New England.

The differences in behavior between Japanese and American mothers provide another contrast. American mothers conceive of their mission as molding their children into active, independent beings by stimulating them and teaching them self-reliance and social skills. Japanese mothers see their task as building a close loyalty to and interdependence on the mother and other members of the family. In line with these values, American mothers put their children in rooms of their own, and they play with their infants to make them vocalize, smile, and laugh. By contrast, Japanese mothers remain very close to their young children; they respond quickly to crying by soothing and quieting more often than stimulating their babies. It is not surprising that American infants are more active, more vocal, and more spontaneous than Japanese infants.

Even within our own society there have been major differences in how mothers have handled their infants over the last 70 years. Government pamphlets published in 1914 containing advice to American mothers told them that because babies had extremely sensitive nervous systems, they should avoid excessive stimulation of the infant. By the 1960s these pamphlets instructed mothers to let their infants experience as much stimulation as they wished, because that was the way the child could learn about the world.

In 1914 mothers were told not to feed or play with the baby every time he cried, because those actions would spoil the infant. A half century later, mothers were told that they should not be afraid of spoiling their baby and that the child would feel trusting and secure if the mother always came to nurture the crying infant. These changes in advice reflect variations in philosophy and in the cultural concept of the ideal child. Contemporary Americans believe it is critical to minimize anxiety in their 1-year-olds and to maximize the baby's comfort and security. Because most children in each generation grow up to function well in their culture, despite different rearing experiences, it is clear that there are many paths to adaptive social development.

Infants respond to other people from the first days after birth. Some of the major changes in social behavior are summarized in Table 3.2 in Chapter 3. By the age of 1 month, infants react to voices and are particularly attentive to faces. Sometime between 2 and 3 months, infants develop a *social smile*—that is, they begin to smile at people. This behavior is often the first clear sign of social responsiveness that parents notice. The social smile is discussed in Box 4.1. Until sometime after 4 months, infants are socially responsive to people in general; they do not usually react differently to familiar and unfamiliar people.

During the second 6 months of life, infants begin to show clear evidence of attachment to particular people in their environment. The person to whom the baby becomes attached is called a *target of attachment*. The first target is usually, but not always, the mother. Within a month or two after the first attachment appears, most infants show attachments to multiple targets, such as the father, brothers and sisters, or grandparents.

CHAPTER 4 / Social and emotional development in infancy
125

BOX 4.1
The social smile

Although infants smile from the first days of life, the exact form of the smile and the conditions that produce it vary with development. The newborn displays a reflex smile that usually involves only the muscles around the mouth and not the muscles around the eyes. This reflex smile, which often occurs in bursts, can occur during irregular sleep or drowsiness. It is also possible to produce this smile by gently touching the infant's cheek or talking to the infant. These responses are regarded as reflex smiles rather than social smiles because they do not occur selectively to the face of another person and because they usually occur when the baby is not in an alert state.

The *social smile* appears at 7 or 8 weeks of age, and by 3 months infants will smile at almost any face. Some smile at a Halloween mask as readily as they do at their parents. The social smile is an important developmental event, because it invites adults to interact with the baby and therefore contributes to the attachment bond. The fact that all human babies show a social smile supports Bowlby's ethological theory hypothesis that smiling, like attachment, is innate in the human species. However, ethological theory does not provide a basis for understanding why the social smile appears at 2 to 3 months. One explanation, based on cognitive functioning, assumes that the onset of the social smile signals the child's emerging ability to recognize stimuli that match its schemata. The face of a stranger alerts the infant and provokes an attempt at assimilation. If the assimilation is successful, the smile will appear. With repeated presentations of a face, assimilation occurs more quickly, and so smiling declines (Sroufe & Waters, 1976).

Although cognitive changes account for the onset of smiling and laughing, once children begin to smile, environmental contingencies and reinforcements influence the frequency of smiling to other people. Gewirtz (1965) studied the patterns of smiling for infants raised in three different environments in Israel. Institutionalized infants living in residential buildings rarely saw their parents and received routine institutional care. Kibbutz infants lived in collective settlements. They were raised in large houses with professional caregivers but were fed and cared for frequently during the first year by their own mothers. Family-reared children were raised in typically Western apartments by their mothers. Figure B4.1 graphs the frequency of smiling to a strange woman's face by infants in these three groups. Frequency of smiling reached a peak in the kibbutz- and family-reared infants a few weeks earlier than in the infants raised in the institution. But for all infants, smiling was most frequent at about 4 months of age. Over the following year, however, the children in the institution smiled less frequently, while those in family care maintained a high rate of smiling. The difference is probably due to the fact that family-reared children received more social feedback than those in institutions.

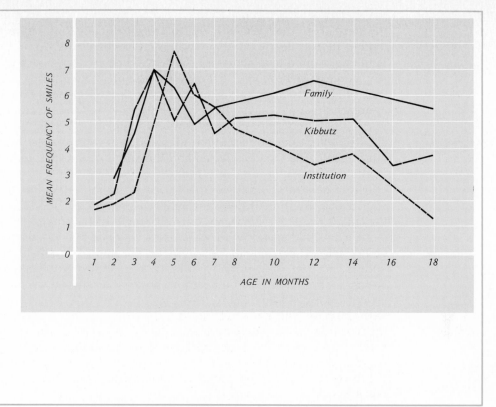

FIGURE B4.1

Frequency of smiling among infants raised in three different environments in Israel — families, kibbutzim, and institutions. Infants in all three environments began smiling at approximately the same time, but the smiling frequency of those in institutions declined over time, probably because they received fewer positive responses from adults (From J. L. Gewirtz. The cause of infant smiling in four child-rearing environments in Israel. In B. M. Foss [Ed.], Determinants of infant behavior [Vol. 3]. London: Methuen, 1965. By permission of the publishers and The Tavistock Institute of Human Relations.)

Signs of attachment

The signs of an infant's attachment to a caregiver are evident in three reliable phenomena. First, a target of attachment is better able to placate and soothe the baby than anyone else. Second, infants are much more likely to approach attachment targets for play or consolation than to approach others. Finally, infants are less likely to become afraid when in the presence of attachment targets than when these people are absent. For example, an unfamiliar woman visited the homes of 1-year-olds and showed the children objects and events that were likely to make them anxious (a large, frightening toy, an unusual sound coming from inside a chair in the room). When the mother was in the room, the child was less likely to cry or show obvious signs of fear than when the mother was not there. The term *attachment* seems appropriate for this set of behaviors, for it conveys the idea that they reveal a special, emotionally toned set of dispositions that infants acquire toward those who care for them.

An attachment has obvious survival value for the infant. For one thing, it permits a feeling of safety and security as the child explores the world and experiences unexpected events. One is likely to see attachment behavior when a child is in a fear-provoking situation. Children may ignore their parents and even prefer to play with a stranger (as long as the parent is present), but when they feel threatened or experience uncertainty, they turn quickly to their mother, father, or other attachment figure.

Infants often look to persons who are targets of attachment for information about the safety or danger of a particular situation. If a 1-year-old is placed on the shallow side of the visual cliff (see Chapter 3) and the mother is standing on the deep side, the child is likely to cross to her if the mother smiles. If the mother shows a fearful face, the child is far less likely to cross and may even cry. Similarly, a child in a laboratory room who begins to approach a novel toy will stop and run to the mother if the mother assumes a fearful face or utters a meaningless phrase in a frightened tone of voice. But the same child will continue to approach the toy if the mother smiles or says something in a reassuring tone of voice (Klinnert, Campos, Sorce, Emde, & Svejda, 1983).

Parental practices and attachment

Although the human infant appears to have an innate tendency to form attachments, the targets selected and the strength and quality of those attachments depend partly on the parents' behavior in relation to the child. Recent efforts to determine what parental qualities are important for attachment have shown that attachment does not result only from parental actions that satisfy the child's need for food, water, warmth, and relief from pain. The sheer amount of time the child spends with the parent also seems not to determine the quality of the child's attachment. For example, a group of Swedish children whose fathers had been their primary caregivers for some part of infancy showed no stronger attachment to their fathers than children whose fathers had been away working full time (Lamb, Hwang, Frodi, & Frodi, 1982). Similarly, infants with mothers who are employed full time seem to be as strongly attached to them as infants whose mothers are at home all the time. The old adage that the quality rather than the quantity of parenting is important seems to fit the facts in this case. Some theorists have proposed that the first step in attachment is a process of *bonding* immediately after birth. This process is discussed in Box 4.2.

What qualities of social interactions between parent and child are most important for the development of attachment? One primary dimension has been variously described as sensitivity, synchrony, and reciprocity. Two components are involved. The first is a sensitivity and responsiveness to the infant's signals, whether they are cries, glances, smiles, or vocalizations. Parents of strongly attached children generally respond quickly and positively to their children's social overtures and initiate playful, pleasant exchanges in ways that fit the baby's mood and cognitive abilities. The important dimension of sensitive interaction is the ability to act in harmony with the child's signals and behaviors (Ainsworth et al., 1978). Consider examples of two parents who show equal amounts of affection and interaction with their children but differ in their sensitivity:

Darcy, an 18-month-old, is playing with some toys on the floor. Her mother finishes some work at her desk and turns to watch Darcy. She comments, "Those are nice blocks, Darcy. You are making a fine tower with them." Darcy smiles. Mother picks up a book and begins to read. In a few minutes, after finishing her tower, Darcy walks to Mother with a children's book in her hand, saying, "Book," and trying to crawl into Mother's lap. Mother takes Darcy in her lap, puts down her own book, and says, "Do you want to read this book?" Darcy says yes, and Mother reads.

Stacy, another 18-month-old, is playing on her living room floor when her mother finishes some desk work. Mother says, "Come here, Stacy. I'll read

BOX 4.2
Early bonding

In both the popular and professional press, some people have suggested that a critical process of "bonding" between mother and child takes place during the first hours after birth. American hospital practices of placing the infants in a separate nursery and taking them to their mothers only for feeding have been heavily criticized because they prevent the mother and infant from establishing an emotional bond during the first postnatal hours. Partly as a result, some hospitals now allow mother and infant some time together immediately after birth, encourage "rooming in" (in which the infant stays in the mother's room instead of the newborn nursery), and have developed programs to involve parents in caregiving for premature babies.

We can ask two questions about early contact between parent and infant: Does it foster attachment or bonding? Is it critical for optimal development? The answer to the first question is a qualified yes, at least in the short run, but long-term effects are more difficult to demonstrate. The answer to the second is no.

These questions were the subject of an experimental investigation in Germany in which some mothers had "early contact" with their infants. The babies were placed in the mother's arms on the delivery bed for at least 30 minutes after birth. The remaining mothers received the standard hospital procedure. Half of each group had "extended contact" — the mothers kept the babies in their rooms for about 5 hours a day in addition to regular feeding. The mothers without extended contact had their babies with them for feedings 5 times a day for about 30 minutes per feeding. The early-contact mothers showed more tender touching and cuddling toward their babies during the first 5 days than did the mothers without early contact. But the differences had disappeared by the time the babies were 8 to 10 days old. Furthermore, early contact was effective only for mothers who had planned pregnancies, suggesting that the effects depended on the mother's attitude about the birth. There were no differences between the mothers who had extended contact and the mothers who did not (Grossmann, Thane, & Grossmann, 1981). In another investigation, babies who were hospitalized after birth because of prematurity or illness showed patterns of attachment at 12 months that were similar to those found in other, earlier studies. Apparently the early separation of parents and children did not lead to long-term problems (Rode, Chang, Fisch, & Sroufe, 1981).

Although early mother-child contact may not be critical for emotional bonding, placing the baby near the mother immediately after birth is emotionally satisfying to some parents and may contribute to a harmonious beginning in their relationship with the child. On the other hand, parents need not feel they are depriving their newborn of some critical experience if they do not have early contact. Some mothers are exhausted after birth and are relieved to have someone take care of them and their baby. Adopted infants have their first contacts with the adoptive mother days, months, or even years after birth, yet strong emotional bonds between child and mother can be established.

your book to you." Stacy looks up but continues building a block tower in which she is apparently engrossed. Mother goes to Stacy and says, "Let's read now," picking her up and giving her a hug. Stacy squirms and whimpers. Mother puts her down, and Stacy returns to her tower. Later, having finished her tower. Stacy picks up the book and tries to crawl in Mother's lap, saying, "Book." Mother says, "No, you didn't want to read when I was ready. I'm busy now."

These two mothers provide their children with equal amounts of attention, but the first is more sensitive and responsive to the child than the second.

A second parental characteristic associated with a strong attachment can be described as warmth, supportiveness, and gentleness. Parents of strongly attached children use warm tones and gentle commands when giving directions, and they support the child's behavior with positive comments when appropriate (Londerville & Main, 1981; Pastor, 1981).

Father's behavior with infants   Most infants develop clear attachments to fathers as well as mothers, and some social critics have suggested that infants could benefit from having frequent care from their fathers as well as their mothers. Two questions about the role of fathers have occupied recent research: Do fathers have the capacity to provide appropriate and sensitive care to infants? What kind of interactions do fathers typically have with their infants? Observations of fathers in standardized situations reveal that they show as much sensitivity, affection, and skill as their wives when feeding and holding their newborn infants (Parke & Tinsley, 1981).

Although there are many similarities between the behaviors of mothers and fathers toward infants, there are some differences. Fathers engage infants in physically active play more often—throwing the baby into the air, for example. Mothers more often use toys in their play and typically provide more physical contact (Parke & Tinsley, 1981). Even in a group of Swedish families where some fathers had primary caregiving responsibilities, mothers still directed more affection and attention to their infants than did fathers (Lamb et al., 1982).

Most observers of the American scene are aware that increasing numbers of women with young children are employed outside the home. By 1980, over one-third of the women with children 3 or under were employed, and more mothers are joining the work force each year. Similar trends are present in most western European nations, and maternal employment has been the norm in many eastern European countries, the Soviet Union, and China for some time. Because fathers rarely take primary responsibility for child rearing, the fact of maternal employment has created a need for new child-care arrangements. As a nation, however, we have been skeptical of the possibility that high-quality care for infants and toddlers could be provided in group settings. Until recently, a number of states refused to license day-care centers for children under 3 years of age.

Why is there such a strong belief that infants may be psychologically handicapped by group care? One reason is the prevalent assumption that infants need one major caregiver to whom they can develop a strong attachment; being cared for by different people may disrupt the attachment process and create anxiety. We might call this the "one mother" hypothesis. A second reason is the belief that infants will receive less attention, affection, and stimulation in group care than at home. As a result, their social and cognitive development may be retarded. In the minds of many, group care conjures up images of institutions with 50 babies lying in a row of cribs sucking propped-up bottles. We can call this the "stimulus deprivation" hypothesis.

However, research to date has shown that psychologically sound group care for infants can create conditions for healthy development, just as some home environments do. What seems to be important is consistent nurturance, frequent social interaction, opportunities for exploration and stimulation, and a small enough child-adult ratio (about 3 to 1) for each infant to receive prompt attention and frequent interaction with responsive adults. Infants on Israeli kibbutzim, who spend most of their time in group care and only a few hours a day with their parents, become attached to their parents, and their emotional development is very similar to home-reared Israeli children. Children who spend all day in adequate group care seem to form secure attachments to their mothers as well as to their caregivers, if their caregivers are involved and interact with them frequently (Anderson, Nagel, Roberts, & Smith, 1981).

In one of the most extensive studies of the effects of day care on infants, 30 Caucasian and 30 Chinese-American children from $3\frac{1}{2}$ to 29 months of age were studied. Half the children in each ethnic group attended a day-care center 5 days a week for about 26 months, while the others (matched with the first group on social class and sex) were raised at home and did not attend a day-care center. The two groups showed similar growth of language, perceptual skills,

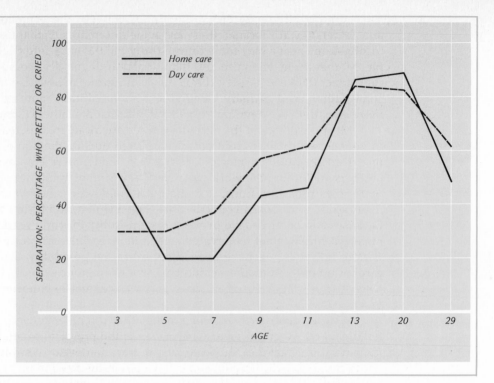

FIGURE 4.3

Percentage of children who attended infant day-care centers and infants who were raised at home full time who fretted or cried when their mothers left the room in a laboratory procedure. The similar patterns suggest that fear of separation from the mother is based on maturational, developmental changes that occur in similar ways for children with different histories of separation from their mothers. (From J. Kagan, R. B. Kearsley, & P. R. Zelazo. Infancy: Its place in human development. Cambridge, Mass.: Harvard University Press, 1978. By permission.)

and quality of attachment to the mother. In addition, Figure 4.3 shows that the occurrence of separation anxiety, a common fear, was similar for the day-care and home-reared children across the period from 4 to 29 months of age.

In one test situation, a day-care teacher and mothers were present in the same room. The day-care children and those raised entirely at home consistently went to their mothers for comfort when they were bored, tired, or distressed. Despite the fact that the day-care teacher spent many hours with the children, the children seemed more attached to their mothers than to the day-care teacher (Kagan, Kearsley, & Zelazo, 1978).

On occasion, day care enhances an infant's development. This is particularly true when the child comes from a family environment where opportunities for exploration and varied experiences are limited. In one experiment, infants from poverty families who were identified as being "high risk" for developmental or learning problems were enrolled in a day-care program beginning at 6 to 12 weeks. They were compared with a control group of children from similar backgrounds raised at home. At 20 months of age, the children in the day-care group had more advanced speech and communication skills than the children in the control group (O'Connell & Farran, 1982).

It is not necessary to have one caregiver assigned to a particular infant in a day-care center. In an experimental day-care program at the University of Kansas, the infant and toddler centers are divided into zones. Each caregiver is responsible for one zone and takes care of the children in that area. In the infant center, for instance, one adult does the diapering, another does feeding, one or two more interact with babies in the play area, and so on. The advantage of this organization is that the caregiver does not have to disrupt ongoing activities with two or three infants in order to tend to the wet diapers or hunger of one child. The adults rotate through the zones, so children experience several caregivers regularly.

But if a day-care center fails to provide varied stimulation and nurturance, the children who attend it will suffer. In one study, 2-year-olds attending unlicensed day-care centers with only one adult for every two dozen babies showed retarded cognitive development. In this sense, the stimulus deprivation hypothesis is valid. However, there is nothing inherently depriving about group care.

When young children come from reasonably supportive families, and group care programs provide a variety of experiences and an involved and nurturant staff, children's intellectual, cognitive, and social development does not seem to deviate from home-reared children in any obvious way. If there are differences in the parental attachments, cognitive capacities, or emotional characteristics between children raised in day care and home-reared children, the differences are subtle and escape current strategies for detecting them.

Residential institutional care for young children—orphanages or homes for children whose parents are unable to take care of them—is sometimes necessary in the United States and is more common in poorer countries. For children growing up under these circumstances, the number of adults available to care for the children, nurturant caregiving, and intellectual stimulation in the institution are critical factors in the children's development. However, it is less clear whether there are long-term consequences of the fact that the infant and young child have no consistent and central attachment figure, a condition that occurs in some institutions. There is little good research on this question, but there is some evidence that children who have grown up in institutions are more dependent, seek more attention from adults, and are more disruptive in school than comparable groups of home-reared children. They do not necessarily, however, show a higher rate of severe emotional problems (Rutter, 1979).

Children who have experienced relatively deprived environments in infancy (either at home or in an institution) retain a capacity for recovery if they are removed to a more varied, challenging, and nurturant setting early in life. For example, a group of severely malnourished female Korean orphans between 2 and 3 years of age were adopted by middle-class American families. Six years after joining their adopted families the children were functioning well in elementary school; they surpassed the expected mean height and weight for Korean children, and their average IQ was 102, which was 40 points higher than the average IQ scores reported for similar Korean children returned to their original, deprived home environments (Winick, Meyer, & Harris, 1975).

Thus far, we have mentioned some behaviors that indicate attachment, such as approaching the target of attachment or becoming calm and unafraid in that person's presence. We have discussed the advantages or consequences of attachment and the experiences that facilitate it. But we have not yet described in full any standard procedure for evaluating the strength or quality of infants' attachments. Currently, the most popular strategy for assessing attachment for research purposes is a laboratory procedure called the Strange Situation. Invented by Mary Ainsworth, a leading theorist, it utilizes both separation reactions and the extent to which the child approaches and is calmed by the attachment target after mild stress.

The Ainsworth Strange Situation   This procedure consists of a series of seven 3-minute episodes during which infants are observed with the mother, with a stranger, with the mother and a stranger, and alone, as shown in Table 4.1.

TABLE 4.1	Episode	Event initiating episode	Persons present during episode
Episodes in the Strange Situation	1	Parent and infant enter room	Parent and infant
	2	Stranger joins parent and infant	Parent, infant, and stranger
	3	Parent leaves room	Infant and stranger
	4	Parent returns to room; stranger leaves	Parent and infant
	5	Parent leaves	Infant alone
	6	Stranger returns	Infant and stranger
	7	Parent returns; stranger leaves	Parent and infant

The two key episodes are episodes 3 and 5, those in which the mother leaves the child, first with the stranger and then alone. Several minutes later, she returns to be reunited with her child. Both the intensity of the child's distress following the mother's departure and the type of behavior shown when she returns are used as indexes of the infant's attachment to her.

Three major patterns have been described. In general, children who show mild protest following the mother's departure, seek the mother when she returns, and are easily comforted by her are called *securely attached*. Children who do not protest the mother's departure and who play contentedly while ignoring the mother upon her return are usually classified as *avoidant and insecurely attached*. Finally, children who are seriously distressed when their mothers leave and who, after the mother returns, alternately cling to her and push her away are called *resistant and insecurely attached*. In samples of middle-class American 1-year-olds, about 70 to 75 percent are usually classified as securely attached, about 15 to 20 percent are classified as avoidant, and about 10 percent are resistant.

Although the Strange Situation may seem artificial, classifications based on it do predict other qualities that theoretically should be related to the security of children's attachment. Children classified as securely or insecurely attached in the Strange Situation when they were 12 to 18 months old were observed at later ages ranging from 21 months to 5 years. Securely attached children were generally more socially outgoing with adults and with other children, more cooperative and compliant with their mothers and with strange adults, better able to cope with stress, and more curious than children classified as insecurely attached (Arend, Gove, & Sroufe, 1979; Londerville & Main, 1981; Pastor, 1981; Waters, Wippman, & Sroufe, 1979). Furthermore, when securely attached children were observed in their own homes, they sought physical contact with their mothers less often than children classified as insecurely attached (Clark-Stewart & Hevey, 1981).

Children who have experienced neglect or serious abuse behave in the Strange Situation as if they were insecurely attached, as theoretical considerations would predict. One study compared 18-month-old infants who were maltreated with infants from the same lower-social-class background who were not subject to parental abuse. Fully 62 percent of the maltreated children were classified as insecurely attached, compared with only 24 percent of the nonabused group (Rosen, 1982).

Limitations of the Strange Situation   Although these scientific findings indicate that the Strange Situation may be a sensitive index of the quality of attachment, other information suggests caution in interpreting children's behavior in this situation as an indication of security or insecurity. First, a recent study has shown that many children change their attachment classifications over the 7-month period between 12 and 19 months. Some insecurely attached 12-month-olds were classified as securely attached at 19 months, while one-third of the securely attached 1-year-olds were insecurely attached 7 months later. The changes were sometimes associated with changes in family circumstances, such as the mother's beginning employment, but children who experienced such changes were just as likely to shift from insecure to secure as the other way around (Thompson, Lamb, & Estes, 1982).

Second, long-term study of mothers and children found no differences in the incidence of secure or insecure attachments at 1 year between children of normal mothers and those growing up with mothers who had serious mental and emotional disorders. Many of the emotionally disturbed mothers were not as lively or attentive to their infants as the normal mothers, yet the children born to these parents were not more likely to behave as if they were insecurely attached (Sameroff, Seifer, & Zax, 1982).

The central determinants of whether a child will be labeled securely or insecurely attached are whether the child cries when the mother leaves and the child's reaction when the mother returns. These two factors are not independent. Children who do not cry when the mother leaves because they are not anxious or upset by the departure are also unlikely to approach the mother for comfort when she comes back. That is, a child who is not very upset and is cheerfully involved in play has no reason to approach the mother when she comes into the room, yet such children are likely to be classified avoidant and insecurely attached.

Some children classified as avoidant may have been socialized to control anxiety in unfamiliar situations. For example, only one-third of a group of 1-year-old middle-class German children observed in the Strange Situation were classified as securely attached. Almost half were classified as avoidant because they did not greet the mother when she returned. Should we conclude that many more German than American children are insecurely attached?

Probably not. The authors of this study wrote that their 1-year-old subjects may have received "a strong push in the direction of affective reserve" from their parents and other adults in the German culture (Grossmann, Grossmann, Huber, & Wartner, 1981, p. 179).

A similar finding emerged for American children. When a large number of 1-year-olds were observed in the Strange Situation, some were classified as securely attached and others as avoidant because they were minimally distressed after their mother's departure. Observations of these children and their mothers at home showed that the mothers of both groups were equally accepting and sensitive to their children's needs. But the mothers of the children who were classified as securely attached were more protective, considered their infants less self-reliant, and felt irreplaceable in their children's lives. By contrast, many mothers of the babies who were classified as avoidant encouraged autonomy and control of fear in their infants. It is probably not a coincidence that these less distressed children were better able to deal with the anxiety created by maternal departure in the laboratory (Hock & Clinger, 1981).

These results could be interpreted as indicating that nurturant, protective mothers create securely attached infants while less protective ones create insecurely attached children. But one could interpret the same results as indicating that protectiveness produces infants who are less able to cope with the uncertainty created in the Strange Situation. Both groups of infants probably often have emotionally secure attachments to their mothers.

Temperamental differences among infants in vulnerability to anxiety and uncertainty also contribute to the child's behavior in the Strange Situation. Infants who easily become very upset by unexpected events, such as the mother's departure, work themselves into an extreme state of upset and, as a result, often push the mother away when she returns as they continue to sob in her arms. These children are often classified as resistant and insecurely attached. Japanese infants often show this extreme distress (Miyake and Takahashi, 1983), probably in part because most Japanese infants have had little experience of being apart from their mother, but also perhaps because of biologically based characteristics. One-year-old Japanese children classified as resistant and insecurely attached were more irritable and fearful than securely attached children from the first days of life through the first birthday. Similarly, Chinese-American infants, whether being cared for totally at home or partially in a day-care center, were more likely to cry following maternal departure in an unfamiliar place and more likely to cling and to remain proximal to the mother in unfamiliar situations than Caucasian infants of the same social class (Kagan et al., 1978).

The suggestion that there is a biological basis for vulnerability to anxiety is supported by individual differences in physiological responses. In one study, the amount of urinary cortisol excreted by infants was measured under both stressful and nonstressful conditions. Urinary cortisol is a chemical secreted by the adrenal cortex, and it is one of the body's reactions to anxiety and emotional upset. As shown in Figure 4.4, infants with a general tendency to secrete high levels of cortisol also showed intense separation distress when their mothers left (Tennes, 1982).

FIGURE 4.4

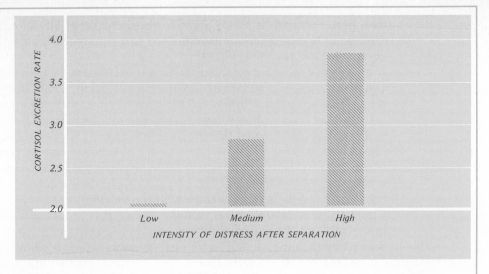

Rate of cortisol excretion on a nonstressful day in 1-year-old infants who subsequently showed low, medium, or high levels of distress and upset following the mother's departure. The results suggest that infants who are very distressed when their mothers leave are temperamentally predisposed to fearful responses. (From K. Tennes. The role of hormones in mother-infant transaction. In R. M. Emde & R. J. Harmon [Eds.], The development of attachment and affiliative systems. *New York: Plenum, 1982, p. 77. By permission.)*

These facts suggest that the child's behavior following separation and reunion reflects, in part, both temperamental differences among children in susceptibility to distress and differences in socialization patterns. The variations in attachment behavior in the Strange Situation produced by temperament and experience may not necessarily indicate insecurity or security of the emotional tie to the mother. Because temperamental qualities affect many aspects of infant behavior, we now turn to an examination of this source of differences among infants.

TEMPERAMENTAL DIFFERENCES IN INFANTS

Any mother, father, or nurse in a newborn ward will tell you that there are obvious differences among infants that can be seen even from the first days of life. Some cry a lot, some are quiet; some sleep on a fairly regular schedule, others wake at irregular hours; some are constantly wriggling, others lie in their cribs quietly for long periods of time. It is possible, of course, to create excessively irritable or active babies by certain handling regimens in the home. But there is good reason to believe that some babies are born with a bias toward certain moods and reaction styles. These constitutionally based biases are called *temperament.*

Psychologists have been interested in temperamental qualities for two reasons. First, if some qualities are based on inherited or prenatally acquired dispositions, these patterns might be resistant to change as the child grows. Second, children influence their parents as well as vice versa; thus, babies with different temperaments provoke different parental reactions and, encountering

similar experiences or child-rearing practices, react in different ways. Experiments with 13 species of monkeys demonstrate that traumatic experiences have markedly different effects on infants with different temperamental predispositions, and the same could be true for human beings. For example, rhesus monkeys emerge from total isolation during the first 6 months of life with seriously deviant social behavior; crab eater monkeys show minimal disruption; and pigtail monkeys display intermediate levels of disturbed social behavior (Sackett, Ruppenthal, Fahrenbruch, Holm, & Greenough, 1981). Similar findings occur for different species of dogs. The social behavior of beagles is seriously affected by 12 weeks of isolation, while terriers show little reaction to the same experience (Fuller & Clark, 1968). The genetic differences among species of dogs create dispositions that lead the animals to react to isolation in different ways.

Infants vary in a large number of physiological and psychological characteristics—irritability, average duration of naps, vigor, duration of smiles. Two criteria have been used to assess which temperamental dimensions are most important: They are stable over time, and they are based on inherited or prenatal, physiological factors. However, only a very small set of temperamental dimensions has been studied by scientists; these include activity, fussiness, fearfulness, sensitivity to stimuli, attentiveness, and vigor of reaction. These dimensions were selected in part because they are relatively easy to observe and intuitively seem likely to be related to the child's future adaptation. These are reasonable criteria to employ when a new area is being explored.

The pioneering studies of temperament were carried out by Alexander Thomas and Stella Chess (1977), and their influential work continues to be widely cited. They conducted detailed interviews with a sample of mothers every 3 months for the first 2 years of their infants' lives and less frequently until the children were 7 years old. The dimensions of temperament that emerged from the interviews were qualities that were salient for the parents. These were actively level, rhythmicity (regularity of sleep and eating), fussiness, distractibility, attention span, intensity, threshold of responding, and readiness to adapt to new events such as new foods, new people, and changes in routine (Thomas & Chess, 1977).

Using ratings of infants on these temperamental qualities, the researchers classified the babies as *easy, difficult,* and *slow to warm up.* The easy children, who comprised about 75 percent of the sample, were happy, regular in sleep and eating, and adaptable infants who were not easily upset. The difficult children (about 10 percent) were often fussy, irregular in their feedings and sleeping habits, fearful of new people and situations, and intense in their reactions. The slow-to-warm-up babies (about 15 percent) were relatively inactive and fussy and tended to withdraw or to react negatively to novelty, but their reactions in new situations gradually became more positive with experience. By age 7, more "difficult" infants had developed serious emotional problems than infants in the other two groups. It is likely that the parents of these hard-to-manage children sometimes responded to their behavior with frustration and hostility, thus increasing the irritability that was an original characteristic of the infants. Most scientific study of infant temperament has focused on activity level, fearfulness (especially with people), and irritability. These characteristics assume special importance if they persist into childhood.

Activity level   Squirmy, wiggly babies do not necessarily grow up to be the terrors of the preschool yard who run full tilt everywhere they go. Although very active newborns tend to be more active than most other children during the first year, there is little preservation of this quality into later childhood (Moss & Susman, 1980; Rothbart & Derryberry, 1981).

Genetic influences on dimensions of temperament are best studied with twins. The rationale for this strategy is similar to the one described in Chapter

BOX 4.3

*Living with a
difficult
temperament*

When parents realize an infant's behavior is determined partly by the child's temperament rather than wholly by what the parents do, they can work more effectively toward a positive outcome for the child. One of the most difficult babies in Thomas and Chess's (1977) sample typically showed intense irritability and withdrawal to new situations and was slow to adapt to anything that was unfamiliar. He showed this tendency with his first bath and with his first solid foods. He also reacted negatively to the first days in nursery and elementary school and on his first shopping trip with his parents. Each of these experiences evoked stormy responses and much crying and struggling. However, his parents learned to anticipate the boy's reactions. They learned that if they were patient and presented new situations gradually and repeatedly, eventually the boy adapted to them. His parents did not interpret his difficulties as reflecting on their effectiveness as parents. As a result, this boy never became a behavior problem, even though most children with this temperamental style are at risk for psychological problems.

During later childhood and adolescence, this boy was fortunate in avoiding many radically new situations. He lived in the same community and went through high school with the same friends. However, when he went to a college away from home, he was confronted with new situations, new friends, and a complex relationship with a female student with whom he was living. Now his earlier temperamental tendencies to withdraw and show intense negative reactions were expressed. However, after a discussion with Dr. Thomas, who explained to the young man his temperamental history and some techniques he might use to adapt to college, the young man's difficulties disappeared, and by the end of the year he had adjusted well again. When told that similar negative reactions might occur in the future, he said, "That's all right. I know how to handle them now" (Thomas & Chess, 1977, pp. 165–167).

2 in the discussion of the genetic bases of intelligence. One of the largest groups of twins studied was part of an investigation called the Collaborative Perinatal Project, in which 350 pairs of twins were observed at birth, 8 months, 4 years, and 7 years of age. Half the twins were identical and half were fraternal. When the babies came into the hospital for testing, trained observers rated their behavior for activity level, sociability, irritability, and other temperamental characteristics.

Analysis of the findings showed a moderate genetic contribution to activity level at 8 months, but not at later ages. That is, the identical twins were more similar to one another in activity level at 8 months than were the nonidentical twins, but not at 4 or 7 years (Goldsmith & Gottesman, 1981). Other scientists have also found only slight support for the notion that differences in activity level are genetically based (Plomin & Foch, 1980).

Irritability

Differences among infants in crying, fussiness, and general irritability during the first 6 months are not enduring. But extreme irritability in infants older than 7 months tends to be modestly preserved for the next year or 2 (Rothbart & Derryberry, 1981: Thomas & Chess, 1977). There is very little evidence regarding the physiological bases for irritability, although it is likely that babies who cry a lot in the first 3 or 4 months may suffer from a specific physical discomfort, like colic. Perhaps that is why irritability in the first few months does not predict later behavior.

Inhibition and fearfulness

What parents call fearfulness or shyness, psychologists call *inhibition to the unfamiliar:* an initial timidity, quietness, and withdrawal in response to unfamiliar people, places, or objects. This dimension of temperament shows some stability, at least from the first birthday through the early childhood years. More important, a tendency toward inhibition is related to other characteristics that lend a coherence to its status as a temperamental quality.

The signs of an inhibited child appear in clearest form around the first birthday because such children are particularly susceptible to fear of strangers and to other fears that are typical of this age period (see Chapter 3). At this age, some infants will stop playing, become quiet, and assume a wary facial expression or cry when an unfamiliar adult approaches them. Other infants are less likely to be wary and will often smile, clap, and allow the unfamiliar adult to play with them, showing little or no sign of inhibition. The inhibited child may recover after 5 or 10 minutes and play with the stranger with considerable pleasure. Although the inhibition in response to an unfamiliar event is usually of short duration, the tendency to respond in this fashion is a stable characteristic of the child during the second and third years. There is reason to believe its persistence is greater in boys than girls, for fearful 1-year-old boys were likely to be fearful when they were 6 to 8 years of age — 7 years later — while this degree of stability was not present among girls (Bronson, 1970).

In one study, the reactions of a large number of 21-month-old children to situations designed to provoke uncertainty were filmed on two different occasions. Behavioral signs of inhibition (withdrawal, clinging to the mother, proximity to the mother, crying, and failure to play) were evaluated from the film records. The most and least inhibited children were then taken to another laboratory where their heart rates were recorded while they watched slides of familiar and unfamiliar scenes and listened to spoken phrases and to recordings of environmental sounds. The extremely inhibited children showed higher and less variable heart rates than the extremely uninhibited children, especially when confronted with the less familiar scenes and spoken phrases that were most difficult to understand. It appears that the inhibited children had a higher average level of arousal of the sympathetic nervous system (see Figure 4.5).

During home visits when the children were 31 months old, those who had been inhibited at 21 months were less likely to interact with an unfamiliar woman and more likely to stay close to their mothers. Additionally, children who were classified as inhibited at 21 months clung to their mothers and did not initiate interactions with another child when they were in a playroom with

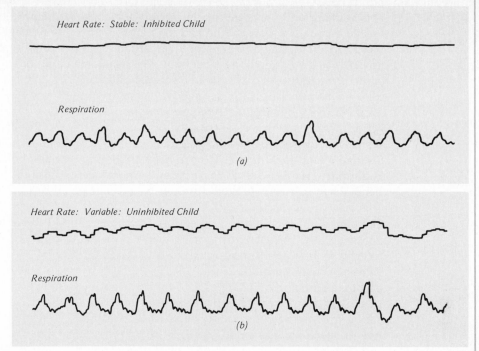

FIGURE 4.5

The heart rate and respiration patterns of an inhibited and an uninhibited child while looking at pictures. Both children have similar patterns of respiration. The inhibited child has a stable heart rate (top pattern), while the uninhibited child has a variable heart rate (bottom pattern). The peaks of the heart rate correspond to the peaks of the respiration cycles for the uninhibited child but not for the inhibited child. (From C. Garcia Coll, J. Kagan, & J. S. Reznick. Behavioral inhibition in young children. Child Development, 1983, in press. By permission.)

Heart Rate: Stable: Inhibited Child

Respiration

(a)

Heart Rate: Variable: Uninhibited Child

Respiration

(b)

their mother and an uninhibited child of the same age and sex (Garcia Coll, Kagan, & Reznick, 1984). If this characteristic remains part of the child's personality and persists until school entrance, it could influence the child's pattern of friendships and perhaps the amount of anxiety experienced in the classroom.

In summary, there are individual differences among infants in the temperamental dimensions of activity level, irritability, regularity, and fearfulness or inhibition in response to new or unfamiliar events. Many of these differences show some stability over time, and some of them are associated with individual differences in patterns of physiological responding. The long-term consequences of temperamental differences for the child's later behavior depend, however, on the experiences that the child encounters. We turn now to discuss the interactive influences of temperament and parental practices on children's behavior.

The principle of bidirectionality

The reciprocal influence of parental behavior and infant temperament forms the basis for the very important principle of *bidirectionality* in development. The principle states that the parent-child relationship goes both ways: Parents influence children, and children influence parental behaviors. Another way to state this is to say that children's development is a product of the interaction between their own characteristics and those of the people who socialize them.

One example of this principle is a family that included two children born a little over a year apart. The older child, a boy named Elliott, was a cuddly baby who smiled readily and was very socially responsive. His mother and father smiled and talked to him a great deal. He was also very active. By 9 months, he was walking and soon getting into everything. He required a lot of attention just to ensure his safety. If he had been observed in the Strange Situation, he would probably have been scored as securely attached. His younger sister, Susan, was a quieter, more sober baby. She watched people intently but did not smile so readily. As a result, her parents talked to her less than they had to Elliott. She was also relatively inactive, seeming content to sit and watch others much of the time. She received less attention and less practice in social interaction, which may have contributed to her quiet manner. She also seemed less distressed by separation and might have been classified as avoidant in the Strange Situation. Elliott and Susan had different patterns of behavior from the beginning, and as a result, their parents treated them differently. The parents' behavior in turn encouraged different patterns of social responding.

The emotions we call fear, joy, sadness, loneliness, and guilt are best viewed as names for combinations of specific external events, thoughts, and changes in internal feeling due to physiological changes. The external event might be the sight of a charging bull; the thoughts could be anticipations of pain and injury; and the physiological changes could include an increase in adrenaline or heart rate. That complex state is usually called *fear.* As another example, when one sees a frown on the face of a friend, expects a sign of rejection, and notices a rise in heart rate, the emotion might be called *social anxiety.*

The measurement of emotion

Parents often infer infants' emotional states from their behavior, sometimes in conjunction with the situation the infant is experiencing. For instance, if an elder sister takes away a toy and a baby cries, a parent might infer that the infant was angry or frustrated. Psychologists use behavioral reactions as one index of emotion, but they also measure physiological responses. For older children and adults, they try to assess the third component described above, the person's thoughts or descriptions of the feelings experienced.

None of these three measures alone is sufficient to classify an emotional state. In the first place, no single behavior or physiological reaction can be used as an index of emotion, because any one reaction can reflect different emotional states. A rise in heart rate accompanies a smile as well as crying. Second, the same observable behavior can be associated with different internal physiological reactions or thoughts. Children threatened with punishment may all hang their heads and look wary, but one may have a rise in heart rate, another stomach contractions, a third increased muscle tension. Thus, a complete assessment of an emotion requires behavioral and physiological measures and, when possible, a report by the person describing how she or he feels.

Infant emotions

The emotional states of infants differ from those of adults, partly because infants do not consciously evaluate their feeling states the way adults do (and, of course, they cannot describe their feelings to others). Adults are often aware of and therefore evaluate changes in their internal feeling states, and these evaluations form an important core of emotion. Thus, it is useful to differentiate between the emotions of infants, on the one hand, and those of adults, on the other. The distinction between the biological state of disease and the psychological state called illness is analogous to the difference between the emotional states of infants and adults. Certain biological changes in the body are regarded as diseases—like cancer or tuberculosis—whether or not the patient has any conscious recognition of the changes in internal function. On occasion, people become aware of the biological changes, and if they evaluate them as stemming from a pathological process, they will regard themselves as having an illness. The recognition that one is ill has important consequences, for it creates a novel psychological state that could either exacerbate or reduce the symptoms of the disease. People may become depressed, irritable, or fatigued simply because they are aware of a diseased biological state. Similarly, when older children or adults become aware of their internal feeling states, they evaluate them and, in so doing, create emotional states that are not possible in the infant.

During the first 3 to 4 months, infants display many reactions suggesting emotional states. One is characterized by motor quieting and heart rate deceleration in response to an unexpected event. Psychologists might call this state "surprise in response to the unexpected." A second set of changes is characterized by increased motor movement, closing of the eyes, heart rate increase, and crying; these changes occur in response to pain, cold, and hunger. Scientists might name this combination "distress in response to physical privation." A third set that includes decreased muscle tone and closing of the eyes after feeding might be called "relaxation to gratification." A fourth pattern includes increased movement of the limbs, smiling, and excited babbling when a moderately familiar event or social interaction occurs. Psychologists might call this profile "excitement to assimilation of an event," although parents would be more likely to label it "joy" or "happiness." In each of these examples, the name of the emotion should contain a reference to its source—for example, "surprise in response to the unexpected" or "distress in response to physical privation."

During the period between 4 and 10 months, new emotional reactions appear. One of these, described in Chapter 3, is fear of the unfamiliar. When they encounter a strange person or an unfamiliar event, infants about 8 months old sometimes respond with a facial expression that adults perceive as fearful—mouth retracted, eyes widened, brows raised. At the same time, they stop playing and may cry. Much younger infants pay attention to similar strange events but rarely seem frightened or cry. Another emotion shown by around 8 months, which we might call "anger to frustration," is signaled by crying and resistance when an activity is interrupted or an interesting object disappears.

During the first year of life, infants also respond to signs of anger or happiness in another person (Kreutzer & Charlesworth, 1973). Mothers who kept records of their children's reactions to the strong feelings of others reported that their 1-year-olds became upset and moved away when someone showed anger but displayed either affectionate or jealous behavior when they saw affection between others (Zahn-Waxler, Radke-Yarrow, & King, 1979).

Once children have developed strong attachments to other people, they may show signs of sadness if they are separated from those people for a long time. For instance, a 1-year-old whose mother has to be in the hospital for several days may become irritable, cry a lot, refuse to play, or show irregular eating and sleeping patterns.

Because many of these emotions appear to be universal, some theorists have proposed that they evolved because they have adaptive value for the young child's survival. For example, wary and fearful reactions to unfamiliar people and places may protect a child from harm during the period of development when first learning to crawl and walk independently. Inhibition of action may prevent the child from approaching dangerous objects, and the child's crying is likely to bring a protective adult. The adaptive function of sadness after loss of an attachment object is less obvious, but the positive feeling manifested when the attachment figure is close may keep children physically near familiar people who will care for them. They may also learn to associate unpleasant feelings with separation from the family group and, as a result, stay close to parents and older siblings. As children get older and are physically and psychologically able to move farther away from adult supervision, their fears of the unfamiliar gradually decline. Even at age 3 or 4, however, sadness when temporarily separated from parents may keep the child close to the family.

Although the similarity observed in the development of infants' emotions suggests that maturational factors are at work, emotional expression is also influenced by learning. As children mature, they begin to interpret and label their feeling states, often using concepts taught by other people. For example, two children are fighting over a toy; the parent takes the toy away, and the children scream loudly. One parent might tell the children they are angry, another might say they are afraid of the punishment that is imminent, and a third might tell them they feel shame for doing something wrong. The children might learn to associate their feelings and the situation with the labels "anger," "fear," or "shame." The next time they have the same or similar feelings in a similar situation, they may apply the label they learned earlier.

SUMMARY

Three major theories of infant social development emphasize the parent-child relationship as a critical influence. According to psychoanalytic theory, infants' striving for sensory pleasure leads them to invest emotional energy, called libido, in the people who provide them with pleasure through gratifications such as feeding. Other theories derived from psychoanalysis stress the formation of trust during infancy when the child experiences consistent care from the mother. Social learning theory also contains the hypothesis that the parents' role in reducing biological drives, such as hunger and thirst, is the basis for the child's emotional bond with the parent. Both of these theories were challenged by studies of monkeys showing that infant monkeys were more attached to a soft, comfortable artificial mother than to a wire mother that fed them.

A third theory, which has stimulated recent studies of infants' attachment to their parents, is based on ethology. The field of ethology entails studying animals in their natural environments and observing regular behavior patterns. Theorists have proposed that human infants are genetically prepared to form attachments to their caregivers and that these attachments are adaptive in the evolutionary sense because they help to assure that adults will care for young children. Attachment is viewed in this theory as an important foundation for healthy social and emotional development later in life. It affects social development by making children receptive to acquiring the standards and values of their caregivers, typically their parents.

In the first few months of life, children respond to people with smiles, coos, and eye contact, but they do not show clear differentiation among people. The first major social behavior is the social smile, which appears between 2 and 3 months. During the second 6 months, children begin to respond to particular people, the targets of attachment. They approach the people to whom they are attached and are easily comforted by them.

Attachment is built from the interactions between the infant and the caregiver. The quality of the interactions, rather than the amount of time, seems to be important. The strongest and most secure attachments seem to occur when the caregiver is sensitive and responsive to the infant's signals and provides nurturant and supportive care. Mothers, fathers, and others close to the baby are often targets of attachment.

As more mothers of infants are employed outside the home, more infants spend a significant part of their time in day care. While many critics have worried that day care would disrupt the attachment to the mother or would deprive the child of important experiences, the available evidence shows that infants in good-quality day care do not differ in any measurable way from those who stay at home with their mothers full time. In families where there is limited opportunity for care and intellectual stimulation, infants appear to benefit from day care.

Some theorists believe that infants establish different qualities of attachment as a function of different patterns of interactions. One of the important dimensions of attachment is security or insecurity. One standard situation for measuring attachment has been used to classify infants as securely or insecurely attached. Children classified as secure show better social adjustment in the preschool years and have more supportive relationships with their mothers. On the other hand, some children classified as insecure are also often emotionally healthy and have sensitive, warm mothers. They seem to behave differently than the "secure" children partly because of temperamental predispositions or because their parents have socialized them to be independent.

Some individual differences in activity level, irritability, fearfulness, and inhibition in new situations arise from predispositions with which the infant enters the world. Such dimensions are called temperament. Temperamental qualities of early infancy may have some stability over time, but qualities that are evident at 1 year are more stable over the next few years. Inhibition in unfamiliar situations is one quality that has some physiological correlates and appears to be most enduring. These temperamental qualities always interact with the child's experience, however. The principle of bidirectionality is a statement that parent-child influences operate in both directions; the child's qualities affect the parent, and vice versa.

REFERENCES

Ainsworth, M. D. S., Blehar, M. C., Waters, E., & Wall, S. *Patterns of attachment: A psychological study of the strange situation.* Hillsdale, N.J.: Erlbaum, 1978.

Anderson, C. W., Nagel, R. J., Roberts, W. A., & Smith, J. W. Attachment to substitute caregivers as a function of center quality and caregiver involvement. *Child Development*, 1981, *52*, 53–61.

Arend, R., Gove, F. L., & Sroufe, L. A. Continuity of individual adaptation from infancy to kindergarten: A predictive study of ego resiliency and curiosity in preschoolers. *Child Development*, 1979, *50*, 950–959.

Behlmer, G. K. *Child Abuse and moral reform in England.* Stanford, Calif.: Stanford University Press, 1982.

Belsky, J. Early human experience: A family perspective. *Developmental Psychology*, 1981, *17*, 3–23.

Bowlby, J. *Attachment* (Vol. 1): *Attachment and loss.* New York: Basic Books, 1969.

Bronson, G. W. Fear of visual novelty. *Developmental Psychology*, 1970, *2*, 33–40.

Clark-Stewart, K. A., & Hevey, C. M. Longitudinal relations in repeated observations of mother-child interaction from 1 to 2½ years. *Developmental Psychology*, 1981, *17*, 127–145.

Crockenberg, S. B. Infant irritability, mother responsiveness, and social support influences on the security of the infant-mother attachment. *Child Development*, 1981, *52*, 857–865.

Erikson, E. H. *Childhood and society* (2nd ed.). New York: Norton, 1963.

Freud, S. *An outline of psychoanalysis.* Standard editor of the works of Sigmund Freud. London: Hogarth Press, 1964.

Fuller, J. L., & Clark, L. D. Genotype and behavioral vulnerability to isolation in dogs. *Journal of Comparative and Physiological Psychology*, 1968, *66*, 151–156.

Garcia Coll, C., Kagan, J., & Reznick, J. S. Behavioral inhibition in young children. *Child Development*, 1984.

Gewirtz, J. L. The cause of infant smiling in four child-rearing environments in Israel. In B. M. Foss (Ed.), *Determinants of infant behavior* (Vol. 3). London: Metheun, 1965.

Goldsmith, H. H., & Gottesman, I. I. Origins of variation in behavioral style. *Child Development*, 1981, *52*, 91–103.

Grossmann, K., Grossmann, K. E., Huber, F., & Wartner, U. German children's behavior toward their mothers at 12 months and their fathers at 18 months in the Ainsworth Strange Situation. *International Journal of Behavioral Development*, 1981, *4*, 157–181.

Grossmann, K., Thane, K., & Grossmann, K. E. Maternal tactual contact of the newborn after various post-partum conditions of mother-infant contact. *Developmental Psychology*, 1981, *17*, 158–169.

Harlow, H. F., & Harlow, M. K. Learning to love. *American Scientist*, 1966, *54*, 244–272.

Hock, E., & Clinger, J. B. Infant coping behaviors: Their relationship to maternal attachment. *Journal of Genetic Psychology*, 1981, *138*, 231–243.

Kagan, J., Kearsley, R. B., & Zelazo, P. R. *Infancy: Its place in human development.* Cambridge, Mass.: Harvard University Press, 1978.

Klinnert, M. D., Campos, J., Sorce, J. F., Emde, R. N., & Svejda, M. J. Social referencing. In R. Plutchik & H. Kellerman (Eds.), *The emotions in early development.* New York: Academic Press, 1983.

Kreutzer, M. A., & Charlesworth, W. R. *Infants' reactions to different expressions of emotion.* Paper presented at the Society for Research in Child Development, Philadelphia, 1973.

Lamb, M. E. The development of father-infant relationships. In M. E. Lamb (Ed.), *The role of the father in child development.* New York: Wiley, 1981.

Lamb, M. E., Hwang, C. P., Frodi, A. M., & Frodi, M. Security of mother and father infant attachment and its relation to sociability with strangers in traditional and nontraditional Swedish families. *Infant Behavior and Development*, 1982, *5*, 355–368.

Londerville, S., & Main, M. Security of attachment and compliance in maternal training methods in the second year of life. *Developmental Psychology*, 1981, *17*, 289–299.

Lorenz, K. Z. *The foundations of ethology.* New York: Springer-Verlag, 1981.

Moss, H. A., & Susman, E. J. Longitudinal study of personality development. In O. G. Brim & J. Kagan (Eds.), *Constancy and change in human development.* Cambridge, Mass.: Harvard University Press, 1980.

Miyake, K., & Takahashi, T. Unpublished manuscript, 1983.

O'Connell, J. C., & Farran, D. C. Effects of day care experience on the use of intentional communicative behaviors in a sample of socio-economically depressed infants. *Developmental Psychology*, 1982, *18*, 22–29.

Parke, R. D., & Tinsley, B. R. The father's role in infancy: Determinants of involvement in caregiving and play. In M. E. Lamb (Ed.), *The role of the father in child development*. New York: Wiley, 1981.

Pastor, D. L. The quality of mother-infant attachment in its relationship to toddlers' initial sociability with peers. *Developmental Psychology*, 1981, *17*, 326–335.

Plomin, R., & Foch, T. T. A twin study of objectively assessed personality in childhood. *Journal of Personality and Social Psychology*, 1980, *39*, 680–688.

Rode, S. S., Chang, P., Fisch, R. O., & Sroufe, L. A. Attachment patterns of infants separated at birth. *Developmental Psychology*, 1981, *17*, 188–191.

Rosen, K. S. The relationship between affect and cognition in maltreated infants. Unpublished manuscript, 1982.

Rothbart, M. K., & Derryberry, D. Development of individual differences in temperament. In M. E. Lamb & A. L. Brown (Eds.), *Advances in developmental psychology* (Vol. 1). Hillsdale, N.J.: Erlbaum, 1981.

Rutter, M. Maternal deprivation, 1972–1978: New findings, new concepts, new approaches. *Child Development*, 1979, *50*, 283–305.

Sackett, G. P., Ruppenthal, G. C., Fahrenbruch, C. E., Holm, R. A., & Greenough, W. T. Social isolation rearing effects in monkeys vary with genotype. *Developmental Psychology*, 1981, *17*, 313.

Sameroff, A. J., Seifer, R., & Zax, M. Early development of children at risk for emotional disorder. *Monographs of the Society for Research in Child Development*, 1982, *47*, (7).

Sears. R. R., Maccoby, E. E., & Levin, H. *Patterns of child rearing*. New York: Harper & Row, 1957.

Sorce, J. F., Emde, R. N., & Frank, M. Maternal referencing in normal and Down's syndrome infants. In R. N. Emde & R. J. Harmon (Eds.), *Attachment and affiliative systems*. New York: Plenum, 1983.

Sroufe, L. A., & Waters, E. The ontogenesis of smiling and laughter: A perspective on the organization of development in infancy. *Psychological Review*, 1976, *83*, 173–179.

Tennes, K. The role of hormones in mother-infant transaction. In R. N. Emde & R. J. Harmon (Eds.), *The development of attachment and affiliative systems*. New York: Plenum, 1982.

Thomas, A., & Chess, S. *Temperament and development*. New York: Brunner/Mazel, 1977.

Thompson, R. A., Lamb, M. E., & Estes, D. Stability of mother-infant attachment and its relationship to changing life circumstances in an unselected middle-class sample. *Child Development*, 1982, *53*, 144–148.

Tinbergen, N. *The study of instinct*. Oxford: Oxford University Press, 1951.

Waters, E., Wippman, J., & Sroufe, L. A. Attachment, positive affect, and competence in the peer group. *Child Development*, 1979. *50*, 821–829.

Watson, J. *Psychological care of infant and child*. New York: Norton, 1928.

Whiting, B. B. (Ed.). *Six cultures: Studies of child rearing*. New York: Wiley, 1963.

Whiting, B. B., & Whiting, J. W. M. *Children of six cultures: A psychocultural analysis*. Cambridge, Mass.: Harvard University Press, 1975.

Winick, M., Meyer, K. K., & Harris, R. C. Malnutrition and environmental enrichment by early adoption. *Science*, 1975, *190*, 1173–1175.

Zahn-Waxler, C., Radke-Yarrow, M., & King, R. A. Child rearing and children's pro-social initiation toward victims of distress. *Child Development*, 1979, *50*, 319–330.

CHAPTER 5

The transition to childhood: the second and third years

*D*uring the 6 months that follow the first birthday the child is transformed. Speech replaces gestures and babbling as a way to communicate desires and ask questions. Play becomes more spontaneous and contains copies of meaningful life experiences and imitations of parents, siblings, and other children. Behaviors that violate the parents' standards about hitting, soiling, and destruction of property are followed by anxiety or shame. Speech, symbolism, imitation, and morality—which are among the most distinctive characteristics of human nature—have suddenly become part of the child's profile. A few months later, children use their own names and the personal pronouns *I, me,* or *my,* indicating that they have attained self-awareness or self-consciousness. At this time children also gain a capacity for empathy, reacting with sorrow and concern for the feelings of others, such as a dog whining in pain or a mother with tears on her cheeks. This chapter considers the emergence of all of these qualities except speech, which will be discussed separately in Chapter 6.

SYMBOLIC
FUNCTIONING

By the end of the first year, children can recognize and retrieve the past, categorize events, and generate ideas of what might happen in the immediate future. The next victory, which occurs soon after the first birthday, is the capacity to treat an object as if it were something other than it is—a talent for pretend play.

As explained in Chapter 3, psychologists assume that during much of the first year children react to new events by creating schemata whose features correspond to those in the original event. But after the first birthday, children transform experience and impose their own ideas on objects, rather than simply adjusting their actions to an object's physical properties. In the hands of a 10-month-old, a rubber ball is an object to squeeze and to throw and a cup something to hold and put to the mouth. However, by the second birthday children invent new and often original uses for these and other objects. They treat a ball as a piece of food, a cup as a hat, a plate as a blanket, or a ball of yarn as a balloon. Children are now capable of *symbolism;* they can both create and accept an arbitrary relation between an object and an idea that is fairly remote from the actual physical qualities of the object.

For example, a verbally precocious 26-month-old girl was playing with a set of toys that included two small dolls, a small bed, and a very large bed. After she had placed one of the small dolls on the small bed, she scanned the rest of the toys and noted that she needed another bed. She looked directly at the very large bed, touched it, but did not pick it up. After almost 2 minutes of study of the available toys, she finally selected a small wooden sink, about 4 inches long, placed the second small doll in it, and put this arrangement next to the other small bed, which already had its doll. Apparently satisfied, she declared, "Now Mommy and Daddy are sleeping."

We can explain the rejection of the large bed (an appropriate object) in favor of the sink, which she knew was not a bed, by suggesting that the child had an idea of the appropriate size of the two beds—both had to be small, like the dolls. In order to have her behavior conform to that idea, the girl distorted reality a bit and used an object that belonged to another category because its size matched her idea of what was appropriate. In treating the sink as a bed she revealed her talent for symbolism (Kagan, 1981).

Symbolic ability develops in phases. Around 12 months, children will treat a toy cup as if it were a real cup and drink from it, or place a small wooden doll on a piece of wood as if the doll were a baby and the piece of wood a bed. Although the degree of distortion imposed on these objects is minimal, no 7-month-old would behave this way. By the middle of the second year, children go one step further and impose new functions on objects. They might turn a doll upside down and treat it as a salt shaker or play with a wooden block as if it were a chair. Many 2-year-olds seem capable of simple metaphor. They will treat two wooden balls, differing only in size, as if they were a parent and child, for example.

FIGURE 5.1

(a)　　　　(b)

Once children become capable of imposing a symbolic meaning on events and the qualities they share, representations of experience become expanded. A woman with a bandaged eye is more than a physical event. She is a person in pain, someone to feel sorry for, and the bandaged eye is an event that has a cause to be discovered. This change in cognitive frame is not due only to new experiences. Parents do not suddenly treat the child differently at the end of the first year, and they continue to feed, clean, converse, and play with their children. Moreover, balls, bottles, and beds do not suddenly acquire new physical properties. The emergence of symbolic functioning in this period, like the improvement of retrieval memory at 8 months, is probably due to special changes in the central nervous system.

Children's drawings

Children's drawings become more symbolic during the second and third years, and they show a regular growth in complexity and sophistication. Children begin to scribble sometime in the second year but rarely try to draw familiar objects. Although their drawings do not portray any specific objects, if they are asked they may call a set of scribbles a dog, a cat, or a person. But by 3 years of age, children create symbolic forms that look like animals or people (see Figure 5.1). In one study, an examiner drew a schematic face on a piece of white paper, as illustrated in Figure 5.2. She then gave the child a piece of paper and told the child to make that drawing. The growth sequence was very similar for children from different cultures. The first attempt to copy the face, around 16 months, usually resulted in a scribbling of parallel lines. During the next phase, which began to appear by about 20 months of age, children created an approximation of a crude circle but included no internal elements to represent the eyes, nose, or mouth. By the second birthday, most middle-class American children were able to draw a circle, and by 30 months, most children attempted to place a few dots or lines inside the circle to represent parts of the face (Kagan, 1981) (see Figure 5.3).

Symbolic play with objects

Although the concept of *play* has been used for many years, it is more difficult to define than most psychological ideas. Catherine Garvey (1977) lists the criteria most observers use in defining play:

FIGURE 5.2

A picture of a face that
an adult examiner
drew on a piece of
paper and showed to
young children. (After
J. Kagan. The second
year. *Cambridge,
Mass.: Harvard Uni-
versity Press, 1981.)*

FIGURE 5.3

Drawings made by
children of four dif-
ferent ages when they
were asked to draw
one like the examiner's
picture in Figure 5.2.
At 16 months, chil-
dren made scribbles of
parallel lines; older
children copied the
circle; the oldest chil-
dren tested added a
few internal elements
representing parts of
the face. (From J.
Kagan. The second
year. *Cambridge,
Mass.: Harvard Uni-
versity Press, 1981.)*

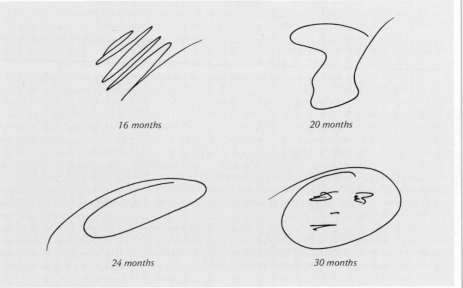

16 months   20 months

24 months   30 months

1. Play is pleasurable and enjoyable.
2. Play has no extrinsic goals. The child's motivations are subjective and serve no practical objective.
3. Play is spontaneous and voluntary, freely chosen by the player.
4. Play involves some active engagement on the part of the player.

Like Garvey, most authors emphasize that play is a voluntary, spontaneous activity that does not have a real-world goal. Because our interest here
is children's capacities for manipulating symbols, we discuss only one type of
play, a set of behaviors called *symbolic acts with objects* (see also Chapter 9).

Beginning in early infancy, children manipulate objects, usually small ones (a rattle, a cloth ball), for reasons that have nothing to do with biological needs like hunger, thirst, and warmth. During the second year, these manipulations often reproduce acts children have seen adults perform, such as talking on a telephone or drinking from a cup. These are early instances of symbolic acts.

An interesting change occurs late in the second year. At this time, children begin to replace themselves with a toy as the active agent in play. For example, a child may put a toy bottle to a doll's mouth rather than to her own mouth, or place a toy telephone beside an animal's head rather than her own head. The toys now change their role from participants in the child's sensorimotor schemes to symbolic agents in a play the child is both inventing and directing. This change in symbolic play with objects occurs at about the same time in American children, in children living on islands in the Fiji chain, and in children living in Vietnamese families that have recently immigrated to the United States (Kagan, 1981).

Theorists have disagreed about both the causes and the purposes of play and have found it necessary to distinguish play that is *exploratory* (shaking a rattle) from play that is *constructive* (building a tower of blocks). A third major category is *pretend play*, in which a child assumes the role of another person,

such as a parent (McCall, Parke, & Kavanaugh, 1977). Some theorists believe that pretend play, especially, can reflect the child's attempt to cope with anxiety and conflict, a popular hypothesis derived from psychoanalytic theory. For example, the child might act out in play an interaction between a mother and a baby doll. Perhaps he will take very good care of the doll because he himself feels deprived of love, or perhaps he will scold and punish the doll because he is trying to work through pressures of his own socialization. Although acting out psychic conflicts clearly can be one reason for play behavior, such conflicts do not account for most play.

Other investigators contend that play is a prerequisite for later skills — practice for tomorrow. Jerome Bruner, for example, believes that play is crucial for the development of intellectual skills (Bruner, Jolly, & Sylva, 1976). In play, children can experiment without interference, and in so doing they may build complex abilities. Playing with crayons and paper facilitates drawing skills; manipulating blocks teaches the child something about mechanics; playing with objects promotes the ability to generate new ways of using these objects. For example, in one study, children who had played with a set of sticks and colored chalk solved a "problem" that required them to clamp two sticks together to get the chalk out of a box. They were as quick and efficient as children who had watched someone else solve the problem (Sylva, Bruner, & Genova, 1976). The effects of play on cognitive development are discussed in Box 5.1.

Play with children

As children begin to play with objects in a more symbolic manner, their reactions to other children also change. Prior to 12 months, a meaningful interaction between two children is rare. Ten-month-olds treat each other as if they were animate toys; they pull at each other's hair, poke at their eyes, and babble to them. But by 18 to 20 months, children can cooperate and take turns with a playmate. In addition, they initiate play with each other, and arguments become more frequent and more intense.

During the middle of the second year, there is a brief period of initial shyness with an unfamiliar child, which contrasts sharply with the spontaneous behavior of the 10-month-old. In one study, each child played in a pleasant room for 20 minutes while the mother sat nearby. Then an unfamiliar child of the same sex and age came into the room with his or her own mother. Children under 1 year continued to play happily with their toys and did not retreat to their mother when the unfamiliar child entered the room. Occasionally a 10-month-old would crawl to the other child and explore her hair, face, or clothes. But a few months after the first birthday, the children showed signs of inhibition. They stopped playing, retreated, and clung to the mother while staring at the other child, although they rarely cried. By 2 to $2\frac{1}{2}$ years of age, this inhibition had begun to decline (Kagan, 1981).

This brief period of apprehension in the presence of an unfamiliar child can be considered a counterpart to stranger anxiety, the distress infants begin to show at about 8 months when confronted with an unfamiliar adult. The question of why it emerges 5 months later, at 13 months instead of 8, interests cognitive psychologists because it relates to infants' development of schemata and expectations. Since most infants are cared for by and interact most often

BOX 5.1

*Does play
promote
cognitive
development?*

One of the popular hypotheses in developmental psychology is that play facilitates intellectual development. The evidence for this claim comes from studies showing that children who have no toys and little opportunity to play with other children are cognitively behind their age-mates. Additionally, children from economically disadvantaged families appear to engage in less pretend play at nursery schools than middle-class children do. Thus, some psychologists believe that one reason many lower-class children have learning problems after they enter school is that their play experiences have been less frequent, less complex, and less varied than those of most middle-class children.

But, some anthropologists have reported cultures in which no make-believe play occurs, even though in most cultures children do play symbolically. Hopi children conduct pretend rabbit hunts and make believe that they are modeling pottery the way their parents do. Israeli children whose families come from Middle Eastern communities show much less make-believe play than do Israeli children whose families have emigrated from Europe. Thus, there are important cultural and class differences in the amount of play.

If play is important for full intellectual development, the introduction and stimulation of play may be one means to promote cognitive development. Phyllis Levenstein, one of the important promoters of the advantages of play, has developed a program for bringing toys to economically disadvantaged children. Mothers are taught how to use these toys to play with their children. In this program, the toys are a vehicle to promote pleasant, stimulating interactions between mothers and children. Because verbal stimulation and affectionate interactions are known to promote children's cognitive development, the beneficial effects of the program may be due to this feature rather than to the toys alone.

Appropriate toys can help slightly older children to learn positive social behavior in preschool. Disadvantaged children attending Head Start programs watched television programs promoting positive behaviors such as helping, sharing, and cooperation. In some class-rooms, there were toys, puppets, records, and dolls that were similar to the characters and themes on the television program; other classrooms had toys that were not related to the social themes of the TV program. When the toys supplemented the television messages, children adopted some of the social behaviors being taught; the toys apparently helped them to practice the behaviors they had been taught (Friedrich-Cofer et al., 1979).

Although these and other studies show that toys can be used effectively in combination with parents, teachers, or television pro-grams to promote children's development, there is little evidence at present that the availability of toys alone contributes to the cognitive or social development of disadvantaged children.

with adults, perhaps they develop well-articulated schemata for adults, expectations about how adults will behave, and a set of responses they can make to adults early in the first year. The average infant has less regular contact with other infants and, therefore, may have less well developed schemata for them by the age of 8 months. By 14 months, however, the child may have matured enough to generate questions during an encounter with an unfamiliar child, questions such as "What should I do with her?" "What will she do to me?" "Will she take my toy?" If the child has no obvious answer to these self-generated inquiries, she becomes apprehensive, stops playing, and may retreat to the mother. After the second birthday, the apprehension and uncertainty are resolved, partly because the child has learned how other children behave and how to behave toward them. At this point the child is able to enter into reciprocal play with another child and to use the other child as a model.

Frequent contact with other infants does not prevent timidity upon first meeting an unfamiliar child. Israeli infants who were raised in an infant house on a kibbutz with a half dozen other infants showed the same degree of apprehension with an unfamiliar child early in the second year of life as Israeli infants who were raised in an apartment. By 29 months, the kibbutz-reared children showed less apprehension than apartment-reared youngsters when exposed to an unfamiliar child. The extensive daily interaction with other children hastened the decline of the inhibition (see Figure 5.4).

Two-year-olds will work together at a doll house, talk to each other on the telephone, and imitate each other in jumping off a couch. But they do not play

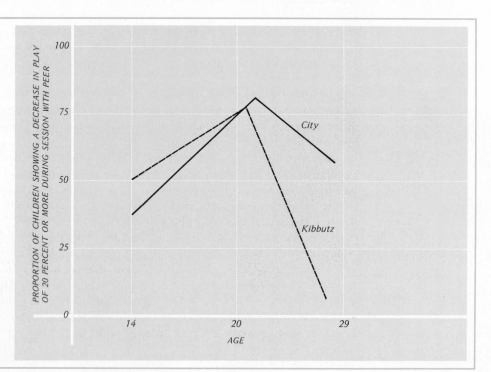

FIGURE 5.4

Changes in social inhibition with an unfamiliar peer. Children around 20 months old showed a decrease in play (suggesting inhibition when with an unfamiliar child in a playroom. The tendency to be inhibited with an unfamiliar peer appeared to decline at an earlier age for kibbutz children who had frequent experience in group settings with other children than for home-reared city children. (From M. Zaslow. Comparison of kibbutz and home-reared children. Unpublished doctoral dissertation, Harvard University, 1978. By permission.)

games with rules, and their play episodes last only a few minutes. Nevertheless, interactive experiences with other children facilitate cooperative play later on (Kagan, 1981; Mueller & Brenner, 1977).

Although the play of boys and girls is basically similar, boys are more likely to engage in rough-and-tumble play with vigorous and aggressive behavior. Girls are more likely to act out social themes that are less vigorous and physically active. These are average differences between the sexes as groups; individual girls who like very vigorous play and boys who enjoy social themes are not hard to find (Maccoby & Jacklin, 1974).

IMITATION

Developmental course

Imagine a scene in a typical home. A father is playing with his 3-month-old baby. The baby is propped in an infant seat while father faces her. Father sticks out his tongue, and the baby sticks out hers. Father smiles, and the baby smiles back. Father then delightedly tells his friend, who is watching, that his daughter imitates everything he does. But is the infant imitating the father?

Imitation has two defining characteristics. First, it must duplicate the behavior shown by the model. Second, it must be selective; that is, the response we call imitative must occur after a particular behavior by the model and not under a large number of other stimulus conditions. For example, if the baby described above also smiles to the father's voice or the shaking of his head, then her smiling when he smiles is not selective. Although some psychologists have claimed that newborns or babies in the first month will imitate adults' facial gestures, such as opening their mouths, there is still controversy about whether these responses represent selective imitation (Hayes & Watson, 1981; Meltzoff & Moore, 1977). Two-month-olds will stick out their tongues when a person sticks out his or her tongue at them, which looks like imitation, but they will also stick out their tongues when an adult moves a slender object like a pencil toward their mouths (Jacobson, 1979).

However, there is no doubt that selective imitation does occur by 7 or 8 months of age and that it becomes both more frequent and more complex during the next several years. One-year-old infants imitate novel gestures, sounds, and other behaviors that they see and hear, although they are more likely to imitate behaviors they can see themselves carry out (like a hand movement) than acts they cannot see themselves perform (like tongue protrusion).

Delayed imitation becomes possible not long after the first birthday, though it is relatively infrequent before about age 2. A 15-month-old stares quietly while her mother dials a telephone and, a few minutes, hours, or perhaps weeks later, repeats the essential form of that act. The motor coordinations necessary for dialing the telephone were in the child's repertoire long before the imitative act occurred. Similarly, a 20-month-old watches as a laboratory researcher puts a wooden block on a small slab of wood and says, "This doll is very tired, and we must put it to bed. Night-night, dolly." The child fails to imitate any part of that sequence during the next 20 minutes. But when she enters the same room 1 month later and sees the same set of toys, she immediately puts the wooden block on the slab of wood and says, "Night-night."

Imitation increases in frequency between 1 and 3 years of age, but the likelihood of imitating a particular response depends on the type of behavior. Children between 1 and 3 years of age were given an opportunity to imitate a variety of motor acts (for example, an adult moved a rectangular block along a table) and social behaviors (the adult placed a screen in front of her face and peeked around the side twice). A third kind of imitation required the coordination of two separate actions in one motor sequence (the adult lifted a small brass cup on a string and struck it 3 times with a metal rod). The frequency of imitation of each of the three classes of acts is shown in Figure 5.5. The motor behaviors were imitated most readily, with 2-year-olds imitating about 80 percent of all the acts modeled; the social behaviors were next most frequent. Imitation of the coordinated sequences occurred rarely before 18 months, but increased between $1\frac{1}{2}$ and 2 years.

The children watched televised models as well as live models. Before the second birthday, children imitated the televised models less often than they did the live adults, but by their third birthday they imitated both live and televised models equally often (McCall et al., 1977). These findings demonstrate that young children imitate a broad range of behaviors and that they acquire information presented by television at an early age.

Explanations of imitation

The capacity to imitate another person is a major reason for the advanced intellectual and technological development of the human species, for imitation is an efficient way to learn new actions. Two questions can be asked regarding imitation by young children. The first is, why do children imitate at all? Contemporary theorists suggest that imitation is a universal maturational phenomenon, "a capacity that is built into the human species" (Yando, Seitz, & Zigler, 1978, p. 4). Indeed, imitation in the young child may be analogous to the swimming of fish and the flying of birds, both of which represent basic abilities that appear early in development.

The second question is, why do children imitate some models more than others or some behaviors more than others? Children possess many more

FIGURE 5.5

Percentage of actions imitated by children from 12 to 24 months. Actions were classified as motor, social, or coordinated behaviors. Children imitated motor actions earliest and most frequently, then social behaviors. Coordinated-action sequences were rarely imitated before 24 months. (From R. B. McCall, R. D. Parke, & R. D. Kavanaugh. Imitation of live and televised models by children one to three years of age. Monographs of the Society for Research in Child Development, *1977, 42 [No. 5]. © The Society for Research in Child Development, Inc. By permission.)*

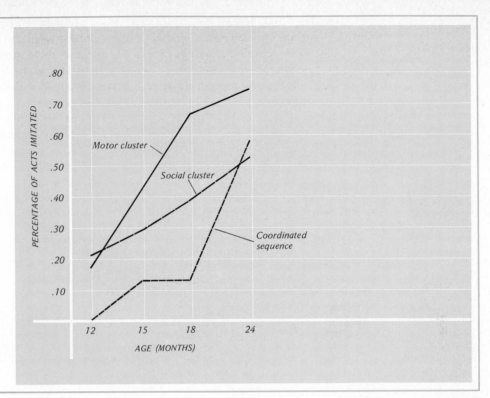

schemata for the behavior of other people than they ever duplicate in their own actions. Why do they imitate only a small number of the many acts they have observed? There are several hypotheses about the determinants of imitation. It is clear that multiple processes are involved and that imitation may serve different functions in infants, toddlers, and older children. For this reason, the bases for imitation at one age may be different from those that are most influential at another age.

The influence of uncertainty One possible influence on imitation during the first 2 years of life is the child's degree of uncertainty about his ability to execute the act that was witnessed. Observations of children suggest that they are most likely to imitate behaviors that they are in the process of mastering. They seem least likely to imitate acts that are thoroughly mastered and those so complex that they do not feel able to attempt them. A woman picking up a telephone is an appealing model for a 15-month-old but not for a 6- or 36-month-old—both of whom possess the motor capability to pick up a toy telephone. The 15-month-old is moderately uncertain about her ability to perform the response, but the 6-month-old has no expectation of carrying out the act, and the 3-year-old is too certain she can implement it. Similarly, 2-year-olds in the very early stages of speech are more likely to imitate an unfamiliar word applied to an unfamiliar object (an adult points to an odd piece of wood and says, "That's a tobo") than a familiar word for a familiar object ("That's a cup") (Leonard, Schwartz, Folger, Newhoff, & Wilcox, 1979).

If children in the second year are uncertain of their ability to perform a witnessed act, they may show signs of distress. In one series of observations, many 2-year-olds stopped playing, protested, clung to their mother, and even cried after they watched a researcher display actions that were a little too difficult to assimilate or to remember well (Kagan, 1981). The distress reactions typically seen between 18 and 24 months did not occur when the acts modeled were either easy to imitate or far beyond the child's ability (see Figure 5.6).

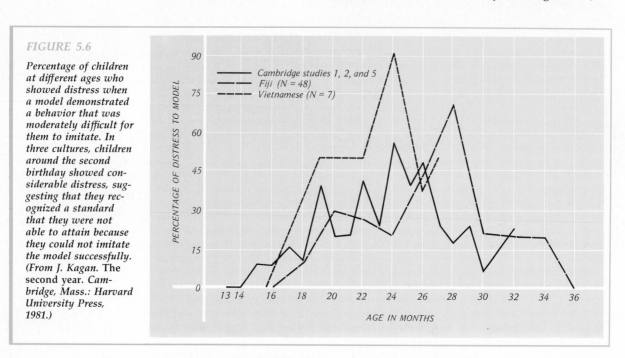

FIGURE 5.6

Percentage of children at different ages who showed distress when a model demonstrated a behavior that was moderately difficult for them to imitate. In three cultures, children around the second birthday showed considerable distress, suggesting that they recognized a standard that they were not able to attain because they could not imitate the model successfully. (From J. Kagan. The second year. Cambridge, Mass.: Harvard University Press, 1981.)

Imitation to promote social interactions When an infant imitates a parent, the parent often smiles, exclaims how wonderful and intelligent the baby is, and imitates the baby in return. The responsiveness of the parent may reinforce the baby's imitative behavior. Such social reinforcements increase the baby's general tendency to imitate, as well as influence which behaviors the baby chooses to imitate. Children are more likely to imitate an action that has received approval, such as eating with a spoon, than a response that is ignored, such as banging two forks together.

Imitation to enhance similarity to another A third basis for imitation emerges as the child enters the third year and begins to imitate specific persons rather than particular acts. By the second birthday, most children are aware that they have qualities that make them more similar to some people than to others (for example, the boy recognizes that he and the father share the properties of short hair, trousers, and similar genital anatomy). The recognition of similarities to the father and other males leads the boy to assume that he belongs to a common category with other males. Correspondingly, girls assume that they belong to a common category with other females. This insight provokes each child to make an active effort to search for additional similarities to other people in order to make firm the category to which they belong. They do this by imitating the actions of those people (see Chapter 10 for further discussion).

Emotional arousal as a basis for imitation   Children will imitate their parents more often than other adults. One reason may be that parents are a more continuous source of emotional arousal—both pleasant and unpleasant—than most other people. Persons who have the power to arouse the child emotionally—whether to joy, uncertainty, anger, or fear—recruit the child's attention, and as a result the child learns their actions more thoroughly than those of people who command less attention. A similar process occurs among children playing together. When pairs of unacquainted 2-year-olds play together, it is often the passive, quieter child who imitates the more dominant, active, loquacious one. The inhibited youngster appears apprehensive about losing a toy to the other and watches the dominant child vigilantly. When the dominant one performs an action that lies in the sphere of possible mastery of the passive child (for example, jumping off a table), the latter is likely to imitate that act within the next few minutes.

Imitation to gain goals   Imitation can be a self-conscious attempt to gain pleasure, power, property, or any one of a number of other desired goals. For example, a child who is trying to build a house with blocks may watch carefully as another child or adult builds a similar structure, and then imitate those actions. Or a 3-year-old may imitate the bullying behavior of another child because that behavior succeeds in getting desired toys away from other children. This basis for imitation typically emerges after the second birthday. Now it is appropriate to say that children are "motivated to imitate another," because they have an idea of a goal to be gained through the imitative act.

In summary, imitation may occur because of response uncertainty, social reinforcement, a desire to be more like another person, or a desire for particular goals. The behaviors imitated during the first 3 years of life depend partly on the child's level of cognitive development, which determines what behaviors the child perceives as challenging but not impossible. The motivation to be similar to another and the degree of emotional arousal induced by another person determine who the child will imitate, and the motivation for certain goals determines what will be imitated.

<table>
<tr><td>A MORAL SENSE
AND THE
EMERGENCE OF
STANDARDS</td><td>During the last 6 months of the second year, children begin to create idealized representations of objects, events, and behaviors. Toys should be without cracks, shirts should have all their buttons, and clothes should have no rips. These representations are called standards. At the same time, children acquire</td></tr>
</table>

standards about correct and incorrect behavior in specific situations, often dealing with cleanliness, control of aggression, and obedience to parents. These standards are the beginning of the child's understanding of right and wrong, good and bad; they are the first step in the developing sense of morality.

If events match children's standards, they may smile, but events that violate a standard may produce signs of anxiety or distress. For example, children will point to broken objects, torn clothing, missing buttons, and reveal in their voice and face a mood of concern. They will point to a crack in a plastic toy and say, "Oh-oh," "Broke," or "Yukky." In one study, 14- and 19-month-olds were brought to a laboratory playroom containing a large number of toys, some of which were purposely flawed (a doll's face was marked with black crayon, the clothes on another doll were torn, the head of an animal was removed). None of the 14-month-old infants paid any special attention to the damaged toys, while over half the 19-month-olds showed obvious preoccupation with them. They brought them to their mother, pointed to the damaged part, stuck their finger in the place where an animal's head had been removed, or, if they could talk, indicated that something was wrong by saying "fix" or "broke." Additionally, parents often report that during the few months before the second birthday, children suddenly show a concern with dirty hands, torn clothes, and broken cups.

Parents do not suddenly begin to punish destruction of property or dirty hands at 18 months; so why do the signs of concern appear at this age? It seems that children are developing the ability to infer that events have causes (even when they do not observe the cause). For example, a 21-month-old child sees a baby crying and immediately assumes the baby is hungry or hurt. When children react emotionally to a broken toy or a shirt without a button, they are assuming that the flaw is not an inherent property of the object but has been caused by something or someone. For example, American 2- and 3-year-olds, as well as Mayan children living in villages in the Yucatan peninsula, looked longer at a picture of a human face with distorted features than at a normal face. The children's verbalizations—"What happened to his nose?" or "Who hit him in the nose?"—implied a concern with the forces that might have damaged the face and inferences as to the events that might have produced the distortion. These observations suggest that by the second birthday children are ready to treat events that violate their standards with concern and to assume they were produced by some external force (Kagan, 1981).

The fact that children not only notice flaws in objects but often become distressed about them suggests that their standards are ideal representations of the "right" or "correct" way things should be. In some cases, they may have learned that breaking toys is followed by parental criticism or punishment. Signs of parental disapproval—whether a frown, a verbal chastisement, or a slap on the rear—produce an unpleasant state probably resembling anxiety. This unpleasant state could become associated with the child's mental representations of the acts that break toys or tear buttons from shirts. Hence, when a child guesses that the broken doll on the carpet resulted from someone's behavior, an emotional reaction is elicited. However, in many instances, children's concern over broken toys and buttonless shirts does not seem to require any prior experience of parental disapproval. It seems to be an inherent part of the formation of standards.

At about this same time, around the second birthday, children also display distress if they are unable to meet standards of behavior imposed by others. As mentioned earlier, when a researcher demonstrates acts that are hard to perform or remember, 2-year-old children from diverse cultural settings show distress. They may cry, throw toys around the room, or ask to go home. We suggested earlier that the children's upset was due to their recognition that they could not meet the standard represented by the model's behavior.

But why did the 2-year-olds feel that they should try to imitate the model? It is possible that past parental punishments for violations of standards about aggression or cleanliness lead 2-year-olds, but not younger children, to ask themselves, "What does the adult want?" and to infer that the adult model wants them to imitate her. In one study, 2-year-olds and 16-month-olds observed a model who, without any toys, pretended she was talking on a telephone or drinking from a cup. After she left the room, some of the 2-year-olds, but none of the 16-month-olds, imitated these behaviors. The response was in the younger child's repertoires, for the 16-month-olds imitated those acts when they were modeled with real toys. But the younger children may not have been mature enough to infer that the adult wanted them to duplicate that behavior and so did not do so when no toys were available.

Another phenomenon implying that children possess standards of correct and incorrect performance is the appearance of a smile when they meet a self-imposed standard that requires the investment of effort. Children who take 5 minutes to complete a six-piece puzzle often smile following success. They do not look at the mother while smiling; rather, it is a private response reflecting the recognition that they have met the standard they initially set for themselves.

In summary, 2-year-old children begin to evaluate actions and events as good or bad, and they often show distress when events do not meet their standards. These capacities are common to children from many cultures, probably because they result from cognitive developmental changes occurring around the second birthday. Children's use of standards to evaluate events and behavior is the beginning of their moral sense of right and wrong (see also Chapter 9 and Chapter 14). The question of the child's innate morality is discussed in Box 5.2.

SELF-AWARENESS

Each of us is familiar with the experience of reflecting upon our feelings and thoughts, knowing whether we are able to solve a particular problem, and initiating or inhibiting a goal-directed sequence of behaviors. In popular language, we are conscious of our qualities and potentials for action.

The last half of the second year is a time when children begin to be aware of their own properties, states, and abilities. Observations of children in our own and other cultures reveal the appearance of a set of behaviors that invites the label *self-awareness*. The source and nature of this self-awareness have long been subjects of debate among philosophers. Contemporary neurophysiologists believe they will be able, eventually, to account for this state as a product of complex patterns of neuronal discharge in the central nervous system.

Directing the behavior of others

The 2-year-old begins to direct the behavior of others. The child puts a toy telephone to the mother's ear, indicates he wants her to move to another chair, requests help with a problem, or asks the mother to make a funny sound. These directives to adults are not aimed at obtaining a specific material object: The child does not want a cookie or a toy. Rather, the child's goal seems to be

BOX 5.2
*Are children
innately moral?*

Must children learn a moral sense, or are they innately prepared to be sensitive to right and wrong? Mothers around the world from many different cultures begin to hold their children responsible for their actions by the second or third birthday. For example, mothers living in the Fiji Islands comment that their children naturally become more responsible after their second birthday, when they acquire a sense of right and wrong, which the Fijians call *vakayalo.* At the end of the nineteenth century, James Sully wrote that the child has an "inbred respect for what is customary and wears the appearance of a rule of life," as well as an "innate disposition to follow precedent and rule which precedes education" (1896, pp. 280–281). Sully, like most nineteenth-century observers, believed it obvious, even to a child, that causing harm to another person is wrong and immoral. The child does not have to learn that hurting other people is bad; it is an insight that inevitably accompanies growth.

Children seem to develop standards on aggressive behavior early in life. For example, many 2- and 3-year-olds are jealous and resentful toward younger siblings, yet they rarely do serious harm to a young infant. When that does occur, it makes headlines because it is a freak event. It appears that most children have begun to establish standards about aggressive behavior by the second birthday, and they realize at some level that hurtful behavior is wrong. Modern theorizing about developmental changes during the second and third years of life suggests that children develop many intellectual capacities that may make them sensitive or ready to absorb the rudiments of moral standards in their society. In this period, children begin to understand that events have causes, even when those causes are not immediately observable, and they can hold an idea or plan of action over a longer time span. They often develop an appreciation for standards of behavior and begin to apply them.

Of course, moral standards are acquired from the people around the child. In fact, initial inhibitions on behavior such as aggression may be removed if the child is taught that aggression is acceptable. Nevertheless, even 3- and 4-year-olds distinguish "moral" wrongs that result in harm to people from violations that merely involve a social convention (such as eating with a spoon). The initial readiness to acquire those standards and the sensitivity to violations that hurt people or destroy objects appear to arise partly from cognitive developmental changes that have a maturational base.

simply to influence the adult's behavior. Because children would not issue commands if they did not expect parents to obey them, it is reasonable to assume that children are aware of their ability to influence other people.

Describing one's own behavior

When children begin to speak three- and four-word sentences that contain verbs, usually after the second birthday, they often describe their own actions as they are performing them. A child says, "Go up," as he climbs up on a chair; "I fix," as he tries to rebuild a fallen tower of blocks; or "Want cookie," as he goes to the kitchen. Because children are more likely to describe their own activities than the behaviors of others, we assume they are concerned with their own activities. When children first begin to speak, they are most likely to call out the names of objects whose meanings they are just mastering, as if knowing the name of something is exciting and leads to the spontaneous utterance. Two-year-olds are gaining a new insight, a new awareness of their own abilities to act, to influence others, and to meet self-imposed standards. These ideas, like the realization that one knows the names of objects, are exciting. As a consequence, children describe their behavior as they perform it (see Table 5.1).

TABLE 5.1

Examples of behaviors that show self-awareness

Behaviors that direct others	Statements describing child's own behavior
Child hands a doll and bottle to the mother, indicating that she wants her mother to feed the doll.	"My book."
	"I sit."
Child requests her mother to take her feet off the sofa and put them on the floor saying, "En ya shoe."	"Tina eat."
	"Me fix."
Child wants the examiner to move to the other side of the couch and points to the place where she wants the examiner to sit.	"Up chair."
	"I go."
	"I do."
Child wants the observer and the mother to hug a toy bear as the child had done moments earlier.	"I play."
Child wants the mother to bite a toy animal.	

Self-recognition

The emergence of self-awareness during the second year is also evident from children's recognition of themselves in a mirror (Lewis & Brooks-Gunn, 1979). Some of the research demonstrating self-recognition and self-awareness is described in Box 5.3.

A sense of possession

Social interactions between children provide additional signs of self-awareness. Two 3-year-old boys, total strangers, were playing on opposite sides of an unfamiliar room with their mothers present. During the first 20 minutes of play, one boy, Jack, took toys from Bill on four separate occasions. Each time Bill did nothing. He did not protest, cry, whine, retaliate, or retreat to his mother for help. But after the fourth seizure, Bill left his toys, walked across the room, took a toy Jack had been playing with earlier, and brought it back to his own play area. Several minutes later, while Bill was playing with a wagon, Jack tried to take it. This time Bill held on and successfully resisted Jack's attempts at appropriation.

Why did Bill resist Jack on the fifth occasion when he had not done so on the first four? One reason may be that the continued experience of losing toys

BOX 5.3

*Two-year-olds'
understanding
self*

By age 2, children acquire the beginnings of a concept of *self*. One facet of self-awareness during the second year was revealed in a simple experiment conducted by Michael Lewis and Jeanne Brooks-Gunn (1979). Children from 9 to 24 months of age were first allowed to look at themselves in the mirror. Then, their mothers surreptitiously marked their noses with rouge, and the children were allowed to look at themselves in the mirror again. Children younger than about 18 to 21 months of age did not touch their nose or face when they saw the rouge in their reflected image, but by 24 months of age two-thirds of the children put their finger to their nose.

Soon after children point to their rouge-colored nose, they begin to use the pronouns *I, me,* and *you,* suggesting that they are now distinguishing clearly between the self and other people. Seymour Epstein of the University of Massachusetts describes an interesting episode:

A little girl named Donna who was two years old was seated at the table with some relatives who were visiting. She was asked to point to Aunt Alice, and she did so correctly. Then there was a game in which they asked the little girl Donna to point to various people. Then someone said, "Point to Donna." The child was confused and initially pointed at random. Then her mother said, "You know who Donna is. Point to the little girl everybody calls Donna." Now Donna had a great insight, and she pointed unhesitatingly to herself. (Epstein, 1973, pp. 412–413.)

Three-year-old children may have a concept of a private thinking self that is not visible to an outside observer. Here is an example of an exchange between an adult and a 3-year-old child.

The examiner asks, "Can I see you thinking?" The child says, "No." The examiner says, "Even if I look in your eyes, do I see you thinking?" The child replies, "No." "Why not?" asks the examiner. The child says, " 'Cause I don't have any big holes." The examiner says, "You mean there would have to be a big hole there for me to see you thinking?" The child nods. (Flavell, 1978, p. 16)

A strong argument for the contribution of maturation to the emergence of a sense of self is seen in the longitudinal study of a deaf child (born of deaf parents) who was learning to communicate with American Sign Language. In the middle of her second year, the same time that hearing children begin to describe their actions as they are doing them, this deaf child began to use signs that made reference to herself (Petitto, 1983).

finally provoked in Bill an idea of personal possession, even though he was playing with these toys for the first time. When objects are lost or seized, the child may try to reaffirm his sense of possession by resisting or taking the other child's toys. These theoretical arguments are based on the assumption that the child has a concept of a "self" that can possess objects, even temporarily, and maintain control over them.

Empathy

The emergence of self-awareness is accompanied by an improved ability to appreciate the perceptions and feelings of others. In one study, children 18, 27, and 36 months of age were visited at home and allowed to play with either a pair of ski goggles they could see through or a pair of goggles that was opaque and therefore gave a sense of blindness. A day later, each child came to a laboratory setting and watched the mother put on the opaque goggles. The 2- and 3-year-old children who had previous experience with the opaque goggles behaved as if they believed their mothers could not see. They tried to remove the goggles and make no gestures toward the mother. These behaviors suggest an awareness that the mother was experiencing the state they had experienced earlier (Novey, 1975).

The ability to infer the emotional state of another is revealed in the behavior of children when they see another person hurt or in distress. Mothers who kept diaries on their children's everyday behavior reported a major change in the child's actions during the last half of the second year. At this time, children show an increased tendency to hug or kiss a person who has been hurt or

to give a victim a toy or food. These prosocial or helpful behaviors were relatively rare during the first part of the second year (Radke-Yarrow, Zahn-Waxler, & Chapman, 1983).

The fact that most 2-year-olds are capable of inferring a psychological and emotional state in another person implies that children can recall their own earlier emotional experiences and act on that information. It seems reasonable to conclude that children are now conscious of their private experiences.

Summary of developmental changes

The child's recognition that the self can meet self-generated or externally set standards seems to provoke the desire to do so. That is, the awareness of standards about correct and incorrect behavior and of one's ability to solve problems seems to strengthen children's motivation to solve a variety of problems set by adults. Once children are conscious of the fact that there is a correct answer, they feel obligated to meet that standard. And most children during the last months of the second year do show improved performance on problems set by adults, such as remembering the location of a toy hidden under one of six cups.

Finally, during the last part of the second year, children start to play with objects and other children in coherent and thematic play sequences that last much longer than they did earlier. The prolonged play themes suggest that the ability to sustain an action plan for a relatively long period of time is a major characteristic of this developmental period. The psychological competence we call "working memory" (see Chapter 3) has improved enough to prevent children from forgetting a goal they began to pursue a minute or two earlier.

The capacity to hold cognitive representations in active or working memory for a long time may be an essential forerunner of self-awareness. A 3-month-old baby who can recognize events becomes a 1-year-old who can retrieve events, and an 18-month-old who can anticipate events, and finally a 2-year-old who knows what she can do, how she feels, and how she is similar to and different from other people.

FAMILY INTERACTIONS IN THE SECOND AND THIRD YEARS

Although many of the competences of the second year—symbolism, imitation, appreciation of standards, self-awareness—will emerge in any child living in a world of objects and people, their subsequent development depends on the individual's experiences. For young children, the most important experiences occur within the family. What are these important experiences and which of them facilitate or hinder the growth of these competences?

Many discussions of child rearing seem to be based on the premise that parents act on totally malleable young organisms and so bear most of the responsibility for their children's behavior and personalities. However, some parents see themselves as holding the reins of a high-spirited animal charging through a forest. They try to monitor the speed and direction a little but believe that some of the child's growth is beyond their control. This latter view is consistent with current assumptions that children play an active role in their own development (see Chapter 1) and that parent-child influences are bidirectional (see Chapter 4).

Each phase of development leads to changes in children's surface behavior, and thus children of different ages present different sets of problems to their parents. During the first year, excessive irritability, sleeplessness, and feeding problems are likely to dominate parents' concerns. During the second year, when the child has become mobile and self-aware, the possibilities of physical harm, destructiveness, and aggression overpower earlier worries. By the third year, disobedience, resistance to routine, poor social skills, and slow growth of verbal ability ascend to the top of the hierarchy of parental preoccupations in many American families. To the extent that each type of behavior provokes a different pattern of corrective action by parents, the changing profile of parental behavior is partially controlled by the child.

The child-rearing techniques parents choose depend in part on their beliefs about development and on the qualities they regard as most important for children to acquire. In modern America, parental ideals for 3-year-olds include cognitive skills, sociability, emotional security, self-confidence, obedience, and control of aggression. A little later, parents hope to see gains in independence, autonomy, motivation for mastery, a capacity for solitude, and a willingness to compete with others and defend the self against attack and domination.

Parents believe that the early development of these qualities will help their children adapt to the social and cognitive challenges they will confront as adolescents and young adults. Hence, when a 2-year-old's behavior violates the parent's standards for children that age, the parent moves into action. If the 2-year-old is too timid with other children, the mother may initiate a play group or enroll the child in nursery school. If the child is too dependent on the mother, she will encourage the child to play alone.

There are, therefore, two complementary bases for parental socialization practices. One is the changing profile of behavior in the child; the other is the parents' view of the ideal behaviors for the child at that stage of development, which depends in part on the parents' ideals for the future.

Socialization is the process by which children learn the standards, values, and expected behaviors for their culture or society. In the toddler years, the parents are the principal *agents of socialization*. Socialization occurs through parents' serving as models of behavior, expressing acceptance and warmth, providing restrictions or freedom, and punishing unacceptable behavior.

Observation of role models   As discussed earlier, children begin to imitate others in the second year of life. Hence, observation becomes one means of socialization. Adults assume that if young children simply see what others do, they will learn what is correct and practice it. This is true for many standards. But for some standards, observation alone, without some sign from parents indicating that the behavior is approved or disapproved, may not work. For example, it is difficult to learn through observation alone that honesty, persistence, and loyalty to one's beliefs are desirable standards.

Observation is most effective when people display the desirable behavior consistently. If a parent sometimes uses harsh physical punishment (slapping the child, for example) and sometimes controls that aggression, the child is unlikely to accept control of aggression as the proper way to behave, because the child sees how effective aggression is in controlling others. But if a child never sees physical aggression at home, nonaggressive ways of handling frustration will be learned as the appropriate standard. Of course, the child is likely to observe physical aggression elsewhere, among playmates or perhaps on television. In societies like ours, where there is so much behavioral diversity, observation of the parents alone is not always sufficient to override other socialization influences. Parents try to deal with this problem by adding other strategies to their use of modeling; for example, they express approval and disapproval of the child's behavior (see Chapter 11 for further discussion of these techniques).

Love and acceptance   The attachment relationship that began in the first year (see Chapter 4) forms an important basis of socialization in the toddler years. As we noted earlier, a strong attachment is facilitated by parents who are sensitive and responsive to the child's needs and who are generally warm and accepting. Parents may communicate their belief in the child's value, goodness, and ability in many ways. Physical affection, delight in the child's accomplishments, and playful interaction are frequent in our culture; other means of communicating the same basic message prevail in some other cultures.

Parents' acceptance of the child's value may be particularly important for the self-image the child forms during the initial period of self-awareness. If children feel valued and loved, their self-images are apt to be positive and they are likely to feel confidence in their emerging abilities.

Restriction versus permissiveness   For many parents, the issue of restricting their children's actions arises for the first time in the toddler period. As children become physically mobile, they run, climb, poke their fingers into strange places, spill things, pull objects out of cupboards and drawers, and put almost

anything they find in their mouths, to name only a few possibilities. Many of these behaviors can be dangerous to the child or destructive to property, so parents must find a way of dealing with them. At the same time, as children develop the rudiments of standards and empathy by the end of the second year, parents begin to feel that they can expect or demand that children learn to control their behavior. The toddler period is one in which parents often set the pattern for the amount and kinds of control they will exert over their children's behavior.

The issue of restriction or control poses a dilemma for many American parents because they worry that curbing children excessively will make the children overly fearful of them or of authority in general. They value a child's freedom to exercise his own will and occasionally to be a rebel. At the same time, they want their children to obey them. As a result, they may sometimes be inconsistent in responding to disobedience and aggression, with the result that these behaviors are encouraged.

The dilemma about restriction grows partly out of the Western, particularly American, celebration of individual freedom. During the last part of the nineteenth century, American and European scholars urged parents to allow their children some freedom to disobey and develop independence from the family. James Sully, who wrote as the nineteenth century came to a close, reintroduced John Locke's declaration, "Children love liberty, and therefore they should be brought to do the things that are fit for them without feeling any restraint laid upon them." Sully declared that the children resented any check on their impulses. A physician friendly to Freudian theory declared in 1922, "The greatest of all the sins of parenthood is to stand between the child and self-realization — to obstruct his psychological freedom" (Miller, 1922, p. 19).

The effects of restriction on very young children depend on the context and the domains of behavior in which it is exercised. First, most parents restrict some kinds of behavior but not others. Some of the domains in which parents may attempt to curb behavior include aggression, destruction of property, messiness at the table, toileting, sexual habits such as masturbation, exploring new places without adequate supervision, and lack of cleanliness. Although some parents make and enforce rules about many of these areas, few parents are highly restrictive across all of them. More typically, parents restrict and prohibit only those behaviors that they care about, those that violate their ideal of child behavior. For example, some may be highly restrictive about matters involving physical safety, while they are permissive about sexual and aggressive behavior. Therefore, though we often speak of restrictive parents, it is more accurate to examine in what areas the parent is restrictive or permissive.

Second, the effects of restrictiveness depend on other components of the parent-child relationship, particularly the level of acceptance and affection. As we noted in Chapter 4, the attachment generated in an affectionate parent-child relationship provides a strong motive for the child to obey the parent in order to maintain that bond. Hence, a child with a strong attachment to the parent may respond more readily to restrictions, even during the toddler period. The long-term impact of restriction imposed in an affectionate context is seen in reminiscences of Japanese adults who grew up in highly restrictive families in which there were strong attachments and bonds of loyalty. A president of a Japanese automotive company recalls his feelings about his father: "Once his anger was over he did not nag or complain, but when he was angry I was really afraid of him. His scolding was like thunder. . . . I learned from my father how to live independently, doing everything on my own. He was the greatest model for my life" (Wagatsuma, 1977, p. 199).

Third, restrictiveness does not necessarily imply that a parent is punitive. A parent may patiently, but consistently, stop a young child from opening the refrigerator or putting her hand into a light socket with a gentle "no." Even though 1- and 2-year-old children often do not understand elaborate explanations, some brief verbal reason may be helpful in teaching the child (for instance, "Hitting hurts Mommy"). In many cases, the child learns as well or better from these mild "punishments" as from more severe yelling or slapping.

Punishment Harsh punishment may have other consequences beyond those of restrictiveness, and it may be relatively ineffective in producing behavior control in the child. For example, some behaviors that concern parents in the toddler period are likely to decline if they are ignored. Children between 1 and 3 often throw "temper tantrums." They lie down on the floor, cry, beat against objects, and the like. In many cases, children will stop the behavior in a few moments if adults ignore it. If a parent becomes harshly punitive by hitting the child, the behavior often escalates rather than stops.

Although harsh punishment has many potential negative effects on children and is usually not the disciplinary method to be recommended, it does not always generate hostility or feelings of insecurity. Particularly as children grow older, their interpretation of the punishment and the social context in which they live affect how they will respond to punitive parents. For example, working-class parents appear a bit more harsh when they scold their children than middle-class parents, but their behavior may be seen as appropriate in their own social milieu. The resilience of some children with punitive parents is suggested by interviews with adults who had been studied throughout their childhood. Observers had described some children's parents as excessively punitive—they spanked their children a lot and imposed heavy penalties for small misdeeds. Twenty years later, these adults were productive, happily married, without symptoms, and they considered their parents' practices to have been in their own interests (Kagan & Moss, 1962).

In summary, the most effective and beneficial methods of socializing the toddler include acting as a consistent model of desired behavior and establishing a warm, affectionate relationship with the child during the opening years. As children begin to exhibit behavior that parents want to change, parents need to think carefully about what behaviors they do and do not want to socialize. Then, they can use verbal disapproval and provide reasons for restrictions. Physical punishment may be less effective than consistent reprimands and gentle interventions (such as pulling the child's hand away from a hot stove). The effects of any of these child-rearing practices depend, however, on the social context in which they occur.

SUMMARY

Many important competences appear for the first time during the second and third years of life. First, the child becomes capable of symbolic functioning. This capacity to treat an object as if it were something other than it is is often evident in pretend play. Once the child becomes capable of imposing a symbolic meaning on experience, representations become expanded, and the child reacts to events in a more complex way. Children's play may be exploratory, constructive, or pretend—playing the role of another person. When 2-year-olds play with an unfamiliar child, there is often a brief period of apprehension or shyness, perhaps as a result of the maturation of cognitive competences.

Imitation of others increases in frequency between 1 and 3 years of age. The conditions that promote imitation include uncertainty over the ability to reproduce a particular act, the desire to promote certain kinds of social interaction, the motive to be similar to another person, and the desire to gain goals that a model has attained.

During the last 6 months of the second year, the child first becomes aware of standards of correct and incorrect behavior. Children often become upset by violations of standards about aggression and destruction. They also smile when they meet a self-imposed standard on a task that requires the investment of effort. Children acquire standards for the "correct" state of objects and events; for example, they notice broken toys or torn clothes, and show some distress or concern about what caused the problem.

Finally, the first sense of self-awareness emerges during the second year of life. This new ability is revealed in the fact that children begin to direct the behavior of others, they begin to describe their own actions, they show a sense of possession, and they are able to recognize themselves. Further, most 2-year-olds are capable of empathizing with the emotional state of another person, suggesting that they are conscious of their own private experiences.

Although these qualities develop in almost all children, there is variation among 2- and 3-year-olds due, in part, to experiences in the family. These experiences are the product of different techniques of socialization used by parents, including acting as models of behavior, creating a warm, affectionate relationship, deciding on behaviors to restrict or permit, and punishing violations.

The presence of a love relationship between parent and child is an important force in socialization, because children are reluctant to threaten the bond of attachment and love to the parents. Although parents vary in the degree to which they restrict the child's behavior and punish violations, the effects of restriction and punishment depend on the quality of the relationship between child and parent. Hence, most psychologists advise parents to establish an affectionate relationship with their child during the opening years, to decide on the behaviors they wish to socialize, to use gentle but consistent reprimands, and to provide the child with reasons when they prohibit the actions they view as undesirable.

REFERENCES

Bruner, J. S., Jolly, A., & Sylva, K. *Play: Its role in development and evolution.* London: Kenwood, 1976.

Epstein, S. The self-concept revisited. *American Psychologist,* 1973, *28,* 404–416.

Flavell, J. H., Shipstead, S. G., & Croft, K. What young children think you see when their eyes are closed. Unpublished report, Stanford University, 1978.

Garvey, C. *Play.* Cambridge, Mass.: Harvard University Press, 1977.

Jacobson, S. Matching behavior in the young infant. *Child Development,* 1979, *50,* 425–431.

Kagan, J. *The second year.* Cambridge, Mass.: Harvard University Press, 1981.

Kagan, J., Kearsley, R. B., & Zelazo, P. R. *Infancy: Its place in human development.* Cambridge: Harvard University Press, 1978.

Lewis, M., & Brooks-Gunn, J. *Social cognition and the acquisition of self.* New York: Plenum, 1979.

Leonard, L. B., Schwartz, R. G., Folger, M. K., Newhoff, M., & Wilcox, J. M. Children's imitation of lexical items. *Child Development,* 1979, *50,* 19–27.

McCall, R. B., Parke, R. D., & Kavanaugh, R. D. Imitation of live and televised models by children one to three years of age. *Monographs of the Society for Research in Child Development,* 1977, *42*(5).

Maccoby, E. E., & Jacklin, C. N. *The psychology of sex differences.* Stanford, Calif.: Stanford University Press, 1974.

Meltzoff, A. N., & Moore, M. K. Imitation of facial and manual gestures by human neonates. *Science,* 1977, *198,* 75–78.

Miller, H. C. *The new psychology and the parent.* London: Jarrolds, 1922.

Mueller, E., & Brenner, J. The origin of social skills in interaction among play group toddlers. *Child Development,* 1977, *48,* 854–861.

Novey, M. S. *The development of knowledge of others' ability to see.* Unpublished doctoral dissertation, Harvard University, 1975.

Petitto, L. *From gesture to symbol.* Unpublished doctoral dissertation, Harvard University, 1983.

Radke-Yarrow, M., Zahn-Waxler, C., & Chapman, M. Children's pro-social dispositions and behavior. In P. H. Mussen & E. M. Hetherington (Eds.). *Handbook of child psychology:* (Vol. 4): *Socialization, personality, and social development.* (4th ed.). New York: Wiley, 1983.

Stern, W. *Psychology of early childhood* (6th ed.). (A. Barwell, trans.) New York: Henry Holt, 1930.

Sully, J. *Studies of childhood.* New York: Appleton, 1896.

Sylva, K., Bruner, J. S., & Genova, P. The role of play in the problem solving of children three to seven years old. In J. S. Bruner, A. Jolly, & K. Sylva (Eds.), *Play: Its role in development and evolution.* London: Kenwood, 1976.

Vandell, D. I., Wilson, K. S., & Whalen, W. I. Birth order and social experience differences in infant peer interaction. *Developmental Psychology*, 1981, *17*, 438–445.

Wagatsuma, H. Some aspects of the contemporary Japanese family: Once Confucian, now fatherless. In *The Family, Daedalus*, 1977, *106*, 181–210.

Yando, R., Seitz, V., & Zigler, E. *Imitation in developmental perspective.* Hillsdale, N.J.: Erlbaum, 1978.

part **T** *hree*

THE CHILDHOOD YEARS: LANGUAGE AND COGNITIVE DEVELOPMENT

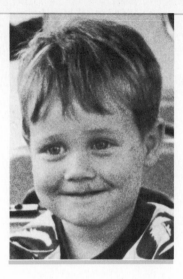

CHAPTER 6

Language and communication

*W*hen she was 18 months old, Eve, a little girl whose speech was being studied and recorded, produced many two-word sentences; for example:

"Right down."
"Mommy read."
"Look dollie."

Just 9 months later, at the age of 27 months, she communicated with much more complete and complex sentences, including these:

"I go get a pencil 'n' write."
"We're going to make a make a blue house."
"How 'bout another eggnog instead of cheese sandwich?" (Brown, 1973)

The contrast between her utterances at 18 months and the sentences she spoke at 27 months highlights the speed with which language skills are acquired and improved. In this chapter we will encounter many other examples of the remarkably fast progress young children make in learning language and in communicating (see Box 6.1).

In the short span of $2\frac{1}{2}$ or 3 years, children progress from uttering their first word, usually when they are approximately 12 to 18 months of age, to speaking fluently in well-formed, grammatically correct sentences, and using new words in grammatically correct ways. Consider this short segment of conversation between two 4-year-olds enjoying pretend play:

Ann: Mommy, mommy, I got new friends called dool, sol, ta.
Mary: Dool, sue, and ta?
Ann: Those are funny names, aren't they?
Mary: No, it's Poopoo, Daigi, and Dia . . . Diarrhea.

Without specific instruction, children somehow acquire a working knowledge of the rules of grammar, or *syntax*, of their language by the time they are 4 or 5. That is, they use many rules of syntax correctly in their own speech. These rules govern how words should be inflected (as by adding endings such as -*s* or -*ing* to indicate a plural noun or progressive verb), how tenses should be formed, and how words should be organized into sentences.

BOX 6.1
*A brief overview
of language
development*

Language is acquired with amazing rapidity, particularly after children speak their first word, usually sometime around the end of the first year. Examples of major advances in language development are presented here. Compare the samples of the 18-month-old's typical two-word combinations, the 2½-year-old's relatively complex utterances, and the conversations between 4-year-olds at play. In the short span of approximately 30 months, the child has progressed from the most primitive telegraphic sentences to the expression of complex ideas phrased in words and structures that are remarkably adultlike.

Ages	Language charactcristics	Examples
4–8 months	Babbling	baba dada gagaga
12 months (approximately)	First understandable words	Mommy dog dirty yes
18 months	Two-word combinations	Mommy soup[a] my pencil drink juice
24–30 months	Longer, more complex utterances with elaboration of different parts of sentence	That why Jackie cried.[a] Put my pencil in there. What is that on the table?
	Children converse, talking to each other in simple sentences, taking turns, but not always responding to each other directly	(Conversation between Susie, 35 months old, and Jackie, 38 months, each playing with a can of play-dough.)[b]

(Jackie hums.)
Susie: Very bad, Jackie, you're very bad.
Jackie: My singing wasn't bad!
Susie: No, *you* are bad.
Jackie: Me?
Susie: Mm-hmm. *(She puts her can of play-dough next to Jackie's)* We have the same things.
Jackie: Mm-hmm. *(takes Susie's can)*
Susie: No! Mine!
Jackie: (gives can back) Look at funny. *(reaching can)*

[a] These are samples of the speech of Eve, one of the children Brown (1973) studied, recorded at ages 18 months and 27 months.

[b] The conversations of the 3- and 4-year-olds are taken from videotapes of peer interactions, courtesy of Susan Ervin-Tripp and Nancy Budwig.

		Susie: You're funny.
		Jackie: I'm funny.
4 years	Utterances longer and more complex; conversation in which utterances are related to each other, more adultlike	(Jane & Kate are playing "tea party")[b]
		Jane: Let's pretend when mommy's out.
		Kate: Oh, yeah. Well, I'm not the boss around here. . . . My mom is. Pretend we are the bosses.
		Jane: Yeah.
		Kate: Us children aren't the bosses.
		Jane: When I grow up and you grow up, *we'll be the bosses!* Hoah!
		Kate: Mm-hmm. But maybe we won't know how to punish.
		Jane: I will.
		Kate: How?
		Jane: I'll spank 'em. That's what my mom does.
		Kate: My mom does sometimes too.

As children are mastering syntax, their understanding of the *meaning* of words and sentences *(semantics)* is also expanding very rapidly. Their larger vocabularies are apparent both in what they understand and in what they say. By the age of 6, the average American child has a vocabulary of approximately 14,000 words (Carey, 1977).

To communicate effectively requires more than following grammatical rules and knowing the meanings of words. Children also need to learn how to use language in interactions with others, to make clear their intentions, and to accomplish goals. *Pragmatics* is the study of such aspects of language as rules of conversation, polite forms of address for individuals of different social statuses, language appropriate for peers and adults—in short, the rules governing the use of language in social contexts. Children rapidly acquire an understanding of many pragmatic aspects of language. For example, by age 4 or 5, they simplify sentences when speaking to younger children, and they often use first and last names appropriately.

What accounts for such remarkable and swift progress in the knowledge and use of language? How are the rules of linguistic structure acquired and used in speaking, understanding, thinking, remembering? To what extent does language development depend on biological factors? Can specific instruction given early in life improve a child's linguistic ability? These and related questions have been the concern of developmental *psycholinguists*, psychologists and linguists who study the skills and knowledge that children must have in order to use their own language effectively and correctly. A rich body of data about language acquisition has accumulated, but many basic questions about underlying processes remain unanswered. These unanswered questions are the subjects of some thought-provoking theories that will be reviewed in this chapter.

In surveying the major research findings and ideas about language development, we begin with the infant's capacity to discriminate and produce sounds and then to understand and speak single words. Next we will look at how youngsters combine words into sentences, extend their knowledge of word meaning and grammar, and produce more complex linguistic constructions. After reviewing major theories that attempt to explain the acquisition and growth of language, we will turn to language as communication (pragmatics) and to the relation between language and thought.

EARLIEST COMPREHENSION AND SPEECH

Sound discrimination and production

The basic units of a language are words. But each word is made up of *phonemes*, individual speech sounds that correspond roughly to the letters of the alphabet. Each language has its own rules governing the combination of phonemes, permitting some combinations and prohibiting others. In English, for example, there are no words beginning with *ng*, *zb*, or *tn*, although these sound combinations occur in other languages. In order to understand and communicate, children must be able to hear and produce the particular sounds and combinations of sounds of their language as adults do.

As if to make this task more difficult, adults do not always pronounce the same phoneme in precisely the same way; the /b/ sound in *baby* probably differs in small and subtle (but to adults irrelevant) ways each time we say it. As adults we readily discriminate between sounds in different phoneme categories, such as /p/, /b/, /t/, /d/, /k/, and /g/, but we ignore differences between two sounds in the same category. At the age of 1 or 2 months, infants make the same category discriminations, reacting differently even to such similar phonemes as /p/ and /b/, and /d/ and /t/ (Eimas, 1975).

Newborns can tell speech from other sounds in the environment and respond to it differently. By the age of 3 months, infants distinguish between their mother's voice and that of other females. This finding suggests that just as birds are biologically prepared to differentiate the song of birds of their own species from the songs of birds of other species (presumably because of the structure of their central nervous systems), human infants are prepared by their biology to discriminate speech from other sounds and, perhaps, to differentiate among different people's voices.

From birth on, infants produce a variety of crying sounds. Parents can sometimes identify their young infant's cries of hunger, pain, or boredom accurately, but they may be judging more by what they know of the situation than by the baby's cries. However, by the time babies are 7 or 8 months old, their parents correctly differentiate between cries of hunger, request, greeting, and surprise (Ricks, 1975).

By the end of the second month, infants begin to laugh and coo, making soft, low vowel (often *oo*) sounds in response to others. This responsive vocalizing may be the beginning of "taking turns," as parents and babies do in conversations later on (Trevarthen, 1974).

At about 5 or 6 months, *babbling* begins. Infants combine vowel and consonant sounds in strings of syllables like *bababa* and *dadada* that sometimes sound like real speech, with rising and falling intonations. Babbling generally increases until the infant is between 9 and 12 months of age, then decreases after the first real words are produced. However, many youngsters continue to babble when communicating with parents or "talking" to dolls or other toys. The amount and frequency of babbling do not predict later linguistic achievement; neither of these measures is correlated with early speech or with the skillful use of language at age 4 or 5.

Maturation rather than learning determines the onset of babbling. Deaf children who cannot hear their own or others' sounds begin to babble at the same age that hearing children do, and the form of their babbling is very similar (though perhaps a bit more monotonous). However, in hearing children, babbling continues and increases in frequency over time. It gradually declines in deaf children, suggesting that continuation of babbling depends on feedback (children hearing themselves) and on social stimulation (hearing others responding to them). If a child's vocalizations are rewarded by attention, the frequency of babbling increases, but the types of sound produced do not change.

In the second half of the first year, babies begin to exhibit clear intentions of communicating. Before the first real word emerges at about the age of 12 months, needs for help are signaled by gazing at a potential helper (adult or other child), gesturing, pointing, and vocalizing. An infant who wants a drink of water may glance at the mother, make some sounds, and point toward the kitchen sink. Objects may be used as a means of attracting attention—for example, a child may extend an arm while holding a toy, not intending to give the toy away but to evoke a response from an adult. There is no single moment at which words become symbols or representations of events. Gradually, random sounds give way to vocalizations that are signals and then to words that refer to actions, objects, or events (Bates, Camaioni, & Volterra, 1975).

First words

Comprehension   Infants *know* and *understand* more words than they actually *utter*. That is, comprehension develops earlier and more rapidly than production. Infants frequently respond to questions and instructions like "Where is your bottle?" or "Pat the doggy" with gestures and actions before they say any words (Huttenlocher, 1974; Sachs & Truswell, 1978).

According to one study, children understand 50 words, on the average, before they are able to produce 10; in this early period, comprehension vocabulary is 5 times as great as productive vocabulary. The babies in this study did not speak 50 words until 5 months after they could understand that many. Early in the second year, children added more than 20 new words per month to their comprehension vocabulary and 9 new words per month to their production vocabulary (Benedict, 1979).

A child's level of comprehension has little relation to the maturity of speech production. A child who says very little may understand a great deal more than a child who produces many words and more complex constructions (Benedict, 1979; Kagan, 1982).

Production   First words are generally spoken around the time of the child's first birthday, although many normal infants do not start to talk until many months later than that. Others begin well before 1 year of age. Typically, a baby's first words are one or two syllables, often a duplicated pair as in *mama* or *dada.* The most common sounds used in first words are the consonants *p, b, v, d, t, m,* and *n* and the vowels *o* (as in *drop*) and *e* (as in *week*).

On the average, the vocabulary a child uses by the age of 18 months includes about 50 words. These words generally refer to things that are important or salient to the child: actions or activities *(give, bye-bye, up),* important people *(mama, daddy, baby),* food *(juice, milk, cookie),* body parts *(ear, eye, nose),* clothing *(shoe, hat, sock),* animals *(dog, cat, Rex),* household items *(cup, spoon, light),* and vehicles *(car, boat, train).* Objects that are simply "there" (tables, stoves, windows) are seldom named, but because infants are interested in action, labels for things that move, change, or can be acted on *(truck, toy, blanket, key)* are common (Clark, 1979; Greenfield & Smith, 1976; Nelson, 1973). Some words that appear often in vocabularies of first words — *yuck, ouch, want, hungry* — suggest that infants also have some understanding of people and mental states as well as of objects and actions (Bretherton, McNew, & Beeghly-Smith, 1983).

An infant's one-word utterances can be used in conjunction with gestures and intonations to communicate many ideas and observations, make requests, and express emotional states such as surprise. At other times, children seem to be experimenting with words simply to test or master their meaning or to map their thoughts onto words.

To interpret a child's intention or meaning fully, we need to consider the circumstances and the context of the utterance. "Ball," spoken as a child points to a red ball on the floor, may simply call attention to the toy or communicate surprise at finding a ball. Or the word may be used to comment on its movements, or to tell the listener that the ball belongs to the baby. If the youngster repeats "Ball, ball," emphatically while reaching out toward it, he is obviously asking for help in getting it. The child seems to have a concept of the whole situation, though he cannot yet express his thoughts in a sentence.

DEVELOPMENT OF WORD MEANING

Many new words and their meanings are acquired through elaborate "naming rituals" that parents indulge in with their babies from the time a child first utters something that sounds like a word (Ninio & Bruner, 1976). Parents point to objects, name them, and correct the child's attempt to repeat the names. Often babies establish effective routines for eliciting the names of objects from their parents — "Uh?" "What's dat?" Simply hearing a word used to label an object a few times is often sufficient for a child to learn its meaning and begin using it (Carey, 1977; Leonard, 1976).

As adults, we can label objects at several different levels of generality. A pet is Prince, a Dalmatian, a dog, a mammal, an animal. Most of the terms of reference children learn first are at an intermediate level of generality. Children of 1 to 3 years old are likely to call a beagle a *dog* rather than a *beagle* (more specific) or an *animal* (more general).

Parents and nursery school teachers usually name objects at this intermediate level for 2- or 3-year-olds, although they may use other terms when speaking with adults. Thus, a mother speaks of Buicks, Chevrolets, and Fiats to her friends but labels these vehicles *cars* when speaking to her youngster. This way of naming things is practical, for it provides children with the terms they are most likely to need at this age. The young child has no need to distinguish between Fiats and Buicks; they are equivalent as far as the child is concerned (Anglin, 1977; Brown, 1958).

Hypothesis testing

A single word in a child's vocabulary may refer to both object and action. Some children say "door" as a door opens or closes, while others say "open" to refer to these actions (Clark, 1979). Clark suggests that when children hear a new word, they make a preliminary hypothesis about its meaning and then test the hypothesis as they use the word. If necessary, they gradually modify their original ideas about the meaning of the word to make them coincide with those of adults (Clark, 1979).

Children use their general knowledge about the world and clues provided by adults' actions when formulating hypotheses about what words mean. For example, if a father acts out the instruction "Pat the dog," his child will consider the nonverbal cues and probably formulate a correct hypothesis about the meaning of *pat*. But consider another young child. As his mother wheeled his stroller past a certain sunny spot, she would often look up at the sky and comment, "What a lovely afternoon." For some time this child thought that *afternoon* was the label for the television aerial on a neighbor's roof (de Villiers & de Villiers, 1978).

Overextensions

Often the meanings children attach to words initially are quite different from adult meanings. Some are *overextensions*. *Doggie* may be used to refer to cats, cows, horses, rabbits, and other four-legged animals as well as dogs; *Daddy* may refer to all men. *Moon* or *ball* may designate many objects that are round—cakes, oranges, the letter *o*. Overextensions are usually based on perceptual similarities in shape, size, sound, texture, or movement (Bowerman, 1976; Clark, 1973), although some are based on similarity in function (Nelson, 1974).

Children also overextend the meanings of common early words that do not refer to objects and cannot be generalized on the basis of perceptual or functional similarities, such as *more, all gone, up, on, off, there*. They use these words in a wide variety of contexts and in relation to many different objects and activities. For example, one child used *on* and *off* in getting her socks off, getting on or off a string horse, pulling beads apart and putting them together, unfolding a newspaper, pushing hair out of her mother's face, opening and closing boxes with lids, putting lids on jelly jars or caps on bottles. Apparently the meanings of these prepositions were generalized to virtually any act involving separation or coming together of objects or parts of objects.

Other overextensions may be based on similarities in subjective reactions. For instance, a 12-month-old girl exclaimed "There!" whenever she felt she had completed a project such as placing the last peg into a pounding board, climbing down off a high bed, or seeing that her mother had finished dressing her (Bowerman, 1982).

Some words are at first *underextended*, that is, defined too narrowly. For example, one 9-month-old used the word *car* to refer exclusively to cars moving on the street below, not to cars standing still or to pictures of cars (Bloom, 1973). For some children the word *kitty* at first refers only to the family's pet cat. Later the word may be extended to include other cats and possibly, through over-extension, also dogs or cows (Clark, 1973; Kessel, 1970). Like overextended meanings, underextensions can be viewed as hypotheses that are modified until the child's meaning matches the adult's.

Overextensions are more common in the production of speech than in comprehension. A child who overgeneralizes *apple,* applying that word to balls, tomatoes, and other round objects, has no difficulty in pointing to the apple in a set of pictures of round objects (Gruendel, 1976; Thompson & Chapman, 1975). Overextended definitions usually last only a short time, fading out as new words enter the child's vocabulary. When the child learns the word *cow* and understands that this animal has features such as moo sounds and horns, the meaning of *cow* is differentiated from the meaning of *dog* (Clark, 1973).

Some overextensions are based on a chain of associations with the original object or event the word referred to. One child first learned to use the word *kick* when she kicked a ball with her foot and thus moved it forward. Within a few months she extended the use of the word to a moth fluttering on a table, making a ball roll by bumping it with the front wheel of her kiddy car, and pushing her chest against the sink. These events are not similar to each other, but each shares one or more features with the original situation in which the child applied the word *kick*. The moth moved limbs (wings); the kiddy car made sharp contact with the ball and propelled it. The child shifted from one feature of the original event to another in her successive uses of the word (Bowerman, 1982).

Extensions of meaning can perhaps be most readily understood in terms of the prototypes or "best examples" of concepts that adults use in forming categories. For example, robins are generally regarded as prototypes of the category

birds, and as better examples of that category than penguins or ostriches (Rosch & Mervis, 1975). It has been hypothesized that when children hear a word for the first time, they assume it is a prototype, a "best example" of some concept. The child identifies the attributes of the prototype and then extends the word to refer to other actions or objects that share one or more of those attributes. The young child's extension of the word *kick* described in the preceding paragraph is an illustration of this process (Bowerman, 1982).

EARLY SENTENCES AND DEVELOPING GRAMMAR

When their speaking vocabularies reach 50 words, at about 18 months to 2 years of age, children begin to put two words together: *see doggie, where Daddy, allgone shoe, throw ball, make cake, more car* (meaning "drive around some more"). After the first two-word combinations appear, the number of different word combinations increases slowly, then suddenly spurts ahead. For example, one boy spoke his first two-word combinations at 19 months and used 14 different two-word combinations during that month. In the following 6 months, the number of different two-word combinations the child used was 24, 54, 89, 250, 1400, and more than 2500, respectively (Braine, 1963).

Telegraphic speech

Children's earliest two-word combinations seem to be abbreviated versions of adult sentences consisting primarily of nouns, verbs, and a few adjectives. Like a telegram, they contain only essential words, generally omitting prepositions (e.g., *in, on, under*), conjunctions *(and, but, or)*, articles *(a, the)*, auxiliary verbs *(have, may, did, is)*, and inflections (endings to indicate plurals or verb tenses).

If you ask a child between the ages of 2 and 3 to repeat a simple sentence such as "I can see a cow," the response is likely to be telegraphic: "See cow" or "I see cow." Although some words are omitted, there is evidence of regularity and rule-following. The most important words are repeated, and correct word order is preserved. Almost all of children's first two-word sentences show systematic and appropriate word order. From the very start, children follow simple rules of grammar. They express fundamental grammatical relationships between subject, verb, and object of the verb by ordering these parts of speech correctly in their earliest sentences (for example, "I getting ball"). "The model sentence is processed by the child as some kind of construction and not simply as a list of words" (Brown, 1973).

Telegraphic sentences express a broad range of meanings. The child's intentions can be inferred from word order and also from the situation. Samples of early speech by children speaking widely different languages—English, German, Russian, Finnish, Turkish, and Luo (spoken in Kenya)—demonstrate "a striking uniformity across children and across languages in the kinds of meanings expressed in simple two-word utterances" (Slobin, 1971). The range of semantic relations or meanings typical of early speech is shown in Table 6.1. The resemblance in the contents of the two-word utterances of children speaking vastly different languages suggests that early utterances arise from universal cognitive developmental changes and from the framework of the child's thoughts, actions, and social interactions. Speech arises from experiences with objects, activities, and interactions with other people that are common to many cultures (Slobin, 1971).

TABLE 6.1	Locate, Name:	see doggie, book there
Meanings expressed in telegraphic speech	Demand, Desire:	more milk, want candy
	Nonexistence:	allgone milk
	Negation:	not kitty
	Possession:	my candy
	Attribution:	big car
	Agent-Action:	mama walk
	Action-Object:	hit you
	Agent-Object:	mama book
	Action-Location:	sit chair
	Action-Recipient:	give papa
	Action-Instrument:	cut knife
	Question:	where ball?

Source: Slobin, 1972.

Expansions of telegraphic utterances   After their first telegraphic statements, children flesh out their sentences with less critical words such as articles and prepositions. Inflections, omitted earlier, are incorporated (Bowerman, 1982). Short sentences are expanded at first by "plugging in" more components. Consider this sequence of statements by 2-year-old Jeff: "Sit down. . . . Jeff sit down. . . . Jeff sit down [pause] chair." The first version consists of a predicate ("sit down"). It is expanded to include the subject ("Jeff"), then to include the adverb "chair" (his version of the adverbial phrase "in the chair"). Jeff has applied his knowledge of the grammatical rules that govern the ordering of words in English: agent (the actor) — action — object — location (where) (Brown, 1973).

Children seem to begin using articles, prepositions, inflections, and auxiliary verbs in a regular order. In a longitudinal study of three youngsters, Roger Brown identified a sequence running from simple to complex. For example, all three children used the progressive *-ing* form of verbs before they used auxiliary verbs such as *am* and *is*. Thus, the children said "I going" and "She going" before they said "I am going" and "She is going." Initially, a newly acquired form of a word may not be used often, but over 2 or 3 years the frequency of correct usage increases to roughly an adult level.

Overregularization   Paradoxically, one way children show their developing knowledge of grammatical rules is by making errors. *Overregularization* is the tendency to avoid irregular forms of verbs and plural nouns and use regular forms only. It is illustrated by a 3-year-old's comment, "The mouses runned away." This speaker knew that plurals are formed by adding *-s* to singular nouns and that the past tense of a verb is formed by adding *-ed* to the present — two important rules for English-speaking children to learn, even though they do not always hold. Before children learn such rules, they often use irregular forms correctly. A year earlier, the 3-year-old quoted above might have pointed to several mice and said, "Mice." But for some time after learning the rules, children tend to ignore or avoid the irregularities of adult speech (Slobin, 1971).

Complex sentences   When simple sentences about four words long have become common and inflections are being mastered — generally sometime between the ages of 2 and 3 — complex sentences begin to appear spontaneously in children's speech. These sentences may consist of two or more simple sentences joined by the conjunction *and* (for example, "You call and he comes") or one thought embedded in another (for example, "I hope I don't hurt it"). Some complex sentences contain *wh* clauses (what, who, where, when), such as, "I know where it is" and "When I get big, I can lift you up."

To construct complex sentences, children have to learn the rules of combining larger groups of words (phrases, clauses, and even sentences) and using connective words (e.g., *and, but, because*). *And* is generally the first and most frequently occurring connective in a child's vocabulary during the third year. *Because, what, when,* and *so* are also used frequently, while *then, but, if,* and *that* appear less frequently (Bloom, Lahey, Hood, Lifter, & Fiess, 1980).

Children's early complex sentences express a number of different meanings. The order of appearance of semantic relations is fairly constant, although some children begin the sequence earlier and move through it faster than others. Additive relations (e.g., "You can carry that and I can carry this") are expressed first, followed by temporal and causal statements ("You better look for it when you get back home," "She put a Band-Aid on her shoe and it maked it feel better"). Relations of contrast or opposition ("I was tired but now I'm not tired"), object specification ("The man who fixes the door"), and notice ("Watch what I am doing") appear still later. During the third year, progress in the use of complex sentences is usually slow and steady, with no sudden leaps forward or abrupt changes from one form to another (Bloom et al., 1980).

Questions   Advances in linguistic development are also reflected in gradual but regular improvement in the production and comprehension of questions. Two-year-olds understand *yes* and *no,* as well as *where, who,* and *what* questions, and generally answer them appropriately. These questions pertain to people, objects, and locations — precisely the things that children are interested in and talk about in their first sentences. At this age, *when, how,* and *why* questions are answered as though they asked *what* or *where.* (Q: When are you having lunch? A: In the kitchen. Q: Why are you eating that? A: It's an apple.) However, by the age of 3 (approximately), children begin to respond to *why* questions appropriately (Ervin-Tripp, 1977). The frequency of correct answers to all types of *wh* questions increases with age between 3 and 5 (Tyack, 1966).

The first yes-no questions that children produce are simply assertions ending with a rising pitch ("Mommy's sock?"). *What* and *where* are the earliest and most frequent *wh* words in the young child's spontaneous questions. *Why, how,* and *when* begin to appear at around 3 and are used increasingly in the next 2 years (Tyack & Ingram, 1977). At first *wh* words are simply attached to the beginning of the sentence without transforming word order, and questions are simply marked by adding an interrogative intonation ("What Mommy doing?" "Where Daddy go?" "Why John can't eat cookie?").

When children begin to construct more complex sentences, they also invert the auxiliary verb and noun in yes-no questions properly ("Are you going to help me?"). However, they still fail to make this inversion in the *wh* questions ("Sue, what you have in your mouth?" "Why kitty can't stand up?"). *Wh* questions are more complex grammatically than the yes-no questions, requiring two operations: inserting the question word and inverting the subject and verb. At this stage, the child can perform each of these operations separately but cannot yet combine them in the same sentence.

Deictic words   *Deictic* words are words, such as *here, there, this, that, mine,* and *yours,* that refer to the location of objects in relation to the speaker. Children's comprehension and production of these words shows that young children are capable of taking the point of view of others. Two-year-olds clearly understand the perspective of the speaker when interpreting the words *here* and *there.* If a mother says to a child on the other side of the room, "Your toy is over here," the child moves to the mother's side of the room to get it. Furthermore, *this, that,* and *there* — often pronounced *dis, dat,* and *dere* — are used with appropriate meaning by infants in their second year. Yet findings from laboratory studies indicate full understanding of these terms is not achieved until some years after they first appear in the child's speech — a case of production being prior to comprehension (de Villiers & de Villiers, 1977).

In one study, a child between 2 and 5 years of age sat at a table opposite the experimenter. Facing a low wall across the center of the table, they played a game together. Each player had an overturned cup and, while the child's eyes were closed, the experimenter hid a piece of candy under one of the cups. The experimenter then gave the child clues such as, "The candy is on *this* side of the wall" (or *"under my cup"* or *"here"* or *"in front of the wall"*). To obtain the candy the child had to translate the partner's viewpoint into his own—"*this* (the experimenter's) side of the wall" was, from the child's perspective, *that* side. All children readily distinguished the contrast between *mine* and *yours,* but 2-year-olds had difficulty when a shift of perspective was required. Three-year-olds were adept at taking the speaker's perspective, however, correctly interpreting *this* and *that, here* and *there,* and *in front of* and *behind* (de Villiers & de Villiers, 1974).

In this game situation, the deictic word had a fixed reference point, the wall between the child and the experimenter. Other researchers have found that preschoolers appropriately restrict their use of *this* to near objects but have difficulty comprehending *this* and *that* when there is no fixed reference point. Many 7-year-olds also seem to misunderstand these terms when they do not share the speaker's perspective (Webb & Abrahamson, 1976).

Passive sentences   Passive sentences like *the cat was chased by the dog* are more complex structures than active sentences, appearing relatively infrequently even in adult conversation. It is therefore not surprising to find that youngsters find passive sentences more difficult to understand and produce than active ones.

Using toys, the 2- and 3-year-old participants in one study had no difficulty acting out the sentence "The truck hits the car" correctly. But in response to the passive statement "The car is hit by the truck," they again made the car hit the truck. Apparently, they interpret the first noun in a sentence as the agent or actor (Bever, 1970).

These findings were replicated in a more thorough study in which children between 2 and 5 years of age were asked to use puppets to act out a variety of active and passive sentences. Some sentences referred to probable events ("The mother feeds the baby"), some dealt with improbable events ("The bear was chased by the mouse"), and some were "reversible"; that is, the positions of actor and object of action could be reversed to describe another equally likely event: For example, "The truck was followed by the car" is just as likely as "The car was followed by the truck" (Strohner & Nelson, 1974).

In interpreting and acting out these sentences, 2- and 3-year-olds were not guided by grammatical structure but used a "probable events strategy." That is, they knew whether events described in the sentences were likely to occur, and they responded in accordance with this knowledge, acting out active or passive sentences that pertained to probable events correctly. However, they acted out about 90 percent of the improbable sentences incorrectly. For example, both "The frog chases the alligator" and "The alligator was chased by the frog" were actually acted out with the alligator chasing the frog. Like the participants in the earlier study, these 2- and 3-year-olds had more difficulty understanding passive sentences than active ones. They acted out most of the active reversible sentences ("The truck hit the car") correctly but were successful on only 30 percent of the passive ones ("The car was hit by the truck").

Like the younger children, 4-year-olds found probable sentences easier to interpret than improbable ones, but the differences were not as great. Perhaps by the age of 4, children are better able to analyze the grammatical structure of sentences and so have less need to rely on other cognitive strategies such as assessments of probability. Five-year-olds had no difficulty with probable or reversible sentences, either active or passive, but they made errors in interpreting improbable passive sentences. Apparently by this age, the children relied more heavily on the syntactic information—the structure of the sentence—in making their interpretations (Strohner & Nelson, 1974).

Metalinguistic awareness

The speech of 4- or 5-year-olds demonstrates a remarkable mastery of complex rules of grammar and meaning. To what extent are children conscious of these rules? As cognitive competence advances, *metalinguistic awareness* expands. Language itself becomes a topic the child reflects on, seeks to understand, and talks about.

Preschool children differentiate between sounds that are real words and those that are not, regarding *apple* as a word and rejecting *oope*. However, young children do not understand that words are assigned to objects arbitrarily, by custom rather than by necessity. If you ask a preschooler, "Could you call a *dog* a *cow* and a *cow* a *dog*?"The child is likely to reply, "No, dogs bark and cows give milk." The attributes of the object are thought to be inherent in the word (Vygotsky, 1962).

Two-year-olds can recognize some grammatically incorrect sentences. When presented with a series of sentences such as "Eat the cake" and "Lock the open," they can tell the difference between the well-formed and deviant ones, though their discrimination is far from perfect (Gleitman, Gleitman, & Shipley, 1972). When asked to correct a deviant sentence, many youngsters suggested changes in meaning rather than just grammar, changing *house a build* to *live in a house,* for example. With increasing linguistic maturity, the children shifted from corrections that changed meaning to corrections of word order (de Villiers & de Villiers, 1974).

"Spontaneous repairs"—instances in which a child makes a speech error, recognizes it, and spontaneously corrects it—provide further evidence that the child is thinking about grammatical rules. A girl of 3 said, "She—he didn't give her any food." She began her sentence with the wrong word, giving the object the action, and then corrected herself (Clark & Anderson, 1979).

A detailed study of how French-speaking children deal with various grammatical elements led one investigator to conclude that children younger than about 8 characteristically treat a word as though it had only one function (Karmiloff-Smith, 1979). One of her analyses focused on the French definite article *les*, which has two functions, simultaneously marking (indicating) both *plural* and *total* (all); for example, *les livres* ("the books") refers to all the books present. Children under 5, in the first phase, use the article *les* frequently but only for marking plurals. The sentences of children between 5 and 8 contained more markers than necessary; children said *tous les livres* ("all the books") to indicate the total number, even though *les livres* by itself was sufficient to express this. Many other examples of redundancy or overmarking occurred in the speech of children of this age, particularly if there were any ambiguities in the situation. One child said in French, "The girl pushed a dog and then also the boy he repushed once more the same dog." The investigator believes that while overmarking, the child is experimenting, attempting to understand the different meanings of words and to organize them in a structured, coherent way.

After the age of 8, the child is fully aware of all the marker attributes of words and understands that some words have several functions, so redundancy and overmarking are substantially reduced. The child has attained a more mature, abstract level of linguistic competence closely linked to increasing metalinguistic awareness; the child reflects more on language and makes judgments that rely on the language itself, as adults do (Karmiloff-Smith, 1979).

With greater metalinguistic awareness comes the appreciation of ambiguity, or the comprehension of the fact that certain words, phrases, or sentences can mean different things in different contexts. Ambiguities in language and understanding of the different meanings of words underlie the ability to create metaphors and jokes (see Box 6.2).

THEORIES OF LANGUAGE ACQUISITION

What accounts for the rapid improvement in children's comprehension and use of complicated grammatical structures and rules? What role, if any, do innate mechanisms play? Is the child *active* in the process of language acquisition, searching for rules and regularities, formulating and testing hypotheses about grammar and meaning? Are reinforcement and modeling of major importance? To what extent is progress in language dependent on the growth of cognitive capacities? Do parents and others interacting with the child influence the course of linguistic development?

All these are critical questions for which there are at present no fully satisfactory answers. However, a number of rich and interesting—as well as controversial—theories about these issues have been proposed. No single theory provides a sufficient or adequate explanation of all the processes underlying the acquisition of language; each represents a different approach to the issues, and each basically deals with a different aspect of language development.

Learning theory

During the first half of this century, learning theory dominated American psychological thinking and research. Learning theorists viewed reinforcement (reward) and imitation of models as the principal mechanisms governing the acquisition and modification of most behavior, including language. Learning theory, as was pointed out earlier, stresses *nurture* rather than *nature* as the most powerful influence on development. Partly for this reason, it does more to explain language *performance* (speech production) than to explain the competencies underlying *comprehension.* For example, according to learning theory, the change from babbling to saying words is the outcome of parents' and others' selectively rewarding the child for producing sounds that resemble words; words therefore become prominent in the child's vocalizations. Analogously, children learn to speak grammatically because they are reinforced when they utter correct sentences and not when they speak ungrammatically. In short, learning theorists held that children speak in ways that increasingly conform

BOX 6.2
Humor

As their metalinguistic awareness advances, children begin to think about, talk about, and "play with" words and language forms. Much of our appreciation of humor depends on comprehension of linguistic ambiguities and our awareness that many words have more than one meaning and can be used in different ways.

Children under the age of 7 or 8 tend to regard words as having only one meaning; consequently, they do not find jokes based on word play to be funny. In one study, first- and second-grade children were asked to indicate which answer to a riddle was funnier, a joking answer or a factual one. Consider the riddle "Why did the old man tiptoe past the medicine cabinet?" A joking answer is "Because he didn't want to wake up the sleeping pills"; a serious one is "Because he dropped a glass and didn't want to cut his foot." First-graders chose the serious answer as funny just as often as the joking answer, but second-graders preferred the joking answer (McGhee, 1974).

The humor in riddles and jokes may be based on several kinds of linguistic ambiguity. The kind of jokes and riddles that children first consider funny, beginning at ages 6 or 7, depend on *phonological ambiguity,* that is, the situation in which the same sound can be interpreted in different ways.

> Waiter, what's this?
> That's bean soup, Ma'am.
> I'm not interested in what it's been; I'm asking what it is now.

Appreciation of the humor in lexical ambiguity, involving double meaning, develops soon afterwards. Most 7- and 8-year-olds enjoy jokes such as the following.

> Order! Order in the court!
> Ham and cheese on rye, please, Your Honor.

Not until the ages of 11 or 12 do children understand jokes based on ambiguities in grammatical structure or on different semantic interpretations, such as these.

> *I saw a man-eating shark in the aquarium.*
> *That's nothing. I saw a man eating herring in a restaurant.*

> *Call me a cab.*
> *You're a cab.* (McGhee, 1979; Schultz & Horibe, 1974)

with adult speech because this is the behavior that environmental reinforcers shape and maintain.

Learning theorists emphasize the roles of observation, modeling, and imitation in language acquisition. Certainly children imitate what they hear their parents (models) say, and thus add new words and ways of combining words to their language repertoires. Children cannot acquire a vocabulary or the grammatical structure of their language without exposure to models; children in America learn English, and children in China learn Chinese. They gather information about their own language by hearing others speak it.

Children can also be taught to use complex, grammatical forms—for example, correct and incorrect inflections for plurals and verbs, correct ways to order words in sentences—through modeling. In experimental studies demonstrating this aspect of imitative learning, young children have been taught to produce difficult constructions such as sentences with passive verbs, prepositional phrases, adverbs, correct tenses, and conjunctions (Sherman, 1971). After observing a model, children produced responses similar to the ones they had observed but not exactly the same; that is, they generalized the responses acquired through observation to new linguistic responses.

Criticisms of learning theory   Developmental psycholinguists point out that learning theory does not describe or explain the underlying capacities that enable a child to acquire linguistic knowledge and skills. Reinforcement alone cannot account for the astonishing rate of language development; we can hardly imagine what an enormous number of utterances would have to be rewarded if progress depended on that alone. Nor, they argue, can reinforcement fully explain the acquisition and use of the rules or principles of grammatically correct speech. When an utterance is not reinforced, the child has no way of knowing what was wrong or how to correct the error. When it is reinforced, she has no information about what was correct. The real problem, the psycholinguists argue, is to understand how children come to understand the principles for ordering words and parts of words so that they make sense (Slobin, 1971). Furthermore, observational studies have cast serious doubt on the assertion that parents and other adults reinforce grammatically correct statements. Apparently parents are much more interested in the truth, cleverness, or appropriateness of what children say than in the correctness of their grammar. When a child in one study said, ''Her curl my hair,'' her comment was approved (rewarded) because her mother was curling the little girl's hair. But another child's grammatically impeccable ''There's the animal fun house'' was disapproved (punished) because she was looking at a lighthouse.

Developmental psycholinguists also argue that observation and imitation do not fully explain language acquisition. For one thing, some of a child's first two-word utterances are unique and creative combinations of words that adults are unlikely to use (''allgone bye-bye''). Similarly, when children overregularize (''The mouses runned''), they use language forms that they are unlikely to have heard from adults. When children are observed at home, some children imitate the utterances of others a great deal and some do not, but the amount of imitation is not correlated with rate of language acquisition (Bloom, Hood, & Lightbown, 1974).

Clearly, imitation and observation of others play a role in language production, but simple imitation of others' speech cannot be the principal means of acquiring language. Children appear to extract principles from the language they hear others speaking, and what they learn at any given time depends on their level of cognitive development as well as the types of models or reinforcers they experience. As discussed in Chapter 5, children usually imitate language forms that are moderately familiar to them rather than forms that are entirely new or completely mastered. Some children imitate new words if the words appear in grammatical constructions they have already mastered, while others imitate new constructions if they contain familiar words (Bloom et al., 1974). It may be concluded that observation and imitation play a role in language production but are not sufficient to account for language learning.

Nativist theory   The nativistic view of language acquisition stresses innate, biological determinants of language—the influence of *nature* rather than *nurture*. This view is more concerned with explaining children's *competence* to understand

and use language rather than with influences on performance (how and when they speak). Many developmental psycholinguists argue that young children are not taught grammar; rather, they hear words and sentences from which they somehow infer or abstract complex rules. The task is so complex that it could not be accomplished unless the child's mind was somehow predisposed or "set" to process linguistic input (the language the child hears) and derive grammatical rules from it.

Noam Chomsky, a leading proponent of this point of view, maintains that humans possess an inborn brain mechanism that is specialized for the job of acquiring language. Chomsky has called this mechanism a *language acquisition device* (LAD) (Chomsky, 1957, 1959). The evidence cited for an innate language mechanism includes the universality and regularity of trends in the production of sounds, discussed earlier. Also, regardless of the language they are learning, children progress through the same sequence: babbling, saying their first word at 1 year, using two-word combinations in the second half of the second year, and mastering most grammatical rules of their language by the age of 4 or 5. First words and sentences in all languages express the same basic set of semantic relationships listed earlier in Table 6.1.

Some nativist theorists believe that the brain is especially "ready" for language acquisition between the age of 18 months and puberty; that is, they believe there is a *sensitive period* (see Chapter 4) for language acquisition. "Within this period language acquisition is expected to proceed normally but outside it language acquisition is difficult if not impossible" (Elliott, 1981, p. 23). Informal evidence for this view includes the observation that adult immigrants generally find learning a new language difficult and almost always retain a foreign accent. Their preadolescent children, in contrast, learn their second language quickly, make few errors, and speak without accents (Labov, 1970).

To test the sensitive period hypothesis directly, we would need to determine whether a person who had not learned any language before puberty could do so later on. But where could one find such a person except among the severely retarded? Amazingly, a girl of 13 who had been isolated by her parents and knew very little language was discovered in Los Angeles in 1970. Box 6.3 presents an account of her history and her language learning. Genie's history demonstrates partial support for the sensitive period hypothesis. She did not acquire language in the same way a preschool child would. But her progress demonstrated that a great deal of language learning can occur after puberty.

Cognitive theory

Other theorists, though they may not subscribe to the idea of an inborn mechanism specialized for language acquisition, nevertheless maintain another kind of nativistic view. For them language development is dependent on certain cognitive, information-processing, and motivational predispositions that are inborn. These theorists assume that children are inherently active and constructive and that internal forces rather than forces in the external environment are chiefly responsible for creativity, problem solving, hypothesis testing, and children's efforts to find regularities (rules) in the speech they hear.

BOX 6.3

Genie: Language
acquisition after
puberty

When Genie was brought to the attention of the authorities, she was $13\frac{1}{2}$ years old and past puberty, but she was so malnourished that she weighed only 60 pounds and looked like a young child. She was mute, incontinent, and unable to stand erect. The story of her life was almost incredible. Her tyrannical father believed she was retarded because she was slow in learning to walk (actually this was due to a hip deformity). When she was 20 months old, he locked her into a small, closed room, keeping her tied to a potty chair or lying in a covered crib, and imprisoned her there until she was discovered almost 12 years later. Her mother, who was almost blind, came into the room for only a few minutes a day to feed her. No one spoke to Genie, and she heard few sounds, although her father and older brother occasionally barked at her like dogs. Her father beat her if she made noises or sounds.

After her rescue she went to live in a foster home, where she heard normal language, although she had no special speech training at first. Within a short time, she began to imitate words and learn names, at first speaking in a monotone or a whisper, but gradually raising her voice and using more varied tones. Her language development was in many ways similar to that of a young child, although in some respects she progressed at a faster rate. She began to produce single words spontaneously about 5 months after she went to live in the foster home and began to use two-word utterances about 3 months after that. Her earliest two-word combinations expressed the same relationships that young children expressed first, for example, agent-action, action-object, possession, and location. Bit by bit, she produced longer sentences.

Her conceptual development appeared to be more advanced than her language development. From the start, she generalized words appropriately for specific objects to the class (for example, applying the label *dog,* first applied to a household pet, to all other dogs), and she did not overextend or underextend her early words. Words for colors and numbers, which generally appear relatively late in the normal child's language acquisition, were parts of Genie's early vocabulary.

Nevertheless her language development was deficient in some respects. Five years after she began to acquire language and extensive speech training, her speech was essentially telegraphic. She was still unable to use negative auxiliaries correctly (such as *haven't, isn't, hadn't*), had difficulty forming past tenses (using *-ed* endings), asked no spontaneous questions (although she asked questions she was specifically trained to ask), could not combine several ideas in a sentence, and confused opposite words such as *over* and *under.* In addition, she performed poorly on tests of comprehension (Curtiss, 1977).

Clearly, Genie was able to acquire some basic language after puberty, that is, after the end of the so called "sensitive period" for language acquisition. She failed to master some important features of grammar, and "her development [was] laborious and incomplete, but the similarities between it and normal acquisition outweigh the differences" (de Villiers & de Villiers, 1977, p. 219).

Dan Slobin has proposed that children in all societies are equipped with certain information-processing abilities or strategies that they use in learning language. His cross-cultural studies of language acquisition convinced him that children formulate and follow a set of "operating principles." One operating principle is "Pay attention to the ends of words." Children find ends of words more salient than beginnings and middles, perhaps for reasons of attention and memory. Ways of marking (indicating) place or position that come after the noun, such as suffixes, are easier for children to learn than markers placed before the noun. In Turkish, a suffix marks place (the equivalent of *pot stove on*), whereas in English, the preposition comes before its object *(pot on stove)*. Turkish-speaking children learn these place markers before English-speaking children do (Slobin, 1979).

Another operating principle is "Pay attention to the order of words." Word order in children's early speech reflects the word order of the adult speech the child hears. Children also seem to have strong preferences for consistent and regular systems: A third operating principle is "avoid exceptions." Hence, as explained earlier, overregularization is common in children's early speech *(bringed, goed, deers)*.

"These operating principles are, of course, only a sketch of what might be a theory of language acquisition" (Slobin, 1979, p. 110). The important point is that infants appear to possess strategies for analyzing and interpreting events in the world around them, including speech. By means of these strategies, they acquire knowledge of the structure of language, which then is used in the process of learning to speak and to understand.

Piaget and his followers maintain that cognitive development directs language acquisition, that the development of language depends on the development of thought rather than vice versa (Piaget, 1967). To support their view, they point out that infants show sensorimotor intelligence before any language appears (Sinclair, 1971). Language acquisition does not begin until a number of important cognitive abilities, such as object permanence, have emerged. Furthermore, infants interpret the world about them, form mental representations, and categorize objects and events before they utter even their first words. They identify regularities in the environment and construct a system of meanings before they have acquired productive language (Bowerman, 1981).

By and large, children's earliest utterances pertain to things they already understand. Children talk about what is interesting to them and attracts their attention (Greenfield, 1979) and about what they know about people, objects, events, and relationships (Brown, 1973). In other words, the children's cognitions—their thoughts, perceptions, and modes of interacting with others—develop first. "Linguistic development is, in good part, learning how what you already know is expressed in your native language" (Flavell, 1977, p. 38). "The meanings expressed in children's earliest word combinations and the rules for combining words must be explained in terms of the child's knowledge of real world objects, i.e., that objects exist, cease to exist, recur, can be acted upon, and are associated with peoples' activities" (Rice, 1983, p. 9). Language, according to this line of argument, is "mapped onto" the child's existing cognitive categories and knowledge.

A major issue raised in these theories is the relationship between language and other cognitive processes such as thinking, concept formation, remembering, and problem solving. The relationship between language and thought is very complex, the subject of much philosophical discourse and controversy. Certainly words and sentences play significant roles in our everyday reasoning, in problem solving, and in coding and storing knowledge. However, other forms of mental representation also exist. Einstein did much of his scientific thinking by means of visual images and mathematical symbols. Composers think in musical notes and auditory images, and painters often think in abstract visual modes.

As cognitive competence increases between infancy and the age of 4, the child's language abilities also expand enormously. Understandably, a question of priority arises: Do cognitive achievements stem from advances in linguistic ability? Or, are cognitive achievements *prerequisite* for higher competence in language? These questions have provoked vigorous debates.

Cognition preceding language

As we noted earlier, Piaget and other cognitive psychologists maintain that language development is an aspect of cognitive development and thus reflects, rather than directs, cognitive progress (Sinclair, 1971). For them, language is not a necessary forerunner of cognitive growth; on the contrary, it is cognitive development that guides language acquisition.

Research by some of Piaget's followers indicates that teaching or training children to talk about problems or concepts does *not* stimulate new cognitive understanding (Sinclair, 1971). One of Piaget's coworkers trained a group of 4- to 6-year-old children to use verbal comparisons such as *more* and *less* correctly. After the training, the children were given tests to see whether they knew that the quantity of water was unchanged when it was poured from one beaker into a taller, thinner one. The responses of the trained children demonstrated that training did not enhance their mastery of the quantitative concepts needed to pass this test. On the basis of this and similar experiments, Piagetian researchers concluded that language "does not influence intellectual development in any direct, general, or decisive way" (Furth, 1966, p. 160).

Words and labels may be very useful in thinking and problem solving, but they are not essential to these processes. Deaf children perform many types of cognitive tasks and solve most problems as well as hearing children, though they are generally retarded in language development and some progress slowly at school. The deaf may rely on nonverbal symbolic systems—perhaps images or pictorial representations—in thinking and problem solving (Furth, 1966).

Underlying cognitive understanding may be related to the production and comprehension of words in different ways. An experimenter trained two groups of 2- and 3-year-old children to label the colors red, green, and yellow accurately. One group already understood color concepts but did not know color words before the training began; this was demonstrated by their ability to categorize objects by color. The other group could not do this. When the training was completed, all the children responded correctly to the question "What color is this?" when shown objects of different colors. However, only the children who had prior knowledge of color concepts responded appropriately to the instruction "Give me the red one." Apparently, the children with prior conceptual understanding spontaneously learned to comprehend color terms whereas the other children did not. The latter, although able to name the colors correctly after training, did not comprehend the color concept. The training had influenced their production but not their comprehension of color labels (Rice, 1980).

Most developmental psychologists agree that cognitive advances are fundamental for language development. However, an important question is still unanswered: "Of all the things that young children know about their world, which are relevant for language?" (Rice, 1983, p. 4). For example, object permanence, early symbolic play, and mental representation (discussed in Chapter 5) do not appear to be related to early linguistic achievements in the way that cognitive theory predicts (Bates, Benigni, Bretherton, Camaioni, & Volterra, 1979; Corrigan, 1978; Folger & Leonard, 1978). Nevertheless, the general point holds. In order to communicate as well as they do, young children have to have some knowledge of the social world and some understanding of their own and others' psychological functioning needs and abilities. Cognitive processes undoubtedly underlie many of the linguistic achievements we have been discussing.

Influences of language on cognition

Language may play a more critical role in acquiring some concepts and cognitive skills than in others. Children's knowledge of language may contribute to their understanding of concepts that are not based on physical properties of objects. Psycholinguists generally agree, for example, that language is of paramount importance in understanding social concepts related to status and role, such as *friends, teachers, aunts and uncles, doctor, clergyman.* These social concepts are harder to learn than object categories such as *fruit, dog,* or *car.* The language used in interacting with people signals their social status. Children acquire knowledge of social concepts and social relationships by observing the markers used in talking with others, including greetings ("Hi" or a formal "Good morning"), terms of address (first names, Sir, Doctor), style of speech, content of conversation, and phrasing of requests and directives. Variations in these features of language introduce the child to social distinctions and social categories (Bowerman, 1981; Ervin-Tripp, 1976; Rice, 1983).

Verbal mediation There is little doubt that language aids immeasurably in refining or extending knowledge of the world, in acquiring new information, in storing what has been learned (memory), and in solving problems. Soon after learning to speak, children begin to use words as mediators of action. A *mediator* is a covert (internal) response that intervenes between a stimulus and an overt response. This covert response, which may be a word or a label, thus becomes the immediate stimulus for the response. For example, once a child has learned to apply the word *candy,* he is apt to behave in predictable ways toward everything with this label. When an adult introduces a new object and says, "Have a piece of candy," the child reacts as he has toward other things labeled *candy,* taking it joyfully and popping it into his mouth. Verbal mediation is ordinarily adaptive, for it guides the child to appropriate responses to new stimuli or situations.

Verbal mediation may help children remember and imitate the behavior of models and facilitate problem solving. Once they have some mastery of language, children are apt to formulate verbal rules that guide their performance in many situations. In a learning experiment, a child may have to choose one of several boxes to obtain a prize (a trinket or a piece of candy). After a few trials she may be able to say to herself, "The prize is in the biggest box," and thus direct her behavior to receive a reward on each trial. Children who have learned verbal descriptions of correct and incorrect responses in experimental settings can rehearse these descriptions and are able to retain the appropriate responses over long periods of time and over changes in situations (Flavell, 1977).

Memory and problem solving Experiences are often represented mentally by words and sentences; they may also be retrieved from memory through language cues. This was demonstrated in a classical experiment in which two groups of subjects were shown stimulus figures but given different labels for them. With one group the figure ⌒⌐ was labeled *beehive;* with the other, it was labeled *hat.* Later, the subjects were asked to draw the figures from memory. Those who coded the figure as a *beehive* tended to distort the figure so that it looked like this: ⌒ , whereas those who had been given the label *hat* tended to draw it in this way: ⌓. The participants' memory of the image was strongly affected by the word or label assigned to it. Apparently, the verbal label was remembered (stored and retrieved), and the figure was reconstructed to conform to that label (Carmichael, Hogan, & Walter, 1932).

Complex problems may be solved more easily if verbal mediators are used to label the component parts and to guide actions. In one Russian study, children were shown pictures of butterfly wings and told to match these with similar ones in a large display. The matchings were to be made on the basis of the patterns of wing markings. The children at first found this task perplexing because they had trouble separating the pattern from the color of the wings. An experimental group was then taught labels (the words for *spots* and *stripes*) to describe the various patterns, while a control group was not given any descriptive labels. After learning these labels, the experimental group made more accurate matchings than they had earlier. Even the younger members of the experimental group performed better than the older children of the control group (Liublinskaya, 1957). Clearly, attaching labels to these stimuli gave them some distinctiveness that made the matching task easier.

Spontaneous verbalizing can also aid children in problem solving. A group of 9- and 10-year-olds were instructed to verbalize while performing a task in which disks had to be moved from one circle to another in a small number of moves. A control group was not given these instructions. The children in the experimental group solved the problems more quickly and efficiently than those who did not. Verbalization during practice had the effect of stimulating the participants to think of new reasons for their behavior and thus facilitated "both the discovery of general principles and their employment in solving successive problems" (Gagné & Smith, 1964, p. 18).

ENVIRONMENTAL INFLUENCES ON LANGUAGE

The major theories of language development lead to different hypotheses about the importance of environmental influences on children's language development. Learning theorists suggest that opportunities for reinforcement and observation of models should be important determinants of language development. Nativist and cognitive-developmental theories suggest that opportunities to hear spoken language and to be active in exploring and learning about the environment are important but that specific reinforcements or training are not essential to successful learning of language. Research on environmental influences has investigated how parents talk and respond to their young children as well as differences among social-class and cultural groups.

Adult teaching and language learning

Children learn language in social settings — by communicating with other people, at first usually the mother and other adult caregivers. Many theorists have assumed it is the mother who shapes the child's early linguistic environment to a large extent. Does the way a mother talks influence her child's language development? The question has theoretical importance because it relates to the impact of environmental inputs on language development.

When talking to their babies, mothers usually use a language that is different from the one they use in adult discourse. A special vocabulary (including words like *tummy* and *choo-choo*) and several other distinctive features characterize mothers' talk to babies, referred to as *motherese*. The pitch of the voice tends to be higher, and intonation is exaggerated. Sentences are short, simple, and grammatically correct; they contain fewer verbs and modifiers, function words, subordinate clauses, and embeddings. There are more questions, imperatives, and repetitions, and speech is more fluent and intelligible (Newport, 1977; Snow, 1974; Vorster, 1974).

A number of studies indicate that motherese may facilitate early language development. In one study, the speech of mother-child pairs in their homes was recorded twice, first when the babies were 18 months old (at the one-word stage) and again 9 months later, after they had begun talking in sentences. If a mother used relatively simplified language when speaking to her 18-month-old (many yes-no questions and a high proportion of nouns relative to pronouns), her child was likely to show a high level of linguistic competence at 27 months (longer sentences and more verbs, noun phrases, and auxiliary verbs). The children of mothers who used longer and more complex sentences during the first observation progressed more slowly. These investigators concluded that motherese may be an effective teaching language for very young children (Furrow, Nelson, & Benedict, 1979).

Another investigator, working with children somewhat older, compared the speech of mothers whose children had accelerated speech development with that of mothers whose children were making normal progress in language. Although the sentences that the two groups of mothers used in talking to their children did not differ in simplicity or length, mothers of accelerated children spoke more clearly, made fewer ambiguous or unintelligible statements, let their children lead in conversation, and responded to the children's utterances with related contributions. In effect, they tailored what they said to what the child said, often repeating or expanding the child's statement. For example, such a mother might respond to the child's "Eve lunch" with "Yes, Eve is having lunch now."

The effect of different kinds of maternal speech undoubtedly vary with the age and language ability of the child. The data do suggest, however, that the mother's sensitivity to the child's language ability, intentions, and meanings—and her adjustments of her responses to take account of these factors—can stimulate the child's linguistic progress. Caregivers other than the mother also provide important language stimulation, particularly when children are in day care. Observations of adult interactions with 3-year-old children were carried out in 10 day-care centers in Bermuda. Virtually all the children in Bermuda are in day care—90 percent by the second year of life—so these children in effect represent the entire population. Children in centers where adults talked often to them had more advanced vocabularies than those in centers with relatively little adult conversation (McCartney, Scarr, Phillips, Grajek, & Schwarz, in press).

A well-controlled experimental study shows how specific training can accelerate the child's acquisition of complex grammatical forms. Before the experiment began, the 28-month-olds in the study did not spontaneously use either tag questions ("I found it, didn't I?") or negative questions ("Doesn't it hurt?"). They also did not use future or conditional verbs ("He will eat it," "He could find it"). One group of children was given five training sessions demonstrating the use of questions, while another group had five sessions emphasizing verb forms. The intervention or training consisted of recasting or rewording the child's sentences in the form to be acquired. For instance, when a child in a question training session said, "You can't have it," the experimenter would reply, "Oh, I can't have it, can I!" In a verb training session, the experimenter would answer a question like "Where it go?" with "It will go there."

The training proved to be effective. All the children exposed to tag and negative questions acquired the ability to frame and produce such questions, but they made no progress in the use of future or conditional verbs. Similarly, all children in the verb training group produced new verb constructions, but they did not add tag or negative questions to their language repertoires. The two groups of children showed the same degree of progress on other measures of language development, such as length of utterances and number of words used. Training by means of rephrasing or recasting sentences apparently had very specific, selective effects (Nelson, 1975).

The findings of these studies may be interpreted as supporting the learning theory view that environmental input has great importance in language development. At the same time, it should be noted that these studies dealt only with the *facilitation* of linguistic development after children had acquired some basic language skills. The studies do not show that special environmental input (motherese, training) is *necessary* for language acquisition, nor do they provide any evidence contradictory to the nativists' assertion of a biological basis of language development.

Social-class language differences

Children from middle-class families generally score higher than those from lower-income families on practically all standard measures of linguistic ability—vocabulary, sentence structure, sound discrimination, and articulation (Templin, 1957). One basis for these differences may be different types of speech used by mothers in these social-class groups. In some early work on this issue, an English educational sociologist described two patterns of verbal interaction (Bernstein, 1970). Lower-class mothers, he reported, typically use a *restricted language code,* talking to their children in short, simple, easily understood sentences that refer primarily to here-and-now events. Middle-class mothers, on the other hand, use an *elaborated code* in disciplining their children, teaching them moral standards, and communicating feelings and emotions. Although the simpler codes might be useful to very young children, the more complex codes used by middle-class mothers could enable older children to be more oriented toward abstractions, generalizations, and social relationships. Lower-class children might think in more concrete and less conceptual terms and be more likely to have difficulty in school and in tests of cognitive ability.

These arguments have been questioned for several reasons. For one thing, the investigator failed to differentiate between language *performance* and *competence* (the knowledge necessary to use the language); he assessed only performance. Lower-class children may possess the basic competence for an elaborated code but not use one because, in their view, it is "fancy," effeminate, or too closely associated with school and the values it represents. When lower- and middle-class boys were instructed to write an informal letter to "a close friend" and an official letter applying for funds to make a trip, there were virtually no differences between the formal letters of the two groups (Robinson, 1965). The lower-class boys were able to use an elaborated code when it was required; they possessed competence and knowledge, even though they ordinarily used a "tough" restricted code.

Speech forms and dialects that depart from standard middle-class language may be erroneously perceived as lacking complexity and richness because investigators do not understand them fully. The speech of some lower-class American blacks is sometimes described as grammatically simpler, less differentiated, and more concrete than standard English. It includes statements like "He going home," "Didn't nobody see it," "He be working" (to mean that he generally works), and "John, he say, here I come" (Dale, 1976). From a linguistic point of view, the differences between so-called black English and standard English are only superficial ones. Both are dialects, alternative versions of the same English language, and although they have somewhat different rules, they have a great deal in common. The two dialects are functionally equivalent in that both enable a speaker to convey a wide range of information, thoughts, emotions, and concepts. Furthermore, the language the black child uses with family and friends is rich and fluent, no less differentiated or complex than standard English (Johnson, 1977). Black children express the same meanings, have similar vocabularies, use the same logic, and can learn abstract concepts as well as anyone who learns standard English (Labov, 1970).

COMMUNICATION AND CONVERSATION

One of the most important functions of language is communication. Effective communication requires not only a knowledge of the rules of grammar (syntax) and the meanings of words (semantics) but also the "ability to say the appropriate thing at the appropriate time and place to the appropriate listeners and in relation to the appropriate topics" (Dore, 1979, p. 337): an understanding of pragmatics in the use of language. We consider in this section how children learn to use language in social contexts to converse and communicate.

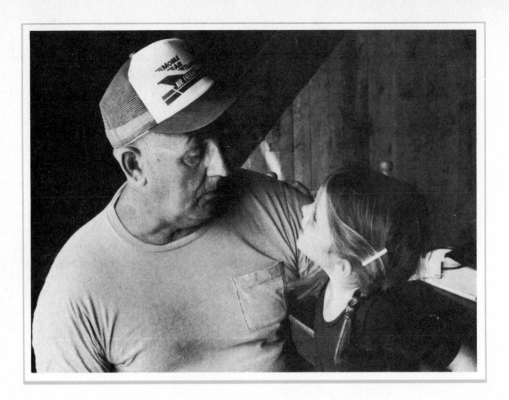

As we have seen, babies communicate before they speak, using actions and gestures to express emotional states and to get help in gratifying needs. Babies will reach toward an object they want, hand a mechanical toy to an adult so that the adult will start it, and shake their heads or make pushing gestures to indicate refusal (Chapman, in press; Pea, 1980). The child's earliest intentional vocal communication may accompany these gestures. Other early communicative sounds draw attention to objects or events or serve as part of a ritual game such as waving goodbye or playing peek-a-boo. These actions and vocalizations may be the precursors of communication through language (Bruner, 1975).

With words and sentences, children can communicate much more efficiently and converse more effectively. Competence in conversation draws on many social, speaking, and listening skills: taking turns; recognizing one's own turn to speak; taking account of the listener's competence, knowledge, interest, and needs; refraining from dominating the interaction or interrupting one's conversational partners; recognizing when a message is not understood and clarifying ambiguous statements; signaling attention and willingness to continue the interaction by nonverbal means such as eye contact; and more (Dore, 1979).

Do young children possess the cognitive capacities needed to develop these communication skills? Piaget's observations led him to conclude that they do not; he stated that early speech is essentially noncommunicative or *egocentric* (Piaget, 1926). Children this age, Piaget said, are not aware that a listener's point of view may be different from their own. They talk as if they were thinking aloud, often describing their own actions, and they engage in "collective monologues" in which two children each follow a line of conversation with little evidence that they are responding to the other's comments. (Sara: "Here goes my train." Sally: "The horse is hurt." Sara: "It's going faster.") Not until the age of 6 or 7 is egocentric speech replaced by "socialized" speech, which takes into account the viewpoint of the listener and thus makes real dialogue possible (Piaget, 1926).

Early verbal exchanges

It is now generally agreed that Piaget grossly underestimated young children's competence in communicating. Two-year-olds speak directly to each other and to adults, usually in staccato utterances referring to familiar objects in the immediate environment. Most messages bring adequate responses; if they do not, the communicator is likely to repeat the message. Short utterances are typical, but lengthier, more elaborate communications occur in some play situations, for example, when children try to cooperate in moving a piece of furniture from one place to another (Wellman & Lempers, 1977).

In conversations initiated by adults, 2-year-olds often simply repeat what the adult says. Three-year-olds take turns with an adult conversational partner, and about half of their responses add new and relevant information to what the

adult has said. The conversation is short, however, seldom continuing for more than two turns (Bloom, Rocissano, & Hood, 1976). In talking with other 3-year-olds, children sometimes sustain much longer turn-taking sequences. One pair of 3-year-olds in a study took 21 turns, asking and replying to questions about a camping trip one of them was going to take (Garvey, 1975, 1977).

By 4, children are capable of remarkable flexibility and know how to make major adjustments in their conversational strategies when their audience requires it. The 4-year-olds in one study were observed talking to 2-year-olds, to peers, and to adults during spontaneous play and while explaining how a toy worked. When talking to 2-year-olds, they used simpler, shorter sentences and more attention-getting words like *hey* and *look* than they did when talking to adults or other 4-year-olds. Sentences addressed to adults and peers were longer and more complex, containing more coordinate and subordinate clauses (Shatz & Gelman, 1973).

Questions and requests

Beginning at about age 3, children's spontaneous conversations include *contingent queries,* that is, questions about what another child has said or done. These questions are frequently requests for elaboration, clarification, or explanation, the most common being "what?" or its synonym "Huh?"

Lenny: Look it, we found a parrot in our house.
Phil: A what?
Lenny: A parrot. A bird.
Phil: Wow!

In this conversation—a representative interaction between 3-year-olds—the query "A what?" (spoken with rising intonation) was clearly a request for repetition. After making his inquiry, the listener gave the speaker his turn to respond, and the speaker gave the expected response plus an expansion. The listener then responded, acknowledging that the speaker's initial statement had been clarified (Garvey, 1975).

The forms of contingent query are mastered by the time the child has fluent speech, that is, by the age of 3 or 4. These queries are successful in keeping conversations of preschool children going. The findings of one study show that 66 percent of the queries received appropriate responses, 20 percent elicited some other relevant reply, and only 14 percent went unanswered (Garvey, 1975).

Young children often intentionally elicit contingent questions from others in order to maintain the listener's attention and to set the stage for something they want to say.

Arnie: Do you know what I want to be when I grow up?
Ken: What? *(spoken with falling intonation)*
Arnie: I wanna be a fireman.
Ken: Oh.

In naturalistic play and conversation, preschoolers not only ask questions but make requests. The younger and older children in one study produced equal numbers of direct requests (e.g., "Give me the hammer"), but older chil-

FIGURE 6.1

Drawings used in a study in which one child had to describe a drawing to another who could not see it. By age 7 or 8, children provided descriptions that were clear and specific enough for the listener to choose a matching drawing from an array. (Reprinted from S. Glucksberg & R. M. Krauss. What do people say after they have learned how to talk? **Merrill-Palmer Quarterly,** *1967, 13, 309–316. By permission of the* **Wayne State University Press.** *Copyright 1967,* **The Merrill-Palmer Institute of Human Development and Family Life.)**

Later communication skills

dren (over 4) made twice as many indirect requests ("See if you can hand me the hammer") as younger ones. Indirect requests were more successful; that is, they brought compliance 75 percent of the time, while only half the direct requests produced the desired effect. Many children's requests were accompanied by justifications. One child asked another to stop leaning on her by saying, "Stop it. You hurt my hip." As is usually the case, the listener's reactions demonstrated clear awareness of the meaning of the speaker's request.

Understanding *indirect* requests requires considerable communicative competence, but even preschoolers can do it:

Jan: I need a pencil.
Laurie: Here. *(tosses a pencil to Jan)* (Garvey, 1975)

In their everyday experiences, young children hear many indirect requests phrased as statements. Coming from a parent or teacher, "It's clean-up time" and "I shouldn't see that on the table" are correctly interpreted as requests for action. Clearly, the child's valid inferences are not based solely on knowledge of language but also on understanding the speaker's intentions, sensitivity to the speaker's status and needs, *plus* knowledge of the social rules that obtain in this context (Elliot, 1981; Ervin-Tripp, 1977).

The normal give-and-take of children's conversation seems to contradict Piaget's ideas about the egocentricity of young children's language. In this conversation between 4-year-olds, note the subtlety of Lisa's understanding of Jane's perspective.

(Lisa approaches a large toy car that Jane has been sitting on.)
Lisa: Pretend this was my car.
Jane: No.
Lisa: Pretend this was our car.
Jane: All right.
Lisa: Can I drive our car?
Jane: Yes, O.K. *(smiles and moves away from the car)*
Lisa: (turns wheel and makes driving noises) (adapted from Garvey, 1975, p. 42)

With increasing cognitive competence and expanded knowledge of the world, children become more skillful communicators. Listening skills also improve, and children do better at detecting ambiguities in messages and asking for clarification (Asher, 1978).

Researchers often study children's communication by having pairs of children play a game that requires an exchange of information. For example, the children may sit opposite each other at a table with a barrier across it so that they cannot see each other. In one such study, each child was given a peg and a set of blocks that could be stacked on the peg. The blocks contained distinctive but hard-to-describe drawings like those shown in Figure 6.1. The task of one child, the speaker, was to pick up a block, describe the drawing on it to the other child, and put it on the peg. The listener's task was to choose the block that matched the speaker's description and put it on the peg, to that at the end of the game the blocks would be stacked on both pegs in the same order.

All the children played the game eight times. The first time, all performed poorly. The older children improved rapidly, however, performing without error by the eighth game. Kindergarten children continued to make many mistakes throughout the series. Young children's messages often showed no awareness of the kind of information the other player might find meaningful. For example, they might describe the drawing on a block by saying "Mommy's dress" or "Daddy's shirt." If the listener asked for more information, a young speaker was likely to repeat the description already given or to remain silent. Older speakers gave fuller, more informative descriptions. They also reacted more appropriately to feedback from the listener. If the listener said, "I don't know which one you mean," an older speaker was likely to give a new description or add more details (Glucksberg & Krauss, 1967; Krauss & Glucksberg, 1969).

As their conversational skills improve, children become more effective listeners. Compared with preschoolers, older children consider what the speaker says more carefully and are better able to evaluate whether they understand, that is, whether the speaker's statements are adequate, informative, or ambiguous. They do a better job of asking for information to reduce ambiguity and uncertainty. Experiments show that this skill can be augmented simply by instructing children to ask questions freely whenever a message is not entirely clear (Patterson, Massad, & Cosgrove, 1978).

SUMMARY

Infants begin to babble, pronouncing strings of syllables like *bababa* at about 5 or 6 months and typically utter their first understandable word sometime around the end of the first year. Comprehension develops earlier and more rapidly than production, however, and infants frequently respond to questions and instructions with gestures and actions before they say any words. Six months to a year after uttering their first word, when their speaking vocabularies include about 50 words, children start to form two-word sentences. These are generally telegraphic versions of adult sentences, consisting largely of nouns and verbs plus a few adjectives but omitting prepositions, conjunctions, articles, and auxiliary verbs. Yet even these first two-word sentences manifest systematic regularity of word order, and from the very start, the child expresses the basic grammatical relationships of subject, predicate, and object. Children of many cultures, speaking different languages, express the same meanings in their earliest sentences, including such basic semantic relations as identification, location, negation, agent-action, and agent-object. The circumstances and context of an utterance must be considered in interpreting fully the child's intention or meaning.

As the child's sentences become longer and more complex, some little words and word endings (inflections) are added—a few prepositions and articles, forms of the verb *to be,* plurals, and possessives. Although there are striking individual differences in the *rate* of acquisition of these grammatical forms, there is an amazing uniformity in the *order* in which they emerge. Only 30 months (approximately) after children utter their first sentences—that is, between the ages of 4 and 5 years—they are capable of using full, complex, adultlike sentences that demonstrate near mastery of the rules of grammar in their own language.

By the age of 6, most American children have vocabularies of between 8,000 and 14,000 words. The meanings that children first assign to the words are frequently different from those of adults. Many are overextensions or over-generalizations (definitions that are broader or more general than those of adults), based on similarities in appearance, function, or subjective reactions. Some words are underextended, or defined too narrowly.

During the period between kindergarten and high school, vocabulary increases rapidly, speech performance improves, syntax becomes more complete, a greater variety of grammatical structures is used, and the meanings assigned to words become more adultlike. At the same time, the child's metalinguistic awareness expands, and language itself becomes a topic for the child to reflect on, understand, talk about, and "play with." By the age of 8, children understand that some words have several meanings and functions, and this understanding is the basis for the appreciation and creation of jokes and metaphors.

Learning theorists have attempted to explain language acquisition in terms of reward, punishment, and imitation of verbal responses. However, most psycholinguists do not believe that these mechanisms can account fully for the amazingly rapid development of children's comprehension and use of language or their ability to create novel sentences at a very early age. Chomsky's nativistic theory holds that humans possess a built-in or prewired system, a language acquisition device (LAD), that enables the child to process language, construct rules, and understand and produce appropriate grammatical speech. Other theorists maintain that language development is dependent on the individual's inherent tendencies toward activity and construction, as well as cognitive information-processing and motivational predispositions. Research studies indicate that various kinds of environmental input *facilitate* language development, but there is no evidence that any special kind of training is necessary for language acquisition.

Language generally enhances cognitive functions such as thinking, reasoning, problem solving, and coding and storing knowledge (memory). However, cognitive thought processes are not completely dependent on language, for many deaf children, although deficient in language skills, solve cognitive problems well. Verbal mediators such as labels are helpful in many cognitive tasks, but other mediators, such as images and pictorial representations, are also used frequently.

Competence in conversation and communication involves many social as well as language and listening skills. By the age of 3, children sustain coherent conversations, taking turns in talking, not only in play but also in goal-directed activities. They ask each other relevant questions and make direct and indirect requests for elaboration and explanation. Within increasing cognitive competence, more sophisticated comprehension of syntax and semantics, and expanded knowledge of the world, children become more skillful communicators.

REFERENCES

Anglin, J. M. *Word, object, and conceptual development.* New York: Norton, 1977.

Asher, S. R. Referential communication. In G. J. Whitehurst & B. J. Zimmerman (Eds.), *The functions of language and cognition.* New York: Academic Press, 1978.

Bates, E., Camaioni, L., & Volterra, V. The acquisition of performatives prior to speech. *Merrill-Palmer Quarterly,* 1975, *21,* 205–226.

Bates, E. *Language and context: The acquisition of pragmatics.* New York: Academic Press, 1976.

Bates, E., Benigni, L., Bretherton, I., Camaioni, L., & Volterra, V. *The emergence of symbols: Cognition and communication in infancy.* New York: Academic Press, 1979.

Benedict, H. Early lexical development: Comprehension and production. *Journal of Child Language,* 1979, *6,* 183–200.

Bernstein, B. A sociolinguistic approach to socialization: With some reference to educability. In F. Williams (Ed.), *Language and poverty: Perspectives on a theme.* Chicago: Markham, 1970.

Bever, T. G. The cognitive basis for linguistic structures. In J. R. Hayes (Ed.), *Cognition and the development of language.* New York: Wiley, 1970.

Bloom, L. M. *One word at a time: The use of single word utterances before syntax.* The Hague: Mouton, 1973.

Bloom, L. M., Hood, L., & Lightbown, P. Imitation in language development: If, when, and why. *Cognitive Psychology,* 1974, *6,* 380–420.

Bloom, L., Lahey, L., Hood, L., Lifter, K., & Fiess, K. Complex sentences: Acquisition of syntactic connectives and the semantic relations they encode. *Journal of Child Language,* 1980, *7,* 235–261.

Bloom, L., Rocissano, L., & Hood, L. Adult-child discourse: Developmental interaction between linguistic processing and linguistic knowledge. *Cognitive Psychology,* 1976, *8,* 521–552.

Bowerman, M. F. Semantic factors in the acquisition of rules for word use and sentence construction. In D. M. Morehead & A. E. Morehead (Eds.), *Normal and deficient language.* Baltimore: University Park Press, 1976.

Bowerman, M. F. Cross-cultural perspectives on language development. In H. C. Triandis (Ed.), *Handbook of cross-cultural psychology.* Boston: Allyn & Bacon, 1981.

Bowerman, M. F. Starting to talk worse: Clues to language acquisition from children's late speech errors. In S. Strauss (Ed.), *U-shaped behavioral growth.* New York: Academic Press, 1982.

Braine, M. D. S. The ontogeny of English phrase structures: The first phase. *Language,* 1963, *39,* 1–13.

Bretherton, I., McNew, S., & Beeghly-Smith, M. Early person knowledge as expressed in gestural and verbal communication: When do infants acquire a "theory of mind"? In M. E. Lamb and L. R. Sherrod (Eds.), *Infant social cognition.* Hillsdale, N.J.: Erlbaum, 1983.

Brown, R. How shall a thing be called? *Psychological Review,* 1958, *65,* 14–21.

Brown, R. *A first language: The early stages.* Cambridge, Mass.: Harvard University Press, 1973.

Bruner, J. S. From communication to language: A psychological perspective. *Cognition,* 1975, *3,* 255–287.

Carey, S. The child as word learner. In M. Halle, J. Bresnan, & G. A. Miller (Eds.), *Linguistic theory and psychological reality.* Cambridge, Mass.: MIT Press, 1977.

Carmichael, L., Hogan, H. P., & Walter, A. A. An experimental study of the effect of language on reproduction of visually perceived form. *Journal of Experimental Psychology,* 1932, *15,* 73–86.

Chapman, R. Issues in child language acquisition. In N. Lass, J. Northern, D. Yoder, & L. McReynolds (Eds.), *Speech, language, and hearing: Normal processes and clinical disorders.* Philadelphia: Saunders, 1982.

Chomsky, N. *Syntactic structures.* The Hague: Mouton, 1957.

Chomsky, N. (Review of *Verbal behavior* by B. F. Skinner.) *Language,* 1959, *35,* 26–58.

Clark, E. Building a vocabulary: Words for objects, actions, and relations. In P. Fletcher & M. Gorman (Eds.), *Language acquisition.* Cambridge: Cambridge University Press, 1979.

Clark, E., & Anderson, E. S. *Spontaneous repairs: Awareness in acquiring language.* Paper presented at a meeting of the Society for Research in Child Development, San Francisco, 1979.

Clark, E. V. What's in a word? On the child's acquisition of semantics in his first language. In T. E. Moore (Ed.), *Cognitive development and the acquisition of language.* New York: Academic Press, 1973.

Coates, B., & Hartup, W. W. Age and verbalization in observational learning. *Developmental Psychology*, 1969, *1*, 556–562.

Corrigan, R. Language development as related to stage 6 object permanence development. *Journal of Child Language*, 1978, *5*, 173–179.

Curtiss, S. *Genie: A psycholinguistic study of a modern-day "wild child."* New York: Academic Press, 1977.

Dale, P. *Language development structure and function* (2nd ed.). New York: Holt, Rinehart and Winston, 1976.

de Villiers, P. A., & de Villiers, J. A. On this, that, and the other: Nonegocentrism in very young children. *Journal of Experimental Psychology*, 1974, *18*, 438–447.

de Villiers, P. A., & de Villiers, J. A. Semantics and syntax in the first two years: The output of form and function and the form and function of the input. In F. D. Minified & L. L. Lloyd (Eds.), *Communicative and cognitive abilities: Early behavioral assessment.* Baltimore: University Park Press, 1977.

de Villiers, J. A., & de Villiers, P. A. *Language acquisition.* Cambridge, Mass.: Harvard University Press, 1978.

Dore, J. Conversation and preschool language development. In P. Fletcher & M. Gorman (Eds.), *Language acquisition,* Cambridge: Cambridge University Press, 1979.

Eimas, P. D. Developmental studies of speech perception. In L. B. Cohen & P. Salapatek (Eds.), *Infant perception.* New York: Academic Press, 1975.

Elliot, A. J. *Child language.* Cambridge: Cambridge University Press, 1981.

Ervin-Tripps, S. Speech acts and social learning. In K. H. Basso & H. Selby (Eds.), *Meaning in anthropology.* Albuquerque: University of New Mexico Press, 1976.

Ervin-Tripp, S. Wait for me, rollerskate. In C. Mitchell-Kernan & S. Ervin-Tripp (Eds.), *Child discourse.* New York: Academic Press, 1977.

Flavell, J. H. *Cognitive development.* Englewood Cliffs, N.J.: Prentice-Hall, 1977.

Folger, M., & Leonard, L. Language and sensorimotor development during the early period of referential speech. *Journal of Speech and Hearing Research,* 1978, *21*, 519–527.

Furrow, D., Nelson, K., & Benedict, H. Mothers' speech to children and syntactic development: Some simple relationships. *Journal of Child Language,* 1979, *6*, 423–442.

Furth, H. G. *Thinking without language.* New York: Free Press, 1966.

Gagné, R. M., & Smith, E. C. A study of the effects of verbalization on problem solving. *Journal of Experimental Psychology,* 1964, *63*, 12–18.

Garvey, C. Requests and responses in children's speech. *Journal of Child Language,* 1975, *2*, 41–63.

Garvey, C. *Play.* Cambridge, Mass.: Harvard University Press, 1977.

Gleitman, L. R., Gleitman, H., & Shipley, E. F. The emergence of the child as grammarian. *Cognition,* 1972, *1*, 137–164.

Glucksberg, S., & Krauss, R. M. What do people say after they have learned how to talk? *Merrill-Palmer Quarterly,* 1967, *13*, 309–316.

Greenfield, P. M. *The role of perceptual uncertainty in the transition to language.* Paper presented in a symposium at the biennial meeting of the Society for Research on Child Development, San Francisco, March, 1979.

Greenfield, P. M., & Smith, J. H. *The structure of communication in early language development.* New York: Academic Press, 1976.

Gruendel, M. M. *Concepts, categories, and early word use: Overextension reconsidered.* Paper presented at the First Annual Boston University Conference on Language Development, 1976.

Huttenlocher, J. The origins of language comprehension. In R. L. Solso (Ed.), *Theories in cognitive psychology.* Hillsdale, N.J.: Erlbaum, 1974.

Johnson, R. P. Social class and grammatical development. *Language and Speech,* 1977, *20*, 317–324.

Kagan, J. *The second year: The emergence of self-awareness.* Cambridge, Mass.: Harvard University Press, 1982.

Karmiloff-Smith, A. Language development after five. In P. Fletcher & M. Gorman (Eds.), *Language acquisition.* Cambridge: Cambridge University Press, 1979.

Kessel, F. S. The role of syntax in children's comprehension from ages six to twelve. *Monographs of the Society for Research in Child Development,* 1970, *35*(6, Whole No. 139).

Krauss, R. M., & Glucksberg, S. The development of communication: Competence as a function of age. *Child Development,* 1969, *40,* 255–266.

Labov, W. The logic of nonstandard English. In F. Williams (Ed.), *Language and poverty: Perspectives on a theme.* Chicago: Markham, 1970.

Leonard, L. B. *Meaning in child language.* New York: Grune & Stratton, 1976.

Liublinskaya, A. A. The development of children's speech and thought. In B. Simon (Ed.), *Psychology in the Soviet Union.* Stanford, Calif.: Stanford University Press, 1957.

McCartney, K., Scarr, S., Phillips, D., Grajek, S., & Schwarz, J. C. Environmental differences among day care centers and their effects on children's levels of intellectual, language, and social development. *American Journal of Orthopsychiatry,* in press.

McGhee, P. E. The role of operational thinking in children's appreciation of humor. *Child Development,* 1971, *42,* 733–744.

McGhee, P. E. *Humor: Its origin and development.* San Francisco : Freeman, 1979.

Nelson, K. Structure and strategy in learning to talk. *Monographs of the Society for Research in Child Development,* 1973, *38* (Whole No. 149).

Nelson, K. Concept, word, and sentence: Interrelations in acquisition and development. *Psychological Review,* 1974, *81,* 267–285.

Nelson, K. Individual differences in early semantic and syntax development. In D. Aaronson & R. W. Rieber (Eds.), *Developmental psycholinguistics and communication disorders. Annals of the New York Academy of Science,* 1975, *263,* 132–139.

Newport, E. L., Gleitman, H., & Gleitman, L. R. Mother, I'd rather do it myself: Some effects and non-effects of maternal speech style. In C. E. Snow & C. A. Ferguson (Eds.), *Talking to children.* Cambridge: Cambridge University Press, 1977.

Ninio, A., & Bruner, J. *The achievement and antecedents of labelling.* Unpublished paper, Hebrew University, Jerusalem, 1976.

Papandrapoulou, I., & Sinclair, H. What is a word? Experimental study of children's ideas on Grammar. *Human Development,* 1974, *17,* 241–258.

Patterson, C. J., Massad, C. M., & Cosgrove, J. M. Children's referential communication: Components of plans for effective listening. *Developmental Psychology,* 1978, *14,* 401–406.

Pea, R. D. The development of negation in early child language. In D. R. Olson (Ed.), *The social foundations of language and thought: Essays in honor of Jerome S. Bruner.* New York: Norton, 1980.

Piaget, J. *The language and thought of the child.* London: Routledge & Kegan Paul, 1926.

Piaget, J. Language and thought from the genetic point of view. In D. Elkind (Ed.), *Six psychological studies.* New York: Random House, 1967.

Rice, M . *Cognition to language.* Baltimore: University Park Press, 1980.

Rice, M. Cognitive aspects of communicative disorders. In R. H. Schiefelbusch & J. Picka (Eds.), *Communicative competence: Acquisition and integration.* University Park, Md.: University Park Press, 1983.

Ricks, D. M. Vocal communication in preverbal normal and autistic children. In N. O'Connor (Ed.), *Language, cognitive deficits, and retardation.* London: Butterworth, 1975.

Robinson, W. P. The elaborated code in working-class language. *Language and Speech,* 1965, *8,* 243–252.

Rosch, E., & Mervis, C. B. Family resemblances: Studies in the internal structure of categories. *Cognitive Psychology,* 1975, *7*(4), 573–605.

Sacks, J., & Truswell, L. Comprehension of two-word instructions by children in the one-word stage. *Journal of Child Language,* 1978, *5,* 17–24.

Schultz, T. R., & Horibe, F. Development of the appreciation of verbal jokes. *Developmental Psychology,* 1974, *10,* 13–20.

Shatz, M., & Gelman, R. The development of communication skills: Modifications in the speech of young children as a function of the listener. *Monographs of the Society for Research in Child Development,* 1973, *38* (Whole No. 152).

Sherman, J. Imitation and language development. In H. W. Reese & L. Lipsitt (Eds.), *Advances in child development and behavior.* New York: Academic Press, 1971.

Sinclair, H. Sensorimotor action patterns as a condition for the acquisition of syntax. In R.

Huxley & E. Ingram (Eds.), *Language acquisition: Models and methods.* New York: Academic Press, 1971.

Slobin, D. I. *Psycholinguistics.* Glenview, Ill.: Scott, Foresman, 1971.

Slobin, D. I. Seven questions about language development. In P. C. Dodwell (Ed.), *New horizons in psychology* (Vol. 2). Baltimore: Penguin, 1972.

Slobin, D. I. *Psycholinguistics* (2nd ed.). Glenview, Ill.: Scott, Foresman, 1979.

Snow, C. E. *Mother's speech and research: An overview.* Paper presented at the Conference on Language Input and Acquisition, Boston, 1974.

Strohner, H., & Nelson, K. E. The young child's development of sentence comprehension: Influences of event probability, nonverbal context, syntactic form, and strategies. *Child Development,* 1974, *45,* 567–576.

Templin, M. C. Certain language skills in children. *Institute of Child Welfare Monographs* (Serial No. 26). Minneapolis: University of Minnesota Press, 1957.

Thompson, J. R., & Chapman, R. S. Who is "Daddy"? The status of two-year-olds' overextended words in use and comprehension. *Papers and Reports on Child Language Development* (Stanford University), 1975, *10,* 59–68.

Trevarthen, C. Conversations with a two-month-old. *New Scientist,* 1974, *62,* 230–233.

Tyack, D., & Ingram, D. Children's production and comprehension of questions. *Journal of Child Language,* 1977, *4,* 211–224.

Vorster, J. Mother's speech to children: Some methodological considerations. *Publications of the Institute for General Linguistics* (No. 8). Amsterdam: University of Amsterdam, 1974.

Vygotsky, L. S. *Thought and language.* New York: Wiley, 1962.

Webb, P. A., & Abrahamson, A. A. Stages of egocentrism in children's use of "this" and "that": A different point of view. *Journal of Child Language,* 1976, *3,* 349–367. Wellman, H. M., & Lempers, J. D. The naturalistic communicative ability of two-year-olds. *Child Development,* 1977, *43,* 1052–1057.

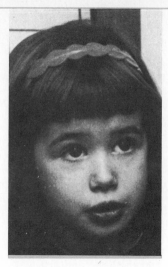

CHAPTER 7

Cognitive development

Cognition is a central topic in human development, so complex it cannot be fully discussed in one or two chapters. You have already encountered some cognitive processes and achievements. The cognitive processes of perception, memory, and categorization, as well as Piaget's ideas about sensorimotor intelligence during infancy, were described in Chapter 3. The first evidence of symbolism and inference was considered in Chapter 5, and the early growth of language as it relates to cognitive capacity in Chapter 6. This chapter amplifies our understanding of cognitive processes during childhood and early adolescence.

COGNITION: MEANING AND ISSUES

Cognition is a broad and inclusive concept that refers to the mental activities involved in the acquisition, processing, organization, and use of knowledge. The major processes subsumed under the term *cognition* include detecting, interpreting, classifying, and remembering information; evaluating ideas; inferring principles and deducing rules; imagining possibilities; generating strategies; fantasizing; and dreaming. The developmental psychologist is concerned with two key questions about cognitive processes. First, what major changes in cognitive functioning occur as children grow? Second, what factors account for these changes?

Maturation and experience

Two different theoretical approaches to these questions are presented in this chapter. The first is Piaget's influential theory, which focuses primarily on reasoning and problem solving and gives less attention to perception, memory, fantasy, and dreaming. The second, usually called the information-processing approach, is relatively new. Psychologists working in this tradition focus their attention on age changes in perception, memory, inference, evaluation, and the use of rules. Before discussing these two approaches in detail, we consider two critical problems or controversies that dominate contemporary study of cognitive development.

One of these problems stems from the fact that it is still not possible to separate the consequences of maturation of the brain, on the one hand, from the consequences of active experience, on the other. Although most psychologists believe that manipulation of objects and reciprocal interactions with people during the early years contribute substantially to cognitive development, some intellectual advances may be attributable primarily to changes in the central nervous system. Babies born without arms or legs because of toxic drugs their mothers took during pregnancy show normal growth of many cognitive abilities, even though these children are not able to play with toys or use their own fingers. However, variety of experience does hasten or retard the time of emergence of some basic cognitive processes. Children in extremely isolated areas of the world who have no toys and live in a homogeneous environment with little cognitive challenge may be several years behind American children in developing some important cognitive abilities (Kagan, Klein, Finley, Rogoff, & Nolan, 1979).

Competence and performance

A second critical issue is the distinction between the knowledge and abilities a child possesses, which we call *actual competence,* and the appropriate use of that knowledge and skill to solve problems, which we call *performance.* Children may possess knowledge that they do not use even though the occasion calls for it. To cite a simple example, although a person may forget the name of an acquaintance, we would not conclude that the person did not know the friend's name or lacked a general ability to recall people's names.

The difference between competence and performance was illustrated in a study in which 3- and 4-year-old children were asked to sort objects belonging to different categories (furniture, vehicles, people, and trees). They were asked to put the objects belonging to the same category either on different pieces of paper or into different plastic bags. The children were more likely to sort the items correctly when they placed them in bags than when they put them on separate pieces of paper (Markman, Cox, & Machida, 1981). Thus, a child who failed to put all the toys representing furniture on one piece of paper—a failure in performance—probably nevertheless possessed the competence we call the concept of furniture.

One reason children's performance may fail to reveal their actual competence is that children occasionally misunderstand the problem as stated. Most of the facts about cognitive development are based on children's answers to questions posed by an adult examiner. Children often interpret questions in a way that differs from the intention of the examiner. An answer that is judged incorrect by the examiner may be correct from the child's perspective. Consider the following example.

A 4-year-old child is shown an array containing four toy garages and three toy cars. Each of the cars is in a garage, leaving one garage empty. The examiner asks the child, "Are all the cars in the garages?" A young child typically says no, and the examiner concludes that the child does not know the meaning of *all.* But if the examiner leads up to the test question, first asking several questions that involve only three cars, the child is more likely to answer correctly. In the first instance, the child may assume that if there are four garages, there must be four cars. He reasons, why would there by a garage if there were no car for it? The child may infer that there is a missing car somewhere and conclude that it is not true that all the cars are in the garages. The child understands the meaning of *all* perfectly well; however, he also brought to the problem an assumption the examiner did not count on.

This example is one instance of a more profound issue. Each question—indeed, every communication from one person to another—contains hidden, implicit understandings between speaker and listener. As explained in Chapter 6, communication between members of a particular culture works most of the time because the listener understands the intentions of the speaker. Because children have to learn the assumptions of adult questions, some improvements in cognitive performances with age are due to changes in a very special competence, namely, the child's understanding of the assumptions held by adults.

A different meaning of competence refers to children's ability to acquire a new skill or segment of knowledge, which we call a *potential competence.* When a child fails a problem—let us say she recalls only four of eight words read to her by an examiner—it is hard to identify the source of the poor performance. Was it failure to use an *actual competence* (the child knew the words and registered them as they were read but could not remember them, perhaps because she was distracted by outside noise) or a flaw in the child's *potential competence* (the child is unable to register or recall a list of eight words because she does not know the meanings of some of them, she does not know how to rehearse information, she is unable to sustain focused attention, or for a host of other reasons)?

Suppose, through careful experimentation, we could determine that the child's inferior performance was due to an inability to focus attention for the 20 seconds it took to read the words. How general a name should we give to this lack of potential competence? It is unlikely that this child is unable to sustain attention for 20 seconds to all verbal information in all situations, and just as unlikely that the lack of competence is limited to this particular set of eight words. But elimination of these two extreme alternatives leaves an enormous space in which to find the best description of the child's potential competence or lack of competence.

This hypothetical example illustrates the controversy surrounding the word *competence,* be it actual or potential. Some scientists prefer to enlarge the domain of competence; others wish to narrow it. We favor the more restricted conception, partly because it permits more precise comparisons of different groups of children. Mayan 8-year-olds living in an isolated village in the northwest highlands of Guatemala have great difficulty remembering lists of eight words and the order of a series of eight pictures laid side by side on a table in front of them. Despite many trials and a very patient examiner, most of the children do not recall more than three or four items. American children of the same age recall all eight words and the series of eight pictures. This evidence might lead us to conclude that the Mayan children lacked the potential competence to register and retrieve more than three or four items of symbolic information. But when these same Mayan children were required to memorize the unique associations between 20 different pairs of geometric designs and meaningful ideas (see Figure 7.1), they learned them all after only seven or eight trials (Kagan et al., 1979). Apparently this particular memory task was easier for them than remembering a list of eight unrelated words.

Children differ in their *potential competence* to acquire various skills and domains of knowledge. But given the evidence, it seems wise to conceive of a child's competence—actual and potential—as applying to limited domains rather than very broad ones (Brown, Bransford, Ferrara, & Campione, 1983).

FIGURE 7.1

Designs and their associated meanings which Mayan children learned over a series of repeated exposures. Children learned and remembered these designs better when they were associated with meaningful ideas, but had difficulty remembering a series of unrelated picutres or words. (From J. Kagan, R. E. Klein, G. E. Finley, B. Rogoff, & E. Nolan. A cross-cultural study of cognitive development. **Monographs of the Society for Research in Child Development,** *1979,* **44**[No. 5]. © *The Society for Research in Child Development, Inc. By permission.)*

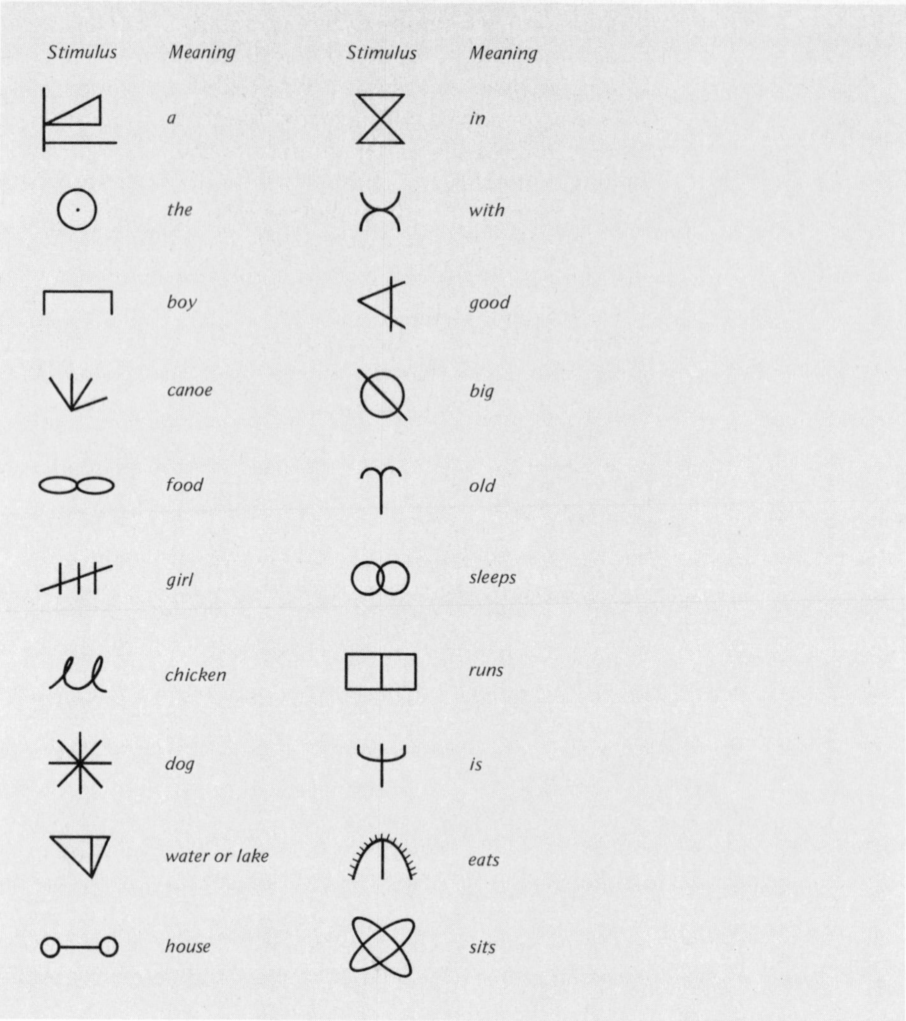

Stimulus	Meaning	Stimulus	Meaning
	a		in
	the		with
	boy		good
	canoe		big
	food		old
	girl		sleeps
	chicken		runs
	dog		is
	water or lake		eats
	house		sits

PIAGET'S THEORY

Jean Piaget was the most influential developmental psychologist of the twentieth century. Largely as a result of his theoretical and empirical work, cognition has held center stage in child development research since 1960. As we shall see, his theory of cognitive growth and change is original, comprehensive, integrative, and elegant.

Piaget died in 1980 at the age of 84. Throughout his long life, he made meticulous observations and records of infants' and children's spontaneous activities, devised many ingenious "tests" of cognitive abilities, and presented problems to thousands of children and adolescents. He was a prolific writer, publishing more than 30 books and 200 articles.

Piaget's ideas have been the source of an untold number of research studies, but they have also generated considerable controversy. As we shall see,

many experts have pointed out weaknesses in Piaget's research and questioned his conclusions. But the criticisms of Piaget have been productive; "much of our most exciting information about intellectual development comes from experimenters whose starting point was either a doubt about one or another of Piaget's conclusions or a desire to defend him against his critics" (Bryant, 1982, p. 2).

Our discussion begins with the fundamental concepts of Piaget's theory, some of which were introduced in Chapter 3. Bear in mind that the theory deals exclusively with cognitive development, beginning with the primitive reflexes and motor coordinations of infancy and extending to the thinking and problem solving of adolescents and adults. Scientific and mathematical abilities are stressed—abstract and logical reasoning, generation of hypotheses, and organizing mental activities into more complex structures. Piaget was not concerned with motives, emotions, personality characteristics, or social behavior, although some psychologists have found his concepts useful in understanding these issues (Block, 1982, Cowan, 1978; Kohlberg, 1969).

In Piaget's theory, knowledge is assumed to have a specific goal or purpose: to aid the person in adapting to the environment. The child or adult does not receive information passively, and thoughts are not simply the products of direct teaching by or imitation of others. Nor is cognitive progress seen as primarily a product of maturation of the brain. Knowledge is acquired and thought processes become more complex and efficient as a consequence of the maturing child's interactions with the world.

Piaget's central thesis is that the individual is active, curious, and inventive thoughout the life cycle. Human beings seek contact and interaction with the environment, search out challenge, and, most important, interpret events. "It is the interpretation, not the event itself, which affects behavior" (Ginsburg & Opper, 1979, p. 67). Children and adults continually construct and reconstruct their knowledge of the world, trying to make sense of experience and attempting to organize their knowledge into more efficient and coherent structures.

The operation

A central concept in Piaget's theory is the operation or the operational structure. *Operations* are "actions which the child performs mentally and which have the added property of being reversible" (Ginsburg & Opper, 1979). An operation can be regarded as a manipulation of ideas that can be reversed (done backwards, so to speak), allowing the person to return mentally to the beginning of the thought sequence. Planning a series of moves in a game of checkers or chess and then mentally retracing one's steps to the beginning of the sequence is an operation. Squaring the number 2 to get 4 is an operation; so is the reverse operation of extracting the square root of 4 to obtain 2. Eight stones can be divided into subgroups of various sizes—for example, four and four, six and two, or seven and one—and then recombined into a single set. In Piaget's theory of cognitive development, the acquisition of operations is at the core of intellectual growth.

Assimilation,
accommodation,
and equilibration

The major mechanisms that allow children to progress from one stage of cognitive functioning to the next are called by Piaget assimilation, accommodation, and equilibration. These mechanisms were briefly introduced in Chapter 3. *Assimilation* refers to the individual's "efforts to deal with the environment by making it fit into the organism's own existing structures—by incorporating it" (Donaldson, 1978, p. 140). That is, a new object or idea is interpreted in terms of ideas or actions the child has already acquired. Assimilation can be seen when a 5-year-old girl has learned that objects that fly in the sky are called birds. Each time the child sees a moving object in the sky, she assimilates that event to her idea of a bird. One day she sees her first low-flying helicopter and tries to assimilate it to her idea of a bird. But the noise, the size, and the shape do not fit her existing idea, and assimilation is not possible.

Piaget suggested that there is a complementary process, accommodation, which is "the individual's tendency to change in response to environmental demands" (Ginsburg & Opper, 1979, p. 18), that is, to modify actions and ideas (schemes) to fit new situations, objects, or information. The 5-year-old girl realizes that she needs a new category for this new object, a helicopter, which cannot be assimilated to her concept of bird. If she questions her parents, they will supply a new word and explain the differences between birds and helicopters, permitting the child to create the new category.

As a result of this new knowledge, the child is temporarily in a state that Piaget calls *equilibrium,* or cognitive harmony. Piaget assumes that all organisms strive for balance in their interactions with their environment. When an individual's equilibrium is disturbed—for example, when something new and interesting is encountered—the processes of assimilation and accommodation function to reestablish it. (The process of establishing equilibrium is known as *equilibration*). The child first attempts to understand a new experience by using old ideas and solutions (assimilation); when these do not work, the child is forced to change her structure or understanding of the world (accommodation).

"This means that when a new event occurs, the organism can apply it to the lessons of the past (or assimilate the events into already existing structures) and easily modify current patterns of behavior to respond to the requirements of the new situation. With increasing experience the organism acquires more and more structures and therefore adapts more readily to an increasing number of situations" (Ginsburg & Opper, 1979, p. 24). As a result of balancing assimilation and accommodation so that neither dominates, mental activities change and cognitive development is advanced.

The processes of assimilation, accommodation, and equilibration function throughout our lives as we adapt our behavior and ideas to changing circumstances. For instance, in studying statistics, we assimilate new information to what we have already learned about mathematics and computation. At the same time, we accommodate to this information, altering our ways of interpreting and organizing quantitative data.

Although all adaptive behavior contains some elements of assimilation and accommodation, the proportions of each vary from activity to activity. According to Piaget, the make-believe play of young children is an example of behavior that is primarily assimilative because the children are not much concerned with the objective characteristics of their playthings. A piece of wood may be a doll, a ship, or a wall, depending on the game being played. By contrast, imitation is mainly accommodation, the child's actions being shaped by what others are doing, that is, by the environment (Donaldson, 1978).

Through interaction with objects and the mechanisms of assimilation, accommodation, and equilibration, children discover very abstract properties of the world that are not inherent in the objects themselves. Piaget provides an excellent example of this process.

> If a child when he is counting pebbles happens to put them in a row and to make the astonishing discovery that when he counts them from the right to the left he finds the same number as when he counts them from left to right, and again the same when he puts them in a circle. He has thus discovered experimentally that the sum (of the number of objects) is independent of the order (of the number of objects). This is a logical, mathematical experiment, not a physical one, because neither the order nor the sum was in the pebbles before he arranged them in a certain manner and joined them together in a whole. (Piaget, 1970, p. 721)

Thus, Piaget insists that some cognitive ideas, operations, and structures are universal, not because they are inherited but because all children's ordinary experiences in the world of objects and people force them to come to the same conclusions and acquire the same cognitive structures. Piaget believes that all children eventually learn to group less abstract categories like *dog* into more abstract categories like *pets* or *mammals*. All children come to realize that all categories can be taken apart into at least two smaller sets; the category animals can be separated into two smaller classes: dogs and all the animals that are not dogs. Similarly, all children come to realize that events can be ordered by their magnitude from the smallest to the largest or the lightest to the heaviest. These rules as well as a great many others develop, Piaget claims, because of the every-

day interactions that children have with objects and people, interactions that through the process of accommodation and equilibration lead to new mental structures.

PIAGET'S
DEVELOPMENTAL
STAGES

Progress in cognitive competence is assumed to be gradual and orderly during childhood, but Piaget delineated a sequence of four qualitatively distinct stages: the sensorimotor stage (0 to 18 months), the preoperational stage (18 months to 7 years), the concrete operational stage (7 to 12 years), and the formal operational stage (12 years onward). The sequence is invariable; that is, all normal children go through the stages in the same order. No child skips from the preoperational stage to the formal operational without going through the stage of concrete operations. This is because each stage builds on, and is a derivative of, the accomplishments of the previous one. At each stage, new, different, more adaptive cognitive capabilities are added to what has previously been achieved.

An underlying common structure of organization gives each stage its unity and differentiates it from other stages. Transition from one stage to the next entails a fundamental reorganization of the way the individual constructs (or reconstructs) and interprets the world. While the order in which the stages emerge does not vary, there are wide individual differences in the speed with which children pass through them. Hence, the ages associated with the stages are approximations or averages. Some children reach a particular stage early, others considerably later.

Sensorimotor stage

During the sensorimotor stage, which is described more fully in Chapter 3, cognitive growth is based on sensory and motor actions. Beginning with actions that are primarily reflex responses, the infant advances through six substages in which goal-oriented actions become increasingly prominent. In the final substage of the sensorimotor period, the child forms mental representations, can imitate past actions of others, and devises new means of solving problems by mentally combining previously acquired schemes and knowledge. In the short period of 18 months or 2 years, "the child has transformed himself from an organism almost totally dependent on reflex and other heriditary equipment to a person capable of symbolic thought" (Ginsburg & Opper, 1979, p. 83).

Preoperational stage

The *manipulation of symbols,* including words, is an essential characteristic of the preoperational stage. It is manifested in delayed imitation (reproducing an action seen in the past) and in children's imaginative or pretend play (Piaget, 1951) (see Chapter 5). A 2-year-old can imitate the marching movement or the broad jump she saw a boy performing yesterday. In play she will use an object to stand for (symbolize) another: A box may be used as a bed, table, chair, automobile, airplane, or baby carriage. She also uses toys as symbols for people and is able to take on make-believe roles herself. Consider the examples of symbolic use of words and objects in the following conversation between two 4-year-old boys:

Joe: Let's use this for a train. (*putting an empty suitcase on his bed*)
Al: Can I get on it?
Joe: Yeah. You're gonna ride on it. Sit here. (*points to one end of the suitcase*). I'm the engineer and I sit here. (*gets on the other end of the suitcase*)

Al: *(sitting at the end of the suitcase he had been assigned)* O.K. Let's go to my Grandma's house in Milwaukee.

These youngsters are already facile in using symbolic responses. And, since their knowledge of language is accelerating rapidly during this period, their ability to use symbolic representation in thinking, problem solving, and creative play will be further enhanced in the next few years.

Nevertheless, the thinking of the preoperational child is limited in several important ways. According to Piaget, it is characteristically *egocentric;* the preoperational child has difficulty imagining how things look from another person's perspective. Piaget designed a model of three mountains that has often been used to study egocentrism. His findings, and those of a later study using a different setup to assess perspective taking, are discussed in Box 7.1. Other limitations in preoperational children's thought are best understood by examining the changes that occur when they enter the stage of concrete operations.

Stage of concrete operations

Sometime between 6 and 8 years of age, children growing up in industrial societies in North America and Europe pass into the stage of concrete operations. Children from less developed or developing countries or those living in extremely isolated areas may enter this stage a few years later. The defining achievement of the stage of concrete operations is the ability to engage in mental operations (as defined earlier) that are flexible and fully reversible. Children at this stage understand certain basic logical rules (called *groupings* by Piaget) and are therefore able to reason logically and quantitatively in ways that were not evident in the preoperational stage. Children in the stage of concrete operations move freely from one point of view to another; thus, they are able to be reasonably objective in evaluating events. They are also able to *decenter,* that is, to focus their attention on several attributes of an object or event simultaneously and to understand the relations between dimensions.

Decentration and conservation   These abilities are demonstrated in Piaget's famous conservation experiments (see Figure 7.2). In one of them, conservation of liquid, the child is shown two identical glasses, both containing the same quantity of fruit juice. After the child acknowledges that both glasses have "the same amount" of juice, the investigator pours the juice from one glass into a taller, thinner glass, and the liquid rises to a higher level. The child is then asked

BOX 7.1

Can the young child take another point of view?

Of the many tasks that Piaget has made famous, one of the most popular is the "three mountains test," which was designed to assess whether a child can take the point of view of another person. In the classic version of the task, a three-dimensional scene is shown to the child. Piaget often used a model of three mountains that are distinguished by their color, the presence of a house on one mountain, and a red cross at the summit of another. The child sits on one side of the table on which the scene is placed. The experimenter then puts a small doll at some other position around the table and asks the child what the doll sees. Young children do not give a verbal description of what they see (it is hard for a child to say that the doll sees a house on top of the mountain on the right). In one version of the experiment, the child is shown some pictures of the scene, each photograph taken from a different angle, and the child has to pick the photograph of the scene as viewed by the doll. In another version, the child is given three cardboard mountains and must arrange them as they would be seen by the doll.

Children under 8 years of age usually do not perform successfully. Most children under 6 choose the photograph or build the model that corresponds to their personal view. Piaget has taken this evidence to mean that young children are egocentric and cannot imagine the perspective of some other individual. In this case, they cannot imagine the doll's perspective.

However, this conclusion contradicts a common observation of many mothers. When 3-year-olds set a table with toy teacups and a doll, they usually place the teacups in the correct orientation with respect to the doll. Further, 3-year-olds are capable of empathizing with the emotional state of another. This real-life evidence suggests that there is something wrong with Piaget's conclusion.

Margaret Donaldson (1978) has described a series of experiments by her colleagues that indicate that Piaget's conclusions are probably incorrect. In one task, two walls are set up to form a cross. Two dolls are used—one represents a policeman, and the other represents a little boy (see Figure B7.1).

Initially, the doll representing the policeman is placed on the scene so that he can see the areas that are marked B and D but cannot

FIGURE B7.1

Scenes shown to preschool children in an experiment designed to assess whether preschool children are egocentric. Children were asked whether a child standing in positions A, B, C, and D could be seen by the policeman or policemen. (From M. Donaldson. Children's minds. *New York: Norton, 1978, pp. 14–15. By permission.)*

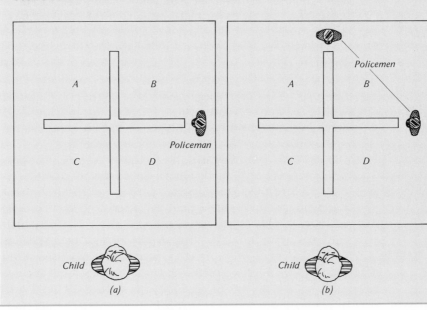

see the areas marked A and C because they are obstructed by a wall (see scene *a*). The experimenter then puts the doll representing the little boy in section A and asks, "Can the policeman see the little boy?" The question is repeated for sections B, C, and D. The policeman is then placed on the opposite side so that he can see A and C but cannot see B and D, and the child is asked to hide the little boy so that the policeman cannot see him. If the child makes any mistakes, the errors are pointed out. Very few mistakes are made.

After this introduction to the task, the test phase begins. A second policeman doll is produced, and each is put in a different position—one at the juncture of A and B and the other at the juncture of B and D, as pictured in scene *b*. The child is told to hide the boy doll so that neither policeman can see the doll. Children can perform correctly only if they can take into account the perspective of both policeman dolls. The question was repeated several times, and each time a different part of the scene was left as the only hiding place for the boy doll. For example, in scene *b* the only place the boy doll could hide would be position C.

Of children between 3½ and 5 years of age, 90 percent placed the doll correctly so that neither policeman could see it. These results indicate that very young children are capable of taking the perspective of another person. How can we reconcile Piaget's conclusions with this result?

First, in Donaldson's experiment the child merely must figure out whether a doll will be visible. There is no need to reason about left and right reversals, as the child would have to in order to, say, reconstruct the scene from the viewpoint of a policeman doll placed opposite him. Moreover, it seems likely that in this task the child understands what he is supposed to do considerably better than in Piaget's mountain task. In Donaldson's experiment, the experimenter took a great deal of care to make sure the child understood the problem. Further, children understand what it means to hide from someone, and it makes some sense that a small boy might want to hide from a policeman. As a result, children confronting the task are motivated and find it meaningful, even at only 3 years of age. Donaldson describes the situation tor the child:

> *The task makes human sense. . . . [The child] apprehends it instantly. . . . The mountains task is at the opposite extreme. Within this task itself there is no play of interpersonal motives of such a kind as to make it instantly intelligible. . . . Thus, the mountains task is abstract in a psychologically very important sense; in a sense that is abstracted from all basic human purposes and feelings and endeavors. It is totally cold-blooded. In the veins of three-year-olds, the blood still runs warm. (1978, p. 17)*

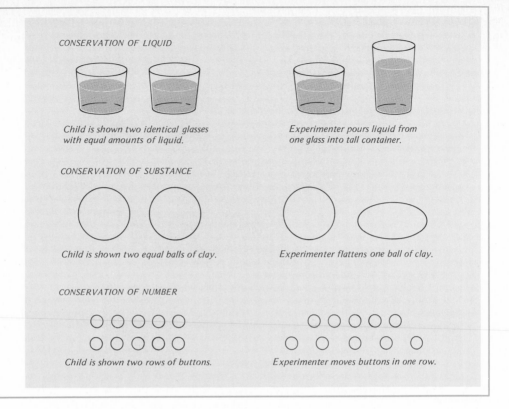

FIGURE 7.2

Illustrations of three types of conservation problems designed to measure children's concrete operational thinking.

CONSERVATION OF LIQUID

Child is shown two identical glasses with equal amounts of liquid.

Experimenter pours liquid from one glass into tall container.

CONSERVATION OF SUBSTANCE

Child is shown two equal balls of clay.

Experimenter flattens one ball of clay.

CONSERVATION OF NUMBER

Child is shown two rows of buttons.

Experimenter moves buttons in one row.

whether the taller glass contains as much, more, or less juice than the other. Preoperational children are likely to answer "more." However, children in the concrete operational stage acknowledge that the amount of liquid remains the same, that a change in one dimension—say the height of a liquid in a glass—can be compensated for by a corresponding change in another dimension—the width. Similarly, children in the concrete operational stage understand that the amount of clay in a ball does not change when its shape is changed (conservation of substance).

In a typical number-conservation experiment, one row of five buttons is lined up directly above another row of five buttons so that the two rows are of equal length. The child agrees that the two rows have the same number of buttons. If, however, one row is shortened by pushing the buttons closer together, the preoperational child is likely to say that the longer row has more buttons. The concrete operational child knows that the rearrangement of buttons does not change their number.

According to Piaget, concrete operational children understand conservation problems because they can perform reversible mental operations (if you poured the liquid back into the short, wide glass, it would again reach the same level as the water in the other short, wide glass) and because they understand two important logical principles. The first, called the identity or equivalence principle, states that if A is equal to B in some attribute (say, length), and B is

equal to C, then it must be true that A is equal to C. One does not have to measure A and C to know that this is true. The second principle is that objects and events have more than one dimension, for example, weight and size, and these dimensions may exist in different relationships. The child knows that a pebble is both small and light, a bowling ball is small and heavy, a balloon may be large although it is light, and a car is large and heavy. Preoperational children pay attention to only one feature of an event at a time (*centration* in thinking)—the height of a glass of water but not the width, for instance. These children do not consider two dimensions simultaneously and thus ignore all but one relevant feature of the conservation task.

Seriation Another characteristic of the concrete operational stage is the ability to arrange objects according to some quantified dimensions such as weight or size. This ability is called *seriation*. An 8-year-old can arrange eight sticks of different lengths in order from shortest to longest. Seriation illustrates the child's grasp of another important logical principle, called transitivity, which states that there are certain fixed relations among the qualities of objects. For example, if A is longer than B, and B is longer than C, then it must be true that A is longer than C. Children in the stage of concrete operations know the validity of that rule even if they have never seen the objects A, B, and C. The competence Piaget calls seriation is critical to understanding the relation of numbers to one another and therefore to the learning of arithmetic.

Relational thinking The concrete operational child appreciates that many terms, such as *taller, shorter,* and *darker,* refer to relationships rather than to absolute qualities. Younger children think in absolute terms and interpret *darker* as meaning "very dark" rather than "darker than another object." If they are shown two light objects, one of which is slightly darker, and are asked to pick the darker one, they may not answer or they may say neither one is darker. Relational thinking is another illustration of the ability to consider more than one event simultaneously because it requires comparison of two or more objects.

Class inclusion The concrete operational child can reason simultaneously about parts and wholes. If an 8-year-old is shown eight yellow candies and four brown candies and is asked, "Are there more yellow candies or more candies?" the child will say there are more candies. However, a 5-year-old given the same problem is likely to say "more yellow candies." This reply, Piaget believed, reflects the younger child's inability to reason about a part and the whole simultaneously.

A child's understanding of class inclusion illustrates the logical principle that there are hierarchical relations among categories. The concrete operational child appreciates that some sets of categories nest or fit into each other. For example, all oranges belong to the category *fruits,* all fruits belong to the category *foods,* and all foods belong to the larger category *edible things.* Moreover, the child can perform an operation and mentally take apart every category of objects and put them back together. The class of foods, therefore, consists of all edible things that are fruits and all of the edible things that are not fruits. Second, the concrete operational child realizes that specific qualities of objects can belong to more than one category or more than one relationship at any one time, a principle called the multiplication of classes or relations. Children appreciate that bananas can belong simultaneously to the category of natural foods and the category of sweet foods, while bread can belong to the category of manufactured foods and the category of starchy foods.

Although operational children have advanced beyond those at the preoperational stage in reasoning, problem solving, and logic, their thinking is still restricted to the here and now of concrete operations. At this stage, children conserve quantity and number and can order and classify real objects and things. But they cannot reason about abstractions, hypothetical propositions, or imaginary events. Further, although they can arrange a series of boxes in order of size, they have difficulty solving abstract verbal problems such as "Edith is taller than Susan. Lily is shorter than Susan. Who is tallest?"

Stage of formal operations In the most advanced stage of cognitive development, which begins at about age 12 and extends through adulthood, the limitations of the concrete operational stage are overcome. The individual uses a wider variety of cognitive operations and strategies in solving problems, is highly versatile and flexible in thought and reasoning, and can see things from a number of perspectives or points of view (Ginsburg & Opper, 1979). The thinking of adolescents is more complex than that of preadolescents, and the range of their intellectual capabilities and activities is much greater.

One of the most striking features of this stage is the development of the

ability to *reason about hypothetical problems*—what *might* be—as well as real ones, and to think about *possibilities* as well as actualities. The concrete operational child mentally manipulates objects and events; in the stage of formal operations, the child can manipulate ideas about *hypothetical* situations. For example, an older child can reach a logical conclusion when asked, "If all Martians have yellow feet and this creature has yellow feet, is it a Martian?" A 7-year-old has difficulty reasoning about improbable or impossible events and is likely to say, "I don't know," or "Things don't have yellow feet."

Another hallmark of problem solving in the stage of formal operations is the *systematic search for solutions*. Faced with a novel problem, an adolescent attempts to consider all possible means of solving it and carefully checks the logic and effectiveness of each one. Planning to drive to the seashore, adolescents can mentally review all the possible routes, systematically assessing which is safest, shortest, and fastest (though they may not always employ this competence in a specific instance).

In formal operational thought, mental operations are *organized into higher-order operations*. Higher-order operations are ways of using abstract rules to solve a whole class of problems. For example, in solving the problem "What number is 30 less than 2 times itself?" concrete operational children are likely to try first one number and then another, using addition and multiplication until they finally arrive at the correct answer. An adolescent combines the separate operations of addition and multiplication into one, more complex operation of an algebraic equation, $x = 2x - 30$, and quickly finds the answer, 30.

During the stage of formal operations, individuals *think about their own thoughts*, evaluating them and searching for inconsistencies and fallacies in logic. A 14-year-old may brood about the following two propositions:

1. God loves humanity.
2. There are many suffering human beings.

These two beliefs seem incompatible and spur the adolescent to look for ways of resolving the tension created by the inconsistency.

In Piaget's investigations of formal operations, conducted in collaboration with his longtime colleague, Barbel Inhelder, children were asked to solve a variety of logical and scientific problems. The problems called for conclusions about the behavior of floating objects, oscillating pendulums, balance beams, and chemical mixtures. For example, in one experiment, children were given five bottles of colorless liquids and instructed to find a way of combining them that would produce a yellow liquid. In attempting to solve this problem, children in the stage of concrete operations use a trial-and-error approach, trying out a number of solutions, generally in an inefficient way. They often test each chemical individually with one or two others but fail to consider all possible combinations. In contrast, adolescents act more like adult scientists or logicians, considering all possible solutions in an exhaustive way, formulating hypotheses about outcomes, and systematically designing tests of the hypotheses. They try all possible combinations of chemicals and draw accurate conclusions through deductive, logical reasoning.

The characteristics of formal operational thinking are also apparent in the preoccupation of many adolescents with theoretical and abstract matters of all sorts—philosophical and political issues such as justice and individual freedom; beauty and aesthetics; religion and moral ideologies. Many adolescents seem to examine and evaluate everything, including their own knowledge, thoughts, ideas, and ways of solving problems. They generate their own theories and question their own integrity, attitudes, and beliefs, searching for consistency and for new values and philosophies of life. Acute concern with "phoniness of ideals" and serious contemplation of the future are adolescent phenomena, rarely seen in children under 10 years of age. Piaget believed that preoccupation with thought is one of the principal manifestations of the stage of formal operations.

Evaluation of Piagetian theory and research

No one has had a greater impact on the field of cognitive development than Piaget. He was a major force in replacing the traditional view of the child as a passive recipient of experience, molded by external forces, with the conception that, from the outset, the child is an active seeker of stimulation, interpreting the world and generating cognitive solutions to problems. By focusing on cognitive *processes*, rather than on factual knowledge, Piaget stimulated psychological research on how knowledge is acquired and how thoughts originate and change. Many of the cardinal concepts of Piaget's theories are accepted by virtually all psychologists—for example, the interactional point of view that cognitive process depends on both maturation and active contact with the world. Nevertheless, many contemporary theorists are critical of some aspects of Piaget's theory and his conclusions about the development of children's abilities.

Basic assumptions   Piaget believed that logical principles provide the basis for mature and effective thought and action. John Locke, in contrast, maintained that a person's most certain knowledge was based on intuitions from perceptual experiences, sources that Piaget regarded as unreliable and characteristic of the less mature child. Some scientists and philosophers dispute Piaget's assumption that knowledge is acquired primarily through active interaction with objects and people. They argue that many of the child's ideas are learned by observation, perception, and reasoning rather than action and, as we have seen, that many cognitive competences develop despite minimal interactions with people or objects.

An important criticism concerns Piaget's assumption that in all cultures children and adolescents learn to apply the rules of Western logic in order to adapt effectively to their environment. This idea is controversial because some cultures use specific logical principles that are not part of Western logic. For example, in Western logic the affirmative statement "The sky is blue" is equivalent in meaning to a double negative, "It is not true that the sky is not blue." Yet in the logical system used in one form of Indian philosophy, these two statements do not have the same meaning.

The concept of stages   The concept of qualitatively different, discontinuous stages of cognitive development is also controversial, as we discussed in Chapter 1. Some investigators think their findings indicate stagelike changes in cognitive functions (Brainerd, 1973b; Neimark, 1975), while others have concluded that "discontinuous and/or abrupt changes in cognitive development,

. . . especially in late childhood and beyond, are difficult to demonstrate convincingly. . . . The cumulative evidence to date on adolescent cognitive development leaves a strong impression of continuous, quantitative, and multidimensional growth and ability. . . . Current evidence for stages is deficient . . ." (Keating, 1980, p. 231).

Furthermore, Piaget and his coworkers have not provided adequate explanations of how children make the transitions from one level of competence to the next. Fundamental concepts such as assimilation, accommodation, and equilibration are not sufficiently precise or detailed to explain *how* particular capabilities—for example, generating mental representations and understanding conservation—are attained.

Egocentrism   Many recent research findings challenge some of Piaget's conclusions about the cognitive powers of preschool children. According to Piaget, preoperational children are *egocentric*, interpreting things only from their own viewpoint, and are unable to adopt others' perspectives or take their needs and capacities into account. As indicated in Box 7.1, however, some recent findings contradict Piaget's. One authority concludes that "there is a clear case for the position that the preschooler can and does take the perspective of others into account. . . . It no longer seems appropriate to characterize the thought of preschoolers as egocentric" (Gelman, 1978, p. 319). For example, as mentioned earlier, 4-year-olds adapt their speech—both what they say and how they say it—to the capacities of their listeners, talking to 2-year-olds in shorter, simpler sentences than they use when addressing peers or adults (Shatz & Gelman, 1973). Most 2½- and 3-year-olds are also able to adopt someone else's perspective in some situations. Children of this age were handed black-and-white photographs of familiar objects one at a time, the face side of the photograph toward them. They were then asked to show the pictures to their mothers, who were seated across a table from them. An egocentric child, unable to understand the mother's perspective, would be expected to show the mother the back of the picture. In fact, all the children turned the fronts of the pictures toward their mothers. This can hardly be considered an egocentric response (Lempers, Flavell, & Flavell, 1977).

Piaget's assertion that children in the preoperational stage do not achieve success in tasks involving conservation, class inclusion, classification, and seriation has also been questioned. Box 7.2 summarizes a number of studies that indicate that the young children do use these operations under certain conditions.

Formal operations   Many psychologists have also questioned Piaget's claim that formal operational thinking and problem solving are universal among normal adolescents and adults. It has been pointed out, for example, that formal operations are seldom used in some nonliterate societies, although it hardly seems possible that any culture could survive without some reasoning about hypothetical situations or abstract propositions. Many adolescents in Western culture apparently have great difficulty solving problems involving abstract logical thinking: Between 40 and 60 percent of college students and adults are unsuccessful in such tasks (King, 1977; Neimark, 1975).

Logical operations   Most of the tests Piaget used in assessing formal opera-

BOX 7.2

Preschool children's operational abilities

Piaget and his research associates conducted many experiments to measure such cognitive operations as *conservation, class inclusion,* and *seriation (transitivity).* According to their findings, these operations are part of the cognitive armamentarium of the child in the stage of concrete operations, but younger (preoperational) children do not grasp them. However, the results of many recent studies indicate that Piaget and his coworkers considerably underestimated or minimized the young child's cognitive competence. As the following examples demonstrate, preschool children can and do use concrete operations.

Number conservation In a replication of one of Piaget's number tasks, an investigator showed children two rows of equal length, each containing five buttons. When he shortened or lengthened one of the rows by arranging the buttons, he found, as Piaget did, that few children (16 percent) between 4 and 6 years of age showed that they understood number conservation (McGarrigle reported in Donaldson, 1978). However, the investigator shortly afterward introduced Naughty Teddy, a mischievous teddy bear that could come out of his box and "mess things up." After Naughty Teddy moved the buttons closer together, most of the children (63 percent) argued that the number of objects had not changed. Under these circumstances, preoperational children demonstrated that they understood number conservation.

In another study, Gelman (1972) showed 3-year-olds two identical plates. One had two small objects on it—for example, two tiny cups—and the other had three objects. After telling the child that one plate was the winner and the other the loser, she covered each with a can. After shuffling the cans around, the examiner asked the child to choose the winner, uncover the display, and tell whether she had chosen correctly. After the child understood the game, the examiner secretly changed one of the displays by adding or subtracting objects or by substituting different colors or even types of objects. When children confronted a changed number of objects—more or fewer—they recognized the change immediately and commented on it. They also recognized changes in type or color of objects and insisted that these changes did not change the number of objects (Gelman, 1972, 1979). Under these circumstances, too, preoperational children showed conservation of number.

Class inclusion In one of Piaget's tests, the child is presented with a bouquet of flowers consisting of four red flowers and two white ones and is asked if there are "more red flowers" or "more flowers." Preoperational children usually answered that there were more red flowers, a response Piaget attributed to the children's inability to decenter, to think simultaneously of a subclass and a whole class.

Is this really the case, or does the child simply misinterpret the question? One investigator showed 6-year-olds four toy cows, three of them black and one of them white. All the cows were laid on their sides, and it was explained that they were sleeping. Two questions were asked: the standard Piagetian question, "Are there more black cows or more cows?" and "Are there more black cows or more sleeping cows?" The investigator argued that the introduction of the adjective *sleeping* would increase the emphasis on the whole class. The hunch was correct. The first question was answered correctly by only 25 percent of the group, while the second question was answered correctly by half the group. In other words, a simple rephrasing of the question enabled many young children to perform class-inclusion tasks successfully (McGarrigle in Donaldson, 1978).

Seriation   Piaget found that preoperational children could not perform seriation or transitivity tasks adequately, but others have shown that, with a little training, preschool children learn to use a rule of transitivity correctly. One investigator read the following premises to 4- and 5-year-olds:

1.   Peter is the same size as David.
2.   David is bigger than you.
3.   You are the same size as John.

The children were then asked, "Is Peter bigger than John?" If the children heard the premises only once, they typically answered incorrectly. But if the premises were repeated until the children had memorized them, three-fourths of the group made the correct inference. Clearly, memory makes an important contribution to the solution of transitivity problems (Trabasso, 1975).

Ingenious investigators have been able to demonstrate that preschool children can use concrete operations by presenting them with tasks that avoided language that might be confusing to a young child or by making sure that other abilities, such as memory, were not hindering children's use of their logical-thinking competencies. In standard measures of number conservation, children are asked whether there are more, fewer, or the same number of objects. Preschool children may not fully understand the words *more* and *same*. When the tasks did not require these verbal responses, or when a meaningful context was provided (Naughty Teddy), young children demonstrated competence in number conservation. In the class-inclusion task, the wording of the original question, "Are there more black cows or more cows?" was apparently confusing. A slight change reduced the confusion and enabled young children to demonstrate that they understood that one class can be a component of another.

tions dealt with traditional scientific and laboratory experiments that most people regard as abstract and isolated from everyday experience. We are much more likely to reason logically about problems (whether concrete or abstract) in our own field of study or interest than about problems in other domains (De Lisi & Staudt, 1980; Falmagne, 1980). The quality of adolescent and adult reasoning apparently varies from problem to problem; this leads us to question Piaget's notion that adolescents and adults possess a broad underlying logical competence or reasoning ability that is generally applied in all problem-solving situations (Flavell, 1977).

Finally, some psychologists feel that Piaget's emphasis on the importance of reversibility, class inclusion, and operations is most relevant to mathematics and physics and less obviously relevant to many natural phenomena that do not show reversibility or obey class-inclusion rules. The relation between the whole and its parts in mathematics is not applicable to living things or the behavior of people; the concept of a crowd is more than the sum of the number of people in the crowd.

Despite these criticisms, Piaget's observations of the sequences in cognitive development seem to be essentially correct. But there is honest controversy over the best way to explain the developmental changes in thought that Piaget and his colleagues have documented. Regardless of the results of future research, it is obvious that Piaget's contributions have been epochal and his influence on developmental psychology without parallel.

INFORMATION-
PROCESSING
APPROACHES

Many psychologists, especially in the United States, use an information-processing approach to understand how the child interprets, stores, retrieves, and evaluates information. In contrast to Piaget and his followers, these psychologists do not have a single, comprehensive theory guiding their research. They focus on understanding specific processes such as perception, memory, inference, evaluation of information, and the use of rules. They also emphasize a wider variety of developmental changes than those stressed by Piaget.

First, they are interested in how children acquire factual knowledge as they mature and how they come to relate different facts to one another. A child learns that the moon is round, circles the earth, is lit by the sun, and is only visible on some nights. He also relates these separate facts to each other and thus comes to understand that the moon's relation to the earth and to the sun determines how much of it is visible on a given night.

Second, these psychologists are interested in how a wide range of cognitive processes change. Children become more planful, better able to monitor their own cognitive performances, and better aware of what they know and do not know. Third, like Piaget, information-processing psychologists are concerned with children's capacity to relate and operate on more units of information simultaneously with increasing age.

The mechanisms that mediate these developmental changes include reinforcement, maturation of the central nervous system, and continuous reorganization of children's knowledge. As noted in Chapter 3, the effects of reinforcement have been observed for many years, but the reasons for these effects are complex. In the framework of information processing, the mechanism of reinforcement is based on the principle that the feedback children receive from successful and unsuccessful solutions leads to a reorganization of their knowledge and changes in their problem-solving behavior. The mechanism of maturation assumes that growth of parts of the brain permits new cognitive talents to emerge: For example, the ability to operate simultaneously on several pieces of information seems to be a derivative of the maturation of the central nervous system.

Finally, the child's mind seems to be continually working on its store of knowledge. As one domain is made more coherent, the mind seems to become freed to work on other areas not yet organized. For example, as a 7-year-old child consolidates the fact that quantity of mass is conserved, regardless of changes in form or appearance, she is free to think about the conservation of volume.

It is helpful to regard cognitive functioning as composed of different processes working on different units of knowledge much as each musician in an orchestra acts in a different way on a particular instrument. Because each cognitive process is selectively associated with certain kinds of knowledge units, we shall organize the discussion around the major cognitive processes.

Perception   Perception can be defined as the detection, recognition, and interpretation of sensory stimuli. A child looks out the window and sees a pattern of light, dark, and colors. From this mosaic the child extracts information; the pattern is perceived as a street scene including people, cars, trees, and buildings. The difference between sensory stimulation on the one hand and information on the other can be appreciated by comparing a scene in a meadow registered by a moving camera and a person. While the camera registers all the colors, shadows, lines, and objects in one plane of the scene, the human being organizes the scene, selecting certain aspects and ignoring the others. The person may make a bright red flower the central element and see the trees merely as background. But the roving camera plays no favorites: All elements emerge as equally important. Furthermore, people relate what they see both to what they saw a few minutes ago and to what they may see in the future—they integrate successive exposures. If a child sees a tree branch move on a windless day, she realizes it cannot be the wind that is moving it and infers from her experience that it must be an animal. As a result, she begins to scan the area for signs of an animal.

The schema   A major cognitive unit involved in perception is the *schema*. A schema is neither an image nor a photographic copy of an event but an abstract representation of the event's distinctive dimensions, as explained in Chapter 3. Like a cartoonist's caricature, it preserves the most essential aspects of the event in a unique pattern. The meaning of a schema is illustrated through a simple exercise. Look out the window for a few seconds, turn away, and then ask a friend to look out the window and name some objects that appear in the scene outside and some that do not. You will be able to tell the friend whether each object named is or is not present in the scene about 90 percent of the time. You can do this because your brief glance at the scene generated a schema for it.

Young children have a remarkable capacity to create and store schemata. Two-year-olds have schemata for many objects in their homes (Ratner & Myers, 1981). For slightly older children, a single glance at a photograph of a totally unfamiliar object or scene can be sufficient to create a schema for it. If 4-year-old research subjects are shown 60 pictures cut from magazines, they typically look at each picture for about 2 seconds. The next day each child is shown 120 pictures, the 60 seen the previous day and 60 new pictures, and is asked to point out the pictures seen on the previous day. The average 4-year-old child will be correct 80 percent of the time. Similarly, when Mayan children 6 to 7 years old who have never seen a telescope or a typewriter are shown color photographs of these objects, a day later they can select them from a long series that includes some photographs they have never seen.

Children's schemata for scenes can contain information about all the objects in the scene and the detailed characteristics of those objects, as well as their relative positions and orientations. In general, children remember best the objects and the spatial relations of the objects to each other but are less accurate in recognizing the detailed properties of those objects (Mandler, 1983). This evidence suggests that the children's schemata for the detailed properties of objects are less well articulated than their schemata for the objects themselves.

According to Gibson (Gibson & Spelke, 1983), all members of a certain category of events share some common qualities and have other qualities that only some members of the category share. All cars have four wheels, doors, and an engine—these are shared, unchanging elements—but cars vary in color, shape, and design—the changing elements. The pattern of unchanging elements forms the basis for the schema. It permits children to recognize an event encountered in the past, even if the event is presented in a very novel way. In one experiment, 10 small luminous points were attached to the limb joints of a person who was filmed in near darkness while he was walking, running, or dancing (Johansson, 1978). The film recorded the group of 10 bright dots, each moving in its own path. Surprisingly, after an exposure as brief as $\frac{1}{5}$ second, schoolchildren perceived a moving person and not a swarm of dots. They were able to do this because they had extracted from past experience a schema representing the unchanging pattern of stimulus elements that occurs when a person is moving.

A major controversy surrounding the nature of a schema is whether the person creates an idealized "average" schema based on all prior exposures to a class of events or whether the mind holds separate schemata for all the exemplars experienced, even though it extracts the dimensions common to all. Support for the idea that children create an abstract average of their experiences that they use to recognize new events is seen in a 5-year-old's ability to recognize a drawing made by an adult but drawn in the child's distinctive style. Four- and 5-year-olds were asked to draw four objects on separate pieces of paper—a man, a flower, a tree, and a bird. An artist then examined the four drawings made by each child and drew two pictures the children had not drawn before—a dog and a house—in each child's unique style (see Figure 7.3). Each child was then shown four drawings, three in the style of other children and one made in the child's own style. Many 5-year-olds were able to select the drawing that was constructed in their style, suggesting that they had developed a schema for it by observing their own previous drawings (Nolan & Kagan, 1980).

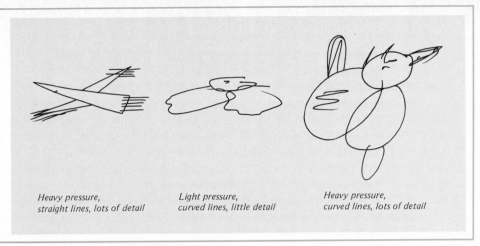

FIGURE 7.3

Styles of drawings of a bird by 5-year-old children, based on different pressures, curved or straight lines, and amount of detail. Children were able to recognize other drawings made in their own styles. (From E. Nolan and J. Kagan. Recognition of self and self's products in pre-school children. **Journal of Genetic Psychology,** 1980, 137, 285–294.)

Heavy pressure, straight lines, lots of detail

Light pressure, curved lines, little detail

Heavy pressure, curved lines, lots of detail

Selection as basic to perception Growing children learn to focus on the most informative aspects of objects and scenes and to ignore the uninformative. They learn to fix their attention on their mother's eyes and voice to detect the parent's mood or search for the presence of a plus or minus sign beside two rows of numbers in order to determine whether they should add or subtract them. Children also learn *where* to search for the information most relevant to the problem they are solving or the goals they wish to attain. The perceived events consist of patterns of light, sound, pressure, and smell, for more than one sensory modality is often used in the perception of a single event.

The specific dimensions used to distinguish one event from another depend on the question the perceiver is trying to answer and the expectations or mental set he has for a particular situation. A boy in the forest who sees a moving object wonders whether it is a bear or a man and searches for a critical feature, like clothing or fur. But the same boy, on a dark street in a large city, hearing footsteps behind him, would expect that the source of the sound was a man, a woman, or a child—it is unlikely to be a bear. Now the presence of clothes would not be critical, and in the dark the child would probably search for differences in the sound of the footsteps. The specific problem children are trying to solve generates a mental set, which in turn sensitizes them to attend to and interpret certain dimensions.

The role of selection and mental set in perception is exemplified by a procedure used by neurologists, called the "face-hands test." The child, whose eyes are closed, is touched simultaneously on one cheek (say, the right) and on the opposite hand (the left). The examiner asks the child to indicate where she was touched. Typically, children under 6 years of age report that they were touched on the face and fail to acknowledge that their hand was also stimulated. Some neurologists assume that this failure indicates an immaturity of the central nervous system that causes sensations from the face to block sensations from the hand. But research findings suggest that the younger child's failure to mention the hand is due to a mental set that led her to expect she would only be touched in one place. If, before the test question, the examiner says, "Sometimes I'm going to touch you only on the cheek, sometimes I'm going to touch you only on the hand, and sometimes I'm going to try to fool you and touch you in two places," the young child reports accurately being touched on both the hand and the cheek. Simply preparing the young child for the possibility of two loci of stimulation changes the pattern of performance completely (Nolan & Kagan, 1978).

Memory   Psychologists distinguish among three types of memory. *Sensory memory* is very brief. If a picture or a sound experienced briefly is not stored or in some way related to existing knowledge within about a second, the information vanishes.

Information in *short-term memory* is available for a maximum of about 30 seconds, usually less. A stranger's name and address stays in short-term memory for about half a minute. If the information is not rehearsed (repeated, silently or aloud) or placed into long-term memory, it will be forgotten. *Long-term memory* refers to knowledge that is potentially available for a long time, perhaps forever. Some psychologists believe that information in short-term memory is transferred to long-term memory through a process of association that links the new material to units already stored in long-term memory. If the incoming information is not associated with existing knowledge, it will not be transferred to long-term memory.

Another basic distinction in memory studies is between recall and recognition. In studies of *recognition,* children are shown a set of pictures or objects, some of which they have seen before, and asked to identify the ones they have seen. Several studies of this type were described in our discussion of perception. In studies of *recall,* children are asked to retrieve all the necessary information: "How many of the things I showed you this morning can you name?"

At all ages, recognition memory is much better than recall memory, but the difference is more pronounced in younger than in older children. A 10-year-old who has been shown a group of 12 pictures can usually recall about 8 of them but can recognize all 12, even if they are included in a much larger set of photographs. A 4-year-old also recognizes all 12 pictures but is able to recall 2 or at most 3. The difference between children and adults is also greater for recall than for recognition memory.

One reason for the poor recall memories of young children may be that they use fewer different types of cognitive units when storing memories than adults do. One of the earliest cognitive units used to represent events is the schema, as explained in Chapter 3. Another early cognitive unit is the image.

Images   Each person's subjective experience provides commanding support for the existence of images, and laboratory data, too, suggest that thoughts and memories sometimes take the form of mental pictures. In one experiment, fourth-grade children and adults were first told the name of an animal; for example, the examiner told the subject to think of cats. The examiner then named a part that could belong to an animal, and the subject had to decide if the part named did or did not belong to cats. Sometimes the part named was a very small but distinctive characteristic of that particular animal (for example, the claws of a cat or the beak of a bird). Sometimes the examiner named a larger part but one that was not a distinctive characteristic (for example, the body of a cat or the tail of a dinosaur). When the subjects were instructed to use imagery to answer the examiner's question, they took longer to decide that the small, distinctive part belonged to the animal than that a large, less distinctive part did. But when they were told specifically not to use imagery in arriving at an answer, both children and adults responded more quickly for the smaller, distinctive part than for the larger, less distinctive one (see Figure 7.4). This study shows that children and adults use images in solving problems.

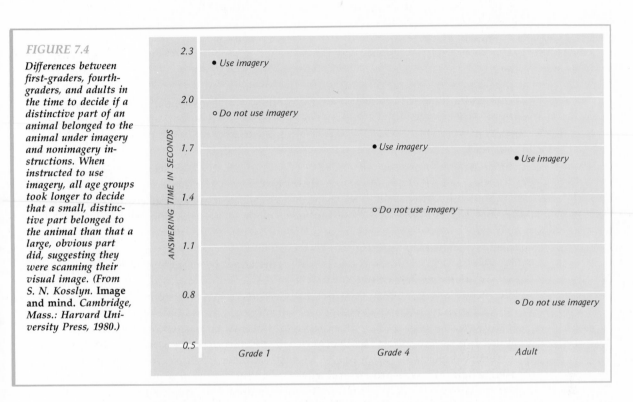

FIGURE 7.4

Differences between first-graders, fourth-graders, and adults in the time to decide if a distinctive part of an animal belonged to the animal under imagery and nonimagery instructions. When instructed to use imagery, all age groups took longer to decide that a small, distinctive part belonged to the animal than that a large, obvious part did, suggesting they were scanning their visual image. (From S. N. Kosslyn. **Image and mind.** *Cambridge, Mass.: Harvard University Press, 1980.)*

Under everyday circumstances, a child's decision to use imagery in recalling information to solve a problem depends on whether that information has become part of a child's conceptual knowledge. Information that is not yet firmly integrated into the child's conceptual knowledge is apt to be recalled by means of images. Because knowledge becomes more conceptual with development, one would expect older children to rely on imagery less often than younger children in many problem situations.

Symbolic concepts A symbolic concept differs from both a schema and an image because the latter two units are faithful to the physical aspects of the event they represent. By contrast, a symbolic concept represents experience more arbitrarily. There is nothing inherent in the word *food,* written or spoken, that suggests that it stands for things that are edible and nutritious.

A symbolic concept is a representation of the qualities that are shared by a set of related but discriminably different events. The concept *food* does not represent any one edible object; it stands for the qualities of being edible and nutritious. Although a concept need not have a word associated with it (children possess a concept of sympathy that they may not be able to describe in words), many concepts do have specific words that name them. In addition, a concept can refer to private feelings and ideas and therefore need not be observable. Examples include the concepts of pleasure, fun, and sadness.

Developmental changes in concepts With development, children's symbolic concepts change in three respects. First, the dimensions that define the concept come to match those that most adults agree are critical. To a 2-year-old, the concept *dog* may stand for a set of stuffed animals he owns. By 5 years of age, most children understand that the concept *dog* refers to animals that live on farms, in houses, or in apartments and have certain sizes and shapes and make barking sounds.

Second, symbolic concepts become more readily available for use in thought. A 3-year-old's concept of *hour* or *day* is much vaguer than that of an 8- or 10-year-old; hence, the younger child does not appreciate how long she will have to wait when her mother says she will be back in an hour. Third, children become better able to describe their symbolic concepts in words. A 4-year-old cannot say very much about his understanding of the concept *love*, although he knows it has to do with a close relationship between people. A 15-year-old can write a 1000-word essay on love, because the attributes have become linked to language and differentiated from similar concepts like attraction, friendship, and loyalty.

Concepts are not static units of knowledge; they are dynamic and constantly changing. The child's mind is continually transforming its conceptual knowledge and, without conscious effort, detecting dimensions shared by two ideas that were originally separate and unrelated. An example of this active use of mind appears in a diary in which a psychologist recorded the speech development of her daughter. At 2 years of age, the girl used the words *put* and *give* correctly. A year later, she began to make occasional errors in which *put* was used when *give* was proper and vice versa. She said "You put me bread and butter" instead of "You give me bread and butter" and "Give some ice in here" instead of "Put some ice in here." It seemed that the two words became closer in meaning. As a result of recognizing this shared dimension, she began to make substitution errors. It is unlikely that the child was taught the shared dimension or was even conscious of it. Rather, she detected it unconsciously as her mind continually worked on its knowledge base (Bowerman, 1978).

As children's understanding of concepts changes, so does the frequency with which particular concepts are used in thought. Children 5, 7, and 10 years old were administered a series of tasks designed to assess their understanding of the concept *living thing* and their tendency to use the concept in a particular problem situation. First, the children were asked to name as many things as they could that were living things. Because all children named some living things, they possessed the concept to some degree (see Figure 7.5). But in a second procedure, the children were asked to remember a list of 20 words that contained 5 words from each of 4 categories mixed together. One of the categories was living things. If the category *living things* was activated, then it was

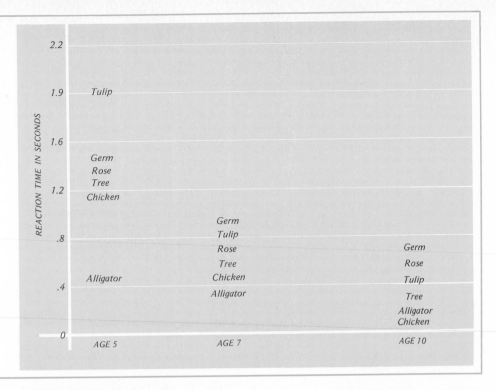

FIGURE 7.5

The time required by 5-year-olds, 7-year-olds, and 10-year-olds to decide if a particular animal or plant belonged to the category living things. *All age groups possessed the category.* (From K. R. Livingston. The organization of children's concepts. Unpublished doctoral dissertation, Harvard University, 1977.)

REACTION TIME IN SECONDS

2.2

1.9   Tulip

1.6

       Germ
       Rose
       Tree
1.2   Chicken

                          Germ
                          Tulip
 .8   Rose   Germ

                          Tree   Rose
       Alligator   Chicken   Tulip
 .4
                          Alligator   Tree
                                                  Alligator
                                                  Chicken
  0
       AGE 5   AGE 7   AGE 10

expected that children would put the words for living things together in their oral recall even though they did not hear them together. Surprisingly, most of the children did not put the words for living things together when they recalled the list of 20 words. Their failure to do so suggests that they did not use the concept they possessed—an actual competence—on this test procedure (Livingston 1977). Because adults in the same situation would have recalled the words for living things together, it is reasonable to conclude that the concept *living thing* is less available for use in the performance of young children.

Working memory   Some psychologists have suggested that the speed with which cognitive units or knowledge can be retrieved from long-term memory improves with age, making it possible for older children to integrate more old and new information during the process that is called *working memory*. Short-term memory lasts about 30 seconds; the more information a person can retrieve from long-term memory in that time, the more transformations he can perform during the approximately 30 seconds when old and new information are available simultaneously in working memory. A larger working-memory capacity makes it possible to solve more complex problems.

Pascual-Leone (1970) believes that, with development, there is growth in the ability to hold information in working memory, which he calls an M space. One can regard an M space as similar to the number of discrete factual units of information (schemata, images, or concepts) that can be operated on in working memory simultaneously. A 3-year-old can deal with one unit of information, a 15-year-old with seven units of information. In an experimental test of this idea, he asked children of different ages to learn different motor responses to different visual stimuli. For example, the children had to clap their hands when they saw the color red but open their mouths when they saw a large cup. Once the children learned these simple associations, they were then presented with two or more visual stimuli simultaneously and had to respond appropriately. The number of correct responses a child could perform corresponds to the maximum number of schemes the child can integrate in her M space. The number of separate acts that could be performed correctly did increase as a function of age among preschool and school-age children, confirming the idea of a larger M space with development.

Metamemory Recall memory also improves with age because of children's growing awareness of what is required to remember information and an increasing ability to assess their own memory capacities (Flavell & Wellman, 1977; Kreutzer, Leonard, & Flavell, 1975). Children's knowledge about memory processes is called *metamemory*. Young children do not always appreciate the strategies and cognitive processes that are required to remember information. When kindergartners were asked, "If you wanted to phone your friend and someone told you the phone number, would it make any difference if you called right away after you heard the number or if you got a drink of water first?" they were just as likely to say they would first get a drink as to phone immediately. By contrast, fifth-graders knew that they could remember the telephone number for only a brief period of time and therefore said they would make the telephone call at once.

In general, children overestimate their ability to recall information but underestimate their ability to recognize something that happened in the past (Yussen & Berman, 1981). As children get older, their predictions of their recall memory become more accurate estimates of their actual performance.

Strategies Performance on memory tests is also affected by *strategies* used during the storage and retrieval of information. These strategies include the organization, elaboration, and rehearsal of information while it is being stored and the systematic search for material being retrieved. With development, children use these strategies more often and more effectively. For example, when asked, "What did you do yesterday?" adults are more likely than children to search their representation of the previous day in a systematic way, beginning in the morning and proceeding mentally through the rest of the day. Children are apt to be more haphazard in retrieving information.

A study of a group of rural Costa Rican 9-year-olds shows that children can improve their recall memory with training in memory strategies. Some of the children were explicitly taught a set of five strategies to aid recall memory. These included *rehearsal* (repeating the names of pictures as each was shown), *association* (linking the pictures, words, or objects in some way), *clustering* (grouping items into categories), *detecting patterns of organization* (for example, noting increasing sizes of items in a row), and *counting* (for example, assigning numbers to sticks of different lengths). One year after training, these children showed a significant memory gain on six different tasks. When compared to an untrained control group, children who had learned strategies were especially good at difficult memory tasks requiring complicated strategies.

Motivation to recall information can produce improvements in memory, partly because it induces children to produce their own strategies. A second group in the study just described was given training in which they were encouraged to try as hard as they could so that they could get a prize. When tested a year later, children who received motivation training performed almost as well as the group that was trained in specific memory strategies (Sellers, 1979).

In conclusion, developmental changes in children's memory performance are influenced by changes in conceptual knowledge, the capacity of working memory, metamemory, and the ability to use strategies. In addition, two influences on recall memory lie outside the child: the nature of the information to be learned and remembered and the requirements of the problem (Brown, 1983). Some children are good at remembering words but poor at remembering geometric patterns. Further, some children can remember the theme of a story but very few of the exact words, while others are better at remembering the exact words than the theme.

Inference
Inference is a process by which cognitive units in working memory are organized according to categories and rules. Inferences permit anticipation of the future and interpretation of the past because they go beyond the information given to generate hypotheses or expectations about other events that might have occurred or might be expected to occur. A 3-year-old's question to his mother is illustrative. "Where does the sun go when it goes into the ground at night?" The child's experience has taught him that all objects that move have a resting place, permanent or temporary. Because the sun appears to be an object that moves, the child infers that it, too, must have a place to rest.

Inferences are based on a perceived similarity between two events. With development, the conditions unique to a particular environment lead some older children to perceive similarities that might be ignored by those growing up in other places. For example, children growing up in subsistence-farming villages with domesticated animals in the village and predators outside treat the quality of being domesticated as an important basis for similarity between animals. Children growing up in urban environments might be slower to perceive this similarity.

Although inferences occur informally throughout the day, when children face formal problems in an academic setting, inference becomes a more conscious process.

Problem solving   Detecting the relation between what the child knows and the elements of a problem is central to generating good solutions. Children were given the following problem: On a cold, windy night, a man is in a log cabin whose four windows have no glass. The only materials in the cabin are some glass bottles, a pot, and a pile of old newspapers. What might the person do to protect himself against the cold?

The key to the solution is to detect the relation between the essential quality of a window without glass, that is, an extension across an open space, and a noncritical quality of a newspaper, that it can be used to cover open spaces. Although all children may know that newspapers can be used in that atypical way, most are unlikely to retrieve that idea and to use that knowledge in this context. This homely example contains a key characteristic in the generation of hypotheses. Most of the time, children and adults solve problems that are routine; that is, the solution is well known. The door is stuck, so one pulls harder. The room is cold; one puts on a sweater. In these and numerous other situations, the person activates rules that have worked in the past. There is almost no thought; the reaction is virtually automatic.

In problems where the solution is not immediately obvious and thought is required, the ideas that are generated first are usually the most reasonable ones. For example, a finger is bruised, but there is no Band-Aid available, so one uses a piece of cloth and Scotch tape. But some problems require the child to think beyond the most likely or expected qualities of objects or events and generate unusual ideas about them. Children are less likely than adults to search for unusual features of objects or events. Children of different ages were shown a tall cylinder holding a few centimeters of water with a small bead floating on the surface. They were then shown a tray containing scissors, string, gum, tongs, a block, and a glass of water and asked to figure out how to get the bead out of the cylinder without turning the cylinder upside down. The string and the tongs were purposely made too short to reach the bead because most children would automatically think of solving the problem that way. The only way to solve the problem was to fill the cylinder with the water in the glass so that the bead would float to the top. Although all children must have seen objects float to the top of containers with liquid many times, very few first-grade children suggested that solution because more reasonable ideas were available, like using the string and gum or using the tongs.

Unusual solutions: creativity   When a child generates a novel but appropriate solution to a problem, the child and idea are called creative. Creativity does not have the same meaning as intelligence. Children are called intelligent if they possess a rich and varied store of schemata, images, symbols, concepts, and rules and use them efficiently and correctly. Children are creative if they use these units in original and constructive ways. Although many intelligent children are not creative, most creative children are intelligent. But their creativity is based on three additional characteristics. They have a mental set to search for the unusual, they take delight in generating novel ideas, and they are not unduly apprehensive about making mistakes. The creative person is somewhat indifferent to the humiliation that may follow a mistake and is willing to attempt mental experiments or high-risk solutions that might fail. Parents and schools can increase the likelihood of creative products among children by displaying a permissive attitude toward mistakes and unconventional ideas.

A study of 10 exceptionally creative girls, selected by their teachers from a large group of adolescents, revealed that the creative girls came from upper-middle-class families who valued intellectual mastery and were less restrictive toward their daughters than most middle-class parents. The girls had learned to read very early, had highly creative hobbies as children (poetry and painting), and described themselves as imaginative (Schaefer, 1970).

Evaluation   Evaluation is the cognitive process of judging the accuracy and appropriateness of one's ideas. Children differ in the degree of care and thoughtfulness they display when they are doing cognitive work, that is, in the extent to which

they use evaluation. Some children accept and report the first idea they think of and act on it after only a brief consideration of its appropriateness. These children are called *impulsive*. Others, of equal talent, devote a much longer period of time to weighing the accuracy of their ideas so that they can reject incorrect conclusions and withhold answers until they are confident their solution is correct. These children are called *reflective*.

Reflection and impulsivity This dimension—called *reflection-impulsivity*—only affects performance in certain problem-solving situations: (a) the child believes an aspect of intellectual competence is being evaluated; (b) the child holds a standard of quality of performance on the task; (c) the child understands the problem and believes he knows how to solve it; (d) several equally attractive responses are available; and (e) the correct answer is not immediately obvious. Hence, the child must evaluate each potential solution if he does not want to make an error. Under these conditions children who are concerned with minimizing error take a great deal of time to examine all alternatives; those who are less concerned with mistakes devote little time to evaluating their initial ideas.

One test that measures this dimension is called the Matching Familiar Figures Test (see Figure 7.6). The child is shown a picture of an object (say, an airplane) and six other pictures of planes. One is identical to the original; the other five are very similar but have minor variations. The child is told to look at the six pictures and pick the one that is exactly like the original. Reflective chil-

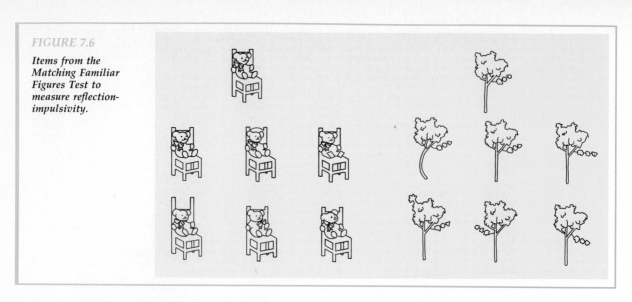

FIGURE 7.6

Items from the Matching Familiar Figures Test to measure reflection-impulsivity.

dren study all the pictures carefully, perhaps for 20 to 30 seconds, before selecting the correct one. Impulsive children make their choices before they have scanned all the pictures carefully, usually respond in less than 10 seconds, and, as a result, make more errors. If the number of alternatives is increased to seven or eight, reflective children prolong their decisions; impulsives continue to respond quickly.

Children generally become more reflective during the elementary school years. In addition, socialization experiences are one important determinant of whether a child will be reflective or impulsive. Japanese children show reflectivity earlier than American or Israeli children (Salkind, Kojima, & Zeiniker, 1978), probably because the Japanese culture communicates to children a concern with careful and correct problem solving earlier and more consistently than American society does.

Children who are reflective on the Matching Familiar Figures Test are also reflective on many other intellectual tasks. They wait longer before discussing a picture, answering an adult who asks them a complicated question, and selecting a problem strategy. They also make fewer errors when asked to report words they heard on a list and are less likely to make errors while learning to read.

Some standardized tests of intelligence have a multiple-choice format: The child must select the correct answer out of three or four alternatives. For example, on the Peabody Picture Vocabulary Test, the child must select one picture from a series that matches the word spoken by the examiner. Other tests of intelligence or vocabulary simply ask the child to remember a specific fact, for example, the definition of a word or the number of pennies in a nickel. Because impulsive children often offer answers without sufficient evaluation, they are likely to obtain lower scores on tests with a multiple-choice format. They are not so handicapped on tests that ask them to retrieve a single piece of information at a time (Margolis, Leonard, Brannigan, & Heverly, 1980).

As might be expected, children with academic problems are a little more likely to be impulsive than comparable groups of children without academic difficulty. Impulsive children are often pessimistic about their ability to solve difficult problems and may adopt a "devil-may-care" attitude. Because they do not believe they can solve the problem, it does not seem useful to take time to weigh each possibility carefully. Academically successful children are more confident, have higher standards for success, and, therefore, believe it is worthwhile to evaluate the potential validity of each solution they generate.

Modifying reflection and impulsivity   Although a tendency to be reflective or impulsive shows moderate stability over periods of 2 to 3 years, it can be modified. After being trained to consider their responses on the Matching Familiar Figures Test and given instructions as to how to scan the pictures in a systematic way, impulsive children showed longer response times and fewer errors than untrained impulsive children.

School-age children who are extremely impulsive should be encouraged to be more concerned with mistakes, while extremely reflective children perhaps should be made less anxious about error so that they can be more spontaneous. Each type of child needs a different experience. Since a child's tendency to be impulsive or reflective influences the quality of performance in school, it is useful for teachers to be sensitized to this characteristic of children.

The use of rules
Another cognitive process, which often completes a problem-solving sequence, is the application of a rule. Rules describe the operations to be performed on information to generate new information. The rule for finding the area of a circle is: Multiply *pi* by the square of the radius. Rules can be generated through inference or learned directly. For instance, children learn many of the rules of grammatical speech by inference; occasionally, these rules are taught to them directly.

An important developmental change in problem solving is the ability to deal with several rules simultaneously. In a study of this ability, children 5, 9, 13, and 17 years of age were presented with a balance beam that had four pegs on each side of the fulcrum and a lever that held the beam steady (see Figure 7.7). The examiner placed individual weights on some pegs on both sides but at different distances from the fulcrum. Then he asked the child to decide whether the beam would balance after the lever was released, allowing the beam to move freely. Young children took only one rule into account. They would count the number of weights on each side and use only that information in deciding whether the beam would balance. If the number of weights was the same, the child predicted the beam would balance regardless of the distance of the weights from the fulcrum. Slightly older children would use at least two rules. If there was an unequal number of weights on each side, they relied exclusively on the number of weights in making their judgments. But if each side had an equal number of weights, they would consider distance from the fulcrum. The most mature children simultaneously took into account the number of weights and the distance of each from the fulcrum in making a correct prediction (Siegler, 1976, 1983).

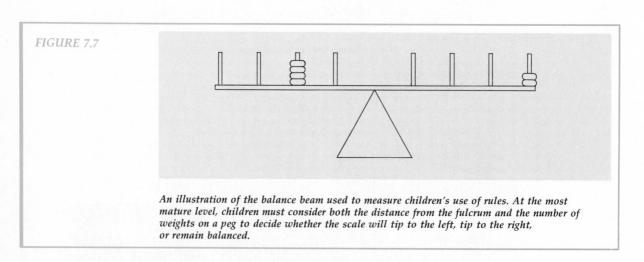

FIGURE 7.7

An illustration of the balance beam used to measure children's use of rules. At the most mature level, children must consider both the distance from the fulcrum and the number of weights on a peg to decide whether the scale will tip to the left, tip to the right, or remain balanced.

One of the common obstacles to generating effective rules is a resistance to giving up old ones that have been useful in the past. A child who believes that all metal objects sink in water may resist a more exact rule relating the density of an object to whether it sinks or floats. She will have difficulty believing that a ship made of steel will float. When the problem situation involves personal concerns with a strong emotional component, resistance to casting aside premises (rules) about people or the self that prevent an insightful solution is even more common. Some of the most painful moments during adolescence occur when beliefs held for years regarding the wisdom of parents, the loyalty of friends, or the trustfulness of teachers are invalidated. The adolescent, with considerable regret, is forced to question a rule that had been a guide to action for a long time.

THE EXECUTIVE PROCESSES: METACOGNITION

One of the most notable changes in cognitive performance between early childhood and adolescence is an increase in number of problem situations in which a particular competence is manifested in performance. Four-year-olds who will inhibit an incorrect response when recalling the location of a hidden toy may not behave reflectively on the Matching Familiar Figures Test. Why is this so? One reason is that 4-year-olds do not yet appreciate the fact that 10 seconds of reflective delay on the Matching Familiar Figures Test is adaptive. They are deficient in *metacognition,* which refers to children's knowledge about and control of their own cognitive functioning. Metamemory, which we defined earlier as children's understanding of how memory works, is one type of metacognition. As children grow, they gradually acquire an understanding of what kinds of competences and cognitive processes are appropriate or necessary for what kinds of situations, when intense effort is required and when it is not, and how to monitor their own mental activity. Several executive processes or metacognitive functions have been described and investigated (Flavell, 1977).

1. *Formulation of the problem and its possible solutions.* The first step in any problem is to generate some idea of the goal to be reached. While a 6-month-old may not have any awareness of a goal, a 2-year-old who needs a dress for her doll will ask her mother directly for the object or initiate a systematic search. A pair of 4-year-olds trying to build a snowman may have difficulty getting the snow to pack into a ball and may give up. Older children will formulate the problem, getting the snow to stick together, and will begin to search for solutions, such as packing it around a solid object. One reason for the change is that older children are familiar with a broader array of problems and, as a result, apply the competence we call formulating the solution to a greater variety of situations.

2. *Awareness of the cognitive processes necessary to solve a problem.* The second executive function, which follows the first, is to be aware of the knowledge and cognitive functions necessary to solve a problem and to adjust one's efforts accordingly. Although 6-year-olds appreciate that recognition of a past event is easier than recalling it (Speer & Flavell, 1979), young children do not understand all the cognitive processes that facilitate recall. For example, kindergarten children seem to be unaware that grouping words by category makes them easier to remember (Flavell & Wellman, 1977; Wellman, 1978). Young children also often fail to realize that focusing attention on information will aid

memory. Four-year-olds who were told that they had to remember a series of photographs for a week did not prolong their inspection times, while 8-year-olds did. Understanding task demands and exercising abilities appropriate to these demands are vital competencies that are applied to an increasing number of problems during the childhood years.

3. *Activation of cognitive rules and strategies.* The third executive function follows naturally from the second. Once the child is aware of the cognitive processes necessary to solve the problem, he should activate them. This becomes easier to do with age, since older children spontaneously search for strategies and apply rules. Consider this string of numbers: 1, 2, 4, 8, 16, 32, 64. An older child is apt to notice that the string of numbers is organized so that each number is twice the preceding number and to use that rule for remembering the sequence or generating new members of the series.

4. *Increased flexibility.* The ability to discard inefficient solutions and search for better ones also improves with age. For example, a 3-year-old who is working on a puzzle may try repeatedly to fit together two pieces that do not belong together and eventually withdraw from the task. An 8-year-old is quick to discard a piece that doesn't fit and search for another that does.

5. *Control of distraction and anxiety.* A fifth executive function is to keep attention focused on the problem, resist distraction, and control the anxiety that mounts when a problem is difficult. Older children can sustain their attention longer and seem better able to prevent fear from interfering with relevant thought.

6. *Monitoring the solution process.* Older children more consistently keep track of their ongoing performance and adjust it to the demands of the task. This function is similar to the cognitive process of evaluation. Monitoring is illustrated in a study in which kindergarten and second-grade children were asked to construct block buildings identical to those described on a tape by another child. Some of the taped instructions (which had been written by the researchers) contained ambiguities, unfamiliar words, or insufficient information. Children were told they could replay the tape as often as necessary in order to complete the block construction. The children were videotaped as they carried out the task to see whether they showed signs of puzzlement and whether they replayed the tape. Older children were more likely than younger children to notice and report inadequate messages. Even though some young kindergarten children showed signs of puzzlement, they were less likely to tell the examiner that the messages were inadequate (Flavell, Speer, Green, & August, 1983).

7. *Faith in thought.* A seventh executive function is the belief that when one is having difficulty solving a problem, it is useful to stop and think in the hope of formulating the correct solution. If an initial solution does not work, young children withdraw effort from the task, in part, because they do not appreciate the usefulness of thought.

8.   *Desire for an elegant solution.* Young children seem to lack a generalized standard for the best—or most elegant—solution to many problems. Although 2-year-olds will, on occasion, want to imitate their mothers' behavior exactly and become upset if they cannot, this concern does not apply to most problems. If 2-year-olds are unsuccessful in building a five-block tower, they do not typically show distress. Indeed, 2-year-olds are impulsive on tests like Matching Familiar Figures, offering a hypothesis quickly, because they do not regard error on this test as a serious violation of a standard. By contrast, 10-year-olds have a general desire to perform with the greatest possible elegance on a great many tasks.

Although many of these executive functions eventually develop in all children, conditions of rearing have a profound influence on their rate of growth. Generally, children growing up in modern societies with good schools and continual exposure to events that challenge existing beliefs show faster development of metacognitive functions. American children perform better than rural Indian children on most memory tests, perhaps because the former group make use of these metacognitive functions. Recall memory for a series of pictures, words, and orientations of dolls was assessed in children living in isolated Indian villages in northwest Guatemala as well as middle-class children living in Cambridge, Massachusetts. The American children reached maximal performance on these tests around 9 to 10 years of age and showed their greatest improvement in performance on most memory tests between 7 and 9 years of age. The children in an isolated village, who had inadequate schools, minimal variety in everyday life, and parents who felt impotent to change their lives, did not begin to approach maximal performance until late adolescence. The children growing up in a more modern Indian village a few kilometers away were in between; they reached maximal performance on the test by 12 to 13 years of age (see Figure 7.8).

School experience contributes to the emergence of executive functions. For example, 5- and 6-year-old children living in jungle villages in Peru or slum settlements in the city of Lima were given different kinds of memory tests. Some of the children in each group attended school, while some did not. The children who attended school did better on all memory tasks, though not on all perceptual tasks (Stevenson, Parker, Wilkinson, Bonnaveaux, & Gonzalez, 1978). In general, schooling has its most beneficial impact on tasks that require children to group objects into abstract categories or to think about hypothetical situations. Such tasks are common in many classroom assignments. When problems require the use of well-established competences with familiar objects and conditions (recognizing the objects in a real-life scene or the important information in a meaningful story, for instance), schooling has much less impact on performance (Sharp, Cole, & Lave, 1979) (see Box 7.3).

A child in whom these metacognitive functions are well developed can approach cognitive problems in a planful, systematic way that permits her to make use of her existing competences more efficiently than a child whose executive functions are not well developed. Children who can formulate a prob-

BOX 7.3

On other ways to count[1]

In the pretechnological societies, where there is no commerce and little need for arithmetical operations, concrete entities such as parts of the body or notches on a stick are used to represent numbers. In an isolated area in New Guinea, a tribe called the Oksapmin have a traditional system for counting based on the body. The Oksapmin count by naming 27 body parts in a conventionally defined order, beginning with the thumb on one hand, which represents the number 1, and proceeding as shown in Figure B7.3 to the small finger of the opposite hand. According to this system, the number 7 is represented by the forearm and by the nose.

FIGURE B7.3

Illustration of the Oksapmin counting system. (From G. B. Saxe. Developing forms of arithmetical thought among the Oksapmin of Papua New Guinea. Developmental Psychology, 1982, 18[4], p. 585. By permission.)

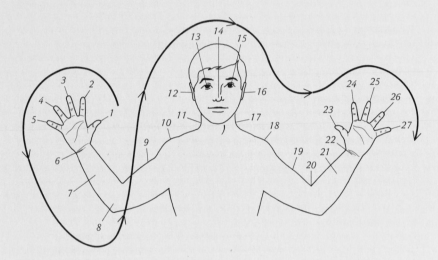

Western currency has entered this community recently, and some Oksapmin men are paid in money (shillings and pounds) for working on tea plantations. Some have returned to their communities and started up small stores. As a result, the Oksapmin have to deal with larger numbers that are not easily operated upon with their original system of counting using parts of the body. The Oksapmin are adapting to these new facts by assimilating the currency system of counting. Rather than using all 27 body parts, a person counts shillings up to position number 20 on Figure B7.3 and might call that 1 pound, reflecting the Australian currency system. To continue the count, the person begins again at the thumb of the first hand—number 1. In one experiment, eight arithmetic problems were administered involving the addition of coins. When asked to add 6 and 8, some adults would enumerate the body parts from the thumb, representing number 1, to the wrist, representing number 6, and then continue counting upwards

[1] Adapted from G. B. Saxe. Developing forms of arithmetical thought among the Oksapmin of Papua New Guinea. *Developmental Psychology*, 1982, *18*, 583–594.

from the forearm, which stands for seven, stopping when they thought the correct answer had been reached. Because it is difficult to keep track of when the second term is completed, the person who used this strategy is typically incorrect. As might be expected, people who owned stores did much better on these problems than people who were not in active commerce. The introduction of money into this economy is gradually changing the way the Oksapmin deal with numbers, providing an example of how historical events can produce changes in cognitive processes.

FIGURE 7.8

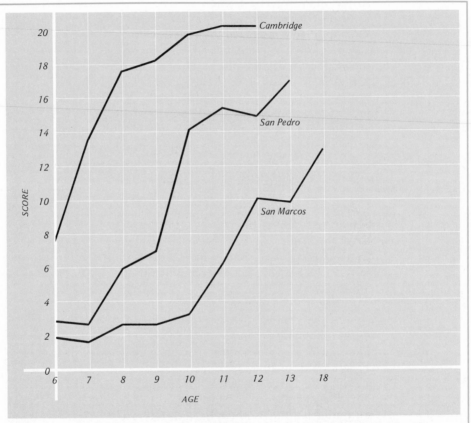

The score on memory tasks achieved by children growing up in Cambridge, Massachusetts, in a modernizing Indian village, and in an isolated Indian village in Guatemala. American children growing up in an urban environment showed their greatest improvement between 6 and 8 years of age. Children growing up in an Indian village with moderately good schooling (San Pedro) showed their greatest performance between 8 and 10 years of age. Children growing up in a very isolated village with inadequate schooling (San Marco) showed their greatest improvement between 10 and 13 years of age. (From J. Kagan, R. E. Klein, G. E. Finley, B. Rogoff, & E. Nolan, A cross-cultural study of cognitive development. **Monographs of the Society for Research in Child Development**, 1979, **44**[No. 5], p. 41. © The Society for Research in Child Development, Inc. By permission.)

lem and its possible solutions, decide what cognitive functions are needed, activate appropriate strategies in a flexible manner, control distraction, monitor their progress in solving the problem, stop to think, and strive for an elegant solution are efficient in their cognitive activities. These qualities are often named by teachers as important for children's progress in school. Cognitive development consists not only of acquiring competences and potential competences in perception, memory, using rules, and the like, but also acquiring the metacognitive capacities to employ those competences appropriately and efficiently.

SUMMARY

Cognition refers to the mental activities involved in the acquisition, processing, organization, and use of knowledge. The developmental psychologist is concerned with two key questions: What major changes in cognitive functioning occur as children grow? What factors account for these changes? No matter what approach one takes to these questions, it is important to distinguish between children's competence (what they know) and their performance (what knowledge they show in a particular situation). Children's ability to acquire a new skill is called their potential competence.

Two important frameworks for the study of cognition are Piaget's theory and information-processing approaches. Piaget assumed that the goal of intellectual development was adaptation. The individual is active, curious, and inventive and acquires knowledge through interaction with the world. The central concept in Piagetian theory is the operation, an action that the child performs mentally and that has the added property of being reversible. The major processes that permit a child to grow from one stage of cognitive functioning to the next are assimilation, accommodation, and equilibration. Assimilation refers to the child's efforts to incorporate information from the environment into existing cognitive structures. Accommodation occurs when cognitive structures change to fit new information. Equilibration is a balance between assimilation and accommodation; thinking tends toward a state of equilibrium.

Piaget's developmental stages include the sensorimotor stage of the first 2 years, the preoperational stage of the preschool years, concrete operations in the years from about 6 to 12, and formal operations in adolescence and adulthood. In the sensorimotor period, cognitive growth occurs through direct sensory and motor experiences. During the preoperational stage, children acquire the capacity to use symbols in their thought, to represent events mentally. Piaget believed that preoperational children are egocentric, that they do not understand that others have different perspectives than theirs.

In concrete operations, many aspects of logical thinking about the world of objects are completed. Children learn to decenter, or to take into account more than one feature of a situation at a time. This ability is demonstrated in tasks measuring conservation of substance, liquid, and number. Concrete operational children understand that the amount of clay or liquid they observe does not change just because its shape or other superficial perceptual qualities change. A second skill of concrete operations is seriation, the ability to arrange objects in order by size or some other quantitative dimension. Third, concrete operations involves understanding relations among objects: concepts such as more, less, darker, and lighter. Finally, children understand that classes of objects are hierarchical—dogs and cats belong to the class *mammals,* and mammals and insects belong to the class *living things.*

In the stage of formal operations, children can reason about hypothetical and abstract possibilities as well as about concrete, physical reality. They search systematically for solutions to problems, they can organize mental operations into higher-order operations, and they can think about their own thoughts. Abstract theoretical, philosophical, and religious ideas come to have some reality in formal operational thought.

Although Piaget's theory has been extremely influential, some psychologists and philosophers have disagreed with some of his assumptions and findings. Not all theorists agree with his premise that knowledge arises from action on the environment or with the assumption that development occurs in discontinuous, qualitatively distinct stages. Empirical studies in recent years suggest, in addition, that Piaget underestimated the cognitive competences of preschool children and perhaps overestimated the abilities of adolescents. A large amount of recent literature shows, for example, that even very young children recognize that others see things from a different perspective than their own. Many adolescents and adults do not demonstrate fully formal operational thought.

The second major approach to cognitive development, information processing, is not one coherent theory but a set of approaches investigating specific cognitive processes such as perception, memory, inference, evaluation of information, and the use of rules. Perception can be defined as the detection, recognition, and interpretation of sensory stimuli. One major cognitive unit involved in perception is the schema, a mental representation of an object's distinctive elements. Perception is selective; children attend to features of a stimulus that they expect or for which they have a mental set.

Three types of memory can be defined: sensory memory for the stimuli one has just perceived, short-term memory lasting about 30 seconds, and long-term memory in which material is stored for later retrieval. Memory can be measured by recognition or recall. At all ages, recognition memory is better than recall, but the difference is more pronounced in younger than in older children. Memory requires the cognitive units of images (pictorial representations of something one has experienced) and symbolic concepts (representations that are symbolic but have no physical similarity to the object represented).

With development, children's memory relies more heavily on symbolic concepts, their concepts come to match those of adults, and they are better able to describe their concepts. They also become capable of integrating more information in working memory. Their metamemory—their awareness of what is required to remember information and ability to assess their own memory capacities—improves, as does their ability to generate and use strategies for remembering things.

Children show improvement in the process of inference, generating anticipations and expectations about implicit information on the basis of what they know. As a result, their problem-solving strategies become more efficient and flexible. When children produce novel and unusual solutions to a problem, they are described as creative.

Evaluation is the cognitive process of judging the accuracy and appropriateness of one's ideas. Individual differences in evaluation of alternative hypotheses are demonstrated by differences in reflection-impulsivity. Reflective children approach problems cautiously, evaluating many possible solutions before producing an answer. Impulsive children respond more quickly and, as a result, make errors more often. Children become more reflective with age. Socialization experiences and anxiety about making errors also contribute to individual differences.

The use of rules is still another cognitive process that becomes more efficient as children develop. Children gradually learn to use combinations of rules rather than focusing on one at a time.

A set of executive or metacognitive processes develops by which children learn to understand and monitor their own thinking and problem solving. As children grow, they gradually acquire an understanding of what kinds of competences and cognitive processes are appropriate and necessary for what kinds of situations, and they learn how to monitor their own mental activity. These executive processes include formulating the nature of a problem and its possible solutions, awareness of the competences necessary to solve it, flexibility, control of distraction and anxiety, self-monitoring, faith in thought, and the desire for an elegant solution. These executive processes are important in enabling children to apply their cognitive competences appropriately and efficiently.

A useful way to conceptualize cognitive development is to view it as the gradual application of the knowledge and competences learned in one situation to an increasingly large domain of problems.

REFERENCES

Ault, R. L. Problem-solving strategies of reflective-impulsive, fast-accurate, and slow-inaccurate children. *Child Development*, 1973, *44*, 259–266.

Block, J. Assimilation, accommodation, and the dynamics of personality development. *Child Development*, 1982, *53*, 281–295.

Bowerman, M. Systematizing semantic knowledge. *Child Development*, 1978, *49*, 977–987.

Brainerd, C. J. Mathematical and behavioral foundations of number. *Journal of Genetic Psychology Monographs*, 1973, *88*, 221–281. (a)

Brainerd, C. J. Neo-Piagetian training experiments revisited: Is there any support for the cognitive-developmental state hypothesis? *Cognition*, 1973, *2*, 349–370. (b)

Brodzinsky, D. M. Relationship between cognitive style and cognitive development. *Developmental Psychology*, 1982, *18*, 617–626.

Brown, A. L., Bransford, J. D., Ferrara, R. A., & Campione, J. C. Learning, remembering, and understanding. In J. H. Flavell & E. M. Markman (Eds.), *Cognitive development* (Vol. 2 of P. H. Mussen (Ed.), *Manual of child psychology.*) Hillsdale, N.J.: Erlbaum, 1983.

Bryant, P. Piaget's questions. *British Journal of Psychology*, 1982, *73*, 157–163.

Cowan, P. A. *Piaget with feeling.* New York: Holt, Rinehart and Winston, 1978.

Decarie, T. G. A study of the mental and emotional development of the thalidomide child. In B. M. Foss (Ed.), *Determinants of infant behavior* (Vol. 4). London: Methuen, 1969.

De Lisi, R., & Staudt, J. Individual differences in college students' performance on formal operational tasks. *Journal of Applied Developmental Psychology*, 1980, *1*, 201–208.

Donaldson, M. *Children's minds.* New York: Norton, 1978.

Falmagne, R. The development of logical competence: A psycholinguistic perspective. In R. M.

Kluovie & H. Spade (Eds.), *Developmental models of thinking.* New York: Academic Press, 1980.

Flavell, J. H. Metacognitive aspects of problem solving. In I. B. Reznick (Ed.), *The nature of intelligence.* Hillsdale, N.J.: Erlbaum, 1976.

Flavell, J. H. *Cognitive development.* Englewood Cliffs, N.J.: Prentice-Hall, 1977.

Flavell, J. H. Cognitive monitoring. In W. P. Dixon (Ed.), *Children's oral communication skills.* New York: Academic Press, 1981.

Flavell, J. H., Speer, J. R., Green, F. L., & August, D. L. The development of comprehension monitoring and knowledge about communication. *Monographs of the Society for Research in Child Development,* 1981, *46*(5, Whole No. 192).

Flavell, J. H., & Wellman, H. M. Metamemory. In R. V. Kil & J. W. Hagen (Eds.), *Perspectives on the development of memory and cognition.* Hillsdale, N.J.: Erlbaum, 1977.

Furth, H. G. *Piaget and knowledge.* Englewood Cliffs, N.J.: Prentice-Hall, 1969.

Gelman, R. Logical capacity of very young children: Number invariance rules. *Child Development,* 1972, *43,* 75–90.

Gelman, R. Cognitive development. In D. W. Porter & M. R. Rosenzweig (Eds.), *Annual review of psychology* (Vol. 29). Palo Alto, Calif.: Annual Reviews, 1978.

Gelman, R. Preschool thought. *American Psychologist,* 1979, *34,* 900–905.

Gelman, R., & Shatz, M. Appropriate speech adjustments: The operation of conversational constraints on talk to two-year-olds. In M. Lewis & L. A. Rosenblum (Eds.), *Interaction, conversation, and the development of language.* New York: Wiley, 1977.

Gibson, E. J., & Spelke, E. S. The development of perception. In J. H. Flavell & E. Martin (Eds.), *Cognitive development* (Vol. 3 of P. Mussen (Ed.), *Manual of child psychology.*) New York: Wiley, 1983.

Ginsburg, H., & Opper, S. *Piaget's theory of intellectual development* (2nd ed). Englewood Cliffs, N.J.: Prentice-Hall, 1979.

Horton, M., & Markman, E. M. Developmental differences in the acquisition of basic and superordinate categories. *Child Development,* 1980, *51,* 708–719.

Hunt, E. On the nature of intelligence. *Science,* 1983, *219,* 141–146.

Johansson, G. Visual event perception. In R. Held, H. W. Leibowitz, & H. L. Tueber (Eds.), *Handbook of sensory physiology: Perception.* Berlin: Springer-Verlag, 1978.

Kagan, J., Kearsley, R. B., & Zelazo, P. F. *Infancy: Its place in human development.* Cambridge, Mass.: Harvard University Press, 1978.

Kagan, J., Klein, R. E., Finley, G. E., Rogoff, B., & Nolan, E. A cross-cultural study of cognitive development. *Monographs of the Society for Research in Child Development,* 1979, *44*(5).

Keating, D. P. Thinking processes in adolescence. In J. Adelson (Ed.), *Handbook of adolescent psychology.* New York: Wiley, 1980.

King, P. *Formal operations and reflective judgment in adolescence and young adulthood.* Unpublished doctoral dissertation, University of Minnesota, Minneapolis, 1977.

Kohlberg, I. Stage and sequence: The cognitive-developmental approach to socialization. In D. A. Goslin (Ed.), *Handbook of socialization theory and research.* Chicago: Rand-McNally, 1969.

Kosslyn, S. N. *Image and mind.* Cambridge, Mass.: Harvard University Press, 1980.

Kreutzer, M. A., Leonard, C., & Flavell, J. H. An interview study of children's knowledge about memory. *Monographs of the Society for Research in Child Development,* 1975, *40* (Whole No. 159).

Lempers, J. C., Flavell, E. R., & Flavell, J. H. The development in very young children of tacit knowledge concerning visual perception. *Genetic Psychology Monographs,* 1977, *95,* 3–53.

Livingston, K. R. *The organization of children's concepts.* Unpublished doctoral dissertation, Harvard University, 1977.

MacKinnon, C. W. Personality and the realization of creative potential. *American Psychologist,* 1965, *20,* 273–281.

Mandler, J. M. Representation. In P. H. Mussen (Ed.), *Manual of child psychology* (Vol. 2): *Cognitive development* (J. H. Flavell & E. M. Markman, Eds.) (4th ed.). New York: Wiley, 1983.

Margolis, H., Leonard, H. S., Brannigan, G. G., & Heverly, M. A. The validity of form F of the Matching Familiar Figures Test with kindergarten children. *Journal of Experimental Child Psychology,* 1980, *29,* 12–22.

Markman, E. M., Cox, B., & Machida, S. The standard object sorting task as a measure of conceptual organization. *Developmental Psychology*, 1981, *17*, 115–117.

Markman, E. M., Horton, M. S., & McLanahan, A. G. Classes and collections: Principles of organization in the learning of hierarchical relations. *Cognition*, 1980, *8*, 227–241.

Messer, S. B., & Brodzinsky, D. M. Three-year stability of reflection-impulsivity in young adolescents. *Developmental Psychology*, 1981, *17*, 848–850.

Neimark, E. D. Intellectual development during adolescence. In F. D. Horowitz (Ed.), *Review of child development research* (Vol. 4). Chicago: University of Chicago Press, 1975.

Newcombe, N., Rogoff, G., & Kagan, J. Developmental changes in recognition memory for pictures of objects and scenes. *Developmental Psychology*, 1977, *13*, 337–341.

Nolan, E., & Kagan, J. Psychological factors in the face-hands test. *Archives of Neurology*, 1978, *35*, 41–42.

Nolan, E., & Kagan, J. Recognition of self and self's products in preschool children. *Journal of Genetic Psychology*, 1980, *137*, 285–294.

Pascual-Leone, J. Mathematical model for the transition rule in Piaget's developmental stages. *Acta Psychologica*, 1970, *63*, 301–345.

Pascual-Leone, J. Compounds, confounds, and models in developmental information processing. *Journal of Experimental Child Psychology*, 1978, *26*, 18–40.

Piaget, J. *Play, dreams, and imitation in childhood.* New York: Norton, 1951.

Piaget, J. *The language and thought of the child.* London: Routledge & Kegan Paul, 1955.

Piaget, J. Piaget's theory. In R. Mussen (Ed.), *Carmichael's manual of child psychology* (Vol. 1) (3rd ed.). New York: Wiley, 1970.

Ratner, H. H., & Myers, N. A. Long-term memory and retrieval at ages two, three, and four. *Journal of Experimental Child Psychology*, 1981, *31*, 365–386.

Rosch, E., Mervis, C. B., Gray, W. D., Johnson, D. M., & Boyes-Braem, P. Basic objects in natural categories. *Cognitive Psychology*, 1976, *8*, 382–439.

Salkind, N., Kojima, H., & Zelniker, T. Cognitive tempo in American, Japanese, and Israeli children. *Child Development*, 1978, *49*, 1025–1027.

Schaefer, C. E. A psychological study of 10 exceptionally creative adolescent girls. *Exceptional Children*, 1970, *36*, 431–441.

Sellers, M. J. G. *The enhancement of memory in Costa Rican children.* Unpublished doctoral dissertation, Harvard University, 1979.

Sharp, D., Cole, M., & Lave, C. Education and cognitive development: The evidence from experimental research. *Monographs of the Society for Research in Child Development*, 1979, *44* (Whole No. 178).

Shatz, M., & Gelman, R. The development of communication skills: Modifications in the speech of young children as a function of listener. *Monographs of the Society for Research in Child Development*, 1973, *38*(2, Serial No. 152).

Siegler, R. S. Three aspects of cognitive development. *Cognitive Psychology*, 1976, *8*, 481–520.

Siegler, R. S. Developmental sequences within and between concepts. *Monographs of the Society for Research in Child Development*, 1981, *46*(2).

Siegler, R. S. Information processing approaches to development. In P. H. Mussen (Ed.), *Manual of child psychology.* (Vol. 1): *History, theories, and methods* (W. Kessen, Ed.). New York: Wiley, 1983.

Speer, J. R., & Flavell, J. H. Young children's knowledge and the relative difficulty of recognition and recall memory tests. *Developmental Psychology*, 1979, *14*, 214–217.

Stevenson, H. W., Parker, T., Wilkinson, A., Bonnaveaux, B., & Gonzalez, M. Schooling environment and cognitive development: A cross-cultural study. *Monographs of the Society for Research in Child Development*, 1978, *175*(43).

Trabasso, T. R. Representation, memory, and reasoning: How do we make transitive inferences? In A. D. Pick (Ed.), *Minnesota symposium on child psychology* (Vol. 9). Minneapolis: University of Minnesota Press, 1975.

Wellman, H. M. Knowledge of the interaction of memory variables. *Developmental Psychology*, 1978, *14*, 24–29.

Yussen, S. R., & Berman, L. Memory predictions for recall and recognition in first-, third-, and fifth-grade children. *Developmental Psychology*, 1981, *17*, 224–229.

CHAPTER 8

Intelligence and achievement

*I*n Chapter 7, we described developmental patterns in children's cognitive processes with a focus on the universals or common features of children's thinking and learning. We turn now to psychologists' efforts to describe individual differences in children's intellectual functioning. We will consider the concept of intelligence and the ways in which children use cognitive processes in real-world learning situations such as school.

All societies place a high value on certain skills and behaviors. The !Kung San of the Kalahari Desert in southern Africa prize superior hunting; South Pacific islanders value outstanding navigation. The specific talents that are celebrated depend on the society's requirements for its maintenance and survival and on the beliefs of its population. Even societies that value mental ability do not necessarily prize the same intellectual talents. The prerevolutionary Chinese valued mastery of the written form of the language; the Sophists of Athens celebrated mastery of oratorical skill; and the Indians of modern Guatemala praise alertness to opportunity. For several centuries, Chinese artists have been praised for copying the style of established masters, while European painters were given recognition for innovation and original departures from earlier works.

To most people, intelligence means the capacity to adapt successfully to the demands and needs of one's culture and environment. Because widely diverse skills are required for success and adaptation in different cultures, it follows that different skills define intelligence in cultures that have different requirements for success. Modern America has come to emphasize the intellectual abilities of language and mathematics. Hence, children and adults who possess these skills are called intelligent.

Because intelligence is so highly valued in our society, the uses of intelligence tests have generated considerable social controversy. For example, in the late 1970s, a judge in California ruled that individual intelligence tests could not be given to a black child if the results would be used to place the child in a special class for children with learning problems (Bersoff, 1981). Despite the many questions raised about intelligence tests, they are widely used.

Intelligence tests are not all alike, and some of the differences among them stem from different theories of intelligence. Although intelligence is one of the oldest and most carefully studied psychological concepts, theorists still disagree on important definitional issues. For example, is intelligence a single quality or ability, or is it a collection of individual skills?

Intelligence can be defined as a very general competence—the ability to learn a wide variety of intellectual skills. It can also be viewed as a collection of moderately general competences, such as "verbal skill" or "numerical skill." Or it can be defined as a large number of specific talents such as "the ability to remember numbers" and "the ability to produce many solutions to anagram problems." Most American and European psychologists who study intelligence favor using a single term (like *intelligence*) to summarize a child's ability to process information efficiently, recall knowledge quickly, and solve problems accurately, regardless of the information or the specific problem involved. They believe intelligence is a general ability that crosses many cognitive domains.

Others contend that a single term such as *intelligence* can obscure the fact that an individual child's abilities are not uniform. Few children are very good or very poor at all cognitive tasks. Most profiles are uneven, and a child who is proficient at finding a subtle difference between two pictures may be poor at comprehending the meaning of a 200-word story or remembering mathematical principles. Among Quechua-speaking children in Peru and Mayan children from Guatemala, there is a poor relation between the ability to remember a pattern of pictures and the ability to remember words or sentences. Children who do well on one of these tasks are not necessarily proficient on the others (Kagan, Klein, Finley, Rogoff, & Nolan, 1979; Stevenson, Parker, Wilkinson, Bonneveaux, & Gonzalez, 1978). Thus, averaging a child's performance across a variety of problems may prevent detection of the child's particular strengths and weaknesses.

This issue—whether intellectual ability is a general quality crossing many tasks and situations or whether specific cognitive abilities must be defined and studied separately—has been debated among psychologists for many years. Persuasive arguments have been presented recently for considering cognitive abilities separately. Partly for that reason, the use of a single IQ score to describe a child's abilities has been seriously challenged.

J. P. Guilford, an educational psychologist, was one of the early advocates of a multidimensional view of intelligence. He proposed a model for the structure of intellect to describe the different types of cognitive abilities that human beings possess. It is illustrated in Figure 8.1.

After examining people's performance on a wide variety of tests, Guilford proposed that intellectual abilities differ in three ways. First, different kinds of *operations* or types of processing are required. Examples of operations are thinking of many different uses for a brick (divergent production) and deciding whether a small furry animal is a cat or a dog (evaluation of information). The second way in which intellectual functions can be classified is according to the *content* of the information processed. For instance, if the operation is remembering, the content might be pictures of toys or words in a song. The third dimension for classifying intellectual abilities is the *product.* One type of prod-

FIGURE 8.1

The Structure-of-Intellect model showing three major dimensions by which intellectual tasks can be classified: operations, contents, and products. The model is designed to show that intelligence involves multiple abilities and to classify those abilities. (From J. P. Guilford. Cognitive psychology with a frame of reference. *San Diego: Edits Publishers, 1979, p. 22. By permission.)*

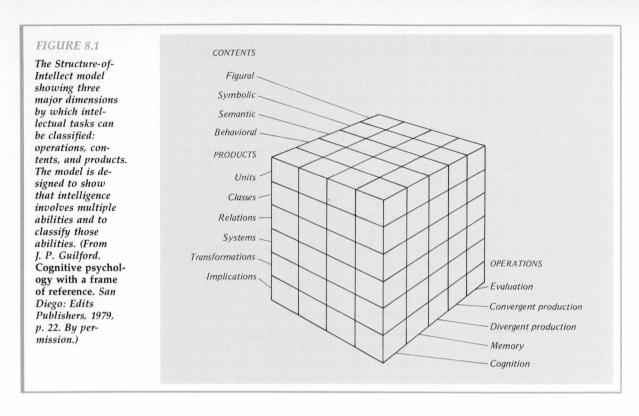

uct is a transformation. If a person imagines what a building would look like upside down, that is a transformation. Another product is seeing implications —for instance, predicting what will happen when blue and red dyes are mixed.

As Figure 8.1 demonstrates, the three dimensions—operations, content, and product—can be crossed to describe performance on a particular task. For example, if the child is asked, "Name as many objects as you can that are both white and edible," the operation is divergent production, the content is symbolic, and the products are units in a class. In Guilford's investigations, testing large numbers of individuals, performance on some of these abilities did not predict performance on others. He therefore argued that intelligence is multifaceted and cannot be conceived as a single ability (Guilford, 1979).

Myths about IQ: What it is and what it is not

The lay public and many professionals have imbued the IQ with almost mystical qualities. It seems to many that the tester peers through a sort of window into the mind and discovers there a number that is predetermined by heredity, fixed for life, and determined by one's innate potential. None of these assumptions is correct. Before turning to the tests themselves, let us examine these assumptions to obtain a more modest and accurate picture of what an IQ score means.

1. *Does an IQ represent innate potential?* An IQ score measures how much you know about certain topics and how well developed certain skills are at the time the test is given, not your innate potential. Your score is obviously influenced by your past experiences with the skills and information contained

in the test. Just as your performance on a reading test depends on your previous experience with reading, your performance on an intelligence test depends on your opportunities to learn and practice vocabulary, information, arithmetic, memory, spatial arrangements, and other skills. Your genetic endowment probably plays a role in how quickly you learn from experience, but that is true for any kind of cognitive achievement, not just IQ.

2. *Is IQ a fixed quality over one's lifetime?* Intelligence test scores are among the most stable human qualities that psychologists measure, but this does not mean that a person's score remains the same throughout life. Even over a few weeks, test scores can vary by as much as 10 points because of changes in motivation, variations in attention, and fatigue. Over longer time periods, there is some stability in intelligence test scores after about age 2. That is, a score at one age predicts scores at later ages. Evidence for this statement comes from two longitudinal studies in which the same children were tested from ages 2 to 18 (Honzik, Macfarlane, & Allen, 1948; Sontag, Baker, & Nelson, 1958). In Table 8.1, correlations of IQs in the preschool and childhood years with scores at ages 10 and 18 are shown. Two generalizations describe the trends shown: (a) As children advance in age, their test scores become increasingly better predictors of later performance. For instance, the correlation between IQs at ages 3 and 5 is .72; between 8 and 10, it is .88. (b) The stability of test scores is greater for shorter than for longer periods of time. That is, the shorter the interval between tests, the higher the correlations between them or the more similar the scores.

TABLE 8.1	Age	Correlation with IQ at age 10	Correlation with IQ at age 18
Correlations between Stanford-Binet IQ during the preschool and middle-childhood years and IQ at ages 10 and 18 (Wechsler-Bellevue)	2	.37	.31
	3	.36	.35
	4	.66	.42
	6	.76	.61
	7	.78	.71
	8	.88	.70
	9	.90	.76
	10	—	.70
	12	.87	.76

Source: Adapted from M. P. Honzik, J. W. Macfarlane, & L. Allen. The stability of mental test performance between two and eighteen years. *Journal of Experimental Education,* 1948, *17.* A publication of the Helen Dwight Reid Educational Foundation. By permission.

Nevertheless, some children show marked changes as they grow. In one longitudinal sample, following children from 2½ to 17 years of age, the difference between the average child's highest and lowest scores was 28.5 points (McCall, Appelbaum, & Hogarty, 1973). Even after age 6, when IQ scores are relatively stable, some children show large changes, increasing as well as decreasing. The average changes between ages 6 and 18 for children in two groups studied at the University of California are shown in Table 8.2. The majority of children shifted 15 points or more, and over one-third shifted 20 points or more.

	GUIDANCE	CONTROL	TOTAL
Change in IQ	N = 114(%)	N = 108(%)	N = 222(%)
50 or more IQ points	1	—	.5
30 or more IQ points	9	10	9
20 or more IQ points	32	42	35
15 or more IQ points	58	60	58
10 or more IQ points	87	83	85
9 or fewer IQ points	18	17	15

TABLE 8.2

Changes in IQ between ages 6 and 18

Source: Adapted from M. P. Honzik, J. W. Macfarlane, & L. Allen. The stability of mental test performance between two and eighteen years. *Journal of Experimental Education,* 1948, *17.* A publication of the Helen Dwight Reid Educational Foundation. By permission.

Larger changes are less common. It would be rare (though not impossible) for a child to shift from a score of 70 to 130 or from 130 to 70. From a practical view, this means we can predict that a child with a high score is unlikely to change to a very low score and vice versa, but we cannot predict with any precision the exact score that a child will have a few years from now.

Large changes in IQ are often related to health, emotional events, personality characteristics, and environmental variables. In one study, children whose IQs increased during early and middle childhood tended to be independent, competitive, and prone to take initiative. Their parents encouraged intellectual accomplishments and used firm but rationally explained discipline. By contrast, parents of children whose IQs decreased used severe punishments in disciplining their children (McCall et al., 1973).

3. *Does IQ measure aptitude rather than achievement?* Because intelligence tests are usually used to predict future performance rather than to measure past accomplishments, some people have drawn a distinction between aptitude and achievement. *Aptitude* is a person's ability to learn a new skill or to do well in some future learning situation. For example, the Scholastic Aptitude Test, given to high school students across the United States, is designed to predict their academic performance in college. *Achievement* tests, on the other hand, are often used to assess "terminal" status—how well a person has done in a particular course or school subject. Standardized achievement tests given in most public school systems are used primarily to provide a yardstick of how well the students have learned reading, math, and other academic subjects. Second, aptitude tests often cover a wide range of content, while achievement tests measure a specific set of information or skills. Both distinctions are matters of degree rather than absolute differences. For example, achievement tests are very good predictors of academic success. Intelligence tests are not more fundamental measures of aptitude than are many achievement tests (Anastasi, 1981).

4. *Does "performance" on an IQ test indicate intellectual "competence"?* Performance on a test consists of the answers given by a child. What most people are interested in, however, is not simply whether the child answers a particular set of questions correctly, but whether the child has certain competences or knowledge. If children perform well on a test, one can be reasonably confident they have the competences it measures. However, as we pointed out in Chapter

7, you cannot infer lack of competence from poor performance. That is, if a child does not answer the questions correctly, one cannot be sure that the competences are lacking—only that the child did not demonstrate them. That fact is one of the most critical points in interpreting intelligence test results. When a child fails to perform a skill, one must exercise caution in concluding that the child is *unable* to do so.

TESTS OF
INTELLIGENCE

The first intelligence tests were created by two Frenchmen, Binet and Simon, for a practical purpose: to predict which children would succeed or fail in school. Their assignment was similar to the task of psychologists who devised tests to select candidates to be trained as fighter pilots. Those psychologists chose test items on which expert, experienced pilots performed better than poor pilots. The quality they were trying to measure was not an abstract, theoretical entity; it was the person's performance in a specific situation. Intelligence tests were created in a similar manner. From a wide variety of questions, Binet and Simon selected those that discriminated children who were doing well in school from those who were not. Not surprisingly, therefore, IQ scores correlate with school achievement.

The Stanford-Binet Intelligence Test

The current Stanford-Binet Intelligence Test is descended from the test developed by Binet and Simon in the early 1900s. It is one of the best known and most widely used intelligence tests for children from 2 to about 16. It contains items measuring information, verbal ability, memory, perception, and logical reasoning. The items are arranged in age levels. The items at the 2-year level include placing simple blocks in a three-hole form board; identifying models of common objects, such as a cup, by their use; identifying major parts of a doll's body; and repeating two digits. At the 6-year level, the child must define at least six words, state the differences between a bird and a dog, and trace the correct path through a maze.

The questions at each level were selected initially by giving many items to a large sample of children. The items assigned to the 3-year level were those passed by about half the 3-year-olds in the initial group, the items placed at the 6-year level were those passed by about half the 6-year-olds, and so on. Because generations of children may change, the test has been restandardized several times. New groups of children have been given the items to find out whether each item still describes the average performance of the age level in which it is placed.

The IQ score is determined by comparing the child's score with averages for others of the same age. An IQ of 100 means a score equal to the average score for children at the age of the child being tested. Another score sometimes derived from an IQ test is a mental age (MA). If a 6-year-old obtains a score equal to that of the average 8-year-old, her MA is 8; if a 14-year-old performs like the average 7-year-old, his MA is 7. The mental age is sometimes used with retarded children to decide what level of educational attainment can be realistically expected. It is no longer used widely, however, because it can be misleading. A 6-year-old with a mental age of 9 does not think or perform in all ways like a 9-year-old with a mental age of 9; similarly, a retarded adult with a mental age of 7 does not perform in all ways like an average 7-year-old.

Figure 8.2 shows the distribution of IQ scores for the population used in standardizing the Stanford-Binet. The test is constructed so that the distribution of scores closely resembles the normal bell-shaped curve, with the center of the curve at IQ = 100 and with higher and lower IQs about equally common. Table 8.3 shows the percentage of individuals in different IQ ranges and the interpretive label for each range.

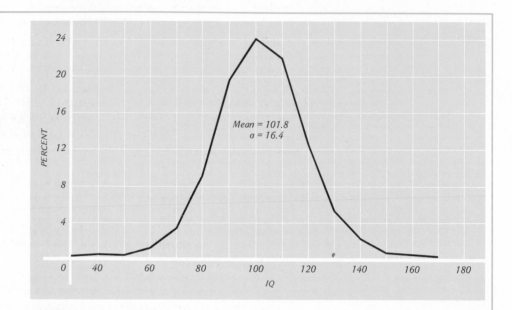

FIGURE 8.2

Distribution of IQs on the Stanford-Binet in the 1937 Terman-Merrill standardization group. (From L. M. Terman & M. A. Merrill. **Stanford-Binet Intelligence Scale: Manual for the third revision of Form L-M.** *Boston: Houghton Mifflin, 1973, p. 18. Copyright, © 1973 by Houghton Mifflin Company, reproduced by permission of the publisher, The Riverside Publishing Company.)*

Mean = 101.8
σ = 16.4

TABLE 8.3

Percent of children at different levels of IQ in the 1937 Standardization Group of the Stanford-Binet

IQ	Percent	Classification
160–169	0.03	
150–159	0.2	Very superior
140–149	1.1	
130–139	3.1	Superior
120–129	8.2	
110–119	18.1	High average
100–109	23.5	Normal or average
90–99	23.0	
80–89	14.5	Low average
70–79	5.6	Borderline defective
60–69	2.0	
50–59	0.4	Mentally defective
40–49	0.2	
30–39	0.03	

Source: L. M. Terman & M. A. Merrill. *Stanford-Binet Intelligence Scale: Manual for the third revision of Form L-M.* Boston: Houghton Mifflin, 1973, p. 18. Copyright, © 1973 by Houghton Mifflin Company, reproduced by permission of the publisher, The Riverside Publishing Company.

Two other major intelligence tests for children are the Wechsler Intelligence Scale for Children — Revised (WISC-R), designed for ages 7 to 16, and the Wechsler Preschool-Primary Scale of Intelligence (WPPSI), for ages 4 to $6\frac{1}{2}$ (Aiken, 1982). The items are arranged in subtests that measure particular skills: vocabulary, similarities and differences, copying designs with colored blocks, and several others. The subtests are grouped to calculate two types of IQ scores: the *Verbal IQ* score, based on items using language (e.g., vocabulary), and the

Performance IQ, based on subtests that do not require language (e.g., assembling parts of a puzzle). The Full Scale IQ is computed by combining the Verbal and Performance scores. Despite the differences in administration, scores on the Stanford-Binet and the Wechsler tests are highly correlated. That is, a child is likely to get similar scores on the two tests.

Group tests of intelligence

Both the Stanford-Binet and the Wechsler tests are individually administered. Because they often take over an hour to administer, they are ordinarily given only when a question exists about a particular child's educational or emotional needs. Group tests of intelligence have been developed for use in schools with large numbers of children. These tests are correlated with individually administered tests, but they are generally less accurate measures of children's knowledge because the testing process does not permit an examiner to be sure all children understand the directions, have enough time to complete each section, and are attending to the task without becoming distracted.

Multidimensional tests of intelligence

The tests discussed so far have been based on the assumption that intelligence is a unitary characteristic—that one or perhaps two scores can describe intellectual ability. As we noted earlier, some theorists have argued that intelligence should be viewed as several separate abilities; they have designed tests based on this multidimensional view. The Primary Mental Abilities Test, designed for elementary school–age children, and the Differential Aptitude Test, designed for older children and adolescents, both contain separate sub-tests for skills such as verbal reasoning, number facility, spatial relations, and perceptual speed. Although scores on many of these sub-tests are correlated with scores on the Stanford-Binet and the Wechsler, multidimensional tests are especially useful when one has questions about specific ability areas such as "Does this child have problems visualizing spatial relationships?" (Anastasi, 1982).

INDIVIDUAL DIFFERENCES IN INTELLECTUAL FUNCTIONING

Individual differences in performance on intelligence tests result from an interaction of genetic endowment and experience. We have already discussed the contribution of genetic factors to individual differences in intelligence (see Chapter 2). We now turn to an examination of environmental influences on intellectual performance.

Environmental influences

What are the important elements of the environment for promoting intellectual functioning? One way to answer this question is to study the environments of children who perform at different intellectual levels and try to identify factors that correlate with IQ. This method has one major flaw, summarized in the adage taught to all introductory psychology students: Correlations do not imply causation. If we find that parents of brighter children behave differently than parents of children who do not perform well, we do not know whether the parents' behavior stimulated the child or whether the parents responded to characteristics of their children. For example, in the United States, the amount of time parents spend helping their children with homework is negatively correlated with the children's school achievement. That is, the poorer students get more help. Does parental help interfere with school achievement? Probably not. It is more likely that poor achievers need or ask for help more often. With these cautions about interpretation, we will examine the evidence.

Some psychologists have tried to evaluate the influence of environment by calculating the correlation between the IQs of adoptive parents and their children. Obviously, children's similarities to adoptive parents cannot be attributed to genetic causes. Such correlations are typically low, around .20 (Willerman, 1979). Highly intelligent adoptive parents have children whose IQs are similar to those of children of less intelligent adoptive parents. Examining the similarity in IQ between parents and children may not be a good way to evaluate environmental influences on children, however, because parents' IQs may not be good indicators of the intellectual stimulation they provide for their children.

More direct measures of the intellectual stimulation provided by parents do predict children's IQs whether they are adopted or not. Burks (1928) rated home environments for the presence of books, magazines, stimulating toys, and parent involvement. These aspects of the home environment predicted children's IQs moderately well for both adopted and nonadopted children. More recently, the home environments of 105 children (78 black, 37 white) were rated on certain social and physical characteristics when the children were 2 years old using a measure called the HOME Index. The children's IQs on the Stanford-Binet were measured at age 3. Children with high IQs turned out, according to the HOME Index, to have mothers who were involved with them, affectionate, and verbally responsive and who avoided restriction and punishment. Their households were organized, and appropriate play materials were available. There were predictable routines such as regular times for naps and meals, but there were also opportunities for variety in the daily routine. The HOME Index predicted children's IQs better than did the family's social status, particularly among black families (Bradley, Caldwell, & Elardo, 1977). In another sample of low-income families, HOME Index qualities measured at 12 months predicted school achievement 5 to 9 years later (Van Doorninck, Caldwell, Wright, & Frankenburg, 1981). In short, these and other investigations suggest that intellectual development is enhanced when parents are affectionate, are verbally responsive, and provide an organized, predictable environment with some possibilities for variety of experience. One feature of the environment that can interfere with intellectual functioning is excessive noise and disorganization. For example, in a group of 39 children who were studied from 12 to 24 months of age, the amount of noise from television, other children, traffic, or appliances was consistently associated with relatively poor performance on tests of intellectual functioning (Wachs, 1979).

Sex differences in intellectual performance

When the Stanford-Binet and some other intelligence tests were constructed, items were discarded if the average performance of boys and girls differed. That is, the tests were constructed to avoid content or skills on which males and females might differ. Nevertheless, in the United States girls have slightly higher IQs in the early years than boys (Broman, Nichols, & Kennedy, 1975). Girls also get better grades than boys throughout all the school years, although the difference decreases in high school and college.

More important, males and females, on the average, have different patterns of performance in different intellectual domains. Females in our culture perform a little better than males on standardized tests of verbal ability — reading, verbal fluency, and verbal comprehension. During elementary school, males and females perform about equally well in mathematics, but males begin to do better in high school, and they clearly excel in college. Males also perform better, on the average, on tasks that require visual-spatial reasoning (for instance, imagining how a cube constructed of black and white blocks would look from another side or being able to read a map) (Huston, 1983; Maccoby & Jacklin, 1974; Meece, Parsons, Kaczala, Goff, & Futterman, 1982). Of course, the averages do not represent all individuals; there are many boys who perform better than many girls on verbal skills, and there are many girls who do well at math and spatial reasoning. Nevertheless, the reasons for the average differences have been hotly argued by scientists.

The patterns of achievement by males and females are consistent with cultural stereotypes about appropriate behaviors for men and women. Children learn very early that reading, art, and verbal skills are stereotyped as feminine, while mechanical, athletic, and mathematical skills are socially defined as masculine (Huston, 1983; Stein & Bailey, 1973). The socialization that boys and girls receive from family, school, peers, and the mass media probably all contribute to the different patterns of intellectual development and ultimate occupational achievement shown by males and females. Although some investigators have tried to demonstrate that genetic and neurological differences between the sexes may account for their performance differences, these efforts have not demonstrated a physiological basis for sex differences in visual-spatial, mathematical, or verbal abilities.

Social class and race
Many of the environmental factors that have the greatest impact on the child's IQ and achievement are associated with the social class and ethnic group of the family. Social class is typically correlated with IQ (average correlation about .50). For example, in a study following 26,760 children from before birth to age 4, the best predictor of IQ at age 4 was the mother's education and her social status. Neither the child's prenatal and birth history nor the child's performance on an infant intelligence scale predicted as well as the mother's education and social class (Broman et al., 1975).

Children from many economically disadvantaged minority groups in both the United States and Europe — many of whom are nonwhite — obtain lower IQ scores and perform less well in school than the average child in the same country. For instance, black children in the United States, who are often from economically impoverished homes, have average IQ scores 10 to 15 points below the average for white children (Broman et al., 1975; Hall & Kaye, 1980).

There has been a great deal of controversy about the reasons for the relatively poor performance of black and other minority children on IQ tests. Arthur Jensen, an educational psychologist at the University of California, suggested that the difference between blacks and whites was the result of genetic factors (Jensen, 1969). Like many other psychologists, we disagree with Jensen's interpretation of the data. The available evidence does not support the conclusion that one race is genetically inferior to another, but rather that black

BOX 8.1
Intelligence and occupational achievement

Melissa is an 8-year-old black female whose mother works as a domestic servant earning the minimum wage and whose father lives in another city. Melissa's score on an intelligence test administered by the school psychologist is 140. Robert is an 8-year-old white male whose father owns a prosperous business and whose mother has a master's degree in English. His score on an intelligence test is 105. Which of these children will probably achieve a higher occupational level in adulthood? Which will earn more money?

If you answered "Melissa," you have some chance of being right. One of the reasons that IQ is emphasized so heavily in our society is the belief that intelligence leads to success. There is, of course, some basis for that belief. In one longitudinal study of children from 3 to 18, the correlation between IQ measured after age 7 and adult occupational and educational attainment was moderately high (McCall, 1977).

But if you answered "Robert," your chance of being right is fairly high. The education of the child's father, which is a good indicator of the family's social class, predicts the child's later occupation even better than childhood IQ (McCall, 1977). Being female or being a member of a nonwhite ethnic minority also makes it fairly unlikely that an individual will achieve high occupational status. Although girls perform slightly better in school than boys, the ultimate occupational status of males is considerably higher than that of females. The average salary of female workers is approximately 60 percent of the average for males. Nonwhite minorities experience difficulties in school achievement for many reasons, but even those who perform well in school often find their occupational opportunities limited.

One reason for these differences is that society provides different occupational opportunities to people of different genders, races, and social-class backgrounds. Other reasons are more subtle: differences in the quality of the schools attended, the expectations communicated by teachers and parents, and the values of the peer group. Whatever the reasons, social class, gender, and race are all important predictors of occupational success. Intelligence as measured on IQ tests is only one of several contributors.

children have lower IQs because of experiences in their families, neighborhoods, and schools as well as the events associated with economic disadvantage and racial discrimination (Scarr, 1981).

Support for this view comes from a study of black children adopted by middle-class white families during the first 2 or 3 years of life. The IQs of the adopted children, shown in Table 8.4, were slightly above average and were similar to those of white adopted children. Children adopted in infancy had

TABLE 8.4	IQ SCORES		
Intelligence test scores of black children adopted by white families	Number	Average	Range
All adopted children			
Black	130	106	68–144
White	25	111	62–143
Other	21	100	66–129
Early adopted children			
Black	99	110	86–136
White	9	117	99–138
Other	(only three cases)		
Natural children	144	117	81–150

Source: S. Scarr & R. A. Weinberg. IQ test performance of black children adopted by white families. *American Psychologist*, 1976, *31*, 732. By permission.

higher averages than those adopted when they were 1 year old or older. The higher the educational level of the adoptive mother, the higher the IQ of the adopted child. The authors of this study concluded: "The major findings of the study support the view that the social environment plays a dominant role in determining the average IQ level of black children and that both social and genetic variables contribute to individual variation among them" (Scarr & Weinberg, 1976).

Genetic explanations have also been offered for social-class differences in average IQ, and similar arguments against such explanations can be offered. Children born to lower-class families in France but adopted by upper-middle-class families were studied. The adopted children had average IQ scores of 110, 18 points higher than their biological siblings who had remained in their lower-class homes. Among the adopted children, there were no IQs under 80; among their biological siblings, 20 percent had IQs below 80. The proportion of school failure was 12 percent for the adopted children and 70 percent for their brothers and sisters who remained with their families (Schiff, Duyne, Dumaret, Stewart, Tomkiewicz, & Feingold, 1978). We cannot conclude that the differences in test performance shown by different social-class and ethnic groups are due primarily to genetic factors.

Difference versus deficit Although we have argued that social experience makes a major contribution to ethnic and class differences in IQ, we must avoid the trap of viewing the minority or lower-class child's social environment as inferior or deficient. That approach is sometimes called the *deficit model*. A more penetrating analysis indicates that nonwhite and lower-class children learn *different* cognitive skills than those most valued in white middle-class society, but that their cognitive and language skills are advanced and sophisticated. Like children in all societies, they learn the skills valued in their culture. For example, linguistic analyses of "Black English" have demonstrated a distinctive, consistent, and complex grammatical structure; it is not an impoverished version of standard English (see Chapter 6).

When one leaves the realms of IQ, achievement tests, and tasks that depend on schooling, there are fewer cognitive differences based on social class, race, or formal education. Preschool and kindergarten boys from middle- and lower-class black and white families were tested on their understanding of mathematical concepts that do not depend on formal symbol systems taught in schools. Tasks were designed to measure the children's understanding of "more," addition and subtraction, basic counting, and conservation of number. There were few differences in performance based on race or social class (Ginsburg & Russell, 1981). Such concepts may be learned without direct instruction through children's everyday interactions with the physical world. These findings suggest that lower-class and nonwhite children do not have generalized cognitive deficits; the tasks on which middle-class whites excel are those that are subject to "teaching" by parents and schools.

Test bias   One implication of the *difference model* is that tests of intelligence are biased against lower-class and minority-group children. That is, the tests sample skills and information that are part of the middle-class culture rather

than skills and information that minority children learn. This problem has been recognized for many years, but there was a resurgence of concern about it during the 1970s, partly because of a number of court cases in which minority parents challenged the use of IQ tests to place their children in classes for the mentally retarded.

The content of most IQ tests is probably more familiar to middle-class white children than to many minority children. For example, a middle-class white child might be more familiar with the word *lecture* than a black child. Although some content bias of this kind undoubtedly occurs, it is not as simple as it appears. Anglo, Hispanic, and black college students rated the items on an IQ test for bias; there was very little agreement among members of each group about which items were biased. Still more disconcerting was the fact that the items the adults thought were biased were not those on which minority children performed poorly (Sandoval & Millie, 1980).

More general differences in life experience probably do make IQ tests difficult for minority children. For many ethnic minorities in the United States, standard English is a second language that is less familiar than the language spoken at home or in their neighborhoods. In addition, minority children may have less opportunity to learn test-taking skills or to be familiar with the process of testing. Finally, fear of failure or lack of confidence in their abilities appears to be especially severe for lower-class and minority children. One group of researchers did a series of studies in which they tried to arrange testing conditions to reduce children's anxiety about failure and make them feel confident and comfortable in the testing situation. The average IQ in these "optimal" testing conditions was about 6 points higher than that of a comparison group tested in the standard way. The beneficial effects of the optimal testing conditions were especially great for economically disadvantaged children (Zigler, Abelson, & Seitz, 1973; Zigler, Abelson, Trickett, & Seitz, 1982). We can conclude that there is some basis for believing that IQ tests do not measure all of the cognitive *competences* of lower-class and minority children as well as they do for middle-class white children.

What is the future of the IQ?

Should IQ tests be used to make educational decisions for any child, particularly a member of a minority group? On the one hand, some people argue that an IQ test does measure the skills needed to achieve in school, even though those may also have a middle-class bias. That is, a test may indicate how much a minority child has learned about the requirements for achievement in the middle-class society represented by schools. In fact, among college students, test scores predict academic performance about as well for minority students as for majority-culture students (Cleary, Humphreys, Kendrick, & Wesman, 1975; Cole, 1981). Furthermore, an "objective" test may provide an opportunity for academically talented minority students to be identified even when teachers do not recognize them. On the other hand, there is considerable danger that teachers and parents will assume that a child who scores low is incapable of learning and will not put forth their best efforts to teach that child.

Two of the points made earlier in the chapter provide a partial solution to this dilemma. First, because intelligence is multidimensional, it is probably more useful to examine tests of specific skills than to rely solely on a single IQ score. Rather than saying a child is intelligent, we might say he is good at language, math, spatial reasoning, creative writing, or artistic composition.

Second, because intelligence tests are basically tests of achievement or learning across a wide range of cognitive domains, the label *IQ* could be replaced by a term such as *school ability* or *academic aptitude* (Reschly, 1981). These labels might avoid the implication that test scores are an index of innate potential or a fixed entity that the person carries throughout life. They might better convey the notion that tests of cognitive performance can be useful for educational diagnosis, while reducing the possibility that children will be stigmatized or considered incapable of learning.

MOTIVATION AND SCHOOL ACHIEVEMENT

Children's achievement in school and in adult life depends not only on their abilities but also on their motivation, attitudes, and emotional reactions to school and other achievement situations. One of the earliest constructs proposed by psychologists to describe this aspect of achievement was *achievement motivation*. "Achievement motivation is an overall tendency to evaluate one's performance against standards of excellence, to strive for successful performance, and to experience pleasure contingent on successful performance" (Feld, Ruhland, & Gold, 1979, p. 45). It is a desire to do well in a particular domain (e.g., football or music) and a tendency to evaluate performance spontaneously. We often infer achievement motivation from *achievement behaviors* such as persisting at a difficult task, working intensely or striving for mastery, and selecting challenging but not impossibly difficult tasks (that is, setting a moderate level of aspiration).

It is easy to see that these achievement behaviors could contribute to school achievement for a child who consistently engaged in them. Consider two children whose IQs are both 100 as they go through the first few grades of school. Sara begins learning to read with enthusiasm. She concentrates on the books and worksheets that the teacher provides, and she persists on problems that are difficult for her. When she goes to a learning center where there is a choice of activities, she selects a book that has some difficult words but is one that she can read. Linda begins with the same skill but is inclined to be distracted from assignments when a teacher is not working with her. When she encounters difficult words, she gives up easily. At the learning center, she chooses a very easy book that she is sure she can read. Over time, Sara will probably learn more reading skills, and she will be better liked by her teachers, than Linda.

Achievement motivation and behavior are not constant across all tasks and situations. Even if we restrict ourselves to discussing school achievement, children's levels of motivation may vary from one subject area to another or from one time period to the next. One child may be very persistent and involved when working on art projects but show little effort in math. Another may read avidly, selecting challenging books, but seek the easiest position when teams are chosen in physical education. Of course, the greatest social concern arises when children show less than optimal motivation in the "hardcore" school subjects, especially reading and math. What determines a child's level of motivation in a particular task area? Psychologists investigating this question have focused on four factors: the *value* that the child attaches to success in that area (attainment value or incentive value), the child's *expectancies* of success, the child's *attributions* about why he succeeds or fails, and the child's *standards of performance* (the scale against which the child evaluates his own performance). We will discuss each of these in turn.

Attainment value

"How important is it to you to do well in music?" "How important do you think math will be in your future work?" "How much would you like to be good at leadership?" Such questions are all efforts to assess attainment value. They are attempts to measure how much value a person attaches to attainment of excellence in a particular area. Attainment value is an important influence on children's selection of activities when they have choices.

Jacquelynne Parsons and her colleagues at the University of Michigan investigated achievement in mathematics for a group of 668 students in grades 5 through 12 using a large battery of questions about motivations and attitudes. All students were assessed on two occasions, a year apart, so some comparisons over time could be made. These investigators were interested in two outcomes: math grades and selection of advanced math courses as electives. Course choice was deemed particularly important because once students discontinue taking mathematics, they are effectively disqualified from later courses of study or college majors that require advanced math. One major reason that males perform better than females on math tests during high school and college is that more males take advanced elective math courses and, as a result, have more training. The findings demonstrated that the value attached to math achievement was the best predictor of students' intention to take advanced math.

Students who considered math important and who thought math would be useful to them in the future were most likely to say they intended to take elective math courses. Girls considered math less useful for their future lives than boys did, suggesting that different levels of attainment value are one reason girls more often discontinue taking math than boys (Parsons, 1982).

Not surprisingly, children who expect to succeed and who believe that they have the ability to perform a task do in fact perform well. For example, in the Michigan study of math achievement, the best predictor of math grades was the student's "self-concept of ability" and expectancies of success in math (Parsons, 1982). Of course, one reason for students' high expectations is past success. But high expectancies in turn can provide children with a feeling of *efficacy*—a sense of competence that is satisfying and motivates them to try harder in the future (Bandura, 1981).

Expectancies and self-perceptions are not solely a result of previous experiences with success and failure. Children with the same level of past performance often evaluate their abilities differently and have different expectations about future success. For example, across a wide range of achievement areas, boys often have higher expectancies than girls, even when their average past performance is similar or lower (Crandall, 1969; Parsons, 1982; Stein & Bailey, 1973). Some research shows that the difference between boys' and girls' expectancies begins even before they enter school (Crandall, 1978).

One reason children with the same level of performance might have different expectancies of success could be that they interpret their successes and failures differently. They may make different *attributions*. Attributions are inferences about the reasons for one's own or someone else's behavior. Whether or not we are aware of it, we constantly make attributions: Mary must be grouchy today because she didn't get enough sleep. If Joe, who is usually a poor student, got an A, it must be an easy course.

The concept of attribution was applied to achievement motivation by Bernard Weiner and his associates (Bar-Tel, 1978; Weiner, 1974). They proposed that people's perceptions of the causes for their own successes and failures were important determinants of achievement behavior and expectancies about future performance. Four major causes for success or failure were identified: (a) ability (or lack of ability), (b) effort (or lack of it), (c) task difficulty (or ease), and (d) luck (good or bad). Examples of each are shown in Table 8.5. As you can see, the four attributions are classified along two dimensions.

TABLE 8.5		Internal	External	Effect on expectancy
Examples of attributions about success and failure	*Stable*	ABILITY	TASK DIFFICULTY	
	Success	"I'm good at math."	"It was an easy test."	Expect future success.
	Failure	"I'm lousy at math."	"It was a hard test."	Expect future failure.
	Unstable	EFFORT	LUCK	
	Success	"I studied hard."	"I guessed right."	Don't know.
	Failure	"I didn't study enough."	"I guessed wrong."	Future could be different.

One dimension is *internal/external.* Ability and effort are internal causes because they originate within the individual and are, to some degree, within that person's control. Task difficulty and luck are external causes because they arise outside the individual and are often beyond one's control. This internal/external dimension is also sometimes called *locus of control.* If people feel that their successes and failures are internally controlled, they are more likely to put forth effort to achieve than if they think that external forces such as fate or other people's actions control what happens to them.

The other dimension is *stable/unstable.* Ability and task difficulty are stable characteristics that are not easily changed. Effort and luck are unstable and can change readily. Attributing success or failure to stable causes is more likely to affect a child's expectancies for the future than attributions to unstable causes. For example, a person who attributes success to ability will probably expect to succeed again and will put forth effort, show task persistence, and select a moderate level of aspiration when a similar task is encountered again. A person who attributes failure to ability or task difficulty will probably have low expectancies and may give up easily or select a very low level of aspiration in future attempts at the task. On the other hand, a person who attributes failure to lack of effort might try harder the next time. Consider the following example of Jennifer, a 12-year-old who is trying to become a good swimmer.

> *Every day, she counts the number of laps she swims and times how long it takes her. Like most of us, she does well on some days and less well on others. If she considers her good days an index of her ability and interprets her bad days as times when she is not trying as hard as she might, she will probably feel good about her swimming abilities. She will also redouble her efforts after a setback or a string of poor performances. On the other hand, if she thinks her good days are flukes of luck or the result of superhuman effort but that her bad days show she really does not have ability to become a high-powered swimmer, she will probably become discouraged. When she hits a string of bad days, she will be inclined to give up and decide she really cannot do it.*

The pattern of maladaptive attributions just described—believing that your successes do not reflect ability and that failures cannot be reversed by effort—has been labeled *learned helplessness* by some psychologists (Dweck, 1975). They propose that some children believe that the causes of failure are outside their control or cannot be changed. As a result, they feel helpless and give up easily when they fail. Such children do not initially experience any more failures or successes than other children, but they interpret them differently.

In a series of studies, Dweck and her associates identified children who experienced learned helplessness by administering a questionnaire asking the children why they succeed and fail in school (Crandall, Katkovsky, & Crandall, 1965). One group, the "mastery-oriented" children, believed that their failures often resulted from lack of effort. The other group, the "learned-helpless" children, attributed failure to other causes such as bad luck, task difficulty, or poor ability. The children were then given individual tests on which they sometimes succeeded and sometimes failed. The mastery-oriented children inter-

preted success as an indication of their ability; after failure, they redoubled their effort and concentrated on strategies for changing their approach to the task. The learned-helpless children did not interpret their successes as signs of ability, and they thought the reasons for failure were beyond their control, so they tended to give up easily (Diener & Dweck, 1978, 1980).

These findings led to a series of studies in which children were trained to attribute their failures to lack of effort rather than lack of ability. Their performance in math improved after training (Dweck, 1975). Teaching children to attribute their successes to ability and their failures to lack of effort may help to improve academic achievement, but only when they have the relevant skills or abilities. A child who tries very hard and fails may feel forced to conclude that the failure results from poor ability and to suffer lowered self-esteem as a result (Covington & Omelich, 1979).

Developmental differences in attributions about achievement   Although adults and older children make the types of attributions described in Weiner's model (Table 8.5), it appears that younger children sometimes do not distinguish clearly between effort, outcome, and ability. When children were shown films about a child who worked hard and one who did not, kindergarten and first-grade children seemed to interpret the outcomes with a kind of "halo": "People who try harder are smarter—even if they fail." Children from 7 to 9 understood that effort was likely to lead to success, but they still did not distinguish ability from effort. For example, they did not conclude that a lazy child who succeeded had higher ability than one who worked hard and did not succeed.

It was not until ages 10 to 13 that most children clearly separated effort and ability (Shantz, 1983).

After reviewing this literature, Shantz (1983) concludes that "children differentiate effort before ability in development; tend to account for success in terms of effort rather than ability; and reward effort more than ability. Why this primacy of effort over ability? The maxim of 'try hard and you will succeed' has been suggested (by Guttentag & Longfellow, 1977) as a frequently taught rule and one which might function to preserve self-esteem since one has more control over effort than ability" (p. 60).

Group differences in attributions　Are the achievement and school problems of some groups related to their attribution patterns? Little is known about the attributions that are typical of children from different social-class or ethnic groups, but there is a large amount of information about sex differences. Among children and adults, males are more apt to attribute their successes to ability, and females more often attribute their failures to lack of ability (Dweck & Reppucci, 1973; Parsons, 1982; Meece, Parsons, Kaczala, Goff, & Futterman, 1982). One reason for these differences is suggested by the fact that women who rate themselves high on "masculine" characteristics such as independence, dominance, and ability to make decisions have attribution patterns that are similar to those of the average male. Compared to women who rate themselves low on "masculine" attributes, their performance on cognitive tasks is less likely to deteriorate after they experience failure and more likely to improve after they experience success (Welch & Huston, 1982). Training girls as well as boys in ways that encourage independence and competitiveness may promote an adaptive pattern of attributions, leading in turn to high expectancies of success.

Standards of performance

When you evaluate your performance, you compare it with a standard of excellence. You may evaluate how well you do something on the basis of your own past performance (e.g., I ran a mile in less time than I have run it before); on the basis of a goal you have selected for yourself (I set a goal of reading 20 books this summer, and I did it); or on the basis of comparisons with others (I was fifth highest in my class on that test). When the standards you adopt are personal or are based on comparisons with your own past performance, they are *autonomous* standards. When they are based on comparisons with other people's performance, they are described as *social comparison* standards (Veroff, 1969). In American society, the emphasis on competition and individual achievement leads to a heavy reliance on social comparison as a basis for evaluating one's performance. Over the first several years of life, children increasingly use social comparison processes to evaluate their performance.

Developmental patterns of achievement motivation

In Chapter 5, we discussed the beginning emergence of standards during the toddler years. As children grow through the preschool and early elementary school years, they develop more refined abilities to think about and adopt standards of performance and to use information about others' performance in their self-evaluations (Ruble, Boggiano, Feldman, & Loebl, 1980). Preschool children (under the age of 5) do show achievement behavior: They persist at tasks and make efforts to master new skills. There is some correspondence between their expectancies of success and their achievement efforts (Crandall,

1978). Compared to elementary school children, however, they more often choose easy over challenging tasks (Stein & Bailey, 1973).

During the first few years of school, several changes occur. First, children's expectancies become more realistic—that is, more closely related to their actual performance (Nicholls, 1978; Ruble, Parsons, & Ross, 1976). Second, children increasingly use social comparison for evaluating their own performance (Feld et al., 1979; Ruble et al., 1980). Third, they set higher levels of aspiration—that is, they choose more difficult tasks (Feld et al., 1979). Fourth, their anxiety about failure on tests and other school tasks increases (Rholes, Blackwell, Jordan, & Walters, 1980; Sarason, Hill, & Zimbardo, 1964).

Whether these changes are due to cognitive development, school experience, or both, we do not know. Cognitive growth probably plays a role in enabling children to conceptualize a standard and compare themselves with it. At the same time, for most American children, elementary school serves as their initiation into the world of grades, evaluations, failures, competition, and clear comparisons with peers. Beginning in first grade, children in most schools are placed in reading and arithmetic groups according to "ability" (current level of skill). They are evaluated on report cards, their papers are graded, and they are tested. These school experiences may teach children to evaluate themselves, to compare themselves with peers, and to be concerned about failure. We turn now to the problem of anxiety about failure to meet academic standards and its effects on children's performance.

Test anxiety

Increasingly, American schools rely on tests—standardized achievement tests, minimum competency tests, and entrance examinations—to make decisions about educational placement and judgments about students' achieve-

ment. During the first few years of school, many children develop a pattern of anxiety about testing that interferes with their performance. Consider an example supplied by Hill (1980). Mark gets nervous before a standardized test. As the teacher reads complicated instructions, he has trouble concentrating. He is nervous about the time limit because he has trouble finishing timed tests (nobody bothered to tell him that children are not expected to finish standardized tests). He notices that some other children are further along than he is. He starts to rush. He manages to finish but gets few problems right. Mark is a child with high test anxiety. He does not perform as well on tests as his teachers think he can.

In one longitudinal study, 713 elementary school children were followed for 4 years. Children with high anxiety performed more poorly than those with low test anxiety. The differences between high- and low-anxiety children became more pronounced as children got older (Hill & Sarason, 1966). How do we know whether the anxiety caused the poor test performance or the history of poor performance led to anxiety? Of course, we do not know with any certainty. Some of both probably occurred.

One reason to believe that anxiety affects performance adversely is that performance of highly anxious children changes when testing conditions are altered. Children were given math problems under four testing conditions: standard instructions that the test measured the children's ability, "diagnostic" instructions that it would tell where they needed help, "expectancy reassurance" instructions in which children were told that no one gets all the problems right, and "normative" instructions in which they were told that individual scores were not important. The performance of children with high, medium, and low test anxiety is shown in Figure 8.3. The highly anxious children per-

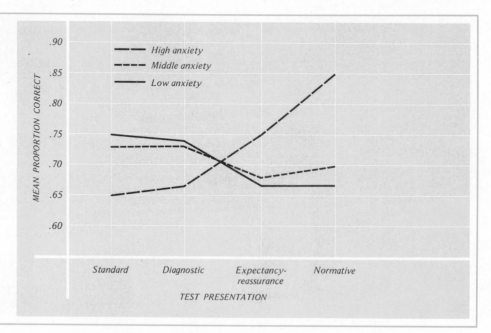

FIGURE 8.3

Test performance of children with different levels of anxiety under four types of test instructions. The diagnostic, expectancy-reassurance, and normative instructions were intended to reduce children's debilitating anxiety, while standard instructions were thought to increase it. (From K. T. Hill, Motivation, evaluation, and educational testing policy. In L. J. Fyans [Ed.], Achievement motivation: Recent trends in theory and research. New York: Plenum, 1980, p. 65. By permission.)

--- High anxiety
--- Middle anxiety
— Low anxiety

MEAN PROPORTION CORRECT

.90
.85
.80
.75
.70
.65
.60

Standard   Diagnostic   Expectancy-reassurance   Normative

TEST PRESENTATION

formed much better when the instructions provided reassurance or removed the threat of individual evaluation (Hill, 1980).

Test anxiety and its debilitating effects may account for some of the group differences in test performance that we have already discussed. Minority-group children (Hispanics and blacks) have higher levels of test anxiety than white children. Girls report more anxiety than boys (Hill, 1980).

A research program conducted by Kennedy Hill at the University of Illinois has been designed to find ways of reducing the negative effects of test anxiety on children. Children are taught about test formats, how to deal with timed tests, and the purposes of testing. Report cards contain specific feedback about strengths and weaknesses instead of letter grades. Children's own accomplishments are emphasized; comparison with others is minimized. These changes are particularly helpful to children with high test anxiety (Hill, 1980).

ENVIRONMENTAL INFLUENCES ON ACHIEVEMENT

Parents and achievement motives

Just as the child's attainment values and expectancies of success are important elements of achievement motivation, so the parents' values and expectancies are influential for the child. In the University of Michigan study of math achievement, the value that parents attached to different areas of achievement influenced their children's values. For example, parents considered math more important for their sons' futures than for their daughters'. The children's attainment values reflected those priorities. Parents also had lower expectancies of success for their daughters than for their sons, despite the fact that boys and girls performed equally well in school. Even more impressive was the fact that, for both boys and girls, the children's expectancies of success were *more* closely related to their parents' expectancies than to their own past performance (Parsons, Adler, & Kaczala, 1982). Parents' perceptions of their children's abilities appear to have a direct influence on the children's confidence and expectancy of succeeding.

Parent expectancies and demands concerning achievement are more likely to raise a child's achievement motivation when parents also make demands for mature behavior. Obviously, such demands need to be appropriate for the child's developmental level. At age 2, a parent might expect the child to use a spoon for eating, to say when she needs to go to the bathroom, or to learn recognize colors and simple shapes. At age 5, a demanding parent might expect that the child eat neatly, ask before interrupting, and learn reading skills. In one study, 4-year-olds were observed in their everyday activities in preschool. Their parents were interviewed at length, and the parents and children were observed together. Children who exhibited high levels of achievement effort and task persistence in preschool had parents who were moderately affectionate but who made demands for mature behavior (Baumrind, 1973).

Perhaps making demands on children and expecting them to do things independently is one way of communicating high expectancies. It may convey the message, "I think you are capable of doing this." Direct observation of parents with their children helps to elaborate our understanding of this process. One group of Dutch children were observed at home with their parents while they performed a variety of tasks. The children had been selected to represent extremes of high and low achievement motivation. Parents of children with

high achievement motivation used more nonspecific help and less specific help than those whose children had low motivation. An example of nonspecific help on a puzzle might be, "Why don't you try turning the pieces around to see if some of them fit that way?" Specific help might be, "Try this piece here." The nonspecific help provides guidance without solving the problem for the child. Interestingly, in the Dutch families—and in another sample of American families—parents were especially likely to give specific help to girls, encouraging boys to solve problems independently (Block, 1979; Hermans, Ter Laak, & Maes, 1972).

Intrinsic motivation   Parents and others often praise achievement effort or offer concrete rewards for achievement ("I'll give you a dollar for every A on your report card.") There are also many school programs based on behavior modification principles in which children receive tokens and other rewards for working at achievement tasks. Although such techniques are often quite effective in producing achievement effort, they may sometimes interfere with the child's own spontaneous interest in a task or activity. A person's motives for performing a task can be *intrinsic* (e.g., the person enjoys mastering new things or finds the task inherently interesting) or *extrinsic* (e.g., another person offers a reward or praise for performing the task). When a child has a high level of intrinsic motivation to engage in a particular form of achievement, extrinsic incentives to do so may, under certain circumstances, lead to reduced intrinsic interest. Some of the findings concerning intrinsic and extrinsic motivation are presented in Box 8.2.

Cultural differences   Some cultural groups emphasize intellectual achievement in the socialization of children more than others. Harold Stevenson and his colleagues carried out a carefully designed comparison of achievement levels and cognitive development for first- and fifth-grade children in Japan, Taiwan, and the United States. By fifth grade, Chinese and Japanese children had higher levels of performance in math and in some areas of reading than American children. The three groups did not differ on various tests of general intellectual ability, and the differences did not appear to be due to the type of mathematics curriculum in the schools. One basis for the superior performance of Chinese and Japanese children may be the emphasis on achievement in socialization by parents, schools, and other parts of the culture (Stevenson, Stigler, Lucker, Lee, Hsu, & Kitamura, 1982).

Head Start and other intervention programs

In the 1960s, a large number of intervention programs were established to enhance intellectual achievement of preschool and elementary school children. The best known of these, and the one that has enrolled the most children, is Project Head Start. The first Head Start programs were run during the summer of 1965 for 500,000 children. The goal of Head Start was to provide economically deprived children with the skills they would need when they entered public school. Although the program was intended to contribute to children's physical, social, emotional, and cognitive development, most of the evaluations of Head Start's success have focused on school-related skills, particularly IQ (Zigler & Valentine, 1979).

In the early years of Head Start, extensive evaluations were conducted. Their results were scrutinized carefully by educators and legislators to determine whether the benefits of the program were sufficient to merit continued support from the federal government. These evaluations consistently showed that children in Head Start programs made significant gains in IQ, vocabulary, and school readiness skills such as understanding letters, numbers, and concepts. The gains were especially large for children with initially low IQs (Horowitz & Paden, 1973; Zigler & Valentine, 1979).

The second conclusion drawn from these early evaluations was less optimistic—short-term gains tended to fade out during the early grades. In many cases, however, these evaluations were faulty because all Head Start programs were grouped together, without attention to the quality of the program, the skills of the teachers, and the like. More important, there were usually no appropriate control groups of children with whom Head Start children could be compared. Often, they were compared to other children in their neighborhoods or in their schools, but, because these control groups had not been selected at the time children entered Head Start, there was some doubt about how similar the two groups had been before they began to participate in Head Start. More recent follow-ups have shown that Head Start children perform better in school and have fewer academic problems than comparable children without Head Start experience, even several years after entering school (Zigler & Valentine, 1979).

The value of early educational intervention has also been supported by a

BOX 8.2

*Turning play
into work*

A professor of child development observed a preschool classroom in which children could earn tokens that allowed them to enter an area containing toys. They earned the tokens by spending a certain amount of time in an area where letters, numbers, or concepts were being taught. The professor complained, "They're teaching children that reading and math are no fun."

Some psychological researchers would agree with this criticism, arguing that children's intrinsic motivation or interest in an activity may be stifled by unnecessary external incentives. In one study, children were observed during free play to determine how much time they spent drawing. Then they were taken to an individual laboratory session where they had an opportunity to draw under one of three conditions: (a) They were told at the outset that they would get a "good player" award for drawing (expected reward). (b) They were allowed to draw and were given a "good player" award unexpectedly after they finished (unexpected reward). (c) They drew without any reward (no reward). Later, they were observed during free play to see how much time they spent drawing. Children in the expected-reward group spent less time drawing than children in the other two groups, as shown in Figure B8.2. It appeared that the experience of drawing in order to receive an award had undermined their intrinsic interest in the activity (Lepper, 1981).

FIGURE B8.2

Mean time spent drawing during classroom free play before and after experimental treatments. In expected-reward treatment, children were told they would receive a reward for drawing. In unexpected-reward treatment, they received a reward after they finished drawing. Those in no-award treatment did not receive a reward. The decline in spontaneous drawing after expected-reward treatment was interpreted as a decline of intrinsic motivation (From M. R. Lepper. Intrinsic and extrinsic motivation in children: Detrimental effects of superfluous social controls. In W. A. Collins [Ed.], Minnesota symposia on child psychology [Vol. 14]. Hillsdale, N.J.: Erlbaum, 1981, p. 170.)

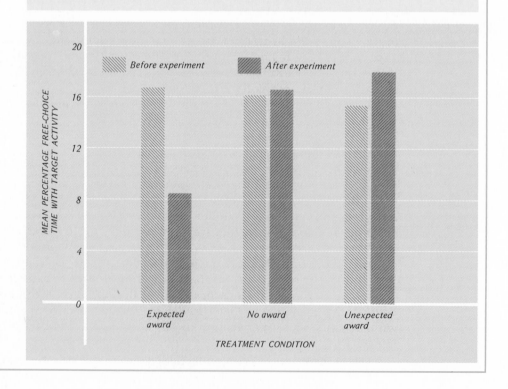

During the school years, grades become an important extrinsic reward. One investigation demonstrated that the practice of grading may reduce intrinsic motivation. Sixth-grade children were given anagrams at four difficulty levels to solve. Half of them were told it was a game, and half were told it was a school task on which they would receive letter grades. Those working for grades chose easier problems to solve, and they manifested less pleasure and more anxiety about failure than the children who thought it was a game (Harter, 1981).

How can these findings be reconciled with the fundamental psychological principle that rewards usually increase behavior? First, the debilitating effects of rewards occur only for activities that are intrinsically interesting to the person—activities that the child will engage in without external pressure. If a teacher or parent wishes to encourage participation in activities that the child does not spontaneously select, external rewards may be effective. Second, because an unexpected reward did not reduce intrinsic interest, it seems that the interference results from the child's perception that he did the task in order to get a reward, not simply from receiving it. (Of course, the next time the reward will be less unexpected.) Third, if the reward is given for exceptionally good drawings rather than just for spending time drawing, children's later intrinsic interest often remains relatively high. In this case, the reward signifies the child's competence and is not just an incentive to do the task.

In short, there are many occasions on which subtle or obvious forms of reward contribute to children's interest and involvement. When a child is already interested, however, superfluous incentives or adult supervision may serve to quash that interest. They may transform play into work (Lepper, 1981).

follow-up study of children who participated in various types of experimental preschool intervention programs in the 1960s and 1970s. These evaluations included control groups of children who did not participate in the program but who were selected and studied for comparative purposes when the experimental groups were enrolled. These studies provide more adequate evaluations of the short- and long-term effects of early intervention than most of the Head Start studies. The results are described in Box 8.3.

Although poor children who have experienced preschool intervention have improved chances to achieve, their performance still tends to be below average. Many children from poor families get progressively farther behind the longer they are in school. For that reason, Project Follow Through was established in 1967 to carry intervention through the first four grades of elementary school. Follow Through consists of special curricula in the schools, special training for teachers, and extra classroom aides to provide individual attention

BOX 8.3
*How long does
a head start last?*

Economically disadvantaged children can gain lasting academic benefits from participating in carefully designed early education programs during their preschool years. In 1976, eleven investigators in different parts of the country who had directed experimental early education programs in the 1960s formed a consortium to follow up their graduates, who were then 10 to 17 years old. Many of these programs were the models on which Project Head Start was based. The programs were selected because they all were initially evaluated with control groups of children selected to be comparable to the children participating in the educational program. Most other Head Start evaluations were difficult to interpret because they lacked such control groups. All children were from low-income families, and over 90 percent of them were black. Each investigator collected information on grade levels, special class placements, achievement test scores, and IQ.

In 1976, the experimental groups (those who had participated in the preschool educational programs) more often fulfilled the achievement requirements of their schools than children in the matched control groups. Experimental children less often repeated a grade or were assigned to special classes for slow learners. They also performed better on reading and mathematics achievement tests during much of elementary school and on intelligence tests for 3 or 4 years after they left preschool. In a few programs, students were followed through the high school years. Those who had participated in preschool programs more often completed high school and were more likely to be employed after high school. Female students from the experimental groups were as likely as the control groups to become pregnant before completing high school, but they more often returned to school after having their babies. Of the experimental group, 25 percent were enrolled in some form of post–high school education, as compared with 3 percent of the control group (Lazar & Darlington, 1982). These findings contradict earlier reports that Head Start programs produced no long-term effects on children's intellectual development. They suggest that carefully designed early education programs can produce lasting benefits for economically disadvantaged children.

to children. Not surprisingly, children who have both Head Start and Follow Through perform better in school than those who have only preschool intervention (Rhine, 1981; Zigler & Valentine, 1979).

Models of early intervention Intervention programs are based on different models of child development that reflect different theories. Those based primarily on learning theory tend to emphasize structured teaching of specific academic skills such as vocabulary and numbers. Others, guided by cognitive developmental theories, stress flexibility and try to provide opportunities for children to develop general processes of logical thinking rather than specific skills. Still others focus on increasing children's achievement motivation and self-confidence. The available evidence shows that all models produce changes in school-related skills.

The largest immediate gains occur for children in the learning-based programs that emphasize structured academic skills, but 1 or 2 years after completion, children from different types of programs show similar gains (Lazar & Darlington, 1982; Zigler & Valentine, 1979). In elementary school, similar structured programs produce higher reading and mathematics scores then more flexible programs that do not concentrate so heavily on reading and arithmetic. That is, curricula that purposely teach specific academic skills are likely to accomplish their mission. However, the more flexible programs produce more independent activity, initiative, and lower absence rates (Rhine, 1981; Stallings, 1975). These findings suggest that the outcomes of different curricula correspond to the aims of their founders. Those who believe that responsibility and independent activity are important are likely to accomplish that goal; those who believe that reading and mathematical skills are central achieve their aim.

We can sum up the results of American social experiments in early intervention with a few conclusions:

1. Early educational intervention can produce an increase in school-related intellectual skills, IQ, and language use. Children who experience early intervention programs enter school with more skills than they would otherwise have had. That advantage can be maintained throughout elementary school by continuing educational intervention, though such intervention is available to only a few children.

2. Some positive effects of well-planned programs last for many years. Early intervention provides a partial counterweight for the downward trend in school performance that frequently occurs among poor children.

3. Models of education based on different assumptions about children's development produce somewhat different outcomes, but they are all effective in helping children to develop intellectual skills.

Intervention with television The late 1960s also witnessed a major effort to use television for teaching disadvantaged children. A group of educators, psychologists, and television writers and producers combined their talents to create "Sesame Street" and "Electric Company." Production techniques from advertising and cartoons were used to package information about reading, cognitive skills, self-esteem, and prosocial behavior. These programs reached a large number of children, many of whom did not have other opportunities for preschool education. Large-scale evaluations, conducted during the first 2 years of broadcasting, demonstrated that children learn letters, numbers, and other cognitive skills from these programs.

In the first of these evaluations, children who watched the program frequently were compared with those who did not. In the second, the researchers used a field-experimental design in which children were randomly assigned to

view or not to view the program at home. The experimental group was given cable connections or UHF sets (necessary to receive the program in their communities), and their mothers were asked to encourage the children to watch the program. The control group did not receive extra TV reception aids or encouragement to view. Both groups of children took a test of cognitive skills before and after the viewing season (about 6 months long). The results of the two evaluations are shown in Figure 8.4. As you can see, the children who watched most often gained significantly more than those who watched infrequently. They learned from watching "Sesame Street" (Bogatz & Ball, 1971; Cook, Appleton, Conner, Shaffer, Tabkin, & Weber, 1975).

Issues in early intervention

Despite the positive findings about early intervention, the whole effort has stimulated controversy. The issues raised are central to child psychology in general, and they are presented here as an illustration of the ways in which some of the general assumptions we discussed in Chapter 1 affect one's position about a practical program for children.

FIGURE 8.4

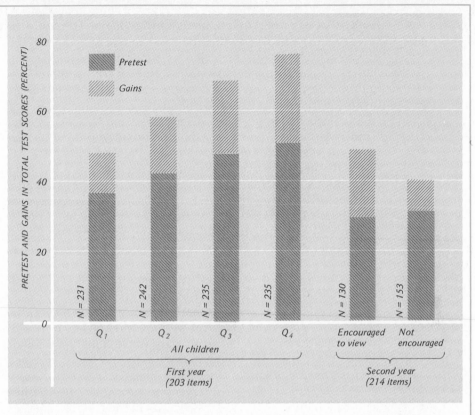

Pretest and gain scores on the test measuring skills taught by "Sesame Street." In the first year, different frequencies of viewing were compared. Viewing quartiles were defined as follows: Q_1, once a week or less; Q_2, two or three times per week; Q_3, three or four times per week; Q_4, five or more times per week. In the second year, experimental "encouraged to view" children were compared with a control group who were not specially encouraged. (Adapted from S. Ball & G. A. Bogatz. The first year of "Sesame Street": An evaluation. Princeton, N.J.: Educational Testing Service, 1970, and G. A. Bogatz & S. Ball. The second year of "Sesame Street": A continuing evaluation. Princeton, N.J.: Educational Testing Service, 1971. Copyright, Children's Television Workshop.)

Environmental versus biological influences on cognitive skills Proponents of early intervention share a belief that environmental forces play a major role in cognitive development. As explained earlier, not everyone accepts that assumption. However, even advocates of genetic determinants of intelligence admit that IQ gains of 10 to 15 points are typically produced by Head Start (Jensen, 1969). An average change of 10 to 15 IQ points would make scores of black children equivalent to those of white children in the United States. In addition, intervention may have more impact on school success and achievement than on IQ (Jensen, 1969).

Passive versus active modes of learning   Proponents of early intervention assume that learning environments can be planned and structured by adults to produce more developmental change than would happen in the ordinary course of events. Obviously, that view is supported by the evidence we have discussed. Some theorists have argued, however, that many important cognitive gains occur through active exploration and manipulation of the objects that are available in all children's environments. All children have opportunities to see that objects fall, appear and disappear, come in different numbers, and have similarities and differences. Adult intervention is not only unnecessary, it may even interfere with the natural process (Ginsburg, 1972).

In some domains of cognitive skill, the evidence supports Ginsburg's contentions. Children do learn the principles of conservation, classification, and logical thinking about their physical world almost universally by middle childhood. For other skills, such as reading, certain forms of language, and many mathematical processes, formal training appears to be important (Sharp, Cole, & Lave, 1979). These skills can be enhanced by early intervention programs.

Stability in development   The third assumption shared by early interventionists is the belief in stability of the cognitive and social skills learned in early childhood. That is, they assume that early experience can make a difference that will endure over time. Yet we have already noted in earlier chapters that children's cognitive skills are not very stable from the preschool years to adulthood. Why, then, do proponents of early intervention expect lasting effects, and why do such affects often occur?

Long-term effects of intervention probably reflect lasting changes in the child's environment as well as changes in the children. Parents often appear to learn new ways to convey skills and encouragement to their children from intervention programs. For instance, in the follow-up study described in Box 8.3, mothers of children who had participated in early intervention had higher aspirations for their children and were more positive about their children's school performance than control mothers. One program contained a strong focus on teaching mothers to provide cognitive stimulation for their children; in follow-up evaluations, the younger sisters and brothers showed some improvement even without attending preschool, presumably because the mothers were practicing the skills they had learned (Klaus & Gray, 1968). Conversely, in the absence of intervention, the lack of stimulation in children's home environments continues over time (Hanson, 1975).

A second reason why a head start may have long-term effects is that children who enter school with reasonably good academic skills, ability to attend, and high motivation to learn may be viewed favorably by teachers who may in turn have higher expectations for their achievement. Such early advantages in school may lead to better achievement, which in turn leads to more self-confidence and more positive school experiences. Contrast this cycle with what might occur for a child entering school who does not know the alphabet, has trouble sitting still, and does not pay attention to directions. Children from early intervention programs may "create" different school environments for themselves.

Intelligence is the capacity to learn and adapt to the requirements for survival in one's culture. In modern Western societies, the ability to use language and mathematical symbols is valued, and skill in these areas is used to define intelligence. Some theorists consider intelligence a single general ability to learn. Others argue that there are many different abilities that fall in different patterns for different individuals. Although IQ remains relatively stable after about age 6, it does not provide a magic window to innate potential. It is influenced by experience and is similar in many respects to a score on an achievement test. Most important, if a child fails to perform a task on an intelligence test, one cannot conclude that she is unable to perform it, only that she did not do so.

Home environments that encourage intellectual development have adults who are affectionate, who talk to the child, and who respond to the child's bids for attention. Stimulating toys and opportunities to explore also contribute to cognitive development. On the average, males and females have slightly different patterns of abilities. Males perform slightly better in math and ability to visualize spatial relationships. Females perform slightly better in verbal skills. Children from minority groups and lower-social-status families perform somewhat less well on intelligence tests than their majority, middle-class counterparts, on the average. The social-class and race differences can be best interpreted as showing *differences* in types of cognitive abilities rather than general *deficits* in cognitive functioning. Middle-class children are more familiar with the material included in tests of intelligence, and they appear to be less often hampered by low self-confidence and anxiety about failure.

Because intelligence tests have often been misused, particularly when making educational decisions about minority-group children, some people have rejected the tests altogether. Such tests can have value if they are treated as one of several predictors of school performance without assuming that the score reflects an innate, fixed set of abilities.

Motivation to achieve in reading, math, art, music, athletics, or other domains affects the child's effort and performance. Achievement motivation is manifested in achievement behavior, such as task persistence and attempts to master new challenges. Four factors that influence achievement motivation and effort in a particular domain are attainment value (the value attached to doing well), expectancies of success, attributions about the reasons for success and failure, and standards of performance. Attainment value often influences the child's choice of activities (e.g., selecting among different elective courses). Expectancies appear to affect the level of performance. Expectancies are at least partly based on attributions about the reasons for past successes or failures. Children can attribute a success or failure to ability (or lack of ability), effort (or lack of effort), task ease or difficulty, or luck (good or bad). Achievement and test performance can also be hindered by anxiety about failure. Parents encourage achievement motivation in children by demanding mature behavior, encouraging children to solve problems on their own, and providing affection and reasoned discipline.

Several intervention programs for preschool and elementary school children have been designed to produce long-term improvement in school performance. These programs have been consistently successful in producing short-term gains in cognitive functioning. The best of them have also led to long-term benefits for school performance. Issues of environmental versus biological influences on cognitive development, passive versus active learning, and stability of intellectual and social skills over time all influence psychologists' recommendations about when and what type of early intervention programs may benefit children.

REFERENCES

Aiken, L. R. *Psychological testing and assessment* (4th ed.). Boston: Allyn & Bacon, 1982.

Anastasi, A. Coaching, test sophistication, and developed abilities. *American Psychologist*, 1981, *36*, 1086–1093.

Anastasi, A. *Psychological testing* (5th ed.). New York: Macmillan, 1982.

Bandura, A. Self-referent thought: A developmental analysis of self-efficacy. In J. H. Flavell & L. Ross (Eds.), *Social cognitive development: Frontiers and possible futures*. New York: Cambridge University Press, 1981.

Bar-Tel, D. Attributional analysis of achievement-related behavior. *Review of Educational Research*, 1978, *48*, 259–271.

Baumrind, D. The development of instrumental competence through socialization. In A. D. Pick (Ed.), *Minnesota symposia on child psychology* (Vol. 7). Minneapolis: University of Minnesota Press, 1973.

Bee, H. L., Bernard, K. E., Eyres, S. J., Gray, C. A., Hammond, M. A., Spietz, A. L., Snyder, C., & Clark, B. Prediction of IQ and language skill from perinatal status, child performance, family characteristics, and mother-infant interaction. *Child Development*, 1982, *53*, 1134–1156.

Bersoff, D. N. Testing and the law. *American Psychologist*, 1981, *36*, 1047–1056.

Block, J. H. *Personality development in males and females: The influence of differential socialization.* Paper given at the annual meeting of the American Psychological Association, New York, September, 1979.

Bogatz, G. A., & Ball, S. *The second year of "Sesame Street": A continuing evaluation* (Vols. 1 & 2). Princeton, N.J.: Educational Testing Service, 1971.

Bradley, R. H., Caldwell, B. M., & Elardo, R. Home environment, social class, and mental test performance. *Journal of Educational Psychology*, 1977, *69*, 697–701.

Broman, S. H., Nichols, P. L., & Kennedy, W. A. *Preschool IQ: Prenatal and early developmental correlates.* Hillsdale, N.J.: Erlbaum, 1975.

Burks, B. S. The relative influences of nature and nurture upon mental development: A comparative study of foster parent–foster child resemblance and true parent–true child resemblance. *The 27th yearbook of the National Society for the Study of Education* (Part 1). Bloomington, Ind.: Public School Publishing, 1928.

Cleary, T. A., Humphreys, L. G., Kendrick, S. A., & Wesman, A. Educational use of tests with disadvantaged students. *American Psychologist*, 1975, *30*, 15–41.

Cole, N. S. Bias in testing. *American Psychologist*, 1981, *36*, 1067–1077.

Cook, T. D., Appleton, H., Conner, R. F., Shaffer, A., Tabkin, G., & Weber, S. J. *"Sesame Street" revisited.* New York: Russell Sage, 1975.

Covington, M., & Omelich, C. Effort: The double-edged sword in school achievement. *Journal of Educational Psychology*, 1979, *71*, 169–182.

Crandall, V. C. Sex differences in expectancy of intellectual and academic reinforcement. In C. P. Smith (Ed.), *Achievement-related motives in children*. New York: Russell Sage, 1969.

Crandall, V. C. *Expecting sex differences and sex differences in expectancies.* Paper presented at the Annual Meeting of the American Psychological Association, Toronto, August 1978.

Crandall, V. C., Katkovsky, W., & Crandall, V. J. Children's beliefs in their own control of reinforcements in intellectual-academic achievement situations. *Child Development*, 1965, *36*, 91–109.

Darlington, R. B., Royce, J. M., Snipper, A. S., Murray, H. W., & Lazar, I. Preschool programs and later school competence of children from low-income families. *Science*, 1980, *208*, 202–204.

Diener, C. I., & Dweck, C. S. An analysis of learned helplessness: Continuous changes in performance, strategy, and achievement cognitions following failure. *Journal of Personality and Social Psychology*, 1978, *36*, 451–462.

Diener, C. I., & Dweck, C. S. An analysis of learned helplessness: II. The processing of success. *Journal of Personality and Social Psychology*, 1980, *39*, 940–952.

Dweck, C. S. The role of expectations and attributions in the alleviation of learned helplessness. *Journal of Personality and Social Psychology*, 1975, *31*, 674–685.

Dweck, C. S., & Reppucci, N. D. Learned helplessness and reinforcement responsibility in children. *Journal of Personality and Social Psychology*, 1973, *25*, 109–116.

Feld, S., Ruhland, D., & Gold, M. Developmental changes in achievement motivation. *Merrill-Palmer Quarterly*, 1979, *25*, 43–60.

Ginsburg, H. P. *The myth of the deprived child*. Englewood Cliffs, N.J.: Prentice-Hall, 1972.

Ginsburg, H. P., & Russell, R. L. Social class and racial influences on early mathematical thinking. *Monographs of the Society for Research in Child Development*, 1981, *46*(6, Serial No. 193).

Guilford, J. P. *Cognitive psychology with a frame of reference*. San Diego: Edits Publishers, 1979.

Guttentag, M., & Longfellow, C. Children's social attributions: Development and change. In C. B. Keasey (Ed.), *Nebraska symposium on motivation, 1977: Social cognitive development*. Lincoln: University of Nebraska Press, 1977.

Hall, V. C., & Kaye, D. B. Early patterns of cognitive development. *Monographs of the Society for Research in Child Development*, 1980, *45*(2, Serial No. 184).

Hanson, R. A. Consistency and stability of home environmental measures related to IQ. *Child Development*, 1975, *46*, 470–480.

Harter, S. A model of mastery motivation in children: Individual differences and developmental change. In W. A. Collins (Ed.), Aspects of the development of competence. *Minnesota symposia on child psychology* (Vol. 14). Hillsdale, N.J.: Erlbaum, 1981.

Hermans, H. J. M., Ter Laak, J. J. F., & Maes, P. C. J. M. Achievement motivation and fear of failure in family and school. *Developmental Psychology*, 1972, *6*, 520–528.

Hill, K. T. Motivation, evaluation, and educational testing policy. In L. J. Fyans (Ed.), *Achievement motivation: Recent trends in theory and research*. New York: Plenum, 1980.

Hill, K. T., & Sarason, S. B. The relation of test anxiety and defensiveness to test and school performance over the elementary school years: A further longitudinal study. *Monographs of the Society for Research in Child Development*, 1966, *31*(2, Serial No. 104).

Honzik, M. P., Macfarlane, J. W., & Allen, L. The stability of mental test performance between two and eighteen years. *Journal of Experimental Education*, 1948, *17*, 309–324.

Horowitz, F. D., & Paden, L. Y. The effectiveness of environmental intervention programs. In B. M. Caldwell & H. N. Ricciuti (Eds.), *Review of child development research* (Vol. 3). Chicago: University of Chicago Press, 1973.

Huston, A. C. Sex-typing. In P. H. Mussen & E. M. Hetherington (Eds.), *Handbook of child psychology* (Vol. 4). *Socialization, personality and social development* (4th ed.). New York: Wiley, 1983.

Jensen, A. R. How much can we boost IQ and scholastic achievement? *Harvard Educational Review*, 1969, *39*, 449–483.

Kagan, J., Klein, R. E., Finley, G. E., Rogoff, B., & Nolan, E. A cross-cultural study of cognitive development. *Monographs of the Society for Research in Child Development*, 1979, *44*(No. 5).

Klaus, R. A., & Gray, S. W. The early training project for disadvantaged children: A report after five years. *Monographs of the Society for Research in Child Development*, 1968, *33*(4, Serial No. 120).

Lazar, I., & Darlington, R. Lasting effects of early education: A report from the Consortium of Longitudinal Studies. *Monographs of the Society for Research in Child Development*, 1982, *47*(2–3, Serial No. 195).

Lepper, M. R. Intrinsic and extrinsic motivation in children: Detrimental effects of superfluous social controls. In W. A. Collins (Ed.), *Minnesota symposia on child psychology* (Vol. 14). Hillsdale, N.J.: Erlbaum, 1981.

Maccoby, E. E., & Jacklin, C. N. *The psychology of sex differences.* Stanford, Calif.: Stanford University Press, 1974.

McCall, R. B. Children's IQ as predictors of adult educational and occupational status. *Science,* 1977, *297,* 482–483.

McCall, R. B., Appelbaum, M. I., & Hogarty, P. S. Developmental changes in mental performance. *Monographs of the Society for Research in Child Development,* 1973, *38*(3, Serial No. 150).

McCartney, K., Scarr, S., Phillips, D., Grajek, S., & Schwarz, J. C. Environmental differences among day care centers and their effects on children's levels of intellectual, language, and social development. *American Journal of Orthopsychiatry,* in press.

Meece, J. L., Parsons, J. E., Kaczala, C. M., Goff, S. B., & Futterman, R. Sex differences in math achievement: Toward a model of academic choice. *Psychological Bulletin,* 1982, *91,* 324–348.

Nicholls, J. G. The development of the concepts of effort and ability, perception of academic attainment, and the understanding that difficult tasks require more ability. *Child Development,* 1978, *49,* 800–814.

Parsons, J. E. Expectancies, values, and academic behaviors. In J. T. Spence (Ed.), *Perspectives on achievement and achievement motivation.* San Francisco: Freeman, 1982.

Parsons, J. E., Adler, T. F., & Kaczala, C. M. Socialization of achievement attitudes and beliefs: Parental influences. *Child Development,* 1982, *53,* 310–321.

Reschly, D. J. Psychological testing in educational classification and placement. *American Psychologist,* 1981, *36,* 1094–1102.

Rhine, W. R. *Making schools more effective: New directions from Follow Through.* New York: Academic Press, 1981.

Rholes, W. S., Blackwell, J., Jordan, C., & Walters, C. A developmental study of learned helplessness. *Developmental Psychology,* 1980, *16,* 616–624.

Ruble, D. N., Boggiano, A. K., Feldman, N. S., & Loebl, J. H. Developmental analysis of the role of social comparison in self-evaluation. *Developmental Psychology,* 1980, *16,* 105–115.

Ruble, D. N., Parsons, J. E., & Ross, J. Self-evaluative responses of children in an achievement setting. *Child Development,* 1976, *47,* 990–997.

Sandoval, J., & Millie, M. P. W. Accuracy of judgments of WISC-R item difficulty for minority groups. *Journal of Consulting and Clinical Psychology,* 1980, *48,* 249–253.

Sarason, S. B., Hill, K. T., & Zimbardo, P. C. A longitudinal study of the relation of test anxiety to performance on intelligence and achievement tests. *Monographs of the Society for Research in Child Development,* 1964, *29* (No. 7).

Scarr, S. *Race, social class, and individual differences in IQ.* Hillsdale, N.J.: Erlbaum, 1981.

Scarr, S., & Weinberg, R. A. IQ test performance of black children adopted by white families. *American Psychologist,* 1976, *31,* 726–739.

Schiff, M., Duyne, M., Dumaret, A., Stewart, J., Tomkiewicz, S., & Feingold, J. Intellectual status of working-class children adopted early into upper-middle-class families. *Science,* 1978, *200,* 1503–1504.

Shantz, C. U. Social cognition. In P. H. Mussen, J. H. Flavell, & E. M. Markham (Eds.), *Handbook of child psychology* (Vol. 3): *Cognitive development* (4th ed.). New York: Wiley, 1983.

Sharp, D., Cole, M., & Lave, C. Education and cognitive development: The evidence from experimental research. *Monographs of the Society for Research in Child Development,* 1979, *44*(1–2, Serial No. 178).

Sontag, L. W., Baker, C. T., & Nelson, V. L. Mental growth and personality: A longitudinal study. *Monographs of the Society for Research in Child Development,* 1958, *23* (Serial No. 68).

Stallings, J. Implementations and child effects of teaching practices in Follow-Through classrooms. *Monographs of the Society for Research in Child Development,* 1975, *40*(7–8, Serial No. 163).

Stein, A. H., & Bailey, M. M. The socialization of achievement orientation in females. *Psychological Bulletin,* 1973, *80,* 345–366.

Stevenson, H. W., Parker, T., Wilkinson, A., Bonnaveaux, B., & Gonzalez, M. Schooling environment and cognitive development: A cross cultural study. *Monographs of the Society for Research in Child Development,* 1978, *43* (No. 175).

Stevenson, H. W., Stigler, J. W., Lucker, G., Lee, S., Hsu, C., & Kitamura, S. Reading disabilities: The case of Chinese, Japanese, and English. *Child Development*, 1982, *53*, 1164–1181.

Terman, L. M., & Merrill, M. A. *Stanford-Binet Intelligence Scale: Manual for the third revision of Form L-M.* Boston: Houghton Mifflin, 1973.

Van Doorninck, W. J., Caldwell, B. M., Wright, C., & Frankenburg, W. K. The relationship between 12-month home stimulation and school achievement. *Child Development*, 1981, *52*, 1080–1083.

Veroff, J. Social comparison and the development of achievement motivation. In C. P. Smith (Ed.), *Achievement-related motives in children.* New York: Russell Sage, 1969.

Wachs, T. D. Proximal experience and early cognitive intellectual development: The physical environment. *Merrill-Palmer Quarterly*, 1979, *25*, 3–41.

Weiner, B. (Ed.). *Achievement motivation and attribution theory.* Morristown, N.J.: General Learning Press, 1974.

Welch, R. L., & Huston, A. C. Effects of induced success/failure and attributions on the problem-solving behavior of psychologically androgynous and feminine women. *Journal of Personality*, 1982, *50*, 81–97.

Willerman, L. Effects of families on intellectual development. *American Psychologist*, 1979, *34*, 923–929.

Zigler, E., Abelson, W. D., & Seitz, V. Motivational factors in the performance of economically disadvantaged children on the Peabody Picture Vocabulary Test. *Child Development*, 1973, *44*, 294–302.

Zigler, E., Abelson, W. D., Trickett, P. K., & Seitz, V. Is an intervention program necessary in order to improve economically disadvantaged children's IQ scores? *Child Development*, 1982, *53*, 340–348.

Zigler, E., & Valentine, J. (Eds.). *Project Head Start: A legacy of the war on poverty.* New York: Free Press, 1979.

part ***F****our*

THE CHILDHOOD YEARS: PERSONAL AND SOCIAL DEVELOPMENT

CHAPTER 9

*T*he development of social cognition

"*H*ow do children conceptualize and reason about their social world—the people they observe, the relations between people and the groups in which they participate? What are the developmental changes in such concepts and reasoning? And how is social cognitive functioning related to social behavior? These are the central questions addressed in the area of social cognitive development" (Shantz, 1983, p. 495).

The study of social cognition has attracted much attention in recent years as psychologists have realized that children's social and emotional reactions depend partly on how they think. Consider the following example:

A 4-year-old takes a bowl of oatmeal away from her 1-year-old brother. She does not like oatmeal, so she assumes she is doing him a favor. He screams, and her father scolds her for being mean to her brother.

The problem in this example is the 4-year-old's failure to take into account her brother's preferences and to recognize that they are different from her own. If her father understood her social cognitive processes, he might praise her for her efforts to be kind but point out that her brother likes oatmeal.

Broadly defined, *social cognition* refers to perception, thinking, and reasoning about humans and human affairs (Flavell, 1977). Investigations of social cognitive development focus on children's knowledge and understanding of the social world—of people, including themselves, and of social relationships. The research reviewed in this chapter emphasizes children's perceptions of themselves and others; thoughts about friends, authorities, and leaders; judgments about moral and social rules; and knowledge of social conventions. Although each topic has unique features, some common principles apply to reasoning in all these domains.

Much of the research on social cognition has been inspired by Piaget's theory and writing. Because investigators of social cognition have been strongly influenced by cognitive developmental theory, it is not surprising that many of them maintain that children's conceptualizations and reasoning about people and social relationships progress through sequences of qualitatively distinct levels or stages. These stages are said to emerge in *invariant order*, although at different rates in different children. Each more advanced stage is built on the preceding ones but has new characteristics and a new organizational structure.

At the most general level, children's social thinking can be described as developing in several interdependent directions: (a) from "surface to depth," that is, from attention to appearances to consideration of more enduring qualities (e.g., from thinking about friends in terms of attractiveness to judgments about personal motives); (b) from simple to complex, that is, from narrow concentration on one aspect of an issue or problem (*centration*) to a broader perspective that takes account of many dimensions simultaneously; (c) from rigid to flexible thinking; (d) from predominant concern with oneself and the here and now to concern with the welfare of others and with the future; (e) from concrete to abstract thinking; and (f) from diffuse, sometimes inconsistent, ideas to systematic, organized, integrated thoughts (Damon & Hart, 1982; Flavell, 1977).

Distinguishing people from objects

Although many principles of cognitive development apply to understanding both the physical and social worlds, children know from very early that living things are different from inanimate objects. Young infants appear to expect interactions from people but not from objects. They become distressed—grimacing, thrashing, and crying—if someone faces them without speaking or moving (Gelman & Spelke, 1981; Trevarthen, 1977). By 5 months of age, infants react to other people's expressions of positive emotions with smiles and cooing but become upset by expressions of anger, fear, and sadness (Kreutzer & Charlesworth, 1973). When an 8-month-old sees another person gazing in a particular direction, the infant is likely to look in the same direction (Scaife & Bruner, 1975).

The qualities that distinguish people from inanimate objects—such as the ability to move independently and the possession of feelings—are recognized early. Infants 24 months old are surprised when a chair seems to move on its own but not when it is moved by someone. Three-year-olds agree that a sentence like "The girl is sorry" is sensible but the sentence "The door is sorry" is not (Keil, 1979).

Rudimentary knowledge and understanding of social relationships are undoubtedly acquired in infants' earliest encounters with their caregivers. For example, from the outset, caregivers respond to children's cries. While being attended to and cooing in response to being spoken to, infants begin to learn about human interactions, about conversation, about "taking turns," and, in a primitive way, about relationships to authorities. In early childhood interactions between peers, children share toys, exchange favors, and even establish such feelings as trust and intimacy (Damon, 1977). They gradually establish concepts of social relationships (friendship, authority) and concepts about themselves and their own identities as a result of social interactions with others.

Understanding others' points of view

Piaget regarded preoperational children as egocentric, unable to understand that their own perspectives, points of view, thoughts, motives, intentions, and attitudes are different from those of others (see Chapter 7). He maintained that egocentrism begins to decline sharply at age 6 or 7, when children enter the stage of concrete operations and recognize that other people have their own thoughts, points of view, and intentions. However, as mentioned in Chapter 7, recent evidence demonstrates that even very young children are not

as egocentric as Piaget proposed. They are frequently aware that others do not see things as they do, and they often modify their behavior to take account of others' needs and interests.

Methods of study   The challenge to Piaget's assertions about egocentrism came about because investigators used new methods to assess children's knowledge. Our conclusions about children's social understanding depend partly on the methods used to study it. Many investigators of social cognition have used variations on Piaget's *clinical method,* a procedure in which the child is asked questions about a story or a hypothetical situation. The interviewer tries to determine what the child thinks about the motives, actions, and intentions of the characters in the story. For example, Selman (1980) has investigated children's ability to take others' perspectives (also called *role-taking ability*) by presenting story dilemmas designed to elicit reasoning about social or moral situations. Here is an example of a dilemma presented to children age 4 to 10, together with some probing questions.

> *Holly is an 8-year-old girl who likes to climb trees. She is the best tree climber in the neighborhood. One day while climbing down from a tall tree, she falls off the bottom branch but does not hurt herself. Her father sees her fall. He is upset and asks her to promise not to climb trees any more. Holly promises.*

Later that day, Holly and her friends meet Shawn. Shawn's kitten is caught up in a tree and can't get down. Something has to be done right away, or the kitten may fall. Holly is the only one who climbs trees well enough to reach the kitten and get it down, but she remembers her promise to her father. (Selman, 1980, p. 36)

Role-taking questions include "Does Holly know how Shawn feels about the kitten? Why?" "How will Holly's father feel if he finds out she climbed the tree?" "What does Holly think her father will think of her if he finds out?" The responses are coded for the child's explanation of the thoughts and feelings of each individual referred to in the dilemma and the relationships among their various perspectives.

To be scored nonegocentric on this measure, children must be able to consider a hypothetical situation and verbalize their thoughts about the situation. Answering questions about people in a hypothetical situation may be more difficult for a child than assuming the point of view of a real person that the child knows. In addition, one of the truisms of developmental psychology is that children often have knowledge that they cannot easily verbalize. Therefore, the fact that children cannot explain how others feel does not mean they do not know or understand those feelings. Suppose, for example, that we could observe a child in a real-life dilemma like Holly's. A preschooler might indicate that she understood her father's perspective by asking permission or by explaining to her father why she climbed the tree. We might assume that she understood Shawn's point of view if she reassured him that the kitten would be all right. When investigators use nonverbal methods, or when they measure children's reactions in real-life situations, they often find signs of perspective taking at an early age.

The fact that our conclusions depend partly on the method used does not mean that studies using hypothetical stories are invalid. It does mean that we must be clear about what is being measured. The stages demonstrated by this method reflect children's ability to reason about abstract social situations *and* to explain their reasoning. Abstract, verbal understanding is an important aspect of development. However, we must not infer that younger children have no understanding of others' perspectives simply because they do not respond to hypothetical, verbal measures in the same way that older children do.

Stages of role taking   With that caution, we will examine the stages of perspective taking or role taking derived from children's responses to Selman's dilemmas. At stage 0, the *egocentric viewpoint,* children fail to distinguish between their own interpretation of an event and what they consider true or correct. For example, in response to the question "How will Holly's father feel when he finds out?" the child says, "Happy, he likes kittens." At stage 1, *social informational role taking* (ages 6–8), children are aware that others have a different interpretation or perspective. At this stage, a child might say, "Holly's father will be mad because he doesn't want her to climb trees." *Self-reflection* is the essence of stage 2 (ages 8–10), when children recognize that each individual is aware of other people's thoughts and feelings. They know not only that someone else has a different perspective but also that the other person can be aware of the child's perspective. For example, a child who was asked, "Will Holly's father punish her?" replied, "She knows her father will understand why she climbed the tree, so he won't punish her." In stage 3, *mutual role taking* (ages 10–12), children can view an interaction between two people from the perspective of a third person, an onlooker, parent, or mutual friend. A child at this stage might say, "Holly and her father trust each other, so they can talk about why she climbed the tree." Finally, in stage 4, *social and conventional system role taking* (ages 12–15+), children realize that there are integrated networks of perspectives, such as an American or a Catholic point of view. "The subject realizes that each self considers the shared point of view of the social system in order to facilitate accurate communication with and understanding of others" (Selman, 1976, p. 306).

Empathy   A special kind of perspective taking, empathy, refers to "shared emotional responses which the child experiences on perceiving others' emotional reactions" (Feshbach, 1978) (see Chapter 5). When Sally sees Tim crying because his cat has been hit by a car, she may feel sad and imagine how it feels to lose one's cat. Her response is empathic. According to one analysis, empathy has two cognitive components and an affective (emotional) component. The cognitive components are the ability to identify and label the feeling states of other people and the ability to assume the perspective of another person. The affective component is a capacity for emotional responsiveness (Feshbach, 1978).

In one of the most widely used measures of empathy, children see slides accompanied by stories about a child in an emotionally arousing situation. For example:

Slide I. Here is a boy and his dog. This boy goes everywhere with his dog, but sometimes the dog tries to run away.
Slide II. Here the dog is running away.
Slide III. This time the boy cannot find him, and he may be gone and lost forever.

The children are then asked, "How do you feel?" (Feshbach, 1978). An empathic response includes both the cognitive understanding of the feelings and perspective of the boy in the story and an emotional response to the boy's suffering.

As discussed in Chapter 5, children first show signs of empathy during the second year of life. Because it appears so early and is fairly universal, some theorists think that empathy is an innate quality of human beings. They argue that people have evolved as creatures who live together and that concern and consideration for others has survival value, just as self-interest does. Others argue that empathy is learned through early conditioning and that the relevant experiences are virtually universal. For example, an infant might cut a finger, see it bleed, and feel it hurt. When she sees someone else cut a finger, she will associate the sight of blood with her own pain.

One of the cognitive components proposed by Feshbach (1978) is the ability to discriminate and label the emotions of others. It develops gradually from the toddler years on. Children as young as 1 year or less respond differently to the joy, anger, and other emotions of people around them, indicating that they can discriminate these reactions (see Chapter 4). By age 3, children can label faces as happy or unhappy, and by age 4 or 5 they can reliably discriminate faces showing joy, fear, anger, and sadness (Borke, 1971; Masters & Carlson, in press).

The second cognitive component, perspective taking, also appears among very young children. Consider the following anecdote.

> Michael, aged fifteen months, and his friend Paul were fighting over a toy and Paul started to cry. Michael let go, but Paul still cried. Michael paused, then brought his teddy bear to Paul, but Paul continued to cry. Michael paused again, and . . . fetched Paul's security blanket from an adjoining room (Hoffman, 1981, p. 73).

Michael was able to understand that the teddy bear, which would probably have comforted him, did not work for Paul. He then found the object that Paul would find soothing. This story also illustrates the point that the capacities of very young children are often underestimated by relying on verbal methods to measure their understanding.

Situational specificity Empathy is not an all-or-none quality of a child. It varies with the situation, the child's experience, and the people to whom the child is responding. In general, children show more empathy for people who are similar to themselves than for those who are dissimilar. For example, they are more empathic to members of their own gender or race than to children of the other gender or a different racial group (Feshbach, 1978) (see Table 9.1). Perhaps it is easier to put oneself in the place of someone who is obviously similar. Children are also more apt to be empathic when they see someone in a situation they have experienced themselves than when they lack that experience (Aronfreed, 1968).

TABLE 9.1		STIMULUS			STIMULUS	
Empathic responses of 6- and 7-year-old children to children of different genders and ethnic groups	Subject	Boy	Girl	Subject	Black	White
	Boy	4.58 (N = 12)	3.64 (N = 11)	Black	3.97	3.53
	Girl	3.45 (N = 11)	5.50 (N = 12)	White	3.34	4.34

Source: From N. D. Feshbach. Studies of empathic behavior in children. In B. A. Maher (Ed.), *Progress in experimental personality research* (Vol. 8). New York: Academic Press, 1978. By permission.

Preschool children rely heavily on situational cues: A 3-year-old seeing a child in front of a birthday cake assumes the child is happy. Older children are more skillful at perceiving "personal cues" (facial expressions, body postures, and the like) and psychological reactions. A 5- or 6-year-old might notice a frown on the birthday child's face and conclude he is not so happy, even though the situation suggests that he should be (Hughes, Tingle, & Sawin, 1981).

Parent practices and empathy   Although almost all children develop the capacity for empathy, some are more prone to respond with empathy than others. Parents' methods of discipline contribute to children's empathy. Discipline that focuses the child's attention on other people's feelings and reactions is especially important in teaching children empathy. An example is a father's saying, "You shouldn't hit Sarah because it hurts her." Very often, such reasoning includes comments designed to get the child to take the perspective of another person: "Your feelings are hurt when you see other children receiving invitations to a party and you are not invited. That is how Joe will feel if you invite others without inviting him." Parents who use this form of discipline frequently have children who are empathic with others and who are likely to show prosocial helping, sharing, and sympathy (Hoffman, 1981; Radke-Yarrow, Zahn-Waxler, & Chapman, 1983).

Perspective taking and social adjustment   Perspective-taking ability increases with age, probably as a function of cognitive development in interaction with the child's social experience. Some children, however, have considerably lower levels of perspective taking than others of their age. Two questions arise about such children: Do they behave differently than children with better skills? Does training in perspective taking improve maladaptive behavior?

Deficiencies in perspective taking are *one* feature of children who are delinquent or show maladjusted behavior. Such children often lack a variety of social problem-solving skills, including the ability to take another person's point of view. Perspective-taking training sometimes helps reduce problem behavior. One extensive training study was carried out with preadolescent delinquent males. Their scores on a measure of role taking were much lower than the scores of nondelinquent males the same age. In the training sessions, the boys wrote and videotaped skits about people their age. The skits were repeated until each person had played the role of each character in the skit. The trained group was then compared to a control group that received no treatment and to another control group that watched movies instead of performing in skits. Those who had received training performed better on the role-taking measure. More important, they had significantly lower levels of delinquent behavior during the 18-month follow-up period after the training ended (Chandler, 1973).

Although training in perspective taking can apparently produce some benefits, it is likely to be much more effective when combined with training in other aspects of social problem solving. An extensive program in social problem-solving skills is described in Box 9.1.

<table>
<tr><td>SOCIAL COGNITION
AND EMOTIONAL
REACTIONS</td></tr>
</table>

Social cognitive abilities such as perspective taking affect not only children's behavior but also their emotional reactions. For example, preschool and elementary school children are frightened by different kinds of television shows. Cantor and her associates at the University of Wisconsin have shown that the differences stem at least partly from differences in children's tendency to take others' perspectives. In one experiment, preschool and elementary school children saw a film of a boy who was attacked by a swarm of vicious bees. In one version, the camera focused primarily on the threatening bees; in another, it focused on the boy's frightened face. Children's physiological reactions were measured as they watched, and they were asked afterward about how frightened they had felt. Older children were frightened by both versions, but younger children were more frightened by the version showing the bees than by the one showing the boy's face. As children become more skilled in taking others' perspectives and empathizing with their feelings, they are more apt to be frightened by seeing a film character's fearful reactions, even when they do not see the source of the fear (Cantor, 1982).

Children may feel happy, sad, angry, or afraid partly because of the interpretations and attributions that they make about their own or other people's behavior. For example, if Karen knocks over a puzzle that Clark has put together, Clark will be angry and may do something mean to her, especially if he thinks she did it deliberately. If he thinks it was an accident, he will be less likely to be angry or to retaliate. Also, Clark will feel proud of his ability to do the puzzle if he attributes his success to ability but will probably feel surprise if he attributes it to luck. If he fails, he will probably feel shame if he attributes the failure to lack of effort. Other people's emotional reactions to children's behavior are also affected by attributions. When a child fails at a school task, the teacher may feel anger if she thinks the child did not try but pity if she thinks the child tried hard and did not succeed (Weiner, in press).

We turn now to how children conceptualize people—themselves and others—and how they conceptualize friendships, authority relations, and other social interactions. Some people have suggested that we are all "naive psychologists." We all have theories about people's personalities, motives, and behavior patterns. Attributions are one form of naive psychology, but there are others. As children develop, they gradually form concepts of what people are like. We will discuss these concepts first as they apply to the self, then as they apply to others.

*Development
of self-concept*

Our self-concepts play a critical part in determining our relationships with others. William James, one of the founders of the discipline of psychology, divided the self into two components, the "me" and the "I." The "me" is "the sum total of all a person can call his" (James, 1892/1961, p. 44), including abilities, social and personality characteristics, and material possessions. The "I" is the "self as knower." According to a later analysis, this aspect of self "continually organizes and interprets experience, people, objects, and events in the purely subjective manner" (Damon & Hart, 1982, p. 844). In other words, the "I" is self-reflective, aware of its own nature. Research in self-understanding encompasses both the "I" and the "me" aspects of self.

The beginnings of self-awareness appear sometime during the second year of life, as explained in Chapter 5. Around 18 months, children recognize their own faces and point to pictures of themselves when their names are called (Damon & Hart, 1982). During the childhood years, children develop a sense of

BOX 9.1

*Training in
interpersonal
problem-solving
skills*

Social cognitive skills, such as the ability to take other people's perspectives, may be important in children's ability to get along well with others. Myrna Shure and George Spivak at the Hahnemann Community Mental Health Center in Philadelphia have proposed that many of the behavioral adjustment problems that children encounter may result at least partly from lack of cognitive skills in interpersonal problem solving. That is, children who are aggressive, impulsive, or extremely fearful of others may lack basic skills in understanding others and dealing with interpersonal relationships. They have developed training programs to teach interpersonal cognitive problem-solving skills to many age groups. The program for preschool children consists of training for "emotional awareness" or awareness of others' feelings and reactions. For example, the teacher directs a game in which one child holds a toy while the other grabs it. The teacher then says, "How did you feel when he grabbed the toy?" Then the toy is handed back. "Now how do you feel?"

An extensive training program in interpersonal cognitive problem-solving skills was evaluated for 2 years during preschool and kindergarten. Children were randomly assigned to an experimental group that received training or a control group that did not. Three types of skills were taught. One skill was *finding alternatives*—generating as many different solutions as possible to a problem situation. For example, children were shown some pictures and told, "Johnny wants a chance to play with this shovel, but Jimmy keeps on playing with it. What can Johnny do so he can have a chance to play with the shovel?" Children were encouraged to think of many different possibilities. A second skill was *anticipating the consequences* of actions. For instance, a child character was described as having taken an object, such as a flashlight, from an adult without asking. Children were asked to anticipate how the adult might react. The third skill was *understanding cause and effect*. In one story, "Debbie is crying. She is talking to her mother." Children were encouraged to speculate about why the events were happening; that is, to suggest that someone may have hit Debbie or that she might have fallen.

Children were tested on cognitive problem-solving skills at the beginning and end of each year. Children who received the training performed significantly better than the untrained control group on all three skill areas. The scores are shown in Figure B9.1.

Teachers also rated the behavioral adjustment of children before and after the training. Before training, one group of poorly adjusted children had difficulty waiting or delaying gratification, were prone to anger and extreme emotional reactions, and were extremely aggressive. Another group were excessively inhibited, showing little emotion or assertiveness. Both types of children were rated as better adjusted after they received problem-solving training than when they did not.

These findings support the notion that social cognitive skills can help children to get along successfully in social relationships. Children who learned cognitive problem-solving skills were likely to show appropriate levels of emotional expression and assertiveness rather than being either very impulsive or extremely inhibited.

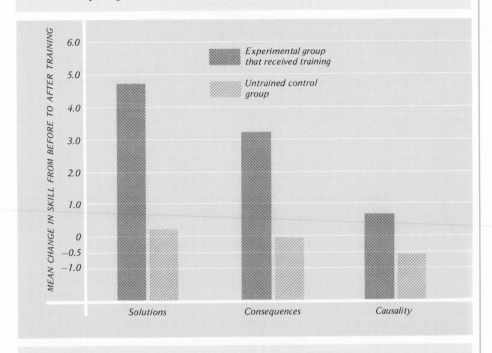

Mean change in children's interpersonal cognitive problem-solving skills for children who received training in preschool and kindergarten and for a control group who did not receive training. Three types of skills were measured: finding alternative solutions in social situations; understanding the consequences of people's actions; and understanding cause-and-effect relationships between actions and outcomes. Children who received training improved significantly more than untrained children on all three skills. They were also rated as better adjusted by their teachers. (Adapted from M. B. Shure & G. Spivack. Interpersonal problem solving as a mediator of behavioral adjustment in preschool and kindergarten children. Journal of Applied Developmental Psychology, 1980, 1, 37. By permission.)

who they are and where they fit in their society. The rudimentary sense of self grows into an elaborated and relatively stable network of self-perceptions and feelings by the time the child reaches the end of elementary school.

Self-concepts are usually measured by asking people to describe themselves or to tell how they are different from others. For example, a child might be asked to tell how he would describe himself in a diary no one else would see or how he would be different if he were his best friend. A teenager might reveal her self-concept if asked to write to a new roommate whom she had never met.

These measures of self-concept are intended to identify the attributes the person considers most important. One person might focus on how kind (or unkind) he is while another might emphasize how interesting (or dull) he is. Self-concept is not identical to self-esteem, though the two are related. Self-esteem, which is discussed in Chapter 10, is based on evaluations and judgments about one's perceived characteristics; self-concept does not imply positive or negative feelings about the self.

There are regular developmental changes in the categories children use when asked to describe themselves. Until about age 7, children seem to define the self in physical terms. They name concrete, observable features of themselves, such as hair color, height, or favorite activities ("I like to play ball"). Inner psychological experiences are not described as being separate from overt behavior and physical characteristics (Broughton, 1978; Keller, Ford, & Meacham, 1978; Selman, 1980).

During middle childhood, descriptions of self shift gradually to more abstract descriptions of facts ("I don't get into fights") and from "physicalistic" to psychological (Damon & Hart, 1982; Harter, 1983; Selman, 1980). Distinctions are made between mind and body, between the private subjective self and external events, and between mental and motivational characteristics and body parts. As a consequence, children begin to think about themselves, to realize that they can monitor their own thoughts and deceive others about their ideas (Broughton, 1978). At this age, a child feels distinct from others because she realizes she possesses unique thoughts and feelings. Children this age seem to be particularly concerned with their own competencies, especially in comparison with others ("I can ride my bike better than my brother can").

These general trends are shown by the responses of children in first, third, and sixth grades to questions about what would change if they became their best friend or when they grew up, or what had changed since they were a baby (see Table 9.2). First-graders most often named external characteristics, such as name, age, and possessions. Older children described their typical behavior. Some sixth-graders also referred to internal feelings and thoughts (Mohr, 1978).

TABLE 9.2

Self-concept at different ages

Responses to the question "What would you have to change about yourself for you to become your best friend?" Numbers are percent of children who gave each category of response.

| | GRADE LEVEL | | |
Type of characteristic described	First	Third	Sixth
External (physical attributes, name, possessions, age)	85	36	8
Behavioral (regular behavior or traits)	5	56	76
Internal (thoughts, feelings knowledge)	10	8	16

Source: Adapted from D. M. Mohr. Development of attributes of personal identity. *Developmental Psychology*, 1978, *14*, 427–428.

In line with the general cognitive changes noted by Piaget and other cognitive theorists, the adolescent's self system is characteristically more abstract, more complex, and more coherent than that of a younger child. In describing the "me," adolescents stress internal, stable, integrated psychological characteristics as well as beliefs, thoughts, and feelings. Typical responses are "I am really friendly, so I can make new friends easily" (Bernstein, 1980, p. 237) or "I am very sensitive to having my feelings hurt" (Harter, 1983; Rosenberg, 1979), and, whereas younger children refer to themselves in terms of present status and activities, adolescents show a real sense of continuity, incorporating their ideas of their present and future selves into self-descriptions.

At the same time, adolescents reveal a "more prominent belief in the 'I's' agency and volitional power" (Damon & Hart, 1982, p. 855), that is, in the self's activity and ability to process and control behavior, thoughts, and emotions. As one adolescent reported, "If I don't like a subject, I won't do anything in the subject. . . . On the other hand, in the subjects I do like . . . my science and mathematics . . . I really work" (Secord & Peevers, 1974, p. 139). Because adolescence is a time of acute self-consciousness and self-awareness, the tendency to evaluate one's own thoughts and feelings is strong, and attempts are made to integrate "the disparate aspects of the self into an internally consistent construct system" (Damon & Hart, 1982, p. 855).

Conceptions of other people

Similar developmental trends appear when children are asked to describe a best friend, a favorite teacher, or a neighbor. When asked, "Tell me about the boy who lives next door" or "What sort of person is Edna?" children younger than about age 7 usually refer to external, concrete attributes such as the person's name, physical characteristics, possessions, and overt behavior. They also frequently use global evaluative adjectives such as *good, bad, mean,* and *nice.*

Beginning in middle childhood, around age 8, children increasingly use abstract adjectives that refer to behavioral traits, psychological characteristics, beliefs, values, and attitudes (Livesley & Bromley, 1973; Peevers & Secord, 1973). During this period, "the child becomes less bound to the surface aspects of people and increasingly abstracts regularities across time and situations and infers motives for behavior" (Shantz, 1983, p. 506).

Around ages 12 to 14, children's descriptions become less concerned with the relationships between themselves and the other individual. Adolescents also use more qualifying terms, such as *sometimes* and *quite,* suggesting that they understand that traits are not fixed and absolute (Shantz, 1983).

Perceptions of motives for behavior Questions such as "What is Sally like?" or "Who are you?" elicit children's perceptions of stable traits of people. In real life, however, people's behavior is "caused" by situational factors as well as enduring traits. Suppose that Rhonda walks down the hall at school ignoring greetings from other children. Susan, who felt snubbed by her, might attribute her behavior to a personality trait ("She's a snob") or to a situational factor ("A teacher just bawled her out"). From age 5 or 6 on, children often assume that both situational and personal factors contribute to people's actions, though the relative weight given to the two types of causes varies.

Adults and older children often attribute other people's behavior to stable traits but offer situational explanations for their own actions. In the example just given, Rhonda might suggest that her behavior is due to the scolding she received from the teacher, while Susan would view it as a sign of an enduring personality trait. One investigation was designed to determine age differences in children's tendency to use personal or situational explanations of behavior. Individuals in five age groups—5, 8, 11, 15, and 20—heard a series of stories about a boy who encountered a dog. In some stories, the boy had previously been fearful in several situations; in others, he had not (the trait of timidity was varied). In some stories, the dog was large and threatening; in others, it was small and cuddly (the situation was varied). Subjects predicted what the boy would do. Although all age groups took into account information about both person and situation, the 5-year-olds gave greater weight to situational factors than did the older children (Ross, 1981).

The tendency of 5-year-olds to weight the immediate situation more heavily than enduring personality characteristics is consistent with their tendency to describe people in terms of external attributes. Their concepts of internal psychological characteristics are not well formed until middle or late childhood.

Processes of developmental change The developmental changes in children's descriptions of themselves and of other people probably arise from their improved abilities to take another person's perspective and to conceptualize inner thoughts and feelings. During middle childhood (roughly ages 6 to 12), children become aware that others form opinions and make judgments about them on the basis of their behavior. Many children become more self-conscious and concerned about what other people think of them during this period.

Another cognitive basis for the developing self-concept is social comparison. We form our concepts of ourselves partly by observing others and comparing ourselves with them. Many theorists have argued that the image of self is a reflection of others' perceptions. As children grow through childhood, they are more likely to make social comparisons and they become more accurate in detecting similarities and differences between themselves and others.

Parents and other adults who understand these developmental changes in children's conceptions of themselves and others may be better able to understand and reason with young children. For example, it is more meaningful to talk with young children about what they like to do ("You paint pictures well") than about more abstract traits ("You are kind to others").

Friends and friendship

Friendships and peer interactions are influenced not only by concepts about individuals but also by children's views of social relationships among people. To investigate children's conceptions of friendship, some researchers have used interview techniques ("Who is your best friend? Why is Nancy your best friend?") (Damon, 1977; Selman, 1980; Youniss, 1981), while others have presented dilemmas in story formats and asked children questions about them (Selman, 1976). In one story dilemma, two girls, Kathy and Debbie, have been friends since they were 5 when a new girl, Jeanette, moves into their neighborhood. Jeanette invites Kathy to go to the circus with her on a day that Kathy has promised to play with Debbie. What will Kathy do? Questions about friendship and social relationships follow.

Integrating the results of several relevant studies that used different tech-

niques, Damon (1977) concluded that between the age of 5 and adolescence children's conceptions of friendship evolve through three major levels. At the first level, typical of 5- to 7-year-olds, friends are the playmates the child sees most frequently, usually neighbors or schoolmates. They share material goods such as food and toys. Friends "act nice" and are "fun to be with." Friendships have no long-lasting or permanent status and are easily established and terminated. "But there is no sense yet of liking or disliking the stable personal traits of another" (Damon, 1977, p. 154). One 5-year-old reported, "When I don't play with them they don't like me" (p. 156). The same youngster finds it very easy to make friends. "Like when I'm doing something and they're doing something else and I walk by they grab me in. They just grab me by the hand and I fly in" (p. 155).

Between the ages of 8 and 11, at level 2, children regard friends as those who assist and share with them, responding to one another's needs and desires and sharing mutual interests. Mutual trust and possession of desirable attributes such as kindness and considerateness are also critical features of friendships. Betty, age 10, likes Karen "because she's nice; she gives me jewelry and candy, and I give her things, too" (Damon, 1977, p. 158).

At level 3, attained at approximately 12 years of age, friendships are judged on the basis of understanding and sharing innermost thoughts, feelings, and other secrets, and they are usually stable over long periods of time (Damon, 1977). Friends help each other with psychological problems such as loneliness, sadness, and fear, and they avoid giving psychological pain or dis-

BOX 9.2
American children's concepts of authority

In Damon's extensive investigations (1977), children between 4 and 11 were told stories about two kinds of social dilemmas and asked questions about solutions. In one, Michele (or Peter, when the story was told to boys) had to choose between obeying her mother, who told her she must clean up her room before going out to play, and disobeying by going on a picnic with friends. In another dilemma, a child authority, the captain of a team, tells Peter (or Michelle) that he can't play the position on the team that he wants.

In the earliest stages, characteristic only of 4-year-olds, children do not regard authority as external. The authority's commands and the child's desires are viewed as similar. Children may assert that they obey because they want to do what they have been told to do. For example, in discussing the captain's decision not to give the child the position he desired, one boy said, "The other kids like him and want to do what he says" (Damon, 1977, p. 182).

Beginning at age 5 or 6, an authority figure is seen as having "an inherent right to be obeyed" because of overall superiority, greater social or physical power, size, strength, or status. Thus, according to Tim, age 5, Peter should clean up his room because his mother told him so and "'cause she is the boss of the house like his father. . . . Mothers and fathers are bigger and they can spank" (Damon, 1977, p. 188).

At age 8, approximately, a more sophisticated view of authority as a reciprocal relationship appears. The authority figure deserves obedience because of past, present, or future assistance to the child. Ben, age 7, says that Peter "should miss the picnic." Why? "Because if his mother told him to do something he should do it. . . . Because if you were sick and asked her for a glass of water, she would do it for you; but if you won't do something for her, she won't do it for you" (Damon, 1977, p. 191).

By age 9, children think obedience to authority is essentially voluntary and cooperative. The authority and subordinate figures are perceived as having equal rights, but the authority has a responsibility for the welfare of the subordinate. Nine-year-old Lisa says, "Her mother knows best . . . her mother went through all these times when she was a kid . . . so now she knows what to tell Michelle to do, what's best for her and stuff. She knows because she has been through it" (Damon, 1977, p. 194).

At the highest level of reasoning, at age 11 or 12, the authority relationship is considered fully cooperative, established by consensus or agreement, and related to specific situations. "Even long-term authority roles (mother, teacher, and so on) are seen as legitimate only in certain appropriate conditions and even then only with agreement of the governed" (Damon, 1977, p. 197). Although special abilities and knowledge are required, the demands of the situation must also be evaluated in accepting someone as an authority. "Mothers know what's best for their kids . . . they know how to bring them up and stuff, they know when to tell a kid no and when to say yes . . . they don't have to know more about everything, just the things that matter in bringing up kids, like what time kids should go to bed at night, what they should eat and that they should clean their room up before they go out on picnics. That doesn't mean they could be president or anything. . . . A president has to know how to get votes and please lots of people" (Damon, 1977, p. 199).

comfort to each other. In the words of one 13-year-old boy, "You need someone you can tell anything to, all kinds of things that you don't want spread around. That's why you are someone's friend" (p. 163). (Children's peer relations are discussed in Chapter 12.)

Authority relationships

While friendship is the major social relationship among peers, authority is the key to the interactions between adults and children. (Of course, there are also hierarchies within peer groups—leader and follower statuses.) Between kindergarten age and adolescence, ideas about relationships with authority change, just as ideas about friendship do. In the earliest stage there is little understanding of the function of authority. This is followed by a stage of obedience to authority in order to achieve goals and to avoid unpleasant consequences. More sophisticated thoughts about authority as a voluntary and cooperative relationship emerge later on. A detailed description of children's changing concepts of authority relations appear in Box 9.2.

MORAL JUDGMENT

Children's ideas about the proper and appropriate functions of authority play an important role in their concepts of the moral and ethical rules by which people should be guided. Rules of morality, based on principles of justice and concern for others, are taught by families, schools, and religious institutions. When American psychologists began investigating morality, they were primarily interested in how children acquire an internalized desire to conform to the moral rules of society and in children's motives for obeying rules. They often ignored the possibility that children might wish to conform to moral rules but have a different understanding of them than adults do. In the domain of morality, as in many others, Piaget laid the groundwork for later research by examining developmental changes in children's cognitions or judgments about moral issues. This line of investigation provided information on how children understand and interpret moral rules. As we review this information on cognitive aspects of morality, keep in mind that we are talking about children's beliefs or ideals, not their behavior. The relation between moral judgments and moral behavior is not very clear, as will be seen later in the chapter.

Piaget's theory

Piaget used interviews to investigate children's moral thought, asking them questions about moral issues or the ethics of characters in stories. For instance, he might ask, "Why shouldn't you cheat in a game?" Or, after telling a story about a mother who gave the biggest piece of cake to her most obedient child, he might question the child about the justice of her action.

Realism versus relativism Piaget concluded that from ages 5 to about 12, a child's concept of justice passes from moral realism to moral relativism. *Moral realism* is a rigid and inflexible notion of right and wrong in which "justice is subordinated to adult authority." *Moral relativism,* which begins at around age 11, is based on the idea that everyone has an equal right to justice and consideration (Piaget, 1932, p. 314).

The moral realist believes that rules are absolute. They are fixed, inflexible, and given by authority. They cannot be changed, and exceptions cannot be made. For example, when children were told a story in which the commands of a parent conflicted with justice or equality, younger children usually chose obedience to adults as the correct course of action. Older children believed that adult authority could be violated in the circumstances described. Younger children did not think it was ever right to tell a lie, whereas older children thought lying might be right under some conditions.

For Piaget, the world of children's games and peer-group interaction was an important arena for moral thinking. At the stage of moral realism, children thought there was one "right" way to play a game. For example, they would argue that you had to land in every square in hopscotch because that was "the way the game is played." Older children recognized that rules could be made and changed by group consensus: "Let's play that you skip every third square." Hence, older children rejected blind obedience to authority and viewed moral rules as the product of cooperation, reciprocity, and interaction among peers.

Intentions versus consequences In the period of moral realism, children judge actions more by their consequences than by intentions. In a classic story used to measure moral judgment, two children are described. Johnny is trying to help his mother by carrying something into the kitchen. When he pushes open the door, he accidently upsets a tray containing 15 glasses, and all the glasses break. A second boy, Billy, while trying to sneak a cookie out of the cupboard, breaks one glass. Which child did the naughtier thing? In the stage of moral realism, children argue that the first boy was naughtier because he broke more glasses. Older children give more weight to the motives or intentions of the person and judge the second boy naughtier because he was trying to steal a cookie.

Recent research has demonstrated that children's understanding of intentions is more complex than Piaget thought. When the consequences of an action are positive, young children give more credit to an actor with good intentions than to one with bad intentions. For instance, children from 5 to 11 years old were asked to judge a boy who emptied a toy box on the floor because he wanted to straighten them (good intentions) or because he was cross and wanted to make a mess (bad intentions). All age groups rated the boy with positive intentions more favorably than the one with negative intentions when an adult praised his actions (positive consequences). All but the youngest children also took into account his intentions when he was scolded by an adult (negative consequences) (Costanzo, Coie, Grumet, & Farnill, 1973) (see Figure 9.1).

FIGURE 9.1

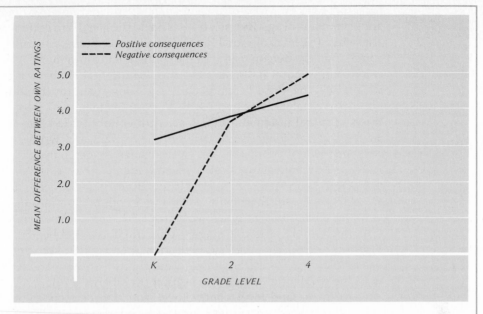

Children's ratings of how good a boy in a story was when he performed an action that resulted in positive or negative consequences. The mean difference is the difference in ratings made when his intentions were positive when they were negative. When the consequences were positive, all age groups rated the boy with positive intentions more favorably than the boy with negative intentions. When consequences were negative, all but the youngest group rated the boys with positive intentions more favorably. (From P. R. Costanzo, J. D. Coie, J. F. Grumet, & D. Farnill. A reexamination of the effects of intent and consequence of children's moral judgments. **Child Development**, 1973, 44, 159. © The Society for Research in Child Development, Inc. By permission.)

Even very young children evaluate intentionally naughty acts as worse than accidental ones. For example, in the story about Johnny and Billy, if Billy deliberately breaks the glass, young children judge him naughtier than Johnny. Parents of preschoolers often hear "It was an accident," and they probably treat a misdeed more leniently if they believe it was unintentional. Children sometimes have difficulty inferring people's intentions accurately, and they weigh damage done in a misdeed heavily in making their judgments. However, they do understand the difference between deliberate and accidental actions at a young age (Karniol, 1978).

Kohlberg's theory

Piaget became increasingly preoccupied with the study of logical and scientific thinking and did not pursue his work on moral judgments. About 30 years after Piaget published his studies of moral development, Lawrence Kohlberg began to extend and amplify Piaget's work. Kohlberg and his associates presented children and adolescents with a series of moral dilemmas and asked them to make judgments about them, articulating their reasoning. The most familiar dilemma is about Heinz, a man whose wife is dying. Heinz does not have enough money to buy the drug that will save her life. The druggist refuses to lower the price or delay payment, so Heinz breaks into the drugstore and steals the drug. The person is asked whether Heinz should have done so and why. The level of moral judgment depends on the structure or kind of reasoning that the person uses, not the content of the judgment. A person could receive a high moral judgment score for saying that Heinz was right or that he was wrong; the score depends on the reasons given for the judgment.

After analyzing responses to these dilemmas, Kohlberg proposed three levels of moral judgment, which are further subdivided into two stages each. At the *preconventional level,* children judge right and wrong primarily by the consequences of actions. In the earliest stage (stage 1), the child's definition of right and wrong states that a person should obey rules in order to avoid punishment. In stage 2, a simple doctrine of reciprocity develops. People should act to meet their own needs and let others do the same, doing what is "fair" or constitutes an equal exchange. The saying "You scratch my back and I'll scratch yours" fits this stage (Colby, Kohlberg, Gibbs, & Lieberman, 1983; Kohlberg, 1976). The child's moral orientation is still primarily individualistic, egocentric, and concrete, although the rights of others are seen as coexisting with the child's rights in some fashion (Kohlberg, 1976).

At the second level, *conventional morality,* the focus is on societal needs, and values take primacy over individual interests. Initially, at stage 3, a child may put strong emphasis on being "a good person in your own eyes and those of others" (Kohlberg, 1976, p. 34), which means having good motives and showing concern about others. Typically, there is considerable emphasis on conformity to stereotyped images of majority or "natural" behavior. Reflecting increased cognitive development, at this stage the intention behind a behavior acquires major importance; one seeks approval by "being good." At stage 4, a *social perspective* takes precedence. The child shows concern not only with conformity to the social order but also with maintaining, supporting, and justifying this order. "Right behavior consists of doing one's duty, showing respect for authority, and maintaining the given social order for its own sake" (Kohlberg & Gilligan, 1972).

At the *postconventional* and *principled levels* (stages 5 and 6), people base moral judgments on principles that they have considered and accepted because the principles are inherently right rather than because society has defined them as right. Kohlberg calls this level a "prior-to-society" perspective. When Martin Luther King said that disobeying segregation laws was morally right because he was obeying a higher law, he was making a postconventional moral argument. Reflecting children's acquisition of formal operational thinking, this level is characterized by a "major thrust toward abstract moral principles which are universally applicable, and not tied to any particular social group" (Kohlberg & Gilligan, 1972). A detailed explanation of each stage appears in Box 9.3.

Over several years of investigation, methods of scoring moral judgments have been refined in an effort to separate the structure of a person's reasoning from the content of the person's values. The resulting findings have caused these investigators to place the average age at which children enter each stage somewhat later than they did in their initial writings (Rest, 1983). Many people score at the preconventional level until well into adolescence, and most adults remain at the conventional level. Stage 5 reasoning is rare, and stage 6 is virtually never encountered. A 20-year longitudinal study following men from early adolescence to their mid-30s demonstrated that the stages do occur in the order proposed by Kohlberg, but change is very gradual. Over 20 years, these men changed on the average less than two stages (Rest, 1983).

Similarities between theories   Both Piaget and Kohlberg proposed that progression through the stages of moral judgment is based on more general cognitive developmental changes, including the increasing ability to take other people's perspectives and the ability to use concrete operations. Cross-cultural studies indicate that formal education also affects the level of moral reasoning that people show. On the average, highly educated people reason at higher stages of moral thought than those with little or no education (Rest, 1983). Education is important probably because it broadens a person's perspective and offers opportunities for abstract thought, not because particular moral values are taught. Well-educated people may also be better able to verbalize on the abstract level required by the higher stages.

Both theorists agree that peer interaction promotes moral development. The young child's interactions with adults encourage moral realism because of the disparity in authority between adult and child. In peer interactions, however, authority differences are minimized. Children gain experience in negotiating about the rules of games and other aspects of group activity that touch on morality. They learn that the group can form and change rules, and they learn to take the perspectives of other people.

BOX 9.3

Six stages of moral judgment

Lawrence Kohlberg (1976) proposed six stages of moral judgment. This table lists those stages and gives some examples and definitions for each stage.

Level and stage	CONTENT OF STAGE		Social perspective of stage
	What is right	*Reasons for doing right*	
LEVEL I – PRECONVENTIONAL			
Stage 1: Heteronomous morality	To avoid breaking rules backed by punishment, obedience for its own sake, and avoiding physical damage to persons and property.	Avoidance of punishment, and the superior power of authorities.	*Egocentric point of view.* Doesn't consider the interests of others or recognize that they differ from the actor's; doesn't relate two points of view. Actions are considered physically rather than in terms of psychological interests of others. Confuses authority's perspective with one's own.
Stage 2: Individualism, instrumental purpose, and exchange	Following rules only when it is to someone's immediate interest; acting to meet one's own interests and needs and letting others do the same. Right is also what's fair, what's an equal exchange, a deal, an agreement.	To serve one's own needs or interests in a world where you have to recognize that other people have their interests, too.	*Concrete individualistic perspective.* Is aware that everybody has his own interest to pursue and these conflict, so that right is relative (in the concrete individualistic sense).
LEVEL II – CONVENTIONAL			
Stage 3: Mutual interpersonal expectations, relationships, and interpersonal conformity	Living up to what is expected by people close to you or what people generally expect of people in your role as son, brother, friend, etc. "Being good" is important and means having good motives, showing concern about others. It also means keeping mutual relationships, such as trust, loyalty, respect, and gratitude.	The need to be a good person in one's own eyes and those of others. Caring for others. Belief in the Golden Rule. Desire to maintain rules and authority that support stereotypical good behavior.	*Perspective of the individual in relationships with other individuals.* Aware of shared feelings, agreements, and expectations that take primacy over individual interests. Relates points of view through the concrete Golden Rule, putting oneself in the other person's shoes. Does not yet consider generalized system perspective.

Stage 4: Social system and conscience	Fulfilling the actual duties to which one has agreed. Laws are to be upheld except in extreme cases where they conflict with other fixed social duties. Right is also contributing to society, the group, or an institution.	To keep the institution going as a whole, to avoid the breakdown in the system "if everyone did it," or the imperative of conscience to meet one's defined obligations. (Easily confused with stage 3 belief in rules and authority; see text.)	*Differentiates societal point of view from interpersonal agreement or motives.* Takes the point of view of the system that defines roles and rules. Considers individual relations in terms of place in the system.

LEVEL III—POSTCONVENTIONAL or PRINCIPLED

Stage 5: Social contract or utility and individual rights	Being aware that people hold a variety of values and opinions, that most values and rules are relative to one's own group. These relative rules should usually be upheld, however, in the interest of impartiality and because they are the social contract. Some nonrelative values and rights like *life* and *liberty*, however, must be upheld in any society and regardless of majority opinion.	A sense of obligation to law because of one's social contract to make and abide by laws for the welfare of all and for the protection of all people's rights. A feeling of contractual commitment, freely entered upon, to family, friendship, trust, and work obligations. Concern that laws and duties be based on rational calculation of overall utility, "the greatest good for the greatest number."	*Prior-to-society perspective.* Perspective of a rational individual aware of values and rights prior to social attachments and contracts. Integrates perspectives by formal mechanisms of agreement, contract, objective impartiality, and due process. Considers moral and legal points of view; recognizes that they sometimes conflict and finds it difficult to integrate them.
Stage 6: Universal ethical principles	Following self-chosen ethical principles. Particular laws or social agreements are usually valid because they rest on such principles. When laws violate these principles, one acts in accordance with the principle. Principles are universal principles of justice: the equality of human rights and respect for the dignity of human beings as individuals.	The belief as a rational person in the validity of universal moral principles, and a sense of personal commitment to them.	*Perspective of a moral point of view* from which social arrangements derive. Perspective is that of any rational individual recognizing the nature of morality or the fact that persons are ends in themselves and must be treated as such.

Source: Adapted from J. Rest, Morality. In P. H. Mussen, J. Flavell, & E. Markman, (Eds.) *Handbook of child psychology* (Vol. 3): *Cognitive development* (4th ed.). New York: Wiley, 1983. By permission.

These ideas have been applied in moral education programs. For example, one high school carried out an experimental program in which a group of students were given responsibility for certain decisions about rules and procedures in the school. The ensuing discussions were intended to promote higher levels of moral thinking. These programs are still being evaluated.

The emphasis on peer interactions in both Piaget's and Kohlberg's theories differs sharply from the more conventional notion that children learn moral values and standards from their parents and other adults. The contradiction is more apparent than real, however. Piaget and Kohlberg are concerned with *how* children think about moral values, not with *what* they think. Children do learn values and moral rules from adults, but peers help them judge and interpret what they are learning at their own level of understanding.

Criticisms of Kohlberg's theory   Kohlberg's theory has had widespread influence and stimulated a great deal of research. It has also been the object of controversy, challenged on many grounds. For example, there is disagreement among psychologists about how universal the stages of moral development are. Kohlberg has argued that his system represents a hierarchy of morality that is universal across cultures. Critics reply that all morality is culturally relative and that it is ethnocentric to argue that one kind of moral thought is "higher" than another. Principled judgments that oppose the laws of a society might not be considered the most advanced form of moral thinking in another culture or another time (Baumrind, 1978).

Another telling criticism is that Kohlberg underestimates the moral knowledge and sensitivity of young children. A number of investigators disagree with Kohlberg's assertion that youngsters base their moral judgments only on reward, avoidance of punishment, and unquestioning deference to authority. On the contrary, according to some, children have a more profound understanding of morality than they are able to articulate, "an intuitive moral competence that displays itself in the way they answer questions about moral rules and in the way they excuse their transgressions and react to the transgressions of others" (Schweder, Turiel, & Much, 1981, p. 288).

Morality versus social convention   In a series of studies, Turiel and his colleagues found that children between 4 and 6 recognize *moral issues* (general principles relating to justice, fairness, and the welfare of others) and distinguish these from *social conventions* (arbitrary rules of conduct sanctioned by custom and tradition, such as type of clothing or use of first name or titles in addressing people). Children between 5 and 11 years of age were told two kinds of hypothetical stories (Weston & Turiel, 1980). One was about a school in which there were no rules about hitting and children were allowed to hit each other. Another was about a school that permitted children to take off their clothes. The children were asked to evaluate these school policies. The majority of children of all ages said that a school should not permit hitting but that a school could allow children to undress.

Analogously, children say that it is wrong to hit or steal (moral issues) even if there are no rules or laws against such acts and no punishment for them. However, addressing teachers by their first names would be right if there were no rules forbidding this. Turiel concluded that social-conventional thinking and morality are distinct conceptual systems (Turiel, 1978, 1983).

In addition to asking children about hypothetical situations, investigators have observed responses to actual rule violations in school groups ranging from preschool to seventh grade. At the preschool level, teachers reacted more often than peers to violations of school rules (social convention), and their comments usually stressed rules, possible punishments, or the need for order. Children as well as teachers responded to moral-rule violations, and their remarks usually emphasized feelings of others or reasons for obeying the rule. Elementary school children responded to both types of transgression, but they made different kinds of responses. These are shown in Table 9.3. When children were asked about the events that had occurred, even the preschool children readily distinguished social conventions from moral rules (Nucci & Nucci, 1982a; Nucci & Turiel, 1978; Smetana, 1981).

TABLE 9.3

Children's responses to transgressions that violated moral rules and transgressions that violated social-conventional rules

Responses were coded from observations of naturally occurring behavior

TYPES OF RESPONSE THAT OCCURRED MOST OFTEN TO MORAL TRANSGRESSIONS

Injury or loss statement. Statements that indicate pain or injury to self or personal loss (loss of property, personal space, etc.).

Evaluation of act as unfair or hurtful. Evaluation that indicates that the behavior causes injustice or harm to others.

Perspective-taking request. Request that the transgressor consider how it feels to be the victim of the act.

Retaliatory act. Action taken by the victim, such as hitting, angry use of abusive language, or commission of a parallel act (e.g., stealing something back from the transgressor), in order to inflict discomfort on the transgressor.

RESPONSES THAT OCCURRED MOST OFTEN TO SOCIAL-CONVENTIONAL TRANSGRESSIONS

Disorder and deviation statement. Indication that the behavior is out of place, is odd, or is creating a mess, disorder, or chaos.

Rule statement. Statements that specify a rule governing the action.

Ridicule. Use of sarcasm or derisive labels to indicate the inappropriateness of the behavior.

Source: Adapted from L. P. Nucci & M. S. Nucci. Children's social interactions in the context of moral and conventional transgressions. *Child Development,* 1982, *53,* 403–412. © The Society for Research in Child Development, Inc. By permission.

Prosocial moral judgment

Moral and social rules can be broadly classified as prescriptive (things one should do) and proscriptive (things one should not do). *Prosocial behavior* is the term often used by psychologists to represent culturally prescribed moral actions such as sharing, helping someone in need, cooperating with others, and expressing sympathy. Judgments about prosocial actions—when no law or rule is involved, but a person must choose between helping another person or benefiting himself—appear to follow a slightly different pattern than judgments about moral violations.

Preschool children were observed in free play. When they did something helpful for another child, the researcher immediately asked them why they had been helpful. They most often said that they were aware of the other child's need or that helping the other child was useful to reaching their own goals. They rarely mentioned punishment or authority (Eisenberg-Berg, 1979; Eisenberg-Berg & Hand, 1979). These findings suggest that the stages of moral reasoning may be different for different kinds of moral content.

In summary, the stages of moral judgment identified by Kohlberg and Piaget appear to describe children's abstract reasoning about issues of justice and fairness, but they cannot always be generalized to other moral issues or rules. In addition, our earlier caution about drawing conclusions from verbal reasoning about hypothetical situations applies to the moral domain. When children are observed in real-life encounters, their behavior indicates considerably more understanding of moral issues than their responses to hypothetical situations might lead one to expect.

Moral reasoning and behavior

The study of children's moral judgment asks what thought processes and criteria they use to decide what is right and wrong, not what moral actions they may take. Still, we would expect the individual's thinking about morality to influence her behavior. Is the child who reasons at a relatively high level more likely to behave in a moral fashion? Do children who give prosocial answers to dilemmas also show prosocial behavior when confronted with another person's need? The answers are frustratingly indefinite. In some instances, people with high levels of moral reasoning behave in altruistic, honest, or principled ways, but that is not always the case.

Even when judgments and behavior are measured in similar situations, children's actions often differ from what they consider right. In one study, children worked in groups of four to make bracelets. Each child was asked to decide the fair way to divide 10 candy bars among the group. When they actually divided the candy, however, they did not follow the patterns they had thought would be most fair. Not too surprisingly, they gave themselves more candy than they had judged "right" (Gerson & Damon, 1978). Clearly, carefully reasoned judgments about what is right constitute only one of many factors that influence behavioral choices. Some others will be discussed in the next chapter.

Knowing the child's level of moral judgment may help parents and others to reason with children persuasively. Consider the following anecdote:

> *Teddy, 10, had promised to attend a movie with his grandmother. Then his friend called to ask him to go skating. He wanted to go skating, but his mother thought that he should keep his promise to his grandmother. She tried first pointing out that Grandma's feelings would be hurt if he did not go with her, but he continued to protest that he wanted to go skating. Mother then said, "You know, Grandma has given you a lot of things and done a lot of nice things for you recently. It's your turn to do something nice for her." Teddy's face suddenly cleared, and he said, "Oh yeah. I guess you're right."*

Teddy was persuaded by reasoning that emphasized an obligation of reciprocity resembling Kohlberg's stage 2. Children will accept reasoning from others when it fits their level of moral judgment more readily than when it does not.

Fitting the moral reasoning to the child's level of understanding influences resistance to temptation even when the adult giving the reasons is not present. Children were left alone in a playroom filled with several toys after being told not to play with some of those toys. One group was given an object-oriented rationale for avoiding certain toys. It was relatively concrete, with a focus on the physical consequences of handling the toy ("the toy is fragile and might break"), and was intended to correspond to immature levels of moral judgment. The second group received a more abstract rationale that stressed ownership ("the toy belongs to another child") and was intended to reflect more advanced forms of moral judgment. The concrete rationale was more effective in inhibiting 3-year-old children's play with the forbidden toys; 5-year-olds inhibited their play slightly more after the property rationale (Parke, 1974) (see Figure 9.2). Because older children were more likely to use abstract moral reasoning, they were also more influenced by such reasons.

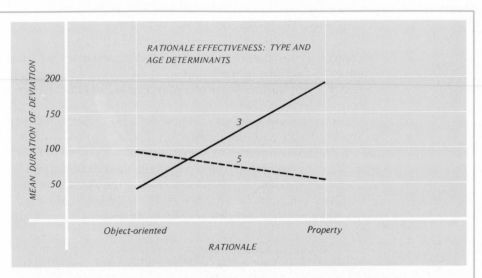

*Duration of deviation from rules when children were left alone with toys and told not to play with some of them. Three-year-olds deviated less often when they were given a reason focused on the physical characteristics of the toys (they might break) than when they were given a more abstract reason emphasizing property (they belong to someone else). Five-year-olds deviated less after the property rationale, presumably because it fit their level of moral reasoning. (From R. D. Parke. Rules, roles, and resistance to deviation: Recent advances in punishment, discipline, and self-control. In A. D. Pick [Ed.], **Minnesota symposia on child psychology** [Vol. 8]. Minneapolis: University of Minnesota Press, 1974, p. 116. By permission.)*

<table>
<tr><td>SCRIPTS AND THE
SOCIAL WORLD</td><td>Social cognition or knowledge is not just abstract reasoning about friendship, self, and morality. It consists also of knowledge about everyday social routines and expected behavior patterns. Social psychologists use the term *scripts* to describe our mental models for sequences of events and appropriate behavior in particular settings (Nelson, 1981; Schank & Abelson, 1977). The script for a social event such as "going to class" specifies our own and other people's ac-</td></tr>
</table>

tions, as well as props, and defines what we are required to do (obligatory actions) and what we *may* do (optional actions). For example, in this script, a lecturer is assumed, as are a blackboard, chairs, desk, notebooks, and pencils (props). Actions include entering the classroom, looking for a seat, getting notebook and pen ready, and quieting down when the professor begins to lecture. Script knowledge enables us to carry out sequences of actions and interactions more or less automatically and to predict others' behavior.

Scripts are so automatic for adults that we are often unaware of their existence until we find ourselves in a strange context where we do not know the script. For example, if you were invited to dinner by a family in Nepal, you would be uncertain as to what to wear, whether it is polite to arrive on time or late, what sequence of events to expect when you arrived, who should enter the dining room first, and so on. Young children enter the world equally ignorant and must learn many scripts during their early years.

Children's knowledge of scripts

Nelson (1981) interviewed children from 3 to 8 years of age about routine activities such as eating dinner at home, going to a restaurant, and going to a supermarket. The children's knowledge of these scripts proved to be extensive and socially accurate. They abstracted essential elements of social events, drew inferences about them, and formulated generalizations about expected sequences and actions of participants.

A girl not quite 5 years of age recounted her knowledge of the restaurant script in this way: "Now, first we go to restaurants at nighttime and we, um, we, and we go and wait for a little while, and then the waiter comes and gives us the little stuff with the dinners on it, and then we wait for a little bit, a half an hour or a few minutes or somethin, and, um, then our pizza comes or anything, and um, (interruption) . . . (So then your food comes . . .) then, we eat it, and, um, then when we're finished eating the salad that we order we get our pizza when it's done, because we get the salad before the pizza's ready. So then when we're finished with all our pizza and all our salad, we just leave" (Nelson, 1981, p. 103).

With age, children enlarge their store of scripts and apply them more appropriately and extensively. By middle childhood, children are "script experts. They readily divide their day into well-defined events (such as recess, math lessons, and art) and can articulate the rules for each event" (Nelson, 1981, p. 109).

Script knowledge is acquired through direct participation in social events and by observing others. Adults occasionally verbalize script elements to children, but most of the learning probably occurs without direct teaching. Television is also a source of scripts for many children and adults, particularly for social contexts such as courtrooms, newspaper offices, and police stations that they rarely observe directly. In fact, the American Bar Association has expressed concern that juries expect the defense to produce courtroom confessions from a guilty spectator, just as television trials do, in order to acquit an accused person.

Script knowledge helps children to enter situations and social relationships comfortably. When children have shared scripts for such activities as going to school or eating lunch, they talk freely, exchange information readily, and keep a conversation going for many "turns" (Nelson & Gruendel, 1979). They are likely to be less communicative and more "egocentric" when there is no shared script, when each has a somewhat different script for an event, or when the situation is novel. Imagine what might happen in a two-child discussion about attending church if one of the children had never been to church or if one had been only to a Catholic church and the other to a synagogue. As Nelson points out, "the talk of adults may also appear egocentric when shared scripts are absent. This will most often happen when the individuals are not aware of the discrepancy; when there is an awareness, adults, unlike young children, are usually capable of repairing, explaining, and thereby establishing a shared perspective" (Nelson, 1981, p. 12).

Play and fantasy   Children practice and rehearse many scripts in fantasy play. Shared scripts provide material for doctor-patient games, pretend telephone conversations, tea parties, and many other play activities. As noted in Chapter 5, fantasy play occurs almost universally among children. For that reason, many people have assumed that it serves important developmental functions. One of those functions may be to practice routines and interactions that will be used for serious purposes later in life. Children's role-playing fantasy is one means by which they rehearse and consolidate scripts that will be useful to them in the future.

Social pretend play (as opposed to solitary play) increases during the preschool years, peaking around age 6 or 7, then declines. As children get older, their play becomes more elaborate and imaginative. When they play roles such as mother and father or teacher and pupil, they become increasingly skilled in relating the two roles to one another (Rubin, 1983). Three-year-olds, for example, might engage in a sequence like the following, where each is pursuing a role but the two are not coordinated:

Molly (playing mother): Here's some food, baby.
Joe (playing baby): I want my ball.
Molly: This cereal is good for you.
Joe: (Crawls on the floor after the ball)

By 5 or 6, the interaction would involve more reciprocity of roles:
Michael (playing teacher): Show me the yellow balloon.
Mindy (playing pupil): That's the yellow one, and that's the red one.
Michael: Very good. Now go wash your hands.
Mindy: No, my hands are clean.

Play can also provide an avenue for adults to understand or modify children's social scripts and expectations. In play therapy, children are encouraged to act out events, and the therapist can respond or participate. Fantasy play can also be used to provide children with new scripts when they are about to experience a new situation. For example, children can be prepared for hospitalization by acting out the scripts of entering the hospital, eating meals, being prepared for surgery, and the like. Knowing the script reduces fear of the unknown and enables the child to enter the situation with greater comfort.

SUMMARY

Children's concepts and reasoning about people and social relationships—their social cognitions—are an important part of their knowledge about the world and an important influence on their social interactions. From infancy onward, children understand that human beings are different from inanimate objects. One of the major developmental accomplishments in understanding people is the ability to take the perspective of others. Although very young children show evidence of understanding others' perspectives, the child's skill and sophistication in correctly knowing how someone thinks and feels develop gradually during childhood and adolescence.

Children's concepts about themselves and about the traits and motives of others also undergo developmental change. Before age 7 or 8, children describe themselves and others using externally observable physical characteristics, such as hair color, or preferred activities, such as a favorite game. As they get older, they use more internal, psychological characteristics to describe themselves and others (e.g., the tendency to be sensitive or power-hungry). Adolescents move to even more abstract characteristics in their self-descriptions.

Children's concepts of morality, justice, and rules form another domain of social cognition. Both Piaget and Kohlberg proposed stages of moral development in which the child moves from orientation to external authority and threats of punishment as criteria for right and wrong to a view that morality is based on group decisions about rules and on the needs and welfare of all people involved. Recent investigations demonstrate, however, that even preschool children distinguish intentional from accidental actions. They also know the difference between rules that are based on principles of justice (such as a rule that forbids hitting people) and rules based on social convention (such as a rule about what time you come to school).

Finally, children gain social knowledge in the form of *scripts*—generally accepted routines for everyday behavior. Children practice such scripts in imaginative play and use them as guides in their interactions with others.

REFERENCES

Aronfreed, J. *Conduct and conscience: The socialization of internalized control over behavior.* New York: Academic Press, 1968.

Baumrind, D. A dialectical materialist's perspective on knowing social reality. In W. Damon (Ed.), *New directions in child development: Moral development.* San Francisco: Jossey-Bass, 1978.

Bernstein, R. M. The development of the self-system during adolescence. *Journal of Genetic Psychology,* 1980, *136,* 231–245.

Borke, H. Interpersonal perception of young children: Egocentrism or empathy. *Developmental Psychology,* 1971, *5,* 263–269.

Broughton, J. Development of concepts of self, mind, reality, and knowledge. In W. Damon (Ed.), *New directions in child development: Social cognition.* San Francisco: Jossey-Bass, 1978.

Cantor, J. *Developmental changes in children's fright responses to television and other mass media.* Paper presented at the Annual Meeting of the International Communication Association, Boston, May 1982.

Chandler, M. J. Egocentrism and antisocial behavior: The assessment and training of social perspective-taking skills. *Developmental Psychology,* 1973, *9,* 326–332.

Colby, A., Kohlberg, L., Gibbs, J., & Lieberman, M. A longitudinal study of moral judgment. *Monographs of the Society for Research in Child Development,* 1983, *48*(Serial No. 200).

Costanzo, P. R., Coie, J. D., Grumet, J. F., & Farnill, D. A reexamination of the effects of intent and consequence on children's moral judgments. *Child Development,* 1973, *44,* 154–161.

Damon, W. *The social world of the child.* San Francisco: Jossey-Bass, 1977.

Damon, W. Exploring children's social cognition on two fronts. In J. H. Flavell & L. Ross (Eds.), *Social cognitive development: Frontiers and possible futures.* New York: Cambridge University Press, 1981.

Damon, W., & Hart, D. The development of self-understanding from infancy through adolescence. *Child Development,* 1982, *53,* 841–864.

Eisenberg-Berg, N. Development of children's prosocial moral judgment. *Developmental Psychology,* 1979, *15,* 128–137.

Eisenberg-Berg, N., & Hand, M. The relationship of preschoolers' reasoning about prosocial moral conflicts to prosocial behavior. *Child Development,* 1979, *50,* 356–363.

Feshbach, N. D. Studies of empathic behavior in children. In B. A. Maher (Ed.), *Progress in experimental personality research* (Vol. 8). New York: Academic Press, 1978.

Flavell, J. H. *Cognitive development.* Englewood Cliffs, N.J.: Prentice-Hall, 1977.

Gelman, R., & Spelke, E. The development of thoughts about animate and inanimate objects: Implications for research on social cognition. In J. H. Flavell & L. Ross (Eds.), *Social cognitive development: Frontiers and possible futures.* New York: Cambridge University Press, 1981.

Gerson, R. P., & Damon, W. Moral understanding and children's conduct. In W. Damon (Ed.), *New directions in child development: Moral development.* San Francisco: Jossey-Bass, 1978.

Grueneich, R. Issues in the developmental study of how children use intention and consequence information to make moral evaluations. *Child Development,* 1982, *53,* 29–43.

Harter, S. Developmental perspectives on the self-system. In P. H. Mussen & E. M. Hetherington (Eds.), *Handbook of child psychology* (Vol. 4): *Socialization, personality, and social development* (4th ed). New York: Wiley, 1983.

Hoffman, M. L. Development of the motive to help others. In J. P. Rushton & R. M. Sorrentino (Eds.), *Altruism and helping.* Hillsdale, N.J.: Erlbaum, 1981.

Hughes, R., Jr., Tingle, B. A., & Sawin, D. B. Development of empathic understanding in children. *Child Development,* 1981, *52,* 122–128.

James, W. *Psychology: The briefer course.* New York: Harper & Row, 1961. (Originally published, 1892).

Karniol, R. Children's use of intention cues in evaluating behavior. *Psychological Bulletin,* 1978, *85,* 76–85.

Keil, F. *Semantic and conceptual development.* Cambridge, Mass.: Harvard University Press, 1979.

Keller, A., Ford, L. H., & Meacham, J. A. Dimensions of self-concept in preschool children. *Developmental Psychology,* 1978, *14,* 483–489.

Kohlberg, L. Moral stages and moralization: The cognitive-developmental approach. In T. Likona (Ed.), *Moral development and behavior: Theory, research, and social issues.* New York: Holt, Rinehart and Winston, 1976.

Kohlberg, L., & Gilligan, C. The adolescent as a philosopher: The discovery of the self in a postconventional world. In J. Kagan & R. Coles (Eds.), *12 to 16: Early adolescence.* New York: Norton, 1972.

Kreutzer, M. A., & Charlesworth, W. R. *Infants' reactions to different expressions of emotion.* Paper presented at the Society for Research in Child Development, Philadelphia, March 1973.

Livesley, W. J., & Bromley, D. B. *Person perception in childhood and adolescence.* London: Wiley, 1973.

Masters, J. C., & Carlson, C. R. Children's and adults' understanding of the causes and consequences of emotional states. In C. Izard, M. Kagan, & R. Zajonc (Eds.), *Emotions, cognition, and behavior.* Cambridge: Cambridge University Press, in press.

Mohr, D. M. Development of attributes of personal identity. *Developmental Psychology,* 1978, *14,* 427–428.

Nelson, K. Social cognition in a script framework. In J. H. Flavell & L. Ross (Eds.), *Social cognitive development: Frontiers and possible futures.* New York: Cambridge University Press, 1981.

Nelson, K., & Gruendel, J. M. *From personal episode to social script: Two dimensions in the development of event knowledge.* Paper presented at a meeting of the Society for Research in Child Development, San Francisco, April, 1979.

Nucci, L. P., & Nucci, M. S. Children's responses to moral and social conventional transgressions in free-play settings. *Child Development,* 1982, *53,* 1337–1342. (a)

Nucci, L. P., & Nucci, M. S. Children's social interactions in the context of moral and conventional transgressions. *Child Development,* 1982, *53,* 403–412. (b)

Nucci, L. P., & Turiel, E. Social interactions and the development of social concepts in preschool children. *Child Development,* 1978, *49,* 400–407.

Parke, R. D. Rules, roles, and resistance to deviation in children: Explorations in punishment, discipline, and self-control. In A. Pick (Ed.), *Minnesota symposia on child psychology* (Vol. 8). Minneapolis: University of Minnesota Press, 1974.

Peevers, B. H., & Secord, P. F. Developmental changes in attribution of description concepts to persons. *Journal of Personality and Social Psychology,* 1973, *27,* 120–128.

Piaget, J. *The moral judgment of the child.* London: Kegan Paul, 1932.

Radke-Yarrow, M., Zahn-Waxler, C., & Chapman, M. Children's prosocial dispositions and behavior. In P. H. Mussen & E. M. Hetherington (Eds.), *Handbook of child psychology* (Vol. 4): *Socialization, personality, and social development* (4th ed.). New York: Wiley, 1983.

Rest, J. R. Morality. In P. Mussen, J. Flavell, & E. Markman (Eds.) *Handbook of child psychology* (Vol. 3): *Cognitive development* (4th ed.). New York: Wiley, 1983.

Rosenberg, M. *Conceiving the self.* New York: Basic Books, 1979.

Ross, L. The "intuitive scientist" formulation and its developmental implications. In J. H. Flavell & L. Ross (Eds.), *Social cognitive development: Frontiers and possible futures.* New York: Cambridge University Press, 1981.

Rothenberg, B. B. Children's social sensitivity and the relationship to interpersonal competence, intrapersonal comfort, and intellectual level. *Developmental Psychology, 1970, 2,* 335–350.

Rubin, K. The development of play. In P. H. Mussen & E. M. Hetherington (Eds.), *Handbook of child psychology* (Vol. 4): *Socialization, personality, and social development* (4th ed.). New York: Wiley, 1983.

Scaife, M., & Bruner, J. S. The capacity for joint visual attention in the infant. *Nature, 1975, 253,* 265–266.

Schank, R. C., & Abelson, R. Scripts, plans, goals, and understanding. Hillsdale, N.J.: Erlbaum, 1977.

Schweder, R., Turiel, E., & Much, N. The moral intuitions of the child. In J. H. Flavell & L. Ross (Eds.), *Social cognitive development: Frontiers and possible futures.* New York: Cambridge University Press, 1981.

Secord, P., & Peevers, B. The development and attribution of person concepts. In T. Mischel (Ed.), *Understanding other persons.* Oxford: Blackwell, 1974.

Selman, R. L. Social cognitive understanding: A guide to educational and clinical practice. In T. Likona (Ed.), *Moral development and behavior: Theory, research, and social issues.* New York: Holt, Rinehart and Winston, 1976.

Selman, R. L. *The growth of interpersonal understanding.* New York: Academic Press, 1980.

Shantz, C. V. Social cognition. In P. H. Mussen, J. Flavell, & E. Markman (Eds.), *Handbook of child psychology* (Vol. 3) *Cognitive development* (4th ed.). New York: Wiley, 1983.

Shure, M. B., & Spivak, G. Interpersonal problem solving as a mediator of behavioral adjustment in preschool and kindergarten children. *Journal of Applied Developmental Psychology, 1980, 1,* 29–44.

Smetana, J. G. Preschool children's conceptions of moral and social rules. *Child Development, 1981, 52,* 1333–1336.

Spivak, G., Platt, J. J., & Shure, M. B. *The problem-solving approach to adjustment.* San Francisco: Jossey-Bass, 1976.

Trevarthen, C. Descriptive analyses of infant communicative behavior. In H. R. Schaffer (Ed.), *Studies in mother-infant interaction.* London: Academic Press, 1977.

Turiel, E. Distinct conceptual and developmental domains: Social convention and morality. In C. B. Keasey & H. E. Howe (Eds.), *Nebraska Symposium on Motivation* (Vol. 25). Lincoln, Nebr.: University of Nebraska Press, 1978.

Turiel, E. *The development of social and moral knowledge.* Cambridge: Cambridge University Press, 1983.

Urbain, E. S., & Kendall, P. C. Review of social-cognitive problem-solving interventions with children. *Psychological Bulletin, 1980, 88,* 109–143.

Weiner, B. The emotional consequences of causal ascriptions. In M. S. Clark & S. T. Fiske (Eds.), *Affect and cognition: The 17th annual Carnegie symposium on cognition.* Hillsdale, N.J.: Erlbaum, 1982.

Weston, D., & Turiel, E. Act-rule relations: Children's concepts of social rules. *Developmental Psychology, 1980, 16,* 417–424.

Youniss, J. *Parents and peers in social development.* Chicago: University of Chicago Press, 1981.

CHAPTER 10

Identity and social development

*D*uring the childhood years, children develop a sense of who they are and where they fit in their society. They form lasting patterns of social interactions with others, and they incorporate the moral and social rules of their culture in a form that enables them to regulate their own behavior. By the time the child reaches the end of elementary school, the rudimentary sense of self that we described in Chapter 5 has become an elaborated and relatively stable network of self-perceptions and feelings. The child has a sense of identity as a male or a female and as a member of social or ethnic groups. The beginnings of empathy and self-control that were evident in the toddler years become major features of the child's personality and behavior during childhood.

In Chapter 9, we discussed concepts of self, of other people, and of moral and social rules using cognitive developmental theories about children's moral reasoning and social cognitive understanding. In this chapter, we will discuss the ways children apply these concepts in their own lives. Social learning theories are often used in research on children's personal and social actions because such theories are concerned with the influence of both cognitive and environmental influences on *behavior*. The role of both cognitive development and social learning will be examined. Children's concepts about sex-appropriate behavior will be examined in relation to sex differences in behavior; their concepts about themselves will be considered in relation to their self-esteem—the feelings and evaluations they have about themselves. Moral judgments will be related to children's ability to guide and regulate their interactions with others and to follow the moral and social rules of their society.

SOCIAL LEARNING THEORY

Social learning theories of social development offer hypotheses about the environmental conditions influencing behavior. Three major processes are proposed: (a) classical conditioning, (b) contingent reinforcement and punishment, and (c) observational learning (Rushton, 1980).

Classical conditioning (described in Chapter 3) occurs when a conditioned stimulus is paired with an unconditioned stimulus. While learning self-control, for instance, a child may learn to use words to avoid forbidden behavior if they are paired with a negative outcome. For example, if a father says "hot" just before a child touches a stove, the father's word becomes a conditioned stimulus inhibiting the tendency to reach for the stove. Ultimately the child may say the word to himself to aid self-control. A little girl was observed starting to reach toward a stove; as her hand went out, she said, "No, no," and pulled her hand back.

The second process is instrumental or operant conditioning (also discussed more fully in Chapter 3). Many types of social behavior are influenced by the positive or negative consequences they produce. Sharing, helping, aggression, and sex-typed behavior are all enhanced by praise or other positive outcomes and are often inhibited by punishment.

The third process is observational learning. Because children do not always imitate the behavior they observe, social learning research has been aimed at discovering the conditions under which children will learn from observation or will imitate what they learn. Albert Bandura (1977) of Stanford University proposed a model containing four steps in learning and imitating a model's behavior. They are illustrated in Figure 10.1. The first step is *attention*. Obviously, the child must attend to the model if any learning is to occur (although attention does not guarantee learning).

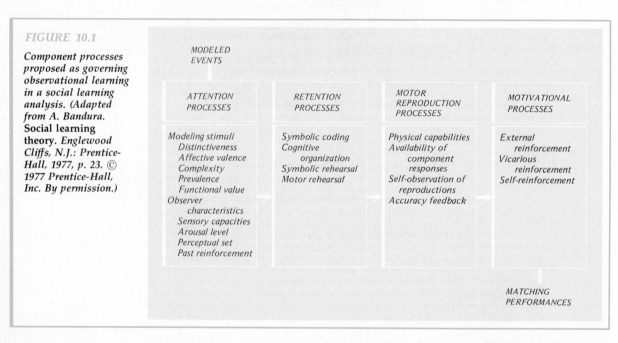

FIGURE 10.1

Component processes proposed as governing observational learning in a social learning analysis. (Adapted from A. Bandura. **Social learning theory.** *Englewood Cliffs, N.J.: Prentice-Hall, 1977, p. 23. © 1977 Prentice-Hall, Inc. By permission.)*

MODELED EVENTS

ATTENTION PROCESSES	RETENTION PROCESSES	MOTOR REPRODUCTION PROCESSES	MOTIVATIONAL PROCESSES
Modeling stimuli	Symbolic coding	Physical capabilities	External reinforcement
Distinctiveness	Cognitive organization	Availability of component responses	Vicarious reinforcement
Affective valence	Symbolic rehearsal	Self-observation of reproductions	Self-reinforcement
Complexity	Motor rehearsal	Accuracy feedback	
Prevalence			
Functional value			
Observer characteristics			
Sensory capacities			
Arousal level			
Perceptual set			
Past reinforcement			

MATCHING PERFORMANCES

The second step is *retention*. The child interprets the model's behavior using her own cognitive skills or categories and stores the information in memory. Hence, what she learns depends partly on her level of cognitive development. In many instances, the process stops here. The child has learned and can remember what the model did. She may not use the information at all in making behavioral choices, or she may interpret it in her own framework and develop somewhat different behavior from that observed. Most important, her behavioral response may occur long after the experience of observing the model. This capacity for delayed imitation means that the effects of observational learning may be difficult to detect. A 10-year-old may watch a roller derby on television; a few years later, on his first visit to a roller rink, he may call on that knowledge and imitate some of the behaviors of the television models.

Only the information that is remembered is available for the step taken by the child in the roller rink, *motor reproduction*. The child's motor and intellectual capabilities for reproducing the response will influence whether or how accurately he does so.

Finally, *motivational processes* are important in determining whether a person will actually perform a behavior. The observed consequences of the behavior for the model are one important influence on children's motivation to imitate. When they see models rewarded, they are more likely to imitate them than when they see them punished, probably because they expect similar consequences for themselves. Not surprisingly, people are also likely to imitate behavior that fits their interests or values and behavior that is exhibited by a model who is attractive, warm, powerful, or high in status.

<table>
<tr><td>

SEX TYPING AND IDENTITY

</td><td>

A child's identity consists partly of an awareness and acceptance of the social categories to which the child is assigned by the culture and partly of individual qualities that are adopted independently. One of the most basic social categories in almost every society is gender. Often the first question asked about a baby is "Is it a boy or a girl?" Our culture and most others define a host of interests, personality attributes, and behaviors as "feminine" or "masculine." Children learn and adopt many of these cultural standards at a remarkably early age.

</td></tr>
</table>

The process of sex typing describes the ways in which biological gender and its cultural associations are incorporated into the child's self-perceptions and behavior. This process has several components. *Gender identity* is the awareness and acceptance of one's basic biological nature as a male or a female. *Sex-role identity* is one's perception or belief that one is masculine or feminine — that is, that one's personality, interests, and behavior conform to one's own definitions of masculinity and femininity. *Sex-role adoption* is the taking on of personality characteristics, preferences, and behaviors that one's culture defines as appropriate for one sex or the other. Sex-role identity describes children's personal and private definition of self, whereas sex-role adoption refers to those psychological characteristics that other people regard as appropriate for one sex or the other, such as aggression or dependency.

Masculine and feminine qualities need not be mutually exclusive. A female might enjoy cooking and repairing cars; she might have a firm sense of her identity as a female even though she has interests that are culturally defined as both feminine and masculine. A male may be both independent and kind — he might regard both of these qualities as consistent with his masculine identity even though others may define kindness as a feminine attribute. In each case, the individual's basic gender identity as a male or a female remains solid and certain; attributes defined by oneself or by others as appropriate for the other sex can be comfortably integrated with a more fundamental sense of self as male or female.

Children develop at least a rudimentary gender identity sometime between 18 months and 3 years of age. They learn to categorize themselves and other people correctly as males or females. Nevertheless, children's understanding of gender during the preschool years is limited. Some anecdotes will illustrate their confusion. A 3-year-old boy upset his parents greatly by announcing that he was going to grow up to be a mommy. Another child became alarmed when he saw his mother dressed in a man's business suit for a Halloween party. He called her a man.

Gender constancy refers to a child's understanding that gender does not change over time and that it remains constant regardless of changes in a person's clothes, activities, or other superficial physical characteristics. Until age 5 or 6, children do not fully understand gender constancy. For example, preschool children sometimes say that if a boy wears a dress or plays with a doll, he will be a girl. In addition, young children pay relatively little attention to genital differences in deciding who is male and who is female. For instance, children watched while pictures of nude children were covered with dresses and long hair or pants and short hair. Young children often said that a figure with female genitals became a boy when wearing pants and short hair or that a male was a girl when wearing a dress (McConaghy, 1979). Some of their confusion may have been due to the methods used. It is possible that they were not able to explain their concepts adequately or that they meant something different than adults mean when they said, "Now it's a girl." They may have meant "Now it looks like a girl." Nonetheless, many efforts to test children's knowledge of gender constancy have led to a similar conclusion: Their understanding is incomplete.

Children's understanding of social expectations for males and females By the time American children reach their third birthday, they not only classify people correctly as female or male, but they also have a remarkable amount of information about social expectations for the two sexes. They know that girls are supposed to play with dolls and dress up like women, while boys are supposed to play with trucks and pretend to be firemen. By age 4 or 5, they know most of the stereotypes for adult occupations. They expect women to be teachers and nurses and men to have a variety of occupations such as pilot and police officer. A young child may adamantly assert that "women can't be doctors" or "men don't change diapers." Preschool children often assume that sex stereotypes are absolute prescriptions for correct behavior, and they sometimes enforce them more rigidly than older people do.

Around age 5, children begin to learn the more abstract, psychological components of sex stereotypes. Boys are believed to be big, loud, aggressive, independent, and competent; girls are thought to be small, quiet, nurturant, obedient, and emotional. These personality traits are probably learned later because they depend on abstract conceptual understanding and because sex differences in related forms of behavior occur less often and are therefore less likely to be observed by children than are differences in dress, play activities, and jobs (Huston, 1983).

Adoption of sex-typed behavior Children's behavior is also sex-typed very early. By age 2, children select toys and activities that fit sex stereotypes. Children in a toddler day-care center were observed during periods when a specially selected set of toys was arranged in their play area. The toys were either masculine, feminine, or neutral, according to adult stereotypes. The amount of time that girls and boys played with each group of toys is shown in Figure 10.2. Even these very young children, particularly boys, selected sex-typed toys (O'Brien, Huston, & Risley, in press). The same pattern occurred when 2-year-old children were observed at home. Girls more often played with soft toys and dolls, asked for help, and dressed up in adult clothes. Boys more often played with blocks and manipulated objects or toys (Fagot, 1974).

In middle childhood, children continue to refine their understanding of social expectations for females and males. At the same time, their thinking

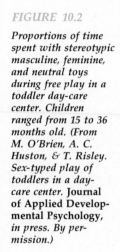

FIGURE 10.2

Proportions of time spent with stereotypic masculine, feminine, and neutral toys during free play in a toddler day-care center. Children ranged from 15 to 36 months old. (From M. O'Brien, A. C. Huston, & T. Risley. Sex-typed play of toddlers in a day-care center. Journal of Applied Developmental Psychology, in press. By permission.)

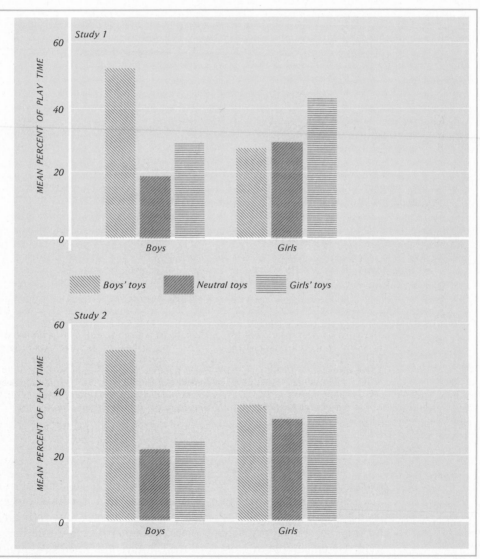

becomes less rigid. They seem more ready than younger children to recognize that people can combine behaviors that are stereotyped as masculine and feminine and to accept departures from sex-role prescriptions. For example, girls from ages 7 to 11 were questioned about whether they thought various activities, qualities, and occupational goals were more appropriate for a man, a woman, or both. Younger children gave more stereotyped answers than older children; older children more often said both. (Marantz & Mansfield, 1977; Meyer, 1980). The patterns appear in Figure 10.3. The greater flexibility of thinking in middle childhood may be partly due to a clear understanding of gender constancy: children now know that their basic gender identity as a girl or a boy will not be altered by violating sex-role stereotypes.

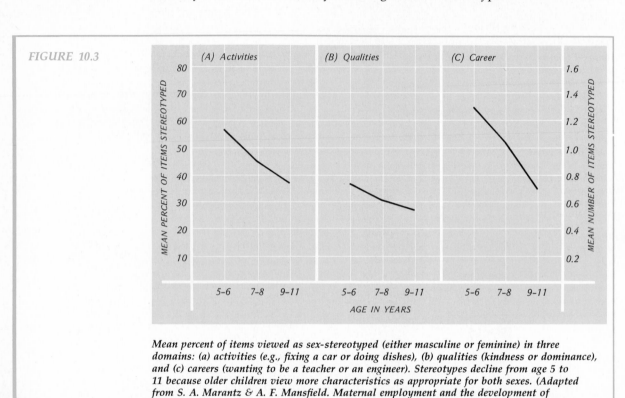

FIGURE 10.3

Mean percent of items viewed as sex-stereotyped (either masculine or feminine) in three domains: (a) activities (e.g., fixing a car or doing dishes), (b) qualities (kindness or dominance), and (c) careers (wanting to be a teacher or an engineer). Stereotypes decline from age 5 to 11 because older children view more characteristics as appropriate for both sexes. (Adapted from S. A. Marantz & A. F. Mansfield. Maternal employment and the development of sex-role stereotyping in five- to eleven-year-old girls. **Child Development,** *1977,* **48,** *672. © The Society for Research in Child Development, Inc. By permission.)*

Children often prefer the activities and roles that are expected for their own sex, but not always. Boys are more attracted to masculine interests and activities than girls are to feminine activities. In fact, many young girls consider themselves tomboys and enjoy "masculine" games and activities, particularly during the elementary school years. Because the male role has greater status than the female role in most societies, children of both sexes are often attracted to things that are defined as masculine.

Androgyny   We stated earlier that it would be hard to find a person with only masculine or only feminine interests and personality traits. The behaviors, roles, and personality characteristics that make up our cultural definitions of feminity and masculinity are diverse and complex. Many people adopt some of each. A boy might, for example, like to play football, yet be gentle and nurturant when handling a puppy. He might also be very independent and enjoy ballet. We must be cautious about using broad labels like "masculine" and "feminine."

A person who combines the psychological qualities that others in the society regard as masculine and feminine is sometimes described as *psychologically androgynous*. Several measures of androgyny have been developed for adults (Bem, 1974; Spence & Helmreich, 1978). Some of these have been adapted for children. The Children's Personal Attributes Questionnaire contains descriptions of masculine and feminine traits, shown in Table 10.1. Children indicate how well they think each description fits them by rating it on a scale from 1 (fits very well) to 5 (does not fit). An interesting finding from this questionnaire is that scores on the masculine and feminine scales are not correlated. That is, a high score on the feminine scale does not necessarily mean a low score on the masculine scale. Children can score high on both, low on both, or high on one scale and low on the other. An androgynous child is one who scores high on both masculine and feminine attributes (Hall & Halberstadt, 1980).

When the concept of androgyny was introduced in the early 1970s, many people argued that it represented a more healthy pattern than traditional sex typing. You can see that the adjectives on both the masculine and feminine

---

TABLE 10.1

Items on the Masculine and Feminine Scales of the Children's Personal Attributes Questionnaire

The child marks how well the item describes himself or herself on a 5-point scale.

Feminine scale	*Masculine scale*
1. My artwork and my ideas are creative and original.	1. It is hard for me to make up my mind about things. (low rating scored as masculine)
2. I do *not* help other people very much. (low rating scored as feminine)	2. In most ways, I am better than most of the other kids my age.
3. I am a very considerate person.	3. I would rather do things for myself than ask grown-ups and other kids for help.
4. I am kind to other people almost all of the time.	4. When things get tough, I almost always keep going.
5. I try to do everything I can for the people I care about.	5. I give up easily. (low rating scored as masculine)
6. I am a gentle person.	6. I am often the leader among my friends.
7. I like art and music a lot.	7. I almost always stand up for what I believe in.
8. I like younger kids and babies a lot.	8. It is easy for people to make me change my mind. (low rating scored as masculine)

Source: J. A. Hall & A. G. Halberstadt. Masculinity and femininity in children: Development of the Children's Personal Attributes Scale. *Developmental Psychology*, 1980, 16(4), 272.

scales represent characteristics that are socially valued and adaptive for many life situations. They should help a person to function well and to cope with many situations. For example, girls who are achievement-oriented and who want to have careers often have masculine interests and personality characteristics, although they do not necessarily lack feminine attributes (Stein & Bailey, 1973). One must keep in mind, however, that the contribution of personality attributes to psychological health depends on their adaptive value in one's cultural group and social setting; for a girl who lives in an urban slum, kindness and gentleness may not be as adaptive as skill in verbal aggression.

How does sex typing come about?

Explanations for sex typing have been proposed by psychoanalytic, social learning, and cognitive developmental theorists. According to psychoanalytic theory, children learn sex typing through a process of *identification* with the same-sex parent that begins at about 4 or 5 years of age. They internalize the masculine or feminine personality characteristics of that parent and adopt many of that parent's values and characteristics.

Social learning theorists have proposed that sex-typed behavior is learned by the same processes that operate for other forms of behavior—instrumental conditioning and observation. They propose that the boys and girls are reinforced and punished for different behaviors from early childhood and that children learn the expected roles for females and males by observing others (Mischel, 1970). They equate identification with imitation and argue that imitation of parents is only one of several possible means by which children learn cultural expectations for males and females. Children have plenty of opportunities to learn the social expectations of their society from the mass media, their peers, teachers, and other adults.

Careful observational studies in homes and preschools support the assertion that parents, teachers, and peers reinforce girls and boys for different kinds of behavior. Parents of children between 20 and 24 months of age more often reacted favorably when children engaged in activities that were "sex-appropriate" than when the children performed behaviors appropriate for the other sex. For instance, they responded positively when girls played with dolls, asked for help, followed an adult around, and helped with an adult task. They reacted positively when boys played with blocks, manipulated objects, and were physically active (see Table 10.2). Parents are often unaware that they treat boys and girls differently. In an interview, many of these parents said they treated both sexes similarly. There was little correlation between their observed behavior and the attitudes expressed in the interview (Fagot, 1978).

Cognitive developmental theorists propose that early patterns of sex-role learning are guided by more general cognitive developmental changes. This view is based on the fact that children acquire knowledge about sex stereotypes very young, almost regardless of their family environments. Lawrence Kohlberg (1966) proposed that children first classify themselves as girls or boys as a part of the general tendency for young children to form categories. They then begin to seek actively for information about the activities, values, and behaviors that distinguish boys from girls. Because young children think in absolute, either-or terms, their stereotypes are fairly rigid. It is a natural step for children to value the patterns associated with their own gender. In effect, a boy says, "I am a

TABLE 10.2

Parents' reactions
to behavior of
toddler boys and
girls

| Child behavior | PARENT REACTION | | | |
	POSITIVE		NEGATIVE	
	To boys	To girls	To boys	To girls
MASCULINE BEHAVIOR				
Block play	.36	.00*	.00	.00
Manipulates objects	.46	.46	.02	.26*
Transportation-toy play	.61	.57	.00	.02
Rough-and-tumble play	.91	.84	.03	.02
Aggression: hit, push	.23	.18	.50	.53
Running and jumping	.39	.32	.00	.07
Climbing	.39	.43	.12	.24*
Riding trikes	.60	.90	.04	.06
FEMININE BEHAVIOR				
Play with dolls	.39	.63*	.14	.04*
Dance	.00	.50	.00	.00
Ask for help	.72	.87*	.13	.06*
Play dress up	.50	.71	.50	.00
Help adult with task	.74	.94*	.17	.06*
Follow parent around	.39	.79*	.07	.07

Note: The proportions in this table represent the percentage of occasions on which parents responded positively (by praising, guiding, comforting, explaining, or joining the child's activity) or negatively (by criticizing, restricting, punishing, or stopping play) when their children engaged in each of the behaviors listed. The information was obtained by observing parents and their 20- to 24-month-old children at home. The asterisks indicate that the difference between treatment of boys and girls was statistically significant.

Source: B. I. Fagot. The influence of sex of child on parental reactions to toddler children. *Child Development*, 1978, 49, 459–465.

boy. Therefore, I want to do 'boy' things." This process is solidified when the child achieves gender constancy.

Once children have acquired concepts of masculinity and femininity, they tend to interpret events in their world according to such gender concepts. They are more likely to attend and remember when someone acts according to sex stereotypes than when those stereotypes are violated (Martin & Halverson, 1981). Because gender concepts guide the child's attention and recall, a cycle can be created by which the child increasingly learns information consistent with those concepts and fails to notice information that does not fit them.

Cognitive developmental theory accounts for the fact that sex stereotypes appear very early and that virtually all children learn them to some extent. It does not account, however, for the fact that boys follow the predicted pattern of valuing and adopting "boy" things, but girls are less likely to value "girl" things. It also does not account for individual differences in the strength and nature of sex typing.

Gender salience One basis for individual differences in adoption of sex-typed interests and behavior may be that the salience or importance of gender concepts is greater for some children than others (Bem, 1981). According to this hypothesis, although all members of a society are well aware of the social ex-

BOX 10.1

Nonsexist child rearing

Using her theory of gender salience, Sandra Bem recently presented a series of proposals for socializing children in a nonsexist manner. She suggested first that gender as a category has assumed too much significance in our culture. It is used even when it is irrelevant. For example, the monitors in an elementary school classroom are one boy and one girl each day; boys and girls are put on opposing teams or are selected alternately for teams. Teachers do not use race, eye color, or any number of other categories to sort children in this way. As a result of the widespread adult attention to gender, it becomes highly salient in children's thinking and assumes more importance than it might otherwise have.

Bem suggests that one way to counteract this pattern is to teach children early that gender is a biological fact, defined by reproductive capacities and by anatomy. Parents can stress that genitals, not clothes or behavior, define you as a girl or a boy. Many parents, even those who teach their children labels for everything around them, avoid labeling genitals or talking directly about biological sex. Yet such labels and discussion enable the child to understand what is critical to being a girl or a boy and what is not. Bem illustrates this point by describing her son Jeremy's experience when he wore barrettes to nursery school at age 4. Several times, another boy told Jeremy he was a girl because "only girls wear barrettes." Jeremy explained that "wearing barrettes doesn't matter. Being a boy is having a penis and testicles." Jeremy finally pulled down his pants to make his point more convincing. The other boy was not impressed. He simply said, "Everybody has a penis; only girls wear barrettes" (Bem, 1983, p. 607).

In addition to teaching that biology defines gender, parents can counteract and try to alter some of the messages about sex stereotypes that children receive from the larger culture. Television programs and storybooks can be selected carefully for very young children. When children encounter traditional themes in books or television, parents and children can discuss them. Parents can point out that it is strange that women so often need rescuing and men so often go on adventures in fairy tales. Parents can also select schools that share and support their own values, and they can make their views known to teachers and administrators in their children's schools.

In discussions with children, Bem suggests that parents stress individual differences—that some boys like to play football and others do not—and point out that people have different opinions about what is right or appropriate. Just as people differ on politics or religious values, they also differ on ideas about sex-appropriate behavior. Finally, children can gradually acquire and understand the value system that their parents hold—that women and men are fundamentally alike in most respects (from Bem, 1983).

pectations for males and females, gender is a particularly salient or important category for some people. They tend to interpret many events in sex-typed terms. Others may judge people and situations according to other categories and pay relatively little attention to gender. Consider Sue, who goes to a picnic in a park where a lot of people are playing Frisbee. She is trying to decide whether to join the game. If gender schemas are salient to her, she might consider whether it is feminine to play Frisbee. She will probably notice whether other girls are playing or think about whether she will be attractive to boys if she plays. Tammy, for whom gender schemas are not very salient, might consider whether she has enjoyed Frisbee in the past, whether she is so uncoordinated that she will look foolish, or whether she sees another activity she prefers. She is basing her decision on criteria unrelated to gender. Both girls might make the same decision, but for different reasons. Some socialization experiences that may encourage or discourage gender salience are discussed in Box 10.1.

Observational learning

Both social learning and cognitive developmental theories emphasize observation as an important means of learning sex typing. Propositions from the two theories can be combined to explain how children learn from observing others. When children observe consistent differences between the behaviors of men and women, they form concepts about what behaviors are masculine or feminine, as proposed in cognitive developmental theory. When the opportunity arises, they tend to imitate the behaviors shown by members of their own gender, as suggested by social learning theory. This process was demonstrated in an experiment in which children watched adults state preferences for sex-neutral items (such as an apple or a banana). Some children saw four men choose one set of items (set A) and four women choose the other set (set B). Another group of children saw three men and one woman choose set A, while three women and one man chose set B. A third group saw two men and two women choose each set of items. Later, all the children had an opportunity to choose items from set A or set B. The results are shown in Figure 10.4. Children in the first (high-consensus) group imitated the choices previously made by members of their own sex; children in the third (low-consensus) group did not. When several models of one gender made the same choice, children apparently concluded that initially neutral preferences were sex-typed. That is, they formed a gender concept, and they imitated behaviors that fit the concept for their own gender (Perry & Bussey, 1979).

In summary, children learn social expectations for the sexes by observing others, and they process that information actively, integrating it with other knowledge they have acquired to construct concepts of gender appropriateness. They learn from many sources other than their parents—the other adults they know and those they see on the mass media. Television may be an especially potent source because children spend many hours each week viewing and because the portrayals of men and women on television are often highly stereotyped. Television women cook, clean, care for children, and try to look beautiful; men are aggressive, adventurous, and successful. Knowledge about social expectations is only one influence on behavior, however. Children's preferences and choices for their own lives also depend on the social value and reinforcement available for different behavioral patterns.

FIGURE 10.4

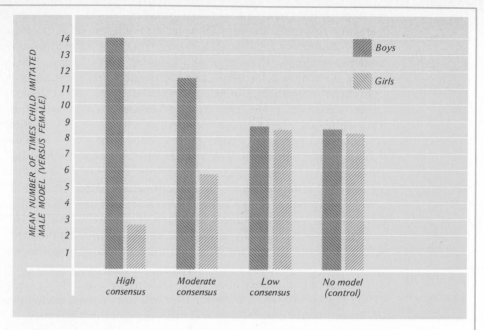

Mean amount of imitation of a male (versus female) model after seeing three levels of "consensus" among several adult models: High consensus — four males displayed one preference while four females displayed another; moderate consensus — three males and one female displayed one preference while three females and one male displayed another; low consensus — two males and two females displayed each type of preference; no model — no models observed. Results suggest that children form a schema or concept that a previously sex-neutral behavior is appropriate for one sex when they see high consensus among models. (Adapted from D. G. Perry & K. Bussey. The social learning theory of sex differences: Imitation is alive and well. **Journal of Personality and Social Psychology,** *1979, 37, 1704. By permission.)*

ETHNIC GROUP AND IDENTITY

Children's self-concepts also include the racial, ethnic, and religious groups to which they belong. Virtually all of the research on ethnic identity has been carried out with black children. Two issues have been explored over the years: how awareness of ethnic or racial differences develops, and how attitudes develop. As early as age 3, both black and white children classify people according to skin color, just as they classify people by gender or by age. They may identify different racial groups before that, but no studies are available for children younger than 3 (Katz, 1976; Powell, 1982).

The group differences that are recognized by very young children are those based on obvious physical characteristics such as skin color and facial features. More subtle differences go unnoticed. Religious identity, for example, generally begins at a somewhat later age than racial identity, partly because there are few if any physical cues for religious preference. Young children are also more likely to understand ethnic distinctions that are emphasized in their culture than ones that are unimportant. In the United States, white children are relatively unaware of differences between light- and dark-skinned Afro-Americans, even though their physical appearance is quite different, while children classify light-skinned Afro-Americans as different from Caucasians.

Minority-group children are aware of ethnic differences earlier than majority-group children. Such differences have more profound social consequences for them, and there is a general tendency in the formation of self-concept for distinctive qualities to be salient. Very short people are more likely to mention height when they define themselves than are people of average stature (McGuire, McGuire, Child, & Fujioka, 1978). Even in adulthood, being black is probably a more salient aspect of one's identity than being white, at least in a predominantly white culture like ours. This is illustrated by one survey of black adolescents. In response to the question "Who are you?" 95 percent mentioned being black or Negro. It would be most surprising to find white teenagers mentioning being white in response to this question (Powell, 1973).

Children's attitudes about their ethnic group appear a little later than their awareness, but still during the preschool years. What those attitudes are is open to question, however. The available research presents mixed results on whether black children have negative self-images or negative attitudes toward their own group. In some investigations, negative self-evaluations appear; in many others, there are no differences between white and black children (Brand, Ruiz, & Padilla, 1974; Harter, 1983; Katz, 1976; Powell, 1982). The discrepancies may be due to measurement problems, geographic differences, and changes in the

social climate over time. Children of the 1970s may have had more positive self-images than earlier generations because of the ''black pride'' emphasized during that period. However, minority children in the 1980s face fewer opportunities and less public concern with their welfare, so such changes could be reversed (Powell, 1982).

Virtually no information exists about ethnic identity for other minorities such as Asian-Americans, American Indians, or Hispanics. We might expect that children's awareness of these groups would depend on the visible physical cues and the social importance of the group distinctions, just as it does for black Americans. We need more information, however, particularly as increasing numbers of children in these groups become part of the American population.

<table>
<tr><td>SELF-ESTEEM</td></tr>
</table>

As children form identities and concepts about themselves, they implicitly assign positive or negative value to their own profile of attributes. Collectively, these self-evaluations constitute the child's self-esteem.

Self-esteem is not identical to self-concept (discussed in Chapter 9), though the two are often confused. The self-concept is a set of ideas about oneself that is descriptive rather than judgmental. Some parts of the self-concept

may be regarded as good or bad, but some may be neutral. The fact that one has dark hair and a soft voice is part of the self-concept, but those qualities are not viewed as good or bad. Self-esteem, on the other hand, refers to one's evaluation of one's own qualities. An example may clarify the distinction. An 8-year-old boy might have a concept of himself as someone who fights a lot. If he values his ability to fight and stand up for himself, that quality might add to his self-esteem. If he is unhappy about his tendency to get into conflicts, then his proneness to aggression might detract from his self-esteem.

Measuring self-esteem

Asking children questions about how much they like themselves and how they evaluate their abilities is a procedure fraught with problems of biased responding. Children may not want to admit that they have undesirable qualities, or, more seriously, they may be unaware of qualities that others consider undesirable. One measure designed to reduce such biases is the Perceived Competence Scale for Children (Harter, 1982). For each question, descriptions of two types of children are presented, and children are asked to decide which group they belong to. For example, "Some kids feel there are a lot of things about themselves that they would change if they could" versus "other kids would like to stay pretty much the same" (Harter, 1979).

Some of the problems in measuring self-esteem are illustrated in a study comparing children's self-evaluations with the evaluations made by their teachers and peers. Three methods were used to assess self esteem: (a) Children ranked themselves in comparison to other members of their class on attributes such as popularity and competence; (b) for triads of classmates, they were asked to say which two were similar and why; and (c) their responses to films of children with different attributes were observed to determine which ones they considered most similar to themselves. The three measures produced moderately consistent scores for many children. However, almost one-third of the children whose peers and teachers rated them as unpopular or incompetent rated themselves as popular and competent. Some children's self-esteem appears to be inflated, at least as compared to other people's evaluations; another possibility is that their self-reports show higher self-esteem than they actually possess (Kagan, Hans, Markowitz, & Lopez, 1982).

Variations in self-esteem

Domain specificity Self-esteem often varies for different domains of behavior. For instance, on the Perceived Competence Scale, there are subscales for three content areas—cognitive, social, and physical skills. A fourth scale measures general feelings of self-worth. Children rate themselves differently in different areas. Their evaluations of their physical skills differ from ratings of social skills, and their general feelings of self-worth do not necessarily depend on how good they feel about their cognitive skills. This fact—that self-evaluations vary for different content domains—is parallel to the point made in Chapter 8 that achievement motivation varies from one kind of task to another. It is a very important point for teachers and others to remember when they work with children.

Developmental changes For children below about age 7, it is difficult if not impossible to measure self-esteem in any meaningful way. Young children show expectancies of success for particular tasks and evaluate themselves in specific situations, but they do not appear to have generalized self-evaluations. If you ask preschool children how good they feel about themselves, they almost always say they are satisfied and happy with themselves, often while giving you a slightly mystified look. By age 9 or 10, children do have a clearly formulated sense of their worth and competence in different areas, and their feelings remain relatively stable over the 10-to-12 age range (Harter, 1983).

Self-esteem and achievement

One reason for widespread interest in self-esteem is the notion that poor self-esteem might account for school failure for some children. Several training programs to improve self-esteem have been carried out in the hope that they would also improve school performance. Such programs have generally failed (Scheirer & Kraut, 1979). One reason is that general feelings of positive self-esteem are not as clearly correlated with school performance as are a child's feelings of competence about cognitive and academic tasks. These programs have failed to realize that self-esteem is domain-specific. In retrospect, it should not be surprising that making children feel good about their athletic skills would not have much effect on their sense of competence in math.

A second, related reason for the failure of training programs is that self-esteem is more likely to be an outcome than a cause of school achievement (Maruyama, Rubin, & Kingsbury, 1981). Children are rational human beings (sometimes), and they judge their competence by their past performance. Simply teaching them to feel good about themselves might reduce some anxiety about failure—and could have other beneficial effects as well—but it is not a very powerful way to change the academic performance of children who are doing poorly in school.

PROSOCIAL BEHAVIOR

One of the major accomplishments of children as they grow older is their increasing ability to regulate their own behavior in ways that conform to the expectations of the society in which they live. In Chapter 5, we discussed the early awareness of standards of behavior. During the early school years, this awareness is elaborated and built on in many ways. Children learn to adopt the standards of their society, to express or suppress impulses in socially acceptable ways, to delay an immediate gratification when a more important goal can be obtained as a result, to consider the needs of other people as well as their own, to cooperate and coordinate their behavior with others, to resist the temptation to do "wrong" things, and to behave in accord with the social rules and conventions of their society. All of these are forms of self-direction.

The moral and social rules that children use to direct their behavior can be broadly classified as prescriptive (things one should do) and proscriptive (things one should not do). *Prosocial behavior* is a term psychologists use to refer to culturally prescribed moral actions such as sharing, helping someone in need, cooperating with others, and expressing sympathy. Such behavior often entails self-control because it requires the person to suppress self-interested responses in favor of actions that serve the needs of other people.

Cooperation

Although helping, sharing, and cooperation are all prosocial, they differ in some important ways. Cooperation is usually defined as two or more people working together toward a common goal. It has been measured in the laboratory using games in which children must work together to win rewards or prizes.

One of these games is the cooperation board shown in Figure 10.5. Even though a player who fails to cooperate cannot win this game, many children behave competitively. In playing games like this one, older children are less cooperative than younger children. Anglo-American children are also less cooperative than Mexican-American children, who are in turn less cooperative than Mexican children living in Mexico (Mussen & Eisenberg-Berg, 1977). The competitive norms of American society appear to be responsible for this cross-cultural contrast.

In the spontaneous play of children, cooperation and competition are not necessarily in conflict. Team sports and partnership games require both forms of behavior, for instance. Cooperation begins in the preschool years; when

FIGURE 10.5

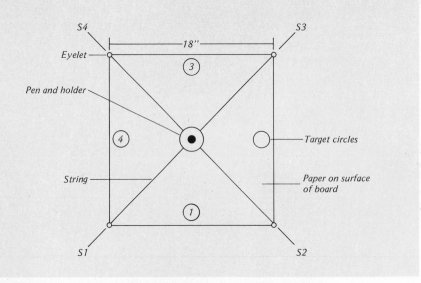

Diagram of a cooperation board. Four children play the game. A pen is suspended at the center, and strings attached to the pen pass through the eyelets at the four corners of the board. The object is to pull the pen through the circles on the board. Because each child controls one string, all must cooperate or work together to move the pen to any of the circles. (From A. Shapira & M. C. Madsen. *Cooperation and competitive behavior of urban Afro-American, Anglo-American, Mexican-American, and Mexican village children.* **Developmental Psychology**, *1970, 3, 16–20.*)

children build something with blocks or engage in fantasy play taking reciprocal roles such as mother and baby, they are cooperating. In a classic study of children from ages 2 through 5, Parten (1932) established that very young children often engage in parallel play (in which two children play with separate objects but are near each other and sometimes talk together). As children get older, they manifest more cooperative play in which they coordinate their activities to attain a mutual goal. Beyond the preschool years, there is little information about the developmental course of cooperation (Barnes, 1971; Radke-Yarrow, Zahn-Waxler, & Chapman, 1983).

Altruism and sympathy

Sharing, helping, and expressing sympathy often require some individual sacrifice, but they do not require as much coordination of one's actions with other people as cooperation does. They also are less likely to be in conflict with competitive motives. In laboratory studies, sharing is often measured by giving children a chance to donate prizes to a charity for poor children. Helping has been measured by exposing the child to cries from a child in the next room to determine whether the child will attempt to see what is wrong or summon an adult. Helping and sharing can also be observed in children's spontaneous play. Altruism tends to increase with age, at least during the school years (Mussen & Eisenberg-Berg, 1977; Rushton, 1980).

Are there prosocial "traits"?   Children do show some consistency in prosocial behavior over these various situations and measures. That is, children who share in one situation tend to share or be helpful in another. The correlations are not high, however, and it is clear that situational influences are also very important in determining when prosocial behavior will occur. Perhaps more interesting, young children who are often helpful and sympathetic to others also engage in other kinds of social interaction frequently, including aggressive and assertive behavior (Radke-Yarrow et al., 1983). The paradoxical relation between prosocial and aggressive behavior is discussed in Box 10.2.

BOX 10.2
Prosocial behavior and aggression: A paradox

A paradox revealed by observational studies of preschool children's behavior is that the children who are most prosocial (helpful, sharing, and sympathetic) also turn out to be among the most aggressive children in the class. For example, observations of natural behavior were carried out in preschool classrooms in two studies. The children in one study were from a mixture of social-class backgrounds in a small city and the surrounding rural area; in the other, they were black and white children from poor urban families. In both studies, children who were more cooperative, generous, and helpful were also more assertive, aggressive, and generally sociable. The correlations between interpersonal aggression and prosocial behavior were .40 and .31 for the two samples (Friedrich & Stein, 1973, 1975).

Why should very prosocial children also be the aggressive members of their classes? One answer seems to be that some children are simply more social than others, so they display more of all kinds of social behavior. A more refined analysis suggests that it may be the moderately aggressive children who are most often helpful and kind; the extremely aggressive children are less often prosocial (Radke-Yarrow et al., 1983). In addition, the pattern is evident primarily for preschool children. During the early years, children assert leadership and dominance in the peer group by verbal and physical aggression as well as by asking or telling others what they want them to do or insisting on their rights in a nonviolent way. As they get older, children probably learn to distinguish socially unacceptable forms of aggression, such as hitting other children, from more acceptable forms of assertiveness, such as giving directions. Among 5- to 8-year-olds, those who were most skilled at understanding others' feelings and motivations were also the children who combined assertiveness and prosocial behavior in their peer interactions. They were socially competent children who were well liked and were often leaders among their peers. By contrast, children who continue to use a lot of physical aggression on their peers in elementary school tend to be rejected and to be deficient in prosocial behavior (Parke & Slaby, 1983).

Cognitive developmental theory suggests that one basis for helping another person may be empathy, the ability to understand and share the other person's feelings or distress (see Chapter 9). There is some evidence that empathy contributes to altruistic behavior, but, like the relation between moral judgment and behavior, the correlations are generally low. Under what circumstances is empathy aroused, and once aroused, when is it translated into altruistic behavior? An example may be useful.

> *Sheldon, a 4-year-old boy, saw a television news story about a family that had lost all its possessions in a fire. A young boy in the family was in tears because his special teddy bear was gone. Sheldon watched the boy intently, then went to his toy box and got out a large, new teddy bear he had just received. He told his father he wanted to send it to the boy on the news.*

This anecdote illustrates some of the conditions under which empathy is most likely to contribute to altruism. First, Sheldon had the cognitive capacity to take the perspective of another child. The child on the television story was crying (a clear sign of distress), and his plight was similar to experiences that Sheldon might have had. Second, Sheldon's empathic reaction was immediate, and he had a concrete idea of what he could do to be helpful. His helpful response might also have occurred had he seen someone else responding helpfully to a similar situation in the past or because another person had been helpful or kind to him in the past when he was in distress (Aronfreed, 1968). As children grow older, their prosocial behavior is more often stimulated by empathy than is the case for young children (Radke-Yarrow et al., 1983; Underwood & Moore, 1982).

How do children develop prosocial behavior? Family and school experiences contribute to prosocial tendencies, but these influences operate in a larger sociocultural context. As the studies of cooperation by Mexican and American children suggest, some cultures value and expect altruism and cooperation more than others.

Parents' altruistic behavior and their treatment of their children affect prosocial behavior. As would be expected from the principles of observational learning discussed earlier, parents who are helpful and do things for other people are likely to have children who are altruistic and helpful, as well. In addition, parents who show empathy and consideration for their children's distress are likely to have children who respond empathically to others. Parental explanations of the effect a child's actions have on other people seem to help children develop prosocial patterns, partly because they tend to increase empathy.

Like other forms of behavior, prosocial behavior can be learned from television programs and books. Several investigations have shown that nursery school children who watched "Mr. Rogers' Neighborhood," a program in which helping, sharing, and cooperation are stressed, showed increased levels of prosocial behavior in their play behavior with other children (Stein & Friedrich, 1975).

The flip side of the moral coin is *pro*scription, the "don'ts" that require children to inhibit unacceptable behavior. Children must learn to obey rules, resist temptation, and restrain themselves from hurting another person or destroying property when they are angry. They must also learn to resist distraction while doing work and to put off attractive immediate rewards in order to obtain larger or more important rewards later.

Ego processes

Many of our concepts about self-regulation originated in psychoanalytic theory. Freud suggested three components of the personality: the id, which represented unconscious drives and impulses; the superego, which represented the conscience or sense of right and wrong; and the ego, which represented the means of balancing or modulating the conflicting demands of one's own needs, one's conscience, and the realities of the outside world. Ego processes include the rational components of the personality. They help people to judge how they can satisfy some of their basic needs (or obtain pleasure) without encountering punishment from the external environment or violating their own moral standards. Consider a child who wants an expensive doll and must save her money to buy it. Ego processes help her avoid stealing or obtaining the doll illegitimately and resist the impulse to buy an attractive hair ornament for which she has the money now. The important function of ego processes is to maintain a balance—both overcontrol and undercontrol are viewed as less healthy than moderate control.

The development of ego processes has been investigated in a longitudinal study following children from age 3 to 11. During the preschool years, the children were observed in free play, tested in the laboratory, interviewed, and assessed indirectly through parent and teacher ratings. Then they were classified according to behaviors like conformity, planfulness, organization, perseverance, resistance to distraction, willingness to delay a reward, and hesitancy about exploring new situations to define their level of *ego control*. Children who showed these behaviors a great deal were called overcontrolling. These children also showed minimal emotional expression and had narrow and unchanging interests. Children who were spontaneous, emotionally expressive, nonconforming, and distractible, tended toward immediate gratification of impulses, had many short-lived enthusiasms and interests, and liked to explore were called undercontrolling. Both extremes have advantages and disadvantages.

It might be most adaptive for a child to be able to shift from greater to less control depending on the situation. For this reason, children were classified on a second dimension, indicating how flexible or adaptable they were. This dimension was called *ego resilience*. Highly resilient children could exercise strong control in some situations and let go in others. A few of these personality characteristics were stable from age 3 to age 7, but many children's levels of control and resilience changed during that age span (Block & Block, 1980).

Cognitive strategies for self-control

Children who are resilient appear to have the ability to exert self-control when needed. What cognitive strategies do children use to resist a temptation or endure a delay in getting something they want? Answers to these questions can be derived from the findings of laboratory experiments.

One means for measuring delay of gratification was a laboratory task in which children were offered the choice between eating a relatively unattractive food (such as a pretzel) whenever they chose or waiting 15 minutes to eat an attractive food (a marshmallow). They were left with both foods and were told they could decide at any time during the 15 minutes to eat the pretzel, or they could wait for the marshmallow. Not too surprisingly, children had more trouble waiting when the rewards were visible than when the rewards were covered by a screen. However, the cognitive strategies they used to deal with the situation were more important than whether the reward was present. For example, one group of children was instructed to think about the delicious taste and feeling of the foods in front of them. Another group was told to imagine that the foods were inedible objects—to pretend that the marsh-mallows were fluffy white clouds making pictures or that the pretzels were logs for a cabin. Children who were instructed to imagine inedible uses for the rewards waited almost twice as long as the ones who were thinking about how good they would taste (Mischel & Patterson, 1978).

Another cognitive strategy children can learn for self-control is self-instruction. Preschool children were offered an attractive reward if they could complete a long and repetitive task (copying letters of the alphabet). They were warned that a talking "clown box" might try to distract them while they worked. Some of them were told to repeat short sentences or "plans," such as "I'm not going to look at Mr. Clown," to themselves when Mr. Clown tried to distract them. They were less distracted and got more work done than children in control groups who were not given plans. It is impressive that very young children can use these self-instructional plans effectively to regulate their own behavior (Patterson, 1982).

A similar technique, *self-monitoring,* has been used effectively to help older children resist distraction and concentrate on their work in school (Pressley, 1979). Sixth-graders in an individualized math curriculum were told to record instances of "off-task behavior" (e.g., talking to others, fooling around) and to use those as a cue to return to work. Children who used this self-monitoring spent more time concentrating on their work and performed better on mathematics tests than control groups (Sagotsky, Patterson, & Lepper, 1978). Self-monitoring and self-instruction are important means by which children learn to control and regulate their own behavior.

Conscience   Many people are particularly concerned that children learn self-control in situations where moral issues are at stake. Prohibitions against hurting others, stealing, cheating, and telling lies are important moral rules in most societies, and adherence to them has special significance. According to both psycho-analytic and social learning theories, children *internalize* moral principles into their own belief system, adopting them as their guides for what is right and wrong. When a child has accepted moral principles and enforces those prin-ciples spontaneously, we say the child has developed conscience. Conscience is more than cognitive judgments about right and wrong; it involves strong affect in the form of guilt when children violate their own moral standards. According to this view, children with a strong conscience should resist the temptation to violate a prohibition even when no one else will know about it because they anticipate feelings of guilt. If they do break a moral rule, they feel guilt, shame, or anxiety. They often confess spontaneously, and they try to make retribution or repair the damage.

Although there is ample evidence that young children often experience guilt when they violate a moral rule, conforming to moral rules does not seem to be motivated primarily by anticipated guilty feelings for violating the rule. Children who are prone to guilt feelings are not any more likely to resist temptation than other children (Hoffman, 1970). In fact, a child with a very solidly internalized moral system may obey moral principles without even considering other possibilities and, as a result, may experience little "temptation" or concern about guilt. For example, children from Mennonite and non-Mennonite families were interviewed about the "shoulds" and "should nots" of behavior. The Mennonite children rarely mentioned the moral religious values of their community prohibiting stealing, lying, killing, and the like. It appeared that these values were so ingrained that they were taken for granted, and the children did not even consider violating them (see Radke-Yarrow et al., 1983).

Situational variations in moral behavior One major issue in trying to understand children's moral behavior is whether honesty is a trait that is consistent across many situations or whether moral behavior is highly situation-specific. The theory that children form an internalized conscience suggests that moral behavior should be consistent across situations—that is, the child who obeys a moral rule in one situation should do so in other situations. The consistency of moral behavior was evaluated in a classic study in which children were observed in school, on the playground, in after-school activities, and in sports. In each situation, honesty, cheating, violating rules, and other moral behaviors were observed. Although the initial reports from this study suggested little consistency across situations, more recent analyses have shown that children were moderately consistent. That is, children who were honest on one test also tended to be honest on another, and children who lied about one event were somewhat more likely to lie about another (Burton, 1963; Hartshorne & May, 1928; Hartshorne, May & Maller, 1929; Rushton, 1980). Consistency was relatively high within one setting (e.g., the classroom); children who were honest on a math test also tended to be honest on a spelling test, and so on. Nevertheless, children were not perfectly consistent, particularly when different settings, such as the playground and the classroom, were compared. If a child was honest in one setting, one could predict the child's behavior in another setting with only moderate success.

Moral behavior is sometimes inconsistent from one situation to another because it depends on the motivations, pressures, reinforcements, and demands of each situation as well as on the conscience of the child. A child who cares a great deal about doing well in math but has little concern about playing basketball well is more likely to cheat on a math test than in a basketball game. Both the person's enduring traits (or moral beliefs) and the characteristics of the particular situation interact to influence moral behavior.

All societies must find ways of preventing their members from injuring, killing, and doing serious harm to one another. All regulate aggressive behavior to some degree, but they vary considerably in the value attached to aggression and the degree to which it is restricted. For example, among American Indian tribes, the Comanche and the Apache raised their children to be warriors, whereas the Hopi and the Zuni valued peaceful, nonviolent orientations. In contemporary America, the Hutterites stress pacificism as a way of life and train their children to be nonaggressive. In the majority American culture, aggression and "toughness" are often valued (Bandura, 1973).

*Definitions
of aggression*

Psychologists of different theoretical persuasions have some basic disagreements about how to define aggression. The issue at the heart of these disputes is whether to define aggression by its observable consequences or by the intentions of the person showing the behavior. Some people define aggression as behavior that hurts or has the potential to hurt another person or an object. It may be physical attack (hitting, kicking, biting), verbal attack (yelling, calling names, derogating), or violation of another's rights (e.g., taking objects forcibly). A strength of this definition is that it is objective: It refers to observable behavior. A weakness is that it includes many behaviors that would not ordinarily be considered aggressive. If a child throws open a door, hitting a person standing on the other side, we would not ordinarily call it aggression unless the child knew the person was there.

According to a second definition, aggression is behavior that is intended to harm another person or object. This definition takes into account the intentions of the actor, but it may be less objective, for it involves inferences about intentions. Furthermore, it excludes some behavior that would normally be called aggressive. A child who pushes another off a swing because she wants to use the swing may not intend to hurt the other, but the behavior would still be considered aggressive by many people. In practice, many researchers use a rough combination of these two definitions. Behavior that is clearly harmful to others is considered aggression, particularly when the child is probably aware of its potential for hurting someone. Intentionally hostile actions are defined as aggression as well.

Some theorists separate *instrumental* from *hostile* aggression. Instrumental aggression is behavior intended to acquire a goal; hostile aggression is behavior intended to hurt someone. Much of the aggression among very young children appears to be instrumental. It centers around property—children grab toys from one another, push each other away from objects they want to play with, and defend their toys against others' efforts to take them. They less often appear to be acting in anger or to be trying to hurt someone or something.

Aggression must also be distinguished from assertiveness. Assertiveness includes defending property or rights (e.g., refusing to allow someone to take a toy) or stating wishes and desires directly. In popular language, we often describe an assertive person as aggressive. For instance, you might describe a salesperson as aggressive if he approaches people with a vigorous sales pitch and does not accept a refusal readily. That person is assertive rather than aggressive. One of the tasks of socialization is to teach children socially acceptable forms of assertiveness while helping them to avoid unacceptable aggression.

Developmental changes

By 12 months of age, children begin to exhibit instrumental aggressive behavior when they are together. Most of their aggression concerns toys and possessions and is directed toward age-mates. Children do attack parents or older children on occasion, but that kind of aggression is relatively infrequent in comparison to attacks on children of approximately their own age. As they reach the preschool and elementary years, aggressive actions become less frequent, and there are changes in the form aggression takes. When aggression occurs, it is more often hostile and less often instrumental. That is, children become less likely to use direct physical attack to achieve instrumental goals. When they do attack someone physically or verbally, they are more apt to have a hostile intent. Verbal aggression also increases with age, at least during the preschool years.

Although a certain amount of aggressive behavior may be acceptable in American society, extremes of aggression lead to problems in the family, in school, and in peer relations. Extremely aggressive children not only display much more frequent aggressive actions, but their behavior is qualitatively different from that of other children. Their aggressive acts are more intense and prolonged than those of the average child. In Figure 10.6, the distribution of aggressive behavior for 100 four-year-old children is shown. The rate of aggressive actions for the children on the high end of the scale is many times the rate shown by the average child. These highly aggressive children also tend to

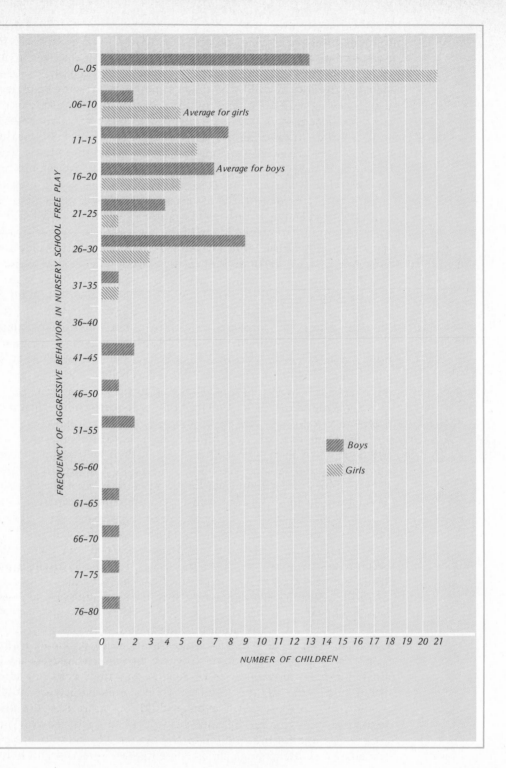

FIGURE 10.6

Frequency of inter-personal aggressive behavior for 4-year-old boys and girls in a preschool class-room. (Adapted from data reported in L. K. Friedrich & A. H. Stein. Aggres-sive and prosocial television programs and the natural be-havior of preschool children. Mono-graphs of the So-ciety for Research in Child Develop-ment, 1973, 38 [4, Serial No. 151].)

persist and escalate their physical and verbal attacks when they get in a fight (Parke & Slaby, 1983).

Stability of aggression

Although children's levels of aggression vary from one situation to another, there are consistent individual differences in proneness to aggressive behavior that persist over time. Children who are highly aggressive in the early years are likely to be aggressive when they reach adolescence and adulthood. Children who are nonaggressive are likely to continue their nonaggression. Some studies have suggested that girls' aggression is less stable over time than boys', but several have demonstrated long-term stability for girls as well as boys (Parke & Slaby, 1983). Of course, children can show temporary periods of increased aggression when stresses such as a new sibling or a parental divorce occur, but extreme aggression that persists for more than a few months often portends a long-lasting pattern of behavior. Moderate aggression gives less cause for concern. Especially in the preschool years, as explained in Box 10.2, it may merely indicate a tendency toward social interactions of all kinds. The stability of aggression suggests that parents, teachers, and others should undertake intervention efforts early if a child shows a problem level of aggression (Fagot & Hagan, 1982; Olweus, 1979; Parke & Slaby, 1983).

Perceived intentions and aggressive behavior

Children judge others' aggression quite differently depending on whether they think it intentional or accidental. Consider the following example of two 9-year-olds:

Jack is running across the playground and bumps into Sam, knocking Sam's arm aside just as he shoots a basket. Sam misses the basket.

Sam's response in this situation will depend partly on whether he thinks Jack bumped him intentionally or accidentally and whether he thinks Jack could have avoided bumping him. Sometime during the preschool years, children begin to perceive others' intentions, particularly obvious differences between accidental and intentional actions as indicated in Chapter 9. As they progress through elementary school, their understanding of others' intentions in aggressive encounters increases. They are more likely to retaliate with aggression when they think an attack on them is intentional than when they consider it accidental.

A study comparing highly aggressive boys with nonaggressive boys shows that the former may have different perceptions of others' intentions than the latter. On the basis of peer and teacher ratings, boys in second, fourth, and sixth grades were classified as highly aggressive or nonaggressive. They were then observed in an experimental situation where they were offered a prize for assembling a jigsaw puzzle. When the puzzle was partly finished, another boy (who was a confederate of the experimenter) took it apart. In one condition, the other boy destroyed it deliberately; in a second condition, it was clearly accidental; in a third condition, the other boy's motives were ambiguous. The subjects then had a chance to "retaliate" by destroying the other boy's jigsaw puzzle. Both the aggressive and nonaggressive boys retaliated when the destruction was deliberate and did not retaliate when it was accidental, but their responses to the ambiguous motives were different. When the other boy's motives were unclear, the aggressive boys retaliated, reacting as if he had acted intentionally. The nonaggressive boys did not retaliate; they reacted as if his actions were accidental (Dodge, 1980).

A highly aggressive child's tendency to interpret others' actions as hostile may be part of a vicious cycle that maintains and increases aggressive behavior. Aggressive reactions in ambiguous circumstances may give the child a reputation that leads others to respond to him aggressively. As a result, the aggressive child in fact experiences frequent hostile attacks by other children, and his belief in others' hostile intentions is supported.

Sex differences

Boys are more often aggressive than girls, a difference noted in most cultures around the world, at almost all ages, and in many animal species as well. Boys are especially prone to use physical aggression, but they also show more verbal aggression than girls do (Maccoby & Jacklin, 1974, 1980; Parke & Slaby, 1983). The differences seem to appear during the second year of life. According to observational studies of toddlers from ages 1 to 3, sex differences in frequency of aggression appear after, but not before, 18 months (Fagot & Hagan, 1982).

Boys are particularly likely to retaliate with physical aggression when they are attacked or when someone interferes with their activities. In one observational study of preschool children, boys were attacked only slightly more often than girls, but they were twice as likely to respond with a counterattack (cited in Parke & Slaby, 1983).

What accounts for such consistent sex differences? Both biological and socialization explanations have been proposed. Some theorists argue that the consistency of sex differences across human cultures and across species is strong evidence for biological influences. Studies testing the relation of sex hormones to aggression, however, have produced ambiguous results. There may be a biological foundation that provides some male children with particularly high potential for learning aggressive behavior, but researchers have made little progress in specifying how such a biological system might operate.

The social experience of boys and girls with respect to aggression is quite different. Aggression is part of the masculine stereotype, and aggressive behavior is expected and often implicitly encouraged for boys. For instance, 1- to 3-year-old boys in preschool received attention for their aggressive actions from adults and peers much more often than girls did (Fagot & Hagan, 1982). The attention was sometimes positive (smiling or joining the child's play) and sometimes mildly negative (stopping the behavior or moving the child to another activity). It is possible, however, that giving any type of attention can encourage behavior more than simply ignoring it.

Television is another source from which children, especially boys, may learn aggressive behavior. The influence of television is discussed in Box 10.3.

Family patterns and aggression

Parents of extremely aggressive children are often hostile and lax in their enforcement of rules and standards and are themselves aggressive. One of the most extensive and sophisticated approaches to understanding the socialization of aggression in the family is the research of Gerald Patterson and his associates at the Oregon Social Learning Center. They have used direct observations in the home and at school to study the patterns of family interaction

BOX 10.3

*Aggression on
television*

Although violence is often regarded as contrary to American values, aggression is also glorified and promoted as a successful means of achieving goals. In television programs, a major means by which such social values are conveyed to children, physical violence occurs on the average about five or six times per hour. In children's programming, especially Saturday morning programs, there are about 25 incidents of physical attack per hour. Aggression by television characters is often rewarded; heroes are as aggressive as villains (Signorielli, Gross, & Morgan, 1982).

Children's aggressive behavior is influenced by these portrayals, as was discussed in Chapter 1. Those who are already prone to aggression are particularly likely to respond aggressively when they watch violent television. In one study, 4-year-old children were observed during free play in nursery school for a 3-week baseline period and were classified as above or below the group average for aggressive behavior. During the next 4 weeks, the children were assigned to groups who watched either aggressive television ("Batman" and "Superman" cartoons), neutral films, or prosocial programs ("Mister Rogers' Neighborhood") for a half hour during each nursery school session. Children who were initially above average on aggression behaved more aggressively in free play after seeing the aggressive television programs than did similar children after seeing neutral programs. Children who were initially below average did not react differently to the two types of programming. These patterns of behavior continued during a 2-week follow-up period after the television viewing sessions were ended (Friedrich & Stein, 1973). Aggression-prone children are likely to become even more aggressive when they watch violence on television (Stein & Friedrich, 1975).

associated with problem behavior in children. The participants are families who are referred to clinics because one or more of their children display conduct problems such as very high aggression, stealing, or other antisocial behavior.

These investigators view the family as a system of interacting members who contribute and respond to each others' behavior. In families with highly aggressive children, the interactions frequently form an escalating pattern of "coercion" that serves to maintain and increase aggressive patterns in the family. When a hostile response occurs, the other family members are likely to do something that increases the probability of additional hostile behavior. For example, a brother yells at his sister; she in turn yells back, calling him a derogatory name; he then hits her; she hits him back; and so on. Similar escalation occurs between parent and child—the child reacts defiantly, and the parent increases the level of threats and punishment.

In Patterson's investigations, children with conduct problems—stealing, aggression, or both—were generally unresponsive to social approval and disapproval. They were unlikely to react to adult efforts to discipline them by mild, verbal means. One reason may be that their parents seem to have used both reward and punishment inconsistently during much of their childhood. Their mothers reacted positively to both deviant and prosocial behaviors. At the same time, these mothers of aggressive children frequently punished prosocial as well as deviant behavior. They were also inconsistent. They reacted harshly on some occasions while ignoring similar behavior at other times (Parke & Slaby, 1983; Patterson, 1976). Other investigators have demonstrated that inconsistent punishment leads to persistence of deviant behavior (Parke & Slaby, 1983).

These maladaptive family patterns can be changed. Patterson and his colleagues (1976) have developed a comprehensive program for retraining parents of highly aggressive children. Behavior modification principles are used in conjunction with the information gained from in-depth observation and study of the interaction patterns that characterize families of highly aggressive children. Parents are first required to study techniques of child management derived from a social learning perspective, such as how to notice and reinforce desired behavior and how to be consistent in enforcing rules. Next, they are taught to observe and record certain child behaviors, both deviant and prosocial. They keep written records of their children's actions along with a record of the events that elicit those actions and the consequences that ensue. In the third stage, they join a parent-training group where modeling and role playing are used to teach methods of reinforcing prosocial appropriate behaviors and reducing deviant behavior. Parents are taught to recognize and reinforce "good" behavior and to use consistent but calm forms of punishment such as "time out" (removing the child from an activity for a specified period of time). These techniques are substituted for their more severe forms of punishment.

Detailed observations in the home have demonstrated that this program is effective in reducing deviant behavior. In some instances, there is an increase in the child's aggressive behavior shortly after the program ends, but one or two extra treatment sessions for the parents usually enables them to return to the more effective pattern of discipline they have been taught. Follow-ups after 1 year show that the beneficial effects of the treatment are reasonably stable. These findings demonstrate that parents can learn more effective, nonpunitive ways of handling their aggressive children and that retraining can be accomplished in a relatively short period of time.

SUMMARY

During the childhood years, children form a distinctive sense of themselves—who they are, what group identities are important to them. Sex-typed identity is one of the first and most important ways in which children define themselves and others define them. During the years from 2 to 6, children learn to label themselves and others as male or female; they also learn social stereotypes for many play and work activities and for personality characteristics such as aggression and gentleness. Masculine and feminine qualities are not mutually exclusive. A person who has high levels of both masculine and feminine traits is called androgynous. In many cases, androgyny is adaptive because it permits the child to function well in a wide range of circumstances.

Social learning theories use the concepts of identification and imitation to explain how children learn sex typing. Girls and boys receive different patterns of approval and disapproval for sex-typed behavior from their parents. Cognitive developmental theories emphasize children's emerging concepts of male and female as basic categories for organizing the social world. They argue that children actively seek information about the qualities defined by society as feminine and masculine and adopt those that are perceived as appropriate for their own sex. Both theories agree that children learn sex roles by observing others and extracting a cognitive concept of femininity or masculinity.

Children's ethnic or religious groups also constitute a part of their identities, particularly for members of minority group in the society in which they live. For instance, American black children form concepts of their ethnic identity in the preschool years.

A child's evaluation of herself—whether she views her own qualities as good or bad—constitutes her self-esteem. Self-esteem differs from self-concept because it includes this evaluative component. Self-esteem is difficult to measure, because one must rely on self-reports. In addition, self-esteem is not just a global quality of the person; it can vary from one area of competence to another. For instance, a person's feelings about his social skills may be different from his feelings about his cognitive skills.

As children learn the standards and expectations of their society, they learn to direct their own behavior. They develop prosocial behavior—those qualities that their society defines as moral or right—and the ability to control antisocial behavior. Prosocial behavior includes cooperation, helping others, being sympathetic, and sharing. The capacity for empathy appears to contribute to children's prosocial behavior, as does parent modeling of such behavior. In natural situations, preschool children who are highly prosocial also tend to be aggressive, probably because they are generally more social than other children.

Self-control has been studied from several viewpoints. One approach has been examination of ego processes in young children, showing consistent differences in children's tendency to inhibit or express impulses. Preschool children can learn cognitive strategies for self-control, such as thinking about something else while they are waiting for a delicious snack. They can learn to repeat instructions to themselves and to monitor their own behavior as methods of self-control. Conscience development during the preschool years leads children to be guilty or anxious when they violate a moral norm, but that guilt does not necessarily lead to resistance to temptation.

Aggression is one frequent outcome of a child's failure to exert self-control. Aggression can be instrumental—designed to obtain a goal, such as getting a toy that someone else has—or hostile—intended to hurt another person. As children get older, the frequency of instrumental aggression declines and hostile aggression becomes relatively more prevalent. Children are more likely to respond to another person's aggression with retaliation when they think it was intentional rather than accidental. Children who are extremely aggressive come from families in which the parents and other children are also aggressive;

minor conflicts often escalate into major ones in these families. The parents are inconsistent and unclear in their enforcement of rules. Mass-media violence also contributes to aggressive behavior, particularly for individuals who are already prone to behave aggressively.

REFERENCES

Aronfreed, J. *Conduct and conscience: The socialization of internalized control over behavior.* New York: Academic Press, 1968.

Bandura, A. *Aggression: A social learning analysis.* Englewood Cliffs, N.J.: Prentice-Hall, 1973.

Bandura, A. *Social learning theory.* Englewood Cliffs, N.J.: Prentice-Hall, 1977.

Barnes, K. E. Preschool play norms: A replication. *Developmental Psychology,* 1971, *5,* 99–103.

Barrett, D. E., & Yarrow, M. R. Prosocial behavior, social inferential ability, and assertiveness in children. *Child Development,* 1977, *48,* 475–481.

Barton, S. L. Developing sharing: An analysis of modeling and other behavioral techniques. *Behavior Modification,* 1981, *5,* 386–398.

Bem, S. L. The measurement of psychological androgyny. *Journal of Consulting and Clinical Psychology,* 1974, *42,* 155–162.

Bem, S. L. Gender schema theory: A cognitive account of sex typing. *Psychological Review,* 1981, *88,* 354–364.

Bem, S. L. Gender schema theory and its implications for child development: Raising gender-aschematic children in a gender-schematic society. *Signs: Journal of Women in Culture and Society,* 1983, *8,* 598–616.

Block, J. H., & Block, J. The role of ego-control and ego-resiliency in the organization of behavior. In W. A. Collins (Ed.), *Minnesota symposia on child psychology* (Vol. 13). Hillsdale, N.J.: Erlbaum, 1980.

Brand, E. S., Ruiz, R. A., & Padilla, A. M. Ethnic identification and preference: A review. *Psychological Bulletin,* 1974, *81,* 860–890.

Burton, R. V. Generality of honesty reconsidered. *Psychological Review,* 1963, *70,* 481–499.

Cordua, G. D., McGraw, K. O., & Drabman, R. S. Doctor or nurse: Children's perceptions of sex-typed occupations. *Child Development,* 1979, *50,* 590–593.

Dodge, K. A. Social cognition and children's aggressive behavior. *Child Development,* 1980, *51,* 162–170.

Fagot, B. I. Sex differences in toddlers' behavior and parental reaction. *Developmental Psychology,* 1974, *10,* 554–558.

Fagot, B. I. The influence of sex of child on parental reactions to toddler children. *Child Development,* 1978, *49,* 459–465.

Fagot, B. I., & Hagan, R. *Hitting in toddler groups: Correlates and continuity.* Paper presented at the Annual Meeting of the American Psychological Association, Washington, D.C., 1982.

Friedrich, L. K., & Stein, A. H. Aggressive and prosocial television programs and the natural behavior of preschool children. *Monographs of the Society for Research in Child Development,* 1973, *38*(4, Serial No. 151).

Friedrich, L. K., & Stein, A. H. Prosocial television and young children: The effects of verbal labeling and role playing on learning and behavior. *Child Development,* 1975, *46,* 27–38.

Hall, J. A., & Halberstadt, A. G. Masculinity and femininity in children: Development of the Children's Personal Attributes Questionnaire. *Developmental Psychology,* 1980, *16*(4), 270–280.

Harter, S. *Perceived Competence Scale for Children.* Denver: University of Denver, 1979.

Harter, S. The Perceived Competence Scale for Children. *Child Development,* 1982, *53,* 87–97.

Harter, S. Developmental perspectives on the self-system. In P. H. Mussen & E. M. Hetherington (Eds.), *Handbook of child psychology* (Vol. 4): *Socialization, personality, and social development* (4th ed.). New York: Wiley, 1983.

Hartshorne, H., & May, M. A. *Studies in the nature of character* (Vol. 1): *Studies in deceit.* New York: Macmillan, 1928.

Hartshorne, H., May, M. A., & Maller, J. B. *Studies in the nature of character* (Vol. 2): *Studies in self-control.* New York: Macmillan, 1929.

Hoffman, M. L. Moral development. In P. H. Mussen (Ed.), *Carmichael's handbook of child psychology* (Vol. 2) (3rd ed.). New York: Wiley, 1970.

Huston, A. C. Sex typing. In P. H. Mussen & E. M. Hetherington (Eds.), *Handbook of child psychology* (Vol. 4): *Socialization, personality, and social development* (4th ed.). New York: Wiley, 1983.

Kagan, J., Hans, S., Markowitz, A., & Lopez, D. Validity of children's self-reports of psychological qualities. In B. A. Maher & W. B. Maher (Eds.), *Progress in experimental personality research* (Vol. 11). New York: Academic Press, 1982.

Katz, P. A. The acquisition of racial attitudes in children. In P. A. Katz (Ed.), *Towards the elimination of racism.* New York: Pergammon, 1976.

Katz, P. A., & Zalk, S. R. Modification of children's racial attitudes. *Developmental Psychology,* 1978, *14,* 447–461.

Kohlberg, L. A cognitive-developmental analysis of children's sex-role concepts and attitudes. In E. E. Maccoby (Ed.), *The development of sex differences.* Stanford, Calif.: Stanford University Press, 1966.

Lepper, M. R. Intrinsic and extrinsic motivation in children: Detrimental effects of superfluous social controls. In W. A. Collins (Ed.), *Minnesota symposia on child psychology* (Vol. 4). Hillsdale, N.J.: Erlbaum, 1981.

Maccoby, E. E., & Jacklin, C. N. *The psychology of sex differences.* Stanford, Calif.: Stanford University Press, 1974.

Maccoby, E. E., & Jacklin, C. N. Sex differences in aggression: A rejoinder and reprise. *Child Development,* 1980, *51,* 964–980.

Marantz, S. A., & Mansfield, A. F. Maternal employment and the development of sex-role stereotyping in five- to eleven-year-old girls. *Child Development*, 1977, *48*, 668–673.

Martin, C. L., & Halverson, C. F., Jr. A schematic processing model of sex typing and stereotyping in children. *Child Development*, 1981, *52*, 1119–1134.

Maruyama, G., Rubin, R. A., & Kingsbury, G. G. Self-esteem and educational achievement: Independent constructs with a common cause? *Journal of Personality and Social Psychology*, 1981, *40*, 962–975.

McConaghy, M. J. Gender permanence and the genital basis of gender: Stages in the development of constancy of gender identity. *Child Development*, 1979, *50*, 1223–1226.

McGuire, W. J., McGuire, C. V., Child, P., & Fujioka, T. Salience of ethnicity in the spontaneous self-concept as a function of one's ethnic distinctiveness in a social environment. *Journal of Personality and Social Psychology*, 1978, *36*, 511–520.

Meyer, B. The development of girls' sex-role attitudes. *Child Development*, 1980, *51*, 508–514.

Mischel, W. Sex typing and socialization. In P. H. Mussen (Ed.), *Carmichael's manual of child psychology* (Vol. 2) (3rd ed.). New York: Wiley, 1970.

Mischel, W., & Patterson, C. J. Effective plans for self-control. In W. A. Collins (Ed.), *Minnesota symposia on child psychology* (Vol. 11). Hillsdale, N.J.: Erlbaum, 1978.

Mussen, P. H., & Eisenberg-Berg, N. *Roots of caring, sharing, and helping: The development of prosocial behavior in children.* San Francisco: Freeman, 1977.

O'Brien, M., Huston, A. C., & Risley, T. Sex-typed play of toddlers in a day-care center. *Journal of Applied Developmental Psychology*, in press.

Olweus, D. Stability of aggressive reaction patterns in males: A review. *Psychological Bulletin*, 1979, *86*, 852–875.

Parke, R. D., & Slaby, R. G. Aggression: A multi-level analysis. In P. H. Mussen & E. M. Hetherington (Eds.), *Handbook of child psychology* (Vol. 4): *Socialization, personality, and social development* (4th ed.). New York: Wiley, 1983.

Parten, M. B. Social participation among preschool children. *Journal of Abnormal and Social Psychology*, 1932, *27*, 243–269.

Patterson, C. J. Self-control and self-regulation in childhood. In T. Field, A. C. Huston, H. C. Quay, L. Troll, & G. E. Finley (Eds.), *Review of human development.* New York: Wiley, 1982.

Patterson, G. R. The aggressive child: Victim and architect of a coercive system. In L. A. Hammerlynck, L. C. Handy, & E. J. Mash (Eds.), *Behavior modification and families: Theory and research.* New York: Bruner Mazell, 1976.

Perry, D. G., & Bussey, K. The social learning theory of sex differences: Imitation is alive and well. *Journal of Personality and Social Psychology*, 1979, *37*, 1699–1712.

Powell, G. J. *Black Monday's children: A study of the effects of school desegregation on self-concepts of Southern children.* Englewood Cliffs, N.J.: Prentice-Hall, 1973.

Powell, G. J. The impact of television on the self-concept development of minority group children. In G. L. Barry & C. Matchell-Kernan (Eds.), *Television and the socialization of the minority child.* New York: Academic Press, 1982.

Pressley, M. Increasing children's self-control through cognitive intervention. *Review of Educational Research*, 1979, *49*, 319–370.

Radke-Yarrow, M., Zahn-Waxler, C., & Chapman, M. Children's prosocial dispositions and behavior. In P. H. Mussen & E. M. Hetherington (Eds.), *Handbook of child psychology* (Vol. 4): *Socialization, personality, and social development* (4th ed.). New York: Wiley, 1983.

Rushton, J. P. *Altruism, socialization, and society.* Englewood Cliffs, N.J.: Prentice-Hall, 1980.

Sagotsky, G., Patterson, C. J., & Lepper, M. R. Training children's self-control: A field experiment in self-monitoring and goal-setting in the classroom. *Journal of Experimental Psychology*, 1978, *25*, 242–253.

Scheirer, M. A., & Kraut, R. E. Increasing educational achievement via self-concept change. *Review of Educational Research*, 1979, *49*, 131–150.

Shapira, A., & Madsen, M. C. Cooperation and competitive behavior of urban Afro-American, Anglo-American, Mexican-American, and Mexican village children. *Developmental Psychology*, 1970, *3*, 16–20.

Signorielli, N., Gross, L., & Morgan, M. Violence in television programs: Ten years later. In

D. Pearl, L. Bouthilet, & J. Lazar (Eds.), *Television and behavior: Ten years of scientific progress and implications for the eighties* (Vol. 2). Washington, D.C.: U.S. Government Printing Office, 1982.

Spence, J. T., & Helmreich, R. L. *Masculinity and femininity: Their psychological dimensions, correlates, and antecedents.* Austin, Tex.: University of Texas Press, 1978.

Stein, A. H., & Bailey, M. M. The socialization of achievement orientation in females. *Psychological Bulletin*, 1973, *80*, 345–366.

Stein, A. H., & Friedrich, L. K. Impact of television on children and youth. In E. M. Hetherington, J. W. Hagen, R. Kron, & A. H. Stein (Eds.), *Review of child development research* (Vol. 5). Chicago: University of Chicago Press, 1975.

Underwood, B., & Moore, B. Perspective-taking and altruism. *Psychological Bulletin*, 1982, *91*, 143–173.

Yarrow, M. R., Scott, P. M., & Waxler, C. Z. Learning concern for others. *Developmental Psychology*, 1973, *8*, 240–260.

CHAPTER 11

Socialization in the family

S ocialization is the process by which children acquire the values, beliefs, and standards of behavior that are expected in their culture. As explained in Chapter 5, this process begins during infancy. During childhood, socialization processes become more complex and diverse.

SOCIALIZATION BY PARENTS

When children are intelligent, polite, honest, or socially well adjusted, their parents are usually given credit. When they are delinquent, neurotic, or poor students, the blame is often placed on parents. Although the family is considered the most important force in children's lives in many societies, particularly the United States, children's interactions with parents and siblings take place within a larger context. Parental socialization practices are strongly influenced by the neighborhood, school, subculture, and wider culture in which the family resides. They are also influenced by the qualities of the child.

The family as system

The relationships of children to parents and other family members can be thought of as a system or network of interacting parts. The family system exists in a set of larger systems—the neighborhood, the community, and the broader society (Bronfenbrenner, 1979). Those systems have effects on children directly and indirectly, through parents' child-rearing practices and attitudes. Consider two 8-year-old boys who live in different parts of the country:

David lives in a high-rise apartment in New York. There are many playmates available at the apartment playground at almost any hour of any day, but he is not allowed to go anywhere except that playground by himself. In fact, David's mother walks to school with him because she is concerned about the heavy traffic on the streets he must cross. David takes for granted the wide variety of skin colors, facial features, and physical characteristics that he sees in the city. He also takes for granted a variety of religious beliefs, and knows that some Jewish friends are not available to play on Saturday, while others are. He frequently goes to children's theater and musical productions, parades, museums, and zoos.

Ladd lives on a ranch in Utah, 20 miles from the nearest town and 5 miles from the nearest neighbor. The 6-year-old daughter of the ranch manager is the only playmate available much of the time. Ladd has a horse, and he is allowed to ride 5 or 10 miles to other houses, being gone from home for

several hours at a time. He loves exploring the countryside on his own. Although his parents are not religious, most of the neighbors are devout Christians, so Ladd does not visit neighbors in his play clothes on Sunday. He has rarely seen anyone with dark skin or facial features that are not Caucasian. His only exposure to music, theater, or the wider world comes from the two commercial television stations that his family set can receive.

The neighborhood and subculture in which each boy lives has a major impact on his experiences, on his ideas about other people's appearances, beliefs, and values, and on the freedom his parents allow him.

The broader society is also part of the context for family behavior patterns. A family pattern that fits comfortably into one society or historical period might be deviant in another and might therefore have different outcomes for the children. For example, in nineteenth-century America, thrashings in the woodshed were expected forms of punishment. A child who was never whipped might have thought his parents were lax and uncaring. In contemporary America, many people consider such punishment cruel and abusive; a child who is whipped might feel mistreated and unloved. Many parents in the United States allow their children to question parental directives and to take part in spirited arguments about rules or moral standards. In Mexico, such behavior would be considered rude and inappropriate; a child who questioned authority would be punished in school and in contacts with other adults (Bronstein-Burrows, 1981).

Within our own culture, people of different social classes have different views about appropriate and acceptable forms of child rearing. For instance, white lower-class mothers are more restrictive and forbid disobedience by young children more often than middle-class mothers (Minton, Kagan, & Levine, 1971). Working-class parents also value conformity to externally imposed standards, whereas middle-class parents put greater emphasis on conformity to internalized standards of behavior (Kohn, 1959). Social class, then is another larger system or context within which the family system operates.

Children's effects on parents

A parent-child relationship evolves over time as two individuals interact with each other. Children's behavior contributes to this interaction just as parents' attitudes and behavior do. This is a restatement of the principle of bidirectionality, which was presented in Chapter 4. An example of the mutual effects of child and parent characteristics appears in an observational study of mother-child interactions for hyperactive and normal children at ages 4 and 8. The hyperactive children, who had histories of physical activity and poor behavior control, asked more questions and were less compliant during play; their mothers were more directive and negative than mothers of normal children. Some of these differences in the mothers' behavior were probably due to their children's initial tendencies to be hyperactive, and the children's behavior was probably influenced in turn by the mothers' responses (Mash & Johnston, 1982).

The effects of children on parents have been demonstrated experimentally in studies in which children's behavior was systematically varied and parents' reactions were observed. One investigator showed parents videotaped episodes of children being dependent (asking for help and having difficulty on a task) or independent (not asking for help) and asked them to respond as they would if their own child exhibited such behavior. When the child was dependent, parents encouraged dependence and gave directions to the child. When the child was independent, parents encouraged independence and were nondirective (Marcus, 1975). Similar patterns occurred when parents were observed with their own children doing easy or difficult tasks (Osofsky & O'Connell, 1972).

One way of thinking about the mutual influence of parents and children is to suppose that parents have upper and lower limits for acceptable behavior. When the child goes above or below those limits, parents respond with efforts to change behavior. For example, a very aggressive child may exceed the parent's upper limit for aggression; the parent will then begin to punish aggression and make efforts to restrain the child's aggressive impulses. The same parent might respond to a very timid child by encouraging more assertive behavior. In many studies of child rearing, it has been demonstrated that aggressive children have parents who use a lot of physical punishment. This pattern could indicate that parents respond to children's aggressive behavior by becoming punitive rather than indicating that children learn aggression from parental punishment (Bell, 1979; Bell & Harper, 1977).

Just as the child's temperament affects the parent, the parent's individual personality characteristics affect responses to the child. For example, a mother who is active and impatient may react to a passive child very differently than a mother who is more passive and patient herself (Bates & Pettit, 1981). Both parent and child bring qualities to their relationship that interact over time.

All parents have an implicit or explicit ideal of what their children should be like—what knowledge, moral values, and behavioral standards they should acquire as they grow. Parents try many strategies designed to move the child toward that goal. They reinforce and punish the child, they use themselves as role models, they explain their beliefs and expectations, and they try to choose neighborhoods, peer groups, and schools that support their values and goals.

The "ideal child" varies from culture to culture, however. Most of the information we will discuss here applies to contemporary American culture because that is where data have been gathered. Some goals of socialization shared by many people in our culture are academic achievement, independence, control of aggression, and skill in social relationships with peers. Therefore, these behaviors are the focus of many investigations of socialization. Other cultures may value different socialization goals or endorse different family patterns.

Psychologists have studied parents' behavior with a variety of methods: direct observation, interviews with parents or with children, ratings by observers, and questionnaires. When different methods produce similar results, we generally have more confidence in the conclusions than when only one method is used. Two dimensions describing important qualities of parenting emerge consistently from different methods: acceptance-rejection and restrictiveness-permissiveness.

FIGURE 11.1

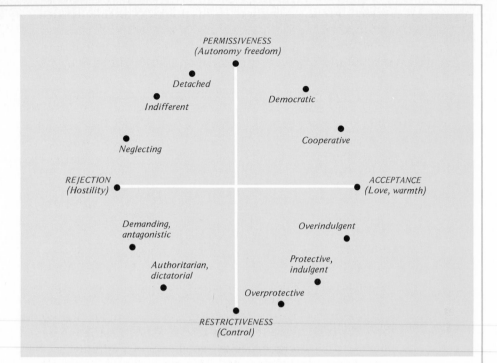

An illustration of the types of child rearing that can be described by classifying parents'
behavior on acceptance-rejection (the horizontal axis) and restrictiveness-permissiveness
(the vertical axis). The labeled points show where parents might fall on the two dimensions.
For instance, a parent who is very restrictive and slightly rejecting is described as authori-
tarian, dictatorial. (Adapted from E. S. Schaefer. A circumplex model for maternal behavior.
Journal of Abnormal and Social Psychology, *1959,* **59,** *226–235. By permission.)*

In Figure 11.1, the dimensions of acceptance and restrictiveness are shown as they combine to form different patterns of parent behavior. The labels in each quadrant of the figure describe how a parent might behave when showing different combinations of acceptance and restrictiveness. For example, a parent who is both accepting and restrictive might be called protective and indulgent. A parent who is rejecting and restrictive might be labeled demanding and antagonistic. A permissive, rejecting parent could be considered indifferent, and a permissive, accepting parent might be described as democratic. The meanings of these rather abstract terms can best be garnered from a closer examination of the types of parent behavior and attitudes involved.

Acceptance　　Acceptance is an attitude toward children that may be mani-fested in different ways depending on the personality of the parent. Accepting parents think their children have many positive qualities, and they enjoy being with their children. They often express affection, but it need not be physical hugging or kissing; it might simply be a smile or a proud look. Mothers' statements in one early study of child rearing exemplify accepting and rejecting attitudes. They were asked what they liked about their child. A mother who was rated warm said, "Everything—how very patient she is, and how understanding. She is very kind." Another said, "I like Sally, being with her, she is an awfully nice child" (Sears, Maccoby, & Levin, 1957, p. 53).

Parents who are not accepting often do not enjoy or even like their children very much. In response to the question "What do you like about your child?" a mother rated low in acceptance said, "He's naughty an awful lot, . . . but I enjoy him. He talks too much sometimes." Another said, "Well, I don't enjoy too many things in him because at the rate he's going, well, he doesn't mind too well; he's got a mind of his own" (Sears et al., 1957, p. 55). In extreme form, this lack of acceptance becomes rejection.

Control   Restrictive parents impose many rules on children, insist on supervising their children closely, and have quite definite standards of behavior to which their children are expected to conform, but they do not necessarily punish often or severely. In fact, a successful restrictive parent has a child who usually complies with rules and does not require frequent punishment. The kinds of rules and restrictions that parents impose depend, of course, on the age of the child. In the preschool years, parents make rules about noise, neatness, play on furniture, obedience, aggressive behavior, nudity, masturbation, and how far from home the child can go alone. Restrictive parents also make demands for mature behavior, good school performance, table manners, and cleanliness. As children get older, parents make rules about being informed where the child is, sexual and aggressive behavior, leisure activities, and friends. They demand good school performance, responsibility in carrying out household jobs, and self-control (Baumrind, 1973; Martin, 1975).

Although parents who are restrictive about one area, such as not hitting adults, also tend to be restrictive about other types of behavior, there are differences in what parents restrict. An example of restrictiveness about aggression appears in a mother's response to a question about what she does when her children get in a fight. "I don't like to see them quarrel. There is no need for it. I don't let it get too bad. I just reprimand them right away" (Sears et al., 1957, p. 242). The same mother may not be restrictive about children's table manners or about how far they can go from home without an adult.

At the other extreme are permissive parents. These parents generally have few rules and make few demands on their children. They do not emphasize learning table manners; they make relatively few demands for mature behavior; they do not restrict noise or play that might damage furniture and household objects; they are not concerned about neatness or obedience; they tend to view aggression, nudity, and masturbation as natural; and they allow their children considerable freedom to play without adult supervision or intervention. A parent rated permissive said she would intervene in a fight between her children "if they're making a terrible amount of noise, or if they're going to do bodily harm to each other. And I don't mean slapping—that doesn't bother me. If one of them picks up a shovel or something, then I'd stop it. Otherwise, I have found that if I sit back and watch without their knowing it, they work it out themselves" (Sears et al., 1957, p. 242).

Effects on children   Although many early studies included attempts to learn about the effects of acceptance or control on children, very few simple associations have been found between these global child-rearing dimensions and children's behavior. Warmth or acceptance is important because it provides a background for parents' efforts to discipline their children and teach them values. In general, warm, accepting parents are more effective than others in transmitting their own values and goals to their children. Extreme rejection is often associated with problem behavior among children (Martin, 1975).

The effects of parental control or restrictiveness vary with the methods that parents use to enforce restrictions. Three broad categories of disciplinary techniques have been studied extensively: power assertion or coercion, inductive techniques such as explanations, and love withdrawal. *Power-assertive* discipline includes physical punishment, shouting, depriving the child of privileges, and using tangible rewards. In general, such techniques rely on the parent's control over things the child wants or on the parent's superior physical strength. *Inductive* techniques, by contrast, include reasoning, praise, and explaining the consequences of the child's actions for other people. Such techniques rely on the communication between the parent and child and on the child's ability to internalize and understand the basis for the parent's demands. *Love withdrawal* includes isolation, expressing disappointment, and shaming or ignoring the child. These techniques are based on the child's need for the parent's love and approval; they threaten the child with loss of love, at least temporarily.

The effects of these methods of discipline are complex for several reaons. First, efforts to discipline children are most effective when the child and parent have a warm, supportive relationship. Second, most parents use a combination of methods; families differ in how much they rely, for instance, on power assertion versus induction, but it is a rare family that does not use some of each. Third, the type of discipline used depends partly on the child's response to initial attempts. In general, parents use mild reprimands and explanations initially. If the child is unresponsive, they gradually escalate to more intense and power-assertive methods. Consider the following example.

> *Deborah and Sharon are playing, and both want to ride the one available bicycle. Their mother tells Sharon, who is riding the bicycle, that she should take turns. Mother explains that it is fair to share the bicycle and that Deborah will feel bad if she does not get a turn (induction). If Sharon gives Deborah a turn, no further discipline is necessary. If Sharon does not give Deborah a turn, then Mother may repeat her instructions. If Sharon continues to ride the bicycle after Mother's inductive attempts, however, Mother will probably resort to power assertion by telling her to get off the bike, or else. If Sharon still refuses, Mother will probably punish her.*

Patterns of parent behavior

Diana Baumrind at the University of California has carried out a series of investigations in which patterns or clusters of parent practices were identified (Baumrind, 1973). The series began with a comparison of parents whose children showed high levels of "instrumental competence" during the preschool years with parents of other groups of children. Competent children were those who rated high in independence, maturity, self-reliance, activity, self-control, exploration, friendliness, and achievement orientation by observers and interviewers. Children with this pattern of behavior (called pattern I) were compared with two other groups. Children who were moderately self-reliant but were discontented, withdrawn, and distrustful were called pattern II. Children who were least self-reliant, explorative, and self-controlled were called pattern III.

To assess parent behavior, the investigators used a variety of procedures, including home visits, observations in structured situations, and parental interviews. Four aspects of the parent's behavior toward the child were evaluated: *control,* that is, efforts to influence the child's goal-oriented activity, modify the expression of dependent, aggressive, and playful behavior, and promote internalization of parental standards; *maturity demands,* pressures on the child to perform at a high level intellectually, socially, or emotionally; *clarity of parent-child communication*—for example, using reason to obtain compliance, asking the child's opinions and feelings; and *parental nurturance,* including both warmth (love, caretaking, and compassion) and involvement (praise and pleasure in the child's accomplishments).

The "scores" of the parents of the three groups of children on these four child-rearing dimensions are shown in Figure 11.2. The parents of mature, competent children (pattern I) scored uniformly high on all four dimensions. Compared with other parents studied, they were warm, loving, supportive, and conscientious, and they communicated well with their children. At the same time, they were controlling and demanded mature behavior from their children. Although they respected their youngsters' independence and decisions, they generally held firm in their own positions, being clear and explicit about the reasons for their directives. This combination of parental control, inductive discipline, and positive encouragement of the child's autonomous and independent strivings was called *authoritative* parental control.

The parents of pattern II children were rated lower on use of rational control. They relied more heavily on power-assertive, coercive discipline, and they were also less warm, nurturant, affectionate, and sympathetic with their children. These parents were called *authoritarian* because they were highly controlling and used power freely; they did not encourage their children to express disagreement with parental decisions or rules, and they provided little warmth.

The parents of the least mature children (pattern III) were permissive, noncontrolling, nondemanding, and warm. They were not well organized or effective in running their household, were lax in disciplining and rewarding their children, made relatively few and then only weak demands for mature behavior, and paid little attention to training for independence and self-reliance. These parents were labeled *permissive.*

In two subsequent studies, Baumrind identified parents who fit the three patterns—authoritative, authoritarian, and permissive—and evaluated their children to determine whether they showed different levels of competence. Two clusters of competent behavior were assessed: *social responsibility,* defined as being friendly, cooperative, and achievement-oriented, and *independence,* defined as being dominant, purposive, assertive, and achievement-

FIGURE 11.2

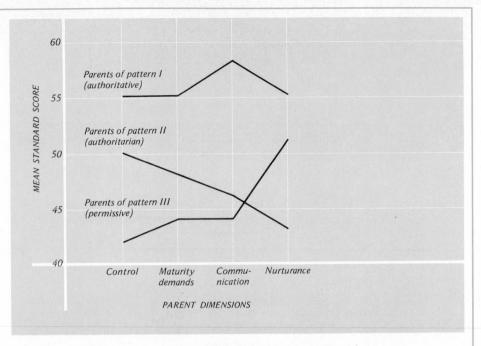

Parents' scores on four dimensions of child rearing. Parents were grouped according to their children's pattern of behavior. Pattern I children were socially competent and mature; pattern II children were moderately self-reliant but somewhat withdrawn; pattern III children were immature. The child-rearing patterns of parents of the three groups of children were called authoritative, authoritarian, and permissive. (From D. Baumrind. Child care practices anteceding three patterns of preschool behavior. **Genetic Psychology Monographs**, 1967, 75, 43–88. By permission.)

oriented. The results indicated that authoritative parenting was associated with social responsibility for boys and with independence for girls.

Because not all parents fit neatly into the three patterns initially identified, two additional patterns of parenting behavior were investigated. *Harmonious* parents were similar to authoritative parents except that they could not be rated on their level of control because they seemed to have control but rarely asserted it. The children simply did what the parents wished without apparent pressure. Daughters in these families behaved much like daughters of authoritative parents; that is, they were relatively independent. The second new pattern was *nonconformist* parenting: permissiveness based on a principled commitment to allowing children freedom to develop. The other permissive parents had little conscious basis for their child-rearing practices and seemed simply to be lax. Boys with nonconforming parents were as competent as those with authoritative parents.

These results make it clear that children's behavior depends on the entire *pattern* of parent behavior more than on a single dimension like warmth or control. Both authoritative and authoritarian parents attempt to control their children's behavior, but with quite different methods. Authoritarian parents rely almost exclusively on power assertion, demanding obedience without question. By contrast, authoritative parents use inductive discipline. They take the child's point of view into account and permit their children to take part in decisions, to question rules, and to influence the course of family interactions. One psychologist has made the interesting suggestion that children in authoritative families exercise more control over their parents than those in other groups (Lewis, 1981). Unlike permissive parents, authoritative parents present clear standards to their children. It appears that similar clarity and control can be gained by families who are thoughtfully and deliberately permissive (nonconformist) and by those who maintain control without exercising it (harmonious).

Authoritative parents may succeed in producing socially competent children partly because they have more confidence in their child-rearing practices than authoritarian or permissive parents (Baumrind, 1973). The children of these parents may also have been more obedient, socially outgoing, and independent from the beginning. Parents with temperamentally "difficult" children feel less confident in their child rearing than those with "easy" children, and they probably vacillate more in their child-rearing practices as they search for some effective means of discipline. We can place some confidence in the efficacy of authoritative child rearing as long as we keep in mind the variability in children's responses.

Parents' use of reinforcement and punishment

If we analyze the ongoing behavior of parents as they interact with their children, we can identify some basic components of the patterns we have described. Parents administer reinforcement and punishment for behaviors such as putting away clothes, hitting another child, and sharing toys. Children also learn from observing what others do and what reinforcements and punishments they receive. Parents serve as models and teachers of attitudes, beliefs, and moral standards. Children learn such beliefs not only through direct instruction and imitation but also through identification with their parents and internalization of parental attitudes and beliefs.

Reinforcement   When a parent praises a child for helping a younger child, gives 50 cents for each A the child receives in school, or lets the child stay up late in return for the child's doing a cleaning job, the parent is using positive reinforcement. Reinforcers can be social (praise, affection) or nonsocial (material goods, special privileges). The effects of social reinforcements such as praise depend partly on the child's relationship with the adult. Praise from a parent who has a warm, accepting relationship with the child is usually more effective than praise from a cold, rejecting parent. On occasion, however, praise from a cold, rejecting parent may have special significance because it is rare.

B. F. Skinner, one of the founders of modern behaviorism, once suggested that parents could rely entirely on positive reinforcement for socializing their children and never have to punish them. Indeed, careful application of the principles of reinforcement can lead to highly effective and humane child rearing (see Hawkins, 1977). Nevertheless, parents' attempts to use reinforcement do not always produce the intended result. One reason is that parents are sometimes inaccurate about what events will be positively reinforcing from the child's point of view. For example, a parent may offer a child money to do a chore when the child would rather have a different reward such as doing something special with the parent.

The effects of reinforcers also depend on children's interpretations or attributions about them. You will recall our earlier discussion of extrinsic and intrinsic rewards (Chapter 8). If children feel that they have complied with the parent's wishes simply in order to get an extrinsic reward, they may be less likely to internalize the behavior. On later occasions, when the reward is absent, they may not exhibit the behavior. For example, if a child works hard in school primarily to earn money for grades, she may be unlikely to develop an internalized sense that learning is important for itself. Similarly, children learn to judge the validity of praise. If they are praised no matter what they do, they will not interpret praise as a meaningful sign of achievement or correct behavior.

Reinforcement is often given unintentionally. A common case of unintentional reinforcement is giving children attention for misbehaving. Take the following example:

> Sally is playing with her friend in one room of the house while her mother works in another room. Sally and her friend decide to play a chase game, running through the room where Mother is. Mother looks up from her work and tells them not to run through there. They run through again, and Mother tells them a little more firmly to stop it. They repeat the action, and Mother gets up from her work, takes them back to the room where they were playing, and suggests that they play with some puzzles there. Just as Mother settles back to her work, they run through again.

What has happened here? Our best guess is that the mother's attention is serving as a positive reinforcer for running through the room where she is. The mother ignored the children when they were playing quietly, but she gave them attention when they ran through her room. She did not intend to reinforce them for running and interrupting her, but that is what she did.

What could this mother do differently? One technique that sometimes works is *extinction*. If attention is reinforcing, then ignoring the behavior may stop it. Mother might pay no attention to the running children. After a few tries, they may stop running because it is not being reinforced. The behavior is extinguished.

If the mother finds it impossible to ignore the behavior (suppose they are about to knock over her good lamp), she could try reinforcing some alternative behavior. She could take them to their quiet game and pay attention to them while they play it. Probably a better strategy would be to tell them she will play with them after a certain period of time *if* they stop running.

Punishment If all the above strategies fail, this mother may need to use punishment to get the children to stop running through forbidden areas of the house. Assuming that the goal of punishment is to persuade children to change their behavior, what will help to accomplish that goal? Certain principles are well established. First, punishment immediately after a forbidden act is more effective than delayed punishment. In fact, the ideal time to stop a behavior is just *before* it occurs (Aronfreed, 1968; Parke, 1977). For example, if a young child repeatedly runs into the street, the best time to administer punishment is when he is just about to step off the curb.

Second, children are more likely to accept and internalize a rule if the severity of the punishment is just sufficient to induce compliance, but not greater. Sending a child to her room for an hour is more severe than sending her for 15 minutes. In several laboratory studies, one group of children were told they would receive a mild punishment for disobeying a rule, and another group were told they would receive a more severe punishment. Both groups complied with the rule, but the mild-punishment group were more likely to internalize the rule as part of their own beliefs (Lepper, 1981). In natural situations, children are more likely to comply when punishments are severe, but severe punishment also tends to inhibit other, desirable behavior (Parke, 1977). Very intense punishments may generate resentment and fear, so children are less likely to accept and internalize the rule that is being enforced.

Third, punishment is most effective when administered consistently and when the behavior being punished is clearly labeled. Telling a child he is being grounded because he was dishonest is less useful than pointing out the specific lie he told his mother. In addition, some of the negative side effects of punishment can be avoided if the adult is calm and does not vent a lot of anger.

These principles are applied in many schools and homes by using "time out," a procedure in which the child is asked to sit on the sidelines of an activity for short periods of time without any attention from adults or other children. It can be administered quickly and calmly, the amount of time can be varied, the reason can be clearly labeled, and it is not physically or emotionally harmful to a child (Hawkins, 1977; Parke, 1977).

Finally, prohibitions and punishments are most likely to be effective if the adult provides a rationale or a reason, that is, uses inductive discipline along with the punishment. Explanations and other forms of inductive discipline lead children to internalize the parents' rules and thus to obey them even when no one will know what they do. For example, if an adult says, "You should stay out of the street because cars can hurt you," a young child is more likely to obey the prohibition later on than if she is simply told not to play in the street. In laboratory studies, giving children a rationale for obeying a rule is more effective in producing compliance than simply punishing them for disobeying it (LaVoie, 1973; Parke, 1977).

Reasoning becomes more effective as children get older. As their level of cognitive development changes, they are more capable of understanding the reasons offered by the parents. When the reasons for parents' rules and disciplinary actions fit the child's level of moral judgment — that is, when they represent the type of reasoning the child might use — then children are more likely to internalize those rules and to comply with them (see Chapter 9).

Negative side effects of punishment Parents and others are justifiably cautious about using punishment because it can have negative side effects. Children learn to imitate the punitive behavior that parents direct toward them. A child who is slapped, spanked, shaken, or shouted at on a regular basis may well learn to use these forms of aggression when trying to assert power over others.

Preschool children in one investigation saw videotapes of parent-child conflicts and were asked what they would do if they were the parent. The methods of discipline they suggested were similar to those that their own parents prescribed in the same situations (Wolfe, Katell, & Drabman, 1982). When parents punish their children, they may be providing long-term training in how to be a parent. Some investigators have suggested that child abuse is transmitted from one generation to the next by this means. Many abusing parents were abused themselves when they were children (Parke & Collmer, 1975).

Another potential problem with punishment is that it may make the child avoid the punishing person. Most children cannot entirely avoid their parents, nor would they want to. Nevertheless, parents have fewer opportunities to provide positive experiences if the child tends to avoid the parents. Extreme avoidance may take the form of running away from home; adolescent runaways often report that their interactions with their families are aversive (see Chapter 14).

The child's role in punishment   The principle of bidirectionality suggests that children contribute to the type and intensity of punishment, not only by their initial behavior or misbehavior but also by their responses to the parent's attempts at discipline. As explained earlier, many real-life disciplinary encounters involve an escalation on the parent's part if the child is defiant or continues a forbidden behavior (Mulhern & Passman, 1981; Parke, 1977; Passman & Blackwelder, 1981).

A similar interaction can be seen in children's relationships with other adults. Children and adolescents who get in trouble with the law often show defiance and rudeness toward teachers and police officers. These adults, in turn, respond punitively. In one program designed to help delinquent youth, such youngsters are trained to respond to adults in a polite, socially accepted manner. One result is that they are less likely to be arrested by police officers or punished in school.

Some characteristics of the child and the child's past behavior have been found to affect the level and type of punishment an adult uses. For example, children who are frequently aggressive in a preschool classroom are more often punished by teachers for aggressive behavior than are other children, even when they do the same thing. Apparently, teachers are "primed" to notice and correct aggression in a child who is frequently aggressive. Partly because of sex stereotypes, adults expect boys to be more aggressive and disobedient than girls, and parents and teachers punish boys more often than they do girls (Maccoby & Jacklin, 1974). Although this difference may be partially due to the fact that boys more often misbehave, that is not the whole explanation. In one study in which parents were observed giving their children positive and negative feedback during a learning task, boys received more punishment for failure than girls, even when their patterns of success and failure were identical (Mulhern & Passman, 1981).

Imitation and identification

Parents socialize their children by example as well as by direct training. Children acquire many of their parents' behavior patterns, idiosyncrasies, motives, attitudes, and values through the processes of imitation and identification. These processes are particularly important in socialization because they occur without any deliberate teaching by the parent or intentional effort to learn

by the child. In fact, children often imitate behavior that parents would rather not teach. The 4-year-old who lets out a few juicy swear words when he bangs his finger with a hammer is demonstrating the power of imitative learning.

The concept of *identification*, derived from Freud's psychoanalytic theory, refers to a process by which a child attempts to incorporate the characteristics of another person. In some senses, children feel that they really are the person they identify with. Through identification, a girl may adopt her mother's attitudes, interests, mannerisms, clothing styles, and behavior patterns. Freud asserted that identification with parents, particularly the parent of the same sex, was the means by which children acquired moral values and masculinity or femininity.

Some theorists distinguish identification from imitation, arguing that imitation is mere emulation of specific observable responses, whereas identification is a more subtle process of incorporating broad, global *patterns* of thought and behavior. Identification also implies a strong emotional tie to the person whose behavior is adopted, while imitation does not. Still another critical feature of identification is the child's perception of similarity between herself and the other person and, as a result of that perceived similarity, the belief that she

shares attributes with that model. Qualities of the model, such as warmth, dominance, competence, and social status, make identification more likely, according to this theory, because the child perceives that she can share these valuable "resources" by identifying with the model. One implication of this view is that identification can lead to antisocial as well as prosocial values — if a parent is a successful criminal, the child may identify with the criminal values and behavior exemplified by the parent.

Other theorists have argued that there is no fundamental difference between identification and imitation. They assert that the process of imitation can account for children's adoption of global patterns of behavior and can be influenced by perceived similarity and other qualities of the model. Part of the controversy revolves around the difficulty of measuring identification. The research investigating the concept, conducted primarily in the 1950s and 1960s, included a variety of measures: laboratory tasks in which children's imitation of parents was observed, comparisons of personality ratings of children and parents by others to determine how similar they were; comparisons of self-ratings of parents and children to determine similarity. In addition, because conscience and sex typing were thought to result from identification, measures of moral behavior and sex typing were often used as well.

These studies supported the theoretical prediction that children would identify most strongly with parents who were warm and dominant and controlled important resources. For example, children with warm parents were rated as more similar to their parents and showed more tendency to imitate them than did children with relatively cold parents. Children emulated parents who were dominant or powerful, either within the marital relationship or in relation to the child. In marriages where power was unbalanced — where one partner made decisions and led the other most of the time — children were more likely to imitate the dominant parent (Hetherington, 1967; Lavine, 1982).

Regardless of which side of this debate they favor, most psychologists agree that much of what children learn from observing their parents and other adults goes well beyond copying behavior. In laboratory studies, children have learned from observing others general rules and principles that they then applied in ways quite different from those they observed (Bandura, 1977). For example, after observing an adult model making moral judgments that represented either the stage of moral realism or moral relativism in Piaget's theory (Chapter 9), children's judgments in response to new moral dilemmas corresponded to the stage used by the model they had seen (Bandura & McDonald, 1963; Cowan, Langer, Heavenrich, & Nathanson, 1969).

Identification and imitation can have long-delayed effects. A child may observe parents' behavior or internalize a moral principle but have no occasion to use that learning until months or even years later. For example, young children learn many adult roles by watching their parents and others. In fantasy play, they often rehearse being a mommy or a daddy or a train conductor or some other role (see the discussion of scripts in Chapter 9). But the end product of this learning may not be apparent until the child is grown and becomes a parent or takes a job.

Thus far, we have talked about family socialization as if the only important people were the parents. Most children have brothers and sisters as well, and sibling relationships affect socialization. A slightly older brother or sister, for example, may be a potent model for imitation and identification. We turn now to a discussion of sibling relationships and influences.

| SIBLINGS |

More than 80 percent of American children have one or more sisters or brothers, and from the first months of life onward almost all children spend a great deal of time watching, paying attention to, and interacting with their siblings. The evidence suggests that, as we would expect, sibling influences are profound, particularly between the ages of 2 and 10.

"Siblings set and maintain standards, provide models to emulate and advice to consider, and act complementary roles in relation to one another through which they both develop and practice social-interaction skills, and serve as confidants and sources of social support in times of emotional stress" (Lamb, 1982, p. 6). In interactions with their siblings, children learn patterns of loyalty, helpfulness, and protection as well as conflict, domination, and competition. These patterns are readily generalized to other social relationships.

The extent to which siblings help shape a child's personality and social development varies with such factors as the child's sex, the sex of the sibling(s), ordinal position, (e.g., first, middle, youngest child in the family), spacing (closeness in age to siblings), total number of children in the family, and parental treatment. As children are added, the structure and dynamics of a family change. Parents are likely to treat their firstborn child differently from the way they treat those born later; their attitudes, expectancies, and skills in child rearing—as well as their anxieties—are modified as a result of experience. In general, parents are more involved with the firstborn, paying more attention and stimulating and talking more to this child. They are also likely to be highly demanding, expecting a great deal from the oldest. Within the family circle, the firstborn generally has only the parents as models and teachers, whereas later-born siblings have both the parents and at least one older child.

Not surprisingly, firstborn children, compared with those born later, tend to be more strongly motivated toward achievement, more affiliative and dependent on others for support, more oriented toward adults and conforming to authority, more conscientious, more prone to guilt feelings, more cooperative, responsible, and helpful, and less aggressive. Attempting to live up to their parents' standards and expectations, these children are high achievers, disproportionately represented among outstanding scientists and scholars in letters and science. However, among very eminent male scientists, firstborns are more reluctant to accept ideas that require them to disagree with a dominant theoretical position. Those with older siblings are more likely to be receptive to creative ideas that are unpopular and ideologically dissonant with the views of the majority. For example, in the nineteenth century, evolutionary theory opposed the popular belief in the biblical explanation of creation. Both Charles Darwin and Alfred Wallace were later-borns, as were over 90 percent of those who favored evolution. The majority of those who publicly opposed the assumptions of evolutionary theory from 1750 to 1870 were firstborns (Sulloway, 1972).

Since older siblings generally are more competent than younger ones and have more power during childhood, later-born children are more likely to suffer from feelings of inadequacy and to be realistic in their self-evaluations. Later-borns are less cautious in their behavior, however; for instance, they tend to participate more in dangerous physical activities. In their interactions with siblings, later-born children acquire important social skills and consider the needs and wishes of their older siblings in order to negotiate with, accommodate, and tolerate them (Bryant, 1982). These social skills apparently generalize to other situations, and later-born children are generally rated by peers as more socially skilled, more sociable and friendly, and more accepting and less demanding of others. Consequently, they are more popular with their peers than firstborn siblings (Miller & Maruyama, 1976).

Sibling relationships

When a second child is born, the older sister's or brother's power is inevitably usurped to some extent. The older child must now compete, often unsuccessfully, for parental attention, rewards, and satisfaction of dependency needs. When mothers are observed with two of their young children, they pay more attention to the younger sibling (Bryant & Crockenberg, 1980).

Although much of the literature on child rearing stresses jealousy or rivalry as the predominant emotion in sibling relationships, recent observational studies show that sibling interactions are much more complex than that. The studies, conducted in homes (as opposed to artificial laboratory settings), provide convincing evidence that siblings as young as 22 months and 8 months manifest "a wide range of complexity of feelings . . . [Each shows] considerable pragmatic understanding of how to annoy and how to console the other" (Dunn & Kendrick, 1982, p. 42). Even at these early ages, siblings spend a great deal of time interacting with and imitating each other, the younger child imitating the older much more frequently. Older siblings frequently made comments about the likes, wants, intentions, and feelings of their baby siblings, demonstrating interest in, and understanding of, the younger one's psychological states. Siblings of the same sex made more friendly approaches and imitated each other more than siblings of opposite sexes. The imitative sequences demonstrate both the attention children pay to each other and the power of the older child as a model for the younger. Nevertheless, ambivalent feelings toward siblings are very common. For example, many older children, although often hostile to the baby, would side with the young child against the mother. "Ambivalence, hostility, comfort and concern were all apparent in the behavior of the elder siblings" (Dunn & Kendrick, 1982, p. 44).

The mother's relationship to the children affected their reactions to each other. For example, friendly relations between siblings are facilitated by mothers who talk to the elder ones about the baby *as a person,* inviting participation in discussions and decision making about the infant's care or reactions (e.g., asking questions such as "Shall we feed him or just let him cry? What do you think he wants?''). The children of these mothers made more positive approaches to each other than did children of mothers who did not discuss the baby in this way. Data from longitudinal studies also indicate that siblings' reactions toward each other are quite consistent over time. Children who generally showed friendly interest in their baby sibling during the first 3 weeks showed more positive social behavior toward that sibling at age 14 months; those who initially reacted to their new siblings by withdrawing were more negative toward that sibling at the later age (Dunn & Kendrick, 1982).

In relationships between siblings of preschool age, the older one tends to be dominant, initiating most interactions that are helpful and cooperative as well as those that are interfering and aggressive. Firstborn males use more physical power techniques in dominating their younger siblings than females; firstborn females are more likely than males to use techniques such as explaining, asking, and taking turns (Sutton-Smith & Rosenberg, 1970). Younger siblings continue to imitate older brothers and sisters more than older ones imitate the younger ones, and the frequency of imitation continues to be higher, if the sibling is of the same sex. In general, playful responses rather than new skills are imitated. Typical examples of imitative behavior are pretending to be a monster, banging Play Dough on the table, pointing a cane like a gun, and repeating various words and phrases (Abramovitch, Peplar, & Corter, 1982).

During middle childhood, older siblings, particularly older brothers, are perceived as powerful and ''bossy'' (Bigner, 1974; Sutton-Smith & Rosenberg, 1968). Some of the power is welcomed, for older siblings often use it to help the younger child (Bigner, 1974). The amount of power and helpfulness attributed to older siblings increases throughout middle childhood.

In European and American cultures, girls in the middle childhood years are likely to help care for younger siblings, a role that girls in other cultures take on earlier. A young child may turn to an older sister if the mother ignores the child's request for help, and the sister frequently gives it (Bryant & Crockenberg, 1980). Taking care of younger siblings fosters prosocial behavior and a sense of social responsibility, a finding replicated in a number of cultures (Whiting & Whiting, 1975).

Sibling influences
We have already noted the strong propensity of younger children to imitate their older siblings, especially those of the same sex. The effects of such modeling are strongly evidenced in a number of findings. For example, boys with older brothers have more masculine interests than girls with older sisters. Girls with older brothers are also more ambitious and more aggressive, have more tomboyish traits, and perform better on tests of intellectual ability than girls with older sisters (Sutton-Smith & Rosenberg, 1970).

As teachers of academic subject matter, older sisters appear to be more skillful than older brothers. Older sisters are more involved, use more directive and deductive methods, offer more explanations, and provide better feedback than older brothers. Brothers use less directive methods in their teaching styles with siblings. Furthermore, younger siblings are more willing to accept an older sister than an older brother in the role of an academic teacher (Cicirelli, 1972, 1973, 1975).

If there is no father in the home, older brothers may be effective models for sex typing in younger boys. The absence of the father is often a disadvantage to a boy; he is likely to be less masculine, more dependent, and less successful in academic performance than boys raised by both parents. However, boys reared without a father but with one or more older male siblings have been shown to be more masculine in behavior, less dependent, and higher in academic aptitude than father-absent boys with older sisters (Santrock, 1970; Sutton-Smith, Rosenberg, & Landy, 1968; Wohlford, Santrock, Berger, & Liberman, 1971).

<table>
<tr><td>

PROBLEMS IN FAMILY FUNCTIONING

</td><td>

Raising children is one of the most difficult and demanding responsibilities of adult life. Yet most people have little preparation or training to be parents. Some adults have emotional problems or life stresses that make it difficult for them to be good parents. We turn now to some extremes of inadequate parenting — parents who subject their children to violence, sexual abuse, or extreme neglect.

</td></tr>
</table>

Child abuse and neglect

Violence toward children has received increasing attention in the press and from social service agencies in the past several years. The line between acceptable corporal punishment and unacceptable violence to children is often difficult to draw, and some would argue that all physical attacks on children are harmful and wrong (e.g., Zigler, 1979). All would agree, however, that extremes of force that injure, maim, or kill children are matters of social and legal concern.

Although exact information about the prevalence of child abuse is virtually impossible to obtain, it is known to occur with disturbing frequency in the United States and western Europe (Parke & Collmer, 1975; Parke & Slaby, 1983). In one survey, most of the parents (73 percent) of children between the ages of 3 and 17 admitted some form of aggression toward their child in the past year, including spanking and slapping. Approximately 3 percent admitted kicking, biting, or hitting the child with a fist; 3 percent admitted threatening the child with a gun or a knife; and 3 percent said they had used a gun or knife against the child at some time. These self-reports, which probably underestimate the true incidence of violent actions, suggest that at least 1 to 2 million children are threatened or attacked with weapons by their parents sometime during their childhood. Mothers were slightly more likely than fathers to spank and hit their children, particularly sons, but fathers and mothers were equally likely to engage in more severe violent actions or to use weapons. Daughters and sons were equally likely to be the targets of such serious attacks (Gelles, 1979).

Child abuse is reported more often for lower-class than for middle-class families, but cases may be less likely to come to official attention when they occur in middle-class families. Adolescent mothers also abuse their children more often than older mothers. Other adults, such as live-in friends, are often involved in cases of child abuse. As illustrated in Box 11.1, child abuse is not a new phenomenon.

Why would parents beat and injure their children? Many observers have suggested that cultural acceptance of corporal punishment is one contributing factor. When parents consider it acceptable to inflict pain for disciplinary purposes, it becomes relatively easy to step over the boundary into abuse. Child abuse is often part of a pattern of family violence. In families where children are beaten, husband-wife violence is common. Some theorists believe that child beating often follows husband-wife violence or that anger at a spouse is deflected onto the relatively defenseless child. In addition, siblings in these families frequently use aggression in their interactions (Parke & Slaby, 1983).

In one investigation, patterns of parent-child interaction were observed directly in the homes of three types of families: (a) those in which at least one child had been physically abused (abuse), (b) those in which a child had experienced such severe neglect (e.g., malnourishment) that the family had been reported to authorities (neglect), and (c) families with no history of abuse or neglect but who were similar to the other families on income and education (control). Interactions such as smiling, praising, affectionate touching, and speaking pleasantly to another person were coded as positive. Negative behaviors included criticism, sarcasm, disapproval, and anger. The rates of positive and negative interaction in each type of family are shown in Figure 11.3. Parents in the abuse and neglect families directed fewer positive and more negative interactions toward their children than did control parents. The children in the neglect families initiated more negative interactions toward their parents and siblings than control children, but abused children, while very negative toward other children, did not initiate frequent negative behavior toward their parents (Burgess & Conger, 1978).

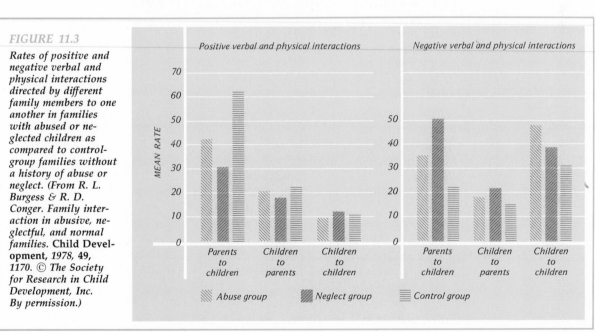

FIGURE 11.3

Rates of positive and negative verbal and physical interactions directed by different family members to one another in families with abused or neglected children as compared to control-group families without a history of abuse or neglect. (From R. L. Burgess & R. D. Conger. Family interaction in abusive, neglectful, and normal families. **Child Development**, 1978, 49, 1170. © The Society for Research in Child Development, Inc. By permission.)

Although no outstanding personality characteristics typify abusing parents, they tend to be socially isolated individuals who restrict their children's contacts with others. Many are poorly educated, young, and poor. Social isolation and poverty often prevent such parents from receiving support from extended family, friends, and community resources. Stresses on parents, which often result from social causes such as low income, unemployment, and lack of

BOX 11.1
*An early report
of child abuse*

The rise in the frequency of parental abuse of children is generating appropriate moral outrage among many contemporary Americans. Although it is not completely clear why there has been such a major increase in the last decade, one possibility is the increased mobility of young parents and the rising number of single-parent families without economic or emotional resources. Many parents are now living with major stresses, both emotional and financial. Some of these same conditions were present in England about a century ago when a sharp rise in parental abuse toward children led to the establishment of the National Society for the Prevention of Cruelty to Children. The Liverpool branch of the society was founded in 1883. A letter from an adolescent girl to an agency official is printed below.[1]

June 2.'98

Anne Purcell states

I am 13½ years of age and live with my father at 2 Underwoods Buildings, Regent Street, York.

My mother died a year ago next month.

Father is a Bricklayer's labourer, he goes to work at 6 a.m., and leaves work at 5.30 p.m. He comes home to dinner at 12.10 p.m.

I have been left school for a long time now and keep fathers house for him and mind my brother, Charlie, aged 6 years, Lucy 3 years, and the baby 13 months. I cook the dinner and do all the work of the house, but father makes his own bed.

Mʳˢ Camidge comes at the end of the week and bakes the bread and does the washing—Sometimes she comes on Thursdays, but mostly on Fridays.

Father only takes drink at the end of the week.

I am very much afraid of my father. He swears and shouts at me and hits me with his hands. On Tuesday May 17ᵗʰ, between 6 & 7 p.m., my brother who had come from soldiering asked for a handkerchief—I said there was one in the drawer but could not find it. My father then hit me with his hand, and when my brother had gone out, my father beat me with the strap he wears round his body and bruised my arm. The strap has a buckle to it.

Last night about 5.30 p.m., father came home. I took baby off the couch and my father saw it had dirtied on it. He took a towel and hit me with it, and when I put baby in the chair, he took off his strap and beat me as hard as he could over my arm & back with the buckle end of it—I did not scream out—I dare not for he would have hit me more. He hit me three or four times. My arm hurts me now, and nursing the baby makes it worse.

When he went out last night, after beating me, he said when he came back he would thrash me with a stick that would make me feel. I sit up late at night as I do not like to go to bed until father gets home.

> *After you and the policeman had left this dinnertime, my father asked me who I had told about him beating me—I said "The neighbours"—He then put his fist in my face and said—"If you go out this afternoon I'll cut you in two." He swore at me and said "You are going away you little B——. and a B——y good job."*
>
> *My arm is in great pain now.*

[1] From G. K. Behlmer. *Child abuse and moral reform in England, 1870–1908.* Stanford, Calif.: Stanford University Press, 1982, pp. 234–235.

child care services, also increase the likelihood that they will abuse their children (Parke & Collmer, 1975). Using a longitudinal analysis of two metropolitan communities, one study demonstrated that the rates of child abuse increased as the rates of unemployment went up. The changes in child abuse followed the changes in employment by a few months, suggesting that the stresses of unemployment build over time (Steinberg, Catalano, & Dooley, 1981).

In many families, one child seems to be singled out for more physical abuse than the others. When social stresses and parent attributes create the potential for child abuse, some children seem to be more likely to receive abuse than others. Children who are physically unattractive, who are hyperactive, or who misbehave a great deal are likely targets of abuse, perhaps because they are particularly annoying to parents. Infants with low birth weight are also frequent targets of abuse, perhaps because they cry more and require more frequent attention than other infants (Parke & Collmer, 1975).

Sexual abuse   The prevalence of sexual abuse (genital fondling, sexual intercourse, and other forms of sexual interaction with children) is even more difficult to estimate than the frequency of violence to children. The Children's Division of the American Humane Society reported 5000 cases in 1972, but these probably represented a small fraction of the total. Adolescent females are the most frequent victims of sexual abuse by other family members. Of the clients seen in one metropolitan treatment center, 25 percent were under 5 years old, 25 percent between 5 and 10, and 50 percent over 10. About 75 percent of the cases of incest are father-daughter incest. Children who are sexually abused are often physically abused as well.

Clinicians who treat sexually abused children report that, like physically abused children, they are often forced into social isolation from their peers. Other members of the family, including the other parent, are often aware of the sexual activity involving the child and sometimes implicitly encourage it. Children are fearful of losing the love and acceptance of both parents if they object or refuse to participate (Kempe & Kempe, 1978).

Treatment   Abusive parents can learn to deal with their children in new ways. Several treatment programs have been carried out to teach parents more effective and less violent methods of discipline through role playing, modeling, and home visits. The retraining program designed by Patterson for parents of highly aggressive children (see Chapter 10) is one example of an effective program for abusive parents.

Child abuse can be treated at the community level by providing resources and support systems for families under stress. The rates of child abuse decline when there are supports such as employment and educational opportunities for mothers and children, support groups for parents, child-care facilities, homemaker services, and hotlines (Parke & Slaby, 1983).

Parent education

Potentially abusive parents are not the only ones who can benefit from parent training. We often assume that the capacity to love and discipline children is intuitive or inborn, but several programs have demonstrated that people can be taught to be more effective parents. Families who have a high risk of abusing their children (e.g., adolescent mothers, low-income single parents, parents of low-birth-weight babies) may be helped by such interventions before abusive patterns begin rather than after the fact.

In one large experiment, parent-child development centers were established in three cities to train low-income mothers in parenting skills. Black, Hispanic, and Anglo mothers of infants participated in weekly sessions in which they were taught principles of child development and child rearing, home management, nutrition and health, and personal development and given information on community resources until their children were 3 years old. In each city, a control group of mothers and children were tested for comparison to the trained mothers.

The most important evidence of the effects of parent training came from direct observations of the mothers with their children. Mothers who had been trained were more affectionate and warm toward their children, used more praise, were less critical and interfering, and used language in a more informative way than control mothers. They asked questions and provided appropriate play materials. Their children, in turn, performed better on several scales measuring intellectual development and showed more happy, cooperative behavior when they were with their mothers than children in the control group (Andrews, Blumenthal, Johnson, Kahn, Ferguson, Lasater, Malone, & Wallace, 1982).

STRUCTURE OF THE FAMILY

The stereotypic image of a family shows a married couple and two or three children. Yet, increasingly, American children do not grow up in such families. The family arrangements of United States children from 1960 to 1978, with projections to 1990, are shown in Figure 11.4. The main trend apparent in this figure is that more and more children are living with a single parent, usually the mother, who is separated, divorced, or widowed or has never married.

In divorced families, about 90 percent of the children live with their mothers. Despite the fact that it has become more legally and socially acceptable for fathers to have primary or joint custody, the proportion of divorced fathers with custody has changed very little since 1960 (Glick, 1979). As the divorce rate has increased, so has the rate of remarriage. As a result, more children are living with a stepparent (usually a stepfather), and they may also have a non-

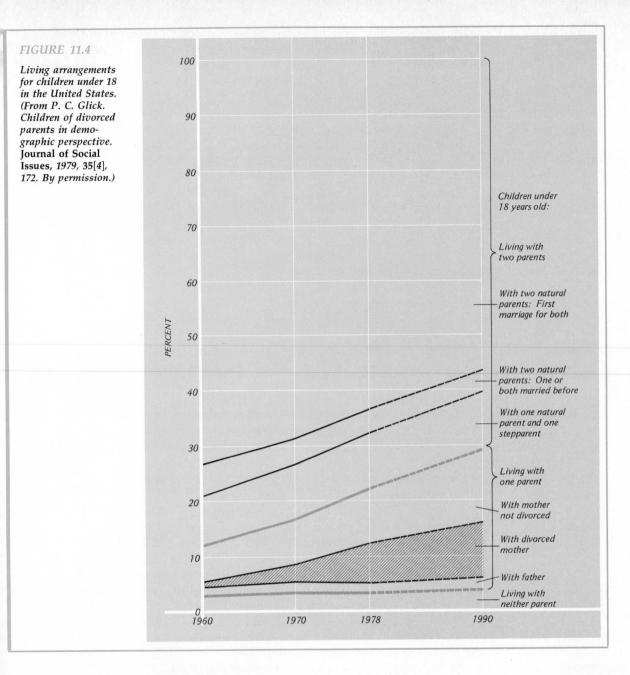

FIGURE 11.4

Living arrangements for children under 18 in the United States. (From P. C. Glick. Children of divorced parents in demographic perspective. **Journal of Social Issues,** *1979, 35[4], 172. By permission.)*

Children under 18 years old:

Living with two parents

With two natural parents: First marriage for both

With two natural parents: One or both married before

With one natural parent and one stepparent

Living with one parent

With mother not divorced

With divorced mother

With father

Living with neither parent

PERCENT

1960   1970   1978   1990

resident stepparent (for example, the father's wife for children who live with their mother). When divorced parents remarry, children sometimes acquire a complicated network of family relationships including not only stepparents, but stepsiblings, half-siblings, and extra sets of grandparents, aunts, uncles, and cousins.

The proportions in Figure 11.4 show general trends. In understanding individual children, it may be more important to ask how many children will experience divorce or single parenting at some point in their lives. In 1976, it was estimated that about 28 percent of children would experience a parent divorce sometime before they reached age 18. By 1990, the figure is expected to reach 32 percent. These figures are much higher for black Americans and for poor people from many ethnic groups (Glick, 1979).

Major changes in family structure and roles have also occurred in many two-parent families that remain intact. First, families are becoming smaller. The birth rate in the United States increased after World War II to a peak in 1957; it has been gradually declining since that time, leveling off at slightly below two children per family in the late 1970s and early 1980s. As a result, there are more one- and two-child families and fewer large families than in the previous generation. Second, parents are slightly older when they have their first child than in the 1950s and 1960s, and many employed couples wait to have their first children when they are in their mid- to late 30s (see Box 11.2).

The trend toward increasing maternal employment, discussed in Chapter 4 in connection with infant day care, also has important effects on family functioning. As noted earlier, roughly one-third of the women with preschool children are presently employed at least part-time, and many women hold an outside job continuously throughout their children's youth. The effects of maternal employment on children and family roles are discussed later in this section.

Of course, single parents are often employed as well. As most divorced mothers provide the principal economic support for their children and themselves, it is hardly surprising that large numbers of them (77 percent) are employed. However, the income of single mothers (like that of women generally) is well below that of men. As a result, in 1983, it was estimated that 25 percent of all children in the United States lived in households with incomes below the poverty line established by the federal government. Many others grow up in households with very limited incomes (VanDusen & Sheldon, 1976).

What do these changes in family structure mean for children? Social commentators lament the dissolution of the family and make dire predictions about the consequences for the children of the coming generation. Family structures that depart from the norm are often considered deviant and abnormal, and children are expected to be adversely affected by single parenting, divorce, and maternal employment. Yet, since many American children are being raised in such "nontraditional" families, it seems most useful to view them as normal and to examine the kinds of parent behaviors and social support systems that contribute to healthy development in various family structures.

Children with single parents

The effects of growing up in a mother-only household depend on the child's sex, the child's age when the father left the home, the reason for the absence of the father (e.g., divorce, death), the mother's attitudes, and whether other adults or older siblings can fill in for the father in some ways.

Boys are affected by father absence considerably more than girls. Boys in father-absent families are often less interested in "masculine" toys and activities than boys in two-parent homes, but the two groups usually do not differ much in rates of dependency. Father-absent boys are sometimes more aggres-

BOX 11.2
*Parents' age
and quality of
parenting*

"I want to have my children young, so I can be energetic enough to do things with them." "I want to wait until I have started my career and traveled a little before I get tied down to children." These statements reflect various opinions about the optimal age for parents to have children. In recent years, there has been an increase in adolescent pregnancy, resulting in very young mothers, as well as an increase in the number of women who have their first child after age 35. Fathers, of course, can range from adolescence to middle age when their children are born. Although the quality of parenting depends on many qualities of the person, one variable that appears to make a difference is the parent's age.

On the whole, parents who have their first child when they are older are more attentive, warm, and satisfied with being a parent than are people who begin their families early. In one investigation of women from 16 to 38 who had babies, the older women were more satisfied with being a parent. When they were observed with their babies 4 months after birth, the older mothers showed more positive affect and interacted with their babies more sensitively. These patterns were true for women having their first baby; older women who already had two children were less attentive and affectionate than younger mothers. Studies of older children show that cognitive and intellectual development is somewhat more advanced for children of older mothers, even when education differences among mothers are taken into account (Ragozin, Basham, Crnic, Greenberg, & Robinson, 1982). Fathers who have their first child relatively late (after age 35) are also warmer and more involved with child rearing than are young fathers (below age 25) (Nydegger, 1973).

These findings suggest that, for many people, waiting to have children may be a good idea. Both men and women may gain more maturity and sensitivity as they get older. In addition, they may have established themselves in their careers, saved a little money, and pursued some of their personal goals and interests so that they have more time and resources for child rearing. Obviously, this generalization does not apply to everyone. Some people are attentive, mature parents at a young age. It is clear, however, that negative stereotypes about older parents are incorrect. Many people get better qualified to be parents as they grow older.

sive and anxious than father-present children (Biller, 1971; Huston, 1983). Most clear differences between father-present and father-absent boys occur for boys whose fathers were absent during the first few years of life. In one investigation, Israeli 2-year-olds whose fathers were killed before they were born were compared with children in two-parent families. The boys living with widowed mothers were more dependent, more anxious about separation, more aggressive, and less autonomous than father-present boys (Levy-Shiff, 1982). In studies of older children, only boys whose fathers had been absent since their preschool years showed less masculine interests and behavior when compared to father-present boys (Biller, 1971; Drake & McDougall, 1977; Hetherington, 1966).

Although girls who grow up in mother-only families show few behavior or personality differences from those in two-parent families, intellectual skills, particularly quantitative skills, appear to be influenced for both sexes. Father-absent children often perform less well in school and on measures of cognitive skills than father-present children, but this pattern may be partly due to income and social-class differences. More interesting, because it cannot be explained by social class, is the frequent finding that quantitative skills are more adversely affected by father absence than verbal skills for both boys and girls (Shinn, 1978). These deficits appear to be partially alleviated by having a substitute or stepfather at home (Chapman, 1977; Shinn, 1978). Why a male adult, father or otherwise, should affect children's quantitative skills is open to question. Because math and number skills tend to be stereotyped as masculine in our society, it may be that male adults more often play games involving math, help children with math homework, or simply demonstrate comfort with computations, whether they are paying bills or measuring materials for carpentry.

Divorce

Because most single-parent families in modern America result from divorce, change and adaptation in divorcing families has been the focus of recent investigations instead of the narrower issue of father absence. The experience of divorce is stressful for all family members, and children's behavior reflects that stress. In one extensive longitudinal study, 4-year-old children and their parents were studied 2 months, 1 year, and 2 years after the parents were divorced. Children in intact families were studied for comparison purposes. The data consisted of observations of the children in school, observations of interactions with their parents, personality tests, and interviews with the parents and children.

Boys were more adversely affected by divorce than girls, and the negative effects lasted longer. After divorce, boys often became unruly, aggressive, lacking in self-control, yet dependent and anxious. Their play patterns in school as well as their behavior at home were less mature than those of children from intact families. These trends increased for 2 months to 1 year, but by 2 years after the divorce, many of the problem behaviors associated with it had declined. Girls showed some of these reactions initially but were similar to children from intact families after 2 years.

Some of the reasons for children's problems were apparent in the analysis of the overall family patterns. Particularly during the first year following the divorce, the parents felt a considerable amount of anxiety, loneliness, and stress. Most families had financial problems because of the increased cost of supporting two households, and many mothers took outside jobs. These women often felt overloaded as a result of trying to carry out the household and family duties of both parents, begin a new job, and adjust to a much reduced income. In this study, as in other samples, fathers saw their children often during the first few months after the divorce, but the frequency of contacts in many families dropped dramatically after that (Clingempeel & Repucci, 1982; Hetherington, Cox, & Cox, 1982). In national samples, the majority of fathers also pay no child support, particularly as the time since the divorce increases.

The parents' relationships with their children often deteriorated, particularly in the case of mothers and sons. Because of their own distress, parents had fewer emotional resources to offer their children at a time when the children also needed extra affection and guidance. Compared to parents from intact families, divorced parents were less affectionate, less consistent in discipline, poorer at communication, and less inclined to make maturity demands (Hetherington et al., 1982). Other observational studies have shown that single mothers often have difficult setting limits and controlling their sons' behavior (Santrock, Warshak, Lindbergh, & Meadows, 1982).

Older children also respond to their parents' divorce with sadness, emotional upset, and disturbed behavior, but the older the child, the better the adjustment to parental divorce. As children get older, they understand interpersonal relationships better, as explained in Chapter 9. They also have more sense of personal control and feel somewhat less vulnerable to the ups and downs of their parents' relationships than very young children (Kurdek, Blisk, & Siesky, 1981).

Father-custody families   Although about 10 percent of the children from divorced families live with their fathers, we know very little about father-only families. In one series of investigations, children from ages 6 to 11 who lived with their fathers were compared with children in mother-custody and two-parent families. Boys in father-custody families were better adjusted than those who lived with their mothers, but girls living with their fathers showed poorer adjustment than girls who lived with their mothers. In both types of families, however, the parents' warmth, calm authority, and other child-rearing practices were more important in predicting the child's behavior than was the sex of the parent (Santrock & Warshak, 1979).

Divorce versus family conflict   The negative effects of divorce on children's functioning could be a result of family conflict as well as separation. Most couples experience marital conflict for some time before they divorce. In fact, some of the problem behavior observed in children following divorce may have begun well before the separation. Even after separation, disputes about finances, visitations, and property often continue. When these conflicts are frequent and openly displayed to children, the children show more behavior problems such as aggression and lack of self-control than they do in families where the divorced parents have a relatively amicable relationship (Emory, 1982; Hetherington et al., 1982).

One important question is whether children suffer more ill effects from conflict in an intact family or from a divorce. Should an unhappily married couple stay together for the sake of the children? The effects of family conflict on children are similar to those observed after divorce, and conflict may have more long-term deleterious effects than divorce (Emory, 1982). In the longitudinal study already described, boys from conflictful intact families showed more aggression and behavior problems than boys from divorced homes by the end of the study, though both groups had more such problems than boys from nonconflictful intact families. The effects of parental conflict were most pronounced when parents argued in front of their children; "concealed" conflicts were less likely to lead to behavior problems (Emory, 1982; Hetherington et al., 1982).

Stepparents   Despite the storybook images of the stepparent as cruel and evil, children often seem to benefit from having one. Boys living with their mothers, particularly, show more socially competent behavior, less anxiety, and fewer cognitive deficits when she remarries than boys living with a single, divorced mother (Shinn, 1978). The effects of having a stepfather are less clear for girls (Santrock et al., 1982). Some of the reasons a stepfather may benefit children are apparent in observations of parent-child interactions. Remarried mothers were more firm and warm with their sons than divorced mothers who had not remarried. A husband provides an important support system for a mother in her interactions with a child. At the same time, he may reduce the mother's work load, financial worries, and loneliness so that she has more time and energy to devote to her children.

Children appear to adjust better to parents' remarriage when they are relatively young or when they are adolescents than during middle childhood. In one follow-up, children between about 9 and 13 had the most difficulty in adapting to a stepparent. The problems were exaggerated if both partners in the new marriage brought children to it (Hetherington et al., 1982).

Maternal employment   What happens to family patterns when a mother is employed full-time away from home? Fathers usually become somewhat more involved in housework and child rearing, but domestic responsibilities are seldom divided equally. Nevertheless, employed mothers are typically more satisfied with themselves and their roles than are nonemployed mothers (Gold & Andres, 1978a, 1978b, 1978c; Hoffman & Nye, 1974). The child in a home where the mother is employed experiences a more egalitarian parent relationship, more care by people outside the family, and more responsibility for household chores than children in other families (Hoffman & Nye, 1974).

Contrary to widespread beliefs that children may be harmed by maternal employment, the evidence suggests that it may have some beneficial consequences for children. Children of employed mothers often have better social and personality adjustment in school, more egalitarian concepts about sex roles, and less traditional stereotypes of male and female activities than children with mothers who are full-time homemakers (Hoffman, 1979; Huston, 1983). One of the most thorough studies of maternal employment is described in Box 11.3.

The effects of maternal employment on children's social and personality

Role changes in two-parent families

BOX 11.3
*Children
with employed
mothers*

Recent studies have helped pinpoint the psychological benefits and problems for children that can accrue from maternal employment. At Concordia University in Montreal, a group of researchers carried out a thorough and extensive study of maternal employment for children at three age levels: 4, 10, and 15. They obtained large samples of boys and girls from middle-class and working-class homes whose mothers were either employed full-time or not employed. When both parents were employed, 4-year-olds were either in day care or private baby sitting. Some of the 10-year-olds were supervised after school, but some were on their own until their parents came home. For each age group, measures of sex-role concepts, social adjustment, and cognitive performance were obtained. Parents responded to questionnaires measuring child-rearing attitudes, sex-role attitudes, parental division of roles in the home, and satisfaction with their present situation.

The results were generally consistent for the three age groups, with a few exceptions. For all groups, children with employed mothers had more egalitarian sex-role concepts than those with nonemployed mothers; that is, they viewed more activities and traits as appropriate for both sexes. In general, children of employed mothers were better adjusted socially; that is, they got along better with other children in school or scored higher on a personality scale measuring adjustment and self-esteem. An exception was 10-year-old boys: Sons of employed mothers were not better adjusted. Cognitive performance was measured with an intelligence test for preschoolers and academic achievement in school for older children. For the most part, there were no consistent differences based on maternal employment except in the preschool sample, where sons of employed mothers scored lower than sons of full-time homemakers.

Parents' attitudes and role divisions in homes where the mother was employed were generally more egalitarian than in families with nonemployed mothers. Household work was divided more equally, and parents expressed feminist attitudes (that is, they said they believed in equal rights for women and equitable division of labor). Many of these findings were replicated when another Canadian cultural group, French-ancestry children, was studied (Gold & Andres, 1978a; 1978b, 1978c).

adjustment are more consistently positive for girls than for boys. Daughters of employed mothers are likely to have higher aspirations for achievement and education, to want a career themselves, and to choose a career that is not traditionally feminine (Hoffman, 1979). These patterns are especially characteristic of girls whose mothers are satisfied with their combination of employment and mothering and consequently serve as models of women who successfully combine child rearing with outside employment. Where negative effects have been found, they occur for boys, especially young ones. Some studies suggest that boys' academic and cognitive skills may suffer when their mothers are employed, but the differences are typically small and inconsistent (Gold & Andres, 1978a, 1978b, 1978c; Hoffman, 1979). One reason for this sex difference is suggested by a recent study comparing the family interactions of employed and nonemployed mothers. There were few differences between the two groups, but there was a tendency for employed mothers to give more attention to their daughters and less to their sons than nonemployed mothers did (Stuckey, McGhee, & Bell, 1982).

On the average, children of employed and nonemployed mothers receive about equal amounts of attention and affection; employed mothers often spend as much or more time doing things with their children as do mothers who are full-time homemakers. They sometimes report enjoying the time with their children more because they are not with them all day every day (Hoffman, 1979).

There are also individual differences among women. Some may be more effective mothers when they have an outside job, while others may be better parents when they are full-time homemakers. A recent analysis demonstrated that mothers who were employed during their child's infancy had different child-rearing attitudes than women who chose not to be employed. The former were less likely to think babies needed exclusive care by their mothers, and they were less likely to need reassurance and guidance from others. In both groups, the mothers who were following a path consistent with their beliefs had more securely attached infants at age 1 than those who were not. That is, the employed mothers who believed others could care for their children and did not need much reassurance had securely attached infants, as did nonemployed mothers who thought their babies needed a mother's exclusive care and who needed reassurance. The children's attachment behavior was not related to maternal employment but to the consistency between the mother's parenting attitudes and her employment situation (Hock, 1980).

Fathers as primary caregivers In a small number of two-parent families, the father is the primary caregiver for the children. Sometimes he stays home full-time with the children while the mother is employed. These families generally report considerable satisfaction with the close father-child relationships that result, but they do experience social pressure because the man's role is unconventional. There is some evidence that fathers who stay home with young children provide added cognitive stimulation and encouragement for achievement. Compared with those from more conventional families, children cared for mainly by their fathers express more sense of control over events around them (internal locus of control), score slightly better on tests of intellectual

development, and have somewhat less stereotyped views about sex roles (Radin, 1982; Russell, 1982; Sagi, 1982).

Fathers who are primary caregivers behave differently from fathers who have less contact with their children, but they do not necessarily behave like mothers. Fathers who are highly involved in raising their children are more nurturant and less punitive than other fathers, but they are also more dominant (Sagi, 1982). Of course, it is impossible to determine whether such characteristics emerge from the experience of primary caregiving or whether they distinguish men who decide to take on child care in the first place.

Other family forms

Extended families, communes, and kibbutzim are examples of family forms that do not fit the two-parent, nuclear family model. In most of these groups, the parent or parents have a special bond and responsibility for the child, but many of the socializing functions of the family are performed by others. The early Israeli kibbutzim were studied extensively because they were a visible social experiment in which children were raised in a residence away from their parents. For many years, kibbutz parents lived in small apartments and the children lived in a children's house with a caregiver. Children spent a few hours a day with their parents. Most kibbutzim were very small communities—usually between 100 and 1000 people—so virtually everyone knew all the children. Many kibbutzim have now returned to a nuclear family pattern in which the children live with their parents and attend child care during the day, but the earlier research is of interest because it provides information about the effects of an unusual variation in the nuclear family structure.

Children in kibbutzim differ little from those raised in nuclear families in Israel. They are a little more peer-oriented and cooperative and a little less competitive, but that could be due to the ideology of the kibbutzim, which emphasizes group and community welfare more than individual achievement. It is clear that this family structure is a healthy and viable one for socializing children (Lynn, 1981).

The effects of variations in family structure, such as single-parent families, families headed by divorced and remarried parents, and families in which the mother is employed and the father is the primary caregiver, depend greatly on cultural context. When such family patterns are relatively common in a society, children probably accept them more easily than when they are rare. In the United States today, a child whose parents are divorced or whose mother has a job is not unusual; many of the child's friends are likely to have similar family situations. There are more support systems available now than 30 years ago, such as day-care centers and after-school programs for children with working parents. Parents may also feel more comfortable and less guilty about such alterations in their lives because they are not alone.

Cultural context and family structure

SUMMARY

Parents are the most important agents of socialization for children, but their influence does not occur in a social vacuum. As a part of the larger society, the family is affected by the norms, values, and expectations of a given culture at a given period of history. Furthermore, socialization of children in the family is a bidirectional process: Attributes of the child interact with the characteristics and child-rearing practices of the parents.

Parents' behavior toward their children can be classified in two broad dimensions: acceptance-rejection and restrictiveness-permissiveness. While these broad dimensions predict some aspects of children's behavior, a more complete picture is obtained when patterns of parent behavior are examined. One pattern, called authoritative parenting, occurs when parents demand mature behavior and enforce rules while explaining reasons for their demands and communicating with their children in an accepting manner. Children whose parents show this pattern are more often socially competent, mature, and responsive than children whose parents are authoritarian or are very permissive.

Parents use reinforcement and punishment in different ways, with varying degrees of success. Positive reinforcement is generally preferable to punishment because it has fewer negative side effects. Quite often, an effective way of inhibiting undesirable behavior is to reinforce some alternative behavior. Both reinforcement and punishment are most effective when the adult and child have a warm, affectionate relationship with each other. Sometimes things that adults think will be reinforcing or punishing to the child are not in fact positive or negative to the child. In those circumstances, the parents' efforts to reward or punish do not have the intended effect. Reinforcement can occur unintentionally when parents pay attention to children's misbehavior. Punishment can be most effective when it occurs immediately after the behavior to be punished, when it is sufficiently intense to inhibit the behavior without being overly intense, when the punished behavior is clearly labeled, and when it is applied calmly and consistently. Providing reasons for the prohibition is important, particularly when the reasons fit the child's level of moral understanding.

Children learn from their parents through processes of identification and imitation as well as by direct teaching. Identification is a subtle process in which the child incorporates broad, global patterns of behaviors and values. Children are most likely to emulate parents who are warm, competent, and powerful.

Brothers and sisters are important family influences. The oldest child in a family is often more adult-oriented, conforming, responsible, and achievement-oriented, whereas a later-born child is often more socially skilled. Older siblings tend to dominate younger ones and to serve as models for them. Sibling rivalry and antagonism occur, but positive, affectionate interactions between siblings are also frequent.

Parents do not necessarily bring maturity or well-developed skills to the task of child rearing, particularly if they are very young, poor, and not well educated. One problem that arises in a distressingly large number of families across all social classes is physical and sexual abuse of children. Both direct training of parents and the development of economic and social support systems can reduce the incidence of child abuse.

A variety of "nontraditional" family structures are becoming increasingly common in the United States as the rates of divorce, remarriage, and pregnancy among unmarried women increase. Boys are more adversely affected than girls by divorce and by living in a household with a single-parent mother, particularly when they are preschool age. Such boys, and to a lesser extent girls, show low levels of maturity and self-control and relatively high levels of anxiety, dependency, and aggression. In some cases, high conflict between parents in intact families appears to produce the same problems for children. Children's adjustment to divorce can be facilitated by frequent contact with the father and reduced conflict between the parents. In general, children's adjustment appears to improve when the parent remarries, particularly in the case of boys who acquire a stepfather.

Many mothers are now employed part-time or full-time during their children's early years and later. Maternal employment appears to promote good social and personal adjustment and to encourage egalitarian concepts of sex roles for both boys and girls. Girls also show higher achievement aspirations when their mothers are employed. When fathers take over primary care of the children or care is shared with a larger community, children develop healthy social and emotional adjustments.

REFERENCES

Abramovitch, R., Peplar, D., & Corter, C. Patterns of sibling interaction among preschool-age children. In M. E. Lamb & B. Sutton-Smith (Eds.), *Sibling relationships.* Hillsdale, N.J.: Erlbaum, 1982.

Andrews, S. R., Blumenthal, J. B., Johnson, D. L., Kahn, A. J., Ferguson, C. J., Lasater, T. M., Malone, P. E., & Wallace, D. B. The skills of mothers: A study of parent-child development centers. *Monographs of the Society for Research in Child Development*, 1982, 42 (Serial No. 198).

Aronfreed, J. *Conduct and conscience: The socialization of internalized control over behavior.* New York: Academic Press, 1968.

Bandura, A. *Social learning theory.* Englewood Cliffs, N.J.: Prentice-Hall, 1977.

Bandura, A., & McDonald, F. J. Influence of social reinforcement and the behavior of models in shaping children's moral judgments. *Journal of Abnormal and Social Psychology, 1963, 67,* 274–281.

Bates, J. E., & Pettit, G. S. Adult individual differences as moderators of child effects. *Journal of Abnormal Child Psychology, 1981, 9,* 329–340.

Baumrind, D. The development of instrumental competence through socialization. In A. D. Pick (Ed.), *Minnesota symposia on child psychology* (Vol. 7). Minneapolis: University of Minnesota Press, 1973.

Bell, R. Q. Parent, child, and reciprocal influences. *American Psychologist, 1979, 34,* 821–826.

Bell, R. Q., & Harper, L. V. *The effect of children on parents.* Hillsdale, N.J.: Erlbaum, 1977.

Bigner, J. J. Second born's discrimination of sibling role concepts. *Developmental Psychology, 1974, 10,* 564–573.

Biller, H. D. *Father, child, and sex role.* Lexington, Mass.: Heath, 1971.

Bronfenbrenner, U. *The ecology of human development: Experiments by nature and design.* Cambridge, Mass.: Harvard University Press, 1979.

Bronstein-Burrows, P. Patterns of parent behavior: A cross-cultural study. *Merrill-Palmer Quarterly, 1981, 27,* 129–143.

Bryant, B., & Crockenberg, S. Correlates and dimensions of prosocial behavior: A study of female siblings with their mothers. *Child Development, 1980, 51,* 529–544.

Bryant, B. J. Sibling relationships in middle childhood. In M. E. Lamb & B. Sutton-Smith (Eds.), *Sibling relationships.* Hillsdale, N.J.: Erlbaum, 1982.

Burgess, R. L., & Conger, R. D. Family interaction in abusive, neglectful, and normal families. *Child Development, 1978, 49,* 1163–1173.

Chapman, M. Father absence, stepfathers, and the cognitive performance of college students. *Child Development, 1977, 48,* 1152–1154.

Cicirelli, V. G. The effect of sibling relationship on concept learning of young children taught by child-teachers. *Child Development, 1972, 43,* 282–287.

Cicirelli, V. G. Effects of sibling structure and interaction on children's categorization style. *Developmental Psychology, 1973, 9,* 132–139.

Cicirelli, V. G. Effects of mother and older sibling on the problem-solving behavior of the younger child. *Developmental Psychology, 1975, 11,* 749–756.

Clingempeel, W. G., & Repucci, N. D. Joint custody after divorce: Major issues and goals for research. *Psychological Bulletin, 1982, 91,* 102–127.

Cowan, C. A., Langer, J., Heavenrich, J., & Nathanson, M. Social learning and Piaget's cognitive theory of moral development. *Journal of Personality and Social Psychology, 1969, 11,* 261–274.

Drake, C. T., & McDougall, D. Effects of the absence of a father and other male models on the development of boys' sex roles. *Developmental Psychology, 1977, 13,* 537–538.

Dunn, J., & Kendrick, C. Siblings and their mothers: Developing relationships within the family. In M. C. Lamb & B. Sutton-Smith (Eds.), *Sibling relationships.* Hillsdale, N.J.: Erlbaum, 1982.

Emory, R. E. Interparental conflict and the children of discord and divorce. *Psychological Bulletin, 1982, 92,* 310–330.

Gelles, R. J. Violence toward children in the United States. In R. Bourne & E. H. Newberger (Eds.), *Critical perspectives on child abuse.* Lexington, Mass.: Heath, 1979.

Glick, P. C. Children of divorced parents in demographic perspective. *Journal of Social Issues, 1979, 35*(4), 170–182.

Gold, D., & Andres, D. Comparisons of adolescent children with employed and nonemployed mothers. *Merrill-Palmer Quarterly, 1978, 24*(4), 243–254. (a)

Gold, D., & Andres, D. Developmental comparisons between ten-year-old children with employed and nonemployed mothers. *Child Development, 1978, 49,* 75–84. (b)

Gold, D., & Andres, D. Relations between maternal employment and development of nursery school children. *Canadian Journal of Behavioral Science, 1978, 10,* 116–129. (c)

Hawkins, R. P. Behavioral analysis and early childhood education: Engineering children's learning. In H. L. Hom & P. A. Robinson (Eds.), *Psychological processes in early education.* New York: Academic Press, 1977.

Hetherington, E. M. Effects of paternal absence on sex-typed behaviors in Negro and white preadolescent males. *Journal of Personality and Social Psychology, 1966, 4,* 87–91.

Hetherington, E. M. The effects of familial variables on sex typing, on parent-child similarity, and on imitation in children. In J. P. Hill (Ed.), *Minnesota symposia on child psychology* (Vol. 1). Minneapolis: University of Minnesota Press, 1967.

Hetherington, E. M., Cox, M., & Cox, R. Effects of divorce on parents and children. In M. E. Lamb (Ed.), *Nontraditional families: Parenting and child development.* Hillsdale, N.J.: Erlbaum, 1982.

Hock, E. Working and nonworking mothers and their infants: A comparative study of maternal caregiving characteristics and infant social behavior. *Merrill-Palmer Quarterly, 1980, 26,* 79–101.

Hoffman, L. W. Maternal employment: 1979. *American Psychologist, 1979, 34,* 859–865.

Hoffman, L. W., & Nye, F. I. *Working mothers.* San Francisco: Jossey-Bass, 1974.

Huston, A. C. Sex typing. In P. H. Mussen & E. M. Hetherington (Eds.), *Handbook of child psychology* (Vol. 4): *Socialization, personality, and social development* (4th ed.). New York: Wiley, 1983.

Kempe, R. S., & Kempe, C. H. *Child abuse.* Cambridge, Mass.: Harvard University Press, 1978.

Kohn M. L. Social class and parental values. *American Journal of Sociology, 1959, 64,* 337–351.

Kurdek, A., Blisk, D., & Siesky, A. E. Correlates of children's long-term adjustment to their parents' divorce. *Developmental Psychology, 1981, 17,* 565–579.

Lamb, M. E. Sibling relationships across the lifespan. In M. E. Lamb & B. Sutton-Smith (Eds.), *Sibling relationships.* Hillsdale, N.J.: Erlbaum, 1982.

Lavine, L. O. Parental power as a potential influence on girls' career choice. *Child Development, 1982, 53,* 658–661.

LaVoie, J. C. Punishment and adolescent self-control. *Developmental Psychology, 1973, 8,* 16–24.

Lepper, M. R. Intrinsic and extrinsic motivation in children: Detrimental effects of superfluous social controls. In W. A. Collins (Ed.), *Minnesota symposia on child psychology* (Vol. 14). Hillsdale, N.J.: Erlbaum, 1981.

Levy-Shiff, R. The effects of father absence on young children in mother-headed families. *Child Development, 1982, 53,* 1400–1405.

Lewis, C. C. The effects of parental firm control: A reinterpretation of findings. *Psychological Bulletin, 1981, 90,* 547–563.

Lynn, D. B. Cultural experiments in restructuring the family. In E. M. Hetherington & R. D. Parke (Eds.), *Contemporary readings in child psychology* (2nd ed.). New York: McGraw-Hill, 1981.

Maccoby, E. E., & Jacklin, C. N. *The psychology of sex differences.* Stanford, Calif.: Stanford University Press, 1974.

Marcus, R. F. The child as elicitor of parental sanctions for independent and dependent behavior: A simulation of parent-child interaction. *Developmental Psychology, 1975, 11,* 443–452.

Martin, B. Parent-child relations. In F. D. Horowitz, E. M. Hetherington, S. Scarr-Salapatek, & G. M. Siegel (Eds.), *Review of child development research* (Vol. 4). Chicago: University of Chicago Press, 1975.

Mash, E. J., & Johnson, C. A. A comparison of the mother-child interactions of younger and older hyperactive and normal children. *Child Development, 1982, 53,* 1371–1381.

Miller, N., & Maruyama, G. Ordinal position and peer popularity. *Journal of Personality and Social Psychology, 1976, 33,* 123–131.

Minton, C., Kagan, J., & Levine, J. A. Maternal control and obedience in the two-year-old. *Child Development, 1971, 42,* 1873–1894.

Mulhern, R. H., & Passman, R. H. Parental discipline as affected by the sex of the parent, sex of the child, and the child's apparent responsiveness to discipline. *Developmental Psychology, 1981, 17,* 604–613.

Nydegger, C. N. *Timing of fatherhood: Role perception and socialization.* Unpublished doctoral dissertation, The Pennsylvania State University, 1973.

Osofsky, J. D., & O'Connell, E. J. Parent-child interactions: Daughters' effects upon mothers' and fathers' behaviors. *Developmental Psychology, 1972, 7,* 157–168.

Parke, R. D. Punishment in children: Effects, side effects, and alternative strategies. In H. L.

Hom & P. A. Robinson (Eds.), *Psychological processes in early education*. New York: Academic Press, 1977.

Parke, R. D., & Collmer, C. W. Child abuse: An interdisciplinary analysis. In E. M. Hetherington, J. W. Hagen, R. Kron, & A. H. Stein (Eds.), *Review of child development research* (Vol. 5). Chicago: University of Chicago Press, 1975.

Parke, R. D., & Slaby, R. G. Aggression: A multi-level analysis. In P. H. Mussen & E. M. Hetherington (Eds.), *Handbook of child psychology* (Vol. 4): *Socialization, personality, and social development* (4th ed.). New York: Wiley, 1983.

Passman, R. H., & Blackwelder, D. E. Rewarding and punishing by mothers: The influence of progressive changes in the quality of their son's apparent behavior. *Developmental Psychology*, 1981, *17*, 614–619.

Radin, N. Primary caregiving and role-sharing fathers. In M. E. Lamb (Ed.), *Nontraditional families: Parenting and child development*. Hillsdale, N.J.: Erlbaum, 1982.

Ragozin, A. S., Basham, R. B., Crnic, K. A., Greenberg, M. T., & Robinson, N. Effects of maternal age on parenting role. *Developmental Psychology*, 1982, *18*, 627–634.

Russell, G. Shared-caregiving families: An Australian study. In M. E. Lamb (Ed.), *Nontraditional families: Parenting and child development*. Hillsdale, N.J.: Erlbaum, 1982.

Sagi, A.: Antecedents and consequences of various degrees of paternal involvement in child rearing: The Israeli project. In M. E. Lamb (Ed.), *Nontraditional families: Parenting and child development*. Hillsdale, N.J.: Erlbaum, 1982.

Santrock, J. W. Influence of onset and type of paternal absence on the first four Eriksonian developmental crises. *Developmental Psychology*, 1970, *6*, 273–274.

Santrock, J. W., & Warshak, R. A. Father custody and social development in boys and girls. *Journal of Social Issues*, 1979, *35*(4), 112–125.

Santrock, J. W., Warshak, R., Lindbergh, C., & Meadows, L. Children's and parents' observed social behavior in stepfather families. *Child Development*, 1982, *53*, 472–480.

Schaefer, E. S. A circumplex model for maternal behavior. *Journal of Abnormal and Social Psychology*, 1959, *59*, 226–235.

Sears, R. R., Maccoby, E. E., & Levin, H. *Patterns of child rearing*. New York: Harper & Row, 1957.

Shinn, M. Father absence and children's cognitive development. *Psychological Bulletin*, 1978, *85*, 295–324.

Steinberg, L. D., Catalano, R., & Dooley, D. Economic antecedents of child abuse and neglect. *Child Development*, 1981, *52*, 975–985.

Stuckey, M. F., McGhee, P. E., & Bell, N. J. Parent-child interaction: The influence of maternal employment. *Developmental Psychology*, 1982, *18*, 635–644.

Sulloway, F. *Family constellations, sibling rivalry, and scientific revolutions*. Unpublished manuscript, Harvard University, 1972.

Sutton-Smith, B., & Rosenberg, B. Sibling consensus on power tactics. *Journal of Genetic Psychology*, 1968, *112*, 63–72.

Sutton-Smith, B., & Rosenberg, B. G. *The sibling*. New York: Holt, Rinehart and Winston, 1970.

Sutton-Smith, B., Rosenberg, B. G., & Landy, F. The interaction of father absence and sibling presence on cognitive abilities. *Child Development*, 1968, *39*, 1213–1221.

VanDusen, R. A., & Sheldon, E. B. The changing status of American women: A life cycle perspective. *American Psychologist*, 1976, *31*, 106–116.

Wallerstein, J. S., & Kelly, J. B. *Surviving the breakup: How children and parents cope with divorce*. New York: Basic Books, 1980.

Whiting, B., & Whiting, J. *Children of six cultures: A psycho-cultural analysis*. Cambridge, Mass.: Harvard University Press, 1975.

Wohlford, P., Santrock, J., Berger, S., & Liberman, D. Older brothers' influence on sex-typed, aggressive, and dependent behavior in father-absent children. *Developmental Psychology*, 1971, *4*, 124–134.

Wolfe, D. A., Katell, A., & Drabman, R. S. Parents' and preschool children's choices of disciplinary child-rearing methods. *Journal of Applied Developmental Psychology*, 1982, *3*, 167–176.

Zigler, E. Controlling child abuse in America: An effort doomed to failure? In R. Bourne & E. H. Newberger (Eds.), *Critical perspectives on child abuse*. Lexington, Mass.: Heath, 1979.

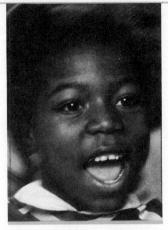

CHAPTER 12

*S*ocialization outside the family

*T*he family plays a central role in the socialization of most children, but as children grow, other socializing influences become increasingly important. In this chapter, we will discuss three major agents of socialization outside the family: schools, peers, and television.

Children of immigrant parents illustrate the importance of socialization beyond the family because the schools, peers, and media to which they are exposed often teach different values and behavior patterns from those of their families. Letifa is a 10-year-old girl whose parents immigrated to the United States from Saudi Arabia. She is the youngest of six children. Her mother wears traditional Saudi dresses, keeps her head covered in public, and generally retreats quietly to the kitchen when a stranger, even a woman, enters the house. She rarely speaks to strange adults, perhaps because her English is not very proficient. Letifa's father wears Western clothes but speaks English with a heavy accent. The family are practicing Moslems, and they speak Arabic at home in an attempt to maintain their culture. Letifa and her older sisters dress in blue jeans and the standard garb of American children and adolescents. They speak English fluently with no trace of an Arabic accent. The older girls drive cars, go to college, and greet visitors to their home readily. The Americanization that is superficially evident in their blue jeans and their ability to look strangers in the eye pervades these girls' values, beliefs, and expectations about human relationships at deeper levels.

Conflicts between traditional family values and peer values sometimes arise. One Sunday afternoon, Letifa wanted to go to a roller skating party with her friends, and her parents wanted her to attend Arabic school. Because Moslems observe a different sabbath than Christians, the scheduling of religious and cultural events is different from the standard pattern in the Midwestern community where she lives.

Letifa attends a school where she is the only Saudi, and her friends are all middle-class white Americans. The family owns a Betamax video recorder, and all the children watch American television. These sources of socialization are largely responsible for the children's marked departures from the patterns of behavior espoused and practiced by their parents.

418

⌈"The school is a social institution reflecting the culture of which it is part, and transmitting to the young an ethos and a world view as well as specific skills and knowledge."⌉(Minuchin & Shapiro, 1983, p. 197). In virtually all industrialized societies, children begin formal schooling sometime between the ages of 5 and 7. The main purpose of such schooling is to teach cognitive skills and information, but school does much more than that. It is a small social system in which children learn rules of morality, social conventions, attitudes, and modes of relating to others. Schools often provide the child's major peer group network; the socializing influence of the school results from the other students as well as from the teachers and school program.

For increasing numbers of children, school begins at age 3 or 4 in a preschool. When nursery schools originated in this country, their purpose was largely social. Children were sent to nursery school for contacts with other children, interesting and creative play activities, and experience with adults outside their families. During the 1960s, the emphasis of many preschools changed to academic skill development, and we now speak of "early education" rather than nursery school. Nevertheless, preschools are different in many respects from elementary schools, which are in turn different from high schools. As we consider the influence of schools on children's social development and motivation, we will often find that different generalizations apply to these various age levels.

We can all think of teachers whom we have liked or disliked, whom we thought were wonderfully stimulating or dreadfully boring, or who inspired us to act like them. Such reactions depend partly on the teacher's personality characteristics, and these attributes affect individual students differently. A teacher that you like may not be the one preferred by your friend. For example, a professor who insults and challenges students may inspire some of them to hard work while driving others into unproductive anxiety reactions.

Male and female teachers Most teachers of young children are female, and most college teachers are male. Throughout school, men more often teach math and science, and they are more often administrators. Women more often teach English and social studies. Some people have argued that young boys have difficulty in the early school years because the elementary school is a female environment. In fact, children do consider many aspects of elementary school to be feminine, and such sex stereotypes can influence motivation and achievement (Dwyer, 1974; Stein & Bailey, 1973). In recent years, there have been efforts to recruit more men into preschool teaching and more women into college and university teaching⌊Male and female teachers value and reinforce similar behavior in the classroom (Fagot, 1981), but it is probably easier for children to use teachers of their own sex as role models.⌉Young boys may think the behavioral demands of school more compatible with masculinity if they see adult men at school meeting those demands. For instance, they may think that sitting quietly trying to master a book is a masculine activity if some of their teachers are men. ⌊Conversely, adolescent females may develop more motivation to pursue math and science if they see women engaged in those fields as high school and college teachers.

Teacher personality [When teachers are warm, flexible, and gentle disciplinarians, students respond with more expression of feeling, open participation in the classroom, and independence (Minuchin & Shapiro, 1983). One problem in evaluating such findings is that warmth and nurturance are very general qualities that may be associated with many other variations in teaching style.

One field experiment provides more precise information because teachers' warmth and nurturance were varied experimentally. Teachers in some preschool play groups were nurturant and friendly; in other groups, the teachers were reserved and matter-of-fact. Both groups of teachers presented a curriculum designed to teach children sympathy and helping behavior. Children's helping behavior in natural situations was observed after the curriculum ended. The children who had been taught by the warm adults were more helpful to others than those who had been taught by the reserved adults. The warmth of the teachers apparently made them more effective teachers and models of empathy and helping (Yarrow, Scott, & Waxler, 1973).

A study that assessed academic performance of fourth-grade students confirmed the good effects of warmth and permissiveness on children with low levels of prior achievement and little academic motivation. Children who had been high achievers, however, learned better in classes where teachers were more reserved and controlling (Soloman & Kendall, 1979).

Teacher expectancies   Both educators and the public were startled in the late 1960s by the publication of a book, *Pygmalion in the Classroom,* in which the authors proposed that teachers' expectancies about a child's abilities could influence how well that child did in school (Rosenthal & Jacobson, 1968). Since that time a large body of research has accumulated showing that teachers' expectancies *can,* under some circumstances, affect learning (Minuchin & Shapiro, 1983; Rosenthal, 1976). They may also affect students' motivation, expectancies of success, and self-esteem.

From kindergarten on, teachers believe that some of the children in their class are brighter and will perform better than others. Although their beliefs are of course based partly on the child's performance, teachers can also be influenced by social stereotypes. For example, in an all-black school in St. Louis, the kindergarten teacher arranged the children in her class at three tables that eventually became three ability groups. The children at table 1, which was closest to the teacher's desk, were from better educated, more middle-class families than the children at table 3, who tended to be from very poor single-parent families. The children were assigned to tables at the beginning of the year, before the teacher had experience with their individual abilities. Because middle-class children often do perform relatively well in school, the teacher probably expected that the children at table 1 would perform better. As a result, she arranged the classroom to promote their achievement, and her expectations were confirmed (Rist, 1970).

How are teacher expectancies communicated to children? For elementary and secondary school children, numerous observational studies in classrooms demonstrate that teachers behave differently with children for whom they have high expectancies than with those they view as less able. First, teachers are friendlier, smile more often, and show more positive feelings toward students they consider bright than toward those they think are less able. Second, when a student for whom they have a high expectancy fails, teachers often ask the question again, perhaps giving clues. They are less likely to press a low-expectancy student after a failure, probably to avoid embarrassing the student. The unintentional message conveyed is that the teacher believes that the high-expectancy student is capable of generating an answer with additional effort but that the low-expectancy student is unable to do so. That is, the teacher is subtly teaching attributions: The high-expectancy student's failure is due to insufficient effort, but the low-expectancy student's failure is due to lack of ability. Third, some teachers interact more with high-expectancy students, partly because such students initiate more interactions with teachers than low-expectancy students do. Other teachers seek out low-expectancy students, especially in one-to-one teaching interactions (Cooper, 1979).

Teachers' praise and criticism Finally, teachers' use of praise and criticism can convey their expectancies. It is not surprising that teachers tend to praise high-expectancy students more than low-expectancy students; the high-expectancy students perform better in school and more often merit praise. However, some teachers are less likely to praise a low-expectancy student, even when that student makes a correct response. In addition, they are more likely to criticize a low-expectancy student than a high-expectancy student, even when both give incorrect responses (Cooper, 1979).

Teachers' praise is most likely to raise students' expectancies when it is contingent on good performance. If teachers praise children indiscriminately (in an effort to make them feel good, for instance), their praise becomes mean-

BOX 12.1

*Guidelines for
effective praise*

Effective praise	Ineffective praise
1. Is delivered contingently.	1. Is delivered randomly or unsystematically.
2. Specifies the particulars of the accomplishment.	2. Is restricted to global positive reactions.
3. Shows spontaneity, variety, and other signs of credibility; suggests clear attention to the student's accomplishment.	3. Shows a bland uniformity, which suggests a conditioned response made with minimal attention.
4. Rewards attainment of specified performance criteria (which can include effort criteria, however).	4. Rewards mere participation, without consideration of performance processes or outcomes.
5. Provides information to students about their competence or the value of their accomplishments.	5. Provides no information at all or gives students information about their status.
6. Orients students towards better appreciation of their own task-related behavior and thinking about problem solving.	6. Orients students toward comparing themselves with others and thinking about competing.
7. Uses students' own prior accomplishments as the context for describing present accomplishments.	7. Uses the accomplishments of peers as the context for describing students' present accomplishments.
8. Is given in recognition of noteworthy effort or success at difficult (for *this* student) tasks.	8. Is given without regard to the effort expended or the meaning of the accomplishment (for *this* student).
9. Attributes success to effort and ability, implying that similar successes can be expected in the future.	9. Attributes success to ability alone or to external factors such as luck or easy task.
10. Fosters endogenous attributions (students believe that they expend effort on the task because they enjoy the task and/or want to develop task-relevant skills).	10. Fosters exogenous attributions (students believe that they expend effort on the task for external reasons—to please the teacher, win a competition or reward, etc.).
11. Focuses students' attention on their own task-relevant behavior.	11. Focuses students' attention on the teacher as an external authority figure who is manipulating them.

| 12. Fosters appreciation of and desirable attributions about task-relevant behavior after the process is completed. | 12. Intrudes into the ongoing process, distracting attention from task-relevant behavior. |

Source: J. Brophy. Teacher praise: A functional analysis. *Review of Educational Research,* 1981, *51,* 26. Copyright 1981, American Educational Research Association, Washington, D.C. By permission.

ingless (Parsons, Kaczala, & Meece, 1982). These and other guidelines, based on research findings, for the effective use of praise are presented in Box 12.1.

One major question is the familiar "chicken and egg" problem: Do teacher expectancies influence performance, or are they merely responses to student differences in achievement? One study suggests that teacher behavior has an effect that is not just an outcome of student differences. Seventh- and ninth-grade math classes were observed, the students' expectancies of success in math were measured, and the teachers' expectancies for each student were assessed. In many classes, boys had higher expectancies of success in math than girls did. The teachers in those classes praised boys for whom they had high expectancies more than high-expectancy girls. In fact, they tended to praise the girls who did not perform well, as though they sought to console those girls for their poor math ability. These patterns are illustrated in Figure 12.1. In other classes, boys and girls had equal expectancies of success. Teachers in those classes treated males and females alike: They praised and criticized both. It appears that the teachers in the two types of classrooms were influencing the girls to set their expectancies at different levels. (Parsons et al., 1982).

Do teachers "like girls better"? Several careful observational studies have been conducted in preschools to find out whether teachers encourage sex-stereotyped behavior. Activities were classified as female-preferred if girls spent more time in them than boys or as male-preferred if boys played in them more than girls. Female-preferred activities generally include dolls, housekeeping play, arts and crafts, and table activities. Boys usually prefer blocks, rough-and-tumble games, and outdoor activities. In general, teachers give more attention and positive reinforcement to both boys and girls who participate in female-preferred activities. It would probably be a mistake to interpret this finding as evidence that teachers value "feminine" behavior. Female-preferred activities are often viewed by teachers as the cognitive curriculum of the preschool. Quiet intellectual games, arts and crafts, and small manipulative activities are important educational experiences for young children, and they often require more adult guidance than blocks and large-motor activities. Therefore, teachers spend more of their time with children in those activities (Fagot, 1978).

In elementary school, there is less choice of activities than in preschool, but teachers typically value and reward quiet, conforming, and obedient behavior. They dislike disruptive, aggressive, or overly dependent behavior. Be-

FIGURE 12.1

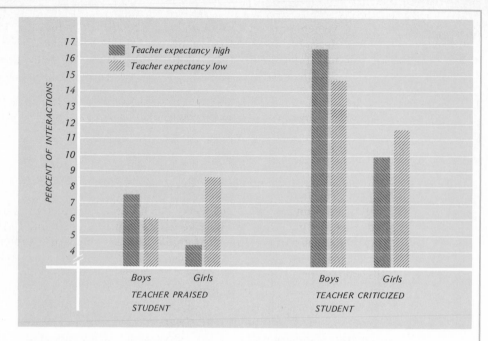

Percent of teacher interactions with students in which teachers praised or criticized the student. The students were classified according to the teachers' expectancies for their level of math performance (high or low) and according to sex. Data were collected during observations of seventh- and ninth-grade math classes. (Adapted from J. E. Parsons, C. Kaczala, & J. L. Meece. Socialization of achievement attitudes and beliefs: Classroom influences. **Child Development,** *1982,* **53,** *328. © The Society for Research in Child Development, Inc. By permission.)*

cause girls more often conform to adult demands, they get in less trouble than boys. Boys receive more punishment, scolding, and criticism for their behavior than girls do. Surprisingly, however, girls do not necessarily receive more praise and positive feedback from teachers. Some teachers take for granted girls' "good" behavior and give relatively little attention to quiet, conforming children; others actively praise and interact with the girls in their classes more than with the boys (Huston, 1983; Maccoby & Jacklin, 1974).

When teachers' attention, praise, and criticism are deliberately made contingent on certain behaviors, there are clear effects. Serbin, Tonick, and Sternglanz (1977) carried out a series of studies in which teachers reinforced children for playing in cross-gender activities—activities that were usually preferred by the other sex. The children increased their rates of play in cross-gender activities but returned to their earlier patterns when the teachers discontinued their reinforcements (see Figure 12.2).

Other researchers have demonstrated that teachers can modify many aspects of children's behavior in the classroom by giving attention when the desired behavior occurs and not attending to the child when the behavior is

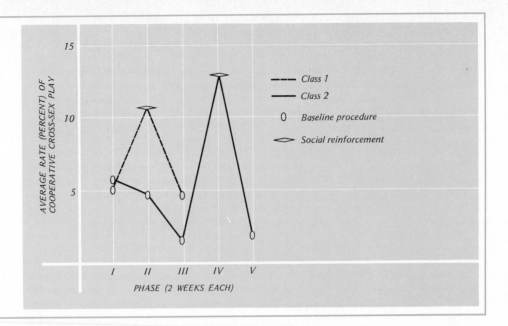

FIGURE 12.2

Frequencies of cross-sex play when teachers reinforced such play and when they did not. (From L. A. Serbin, I. J. Tonick, & S. H. Sternglanz. Shaping cooperative cross-sex play. **Child Development,** *1977,* **48,** *927. © The Society for Research in Child Development, Inc. By permission.)*

absent. For example, a child who is shy and sits away from other children and activities can be drawn into social interaction if teachers smile, talk to her, and praise her on any occasion that she makes an overture to other children. The teacher may sometimes need to suggest that the child join an activity but should not join the isolated child and give her a great deal of attention when she is sitting alone. The attention might reinforce social isolation instead of social participation.

Physical milieu in the school

Space, equipment, lighting, and decoration in classrooms can make a difference in the feelings adults and children have about their school environments. Does the physical milieu of the school also affect children's social interactions, motor behavior, concentration, and learning?

Preschool physical environments Preschools are found in church basements, old houses, unused elementary school classrooms, and many other physical settings. Most states have regulations about the minimum amount of space per child and other aspects of the physical environment. Some researchers have tried to determine whether children's behavior changes as a result of environmental variables such as crowding, number of children in a class, and amount and kinds of equipment. In one series of studies, carried out in Sheffield, England, classroom physical environments were experimentally varied. Children in different play groups were randomly assigned to classes with different environmental characteristics, and behavior was observed over the course of a whole school year. The researchers also tried to separate some of the factors involved in crowding, or density of people. By comparing different types of classes, they were able to separate the effects of three variables: group size, space per child, and amount of equipment per child.

The results, which are consistent with other studies, showed that children in large groups participated in more chasing and rough-and-tumble play as well as more play in "table activities." They spent more time in same-sex interactions but engaged in less fantasy and imaginative play than children in small groups. Density, or space per child, did not have many effects on behavior except when spaces were very crowded (15 square feet per child). Then, there was a decrease in cooperative group play and some increase in aggression. The amount of equipment was more important than the amount of space. When classes had several of each type of plaything, children were less aggressive and less likely to cry than when there were only one or two of each. But, with scarce equipment, children shared equipment and played together more (Smith & Connolly, 1980).

In general, these findings suggest that a preschool classroom that is very crowded or inadequately equipped may produce increased aggression and other kinds of stress for children. On the other hand, small spaces can be carefully organized, and children may learn to share when equipment is limited. In addition, the effects of space and equipment may depend on the child's culture and other experience. For instance, in Holland, where living quarters are typically small, children displayed positive social interactions and little solitary play in preschools with only 12.5 square feet per child (Fagot, 1977).

Elementary school buildings Open-space schools became the "new look" in school construction during the 1960s. These schools were built without interior walls enclosing each classroom. Part of the reason for such construction was to permit "open educational programs" in which children could work individually or in small groups, move from one area to another, and follow flexible schedules. Open architecture by itself, however, appears to have little effect on the children who inhabit it. The type of educational practices that fill the building appear to be more important than the physical arrangement per se, although an open physical space may facilitate an open education program (Gump, 1980). In fact, schools with fairly structured educational programs often reduce the physical openness of the building by using bookcases, file cabinets, wardrobes, and partitions to enclose classroom spaces (Gump & Ross, 1977).

Open education Open education "refers to a set of teaching practices which reflect the belief that children learn best when they can actively explore an environment rich in materials, when they are given the responsibility to make meaningful choices about what is to be learned, and when they are able to interact informally with their teachers and with one another" (Weinstein, 1979, p. 577). Programs called open education differ widely from one setting to another, but they all subscribe to at least some of the following principles: giving students choices of activity, providing individualized and small-group instruction, encouraging students to take initiative in their own learning, providing rich learning materials, deemphasizing grades and individual competition, teaching respect for peers, and viewing the teacher as a facilitator rather than a director of learning. These ideas gained widespread appeal in British and American education during the 1960s and 1970s. By 1980, approximately one-third of the school systems in the United States offered open classrooms as an alternative educational program. Many parents and educators opted for open education because they believed that it would not only help children to

Academic organization of schools

achieve academic competence but at the same time promote enjoyment of learning, self-esteem, curiosity, independence, and a sense of personal control.

The research comparing open with "traditional" programs has produced fairly consistent results. On the average, academic achievement is about equal in the two types of programs. There are no consistent differences in achievement test scores for children attending open and traditional schools. Children in open schools do, however, have more positive attitudes toward school than children in traditional schools and are more independent. Many studies also suggest that open-school students are more creative, more intellectually curious, and more cooperative (see Table 12.1) (Horwitz, 1979; Minuchin & Shapiro, 1983).

TABLE 12.1		RESULTS (PERCENT OF STUDIES)			
Summary of studies comparing children attending open and traditional schools	*Variable and number of studies*	Open better	Traditional better	Mixed results	No significant differences
	Academic achievement (102)	14%	12%	28%	46%
	Self-concept (61)	25%	3%	25%	47%
	Attitude toward school (57)	40%	4%	25%	32%
	Creativity (33)	36%	0%	30%	33%
	Independence & conformity (23)	78%	4%	9%	9%
	Curiosity (14)	43%	0%	36%	21%
	Anxiety & adjustment (39)	26%	13%	31%	31%
	Locus of control (24)	25%	4%	17%	54%
	Cooperation (9)	67%	0%	11%	22%
	Overall average	39%	4%	24%	33%

Source: T. A. Horwitz. Psychological effects of the "open classroom." *Review of Educational Research,* 1979, *49,* 80. Copyright 1979, American Educational Research Association, Washington, D.C. By permission.

Although these studies support the hopes expressed by advocates of open education, they are difficult to interpret because programs labeled "open" or "traditional" differ in so many ways. We can learn more from examining some of the specific dimensions on which they differ. One is the amount of structure or direction provided by the teacher. Another difference is the emphasis on individual competition as opposed to cooperative or group learning. Some research has investigated how these dimensions influence children.

High versus low structure　Teachers' methods can be classified along a continuum from teacher-directed to learner-directed. High levels of structure or teacher direction occur when the teacher tells children which activity or task they should carry out, provides them with directions about how to do the task, gives them written instructions, or provides specific praise or criticism for their performance. At the other extreme, the teacher provides little structure; the children choose activities and tasks, decide how they should be carried out, and rely more on internally generated standards for feeling satisfied or dissatisfied with their work. Of course, there are many points on this continuum, and some people argue that intermediate levels of structure provide opportunities that do not occur at either extreme. Variations in structure can exist within a classroom. Some activities may be closely supervised by teachers, while other activities are relatively unstructured by an adult.

Observations and experimental studies in preschool classrooms show that children in highly structured classes or activities attend well during learning tasks; they comply with teachers' directions, and they turn to the teacher for approval and recognition. They also follow classroom rules and procedures, such as putting away materials, with relatively few reminders from teachers. They spend a lot of time interacting with the teacher and relatively little time in peer interactions.

Low structure, by contrast, encourages positive interactions with peers—helping, cooperation, empathy—as well as aggression, assertiveness, and leadership. Children in low-structure classes and activities also spend more time in fantasy and imaginative play and display more creative and novel behavior than children in highly structured classes (Carpenter & Huston-Stein, 1980; Huston-Stein, Friedrich-Cofer, & Susman, 1977; Smith & Connolly, 1980; Thomas & Berk, 1981)

These patterns were demonstrated in one field experiment in which a preschool classroom was arranged so that some activities were highly structured and others involved little teacher intervention. Children were more prone to lead one another in low-structure situations and to seek attention from adults in high-structure situations (Carpenter, Huston, & Holt, 1981). One might conclude that low structure encourages children to create their own structure in play activity, whereas high structure encourages them to adopt or fit into the structure offered by others.

Both high- and low-structure experiences apparently encourage useful skills for children. It would be a mistake to argue that one or the other is "best." Some children may learn more and feel better in one type of situation or the other. For instance, a child who is easily distracted from school tasks by interactions with other children might do better in a structured classroom, while one who is fearful of authority might flourish in an unstructured situation. Probably many children would benefit from experiences with both high and low structure, so that they can acquire the different social and learning skills promoted by each.

When children are allowed free choice among activities in preschool, girls often select high-structure activities and boys low-structure activities (Carpenter, 1983). Given the fact that both high- and low-structure activities teach children important skills, it may be important for teachers to encourage girls to enter less structured activities and boys to enter more structured activities. For example, in a study of first- and second-graders' creativity, girls benefited more than boys from classes that were relatively unstructured (Thomas & Berk, 1981).

Cooperative learning versus competition

In the traditional American classroom, children sit quietly learning by themselves; they are forbidden to look at another person's paper or talk to other children, they take tests individually, and they receive an evaluation (a grade) that tells them not only how well they have done but how they compare to their classmates. The goal is to promote learning by encouraging individual effort and competition. Encouraging cooperation among students might also promote learning and perhaps lead to better interpersonal relationships among pupils (Johnson, Maruyama, Johnson, & Nelson, 1981). Several programs emphasizing cooperative learning techniques have been developed for use in schools where different ethnic groups were being integrated in the hope that cooperative learning would promote mutual respect and good relations among blacks, hispanics, and anglos.

One type of cooperative program emphasizes a *group reward structure*. For example, in the teams-games-tournaments method, children are placed on study teams of about five people. The teams are carefully matched for previous achievement, and everyone is given reading materials and worksheets covering the same material. Team members study together and quiz each other. Then members of different teams compete in a tournament to see how well they know the information, and the team whose members do best wins an award. Thus, competition is between groups instead of individuals. The essence of this method is that each team member benefits from the successes of the others, so there is a strong incentive to work together (Slavin, 1980).

A second type of cooperative program, the jigsaw method, emphasizes the *task structure*. Children are placed on teams of about six. Each member receives reading material containing one part of what the group must learn. For example, if they are studying the life of Benjamin Franklin, one member learns about his early life, one about his life in Philadelphia, and so on. Then the team meets to teach one another so that they can all pass a test covering the whole life of Benjamin Franklin. They must cooperate, because each person has an essential part of the ''jigsaw'' (Aronson, Blaney, Stephan, Sikes, & Snapp, 1978).

Both types of cooperative learning structures have been successful in improving learning and contributing to mutual concern among students. Children in jigsaw classrooms also showed improved self-esteem, and they liked their classmates better than those in comparison classrooms (Aronson et al., 1978). A description of the jigsaw method as used in one classroom appears in Box 12.2.

Desegregation and integration

School desegregation was originally ordered by the Supreme Court to provide all children in the nation with an equal opportunity for a good education. Thirty years later, we can ask three questions about the results: Does school integration affect learning and achievement? Does school integration influence students' self-esteem, levels of aspiration, and sense of personal value? Does school integration affect the relationships among members of different ethnic groups?

Desegregation does not necessarily lead to integration. Observations of newly desegregated schools have shown that minority students are often resegregated into different classrooms within the school by ability grouping and other means, and social segregation in lunchrooms and on playgrounds is also common. This is one reason why the answers to our three questions are complex. Desegregation by itself has few if any consistent effects on achievement, self-esteem, or intergroup relations.

The cooperative learning techniques that we have already described were developed in many cases to promote positive interactions among members of

BOX 12.2

*A day in a
jigsaw classroom*

One form of cooperative learning is the jigsaw pattern, in which small groups of students work together to teach one another. Each student in a group is responsible for teaching the others some of the facts and information that they all need to learn. The students in the classroom described here were working on colonial America.[1]

Ms. Taylor . . . asked the students to get into their groups and to spend five minutes reviewing before outlining the agenda for this period. . . . Lisa, the team leader, . . . asked, "What are we going to do today?" and the group developed the hour's agenda. When that was accomplished, Lisa asked Kevin to read the previous day's notes on how the group had functioned. Scanning the group-process evaluation cards, Kevin commented that the group needed to improve its ability to stay on the task and not get sidetracked. . . .

For the colonial unit Ms. Taylor had prepared jigsaw activity cards for each particular topic. Lisa passed a card to each person: Mark, Kevin, Amy, Nicole, Jon, and herself. The cards suggested ways that each student could help focus discussion on important issues and directed the student to additional resource information, such as reference books and, for the students who had difficulty reading, tapes. Performance objectives accompanied the material to help the student know specifically what must be presented. For example, the student teaching about Puritanism found on the card, "Each member of your team should be able to name two colonies in which Puritanism was found." Since each student was responsible for teaching different information, each knew that the others were relying on him for his part. . . .

After the five minutes had passed, Lisa called the group back together. . . . Nicole's presentation was to be the first piece in their jigsaw puzzle of information. Her topic was "religious persecution" and she began by asking her groupmates to close their eyes, as was suggested on the activity card. She told them to imagine they deeply believed in a religion, yet the police would not let them go to their church. They were told to try to experience such things as living in England three centuries ago . . . being beaten and put in jail . . . suffering economic losses . . . their children being taught another religion at school . . . deciding to leave . . . sorrow at leaving . . . the tough, perilous trip across the ocean . . . a difficult start . . . hardships, but also schools where their children learned their own religion . . . living, by choice, with people who shared their beliefs, and so on. Although Jon and Amy seemed to have trouble paying attention, the fantasy appeared to help the others prepare for the discussion. Nicole asked them to open their eyes, and . . . read some questions from the activity card: . . . What if you and a friend didn't believe in Puritanism? Should you have to learn that at school, or have to go to a Puritan church?"

A lively discussion ensued, covering the topics suggested by the questions on the activity card. . . .

[Ms. Taylor] was moving from group to group, checking the quality of discussion and behavior. . . . When she came to our group she quietly mentioned to Lisa, the leader, that it did not look as if everyone were participating. (In fact, we had observed that Mark had said nothing and that his chair was pulled back slightly outside the circle.) Ms. Taylor asked Lisa what the group might do to help create an atmosphere where everybody would feel able to participate. After Ms. Taylor left we noted that Lisa interrupted by saying, "Let's wait a second. Are we helping everyone to say whatever they're thinking?"

Kevin responded sharply, "Mark's been off in the clouds again. Why don't you talk like everyone else?"

Amy said, "Quit picking on him. If you weren't talking all the time, maybe he could say something!"

Lisa interrupted to help Mark and the other group members figure out how to make it easier for Mark to share his ideas. They decided to pause briefly between people's comments to make sure that others would have a chance to add their own ideas. They also encouraged Mark to say whatever he wanted, and Lisa and Jon told him that whenever he had talked in the past, they had liked his ideas.

[1] From E. Aronson, N. Blaney, C. Stephan, J. Sikes, & M. Snapp. *The jigsaw classroom.* Beverly Hills, Calif.: Sage, 1978, pp. 62–65. Copyright © 1978. Reprinted by permission of Sage Publications, Inc.

different ethnic groups. In general, they have succeeded. Children in classes using the teams-competition approach or the jigsaw technique have better intergroup relations than comparable classes organized more conventionally (Aronson et al., 1978; Minuchin & Shapiro, 1983; Slavin, 1980). When children from black, hispanic, and anglo backgrounds were placed in groups where cooperation and mutual helping was encouraged, they learned to know one another and to have generally positive attitudes about each other.

Meaningful contact among ethnic groups is more likely in the elementary school, where children spend most of their time in a single classroom, than in junior and senior high school, where they move from class to class. In a longitudinal study of children who entered integrated schools in kindergarten, both black and white children had generally positive attitudes toward the members of each group. Children were asked how much they would like to play with and work with each of their classmates. The average ratings are shown in Figure 12.3. At third, seventh, and tenth grades, children's cross-race and own-race ratings were fairly similar. When they were asked who their best friends were, however, their choices were overwhelmingly members of their own race (see Figure 12.3). In seventh and tenth grades, they also knew more members of

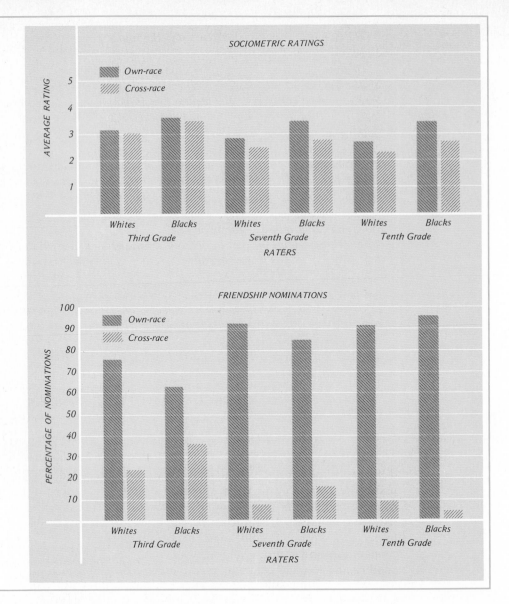

FIGURE 12.3

Ratings of own-race and cross-race peers in integrated classes of black and white children at three grade levels. Sociometric ratings reflect general ratings for how much peers are liked; friendship nominations are for those peers selected as good friends. (From S. R. Asher, L. C. Singleton, & A. R. Taylor. Acceptance versus friendship: A longitudinal study of racial integration. Paper presented at the Annual Meeting of the American Educational Research Association, New York, 1982. By permission.)

their own group than of the other racial group (Asher, Singleton, & Taylor, 1982).

We can give some tentative answers to our three questions about school integration. Although some early studies showed that black children had higher levels of achievement in integrated schools than in segregated schools, more recent evidence shows that integration alone does not lead to improved achievement. Planned programs to promote cooperation and learning in integrated schools have been successful in improving minority children's achievement. No evidence suggests any harmful effects of integration on

achievement by majority or minority groups. Integration does not automatically improve self-esteem, but cooperative, equal-status interactions among children do. Finally, intergroup relations are often positive in integrated schools, but at the upper grades, friendships tend to divide along ethnic lines. Positive intergroup relations are most likely in classrooms where students have similar levels of achievement and social status. Where backgrounds of children are quite different, mutual respect can be fostered by placing the children in cooperative structures where each person has a valued role to play.

Mainstreaming

Legal decisions about educational opportunity have also brought about efforts to integrate children with physical and mental handicaps in regular classrooms. This practice is generally called mainstreaming. Proponents of mainstreaming argue that it provides handicapped children with the best possible opportunity for educational advancement and for normal social relationships with other children. Like school integration, however, mainstreaming by itself does not always achieve these goals. For example, a number of studies have shown that nonhandicapped children in both preschool and elementary school classes interact more with other nonhandicapped peers than with handicapped children (Ipsa, 1981). Self-esteem of handicapped children is not necessarily improved in mainstreamed classes; in some instances, mentally retarded children may feel less confident in classes with normal children than in special classes.

Schools are important in socialization not only because of the teachers, the buildings, and the organization of learning environments but also because they are composed of children who constitute a miniature society for one an-

other. Peers are an important part of children's development from infancy onward. We turn now to examine some of those influences.

PEER RELATIONS
AND PEER
INFLUENCES

Peers (age-mates) contribute in unique and major ways to shaping a child's personality, social behavior, values, and attitudes. Children influence each other by modeling actions that can be imitated, by reinforcing or punishing certain responses, and by evaluating one another's activities and providing feedback to each other. In addition, peer relationships have some subtle impacts on development. For example, children's status in their peer group and the friendships they establish undoubtedly affect their self-concepts. In assessing these effects, we must bear in mind that peer relations are embedded in a larger social context of interaction in the family, in school, and in other organized and informal groups.

Developmental patterns

We cannot determine precisely when peer influences become significant. Many infants have regular contacts with other infants and young children, but the contacts are generally brief, ranging from a few seconds to a minute, and many of them are unreciprocated (Vandell, Wilson, & Buchanan, 1980). "Peer relations exist in babyhood in only the loosest sense" (Hartup, 1983, p. 114). As explained in Chapter 5, social play becomes much more prominent during the second year. Children 2 and 3 years old appear to feel emotionally secure with peers they know, and they are less exclusively dependent on adults.

Most children of preschool age seek out and enjoy their peers. When they find themselves alone, they often try to join ongoing activities with peers (Corsaro, 1981). During the preschool period, social relationships become closer, more frequent, and more sustained than they were earlier. From the age of 3 onward, children prefer, and associate more often with, playmates of the same sex. Eye contact with peers increases, and communication is more effective as children accommodate their language to the level of their partners. They show more involvement in joint efforts, coordinate their activities more effectively, and often collaborate successfully in solving problems (Cooper, 1977). Between ages 3 and 4, there are sharp increases in the strength of attachment to peers and the number of friendships established. Pretend play is more complex and includes more role taking, especially of roles of family members; plots are woven around these roles (Almy, Monighan, Scales, & Van Hoorn, 1983).

Contrast the following two episodes of pretend play, recorded at the same nursery school. In the first, 3-year-old Max and Mary are playing near some open steps in the nursery school playroom. They imitate and instruct each other, but their play is not well coordinated, and each child seems unconcerned with the other's needs or interests.

(Mary climbs to the top step and stands there. Max follows her.)

Mary: My dad made these stairs, Max. Go with me.

(She climbs down and Max follows her. She then crawls under the steps and Max again follows.)

Mary: Me the Nutcracker.

(Nutcracker Suite is playing on the phonograph. Mary bangs her head against the wall several times, Max imitating, as the two of them giggle. Max announces he is a snake and crawls out from under the other step, wriggling on his belly and making hissing sounds. Mary imitates him, crawling out across the room on her stomach and hissing.)

The children in the second episode, Joe and Carl, are just a year older than Max and Mary. Note the coordination of their play and Carl's sophisticated and successful attempt to negotiate in order to resolve a conflict through compromise:

Joe: I'm the father.

Carl: No, I am.

Joe: I want to be the father.

Carl: OK, you could be the father and I'll be the grandfather. Then we can both be fathers. (Almy et al., 1983)

The child's circle of friends widens and the intensity of friendships is likely to increase during the school years. Compared with younger children, schoolchildren interact more with each other and participate in more social activities. More of their behavior is task-related, and their social interactions are generally better organized (Smith, 1977). Cooperation as well as other kinds of prosocial behavior—specifically, sharing and other forms of altruism—increase through the school years, whereas aggression and quarreling decrease. Communication among peers is more effective because of greater understanding of others' motivations and intentions and improved use of feedback from others (Hartup, Brady, & Newcomb, 1981).

During the early school years (ages 6 to 8), informal groups formed by the children themselves predominate, and the school-age child is likely to refer to "the gang." The gang has few formal rules for governing itself, and there is a rapid turnover in membership. Expediency plays a large role in determining group membership.

Later, between the ages of 10 and 14, there is a tendency for children's groups to become more formal, highly structured, and cohesive, with special membership requirements and elaborate rituals for conducting meetings. Even so, the membership may change frequently, and the group itself may not last long. At this time, formal organizations such as athletic teams and scouts become more important, especially for middle-class children. By adolescence, time spent with peers exceeds time spent with adults, including parents (Hartup, 1970; Medrich, Rosen, Rubin, & Buckley, 1982).

Acceptance and rejection by peers

What determines whether children are accepted or rejected by other children, and how does peer acceptance or rejection affect a child? In research on these issues, assessments are made by *observation*, particularly of youngsters at nursery schools, or by *sociometric techniques,* in which children are asked about positive and negative reactions to their classmates through such questions as "Who in the class is your best friend?" "Who would you like to go on a picnic with?" and "Who are the ones that aren't liked by others?"

A number of personality characteristics are correlated with peer acceptance. In general, characteristics that are highly valued in the culture, such as physical attractiveness, are associated with popularity, while negative traits, such as immaturity, are related to rejection (Cavior & Dokecki, 1973; Lerner & Lerner, 1977). Popular children are regarded as friendlier, more outgoing, more adept in initiating and maintaining social interactions, more enthusiastic and helpful, kinder, and more cooperative than those who are unpopular. Rejected children are not necessarily less sociable or friendly than others, but they are more frequently initiators or targets of teasing, fighting, and arguing, and they act in immature, antisocial, disruptive, inappropriate, or deviant ways (Asher & Hymel, 1981; Gottman, 1977). Children who report moderately high self-esteem tend to be accepted by their peers more easily than children who score either very high or very low on self-esteem measures. Exaggerated reports of self-esteem may be inaccurate; in addition, children who say they are wonderful may be perceived as arrogant and may turn other children away (Cook, Goldman, & Olczak, 1978).

These correlational findings must be interpreted cautiously: Which factors are causes and which are effects? Friendliness and helpfulness may augment a child's popularity; disruptiveness and uncooperativeness may lead to rejection. But it is also possible that popularity reinforces and thus enhances a child's friendliness and that rejection may strengthen motives for disruptive and un-cooperative behavior. Among schoolchildren, the status of being "well liked" tends to persist for a long time (1 to 3 years), and unpopularity or rejection does not seem to weaken the associated behavior pattern. Poor relationships with peers during childhood often predict later emotional maladjustment and delinquency (Achenbach & Edelbrock, 1981; Roff, Sells, & Golden, 1972).

Special attachments to friends are a child's most significant peer relationships. Friends are a source of support and security. They serve as confidants, "therapists," models of behavior, and evaluators of the child's action who use different standards from adults. Their rewards and punishments are effective in modifying the child's behavior, and their interactions with the child foster understanding and sensitivity concerning others' thoughts and feelings.

Early friendships are generally fragile, quickly formed and quickly terminated. Preschool friendships are based largely on geographical location (living in the same neighborhood), shared interests and favorite activities, and possession of interesting playthings (Hayes, 1978). In speaking of their friends, schoolchildren stress sharing activities and possessions, helping, cooperation, and absence of fighting (Berndt, 1981; Bigelow & LaGaipa, 1975). By preadolescence, intimacy and loyalty are among the most important criteria in choosing friends, especially among girls. (Children's conceptualizations of friendship were discussed in Chapter 9.)

Children tend to select friends of their own age, sex, and race, as indicated earlier. Cross-sex best friends are rare, and even in integrated classrooms there are usually relatively few close friendships between children of different races (Asher, Singleton, & Taylor, 1982; Kandel, 1978b; Singleton & Asher, 1979). Because children usually attend schools and live in neighborhoods with others who are similar to themselves in social class and parent values, friends are often alike in these ways. However, when children select individual friends, they do not generally resemble each other in intelligence or personality characteristics. They do tend to share interests, attitudes, social orientations (for example, a tendency to seek or avoid social participation), and values (Byrne & Griffitt, 1966; Challman, 1932; Davitz, 1955). As they approach adolescence, within each social class, college-bound children are likely to have college-bound friends, while those who are not planning to go to college choose friends with educational goals like their own (Duncan, Featherman, and Duncan, 1972).

A longitudinal study of adolescent friendships helped to clarify the role of personal similarities in the establishment and maintenance of friendship as well as the influence of friends on children's socialization. Kandel (1978a) assessed the friendship choices, social attitudes, and personality characteristics of high school students twice, at the beginning of the school year and again at the end. She could then examine and compare similarities between friends in three friendship patterns: maintained friendships (friends at the beginning and also at the end of the year), dissolved friendships (friends at the beginning of the year but no longer friends at the end), and newly formed friendships (pairs who were not friends at the beginning but were friends at the end of the year). Resemblances clearly played a role in both the selection of friends and the maintenance of friendships: Children who became friends during the year (selected each other as friends) and pairs who maintained their friendship throughout the year were more alike in behavior and attitudes than pairs of adolescents whose friendships were dissolved during the year. The socializing consequences of friendships were also apparent. Children who remained friends throughout the year were more alike at the end of the year than they had been at the beginning, and new friends adopted each other's char-

acteristics, resembling each other more at the end of the year than they did before they became friends.

Peers as socializing agents

In a very real sense, children live in two worlds, the world of their parents and other adults and the world of their peers. These worlds can exist side by side with remarkably little overlap. The world of peers is a subculture, influenced in many ways by the larger culture but also having its own history, social organization, and means of transmitting its customs from one generation to the next. As many naturalistic and experimental studies show, much of a child's understanding of social behavior and of how to relate to others is transmitted by peers, not by adults.

The influence of peers can be seen dramatically in an unusual situation in which six infants were tragically separated from their mothers in World War II concentration camps and were moved from camp to camp as a group. When they were 3 years old they were placed in a residential nursery in England, but until that time they "had essentially reared themselves; contacts with adults were minimal" (Freud & Dann, 1951, cited in Hartup, 1983, p. 157). Although the children were well taken care of in their new setting, they developed little interest in the adults around them. They wanted to be together all the time and became distressed if any of them was missing from the group. They seemed to have no strong attachments to adults, but their interactions with each other served to socialize them. None of them was deficient, delinquent, or psychotic, and they acquired their new language at a normal rate. They matured into normal, effective adults (personal communication from Dann reported by Hartup, 1983).

The peer group instructs or trains children in critical social skills that cannot be learned in the same way from adults: how to interact with age-mates, how to relate to a leader, and how to deal with hostility and dominance. In later childhood, peers may perform psychotherapeutic functions, helping the child to deal with personal problems and anxieties. Sharing problems, conflicts, and complex feelings may be reassuring; for instance, the discovery that other children are also angry at their parents or are concerned with masturbation may reduce tension and guilt somewhat.

Parents vs. peers   Which are more influential agents of socialization, parents and other family members or peers? The question cannot be answered satisfactorily in any general way. Many behavior patterns learned in the family are reinforced and strengthened through interactions with peers. Other "home-grown" responses may bring ridicule, social ostracism, or abuse from other children; these behaviors will be modified. The power of peers as socializers varies from culture to culture and from one historical era to another. Contemporary American culture seems highly peer-oriented; children are strongly encouraged to interact with peers and are therefore inevitably influenced by them. In general, European children are less likely than Americans to rely on peers for opinions and advice and more likely to rely on adults (Bronfenbrenner, 1970).

Cross-cultural studies show that in some societies—the Soviet Union and China in particular—children and adults share the same social values to a much greater extent than in the United States. In these cultures, peer values—and pressures to conform to those values—serve to maintain the adult system rather than to modify it (Bronfenbrenner, 1970).

Aggression and prosocial behavior   Peers may be particularly important influences on the patterns of aggressive and prosocial behavior that children learn. As we noted in Chapter 10, most aggressive behavior in childhood is directed toward other children, not toward adults. Prosocial behaviors, such as helping, sharing, and expressing sympathy, also are often directed at other children, and they seem to have somewhat different meanings to children when directed toward peers than when they are directed toward adults. A child helping another child has equal competence, whereas a child helping an adult almost always is in a subordinate position.

Detailed observations of nursery schools suggest that aggressive actions—attacks, grabbing others' toys, invasions of territory—are frequently reinforced by other children. Because adults often do not see aggressive actions, relatively few aggressive behaviors receive any response, positive or negative, from teachers. The victims of aggression often yield or withdraw—by giving up a desired toy or a place in line, for instance. When children yield to aggression, the aggressor is apt to repeat the behavior the next time something is wanted. Because aggression is reasonably successful in preschool interactions, some children who are relatively nonaggressive when they enter nursery school become more aggressive while they are there. At first, these children are targets of aggression, but eventually they counterattack, sometimes successfully, and then are less likely to be victims. Thus, it is true, as some parents complain, that children may manifest more aggression after they have attended nursery school than before. However, children do not increase in aggression if they are originally passive and do not interact with others or if they are unsuccessful in counteracting peers' aggression (Patterson, Littman, & Bricker, 1967).

Peers are also readily available models of aggression. In many laboratory experiments, children have observed films of child models making aggressive responses (hitting bobo dolls, striking toys with a mallet, throwing things). In one of these experiments, children who saw child models imitated more aggressive behaviors than children who saw adult models doing the same things (Hicks, 1965). In natural situations, children may more often observe aggression by other children than by adults, particularly forms of aggression that they are capable of copying.

Prosocial responses—friendliness, cooperation, generosity, sharing, helping—may be augmented by peer reinforcement and modeling as well. In preschool classrooms, children who are friendly, helpful, and kind to other children receive more positive responses than those who are not (Hartup, 1983). In laboratory situations, children imitate generosity and helpful behavior when they see other children demonstrating such behavior. It seems reasonable to infer that repeated exposure to prosocial peer models may produce strong, generalized, and enduring prosocial dispositions in the same way that repeated exposure to adult prosocial models does.

Sex typing By the time children reach nursery school age, they have developed some definite ideas about sex-appropriate interests and behavior (see Chapter 10). Partly because preschool children have fairly rigid concepts about what is appropriate for girls and for boys, they reinforce sex-stereotyped behaviors and punish "inappropriate" behaviors more stringently than adults do. In nursery school, boys who play with masculine toys and girls who play with feminine toys are more apt to find friendly playmates and receive positive reactions from their peers. A boy who engages in doll play or dress-up is likely to be teased, or at least ignored, by both boys and girls (Fagot, 1977; Langlois & Downs, 1980).

Children's awareness of peer opinion about sex-typed behavior was illustrated when children were observed in a playroom alone, with a same-sex peer, or with a peer of the other sex. Six toys were available, three of them stereotypically masculine (plastic soldiers, miniature firetrucks, toy airplanes) and three of them feminine (small dolls and doll furniture, a plastic tea set, an ironing board and iron). When peers were present, children were much less likely to play with "sex-inappropriate" toys than when they were playing alone. "In many instances, . . . a child who picked up an inappropriate toy merely looked over at the peer who was busily engaged in drawing and then switched back to an 'appropriate activity' even when the peer gave no overt indication of disapproval" (Serbin, Conner, Burchardt, & Citron, 1979, p. 308). If children do play with "sex-inappropriate" toys, they are sometimes uncomfortable about others' knowing it. One little boy played happily with a plastic makeup set when he was alone; when it was time to return to the classroom, he asked the adult anxiously to be sure that there "wasn't any of that stuff" showing on his face.

Preschool children's tendency to enforce sex stereotypes may counteract parents' efforts to socialize their children to be androgynous or to avoid rigid stereotyping. A child who likes both feminine and masculine play activities is likely to receive criticism and occasional ostracism from peers, but also receives positive reactions. That is, androgynous patterns do not lead to severe rejection. The least accepted children are those who play predominantly with toys and activities stereotyped for the other sex. Girls are less likely than boys to be rejected or criticized for play interests that contradict sex stereotypes. In fact, by middle childhood, a large number of girls consider themselves tomboys and are well accepted by their peers. Boys with exclusively feminine interests, however, are likely to be rejected (Huston, 1983).

Peers can be agents of change in sex stereotypes as well as bastions of conservatism, particularly as children get beyond the preschool years. If school programs, parent values, or other influences lead some members of the peer group to espouse less rigid views about sex stereotypes or to engage in non-stereotyped behavior, others will often follow.

Early in the preschool years, children begin to spend more time playing with peers of their own gender than with those of the other gender. The segregation of boys and girls increases as children get older, until early adolescence. As we noted earlier, it is rare for children in middle childhood to have close friends of the other gender. This segregation of peer groups is one reason why peers encourage sex-stereotyped behavior. A child who plays with girls is likely to be playing feminine games; a child who plays primarily with boys will be playing masculine games.

Social and emotional responses Emotional reactions and social interactions are also subject to change as a consequence of observing peers. For example, children are more likely to laugh and smile in response to humor if they are with others who react in these ways (Brown, Wheeler, & Cash, 1980). An experimental study demonstrates that exposure to sociable peer models can be effective in reducing children's timidity and in stimulating greater social participation. A group of withdrawn nursery school children viewed films showing peer models looking at other children playing, then quietly sharing toys and joining the group's activities and enjoying themselves. When later observed in the nursery school classroom, the children who saw the film were much more outgoing, engaging in many social activities with other children. A control group of withdrawn children who had seen a different, neutral film (about dolphins) remained withdrawn and avoided social relationships with their peers. The intervention—exposure to sociable models—had lasting effects: A month later, the children who had observed the friendly peer models in the film were still having frequent enjoyable interactions with other children (O'Connor, 1969).

Peers may act as "therapists" for children with phobias (intense, irrational fears) by demonstrating (modeling) calm responses to the stimuli and events that frighten the phobic children. Box 12.3 presents an account of a study

BOX 12.3

*Peers as models
of fearlessness*

Since peers are highly effective models of aggression and sex-typed behavior, it is to be expected that they can also help inculcate constructive and cooperative social behavior.

Socially positive effects of peer modeling are evidenced in studies in which children demonstrate calm responses to stimuli and events that frighten other children. In one experiment, some 2- and 3-year-olds who were initially very fearful of dogs and avoided them overcame their fears after exposure to models who approached and played with a dog. The fearful children were assigned to one of four treatment conditions. Group 1, the *model-positive context* group, attended a series of eight enjoyable parties. During each party, a 4-year-old model was ushered into the room and interacted for progressively longer periods as well as more closely and intensely with a dog. Group 2, the *model-neutral context* group, observed the same peer model performing the same sequence of approach responses with the dog, but without parties. The other two groups were controls. Group 3, the *exposure-positive context* group, attended parties during which a dog was brought into the room but did not observe any modeling. Group 4, the *positive context* group participated in the parties but was not exposed to either the dog or the model.

Figure B12.3 shows the performance of the four groups on a pretest, posttest (given 1 day after training was completed), and a follow-up (1 month later). Children in both modeling conditions displayed

FIGURE B12.3

*Mean scores on a
test measuring fearful
children's approaches
to a dog before and
after experimental
treatments and 1
month after treat-
ment. Some children
saw filmed models
playing with dogs
(model treatment).
Other groups expe-
rienced a party at-
mosphere (positive
context) when they
saw the film (model
+ positive context)
or without seeing
the film (positive
context). (From A.
Bandura, J. E. Gru-
sec, & F. L. Men-
love. Vicarious ex-
tinction of avoidance
behavior.* Journal of
Personality and So-
cial Psychology,
*1967, 5, 21. Copy-
right 1967 by the
American Psycho-
logical Association.
By permission.)*

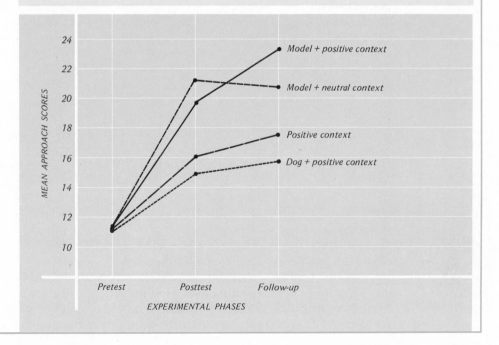

significantly greater and more lasting reduction in avoidance behavior toward a dog than the children in the control conditions. In addition, significantly more of the children exposed to models were willing to play with the dog, even with no one else in the room. The increase in approach responses (or the extinction of avoidance behavior) was generalized from a familiar to an unfamiliar dog (Bandura, Grusec, & Menlove, 1967). In a similar study, some children who were about to receive dental treatment observed a child who was calm while being treated by a dentist. Those who observed this model showed less distress during their own treatment than children who were not exposed to the calm model. Clearly, then, exposure to peer models coping successfully with fearful stimuli can lead to extensive and enduring fear-reduction.

in which 2- and 3-year-olds who were initially very fearful of dogs overcame their fears after exposure to models who approached the dog and played with it.

Peers as schoolteachers   As the studies of cooperative learning indicate, peers can be effective teachers of school subjects. In the Soviet Union, almost all children are given the assignment of tutoring a younger peer. This is regarded not only as a means of instructing the younger child but also as a means of cultivating traits of generosity and social responsibility in the tutor (Bronfenbrenner, 1970).

In this country, children who have been tutored by other children show improvement in reading as well as quantitative skills, and they perform better on standard tests. The greatest benefits accrue when the tutor is somewhat older than the pupil and when the tutoring is conducted on a long-term, one-to-one basis (East, 1976; Linton, 1973).

Some educators maintain that the tutors gain from peer tutoring as much as or more than the children being tutored. The tutor's own motivation and involvement in the subject matter appears to increase, improving the tutor's academic performance. "Tutor benefits are also thought to include increases in self-esteem, prosocial behavior, and [positive] attitudes toward school (both toward teachers and subject matter) since the tutor carries social status, attention from adults, and deference from other children" (Hartup, 1983, p. 163).

TELEVISION AS A SOCIALIZING INFLUENCE

American children spend more time watching television than in any other single activity except sleeping. Although many children and parents consider television a harmless form of entertainment, it is an important socialization agent that influences children's social and cognitive development. Even when children view television merely for amusement, they learn from it. As several scholars have noted, for a child, all television is educational television.

Children begin watching television in infancy. Many parents report that they place their baby in front of the television set, propped in an infant seat, because the television quiets or interests the baby. Six-month-olds show signs of distress when the audio or video transmission is distorted, suggesting that they notice changes in the kind of stimulation emanating from the "magic box" (Hollenbeck & Slaby, 1979). Around age 2 to 2½, children begin to show consistent attention to television programming. They seem to become aware of the people and events being portrayed.

By age 4 or 5, the average child watches over 2 hours of television a day. The amount of viewing increases until late childhood, then declines some during adolescence, probably because adolescents are more mobile and can be away from home more (see Figure 12.4). During the 1970s and early 1980s, the variety of options available on television expanded considerably with cable, pay television, and home video recorders. These options often lead children to spend even more time with television. In addition, video games, which are very popular with children, have many features in common with television.

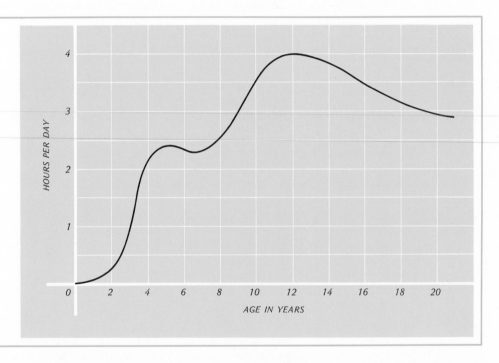

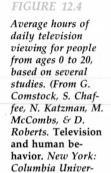

FIGURE 12.4

Average hours of daily television viewing for people from ages 0 to 20, based on several studies. (From G. Comstock, S. Chaffee, N. Katzman, M. McCombs, & D. Roberts. **Television and human behavior.** *New York: Columbia University Press, 1978, p. 178. By permission.)*

What is learned from television?

What a child learns from television depends on both the developmental level of the child and the nature of the programs the child watches. "Little House on the Prairie," "The Dukes of Hazzard," "The Price Is Right," "As the World Turns," "Sesame Street," "Tom and Jerry," and "Jacques Cousteau"— all these shows, and the commercials that accompany them, convey different messages and teach children different things. It is too simple to talk about the effects of television as if they were the same for all children or all shows. Nevertheless, some generalizations are possible because there are some pervasive patterns in American commercial television.

Children can learn both aggressive and prosocial behavior from television (Chapter 1, Chapter 10). They also acquire much of their knowledge about social relationships and social behavior from television. We noted earlier that children learn many "scripts" for different real-life situations from watching television. They learn what people are expected to do on dates, on a military base, at a royal wedding, and in many other situations with which they have little direct experience. In fact, many adolescents, particularly those from poor and minority families, say that they use television deliberately to find out how to act in social situations. The glamorous, adventurous life of many people on television looks attractive, and many young people consider it a better guide for themselves than the everyday existence of their parents (Comstock & Cobbey, 1978).

Children also learn social stereotypes about women, men, minorities, elderly people, and many other groups, including children themselves. The typical lead character on commercial television is a white, middle-class, young or middle-aged man, as are most of the news and sports broadcasters and adults on children's programs. Children and elderly people are seldom shown, and many ethnic minorities are virtually absent from the screen. When such groups are shown, they are often portrayed with little power and unfavorable attributes. These stereotypes are exaggerated on children's programs, where many villains have dark skin and foreign accents and where the male characters take the lead in coping with situations while females remain passive or helpless (Sternglanz & Serbin, 1974; U.S. Commission on Civil Rights, 1977). Children learn from these portrayals, particularly when they have little contact with the group portrayed. For example, white children who knew few black people derived many of their ideas about blacks from television (Greenberg, 1972).

Perhaps more important, portrayals that run counter to prevalent stereotypes can make a significant change in children's views about a group of people. One television series, called "Freestyle," was specifically designed for 9- to 12-year-olds to counteract sex and ethnic stereotypes that might influence career interests. Evaluations of "Freestyle," carried out in several cities, demonstrated that the program was "particularly successful in promoting greater acceptance of girls who engage in athletics and mechanical activities and who assume positions of leadership; of boys who engage in nurturing activities; and of men and women who choose nontraditional careers" (Johnston & Ettema, 1982, p. 204). It was less effective in changing children's behavior, although girls showed some increase in their intentions to participate in athletic and mechanical activities (Johnston & Ettema, 1982).

Factors influencing what is learned

Cognitive development What children learn from television depends partly on their level of cognitive understanding. Although children watch many programs designed for children, most of what they view is intended for adult audiences. The plots, characters, and situations they encounter are often unfamiliar to them, and they have difficulty understanding some of what they see because their cognitive skills for understanding complex stories are not well developed.

First, young children have difficulty *discriminating central, important content* from incidental content that is tangential to the main point. An incidental sight gag (Fat Albert falling flat on his face, for instance) may seem at least as

important as the central theme (he and his gang are trying to help a girl who is unhappy about her parents' divorce). Therefore, the child has trouble following the plot. Second, young children have difficulty *integrating* different elements of a story that occur at different times. For example, a child may not connect the scene of a masked man holding up a bank with a second scene half an hour later of a man being arrested and taken to jail. Third, children have difficulty *making inferences* about events that are not explicitly shown or about the feelings and intentions of characters. When the camera cuts from a scene with soldiers attacking a village to a view of the village in ruins, children may not infer the intervening events well (Collins, 1982). Each of these cognitive capacities—separating incidental from central content, temporal integration, and making inferences—develops gradually during the school years. Most children reach age 9 or 10 before they can employ these skills efficiently in understanding typical adult programs. Therefore, over many years of childhood, children are taking away quite different messages from many programs than most adults would.

Cognitive development also plays an important role in children's understanding of advertising. Television differs from other agents of socialization in that it is primarily controlled by commercial interests. Advertising directed to children is a multimillion-dollar industry. Although many parents and citizens' groups have objected to the amount and kind of advertising that accompanies children's programs, the products advertised still tend to be foods with a higher sugar or fat content, such as sweetened cereals, candy, and snacks, as well as glamorous-looking toys.

Especially during the months before Christmas, toy manufacturers often mount intensive campaigns in which the same ad for a new item or line is shown repeatedly, many times a day. Some ads for toys and other products use slick, attention-getting techniques that are misleading to children. For instance, a boy of 4 persuaded his mother to buy him a brand of shoes he had seen on TV. Arriving home, he put them on, tried a running jump across the living room, and burst into tears. The explanation for his disappointment? When the boys on TV wore those shoes, they were able to jump a 6-foot fence—and in slow motion, too.

Although children can discriminate advertisements from programs by age 3 or 4, they do not fully understand the nature of advertising until age 10 or 11. For example, during elementary school, they come to recognize that ads are aimed at an audience, that ads are made by someone with a persuasive purpose that does not necessarily coincide with the child's welfare, and that ads are staged and scripted. Even a 6- or 7-year-old often takes an ad at face value and is persuaded that a product is desirable. By 10 or 11, children are skeptical of claims in advertisements, and they expect that ads may be deceptive (Robertson & Rossiter, 1974).

Environmental influences   Because most television viewing occurs in a home environment, the people and things in that environment affect what a child learns from television. For example, children learn more from educational television when an adult watches with them than they do by themselves, particularly if the adult labels important events and states inferences (Collins, Sobol, & Westby, 1981; Watkins, Calvert, Huston-Stein, & Wright, 1980). Parents can help children interpret what they see on commercial television, too, by watching with them and offering comments. For example, when young children find remarks or plots confusing, it may be helpful to have their parents explain why a character did something or what that person meant. An older child may be interested in discussing why the president's news conference preempts a baseball game or what values are being conveyed by Archie Bunker.

Parents and teachers can also encourage children's interest in positive messages from television by providing "props" that children can use during play. In preschool classrooms where children watched "Mr. Rogers' Neighborhood," a variety of puppets, dolls, costumes, books, and records from the program were made available during free play. Teachers also directed activities in which the prosocial themes of the television programs were rehearsed. Children who experienced these environmental aids for learning showed increases in positive interactions with one another (Friedrich-Cofer, Huston-Stein, Kipnis, Susman, & Clewett, 1979).

Production techniques   Children's understanding of television messages also depends partly on how those messages are "packaged." Researchers who are concerned about improving children's television have explored what aids to comprehension can be built into programs by using production techniques that fit children's cognitive levels. For example, children generally recall in-

FIGURE 12.5

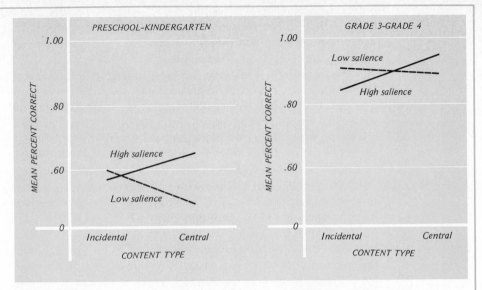

Mean percentage of correct answers for two age groups on questions measuring recall for information in a television program that was central to the plot or incidental to the plot. Each type of information was presented with high-salience production features (high levels of action and special effects) or low-salience production features (little action and some dialogue). Children remembered central plot information better when it was presented with high-salience features than with low-salience features (From S. L. Calvert, A. C. Huston, B. A. Watkins, & J. C. Wright. The relations between selective attention to television forms and children's comprehension of content. **Child Development**, 1982, 53, 606. By permission.)

formation that is presented in visual forms, usually with moderately high levels of movement and accompanying sound effects or music, better than content that is presented verbally. A scene showing a child sneaking around the back of the school to give his teacher some home-made cookies has much more impact than a scene where he tells a friend he's embarrassed to give the teacher cookies (Wright & Huston, 1983). Attention-getting production features can be particularly successful in helping the child to identify central themes and distinguish them from incidental content. An example is shown in Figure 12.5.

Narration that provides important inferences can also help children understand central-content themes. In one study, a "preplay" format was used. Before each section of the program, a short preplay showed the central events while a narrator described them. In most instances, children who saw preplays understood the program content better than a control group (Calvert, 1982).

Towns without television

When television became widespread in the 1950s, many people were afraid that children would lose interest in books and school, families would no longer talk to each other, and people would become passive consumers of entertainment and lose the ability to generate their own amusement. Some social commentators believe that many of these consequences have come to pass;

others argue that television has made remarkably little difference; still others believe that it has begun to realize its positive potential. During the past decade, some empirical evidence has been obtained against which we can evaluate these claims and opinions.

Because television spread so rapidly after its introduction, there have been few opportunities to compare groups who have television available with similar groups who do not have access to television. In British Columbia and Australia, however, two different groups of investigators located towns that did not have television reception and towns that were similar in other respects that did receive television. The main finding in the Australian study was that much of the time that people devoted to television was taken from time previously spent with other media, such as radio and movies. Also, in towns with TV, there were fewer community recreational activities and correspondingly more home-based hobbies such as needlepoint and carpentry (Murray & Kippax, 1978).

In British Columbia, the town without television ("Notel") was compared to a town that received only one channel ("Unitel") and a town that received the three American networks ("Multitel"). A follow-up was conducted 2 years later, after Notel had received television. Possible effects of television on aggressive behavior and sex stereotypes were investigated by comparing the three towns at the beginning of the study and by examining the change in Notel after television was introduced. There were no differences in the frequency of aggression on school playgrounds at the beginning of the study, but children in Notel showed a significant gain after the introduction of television. Children in Notel initially had less stereotyped views about appropriate behavior for boys and girls than children in the other towns before television was introduced, but they evidenced more stereotypes after television reached their community (Williams, in press). It appears that exposure to television led to increases in aggression and sex stereotyping, although the differences in aggression may have been partly a response to the novelty of television.

Television viewing does appear to interfere with reading skills, at least in the early school years. In the British Columbia sample, Notel children performed better on reading tests than the other children when there was no television in their town but declined sharply after television was introduced. These results might have occurred partly because television was new—a novelty effect that would wear off. However, among children in the United States who have grown up with television, heavy viewing is associated with poor reading skills, even when intelligence is controlled. It appears that television displaces reading for many children; heavy viewers are less interested in print media and spend less time practicing reading than light viewers (Hornik, 1981; Morgan & Gross, 1982). Other cognitive skills, such as vocabulary, ability to understand spatial relationships, and math ability, do not appear to be adversely affected by television exposure.

Children also gain much information from watching television, and they can learn cognitive skills as well. For example, a camera can demonstrate visual analysis (finding parts of a complex stimulus) by zooming in on sections of the stimulus and zooming out to show the whole thing. In one study, children who watched several demonstrations of such zooms performed better than a control group on a test of visual analysis (Salomon, 1979). We have already pointed out that children learn letter and number skills from programs such as "Sesame Street" and "Electric Company" (Chapter 8).

Does television make children passive and intellectually lazy? Because children usually watch television for entertainment rather than for educational reasons, they often treat it as an occasion to relax and put forth minimal mental effort (Salomon, 1983). However, children are not passive receivers of incoming stimuli from the TV tube. From a very early age, they make choices about what, when, and how attentively to watch. Their attention is attracted by vivid, rapidly moving productions that contain many audiovisual gimmicks and special effects, but such production features alone are not enough to maintain their interest (Huston & Wright, 1983). They attend to content they can *understand* (Anderson & Lorch, 1983) and to content that is *funny* or *interesting* (Zillmann, Williams, Bryant, Boynton, & Wolf, 1980). They think actively about what they are viewing, perhaps more than adults do.

Form versus content

Television is distinguished from other media by its form, not its content. The *formal features* of television include pace (rate of change), variability (number of different people or places shown), visual techniques (instant replays, special effects), and auditory features (music, sound effects). These can be used to present many types of content. Children's programs and commercials, particularly cartoons, are notable for their forms—the intense bombardment of visual and auditory events that emanate from the screen. The rapid pace, high levels of activity, and visual and auditory gimmicks of Saturday morning "kid-vid" are attention-getting, and, for that reason, they have been adapted (with some important changes) by many educational productions for children. In fact, for preschool children, these formal features of children's programs are more important for maintaining attention than is violent content. That is, a program with very active characters, frequent change of scenes, and high rates of visual and sound effects will hold children's interest well, whether or not the characters show any aggression or violence (Wright & Huston, 1983). This fact is an important argument for reducing violence in cartoons; children would still watch programs with humor and attention-getting formal features.

Some critics have expressed concern that rapid pace and action may stimulate children to be hyperactive and aggressive or to have short attention spans. There is some evidence that viewing programs with these features leads children to be less imaginative than they are when they watch a slow-paced program like "Mr. Rogers' Neighborhood." It is not clear at present when and for whom these effects occur. The advantages of using attention-getting formal features in educational programs appear to outweigh any negative effects (Wright & Huston, 1983).

SUMMARY

Institutions and groups outside the family play an increasingly important role in children's socialization as they grow from infancy through adolescence. In this chapter, we have considered three important socializing influences: schools, peers, and mass media.

Schools are a context for social development as well as a place to learn academic skills. Teachers can influence children's expectancies of success and their self-perceptions by forming expectations about children's abilities and communicating them and by praising and punishing children. In general, teachers value task-oriented behavior, and they try to reduce children's aggression. Male and female teachers tend to behave similarly, but children may use teachers of their own gender as models of the kind of achievement that is appropriate for themselves.

The physical arrangement of a school can contribute to the amount of physical activity and peer interaction. For example, small spaces encourage interaction and reduce running around in preschools, but the effects depend also on the amount of materials available.

In elementary schools, open education is a form of classroom organization in which instruction is individualized and children are given some responsibility for their own learning. Open architecture (no walls between classes) does not necessarily lead to an open-education program. Children in open-education programs make academic progress that is similar to that of children in other types of programs, but they demonstrate more independence and enthusiasm about school.

The amount of structure imposed by teachers in preschools (that is, the degree to which teachers guide and direct children in activities) is related to social behavior. In highly structured situations, children are attentive and compliant and seek recognition from adults. In low-structure situations, children exhibit leadership to one another, aggression, prosocial behavior, and imaginative play. In free play, girls often choose high-structure activities and boys more often choose low-structure activities.

Cooperative learning techniques, in which groups of children work together on an assignment, are useful in promoting integration of different ethnic groups and in promoting self-esteem among children.

Schools are one important place where children have contacts with their peers, form friendships, and participate in social groups with other children. As children grow from infancy through adolescence, peers are increasingly important in their lives. Their interactions become more complex with age.

Acceptance or popularity with peers is relatively stable for a given child over time, at least after the child enters elementary school. In general, characteristics that are highly valued in the culture, such as physical attractiveness, friendliness, social skill, and prosocial behavior, are associated with popularity.

Friendships among children form around shared activities and proximity in the preschool years. By elementary school, friendships become relatively stable and children begin to value internal qualities such as loyalty in their friends.

Peers socialize one another by processes of reinforcement, punishment, modeling, and identification. They often reinforce aggressive behavior in preschool groups, and peers tend to enforce sex-stereotypic play patterns and preferences. Peers can also reinforce prosocial behavior and serve as models for a variety of social behaviors.

Because children spend a great deal of time with mass media, particularly television, they learn a good deal of social information through those media. Television presents violence, social stereotypes, and prosocial actions, to name only a few categories of content. Children's understanding of the world and their behavior are often influenced by the glamorous portrayals of life shown on television.

The child is not a passive recipient of television but an active processor. What children glean from television depends on their level of cognitive development, the people and objects in their environment that may contribute to their understanding, and the production techniques used to convey information.

Television as a medium may have some effects on aggression, sex typing, and reading skills, regardless of its content. Children in communities with television tend to be slightly less aggressive, less sex-typed, and better at reading than children to whom television is unavailable. Television can also convey information in forms that are well suited for children's level of understanding and can teach nonverbal skills quite successfully.

REFERENCES

Abramovitch, R., & Grusec, J. E. Peer imitation in a natural setting. *Child Development*, 1978, *49*, 60–65.

Achenbach, T. M., & Edelbrock, C. S. Behavioral problems and competencies reported by parents of normal and disturbed children aged 4 through 16. *Monographs of the Society for Research in Child Development*, 1981, *46* (Serial No. 188).

Almy, M., Monighan, P., Scales, B., & Van Hoorn, J. Recent research on playing: The perspective of the teacher. In L. Katz (Ed.), *Current topics in early childhood education* (Vol. 5). Norwood, N.J.: Ablex, 1983.

Anderson, D. R., & Lorch, E. P. Looking at television: Action or reaction? In J. Bryant & D. R. Anderson (Eds.), *Children's understanding of television: Research on attention and comprehension*. New York: Academic Press, 1983.

Aronson, E., Blaney, N., Stephan, C., Sikes, J., & Snapp, M. *The jigsaw classroom*. Beverly Hills, Calif.: Sage, 1978.

Asher, S., & Hymel, S. Children's social competence in peer relations: Sociometric and behavioral assessment. In J. D. Wine & M. D. Smys (Eds.), *Social competence*. New York: Guilford, 1981.

Asher, S. R., Singleton, L. C., & Taylor, A. R. *Acceptance versus friendship: A longitudinal study of racial integration*. Paper presented at the Annual Meeting of the American Educational Research Association, New York, 1982.

Bandura, A., Grusec, J. E., & Menlove, F. L. Vicarious extinction of avoidance behavior. *Journal of Personality and Social Psychology*, 1967, *5*, 16–23.

Berndt, T. Age changes and changes over time in prosocial intentions and behavior between friends. *Developmental Psychology*, 1981, *17*, 408–416.

Bigelow, B. J., & LaGaipa, J. J. Children's written descriptions of friendship: A multidimensional analysis. *Developmental Psychology*, 1975, *11*, 857–858.

Bronfenbrenner, U. *Two worlds of childhood: U.S. and U.S.S.R.* New York: Russell Sage Foundation, 1970.

Brophy, J. Teacher praise: A functional analysis. *Review of Educational Research*, 1981, *51*, 5–32.

Brown, G. E., Wheeler, K. J., & Cash, M. The effects of a laughing versus a nonlaughing model on humor responses in preschool children. *Journal of Experimental Child Psychology*, 1980, *29*, 334–339.

Byrne, D., & Griffitt, W. B. A developmental investigation of the law of attraction. *Journal of Personality and Social Psychology*, 1966, *4*, 699–702.

Calvert, S. L. *Improving the comprehensibility of a children's television program: The effects of advance organizer formats on attention and comprehension*. Unpublished doctoral dissertation, University of Kansas, 1982.

Calvert, S. L., Huston, A. C., Watkins, B. A., & Wright, J. C. The relation between selective attention to television forms and children's comprehension of content. *Child Development,* 1982, *53,* 601–610.

Campbell, J. D. Peer relations in childhood. In M. L. Hoffman & L. W. Hoffman (Eds.), *Review of child development research* (Vol. 1). New York: Russell Sage Foundation, 1964.

Carpenter, C. J. Activity structure and play: Implications for socialization. In M. B. Liss (Ed.), *Children's play: Sex differences in the acquisition of social and cognitive skills.* New York: Academic Press, 1983.

Carpenter, C. J., Huston, A. C., & Holt, W. *The use of selected activity participation to modify sex-typed behavior.* Paper presented at the Annual Meeting of the Association for Behavior Analysis, Milwaukee, May 1981.

Carpenter, C. J., & Huston-Stein, A. Activity structure and sex-typed behavior in preschool children. *Child Development,* 1980, *51,* 862–872.

Cavior, N., & Dokecki, P. R. Physical attractiveness, perceived attitude similarity, and academic achievement as contributors to interpersonal attraction among adolescents. *Developmental Psychology,* 1973, *9,* 44–54.

Challman, R. C. Factors influencing friendships among preschool children. *Child Development,* 1932, *3,* 146–158.

Charlesworth, R., & Hartup, W. W. Positive social reinforcement in the nursery school peer group. *Child Development,* 1967, *38,* 993–1002.

Collins, W. A. Cognitive processing in television viewing. In D. Pearl, L. Bouthilet, & J. Lazar (Eds.), *Television and behavior: Ten years of scientific progress and implications for the eighties.* Washington, D.C.: U.S. Government Printing Office, 1982.

Collins, W. A., Sobol, B. L., & Westby, S. Effects of adult commentary on children's comprehension and inferences about a televised aggressive portrayal. *Child Development,* 1981, *52,* 158–163.

Comstock, G., Chaffee, S., Katzman, N., McCombs, M., & Roberts, D. *Television and human behavior.* New York: Columbia University Press, 1978.

Comstock, G., & Cobbey, R. E. Television and the children of ethnic minorities. *Journal of Communication,* 1978, *29*(1), 104–115.

Cook, T., Goldman, J., & Olczak, P. The relationship between self-esteem and interpersonal attraction in children. *Journal of Genetic Psychology,* 1978, *132,* 149–150.

Cooper, C. R. *Collaboration in children: Dyadic interaction skills in problem solving.* Paper presented at the Biennial Meeting of the Society for Research in Child Development, New Orleans, March, 1977.

Cooper, H. M. Pygmalion grows up: A model for teacher expectation communication and performance influence. *Review of Educational Research,* 1979, *49,* 389–410.

Corsaro, W. Friendship in the nursery school: Social organization in a peer environment. In S. R. Asher & J. M. Gottman, *The development of children's friendships.* Cambridge: Cambridge University Press, 1981.

Davitz, J. R. Social perception and sociometric choice in children. *Journal of Abnormal and Social Psychology,* 1955, *50,* 173–176.

Duncan, O. D., Featherman, D. L., & Duncan, B. *Socioeconomic background and achievement.* New York: Seminar Press, 1972.

Dwyer, C. A. Influence of children's sex role standards on reading and arithmetic achievement. *Journal of Educational Psychology,* 1974, *66,* 811–816.

East, B. A. Cross-age tutoring in the elementary school. *Graduate Research in Education and Related Disciplines,* 1976, *8,* 88–111.

Eckerman, C. O., Whatley, J. L., & Kutz, S. L. The growth of social play with peers during the second year of life. *Developmental Psychology,* 1975, *11,* 42–49.

Fagot, B. I. Consequences of moderate cross-gender behavior in preschool children. *Child Development,* 1977, *48,* 902–907.

Fagot, B. I. Reinforcing contingencies for sex-role behaviors: Effect of experience with children. *Child Development,* 1978, *49,* 30–36.

Fagot, B. I. Male and female teachers: Do they treat boys and girls differently? *Sex Roles,* 1981, *7,* 263–272.

Field, T., Roseman, S., Stefano, L., & Koewler, J. H., III. Play behaviors of handicapped preschool children in the presence and absence of nonhandicapped peers. *Journal of Applied Developmental Psychology*, 1981, *2*, 49–58.

Freud, A., & Dann, S. An experiment in group upbringing. *The psychoanalytic study of the child*, 1951, *6*, 127–168.

Friedrich-Cofer, L. K., Huston-Stein, A., Kipnis, D. M., Susman, E. J., & Clewett, A. S. Environmental enhancement of prosocial television content: Effects on interpersonal behavior, imaginative play, and self-regulation in a natural setting. *Developmental Psychology*, 1979, *15*, 637–646.

Gottman, J. M. Toward a definition of social isolation in children. *Child Development*, 1977, *48*, 513–517.

Greenberg, B. S. Children's reactions to TV blacks. *Journalism Quarterly*, 1972, *50*, 5–14.

Gump, P. V. The school as a social situation. *Annual Review of Psychology*, 1980, *31*, 553–582.

Gump, P. V., & Ross, R. The fit of milieu and programme in school environments. In H. McGurk (Ed.), *Ecological factors in human development*. New York: Elsevier North-Holland, 1977.

Harlow, H. F. Age-mate or peer affectional system. In D. S. Lehrman, R. A. Hinde, & E. Shaw (Eds.), *Advances in the study of behavior* (Vol. 2). New York: Academic Press, 1969.

Hartup, W. W. Peer interaction and social organization. In P. H. Mussen (Ed.), *Carmichael's manual of child psychology* (Vol. 2). New York: Wiley, 1970.

Hartup, W. W. The peer system. In P. H. Mussen & E. M. Hetherington (Eds.), *Handbook of child psychology* (Vol. 4): *Socialization, personality and social development* (4th ed.). New York: Wiley, 1983.

Hartup, W. W., Brady, J. E., & Newcomb, A. F. *Children's utilization of simultaneous sources of social information: Developmental perspectives.* Unpublished manuscript, University of Minnesota, 1981.

Hayes, D. S. Cognitive bases for liking and disliking among preschool children. *Child Development*, 1978, *49*, 906–909.

Heller, K. A., & Parsons, J. E. Sex differences in teachers' evaluative feedback and students' expectancies for success in mathematics. *Child Development*, 1981, *52*, 1015–1019.

Hicks, D. Imitation and retention of film-mediated aggressive peer and adult models. *Journal of Personality and Social Psychology*, 1965, *2*, 97–100.

Hollenbeck, A. R., & Slaby, R. G. Infant visual and vocal responses to television. *Child Development*, 1979, *50*, 41–45.

Hornik, R. Out-of-school television and schooling: Hypotheses and methods. *Review of Educational Research*, 1981, *51*, 193–214.

Horwitz, R. A. Psychological effects of the "open classroom." *Review of Educational Research*, 1979, *49*, 71–86.

Huston, A. C. Sex typing. In P. H. Mussen & E. M. Hetherington (Eds.), *Handbook of child psychology* (Vol. 4): *Socialization, personality, and social development* (4th ed.). New York: Wiley, 1983.

Huston, A. C., & Wright, J. C. Children's processing of television: The informative functions of formal features. In J. Bryant & D. R. Anderson (Eds.), *Children's understanding of television: Research on attention and comprehension.* New York: Academic Press, 1983.

Huston-Stein, A., Friedrich-Cofer, L., & Susman, E. J. The relation of classroom structure to social behavior, imaginative play, and self-regulation of economically disadvantaged children. *Child Development*, 1977, *48*, 908–916.

Ipsa, J. Social interactions among teachers, handicapped children, and nonhandicapped children in a mainstreamed preschool. *Journal of Applied Developmental Psychology*, 1981, *1*, 231–250.

Johnson, D. W., Maruyama, G., Johnson, R., & Nelson, D. Effects of cooperative, competitive, and individualistic goal structures on achievement: A metaanalysis. *Psychological Bulletin*, 1981, *89*, 47–62.

Johnston, J., & Ettema, J. S. *Positive images: Breaking stereotypes with children's television.* Beverly Hills, Calif.: Sage, 1982.

Kandel, D. B. Homophily, selection, and socialization in adolescent friendships. *American Journal of Sociology*, 1978, *84*, 427–436. (a)

Kandel, D. B. Similarity in real-life adolescent friendship pairs. *Journal of Personality and Social Psychology*, 1978, *36*, 306–312. (b)

Keniston, K. *The uncommitted: Alienated youth in American society*. New York: Dell, 1962.

Lamb, M. E., Easterbrooks, M. A., & Holden, G. W. Reinforcement and punishment among preschoolers: Characteristics, effects, and correlates. *Child Development*, 1980, *51*, 1230–1236.

Lamb, M. E., & Roopnarine, J. L. Peer influences on sex-role development in preschoolers. *Child Development*, 1979, *50*, 1219–1222.

Langlois, J. H., & Downs, A. C. Peer relations as a function of physical attractiveness: The eye of the beholder or behavioral reality? *Child Development*, 1980, *51*, 1237–1247.

Lerner, R. M., & Lerner, J. V. Effects of age, sex, and physical attractiveness on child-peer relations, academic performance, and elementary school adjustment. *Developmental Psychology*, 1977, *13*, 585–590.

Linton, T. Effects of grade displacement between students tutored and student tutors. *Dissertation Abstracts International*, 1973, *33*, 4091–4092A.

Maccoby, E. E. & Jacklin, C. N. *The psychology of sex differences*. Stanford, Calif.: Stanford University Press, 1974.

Medrich, E. A., Rosen, J., Rubin, V., & Buckley, S. *The serious business of growing up: A study of children's lives outside of school*. Berkeley, Calif.: University of California Press, 1982.

Minuchin, P. P., & Shapiro, E. K. The school as a context for social development. In P. H. Mussen & E. M. Hetherington (Eds.), *Handbook of child psychology* (Vol. 4): *Socialization, personality and social development* (4th ed.). New York: Wiley, 1983.

Morgan, M., & Gross, L. Television and educational achievement and aspiration. In D. Pearl, J. Bouthilet, & J. Lazar (Eds.), *Television and behavior: Ten years of scientific progress and implications for the eighties* (Vol. 2). Washington, D.C.: U.S. Government Printing Office, 1982.

Murray, J. P., & Kippax, S. Children's social behavior in three towns with differing television experience. *Journal of Communication*, 1978, *28*(1), 19–29.

O'Connor, R. Modification of social withdrawal through symbolic modeling. *Journal of Applied Behavior Analysis*, 1969, *2*, 15–22.

Parsons, J. E., Kaczala, C. M., & Meece, J. L. Socialization of achievement attitudes and beliefs: Classroom influences. *Child Development*, 1982, *53*, 322–339.

Patterson, G. R., Littman, R. A., & Bricker, W. Assertive behavior in children: A step toward a theory of aggression. *Monographs of the Society for Research in Child Development*, 1967, *32*(5, Serial No. 113).

Rist, R. C. *The urban school: A factory for failure*. Cambridge, Mass.: MIT Press, 1973.

Robertson, T. S., & Rossiter, J. R. Children and commercial persuasion: An attribution theory analysis. *Journal of Consumer Research*, 1974, *1*, 13–20.

Roff, M., Sells, S. B., & Golden, M. M. *Social adjustment and personality development in children*. Minneapolis: University of Minnesota Press, 1972.

Rosenhan, D. Some origins of concern for others. In P. Mussen, J. Langer, & M. Covington (Eds.), *Trends and issues in developmental psychology*. New York: Holt, Rinehart and Winston, 1969.

Rosenthal, R. *Experimenter effects in behavioral research* (2nd ed.). New York: Irvington, 1976.

Rosenthal, R., & Jacobson, L. *Pygmalion in the classroom: Teacher expectation and pupils' intellectual development*. New York: Holt, Rinehart and Winston, 1968.

Ross, H. S., & Goldman, B. M. Establishing new social relations in infancy. In T. Alloway, L. Krames, & P. Pliner (Eds.), *Advances in communication and affect* (Vol. 4). New York: Plenum, 1976.

Salomon, G. *Interaction of media, cognition, and learning*. San Francisco: Jossey-Bass, 1979.

Salomon, G. Television watching and mental effort: A social psychological view. In J. Bryant & D. R. Anderson (Eds.). *Children's understanding of television: Research on attention and comprehension*. New York: Academic Press, 1983.

Serbin, L. A., Conner, J. M., Burchardt, C. J., & Citron, C. C. Effects of peer presence on sex-typing of children's play behavior. *Journal of Experimental Child Psychology*, 1979, *27*, 303–309.

Serbin, L. A., Tonick, I. J., & Sternglanz, S. H. Shaping cooperative cross-sex play. *Child Development*, 1977, *48*, 924–929.

Signorielli, N., Gross, L., & Morgan, M. Violence in television programs: Ten years later. In D. Pearl, L. Bouthilet, & J. Lazar (Eds.), *Television and behavior: Ten years of scientific progress and implications for the eighties.* Washington, D.C.: U.S. Government Printing Office, 1982.

Singleton, L. C., & Asher, S. R. Racial integration and children's peer preferences: An investigation of developmental and cohort differences. *Child Development,* 1979, *50,* 936–941.

Slavin, R. E. Cooperative learning. *Review of Educational Research,* 1980, *50,* 315–342.

Smith, P. K. Social and fantasy play in young children. In B. Tizard & D. Marvey (Eds.), *Biology of play.* London: William Heinemann Medical Books, 1977.

Smith, P. K., & Connolly, K. J. *The ecology of preschool behavior.* Cambridge: Cambridge University Press, 1980.

Solomon, D., & Kendall, A. J. *Children in classrooms: An investigation of person-environment interaction.* New York: Praeger, 1979.

Stein, A. H., & Bailey, M. M. The socialization of achievement orientation in females. *Psychological Bulletin,* 1973, *80,* 345–366.

Sternglanz, S. H., & Serbin, L. A. Sex role stereotyping in children's television programs. *Developmental Psychology,* 1974, *10,* 710–715.

Suomi, S., & Harlow, H. Early experience and social development in rhesus monkeys. In M. E. Lamb (Ed.), *Social and personality development.* New York: Holt, Rinehart and Winston, 1978.

Thomas, N. G., & Berk, L. E. Effects of school environments on the development of young children's creativity. *Child Development,* 1981, *52,* 1153–1162.

Vandell, D. L., & Mueller, E. C. Peer play and friendships during the first two years. In H. C. Foot, A. J. Chapman, & J. R. Smith (Eds.), *Friendship and social relations in children.* New York: Wiley, 1980.

Vandell, D. L., Wilson, K. S., & Buchanan, N. R. Peer interaction in the first year of life: An examination of its structure, content, and sensitivity to toys. *Child Development,* 1980, *51,* 481–488.

Watkins, B., Calvert, S. L., Huston-Stein, A., & Wright, J. C. Children's recall of television material: Effects of presentation mode and adult labeling. *Developmental Psychology,* 1980, *16,* 672–674.

Weinstein, C. S. The physical environment of the school: A review of the research. *Review of Educational Research,* 1979, *49,* 577–610.

Williams, T. M. (Ed.). *The impact of television: A natural experiment involving three towns.* New York: Academic Press, in press.

Wright, J. C., & Huston, A. C. A matter of form: Potentials of television for young viewers. *American Psychologist,* 1983, *38,* 835–843.

United States Commission on Civil Rights. *Window dressing on the set: Women and minorities in television.* Washington, D.C.: U.S. Government Printing Office, 1977.

Yarrow, M. R., Scott, P. M., & Waxler, C. Z. Learning concern for others. *Developmental Psychology,* 1973, *8,* 240–260.

Zillmann, D., Williams, B. R., Bryant, J., Boynton, K. R., & Wolf, M. A. Acquisition of information from educational television programs as a function of differentially paced humorous inserts. *Journal of Educational Psychology,* 1980, *72,* 170–180.

part **F***ive*

ADOLESCENCE

CHAPTER 13

*A*dolescence:
physical change, mental growth,
and socialization

*A*dolescence has traditionally been considered a more difficult period in development than the middle-childhood years, for both adolescents and their parents. Some 300 years before the birth of Christ, Aristotle complained that adolescents "are passionate, irascible, and apt to be carried away by their impulses" (Kiell, 1967, pp. 18–19). Plato advised that boys not be allowed to drink until they were 18 because of their easy excitability: "Fire must not be poured on fire" (Plato, 1953, p. 14). And in a funeral sermon, a seventeenth-century clergyman compared youth to "a new ship launching out into the main ocean without a helm or ballast or pilot to steer her" (Smith, 1975, p. 497).

Early in the present century, G. Stanley Hall, founder of the American Psychological Association and father of the scientific study of adolescence, introduced his rather romantic notions of adolescence as a period of great "storm and stress" as well as great physical, mental, and emotional potential. A number of prominent clinicians and psychoanalytic theorists still view adolescence as a psychologically disturbed state (Freud, 1969; Josselyn, 1968; Offer, Ostrov, & Howard, 1981). However, empirical investigations of typical adolescents indicate that the extent of adolescent—and parental—turmoil during this period has been considerably exaggerated (Conger, 1977a; Offer, 1975).

Nevertheless, adolescence is a challenging and sometimes difficult stage of life. Why should this be so? The first and most obvious answer is that adolescence, and particularly early adolescence, is above all a period of change —physical, sexual, psychological, and cognitive changes as well as changes in social demands. It seems almost unfair that so many socialization demands— for independence, changing relationships with peers and adults, sexual adjustment, educational and vocational preparation—are made at the same time that individuals are experiencing an almost unprecedented rate of biological maturation. Besides coping with all these developmental changes, adolescents are struggling to achieve an identity of their own—a personal answer to the age-old question "Who am I?"

In this chapter we will examine in some detail the maturational changes of adolescence and their effects on psychological development. We will also explore the basic socialization tasks confronting adolescents and the forces that tend to make these tasks easier or harder. The issues that have been studied

and the methods used to study them are somewhat different than those we have covered in earlier chapters. Questions about the interaction of physical maturation and experience are often investigated for adolescents, but the active or passive nature of the individual is usually not an issue. The methods used are more often self-reports and surveys and less often experiments than in research with younger children, partly because adolescents are presumed to have more capability to respond to questionnaires and interviews.

GROWING UP: PHYSICAL DEVELOPMENT IN ADOLESCENCE

The period we call adolescence may be brief, as in some simpler societies, or relatively prolonged, as in the case of our own technologically advanced society. Its onset may involve abrupt changes in social demands and expectations or only a gradual transition from previous roles. Despite such variations, one aspect of adolescence is universal and separates it from earlier stages of development: the physical and physiological changes of puberty that mark its beginning.

The onset of puberty

The term *puberty* refers to the first phase of adolescence, when sexual maturation becomes evident. Strictly speaking, puberty begins with hormonal increases and their manifestations, such as gradual enlargement of the ovaries in females and testicular cell growth in males. But because these changes are not outwardly observable, the onset of puberty is often measured by such events as the emergence of pubic hair, beginning elevation of the breasts in girls, and increased size of the penis and testes in boys. Sexual maturation is accompanied by a "growth spurt" in height and weight, which usually lasts about 4 years.

Hormonal factors in development   Of critical importance in the orderly regulation of pubertal growth is the *pituitary gland,* located at the base of the brain, to which it is connected by nerve fibers. When the cells of the *hypothalamus,* a central regulating nerve center in the brain, "mature," which happens at different ages in different individuals, signals are sent to the pituitary gland to begin releasing previously inhibited hormones (Grumbach, 1978). Activating hormones released by the pituitary have a stimulating effect on most other endocrine glands, including the thyroid and adrenal glands and the testes and ovaries, which activate their own growth-related and sex-related hormones. The latter include androgens (masculinizing hormones), estrogens (feminizing hormones), and progestins (pregnancy hormones). These and other hormones interact in complex ways to stimulate an orderly progression of physical and physiological development.

Hormonal dimorphism   In the early days of sex-hormone research, when sex differences were conceived of as dichotomous and absolute, it was assumed that females produce only female sex hormones and males only male sex hormones; indeed, the sex hormones were named accordingly. Actually, however, there is overlap, and the hormones of both sexes are present in both men and women (Gupta, Attanasio, & Raaf, 1975; Marshall, 1978). The hormonal difference between the sexes is not a matter of either-or but of the proportions of masculinizing and feminizing hormones. As may be seen in Figure 13.1, as puberty proceeds, the ratio of estrogen levels to testosterone levels increases in females and decreases in males.

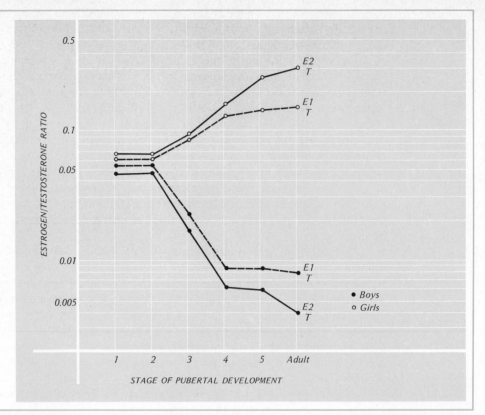

FIGURE 13.1

Mean trends in estrogen/testosterone ratios during pubertal development for girls and boys. Two measures of estrogen level are shown, estrone (E1) and the more potent estradiol (E2). (From D. Gupta, A. Attanasio, & S. Raaf. Plasma estrogen and androgen concentrations in children during adolescence. **Journal of Clinical Endocrinology and Metabolism,** 1975, 40, 636–643. By permission.)

Adolescent growth spurt The term *growth spurt* refers to the accelerated rate of increase in height and weight that occurs with puberty. This increase varies widely in intensity, duration, and age of onset from one child to another, even among perfectly normal children—a fact often poorly understood by adolescents and their parents and consequently a source of needless concern.

In both sexes, the adolescent growth spurt lasts about 4½ years (Faust, 1977; Marshall, 1978). For the average male, peak growth occurs at age 13; in females it is about 2 years earlier, at age 11. In the average boy, the growth spurt begins a few months before his eleventh birthday, though it may begin as early as age 9; similarly, the growth spurt is usually completed shortly after age 15, but may continue until age 17. In girls, the growth spurt usually begins and ends about 2 years earlier. Further slow growth may continue for several years after the growth spurt is completed (Falkner & Tanner, 1978). Because the onset of the growth spurt is so variable, some young people will complete the pubertal growth period in height and weight before others have begun (see Figure 13.2); clearly, *normal* does not mean "average."

Many discouraged parents, with a wary eye on the ever-rising cost of food, have the feeling that rapidly growing adolescents, particularly boys, are "eating us out of house and home." Indeed, the nutritional needs of young people increase considerably during the years of rapid growth, although there

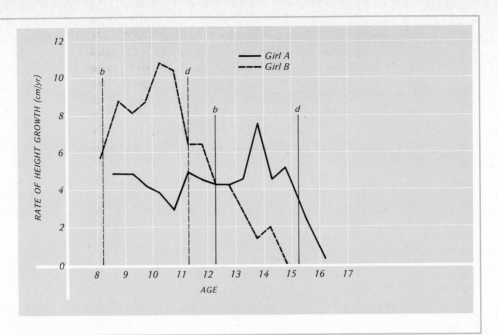

FIGURE 13.2

Differences in timing of the pubertal growth period in height. The early developing girl (A) reached the end (d) of the pubertal period before the late developing girl (B) reached onset (b). Stars indicate onset of menarche. (From M. S. Faust. Somatic development of adolescent girls. Monographs of the Society for Research in Child Development, 1977, 42 [1, Serial No. 169]. © The Society for Research in Child Development, Inc. By permission.)

TABLE 13.1

Recommended daily dietary allowances

	Age	Weight (pounds)	Height (inches)	Calories
Boys	11–14	97	63	2800
	15–18	134	69	3000
	19–22	147	69	3000
Girls	11–14	97	62	2400
	15–18	119	65	2100
	19–22	128	65	2000

Source: National Academy of Sciences, National Research Council. Recommended dietary allowances, revised, 1974. Washington, D.C.: National Academy of Sciences, National Research Council, 1974.

are wide individual variations, depending on such factors as body size and activity level. As can be seen in Table 13.1, on the average, boys need more calories at every age than girls. However, a large, very active girl obviously will have greater nutritional need than a small, inactive boy. Similarly, late maturers need fewer calories than early maturers of the same age.

The shape of things to come   Changes in height and weight are accompanied by changes in body proportions in both boys and girls. The head, hands, and feet reach adult size first. The arms and legs grow faster than the trunk, which is completed last. As the English pediatrician James Tanner says, "A boy stops growing out of his trousers (at least in length) a year before he stops growing out of his jackets" (Tanner, 1971, p. 94). These differences in the rate of growth in different parts of the body largely account for the temporary feelings of awkwardness that some adolescents feel, especially those who are growing fastest. For brief periods, some young people may feel that their hands and feet are too big or that they are "all legs." Of course, thoughtless comments by adults may also produce or intensify feelings of awkwardness.

Sex differences in body shape also are magnified during early adolescence. Although even in childhood girls have wider hips than boys, the difference becomes pronounced with the onset of puberty. Conversely, males develop thicker as well as larger bones, more muscle tissue, and broader shoulders (see Figure 13.3). Partly as a result, males become, and remain, stronger than females (particularly in the upper body) as adolescence proceeds. Other reasons for males' physical strength relative to their size are that they develop larger hearts and lungs, a higher systolic blood pressure, a greater capacity for carrying oxygen in the blood, and a lower heart rate while resting. They are also more resistant chemically to fatigue from exercise (Forbes, 1978; Tanner, 1970).

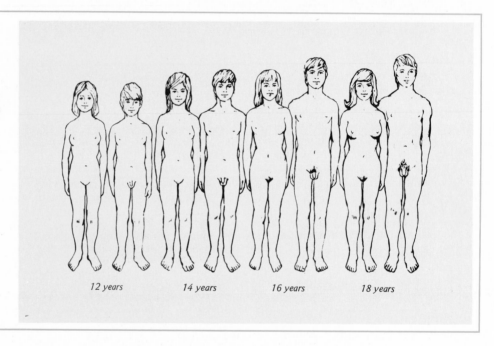

FIGURE 13.3

Body growth and development from ages 12 years to 18 years. (From P. H. Mussen, J. J. Conger, & J. Kagan, Essentials of Child Development and Personality. *New York: Harper & Row, 1980.)*

12 years   14 years   16 years   18 years

SEXUAL MATURATION

As in the case of the growth spurt in height and weight, there are marked individual differences in the age at which sexual maturation begins. While there is some variation within developmental sequences—for example, breast development in girls may appear before or after the development of pubic hair—physical development during puberty and adolescence generally follows a rather orderly progression (Faust, 1977, in press; Tanner, 1970). Thus, a male who has an early growth spurt is more likely to develop pubic hair and other attributes of sexual maturation early; the female who shows early breast development is likely to have early menarche (onset of menstruation). Preadolescents with advanced skeletal (bone) development will probably have an early growth spurt and early sexual maturation (Roche, 1978; Tanner, 1970).

BOX 13.1
Sex differences and sports[1]

In the past decade, there has been an explosion in women's competitive sports. Although almost everyone is aware of the accomplishments of a small band of female superstars in such activities as gymnastics, figure skating, swimming, tennis, and golf (in 1976, Nadia Comaneci was the first Olympic gymnast of either sex to win a perfect 10), many still do not realize how widespread has been the recent growth of women's athletics. Since 1970, for example, the number of female tennis players has risen from 3 million to 11 million. In 1980, more than 1 million girls under the age of 19 were playing soccer, compared to almost none in 1970. Currently, 33 percent of all high school athletes are female—a 600 percent increase in less than 10 years.

What are the implications of adolescent sex differences in physical development for this revolution in women's athletics? Clearly, in some sports men have a physical advantage. On the average, they are 10 percent bigger than women. Because they have broader and stronger shoulders, as well as larger arms with more (hormonally induced) muscle fiber, they have an obvious advantage in sports involving throwing and hitting. And because their legs are generally larger and stronger, and their hips narrower, they are able to run faster.

On the other hand, women often have an advantage where endurance is a factor. Because sustained activity begins to convert body fat to energy, and because women's bodies have a higher percentage of body fat (25 percent of body weight, as compared to about 14 percent for men), women have a relatively greater reserve to draw on. Women also appear able to tolerate heat better than men because of a more efficient system for bringing blood to the body surface for cooling; although the male sweats sooner, the female sweats better. Ever since Gertrude Ederle set a new record for swimming the English Channel, women have dominated the sport of long-distance swimming. In addition to serving as an energy reserve, their body fat provides better buoyancy and insulation against the cold. And their narrower shoulders cut more easily through the water. Similarly, in marathon running, slight-shouldered, strong-legged women have less upper-body weight to carry around. In many sports, of course, skill counts more than other factors. This is clearly true of equestrian sports, diving, figure skating, ballet, and most gymnastics.

Such comparisons as these are interesting physically and physiologically; in a larger sense, however, they are irrelevant. The challenge in all competitive sports, as in many other activities, is to achieve as nearly perfect, coordinated use of one's resources of body and mind as possible. Whether a male basketball player is stronger or a female gymnast more graceful is basically beside the point. As Dr. Dorothy Harris, director of the Center for Women in Sports at Pennsylvania State University, says, "Sports are not for men or women; they are for people."

[1] Adapted from P. S. Wood. Sex differences in sports. *New York Times Magazine*, May 18, 1980, pp. 31 ff. © 1982 by The New York Times Company. By permission.

Sexual development in males   Although testicular cell growth and beginning secretion of male sex hormone begin earlier—typically about age 11½—the first outward sign of impending sexual maturity in males is usually an increase in the growth of the testes and scrotum (the baglike structure enclosing the testes), beginning at about age 12½. There may also be some growth of pubic hair. Approximately a year later, an acceleration in growth of the penis accompanies the beginning of the growth spurt in height. Axillary (body) and facial hair usually make their first appearance about 2 years after the beginning of pubic hair growth, although in a few children axillary hair appears first (Marshall & Tanner, 1970).

A definite lowering of the voice usually occurs fairly late in puberty. In some young men this voice change is rather abrupt and dramatic, while in others it is so gradual that it is hardly perceptible. During this process, the larynx (Adam's apple) enlarges significantly and the vocal cords (which it contains) approximately double in length, with a consequent drop in pitch of about an octave.

During adolescence the male breast also undergoes changes. The diameter of the areola (the area surrounding the nipple) increases considerably (although not as much as in girls) and is accompanied by an elevation of the nipple. In some males (perhaps 20 to 30 percent), there may be a distinct enlargement of the breast about midway through adolescence. Usually, this disappears within a year or so (Bell, 1980). Prepubescent boys may also show a tendency to adiposity of the lower torso, which, again, may suggest feminine body contours to the apprehensive adolescent or adult. Although these bodily configurations typically disappear with time, they may represent a source of needless anxiety for both the adolescent and his parents because of their preoccupation with "masculinity" (Conger & Petersen, 1984). There is no evidence that either of these conditions (in the absence of specific pathology) is related to any deficiency in sexual functioning.

Sexual development in females   The appearance of unpigmented, downy pubic hair is usually the first outward sign of sexual maturity in girls, although the so-called bud stage of breast development may sometimes precede it (Faust, 1977). Budding of the breast is accompanied by the emergence of downy, unpigmented axillary hair and increases in estrogen (female sex hormone) secretion. In the following year, the uterus and vagina show accelerated growth; the labia and clitoris also enlarge. Menarche occurs relatively late in the developmental sequence (about age 12½) and almost always after the growth spurt has begun to slow down (Faust, 1977; Tanner, 1970).

There is frequently a period of a year or more following the beginning of menstruation during which the adolescent female is not yet physiologically capable of conception. Similarly, males are able to have intercourse long before they produce live spermatozoa. Obviously, however, because of significant individual differences, younger adolescents should not assume that they are still "safe" from conceiving because of their age. Some young women are capable of conception within the first year after menarche, the period formerly thought to be safe (Zabin, Kantner, & Zelnik, 1979).

BOX 13.2
*Maturation in
boys and in girls*

Although there may be some individual—and perfectly normal—variations in the sequence of events leading to physical and sexual maturity in boys, the following sequence is typical:

1. Testes and scrotum begin to increase in size.
2. Pubic hair begins to appear.
3. Adolescent growth spurt starts; the penis begins to enlarge.
4. Voice deepens as the larynx grows.
5. Hair begins to appear under the arms and on the upper lip.
6. Sperm production increases, and nocturnal emission (ejaculation of semen during sleep) may occur.
7. Growth spurt reaches peak rate; pubic hair becomes pigmented.
8. Prostate gland enlarges.
9. Sperm production becomes sufficient for fertility; growth rate decreases.
10. Physical strength reaches a peak.

Although, as in the case of boys, there may be normal variations in the sequence of physical and sexual maturation in girls, a typical sequence of events is as follows:

1. Adolescent growth spurt begins.
2. Downy (nonpigmented) pubic hair makes its initial appearance.
3. Elevation of the breast (the so-called bud stage of development) and rounding of the hips begin, accompanied by the beginning of downy axillary (armpit) hair.
4. The uterus and vagina, as well as labia and clitoris, increase in size.
5. Pubic hair grows rapidly and becomes slightly pigmented.
6. Breasts develop further; nipple pigmentation begins; areola increases in size; axillary hair becomes slightly pigmented.
7. Growth spurt reaches peak rate and then declines.
8. Menarche (onset of menstruation) occurs.
9. Pubic hair development is completed, followed by mature breast development and completion of axillary hair development.
10. Period of "adolescent sterility" ends, and girl becomes capable of conception (up to a year or so after menarche).

Normal variations in development Even in today's somewhat more tolerant climate, deviance from group norms in rate of development and physical appearance can still be agonizing for many adolescents and can impair self-esteem (Clausen, 1975; Simmons & Rosenberg, 1975; Tobin-Richards, Boxer, & Petersen, in press). It should therefore be emphasized that the average developmental sequences discussed here are just that—average. Among perfectly normal adolescents there are wide variations in the age of onset of the developmental sequence (and sometimes in the order of events in the sequence). For example, while maturation of the penis may be complete in some boys by 13½, for others it may not be complete until as late as 17 or even older. The bud stage of breast development may occur as early as age 8 in some girls, as late as 13 in others. Age at menarche may vary from about 9 to 16½. The marked differences that occur among normal adolescents in their rates of development are dramatically illustrated in Figure 13.4, which shows the differing degrees of pubertal maturity among three normal males, all aged 14¾ years, and three normal females, all aged 12¾ years.

Psychological aspects of maturation

Many adults forget the more anxiety-laden memories concerning the physical changes of adolescence; even college students are better at remembering events from earlier years than those surrounding the onset of puberty (Conger & Petersen, 1984). Consequently, adults are likely to have only a vague understanding of how acutely aware the average adolescent is of the entire growth process (Bell, 1980). Such awareness, however, is hardly surprising. A clear sense of one's identity as a person requires, among other things, a feeling of consistency and stability of the self over time (see Chapter 14). This is not an easy feeling for adolescents to maintain, faced as they are with the many rapid internal changes of puberty. Unlike younger children, whose physical growth is gradual and orderly, rapidly changing adolescents are likely at times to feel strangers to themselves. Time is needed to integrate these dramatic changes successfully into a newly emerging sense of a stable, self-confident personal identity.

Developmental change and the need to adjust to it cause adolescents to focus concern on physical aspects of the self. However, adolescents' perceptions of their own body ("body image") are not always objective. Prior experience may lead young people to view themselves as attractive or unattractive, loved or unloved, strong or weak, masculine or feminine, regardless of their actual physical appearance and capabilities. Thus, a young man with low self-esteem who is of average overall size and strength may view himself as smaller and weaker than he is. A young woman judged very attractive by peers may view herself as unattractive because she looks like a parent or other relative whom she resents or whom others have denigrated.

Menstruation is much more to the adolescent female than a physiological readjustment. It is a symbol of sexual maturity—of a girl's future status as a woman (Greif & Ulman, 1982; Ruble & Brooks-Gunn, 1982). Because a girl's reaction to menstruation may generalize so broadly, it is vital that her initial experiences be as favorable as possible. Increasing numbers of contemporary girls view the onset of menstruation calmly and look forward to "becoming a woman." In the words of one older adolescent, "It seemed that all my friends

FIGURE 13.4

*Different degrees of
pubertal development
at the same chrono-
logical age. Upper
row: three boys, all
aged 14¾ years. Lower
row: three girls, all
aged 12¾ years. (From
J. M. Tanner. Growth
and endocrinology of
the adolescent. In
J. L. Gardner [Ed.],
Endocrine and ge-
netic diseases of
childhood. Phila-
delphia: Saunders,
1969. By permission.)*

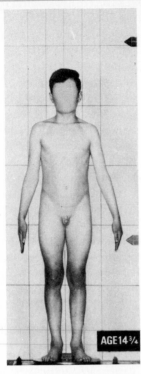
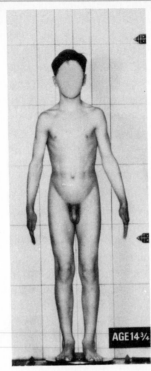
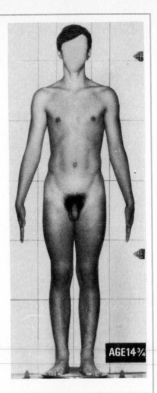

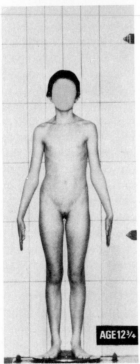
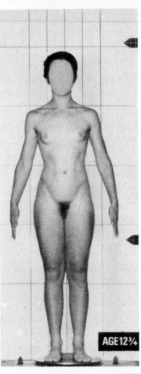
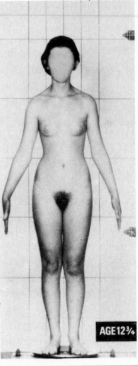

had gotten their period already, or were just having it. I felt left out. I began to think of it as a symbol. When I got my period, I would be a *woman.*" Unfortunately, many other girls view this normal—and inevitable—development negatively. In several studies (Brooks-Gunn & Ruble, 1982, in press; Greif & Ulman, 1982), a majority of preadolescent and adolescent American girls saw the effects of menstruation as negative or at best neutral; most felt that menstruation "is something women just have to put up with." Its most positive aspect was as a sign of maturity; its most negative aspect was "the hassle" of needing to be prepared for its occurrence (Ruble & Brooks-Gunn, 1982).

Why do so many adolescent girls seem to react negatively to the onset of menstruation? One frequent reason is the negative attitudes of others. If a girl's parents and friends act as though she requires sympathy for her "plight" —an attitude indicated by such euphemisms as "the curse"—she herself is likely to react in a similar fashion. Negative initial reactions to menstruation may also stem from physical discomfort, including headaches, backaches, cramps, and abdominal pain. In a recent national health survey, a majority of American adolescent females (aged 12 to 17 years) reported experiences of at least mild pain before or during menses. However, only 14 percent of those with cramps or other pain described it as severe, and relief is now available from several drugs (including aspirin) that inhibit the primary biochemical substance that produces pain (Klein & Litt, in press). Regular exercise, a proper diet (including avoidance of excessive salt, sugar, and caffeine), and sufficient rest can also be helpful.

A number of investigators have reported that postmenarcheal women are somewhat more likely to be irritable and to have negative feelings during the premenstrual and menstrual phases of the menstrual cycle than during other phases (Bell, 1980). As with the physical side effects of menstruation, there is considerable variation from one person to another. In the words of one 16-year old, "My period is no problem and it never really was" (Bell, 1980, p. 35). Others report mood swings, irritability, and a depressed feeling prior to the onset of menstruation. Such fluctuations may be related to changing levels during the menstrual cycle of various female hormones, such as estrogen and progesterone (Bell, 1980; Greif & Ulman, 1982). However, they can also be strongly influenced by psychological beliefs and expectations (Brooks-Gunn & Ruble, in press; Greif & Ulman, 1982). In one study, both premenarcheal and postmenarcheal girls expected others to experience more premenstrual tension and other symptoms than they themselves experienced or expected to experience (Brooks-Gunn & Ruble, 1982). In any event, mood changes associated with the menstrual cycle remain within the normal range of human feelings and reactions. The "raging hormone" myth occasionally used to support arguments against females' assuming stressful jobs presents an inaccurate picture of women's ability to deal effectively with the demands of life throughout the menstrual cycle (Ruble & Brooks-Gunn, 1982; Petersen, in press).

Many negative reactions to menstruation can be avoided or alleviated if parents employ a wise and understanding approach (Bell, 1980). By preparing the child for the onset of menarche ahead of time, seeking medical care for significant physical or psychological side effects, explaining the naturalness of the phenomenon, and showing pride and pleasure in her greater maturity, parents—particularly the mother but also the father—can help to make the onset of menstruation a welcome rather than a feared or hated event. Wardell Pomeroy, a clinical psychologist and coauthor of the Kinsey reports, describes one father "who observed the occasion of his daughter's first menstruation by bringing her flowers and making a little ceremony of the fact that she had now become a young woman. That daughter could not help feeling proud and good about becoming an adolescent" (Pomeroy, 1969, p. 47).

Erection, ejaculation, and nocturnal emission As the onset of menstruation may cause concern to the female, uncontrolled erection and initial ejaculation may surprise and worry some young men. Although genital stimulation, as well as other forms of bodily stimulation, is pleasurable for children, erection and genital stimulation usually carry a greater sense of sexual urgency after puberty. During this period, the penis begins to tumesce very readily, either spontaneously or in response to a variety of stimuli: "provocative sights, sounds, smells, language, or whatever—the [younger] male adolescent inhabits a libidinized life-space where almost anything can take on a sexual meaning" (Stone & Church, 1973, p. 424). Although males may be proud of their capacity for erection as a symbol of emerging virility, they may also be worried or embarrassed by an apparent inability to control this response. They may become apprehensive about dancing or even having to stand up in a school classroom to give a report. They may wonder if other males show a similar apparent lack of control (Bell, 1980; Conger & Petersen, 1984).

The adolescent male's first ejaculation is likely to occur within a year of the onset of the growth spurt (around age 14, although it may occur as early as 11 or as late as 16). First ejaculation may occur as a result of masturbation or nocturnal emission (ejaculation of seminal fluid during sleep, often accompanied by erotic dreams). A boy who had previously masturbated, with accompanying pleasant sensations but without ejaculation, may wonder if the ejaculation of seminal fluid is harmful or an indication that something is physically wrong with him. Others, like this 15-year-old, have no such concern: "I think a first wet dream is a powerful moment. It marks becoming a man. I was really excited about it" (Bell, 1980, p. 15).

Contemporary adolescents are better informed and less likely to be concerned about menstruation and nocturnal emission than those of earlier generations. Nevertheless, many boys and girls, especially in the early years of adolescence, do not gain proper instruction from parents, schools, or peers, and torture themselves with unnecessary fears (Bell, 1980; Conger & Petersen, 1984).

Early versus late maturation in males As we have seen, young people vary widely in the age at which they reach puberty. In general, the psychological effects of early or late maturing appear to be greater among males than among females and are easier to understand. Adults and other adolescents tend to think of the 14- or 15-year-old who looks 17 or 18 as older than he actually is. They are likely to expect more mature behavior from him than they would from a physically less developed male of the same age (Steinberg & Hill, 1978). Because there is less of a height discrepancy between an early maturing boy and most girls his own age (because of the earlier growth spurt in females), he may become involved sooner and with more self-confidence in boy-girl relationships. Furthermore, a physically more developed male has an advantage in many activities, especially athletics. Although a boy who matures much faster than most of his peers may feel somewhat different, he is not likely to feel insecure about the difference. After all, with his more rugged physique, increased strength, and greater sexual maturity, he can assure himself that he is simply changing in the direction society expects and approves.

In contrast, the late-maturing male is more likely to be "treated as a child"—which may infuriate him, even though he may continue to behave immaturely. He is likely to have a harder time excelling in athletics and other activities and in establishing relationships with females. He may wonder when, "if ever," he will reach full physical and sexual maturity.

Not surprisingly, all of this results, on the average, in personality differences between early and late maturers. Extensive, long-term research studies at the University of California found that males who matured late tended to be less poised, more tense and talkative, and more self-conscious and affected in their manner. They were also likely to be more restless, "overeager," impulsive, bossy, and "attention-seeking." Though obviously there are exceptions, late maturers tended to be less popular with peers, and fewer of them were leaders. Early maturers, on the other hand, appeared more reserved, self-assured, and matter-of-fact, and were more likely to engage easily in socially appropriate behavior. They were also more likely to be able to laugh at themselves. Later studies have obtained similar results (Clausen, 1975; Jones, 1954; Mussen & Jones, 1957; Tobin-Richards et al., in press).

On psychological tests, late maturers were found to have more feelings of inadequacy, poorer self-concepts, and more feelings of being rejected or dominated by others. Somewhat paradoxically, they were more likely to combine persisting dependency needs with a seemingly rebellious search for independence and freedom from parental and social restraints (Mussen & Jones, 1957). In other words, late maturers appeared more likely to prolong the typical adolescent independence-dependence conflict than early maturers.

Such differences can easily persist into adulthood. When the subjects of this investigation were followed up at age 33, the average late maturer still emerged as less self-controlled, less responsible, less dominant in relations with others, and more likely to turn to others for support and help. They were also less likely to have jobs or positions in social organizations requiring leadership and supervision of others (Clausen, 1975; Jones, 1957).

Much can be done by parents, teachers, and others to minimize the anxiety and other negative psychological effects of late maturing. They can make a conscious effort to avoid treating a late maturer as younger than he actually is. They can help him to realize that his slower maturation is perfectly normal—that he will indeed "grow up" and be just as physically and sexually masculine as his peers. And they can help him to achieve success in activities where his physical size and strength are not a handicap. For example, while immaturity and smaller physical size can be a handicap for a football player, they may be assets for a diver or a tumbler.

Early versus late maturation in females   Among females, the effects of early or late maturation are generally less extensive and more variable. Although early maturers tend to be somewhat more relaxed, more self-confident, less anxious, and more secure—in short, better adjusted—the differences are not marked and appear to vary with time. For example, in the sixth grade, being more mature than the other girls is usually a disadvantage; at this age, the girls rated most highly in prestige-enhancing personality traits by their peers were those who had not yet reached puberty. By the eighth and ninth grades, however, the girls who had reached puberty were rated somewhat more highly on many positive traits, such as friendliness, leadership ability, enthusiasm, and sense of humor (Faust, 1960). However, there was not much evidence to show that early maturers were significantly better adjusted than late maturers (Clausen, 1975; Tobin-Richards et al., in press).

Why the differences should be greater among males than females is somewhat of a mystery. One reason may be that society favors maturity in adolescent males more clearly and less ambiguously than in females. In young men, early maturing means greater strength and physical prowess and, eventually, active sexual behavior. In young women, it may mean being taller than all the boys and having no one your own age to date.

CHAPTER 13 / Adolescence: physical change, mental growth, and socialization
475

Is sexual activity at an earlier age than peers good or bad? Society often gives females mixed messages on this matter, as do peers. Parents worry that the girl who is sexually attractive at an early age will attract the attention of older boys. If she dates boys who are considerably older, she may not develop strong relations with girls and boys her own age or develop as an individual in her own right. She may also come to feel that she is gaining attention merely as a sex object rather than for who she really is—a complete person. On the other hand, her attractiveness can lend prestige in her own peer group, which may make her social relationships more positive.

In the case of an early maturing female, parents and others should be careful to avoid pressing her into too early sexual relationships. They can help her to develop her own interests and maintain her friendships with peers her own age, assuring her that they will soon catch up.

Parents and others need to assure the late-maturing female of her ultimate physical and sexual maturity, just as in the case of males. If they can help her to realize that there is really no need to rush things along, that in fact gradual maturation can even be useful in allowing her to devote her energies to other important developmental tasks, many unnecessary concerns can be alleviated (Conger, 1979).

ADOLESCENT MENTAL GROWTH

The young person's cognitive abilities also continue to develop, both quantitatively and qualitatively, during the adolescent years. The gains are quantitative in the sense that adolescents are able to accomplish intellectual tasks more easily, more quickly, and more efficiently than at younger ages. They are qualitative in the sense that significant changes also occur in the underlying mental processes used to define and reason about problems (Flavell, 1977; Ford, 1982; Neimark, 1975).

The importance of the changes taking place in adolescence would be difficult to overestimate. In addition to developing *formal operational thinking* (although to varying degrees, as explained in Chapter 7), adolescents are more likely than younger children to be aware of the distinction between simply perceiving something and storing it in memory. They are also more likely to use sophisticated strategies as aids to memory (Flavell, 1977, 1982; Keating, 1980; Neimark, 1975). Their future time perspective is considerably greater than that of younger children, and they are more likely to have what John Flavell (1977) calls ''a sense of the game'': an awareness that much of life consists of anticipating, formulating, and developing strategies for dealing with problems, whether the problem is planning a household budget or estimating the motivations and probable behavior of other people (Flavell, 1977; Flavell & Ross, 1981; Ford, 1982).

Cognitive changes play a critical role in helping adolescents deal with increasingly complex educational and vocational demands. It would be virtually impossible to master such academic subjects as calculus or the use of metaphors in poetry without a high level of abstract thinking or the ability to think about statements that have no relation to real objects in the world.

Many other aspects of adolescent development also depend on the cognitive advances of this period. Changes in the nature of parent-child relationships, emerging personality characteristics, planning of future educational and vocational goals, mounting concerns with social, political, and personal values, even a developing sense of personal identity are all strongly influenced by cognitive changes (Conger, 1977a; Conger & Petersen, 1984).

Hypothetical thought

As we saw in Chapter 7, one of the most important characteristics of formal operational thought is the ability to entertain hypotheses or theoretical propositions that depart from immediately observable events. In contrast to the child, who is preoccupied with the here and now, the adolescent is able to grasp not only the immediate state of things but also the possible state they might or could assume. The implications of this change alone are vast. For example, the adolescent's new-found and frequently wearing talents for discovering a previously idealized parent's feet of clay—for questioning the parent's values, for comparing them with other, more understanding or less conservative parents, and for accusing them of hypocritical inconsistencies between professed values and behavior—all appear at least partly dependent on the adolescent's changes in cognitive ability. "The awareness of the discrepancy between the actual and the possible also helps to make the adolescent a rebel. [The adolescent] is always comparing the possible with the actual and discovering that the actual is frequently wanting" (Elkind, 1968, p. 152).

The relentless criticism by many adolescents of existing social, political, and religious systems and their preoccupation with the construction of (often elaborate or highly theoretical) alternative systems are similarly dependent on their emerging capacity for formal operational thought. A good deal of an adolescent's apparently passionate concern with the deficiencies of parents and the social order and with the creation of "viable alternatives" turns out to be more a matter of word than deed (Conger, 1977a). This is perhaps a reflection of the fact that this stage of cognitive development is still relatively new and not yet fully integrated into the adolescent's behavior.

At the same time, it is important to recognize the positive aspects of the adolescent's newly acquired ability to conceptualize and reason abstractly about hypothetical possibilities. While the younger adolescent may seem to adults to be playing a game of ideas, the exercise is, nevertheless, a vitally important and productive one:

> *Everything will be food for thought, for spoken thought, for passionate discussion, for endless discussions, for peremptory affirmation, and the adult, losing his footing a little in this tidal wave, will often fail to perceive that what he takes to be vain rehashing or sterile questioning of old worn-out problems corresponds in reality, for the youngster, to youthful explorations and true discoveries. (Osterrieth, 1969, p. 15)*

Cognitive aspects of personality development

A preoccupation with thought itself, and particularly with one's own thoughts about oneself, is characteristic of the stage of formal operations. The adolescent girl or boy is likely to become *introspective* and *analytical*. In addition, thought and behavior may appear *egocentric* (Elkind, 1968; Enright, Lapsley & Shukla, 1979). Because adolescents think about themselves a lot, they are likely to conclude that other people, too, are subjecting their thoughts and feelings, personality characteristics, behavior, and appearance to critical scrutiny. This idea may well increase the adolescent's already strong self-consciousness.

Self-consciousness is not always painful, of course. The younger adolescent male who stands before the mirror flexing his muscles and admiring his profile or the female who spends hours applying her makeup or trying some hairstyle or one outfit after another may be dreaming of the dramatic impression that he or she will make on a date or at a party that evening. It is perhaps one of the minor tragedies of adolescent life that when these young people actually meet, each is likely to be more preoccupied with himself or herself than with observing the other (Elkind, 1968).

Cognitive development also plays an important role in the emergence of a well-defined sense of identity:

> By getting away from the concrete, by reasoning, by "concentrating," by trying out hypotheses, he meets up with himself. Who is he, this person who thinks, who adopts an attitude, who speaks his opinion? What is he? What is it in him, what is this center where his ideas are shaped, where his thoughts are produced, where his assumptions are formulated? Is it not himself? (Osterrieth, 1969, pp. 15–16)

Intellectualization may be employed as a psychological defense by some adolescents to deal with troubling anxieties. Intellectualization involves casting into an abstract, impersonal, philosophical form issues that are actually of immediate personal concern. Thus, apparently impersonal, highly intellectual discussions of human sexuality, of the role of aggression in human affairs, of responsibility versus freedom, of the nature of friendship, and of the existence of God may reflect deep-seated personal and emotional concerns. While much of the motivation for the use of intellectualization may be to avoid anxiety, it nevertheless may provide the adolescent with important practice in abstract thought and in formulating and testing hypotheses. In general, intellectualization as a defense is most likely to be employed by bright, well-educated middle- and upper-class youth.

SOCIALIZATION DEMANDS OF ADOLESCENCE

To become truly adult and not just physically mature, adolescents must gradually achieve independence from parents, adjust to sexual maturation, and establish cooperative and workable relationships with peers. In the process of meeting these challenges, the young person must also gradually develop a philosophy of life and a sense of identity. Before adolescents can successfully abandon the security of childhood dependence on others, they must have some idea of who they are, where they are going, and what the possibilities are of getting there (Conger & Petersen, 1984; Erikson, 1968). The fact that in today's changing world these tasks may be more complex and that both parent and child have fewer consistent blueprints to serve as guides in their accomplishment does not fundamentally alter the situation.

Unfortunately, a significant minority of today's young people do not successfully master these developmental tasks or do so only with considerable difficulty. Too many adolescents become delinquent, and the rate of adolescent suicide has increased threefold in the past 25 years. Alcohol and drug use,

school problems, running away, and feelings of alienation and lack of direction
are all too common.

The development of independence is a central task of adolescence, especially in American society, with its strong emphasis on self-reliance. Failure to
resolve the conflict between a continuing dependence and the newer demands
(and privileges) of independence will lead to difficulties in most other areas as
well. Without a reasonable degree of autonomy and separation from parents,
an adolescent can hardly be expected to achieve mature sexual or peer relationships, vocational direction, or a sense of identity, all of which require an image
of oneself as a unique, consistent, and reasonably well integrated person.

Establishing true independence from parents is seldom a simple matter.
Motivations and rewards for independence *and* for continued dependence on
the family are both likely to be strong, leading to conflict and vacillating
behavior. However, the degree of difficulty that an adolescent will encounter
in establishing independence depends in large measure on three things:
(a) general social attitudes toward independence in the adolescent's culture,
(b) the child-rearing practices and models of behavior provided by the adolescent's parents, and (c) interactions with peers and their support of independent
behavior. There are wide variations in patterns of independence training, both
from one culture to another and from one set of parents to another.

In a number of preliterate societies, and even in some culturally isolated
areas of more technologically advanced societies, the task of establishing independence may be less difficult than it is in our own complex, socially fragmented and rapidly changing culture. Among the Mixtecan Indians of Mexico,

for example, socialization is a gradual and informal process (Minturn & Lambert, 1964). Around the sixth or seventh year, the girl begins caring for younger siblings, going to market, helping to serve food and wash the dishes, and perhaps caring for small domestic animals. At about the same age, boys begin gathering produce or fodder in the fields and caring for large animals such as goats or burros.

In such informal ways and largely through example, Mixtecan children gradually learn to take increasing responsibility and to perform the tasks they will assume as adults. There is little anxiety about learning these basic tasks on the part of either parents or children. Parents assume that their children will learn them, and there is no demand or expectation for achievement beyond this. Aggressive competition would be considered unseemly, and nurturance plays a strong role among these people.

At the other end of the continuum, the Mundugumor adolescent of the South Pacific finds the problem of orderly transition from dependence on the parents to the setting up of an independent household infinitely more difficult than Mixtecan or American youth (Mead, 1939). Fathers and sons view each other almost as natural enemies, as do mothers and daughters. Fathers band together with daughters and mothers band together with sons. Consequently, the Mundugumor boy approaches adolescence close psychologically only to his mother, hostile toward his father, and distrustful of girls his own age. The girl, on the other hand, has strong ties to her father, resentment toward the mother, and distrust of her male contemporaries.

There seems little doubt that Mundugumor children, who grow up in a culture that contains much hostility and little tenderness, develop early a kind of hardiness that prepares them somewhat for the demands they must face in adolescence. But this advantage is virtually negated by the fact that the independence demanded of the Mundugumor adolescent is so much more extreme than in most cultures. The prospect of establishing independence is unpleasant and in many ways threatening. In fact, its only really attractive aspect seems to be escape from the hostility of the same-sex parent.

Parent-child relations and the development of independence
Parents play an important part in determining how well an adolescent will be able to meet the demand for increasing autonomy and become a competent, caring, self-reliant adult with a positive self-image. The need for loving and caring parents who are actively involved with their children's development has been well documented. As we shall see further in this and the following chapter, parental hostility, rejection, and neglect consistently occur more frequently than acceptance, love, and trust in the backgrounds of poorly adjusted adolescents with a wide range of problems (Bachman, 1970; Goldstein, Baker, & Jamison, 1980; Rutter, 1980).

Abusing parents Like the younger children described in Chapter 11, adolescents who have been the victims of physical or sexual abuse characteristically have difficulty trusting others and establishing stable emotional relationships, despite a very strong need for love (Helfer & Kempe, 1982; Mrazek & Kempe, 1981). When they do form a social or sexual relationship, they are likely to lapse into distrust at the slightest disappointment. Furthermore, while they may accept their parents' assertions of "bad behavior" at least consciously, they are

also likely to suffer strong underlying feelings of resentment and anger toward their parents—as much from their lack of care and understanding as from their abuse (Steele, 1980). Not surprisingly, a history of child abuse and neglect is common among adolescent runaways and delinquents.

Parental control As explained in Chapter 11, an important dimension of parental behavior is authority and control versus autonomy. Parental behavior patterns vary widely across this range (Baumrind, 1975; Conger, 1977a; Elder, 1980). They may be *autocratic* (parents simply tell their young what to do), *authoritarian* (the child or adolescent can participate but has no voice in decision making), *democratic* or *authoritative* (the young person contributes freely to the discussion of issues relevant to her behavior and may even make decisions, but ultimate authority is retained by parents), *equalitarian* (there is minimal role differentiation between parent and child), *permissive* (the balance in decision making tilts in the direction of the child or adolescent), and *laissez-faire* (the young person is free to subscribe to or disregard parental wishes). Moving from the autocratic to the laissez-faire structure involves a gradual increase in the participation of the adolescent in self-direction and a concurrent decrease in the participation of parents in making decisions concerning the adolescent (Elder, 1980).

A variety of studies here and in other countries have attempted to investigate the relationship between these parental practices and such aspects of adolescent personality and behavior as self-esteem, independence, competence, perceptions of parental attitudes, and sense of identity (Baumrind, 1975; Elder, 1980; Harris & Howard, 1979; Hoffman, 1975; Lewis, 1982). The evidence suggests that democratic or authoritative parents are most likely to have children who as adolescents are self-confident, high in self-esteem, and responsibly independent (Bachman, 1970; Bachman, O'Malley, & Johnston, 1978; Rosenberg, 1965). These adolescents are most likely to feel wanted, to feel that their parents give them enough freedom, and to consider their parents fair and reasonable in their "ideas, rules, or principles about how you should behave" (Elder, 1980, p. 150).

Authoritative parents   Democratic, authoritative parents value both autonomy *and* disciplined behavior. They encourage verbal give and take, and when they exercise parental authority in the form of demands or prohibitions, they explain their reasons for doing so (Baumrind, 1975; Elder, 1980; Hoffman, 1975; Jessor & Jessor, 1977). Such efforts to provide "legitimacy" for the exercise of parental authority are particularly important in the case of adolescents, who are nearing cognitive and social maturity and must soon assume responsibility for their own lives. Authority based on rational concern for the young person's welfare was generally accepted well, whereas "unreasonable," arbitrary authority based on the adult's desire to dominate (or exploit) the adolescent was rejected and led to feelings of anger and, in some cases, depression (Coleman, 1980; Conger, 1977a). Perhaps this description of her parents by a 16-year-old says it best:

> *I guess the thing I think is great about my parents, compared to those of a lot of kids, is that they really listen. And they realize that eventually I'm going to have to live my own life—what I'm going to do with it. A lot of the time when I explain what I want to do, they'll go along with it. Sometimes, they'll warn me of the consequences I'll have to face if I'm wrong, or just give me advice. And sometimes, they just plain tell me no. But when they do, they explain why, and that makes it easier to take. (Conger, 1979, p. 49)*

Autocratic and authoritarian parents   In contrast, authoritarian (or, in more extreme form, autocratic) parents do not feel an obligation to explain the reasons for their directives, and they view unquestioning obedience as a virtue. Some parents may take this stance out of a feeling of hostility or because they cannot be bothered with explanations and arguments. Others, however, do so because they think that this is the way to develop "respect for authority." A mistake they make is that while they may suppress dissent, they usually do not eliminate it; indeed, they are likely to encourage resentment. Adolescents with autocratic parents are less likely to be self-reliant and able to think and act for themselves, probably because they are not given sufficient opportunity to test out their own ideas or take independent responsibility and because their opinions have not been considered worthy of consideration (Elder, 1980; Lewis, 1982). They are also likely to be less self-confident, less independent, less creative, less intellectually curious, less mature in moral development, and less flexible in approaching intellectual, academic, and practical everyday problems. And they are more likely to view their parents as unaffectionate, rejecting, and unreasonable or wrong in their expectations and demands (Conger & Petersen, 1984; Elder, 1980).

Equalitarian, permissive, and laissez-faire parents Parents who are permissive, neglecting, or who assume a false and exaggerated equalitarianism also do not provide the kind of support that adolescents need. Some parents let adolescents "do their own thing," either because they are not involved or do not care (as in the case of neglecting parents). Others seem to have distorted notions of parental responsibility. Among middle-class adolescents, high-risk drug use and other forms of socially deviant behavior occur most frequently among those whose parents say they value individuality, self-understanding, readiness for change, maximizing one's human potential, and equalitarianism in the family, but who actually use these proclaimed values to avoid assuming parental responsibility. Such parents leave their children to drift without offering them dependable models of responsible adult behavior (Conger, 1977a, 1977b). Furthermore, no matter how much children and adolescents may protest at times, they do not really want their parents to be equals. They want and *need* them to be *parents*—friendly, understanding parents, but parents nonetheless, models of *adult* behavior.

In brief, it appears that democratic, authoritative practices, with frequent explanations by parents of their rules of conduct and expectations, foster responsible independence in several ways. First, they provide opportunities for increasing autonomy, guided by interested parents who communicate with the young person and exercise appropriate degrees of control. Second, they promote positive identification with the parents, based on love and respect for the child rather than rejection or indifference. Third, they show by example that autonomy is possible within the framework of a democratic order.

For those who are able to achieve this balance, the results can be rewarding to both parent and child. As an 18-year-old young Chicano woman said of her mother, "She's given me confidence in myself and sometimes she tries to make me understand her point of view. Then when she says something and it's right even though it hurts me, I kind of listen to her even though I pretend I'm not listening, I turn my face; and she makes me believe in myself, even when I'm down" (Konopka 1976, p. 65).

Or this from a 16-year-old male: "My dad's kind of special, I guess. Like, he takes me camping, and he sits down and talks to me about trouble at school. He wants to know what I'm doing, where I'm going. He helps me to learn things, and I admire him for being smart and strong and able to handle problems."

Adolescent sexual behavior

The physical and psychological changes associated with sexual development inevitably require many adjustments on the part of the young person and contribute to a changing self-image. As one 16-year-old expressed it, "When I was 14, my body started to go crazy" (Bell, 1980, p. 73).

Although sexuality in the broadest sense is a lifelong part of being human (even babies love to be held and may fondle their genitals), the hormonal changes accompanying puberty lead to stronger sexual feelings. These feelings are manifested differently in different individuals and in the same person at different times. Some adolescents find themselves thinking more about sex and getting sexually aroused more easily; others are less aware of sexual feelings and more excited by other interests. At the same age, one adolescent may be in

love and going steady, another may be involved in sexual experimentation, and a third may feel that it is much too early for such activities (Conger & Petersen, 1984).

Sex differences   For most boys, the rapid increase in sexual drive that accompanies puberty is difficult to deny and tends to be genitally oriented (Conger, 1980; Miller & Simon, 1980). Self-perceived sex drive in males reaches a peak during adolescence, as does the frequency of total sexual outlet (primarily through masturbation except for the minority of adolescents who are married or living together) (Chillman, 1978).

Among adolescent females, there appears to be a much wider range of individual differences. Some experience sexual desire in much the same way as the average male. But for the majority, sexual feelings are more diffuse and more closely related to the fulfillment of other needs, such as self-esteem, reassurance, affection, and love (Bell, 1980). There is a significant increase in sexual interests and behavior among both sexes during adolescence. Although sexual activity in general—and masturbation in particular—is greater among males than females, the size of the differences has narrowed in recent years (Chillman, 1978; Conger, 1980). In studies of sexual morality, young women typically display more conservative attitudes than young men. For example, among American first-year college students in 1980, two-thirds of the males but only one-third of the females agreed with the statement, "Sex is okay if people like each other" (Astin, 1981). On the other hand, when there is deep involvement, as in living together prior to marriage, differences are much smaller. Only 32 percent of American adolescent females and 21 percent of males said they would not be willing to have intercourse in such circumstances (Norman & Harris, 1981).

In contrast to their Victorian forebears, a majority of today's adolescent females believe that women enjoy sex as much as men, and only 1 in 10 believes that women have less innate capacity for sexual pleasure than men (Conger, 1977a, 1980). This contemporary view is clearly supported by research. The female's basic "physiological capacity for sexual response . . . surpasses that of man" (Masters & Johnson, 1970, pp. 219–220); in addition, sexual behavior (for example, frequency of orgasm) may vary over much wider ranges among females than among males, and even for a particular female at different times (Chillman, 1978; Conger, 1980).

A more complex question involves the conditions under which arousal of a sexual response is likely to occur. In his original studies, Alfred Kinsey (Kinsey, Pomeroy, & Martin, 1948, 1953) argued that men are more easily aroused than women by a wider variety of "psychosexual stimuli," such as nudity, provocative behavior, and erotic books and films. However, the actual situation appears more complicated. In some situations, groups of younger, more liberal, and sexually more experienced females report greater "sexual excitement" in response to a variety of sexual stimuli than older, more conservative, more inhibited, and less experienced males (Wilson, 1971). Furthermore, several studies have found that although males more frequently report subjective feelings of arousal, direct measurements of physiological sexual response do not show substantial differences (Schmidt & Sigusch, 1973). Perhaps conflicts about feelings of arousal still occur more frequently among women, or perhaps physiological sexual arousal—at least below a certain level—is more difficult for women to identify, whereas in men it can hardly fail to be noticed.

In addition, sexuality may be more intimately bound up with other aspects of personality in the case of females. Psychosexual stimulation that cannot be related to the self as a total person because it is perceived as threatening, because it conflicts with existing values, because it is impersonal, or because it is aesthetically offensive may be more likely to "turn off" the average adolescent female than her male peer (Chillman, 1978; Conger & Petersen, 1984). Fantasies of both male and female college students during sexual arousal were most likely to concern petting or intercourse with "someone you love or are fond of" (Miller & Simon, 1980). However, fantasies of sexual activity with strangers for whom they had no particular emotional attachment were almost as frequent for males (79 percent), but not for females (22 percent). Indeed, "doing nonsexual things with someone you are fond of or in love with" was second in frequency for females (74 percent), but not for males (48 percent). For females, "the investment of erotic meaning in both explicitly sexual and nonsexual symbols appears to be contingent on the emotional context. The two genders evaluate the meaning of potentially erotic symbols using distinctive sets of criteria. For males, the explicitly sexual is endowed with erotic meaning regardless of the emotional context. For females, the emotional context is endowed with erotic meaning without regard for the presence or absence of explicitly sexual symbols" (Miller & Simon, 1980, p. 403).

Finally, it may also be that the greater sexual aggressiveness generally manifested by adolescent males is related, at least in part, to vastly greater increases in testosterone levels among males at puberty. It has been demonstrated that this hormone increases sexual and aggressive behavior in both sexes under experimental conditions.

Regardless of the ultimate significance of these and other factors, it seems clear that the lesser sexual activity of female adolescents, and probably to some extent its qualitatively different nature, is *at least partially* attributable to our culture's more restrictive social attitudes toward sexual gratification for women. Although this situation has recently changed significantly in the direction of greater permissiveness, "this permissive message has been given in a limited context. Information about what it means to be sexual and how it is integrated with other aspects of life have been missing" (Petersen & Boxer, 1982). Furthermore, many females are still brought up to be less accepting and proud of their sexuality than males are. Though less rigid than in the past, vestiges of a double standard still remain.

Societal attitudes in other cultures have varied widely. In some societies, such as the Lepcha of India, early sexual activity among both genders was strongly encouraged in the belief that it fostered physical and sexual maturation; in some other cultures, such as the Cuna of the coast of Panama, efforts were made to keep adolescents ignorant of sexual matters until the last stages of the marriage ceremony.

Changing values   Sexual attitudes and values of adolescents in our own culture have been changing significantly for some years. A "new morality" has been developing in the United States and other Western countries. In comparison to earlier generations, today's adolescents show both a greater openness and honesty about sex and an increasing tendency to base decisions about appropriate sexual behavior on personal values and judgment rather than on conformity to institutionalized social codes (Chillman, 1978; Conger, 1980; Conger & Petersen, 1984). In 1980, for example, American high school seniors were asked their reactions to the idea of a man and woman living together without being married. About 1 in 5 said they were experimenting with "a worthwhile alternative lifestyle." Smaller minorities felt either that they were violating a basic principle of human morality or living in a way that was destructive to society. In contrast, nearly half expressed the view that they were "doing their own thing and not affecting anyone else" (Bachman, Johnston, & O'Malley, 1981, p. 190). Approximately three-fourths of contemporary adolescents believe that "it's all right for young people to have sex before getting married if they are in love with each other" (Conger & Petersen, 1984).

How are continuing changes in sexual attitudes and values among contemporary adolescents reflected in their behavior? The answer depends on *what* behaviors one is referring to, and among *which* adolescents. Available information indicates that among males, the number who have engaged in masturbation by age 19 has remained fairly stable since their parents' generation at around 85 to 90 percent (Chillman, 1978; Conger, 1980). But the number who masturbate at younger ages is increasing significantly—about 65 percent currently report masturbating by age 13, as compared with 45 percent in the 1940s. Among females, recent data indicate an increase in masturbation at all ages. By age 13, the incidence is about 33 percent (in contrast to 15 percent in their mother's generation); by age 20, it is about 60 percent (compared to about 30 percent for their mothers at age 20) (Conger, 1980; Haas, 1979). Masturbation is about three times as likely among those who have engaged in sexual intercourse or petting to orgasm as among the sexually inexperienced (Sorensen, 1973).

It seems that these changes in the incidence of masturbation are due largely to more tolerant social attitudes and a decline in myths about the harmful effects of masturbation. Masturbation itself is a normal developmental phenomenon and becomes a problem only when it serves as a substitute for social and other activities in which the young person feels inadequate. But in such instances, masturbation is not primarily a *cause* of the individual's problems but a *response* to them.

Petting does appear to have increased somewhat in the past few decades, and it tends to occur slightly earlier. The major change, however, has probably been in frequency of petting, degree of intimacy of techniques involved, the frequency with which petting leads to erotic arousal or orgasm, and, certainly, frankness about this activity (Chillman, 1978; Conger, 1980; Haas, 1979).

Sexual intercourse among adolescents   A current source of heated social, political, and personal controversy is the extent of premarital sexual intercourse among adolescents. In one well-controlled study, Melvin Zelnik and John Kantner, population experts at the Johns Hopkins University, identified significant increases during the 1970s in premarital intercourse by teenage females living in metropolitan areas (see Table 13.2). In 1979, 50 percent of all 15- to 19-year-old females reported having engaged in premarital intercourse, compared to 30 percent in 1971 and 43 percent in 1976. Not surprisingly, rates were highest for the relatively small number who were married. Premarital intercourse is most likely with future spouses; further, pregnancy often precedes marriage among teenage brides.

Among males aged 17 to 21 in 1979, these investigators found that 70 percent had engaged in premarital intercourse (see Table 13.3). Of these, 56 percent had had intercourse by age 17, and 77 percent by age 19 (Zelnik & Kantner, 1980). Comparable results have been obtained recently in another large, but somewhat less systematically controlled, national sample of adolescents aged 13 to 18 (Norman & Harris, 1981).

When the findings for females are compared with those of their mothers'

TABLE 13.2

Percentage of women aged 15–19 who ever had intercourse before marriage

By marital status and race, United States, 1979, 1976, and 1971

Marital status all age	1979			1976			1971		
	Total	White[a]	Black	Total	White	Black	Total	White	Black
ALL									
%	49.8	46.6	66.2	43.4	38.3	66.3	30.4	26.4	53.7
(N)	(1,717)	(1,034)	(683)	(1,452)	(881)	(571)	(2,739)	(1,758)	(981)
EVER MARRIED									
%	86.7	86.2	91.2	86.3	85.0	93.9	55.0	53.2	72.7
(N)	(146)	(106)	(40)	(154)	(121)	(33)	(227)	(174)	(53)
NEVER MARRIED[b]									
Total	46.0	42.3	64.8	39.2	33.6	64.3	27.6	23.2	52.4
15	22.5	18.3	41.4	18.6	13.8	38.9	14.4	11.3	31.2
16	37.8	35.4	50.4	28.9	23.7	55.1	20.9	17.0	44.4
17	48.5	44.1	73.3	42.9	36.1	71.0	26.1	20.2	58.9
18	56.9	52.6	76.3	51.4	46.0	76.2	39.7	35.6	60.2
19	69.0	64.9	88.5	59.5	53.6	83.9	46.4	40.7	78.3
AGE AT FIRST INTERCOURSE (ALL)									
Mean	16.2	16.4	15.5	16.1	16.3	15.6	16.4	16.6	15.9
(N)	(933)	(478)	(455)	(726)	(350)	(376)	(936)	(435)	(501)

[a] "White" includes the relatively small number of women of races other than black. Except where indicated, the base excludes those who did not respond to the question analyzed in the table. Absolute numbers shown in parentheses are unweighted sample N's.

[b] N is not shown for each single year of age in order to simplify the presentation; N ≥ 87 for each age-race cell among the never-married.

Source: M. Zelnik & J. F. Kantner. Sexual activity, contraceptive use, and pregnancy among metropolitan-area teenagers: 1971–1979. *Family Planning Perspectives*, 1980, *12*(5), 230–237. By permission.

TABLE 13.3

Percentage of men aged 17–21 who ever had intercourse before marriage

By marital status and race, 1979

Marital status and age	Total	White	Black
ALL			
%	70.3	69.6	74.6
(N)	(917)	(567)	(350)
EVER MARRIED			
%	82.7	83.3	72.8
(N)	(74)	(58)	(16)
NEVER MARRIED			
Total	88.9	67.8	74.7
17	55.7	54.5	60.3
18	66.0	83.6	79.8
19	77.5	77.1	79.9
20	81.2	80.7	85.7
21	71.2	68.0	89.4

Source: M. Zelnik & J. F. Kantner. Sexual activity, contraceptive use, and pregnancy among metropolitan-area teenagers: 1971–1979. *Family Planning Perspectives*, 1980, *12*(5), 230–237. By permission.

generation in Kinsey's investigation, they indicate very large increases, particularly at younger ages. Only 3 percent of the women Kinsey surveyed had engaged in premarital intercourse by age 16, and less than 20 percent by age 19 (Kinsey et al., 1953). Furthermore, they demonstrate dramatically that the so-called sexual revolution of the late 1960s has not only continued but expanded in scope. When compared with males of their father's generation, contemporary adolescent males as a whole show little change beyond a tendency to have first intercourse at a slightly younger age. Kinsey found that about 39 percent of males had engaged in premarital intercourse by age 16, 61 percent by age 17, and 72 percent by age 19 (Kinsey et al., 1948). However, as will become apparent, these *overall* findings obscure significant changes taking place among adolescents of higher socioeconomic and educational levels.

Diversity of sexual attitudes and behavior   When considering broad trends in sexual attitudes and behavior, it is important to keep in mind that there are wide variations among different sectors of the population. For example, younger adolescents are typically more *conservative* than older adolescents (Conger, 1980; Haas, 1979). Politically conservative and religiously oriented youth are more conservative in sexual attitudes and behavior than liberal or religiously inactive young people (Chillman, 1978; Zelnik & Kantner, 1980). Cultural differences also exist; for both sexes, premarital intercourse is less common in Canada and the United States than in England, West Germany, and the Scandinavian countries (Conger, 1980).

Economically privileged, more highly educated adolescents and youth are less conservative in their sexual attitudes and values than their less economically favored peers of the same age, although differences are currently decreasing (Chillman, 1978; Conger, 1980). Also, it is among college or college-bound adolescents and youth, especially females, that the greatest changes in sexual behavior have occurred since their parents' generation. In the 1940s, by the age of 21, the incidence of premarital experience among college-educated persons was 49 percent for males and 27 percent for females. In contrast, recent studies show that premarital intercourse among college males has increased to 82 percent; comparable percentages for females range up to a high of 76 percent (Conger, 1980; Conger & Petersen, 1984).

Many experienced young people, particularly older adolescents and youth, appear able to handle their sexual relationships without undue stress. Among American adolescents aged 13 to 19, two-thirds of all nonvirgins stated that sex made their lives more meaningful (Sorensen, 1973). However, other sexually active adolescents report feelings of conflict and guilt, find themselves exploited or rejected, or discover belatedly that they have gotten in over their heads emotionally (Conger, 1980). Especially after the first experience of intercourse, females are far more likely than males to have negative feelings. While males are most likely to report being excited, satisfied, and happy, females most frequently report being afraid, guilty, worried, or embarrassed (Sorensen, 1973).

There are obviously dangers—perhaps particularly for females, who generally have stronger affiliative needs—in assuming that sexual involvement is "okay as long as you're in love" (Chillman, 1978). Encouraged by such a philos-

Among youthful nonvirgins, the majority are involved at any one time with only one person, with whom they share strong affectionate bonds—although one such relationship is often succeeded by another. A small—and predominantly male—minority, however, fall into the category of what Robert Sorensen has labeled "sexual adventurers," who move freely from one sex partner to the next with no feeling of "obligation to be faithful to any sex partner" (Sorensen, 1973, p. 121).

Not surprisingly, these two groups of young people vary significantly in their attitudes as well as their behavior. Most monogamists believe they love and are loved by their partners, believe in openness and honesty between partners, and deny that sex is the most important thing in a love relationship—although they also express greater satisfaction than adventurers with their sex lives. At the same time, their code stresses personal freedom without commitment to marriage, although more than half believe they will or may marry their partner eventually.

Sexual adventurers, in contrast, are primarily interested in variety of experience for its own sake, do not believe that love is a necessary part of sexual relationships, and feel no particular personal responsibility for their partners, although neither do they believe in hurting others. For many adventurers, sex itself is viewed as an avenue to communication; as one young adventurer stated, "Having sex together is a good way for two people to become acquainted."

As a group, monogamists tended to be more satisfied with themselves and life in general, to get along better with parents, and to be more conventional in social, political, and religious beliefs. Despite their greater emphasis on sex as a goal in itself, female adventurers report having orgasm during intercourse less frequently than monogamists.

ophy among peers, adolescents may become more deeply involved emotionally than they can handle responsibly at a particular stage of maturity. Young people may also consciously think that their attitudes are more liberal than they actually are, with the result that involvements may lead to unanticipated feelings of guilt, anxiety, or depression.

Pregnancy and contraception   There also still remain very practical problems, such as the possibility of pregnancy. Despite significant progress during the preceding decade, in 1979 only 34 percent of sexually active young women aged 15 to 19 reported always using contraceptives (up from 17 percent in 1971 and 29 percent in 1976) (Kantner & Zelnik, 1972, Zelnik & Kantner, 1980). Less than half used any form of contraceptive in their first intercourse (see Figure 13.5). Compared to younger adolescents (age 15), older adolescents (age 19) are twice as likely to have used contraception in their most recent intercourse (Planned Parenthood, 1981).

FIGURE 13.5

Percentage of pre-maritally sexually active women aged 15 to 19 from metropolitan areas who always, sometimes, and never practiced contraception, and percentage who practiced at first intercourse, 1976 and 1979. (Adapted from M. Zelnik & J. F. Kantner. Sexual activity, contraceptive use, and pregnancy among metropolitan-area teenagers: 1971–1979. Family Planning Perspectives, 1980, 12 [5], 230–237. By permission.)

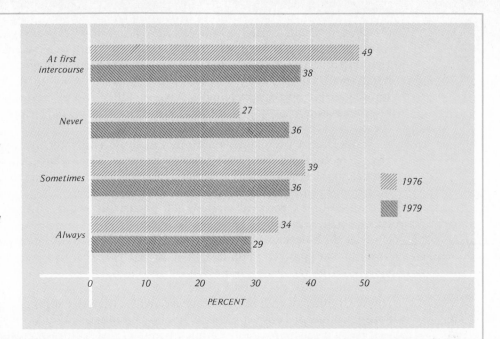

By 1975 over 1 million 15- to 19-year-old women in the United States alone (11 percent of this entire age group) were becoming pregnant each year, two-thirds of them out of wedlock. In 1979, over 16 percent of all women aged 15 to 19 in metropolitan areas of the United States had become pregnant at least once before marriage—up from 13 percent in 1976 and 8.5 percent in 1971. Among sexually active adolescent females, between 1976 and 1979, overall pregnancy rates increased from 30 percent in 1976 to 33 percent in 1979 (Zelnik & Kantner, 1980).

Adolescent pregnancies are more likely to endanger the physical health of both mother and child than adult pregnancies (see Figure 13.6), although the risks could be reduced by adequate prenatal and postnatal care and better nutrition (Petersen & Boxer, 1982).

In addition, teenage mothers (90 percent of whom currently keep their babies) generally face significant problems in other areas. They are twice as likely as their peers to drop out of school, less likely to gain employment, more likely to end up on welfare, less likely to marry, and more likely to be divorced if they do marry. Many are still psychologically in need of mothering themselves and are ill prepared to take on the psychological, social, and economic responsibilities of motherhood; consequently, they are at higher risk for child abuse (Conger & Petersen, 1984; Planned Parenthood, 1981).

Why do so many adolescent women fail to use contraceptive measures? In recent surveys, the major reasons given for not using contraceptives were that

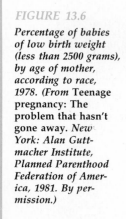

FIGURE 13.6

Percentage of babies of low birth weight (less than 2500 grams), by age of mother, according to race, 1978. (From Teenage pregnancy: The problem that hasn't gone away. *New York: Alan Guttmacher Institute, Planned Parenthood Federation of America, 1981. By permission.)*

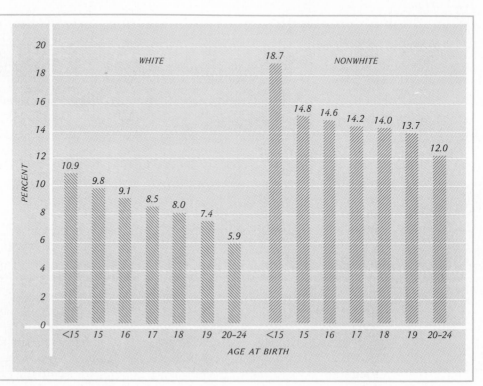

the teenagers thought (usually mistakenly) that they could not become pregnant because of time of month, age, or infrequency of intercourse. Another principal reason was that contraceptives were not available when they needed them. Clearly, better sex education and greater availability of comprehensive family planning services are needed (Planned Parenthood, 1981).

Psychological studies comparing sexually active adolescent females who do and do not use contraceptives have found that those who do not use them tend more often to hold fatalistic attitudes, to be passive and dependent, to take risks, and to deal with anxiety by denying possible dangers (Chillman, 1978). Males who are least likely to employ contraception tend to be either sexually naive or "exploitative," believing that contraception is the female's responsibility (Hornick, Doran, & Crawford, 1979). In contrast, consistent contraceptive use is more likely among adolescents who are older, who are involved in an ongoing relationship, who have high self-esteem and self-confidence, who are doing well in school, who accept their sexuality, and who take a planful and responsible approach to life generally (Chillman, 1978; Hornick et al., 1979; Zelnick & Kantner, 1980).

Contrary to certain popular opinions, only 1 in 15 pregnant adolescents stated that she did not use contraceptives because she was trying to have a baby, and only 1 in 11 said she wouldn't mind getting pregnant. However, among adolescents who are seeking or would not object to pregnancy, a common theme is that of emotional deprivation. In the words of one pregnant 15-year-old: "I guess for once in my life, I wanted to have something I could call my own, that I could love and that would love me." Other related motivations may include being accepted as an adult, getting back at one's parents, "holding" a boyfriend, gaining attention from peers, escaping from school, or just looking for some change in an unrewarding existence (Chillman, 1978).

It seems unlikely that the trend toward premarital intercourse as an accepted practice, and especially toward serial monogamy as the most frequent and the most socially approved pattern among sexually experienced adolescents, will be reversed. Serial monogamy is now practiced by adults of all ages more frequently than in earlier periods. Of all residuals of the youth culture of the 1960s, greater sexual freedom and openness appear to be the most enduring. What one must hope is that those adolescents who do enter sexual relationships can be helped to become mature enough, informed enough, responsible enough, sure enough of their own identities and value systems, and sensitive and concerned enough about the welfare of others so that the inevitable casualties in the sexual revolution can be reduced to a minimum and so that sex as a vital part of human relationships can promote growth toward maturity and emotional fulfillment.

Adolescents and their peers

Peers play a crucial role in the psychological and social development of most adolescents, especially in age-segregated, technologically advanced societies like our own, where entrance into the adult world of work and family responsibilities is increasingly delayed. At the same time, it is important not to overestimate the importance of peers. The tendency of some alarmed adults to attribute to peer group influence everything from changing sexual and social standards to drug use and delinquency is not justified by the evidence.

Interactions with peers serve many of the same functions for adolescents that they do for younger children. They offer opportunities to learn how to control social behavior, to develop age-relevant skills and interests, and to share similar problems and feelings (see Chapter 12). But relations with peers during the adolescent years come closer to serving as prototypes for later adult relationships. Adolescents are also more dependent than younger children on peer relationships simply because ties with parents become looser as independence from parents is achieved. Also, relationships with family members are frequently charged with conflicting emotions during the adolescent period —dependent yearnings existing alongside independent strivings, hostility mixed with love, and conflicts over cultural values and social behavior. For this reason, many areas of the adolescent's life become difficult to share with parents, and parents may have difficulty understanding the adolescent's problems, even though they make an effort and are truly interested in their child's welfare (Conger, 1977a).

In other instances, parental warmth and understanding may be lacking, as in the case of a 16-year-old girl who said of her relationship with her father, "I get along, but, I mean, we're really not that close. Like he's got his business and I've got my school work. He just doesn't seem interested in what I do" (Konopka, 1976, p. 69). In some cases, there may be parental hostility, neglect, or exploitation. In such circumstances, interested and competent peers can provide not only a physical and psychological escape from a difficult family situation but understanding and support as well. They may also serve as role models (Blos, 1979; Conger & Petersen, 1984). For example, a male friend may help to demonstrate to the son of a competitive, authoritarian father that not all relationships between males need be characterized by competition and by patterns of domination and submission.

Of course, there is another side to the coin. Relations with peers during this vulnerable stage of development may also be harmful. For example, an adolescent who is put down, laughed at, or rejected in initial efforts to establish sexual relationships or to join a high school clique may develop anxious, avoidant responses in such situations that will prove difficult to unlearn. Obviously, it is highly desirable that most of the adolescent's experiences with peers be positive, for more than at any other time in life, the young person needs to be able to share strong and often confusing emotions, doubts, and dreams. Adolescence is generally a time of intense sociability, but it is also often a time of intense loneliness. Merely being with others does not solve the problem; frequently the young person may feel most alone in the midst of a crowd, at a party or a dance.

Conformity to peers   A need for peer conformity is clearly observable in middle childhood, though there are wide individual differences at all ages in the strength of this need. Because of the heightened importance of the peer group during adolescence, motivation for conformity to the values, customs, and fads of peer culture generally increases during this period. Most studies indicate a rather rapid rise in conformity needs and behavior during the preadolescent and early adolescent years (9 or 10 to 13 or 14) followed by a gradual but steady decline from middle through late adolescence (14 or 15 on). However, the strength of the need to conform, and to a lesser extent the age at which conformity peaks, may vary with sex, socioeconomic level, parental relationships, and personality factors (Coleman, 1980; Hartup, 1983).

For example, in one study, children and adolescents with a strong tendency for self-blame scored significantly higher on a measure of conformity to peers than those low or medium in self-blame (Costanzo, 1970). Young people who have low status among their peers are more conforming than those with high status (Coleman, 1980). Adolescents with high self-esteem and strong feelings of competence are less conforming than their peers. Females are slightly more conforming than males, except where group pressure is toward misconduct, in which case males appear generally more susceptible (Hartup, 1983).

Parental and peer influences—a false dichotomy?   Many people believe that parental and peer group values are necessarily incompatible and that a sharp decline in parental influence during adolescence is inevitable. But for adolescents there is considerable overlap between the values of parents and peers because of similarities in their cultural backgrounds. In many cases, the differences between parental and peer values may be relatively conspicuous but superficial.

For all these reasons, adolescents need the guidance, support, and communion of their peers. No matter how "understanding" parents and other adults may be, their role is necessarily limited by the fact that the adolescent and his or her peers are struggling to achieve adult status—adults are already there. Young people may not, indeed often do not, know how they are going to accomplish this task successfully. But they know that previous generations of adolescents have done so, and they reason that if they can stick with their peers who, after all, are "all in the same boat," they too will be successful. For example, peer influence is more likely to be predominant in such matters as tastes in music and entertainment, fashions in clothing and language, and patterns of same- and other-sex peer interaction. Parental influence is more likely to be predominant in such areas as moral and social values and understanding of the adult world (Berndt, 1979; Hartup, 1983).

Unusually strong peer group influence in the life of an adolescent may be due as much to a lack of attention and concern at home as to the inherent attractiveness of the peer group (Condry & Siman, 1974; Rutter, 1980). Parental influence is greatest where parental interest, understanding, and willingness to be helpful are highest. In addition, adolescents with such parents are less likely to see a need to differentiate between the influence of their parents and their best friends (Larson, 1972). Finally, we tend to overlook the important fact that the need for rigid conformity to either parents or peers varies greatly from one young person to another (Conger, 1971; Hartup, 1983). More self-confident, more autonomous adolescents may be able to profit from the views and learning experiences provided by both parents and peers without being strongly dependent on either or unduly troubled by parent-peer differences.

Crowds and cliques   Prior to adolescence, peer relations tend to be limited to neighborhood acquaintances and school classmates. However, as the young person enters junior high school and spends more time away from home, the range of acquaintances broadens. For most adolescents, peer relationships fall

into three categories: the broader "crowd"; the smaller, more cohesive, more intimate "clique"; and individual friendships (Coleman, 1980; Dunphy, 1972). Cliques and crowds perform different functions for their members. Cliques can help the young person to keep up to date on current fads and fashions; at a deeper level, they can serve as a somewhat protected, secure testing ground for the young person's developing social beliefs and personal values. In contrast, the larger, more diffuse, more impersonal crowd meets largely on the basis of common interests and shared social activities, such as parties—not because of mutual attraction between individuals, as is true of friends and, to a lesser extent, of cliques. As adolescent development proceeds, there is a gradual shift in emphasis from same-sex to both-sex cliques.

Some individuals, either through choice or through rejection by peers, are isolates—loners who belong neither to cliques nor crowds. Like younger children, adolescents can be remarkably indifferent or even cruel toward other age-mates who do not fit in (Conger, 1977b). For many of these isolated young people, the adolescent years can be a lonely and difficult time.

Individual friendships   Close friends contribute to an adolescent's development in ways the broader peer group cannot. At their best, adolescent friendships can serve as a kind of therapy, allowing the expression of suppressed feelings of anger or anxiety and providing evidence that others have similar doubts, hopes, and fears. As one 16-year-old girl put it, "My best friend means a lot to me. We can talk about things I could never talk about with my parents or other kids—like hassles we're getting or problems we're worried about, and like ideals and things. It really helps to know you're not the only one that has things that bother them" (Conger, 1979, p. 70).

In view of the sensitivity of adolescents to the potential dangers of revealing their inner feelings, it is not surprising to find that they place particular emphasis on the need for security in discussing friendship. Above all, they want a friend to be loyal and trustworthy. Of nearly equal importance, particularly for girls, is that the friend be able to listen and understand at the level of feeling (Bell, 1980; Hartup, 1983; Konopka, 1976).

In the freedom that close friends may have to criticize each other, an adolescent can learn to modify behavior, tastes, or ideas without the painful experience of rejection by others (Bell, 1980; Conger, 1977b; Conger & Petersen, 1984; Konopka, 1976). Furthermore, a friend who "really understands" and who still likes and values one can set to rest nagging doubts about one's own real worth. In short, close friendships help adolescents both define their identity and develop confidence and pride in it.

Unfortunately, the course of adolescent friendships does not always run smoothly. By virtue of their very intensity, they founder more easily than those of most adults (which usually involve more modest demands but also yield more modest rewards). Young people with the greatest number of personal problems may have the greatest need for close friendships but the least ability to sustain them. Even the more stable and rewarding adolescent friendships sometimes blow hot and cold, if only because each friend is in a period of rapidly changing needs, feelings, and problems (Bell, 1980; Coleman, 1980; Conger, 1979).

Close friends are most likely to be of the same age and sex, in the same school grade, and from a common socioeconomic and ethnic background (Hartup, 1983; Kandel, 1978b). Behavioral and attitudinal similarities are not as great. Nevertheless, close friends are generally more similar than acquaintances in intelligence, social behavior, school grades, educational and career goals, conformity to adult expectations, amount of participation in peer group activities, and use of drugs and alcohol (Hartup, 1983; Kandel, 1978a, 1978b, 1981). This is partly because peers who are already similar tend to seek each other out and partly because friends become more similar over the course of their friendship.

However, exceptions are not rare, as in the instance of the studious girl whose best friend is noisy, extraverted, and more interested in outside activities than in school work. Where such an attraction of opposites occurs, it is usually because the young person finds in the friend something felt to be desirable but lacking in herself (Conger, 1979).

Social acceptance, neglect, and rejection   Personality characteristics and social behaviors affect the likelihood of an adolescent's acceptance by peers. In general, as in the case of younger children, adolescents of both sexes who are accepted by their peers are perceived as liking other people. They are rated as tolerant, flexible, sympathetic, lively, cheerful, good-natured, and possessed of a sense of humor. In addition, they act naturally and self-confidently without being conceited; possess initiative, enthusiasm, and drive; and help make plans for group activity (Asher, 1978; Coleman, 1980; Conger & Petersen, 1984; Hartup, 1983). Adolescents who are viewed favorably tend to be those who contribute to others by making *them* feel accepted and involved, by promoting constructive interaction between peers, or by planning and initiating interesting or enjoyable group activities (Savin-Williams, 1980).

Characteristics that are least admired and most likely to lead to neglect or outright rejection are in many ways the opposite of those leading to acceptance and popularity. The adolescent who is ill-at-ease and lacking in self-confidence and reacts with timidity, nervousness, or withdrawal is likely to be neglected by peers and to emerge as a social isolate. The adolescent who reacts to insecurity with compensatory overaggressiveness, conceit, or demands for attention may receive active dislike and rejection. Similarly, the adolescent who is self-centered and unable or unwilling to perceive and act to meet the needs of others, who is sarcastic, tactless, and inconsiderate, and who contributes little to the success of group efforts is likely to receive little consideration in return.

A few individualists, confident of their own goals and interests and possessed of a strong sense of ego identity, may neither need nor seek peer approval. But most adolescents, still judging their own worth to a considerable extent in terms of others' reactions to them, are dependent on the approval of respected peers. Unpopular adolescents are caught in a vicious cycle. If they are already emotionally troubled, self-preoccupied, and lacking in a secure self-concept, they are likely to meet with rejection or indifference from peers. In turn, an awareness of not being accepted by peers and a lack of opportunity to participate in and learn from peer group activities further undermines self-confidence and increases a sense of social isolation.

Clearly, social acceptance by peers is desirable, particularly if it is based on mutual helpfulness and shared interests. In our opinion, however, there is currently an overemphasis, particularly among upper- and middle-class parents, on the pursuit of popularity. Most adolescents, at one time or another, feel that they do not belong, and the pain, however temporary, can be very real; parents' overdetermined insistence on popularity can often compound the young person's difficulties.

Peer relations and later adjustment   In view of the important role played by peer relationships in our society, it should not be surprising to find that peer experiences in childhood and adolescence are significantly related to later adjustment (Hartup, 1983). Children with poor peer relations have a higher probability of adult neurotic and psychotic disturbances, conduct disorders and delinquency, and disturbances in sexual behavior and adjustment than those who get along well with their peers (Hartup, 1983). For example, in one investigation (Cowen, Pederson, Babijian, Izzo, & Trost, 1973), a wide variety of measures were obtained on third-grade children, including intelligence test scores, school grades, achievement test scores, school attendance, and teacher and peer ratings. Eleven years later, those using mental health services were identified through community mental health registers. Of all the measures originally obtained, the best predictors of adult mental health were the peer ratings.

Similarly, delinquency rates among adolescents and young adults and bad-conduct discharges from the armed services are significantly higher among individuals who had difficulty getting along with others as children (Conger & Miller, 1966; Hartup, 1983). "There is every reason to believe, then, that poor peer relations are centrally involved in the etiology of a variety of emotional and social maladjustments" (Hartup, 1983, p. 167).

Adolescent love   When American adolescents were asked if they had ever been in love, 56 percent replied that they had been, 39 percent said they had not, and 5 percent were not sure (Gallup, 1979). Younger adolescent males, aged 12 to 15, were least likely to say they had been in love (47 percent), while older adolescent females, age 16 to 18, were most likely. Among those who said that they had been in love at some point, slightly over half said they were currently in love. Again, females were more likely than males to say they were currently in love (61 percent versus 42 percent), with older females having the highest frequency (69 percent), followed by younger females (49 percent), older males (43 percent), and younger males (38 percent).

In some cases, adolescent romances evolve gradually into stable, committed, long-term relationships; more frequently they are intense emotional experiences that last a while and then change. Nevertheless, during the relationship, the feelings can be just as vital, and the capacity for joy or despair just as great, as in adult love affairs. To be in love with someone who does not reciprocate is painful; it is "even more painful when you are still in love with someone who's no longer in love with you" (Bell, 1980, p. 69). For adults to discuss adolescent "puppy love" as not serious (or even as amusing) indicates a lack of sensitivity—as well as a short memory. Breaking up with a boyfriend or girlfriend can lead to genuine depression. As one 17-year-old described her feelings: "I just feel like my life's over, like there's never going to be anything to smile about again" (Bell, 1980, p. 69). Fortunately, in most cases, the hurt gradually fades, but having a close friend to talk to can be very helpful at such a time.

Instead of breaking up, adolescents sometimes seek to maintain a relationship simply for the security involved. This tends to limit their own continued development: "It's comforting to know that you'll always have a date for the weekend and that someone cares about you and is choosing to spend time with you. But fear—fear of being alone, fear of going out with new people, fear of hurting the other person's feelings, fear of being rejected—is not a healthy basis for a relationship" (Bell, 1980, p. 70).

The young person best prepared for the intimate emotional demands of marriage tends to be one who has been able to try out a variety of social and personal roles. Optimally, this means involvement both with peers of the other sex and with close friends of the same sex in the early years of adolescence (Conger, 1979; Conger & Petersen, 1984).

Up through middle adolescence, young people who have clearly defined educational and vocational plans and who aspire to marriages like those of their parents "tend to be less often in love while in school, are less frequently going steady, and are less apt to plan on being married before they are 21" (Duvall, 1964, p. 228). Adolescents who did not want a marriage like their parents' were significantly more likely to report being in love right now. Young women with high self-esteem tended in adolescence to date more often, but to go steady less often, than those with low self-esteem (Conger & Petersen, 1984; Klemer, 1971). Another investigator (Knox, 1970) found that high school seniors whose parents were living together tended to have a more realistic, less romantic attitude toward love than those whose parents were divorced or who had a deceased parent.

SUMMARY

Adolescence has long been considered a more difficult period in development than the middle-childhood years. However, the concept of adolescence as a psychologically complex stage worthy of scientific study did not emerge until the end of the nineteenth century.

Adolescence is above all a period of rapid physical, sexual, psychological, cognitive, and social change. The physical changes of puberty, including sexual maturation and the adolescent growth spurt, are initiated by an increased output of activating hormones by the pituitary gland. These hormones stimulate other endocrine glands to produce their own growth- and sex-related hormones, including androgens, estrogens, and progestins. The age of onset and the duration of the adolescent growth spurt in height and weight vary widely among normal children. The average age of onset is about 11 in girls and 13 in boys; the growth rate reaches a peak about a year later.

Age at the onset of puberty also varies greatly. In the average boy, sexual maturation begins with an increased rate of growth of the testes and scrotum and the first appearance of pubic hair, followed by the enlargement of the penis, development of body and facial hair, lowering of the voice, sperm production and nocturnal emissions, and an increasingly masculine body build. In girls, the beginning elevation of the breast is usually the first observable sign of sexual maturation. Pubic hair appears, and the uterus, vagina, labia, and clitoris enlarge. Menarche (the onset of menstruation) appears fairly late in the developmental cycle, at around age 13, but with wide individual variations. Conception is usually not possible until a year or so after menarche. The rapid physical changes of puberty make it difficult for the adolescent to achieve a feeling of self-consistency, and time is needed to integrate these changes into a slowly emerging sense of individual identity.

To the adolescent girl, menstruation is a symbol of sexual maturity and womanhood. Because young women's reactions to menstruation may generalize broadly, it is vital that their initial experiences with it be as favorable as possible. A majority of females view menstruation as either negative or at best neutral. In part, this attitude may be due to physical discomfort and hormonal influences on mood, but it appears to be largely due to negative social attitudes. Just as the onset of menstruation may concern adolescent females, uncontrolled erection and initial ejaculation (including nocturnal emission) may surprise and worry young men.

Late-maturing males experience more psychological and social problems in adjustment than early or average-maturing males. Among females, the psychological effects of early or late maturing are considerably less, although early maturers tend to be somewhat more relaxed and self-confident and less anxious than late maturers.

Continuing cognitive development, including the advent of the stage of formal operations, allows adolescents to think more abstractly, to formulate and test hypotheses, and to consider what might be rather than merely what is. These abilities often lead adolescents to criticize parental and social values. Adolescent thought and behavior may also appear *egocentric*; young people at this stage may conclude that others are as preoccupied with their behavior and appearance as they themselves are. Adolescent cognitive development also plays an important role in personality development and in the formation of a clear sense of identity.

Becoming independent of one's family is a basic task of adolescence. It is fostered by *authoritative* parents who value both autonomy *and* disciplined behavior and who provide explanations for their expectations or prohibitions. More difficulties are experienced by children of *autocratic* or *authoritarian* parents, who just tell their children what to do, and *permissive, laissez-faire, equalitarian,* or *neglectful* parents, who may seem (or be) uncaring or irresponsible.

Dealing with sexual maturity is another major adolescent task. Sexual activity, especially masturbation, is more frequent among males than females, although the differences have narrowed somewhat in recent years. Furthermore, young women typically display more conservative attitudes toward sexual matters. Although physiological factors may play a part in these sex differences, they are also attributable to our culture's more restrictive attitudes toward sexual behavior for women.

Premarital intercourse has increased markedly, especially among middle-class youth (and particularly females). Roughly half the young people in the United States have had sexual intercourse by age 17. These figures increase to

77.5 percent of males and 69 percent of females by age 19. However, there is still great diversity among adolescents in sexual attitudes and behavior. In general, adolescents who are younger, politically conservative, and religious are more conservative, while those who are highly educated are less conservative.

Despite significant gains in recent years, slightly over half of all sexually active female adolescents did not use a contraceptive device in their first experience of intercourse, and only a little over one-third consistently use such a device thereafter. As a result, over 1 million 15- to 19-year-old women in the United States (11 percent of this entire age group) become pregnant each year.

Peers play a vital role in the psychological development of most adolescents as ties with parents become weaker. Peers provide an opportunity to learn social skills, to control behavior, and to share similar problems and feelings. Being accepted by peers generally—and, especially, having one or more close friends—may make a great difference in the young person's life. Close friends are likely to be of the same age and sex, to come from similar backgrounds, and to share similar values and goals, but exceptions (the "attractions of opposites") are not rare. Contrary to popular opinion, peers are more likely to reinforce basic parental values than to oppose them, although there are likely to be generational differences in tastes, fads, and customs. Adolescent peer groups include the larger, more impersonal *crowd,* the smaller *clique,* and *individual friendships.* As adolescent development proceeds, there is a shift from same-sex to both-sex cliques.

Many factors affect the likelihood of an adolescent's acceptance by peers, including intelligence, physical appearance and skills, social status, and special talents. Generally, adolescents prefer peers who are cheerful, tolerant, good-natured, and enthusiastic, people who contribute to others by making *them* feel accepted and involved. Poor peer relationships during childhood and adolescence are predictive of adult emotional disorders, delinquency, disturbances in sexual adjustment, and other forms of maladaptive behavior.

A majority of adolescents, particularly older females, state that they have been in love. Adolescent romances frequently involve intense feelings, and breaking up with a boyfriend or girlfriend can be very painful. Adolescents who are able to try out a variety of social and personal roles during adolescence are best prepared, socially and emotionally, for marriage and adult life.

REFERENCES

Asher, S. R. Children's peer relations. In M. E. Lamb (Ed.), *Social and personality development.* New York: Holt, Rinehart and Winston, 1978.

Astin, A. W. *The American freshman national norms for fall 1980.* Los Angeles: American Council on Education and Graduate School of Education, University of California at Los Angeles, 1981.

Bachman, J. G. *Youth in transition* (Vol. 2): *The impact of family background and intelligence on tenth-grade boys.* Ann Arbor, Mich.: Institute for Social Research, University of Michigan, 1970.

Bachman, J. G., Johnston, L. D., & O'Malley, P. M. *Monitoring the future: Questionnaire responses from the nation's high school seniors.* Ann Arbor, Mich.: Institute for Social Research, University of Michigan, 1981.

Bachman, J. G., O'Malley, P. M., & Johnston, J. *Adolescence to adulthood: Change and stability in the lives of young men.* Ann Arbor, Mich.: Institute for Social Research, University of Michigan, 1978.

Baumrind, D. Early socialization and adolescent competence. In S. E. Dragastin & G. H. Elder, Jr. (Eds.), *Adolescence in the life cycle: Psychological change and social context.* New York: Wiley, 1975.

Bell, R. *Changing bodies, changing lives: A book for teens on sex and relationships.* New York: Random House, 1980.

Berndt, T. J. Developmental changes in conformity to peers and parents. *Developmental Psychology,* 1979, *15,* 606–616.

Blos, P. *The adolescent passage.* New York: International Universities Press, 1979.

Brooks-Gunn, J., & Ruble, D. N. The development of menstrual-related beliefs and behaviors during early adolescence. *Child Development,* 1982, *53,* 1567–1577.

Brooks-Gunn, J., & Ruble, D. N. The experience of menarche from a developmental perspective. In J. Brooks-Gunn & A. C. Petersen (Eds.), *Girls at puberty: Biological, psychological, and social perspectives.* New York: Plenum, in press.

Chillman, C. S. *Adolescent sexuality in a changing American society: Social and psychological perspectives.* Washington, D.C.: U.S. Government Printing Office, 1978.

Clausen, J. A. The social meaning of differential physical and sexual maturation. In S. E. Dragastin & G. H. Elder, Jr. (Eds.), *Adolescence in the life cycle: Psychological change and social context.* New York: Wiley, 1975.

Coleman, J. C. *The nature of adolescence.* London: Methuen, 1980.

Condry, J., & Siman, M. L. Characteristics of peer- and adult-oriented children. *Journal of Marriage and the Family,* 1974, *36,* 543–554.

Conger, J. J. A world they never knew: The family and social change. *Daedalus,* 1971 (Fall), 1105–1134.

Conger, J. J. *Adolescence and youth: Psychological development in a changing world* (2nd ed.). New York: Harper & Row, 1977. (a)

Conger, J. J. Parent-child relationships, social change, and adolescent vulnerability. *Journal of Pediatric Psychology,* 1977, *2,* 93–97. (b)

Conger, J. J. *Adolescence: Generation under pressure.* New York: Harper & Row, 1979.

Conger, J. J. A new morality: Sexual attitudes and behavior of contemporary adolescents. In P. H. Mussen, J. J. Conger, & J. Kagan (Eds.), *Readings in child and adolescent psychology: Contemporary perspectives.* New York: Harper & Row, 1980.

Conger, J. J., & Miller, W. C. *Personality, social class, and delinquency.* New York: Wiley, 1966.

Conger, J. J., & Petersen, A. *Adolescence and youth: Psychological development in a changing world* (3rd ed.). New York: Harper & Row, 1984.

Costanzo, P. R. Conformity development as a function of self-blame. *Journal of Personality and Social Psychology,* 1970, *14,* 366–374.

Cowen, E. L., Pederson, A., Babijian, H., Izzo, L. D., & Trost, M. A. Long-term follow-up of early detected vulnerable children. *Journal of Consulting and Clinical Psychology,* 1973, *41,* 438–446.

Dunphy, D. C. Peer group socialization. In F. J. Hunt (Ed.), *Socialisation in Australia.* Sydney: Angus & Robertson, 1972.

Duvall, E. M. Adolescent love as a reflection of teen-agers' search for identity. *Journal of Marriage and the Family,* 1964, *26,* 226–229.

Elder, G. H., Jr. *Family structure and socialization.* New York: Arno Press, 1980.

Elkind, D. Cognitive development in adolescence. In J. F. Adams (Ed.), *Understanding adolescence.* Boston: Allyn & Bacon, 1968.

Enright, R. D., Lapsley, D., & Shukla, D. Adolescent egocentrism in early and late adolescence. *Adolescence,* 1979, *14,* 687–695.

Erikson, E. H. *Identity: Youth and crisis.* New York: Norton, 1968.

Falkner, F., & Tanner, J. M. *Human growth* (Vol. 2): *Postnatal growth.* New York: Plenum, 1978.

Faust, M. S. Developmental maturity as a determinant in prestige of adolescent girls. *Child Development,* 1960, *31,* 173–184.

Faust, M. S. Somatic development of adolescent girls. *Monographs of the Society for Research in Child Development*, 1977, *42*(1), 1–90.

Faust, M. S. Alternative constructions of adolescence and growth. In J. Brooks-Gunn & A. C. Petersen (Eds.), *Girls at puberty: Biological, psychological, and social perspectives.* New York: Plenum, in press.

Flavell, J. H. *Cognitive development.* Englewood Cliffs, N.J.: Prentice-Hall, 1977.

Flavell, J. H. On cognitive development. *Child Development*, 1982, *53*, 1–10.

Flavell, J. H., & Ross, L. (Eds.). *Social cognitive development.* New York: Cambridge University Press, 1981.

Forbes, G. B. Body composition in adolescence. In F. Falkner & J. M. Tanner (Eds.), *Human growth* (Vol. 2): *Postnatal growth.* New York: Plenum, 1978.

Ford, C. S., & Beach, F. A. *Patterns of sexual behavior.* New York: Harper & Row, 1951.

Ford, M. E. Social cognition and social competence in adolescence. *Developmental Psychology*, 1982, *18*, 323–340.

Freud, A. Adolescence as a developmental disturbance. In G. Caplan & S. Lebovici (Eds.), *Adolescence: Psychosocial perspectives.* New York: Basic Books, 1969.

Gallup, G. Gallup youth survey. *Denver Post*, November 20, 1979, p. 36.

Goldstein, M. J., Baker, B. L., & Jamison, K. R. *Abnormal psychology: Experiences, origins, and interventions.* Boston: Little, Brown, 1980.

Greif, E. B., & Ulman, K. J. The psychological impact of menarche on early adolescent females: A review of the literature. *Child Development*, 1982, *53*, 1413–1430.

Grunbach, M. M. The central nervous system and the onset of puberty. In F. Falkner & J. M. Tanner (Eds.), *Human growth* (Vol. 2): *Postnatal growth.* New York: Plenum, 1978.

Gupta, D., Attanasio, A., & Raaf, S. Plasma estrogen and androgen concentrations in children during adolescence. *Journal of Clinical Endocrinology and Metabolism*, 1975, *40*, 636–643.

Haas, A. *Teenage sexuality: A survey of teenage sexual behavior.* New York: Macmillan, 1979.

Harris, I. D., & Howard, K. I. Phenomenological correlates of perceived quality of parenting: A questionnaire study of high school students. *Journal of Youth and Adolescence*, 1979, *8*, 171–180.

Hartup, W. W. Peer interaction and social organization. In P. H. Mussen (Ed.), *Carmichael's manual of child psychology* (Vol. 1) (3rd ed.). New York: Wiley, 1970.

Hartup, W. W. The peer system. In P. H. Mussen (Ed.), *Handbook of child psychology* (Vol. 4): E. M. Hetherington (Ed.) *Personality and social development* (4th ed.). New York: Wiley, 1983.

Helfer, R. E., & Kempe, C. H. (Eds.). *Child abuse and neglect: The family and the community.* Cambridge, Mass.: Ballinger, 1982.

Hoffman, M. L. Moral internalization, parental powers, and the nature of parent-child interaction. *Developmental Psychology*, 1975, *11*, 228–239.

Hoffman, M. L. Moral development in adolescence. In J. Adelson (Ed.), *Handbook of adolescent psychology.* New York: Wiley, 1980.

Hornick, J. P., Doran, L., & Crawford, S. H. Premarital contraceptives usage among male and female adolescents. *Family Coordinator*, 1979, *28*, 181–190.

Jessor, R., & Jessor, S. L. *Problem behavior and psychological development.* New York: Academic Press, 1977.

Jones, H. E. The environment and mental development. In L. Carmichael (Ed.), *Manual of child psychology.* New York: Wiley, 1954.

Jones, M. C. The later careers of boys who were early or late maturing. *Child Development*, 1957, *28*, 113–128.

Josselyn, I. M. *Adolescence.* Washington, D.C.: Joint Commission on Mental Health of Children, 1968.

Kandel, D. B. Homophily, selection, and socialization in adolescent friendships. *American Journal of Sociology*, 1978, *84*, 427–436. (a)

Kandel, D. B. Similarity in real-life adolescent friendship pairs. *Journal of Personality and Social Psychology*, 1978, *36*, 306–312. (b)

Kandel, D. B. *Peer influences in adolescence.* Paper presented at the Biennial Meeting of the Society for Research in Child Development, Boston, April 2, 1981.

Kantner, J., & Zelnik, M. Sexual experiences of young unmarried women in the U.S. *Family Planning Perspectives*, 1972, *4*, 9–17.

Keating, D. P. Thinking processes in adolescence. In J. Adelson (Ed.), *Handbook of adolescent psychology.* New York: Wiley, 1980.

Kiell, N. *The universal experience of adolescence.* Boston: Beacon, 1967.

Kinsey, A. C., Pomeroy, W. B., & Martin, C. E. *Sexual behavior in the human male.* Philadelphia: Saunders, 1948.

Kinsey, A. C., Pomeroy, W. B., Martin, C. E., & Gebhard, P. H. *Sexual behavior in the human female.* Philadelphia: Saunders, 1953.

Klein, J. R., & Litt, I. F. Menarche and dysmenorrhea. In J. Brooks-Gunn & A. C. Petersen (Eds.), *Girls at puberty: Biological, psychological, and social perspectives.* New York: Plenum, in press.

Klemer, R. H. Self-esteem and college dating experience as factors in mate selection and marital happiness: A longitudinal study. *Journal of Marriage and the Family*, 1971, *33*, 183–187.

Konopka, G. *Young girls: A portrait of adolescence.* Englewood Cliffs, N.J.: Prentice-Hall, 1976.

Larson, L. E. The influence of parents and peers during adolescence. *Journal of Marriage and the Family*, 1972, *34*, 67–74.

Lewis, C. S. The effects of parental firm control: A reinterpretation of findings. *Psychological Bulletin*, 1982, *90*, 547–563.

Marshall, W. A. Puberty. In F. Falkner & J. M. Tanner (Eds.), *Human growth* (Vol. 2): *Postnatal growth.* New York: Plenum, 1978.

Marshall, W. A., & Tanner, J. M. Variations in the pattern of pubertal changes in boys. *Archives of Disease in Childhood*, 1970, *45*, 13.

Masters, W. H., & Johnson, V. E. *Human sexual inadequacy.* Boston: Little, Brown, 1970.

Mead, M. *Male and female.* New York: Morrow, 1939.

Miller, P. Y., & Simon, W. The development of sexuality in adolescence. In J. Adelson (Ed.), *Handbook of adolescent psychology.* New York: Wiley, 1980.

Minturn, L., Lambert, W. W., et al. *Mothers of six cultures: Antecedents of child rearing.* New York: Wiley, 1964.

Mrazek, P. B., & Kempe, C. H. *Sexually abused children and their families.* Elmsford, N.Y.: Pergamon Press, 1981.

Mussen, P. H., & Jones, M. C. Self-conceptions, motivations, and interpersonal attitudes of late and early maturing boys. *Child Development*, 1957, *28*, 243–256.

Neimark, E. D. Intellectual development during adolescence. In F. D. Horowitz (Ed.), *Review of child development research* (Vol 4). Chicago: University of Chicago Press, 1975.

Norman, J., & Harris, M. *The private life of the American teenager.* New York: Rawson, Wade, 1981.

Offer, D. Adolescent turmoil. In A. H. Esman (Ed.), *The psychology of adolescence.* New York: International Universities Press, 1975.

Offer, D., Ostrov, E., & Howard, K. The mental health professionals' concept of the normal adolescent. *Archives of General Psychiatry*, 1981, *38*, 149–152.

Osterrieth, P. A. Adolescence: Some psychological aspects. In G. Caplan & S. Lebovici (Eds.), *Adolescence: Psychosocial perspectives.* New York: Basic Books, 1969.

Petersen, A. C. Menarche: Meaning of measures and measuring meaning. In S. Golub (Ed.), *Menarche: An interdisciplinary view.* New York: Springer, in press.

Petersen, A. C., & Boxer, A. Adolescent sexuality. In T. Coates, A. Petersen, & C. Perry (Eds.), *Adolescent health: Crossing the barriers.* New York: Academic Press, 1982.

Planned Parenthood Federation of America. *Teenage pregnancy: The problem that hasn't gone away.* New York: Alan Guttmacher Institute, Planned Parenthood Federation of America, 1981.

Plato. *The dialogues of Plato* (Vol. 4): *Laws* (4th ed.) (B. Jewett, trans.). Oxford: Clarendon Press, 1953.

Pomeroy, W. B. *Girls and sex.* New York: Dell (Delacorte Press). 1969.

Roche, A. F. Bone growth and maturation. In F. Falkner & J. M. Tanner (Eds.), *Human growth* (Vol. 2) *Postnatal growth.* New York: Plenum, 1978.

Rosenberg, M. *Society and the adolescent self-image.* Princeton, N.J.: Princeton University Press, 1965.

Ruble, D. N., & Brooks-Gunn, J. The experience of menarche. *Child Development*, 1982, *53*, 1557–1566.

Rutter, M. *Changing youth in a changing society: Patterns of adolescent disorder.* Cambridge, Mass.: Harvard University Press, 1980.

Savin-Williams, R. C. Social interactions of adolescent females in natural groups. In H. C. Foot, A. J. Chapman, & J. R. Smith (Eds.), *Friendship and social relations in children.* New York: Wiley, 1980.

Schmidt, G., & Sigusch, V. Women's sexual arousal. In J. Zubin & J. Money (Eds.), *Contemporary sexual behavior: Critical issues in the 1970s.* Baltimore: Johns Hopkins University Press, 1973.

Simmons, R. G., & Rosenberg, F. Sex, sex roles, and self-image. *Journal of Youth and Adolescence,* 1975, *4*, 229–258.

Smith, S. R. Religion and the conception of youth in seventeenth-century England. *History of Childhood Quarterly: The Journal of Psychohistory,* 1975, *2*, 493–516.

Sorensen, R. C. *Adolescent sexuality in contemporary America: Personal values and sexual behavior ages 13–19.* New York: Abrams, 1973.

Steele, B. Psychodynamic factors in child abuse. In C. H. Kempe & F. E. Helfer (Eds.), *The battered child.* Chicago: University of Chicago Press, 1980.

Steinberg, L. D., & Hill, J. P. Patterns of family interaction as a function of age, the onset of puberty, and formal thinking. *Developmental Psychology,* 1978, *14*, 683–684.

Stone, L. J., & Church, J. *Childhood and adolescence: A psychology of the growing person* (3rd ed.). New York: Random House, 1973.

Tanner, J. M. Physical growth. In P. H. Mussen (Ed.), *Carmichael's manual of child psychology* (Vol. 2) (3rd ed.). New York: Wiley, 1970.

Tanner, J. M. Sequence, tempo, and individual variation in the growth and development of boys and girls aged twelve to sixteen. *Daedalus,* 1971, *100*(4), 907–930.

Tobin-Richards, M., Boxer, A., & Petersen, A. C. The psychological impact of pubertal change: Sex differences in perceptions of self during early adolescence. In J. Brooks-Gunn & A. C. Petersen (Eds.), *Girls at puberty: Biological, psychological, and social perspectives.* Plenum, in press.

Wilson, W. C., et al. *Technical report of the Commission on Obscenity and Pornography* (Vol. 6): *National survey.* Washington, D.C.: U.S. Government Printing Office, 1971.

Zabin, L. S., Kantner, J. F., & Zelnik, M. The risk of adolescent pregnancy in the first months of intercourse. *Family Planning Perspectives,* 1979, *11*, 215–222.

Zelnik, M., & Kantner, J. F. Sexual activity, contraceptive use, and pregnancy among metropolitan-area teenagers: 1971–1979. *Family Planning Perspectives,* 1980, *12*, 230–237.

CHAPTER 14

Adolescence: identity, values, and problems of adjustment

A central task of adolescence in our society is finding a workable answer to the question "Who am I?" Although this question has preoccupied humankind for many centuries and has been the subject of innumerable poems, novels, and auto-biographies, only in recent decades has it become the focus of systematic psychological concern, initially through the writings of psychoanalyst Erik Erikson (Erikson, 1968). Perhaps it is no coincidence that Erikson had a rich background in art, literature, and education.

Adolescents and adults with a strong sense of ego identity see themselves as separate, distinctive individuals. The very word *individual,* as a synonym for *person,* implies a universal need to perceive oneself as somehow separate from others, no matter how much one may share with them. Closely related is the need for self-consistency, a feeling of wholeness. When we speak of the *integrity* of the self, we imply both a separateness from others and a unity of the self, a workable integration of the person's needs, motives, and patterns of responding. In order to have a clear sense of ego identity, the adolescent or adult also requires a sense of continuity of the self over time. In Erikson's words, "the younger person, in order to experience wholeness, must feel a progressive continuity between that which he has come to be during the long years of childhood and that which he promises to become in the anticipated future (Erikson, 1956, p. 91).

Finally, for Erikson, a sense of identity requires *psychosocial reciprocity*—a consistency "between that which he conceives himself to be and that which he perceives others to see in him and expect of him" (Erikson, 1956, p. 94). Erikson's assertion that one's sense of identity is tied at least partly to social reality is important; it emphasizes the fact that societal or individual rejection can seriously impair a child's or adolescent's chances of establishing a strong, secure sense of personal identity. Erikson's theory of development is explained in Box 14.1.

Any developmental influences that contribute to confident perceptions of oneself as separate and distinct from others, as reasonably consistent and integrated, as having continuity over time, and as being similar to the way others perceive one to be contribute to an overall sense of ego identity. By the same token, influences that impair these self-perceptions foster identity confusion (or identity diffusion), "a failure to achieve the integration and continuity of self-images" (Erikson, 1968, p. 212).

Identity in other cultures

Americans place great emphasis on the development of an individual as an *individual,* probably in part because of America's frontier tradition of self-reliance and independence. In other cultures, such as China and Japan, there is greater emphasis on achieving one's identity and sense of worth through close relationships with others and being a member of an established social order. "Society weighs heavily in the life of the Japanese, and learning to accept the burdens and limitations involved is the major first step on the road to maturity" (Rohlen, 1969, p. 127). Nevertheless, even in cultures that place a relatively heavy emphasis on *group identity* as contrasted with *individual identity,* there is still a need to perceive oneself as a consistent, distinct person who is to some degree separate from others. Indeed, the Japanese language expresses the need for combining individual and group identity in the phrase "putting others inside one's self," which is used to indicate the desirability of empathy and openness toward others.

Problems with identity

Many adolescents find themselves playing roles that shift from one situation or from one time to another and worry about "which, if any, is the real me?" They also self-consciously try out different roles in the hope of finding one that seems to "fit." An adolescent who had three distinctly different hand-

BOX 14.1

*Erikson's eight
stages of
development*

Erik Erikson was a psychoanalytic theorist who proposed major revisions in Freud's ideas about stages of development. Erikson thought that Freud overemphasized the biological and sexual determinants of developmental change and underemphasized the importance of child-rearing experiences, social relationships, and cultural influences on the development of ego or self. He also believed that important developmental changes occurred after childhood. Erikson, therefore, proposed a series of eight stages of development stretching over the entire life span. While many psychologists with an interest in childhood refer to the theory, it has stimulated little research on young children. However, it has been particularly influential in stimulating research on adolescent and adult development. Therefore, the student of adolescence needs some familiarity with its basic concepts.

The eight stages proposed by Erikson are presented in Figure B14.1. Each stage is defined by a developmental task or crisis that needs to be resolved in order to continue a healthy pattern of development. The major concern of the first stage is establishment of trust. Erikson believed that infants developed trust when their world was consistent and predictable—when they were fed, warmed, and comforted in a consistent manner.

The second stage is described as a conflict between developing autonomy or shame and doubt. In the toddler period, children begin to assert independence—they say "no," and they can walk and run where they choose. Toilet training, often begun during this period, can become a battlefield where the child refuses to do what the parent

FIGURE B14.1

The eight stages of development in Erikson's theory. At the left side, the approximate ages or Freudian psychsexual stages corresponding to each stage are listed. The conflicts central to each stage in Erikson's theory are shown on the diagonal. (From E. Erikson. Childhood and society [2nd ed.]. New York: Norton, 1963, p. 273.)

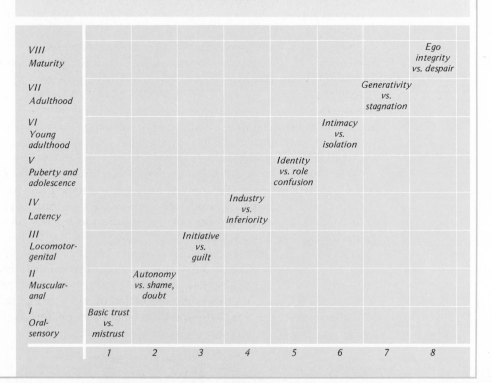

	1	2	3	4	5	6	7	8
VIII Maturity								Ego integrity vs. despair
VII Adulthood							Generativity vs. stagnation	
VI Young adulthood						Intimacy vs. isolation		
V Puberty and adolescence					Identity vs. role confusion			
IV Latency				Industry vs. inferiority				
III Locomotor-genital			Initiative vs. guilt					
II Muscular-anal		Autonomy vs. shame, doubt						
I Oral-sensory	Basic trust vs. mistrust							

wishes. Erikson believed that it was important to give children a sense of autonomy and not to be harsh or punitive during this period. Parents who shame their children for misbehavior could create basic doubt about being independent.

The third stage entails a conflict between initiative and guilt. The child in this stage begins to be task-oriented and to plan new activities. It is a period when masturbation and sexual curiosity are often noticed by parents. The danger in this period, according to Erikson, is that the child may develop excessive guilt about the acts that are initiated.

During the years of middle childhood, children need to solve the conflict between industry and inferiority. Children enter school, begin to perform tasks, and acquire important skills. Achievement and the sense of competence become important; a child who has no particular competences or who experiences repeated failure may form strong feelings of inferiority.

The major conflict in adolescence is identity formation versus role confusion. The young person solidifies many elements of childhood identity and forms a clear vocational and personal identity. Failure to solve this conflict can result in role confusion or diffusion of identity. Erikson acknowledged that identity formation might proceed somewhat differently for males and females because society emphasizes different adult roles for them. He thought that career identity was particularly important for males but that females' identity might center around their future spouse and their role as wife and mother. The changes in women's roles in recent years have led many psychologists to revise this portion of the theory to include career goals as part of female identity as well.

In young adulthood, the major conflict is intimacy versus isolation. Deep, enduring personal relationships need to be formed. A person who does not form such relationships may be psychologically isolated from others and have only superficial social relationships. The most important intimate relationship, according to Erikson, was a committed sexual relationship with a partner of the other sex. Again, this view has been challenged as unnecessarily narrow; some people have argued that many kinds of intimate relationships are important and rewarding.

In middle adulthood, the conflict is generativity versus stagnation. One form of generativity is having children, but being productive and creative in one's work or other activities can also be important. Without a sense of producing or creating, Erikson argued, an adult stagnates and ceases growing.

The final conflict is ego integrity versus despair. People with ego integrity have a sense of order and meaning in life and a feeling of satisfaction with what has been accomplished in their lives. There is a sense of being part of a larger culture or world. Despair can occur when people become afraid of death or when they do not accept the life they have led as satisfying or worthy (Erikson, 1963).

writing styles was asked why she did not have one consistent style. She replied, "How can I write one way till I know who I am?"

The search for identity becomes acute during adolescence, partly because change is the order of the day. During adolescence, the young person is confronted with a host of psychological, physiological, sexual, and cognitive changes, as well as new and varied intellectual, social, and vocational demands. As a result, adolescents are likely to be concerned with how they appear in the eyes of others compared with what they believe themselves to be and with the question of how to connect the roles and skills cultivated earlier with the demands of tomorrow.

Achieving a well-defined sense of individual identity also depends partly on cognitive skills. The young person must be able to conceptualize herself in abstract terms, at times almost like a spectator. The capacity for abstract thinking discussed in Chapter 13 aids the adolescent in the search for an individual identity but makes the search more difficult at the same time. "Such cognitive orientation forms not a contrast but a complement to the need of the young person to develop a sense of identity, for, from among all possible and imaginable relations, he must make a series of ever-narrowing selections of personal, occupational, sexual, and ideological commitments" (Erikson, 1968, p. 245).

Erikson (1968) pointed to two important ways that the search for identity can go wrong. It may be prematurely foreclosed (that is, crystallized too early), or it may be indefinitely extended.

Identity foreclosure Identity foreclosure is an interruption in the process of identity formation. It is a premature *fixing* of one's self-images, which interferes with development of other potentials and possibilities for self-definition. Youth whose identities have been prematurely foreclosed are likely to be highly approval-oriented. They base their sense of self-esteem largely on recognition by others, usually have a high degree of respect for authority, and tend to be more conforming and less autonomous than other youth. They are also more interested in traditional religious values, less thoughtful and reflective, less anxious, and more stereotyped and superficial, as well as less close and intimate in same-sex and other-sex relationships. Although they do not differ from their peers in overall intelligence, identity-foreclosure youth have difficulty being flexible and responding appropriately when confronted with stressful, cognitive tasks; they seem to welcome structure and order in their lives. They tend to have close relationships with their parents (especially in the case of sons and their fathers) and to adopt parental values. Their parents, in turn, generally appear to be accepting and encouraging, while exerting considerable pressure and support for conformity to family values (Bourne, 1978a, 1978b; Donovan, 1975; Marcia, 1980; St. Clair & Day, 1979).

Identity confusion In contrast, other adolescents go through a prolonged period of identity confusion. Sometimes they never develop a strong, clear sense of identity. These are adolescents who "cannot 'find themselves,' who keep themselves loose and unattached, committed to a bachelorhood of pre-identity" (Douvan & Adelson, 1966, p. 16). Like Lenny, the antihero of Romain Gary's novel *The Ski Bum*, who opts for total detachment from family and country, such a person may exhibit "a pathologically prolonged identity crisis," never achieving any consistent loyalties or commitments.

Young people undergoing identity confusion often have low underlying self-esteem and immature moral reasoning. They have difficulty taking responsibility for their own lives. They are impulsive, disorganized in their thinking, and prone to become involved in drug use. Their personal relationships are often superficial and sporadic. Although generally dissatisfied with their parents' way of life, they have difficulty becoming productively involved in fashioning one of their own (Donovan, 1975; Marcia, 1980; Orlofsky, 1978; Waterman, & Waterman, 1974).

Achieved ego identity Searching and confusion may sometimes be beneficial. Individuals who have achieved a strong sense of identity after a period of active searching are likely to be more personally autonomous, creative, and complex in their thinking than those whose identities were formed without a period of confusion. They also show a greater capacity for intimacy, a more confident sexual identity, a more positive self-concept, and more mature moral reasoning. While their relationships with their parents are generally positive, they have typically achieved considerable independence from their families (Bourne, 1978a, 1978b; Hodgson & Fischer, 1978; Orlofsky, 1978; Orlofsky, Marcia, & Lesser, 1973; St. Clair & Day, 1979).

Research comparisons show that young women who have achieved a clear sense of identity "have weighed occupational and ideological alternatives and have arrived at conclusions to which they appear committed, yielded [less] . . . to conformity pressures, and were also less uncomfortable in resisting them" than other groups tested (Toder & Marcia, 1973, p. 292). They chose relatively difficult college majors, and they also manifested few negative feelings, such as anxiety, hostility, or depression, than women without a firm identity status (Marcia, 1980).

Variations in identity formations So far we have been discussing identity formation as though it were a single task at which a young person either succeeds or fails. In reality, the matter is more complex. Patterns of identity formation may vary widely among particular adolescents, or groups of adolescents, as a result of influences that range from parent-child relationships to cultural or subcultural pressures and even the rate of social change. In a simple primitive society, where there are only a limited number of possible adult roles and little social change, identity formation may be a relatively simple task that is quickly accomplished. But in a rapidly changing, complex society like our own, where there is so much choice, the search for identity can be difficult and prolonged (Conger & Petersen, 1984; Erikson, 1968; Marcia, 1980; Waterman, 1982).

Within a particular society, identities may be typical or deviant: The individual may seek personal, social, and vocational roles that are expected and approved by society or more idiosyncratic roles. Some unusual roles are positive and constructive, as in the case of the artist or poet who "marches to a different drummer," or negative, as in the case of the long-term drug addict or "career criminal" (Conger, 1977a; Douvan & Adelson, 1966).

There are many variations in identity formation. The popular stereotype of an acute and fairly prolonged "identity crisis" is probably exaggerated. The belief by some clinical psychologists and others that absence of a period of intense adolescent turmoil portends later emotional disturbance is not supported by research findings (Conger, 1979). Many adolescents form an ego identity without serious "storm and stress."

Gender identity and sex-role identity

Most people acquire *gender identity,* an awareness and acceptance of one's basic biological nature as a male or female, early in life (see Chapter 10). With the notable exception of transsexuals (who typically report having felt, even as children, that they were trapped in a body of the wrong sex), the great majority of people, including most homosexuals, appear content with being male or female and have no desire to change (Green, 1974; Stoller, 1980).

But for those who resent their biological identity (e.g., who resent their sexual nature and their procreative capabilities or who are hostile to their own or the other sex), adolescence can be a particularly stressful and confusing period in development. Rapid sexual maturation calls dramatic attention to the fact that one's gender is a biological fact. Conflicts about gender identity are difficult to deal with and are likely to create significant problems in the development of a confident, secure *overall* identity (Conger & Petersen, 1984).

As explained in earlier chapters, a confident, secure sex-role identity means that you perceive yourself as masculine or feminine according to your own definition of these terms. This does *not* require rigid conformity to sex-role stereotypes. Two young women may both have clear and confident sex-role identities but define them quite differently. One of them may view being a highly independent, competitive corporate executive in a traditionally male business as entirely consistent with a feminine sex-role identity, while another may feel that her feminine identity is best expressed by devoting herself primarily to the roles of wife, mother, and homemaker.

The pattern labeled *androgyny*—a combination of traditional and socially valued "masculine" and "feminine" characteristics in the same individual—has recently come to be viewed as socially adaptive (Bem, 1981; Huston, 1983; Spence & Helmreich, 1978). In one study, four groups were compared: adolescents and youth who scored high on both socially positive masculine characteristics (e.g., independence, assertiveness) and socially positive feminine characteristics (nurturance, understanding)—the androgynous group; those who scored high only on masculine items; those who scored high only on feminine items; and those who scored low on both, referred to as "undifferentiated." As may be seen from Table 14.1, relatively few males or females were "cross-typed"; that is, few males scored highest on feminine items and few females scored highest on masculine items.

TABLE 14.1	COLLEGE SAMPLE			
Percentage of students falling into each of the four personal attributes categories for college and high school samples	**Undifferentiated**	**Feminine**	**Masculine**	**Androgynous**
Males	25	8	34	32
Females	28	32	14	27
	HIGH SCHOOL SAMPLE			
	Undifferentiated	**Feminine**	**Masculine**	**Androgynous**
Males	23	8	44	25
Females	18	35	14	35

Source: J. T. Spence. *Traits, roles, and the concept of androgyny.* Paper presented at the Conference on Perspectives on the Psychology of Women, Michigan State University, May 13–14, 1977. By permission.

Androgynous individuals of both sexes scored highest on measures of self-esteem, followed by the masculine, the feminine, and, lowest of all, the undifferentiated. Androgynous individuals also reported receiving more academic and extracurricular honors than undifferentiated individuals. Female athletes and scientists are more likely to score high on androgyny or on masculinity rather than solely on femininity. Masculine and androgynous self-perceptions characterize young people of both sexes who value and expect to do well in mathematics, formal logic, and spatial skills (Huston, 1983; Nash, 1979; Spence & Helmreich, 1978).

Androgyny in these studies is defined by socially valued attributes. Negatively valued masculine attributes (such as arrogance, greed, hostility) and negatively valued feminine characteristics (such as being gullible, servile, whiny, nagging) have also been measured. Males and females who have such characteristics do not fare well. People with negative feminine characteristics have low self-esteem. They face adjustment problems because they tend to be vulnerable, insecure, and hypersensitive. Individuals with negative masculine attributes tend to be overly aggressive and critical of others (Block, 1973; Spence, Helmreich, & Holahan, 1979).

It seems both socially and personally desirable to permit individuals of both sexes to be "both independent and tender, assertive and yielding, masculine and feminine, allowing people to cope more effectively with diverse situations" (Bem, 1975, p. 62). It should be noted, however, that positive masculine attributes, such as independence and self-confidence, are the most important and adaptive components of androgyny, especially for females (Huston, 1983).

Further, it is important to avoid imposing a new stereotype—even of some "ideal" androgynous balance—on all boys and girls, men and women. A better goal would be to permit each adolescent to develop his or her *unique* potential as a human being, consistent with the rights of others.

VOCATIONAL CHOICE IN A CHANGING WORLD	For most people, young and old alike, vocational identity forms an important part of overall identity (Conger & Petersen, 1984; Erikson, 1968; Marcia, 1980; Orlofsky, 1978). Having a job that society values—and doing it well—enhances self-esteem and the development of an increasingly secure, stable sense of identity. Conversely, being told by society that one is not needed and that meaningful employment is not available (a message being given to large numbers of young people today) can foster self-doubt, resentment, and a loss of self-esteem. It increases the likelihood of identity confusion or even, as in some cases of delinquency or "dropping out," a negative identity (Borow, 1976).

A number of groups, including a panel of the President's Science Advisory Committee, have recommended that young people aged 16 and over be given greater opportunity to become involved in part-time work experiences, including public service participation, in order to prepare them for the job market. A few such programs have been tried and proved successful. For example, in a school in Chicago formerly characterized by a high delinquency rate, students spend half of each day studying academic subjects at their own pace, earning credits when they complete a prescribed amount of work. During the other half, they are employed in business-funded training projects such as renovating buildings in the community. Among the results have been a high rate of attendance and elimination of vandalism (Conger & Petersen, 1984).

The work experiences that most help adolescents make the transition to the world of adult work are those that are relevant to the adolescents' future goals, but such jobs are hard to come by. Recent studies suggest that the jobs most frequently available to adolescents attending school, such as working at fast-food outlets, washing cars, or packing groceries, do have some benefits. They appear to promote a greater understanding of money matters, an increased work orientation, and a somewhat greater feeling of independence.

However, they do little to encourage future educational and vocational aspirations and planning. Some jobs lack challenge and tend to make adolescents doubt the intrinsic rewards of work. Others encourage acceptance of marginal business practices. Finally, while having worked during adolescence appears to have a positive effect on adult employability for high school dropouts, how much difference it makes in the case of full-time students is still unclear (Greenberger & Steinberg, 1981; Hamilton & Crouter, 1980; Steinberg, Greenberger, Garduque, Ruggiero, & Vaux, 1982; Stephenson, 1981).

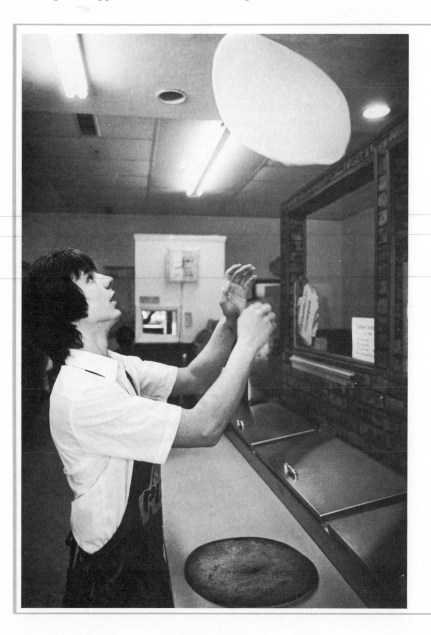

As adolescents leave childhood and approach the time when they must support themselves, they become progressively more realistic about their vocational goals. They begin attempting to match their aspirations and capabilities with available opportunities. In our society, the actual requirements of most jobs and their availability in the labor market are not matters of common knowledge, and young people clearly need help to make intelligent choices. Unfortunately, truly knowledgeable, skilled assistance is rarely available. Consequently, a young person's vocational interests usually develop in a rather unsystematic fashion, guided by such influences as parental desires, suggestions of school counselors (some of whom are poorly informed), accidental contact with various occupations, and the kinds of jobs friends are going into. Social class and sex-typed expectations also play a role.

Socioeconomic influences   Social class influences vocational goals in a variety of ways. For one thing, it helps to determine the kinds of occupations with which the young person will be familiar and, hence, be likely to consider in forming occupational aims. In addition, it plays an important role in determining the social acceptability of occupations. Certain types of occupations are considered appropriate to the members of a particular social class; others are considered inappropriate. Becoming a truck driver, a clerk in a grocery store, or an automobile mechanic may be considered an appropriate choice in a lower-middle-class group but not in an upper-class group. In one well-designed study, all graduating seniors in Wisconsin high schools were asked to state the occupations that they hoped eventually to enter. Their choices were then assigned "prestige scores." Very few students whose families were in the lower third of the socioeconomic-status scale aspired to high-prestige occupations; many students in the upper third did so. Furthermore, the later actual occupational attainments of students of lower socioeconomic status were close to their expectations (Little, 1967).

Some researchers argue that the relative values assigned by adolescents to different occupations vary by social class and that these variations largely account for social-class differences in vocational goals (Caro, 1966). Others argue that both middle-class and working-class youth agree on the relative desirability and prestige of various occupations. Differences in goals, they say, stem less from values than from perceptions of differences in opportunities and general life chances. A girl whose parents are unable to or uninterested in helping her go to college is not very likely to aspire to be a doctor. Similarly, a boy whose parents expect him to go to work upon completion of high school is not likely to spend much time contemplating a career as an engineer (Conger & Petersen, 1984; Stephenson, 1979).

Women and work   One of the most significant changes in American society since World War II has been the rapid rise in the number of women entering the job market. In 1947, only one-third of all women were employed or seeking work outside the home; by 1980, that figure had risen to just over half (two-thirds for 20- to 24-year-olds) (U.S. Department of Commerce, 1981) (see Table 14.2). It is estimated that by 1990, 2 out of every 3 married women, and 3 out of every 4 married women with children living at home, will be in the job market (Smith, 1979).

TABLE 14.2

Married, separated, and divorced women: labor force participation rate, by presence and age of children, 1960–1981

Item	PARTICIPATION RATE (PERCENT)				
	1960	1970	1975	1980	1981
All women	37.1	42.8	37.5	45.5	46.7
Married, husband present, total	30.5	40.8	44.4	50.1	51.0
No children under 18	34.7	42.2	43.9	46.0	46.3
Children 6–17 only	39.0	49.2	52.3	61.7	62.5
Children under 6	18.6	30.3	36.6	45.1	47.8
Separated, total	(NA)	52.3	54.8	59.4	60.8
No children under 18	(NA)	52.3	56.4	58.9	59.9
Children 6–17 only	(NA)	60.6	59.0	66.3	70.0
Children under 6	(NA)	45.4	49.1	52.2	51.0
Divorced, total	(NA)	70.9	72.1	74.5	75.0
No children under 18	(NA)	67.7	69.9	71.4	72.4
Children 6–17 only	(NA)	82.4	80.1	82.3	83.4
Children under 6	(NA)	63.3	65.6	68.3	65.4

Note: Does not include those in the work force seeking work, but currently unemployed.
Source: U.S. Bureau of Labor Statistics, 1982, & U.S. Department of Commerce, Bureau of the Census, *Statistical abstract of the United States, 1982–1983*. Washington, D.C.: U.S. Government Printing Office, 1982.

Despite the dramatic increase in women's participation in the labor force and decreases in sex-role stereotyping, members of both sexes still tend to have relatively traditional, sex-related occupational aspirations (e.g., skilled worker for boys, office worker, nurse, or teacher for girls). However, it is more common for females to aspire to jobs traditionally filled by males, such as business executive, physician, lawyer, engineer, and telephone line worker, than for males to aspire to traditionally feminine occupations (Astin, 1983; Marini, 1978). This sex difference appears due partly to the greater economic and other rewards associated with traditionally male jobs in our society, partly to the greater number and variety of such jobs, and partly to fewer inhibitions on the part of females in aspiring to "masculine" occupations (Conger & Petersen, 1984).

Young women with high-status occupational expectations—typically, those who want full-time careers in traditionally male fields—have less traditional sex-role attitudes than women with more traditional aspirations. They usually plan to marry late, have few children, and work while their children are young. Although most want to be involved with both a career and child rearing, they tend to be somewhat more oriented toward a job than toward children. They are also unlikely to view having children and being able to depend on a spouse's support as important considerations in deciding to marry. A minority plan not to marry or not to have children (Areshansel & Rosen, 1980; L. W. Hoffman, in press; Tittle, 1981).

Female adolescents planning to enter nontraditional careers typically score relatively high on measures of academic ability (particularly in the physical and biological sciences and in mathematics) and have high grades. They are generally independent, assertive, and concerned with exhibiting competence (Areshansel & Rosen, 1980; L. W. Hoffman, in press; Tittle, 1981).

In contrast, the minority of young women planning full-time careers as housewives and mothers endorse strongly traditional values with respect to occupational and domestic roles of men and women. They expect to marry young and have several children, they have relatively low educational aspirations, and they view children and having a spouse to rely on as important. Occupying a middle ground between these two extremes are adolescents who plan to stay at home while their children are young but work before having children and when their children are older (Areshansel & Rosen, 1980; Tittle, 1981).

With the new variety of options for women comes uncertainty among high school women about how to coordinate job and child-rearing roles (Areshansel & Rosen, 1980; Smith, 1979). Such uncertainty reflects a genuine dilemma. Finding workable solutions to the problems of combining children and a career is not easy in today's society.

Parental influences In general, if parents set high educational and occupational goals and reward good school work, their children have high aspiration levels. Working-class adolescents are more likely to seek advanced education and occupational mobility if their parents urge them to than if parents do not exert pressure in this direction (L. W. Hoffman, in press). In one study, *ambitious middle-class males* showed the highest percentage of parental support and encouragement for educational and vocational achievement. *Upwardly mobile working-class males* ranked a close second (Simpson, 1962). In contrast, *unambitious middle-class males* and *nonmobile working-class males* ranked far behind in percentage of parental support.

Father's occupation exerts a significant influence on the career choices of sons, though generally not on those of daughters (L. W. Hoffman, in press; Mortimer, 1976). Some of the reasons sons often choose the same work as their fathers seem obvious: greater opportunity to become familiar with the father's occupation as compared with others, easier access to the occupation, and, in some cases, a strong parental motivation—and sometimes pressure—for the son to enter the occupation. However, it appears that more subtle factors also play a part. For instance, a father may communicate certain values to his son that relate to the father's vocation. A physician might encourage his son to value health, the power of science, service to others, intellectual satisfaction, and high income. Such a process is most probable when the father's job has high prestige, the son has a close relationship with his father, and the father provides a strong *and* positive role model generally (Bell, 1969; Mortimer, 1976).

Maternal role models influence the career choices of daughters and the attitudes regarding appropriate sex and vocational roles for women for both daughters and sons (see Chapter 11). Young men and especially young women with employed mothers perceive smaller male-female differences in such generally sex-stereotyped attributes as competence and warmth-expressiveness than do the sons and daughters of nonemployed mothers. Adolescent daughters of employed mothers more often admire and want to be like their mothers than daughters of nonemployed mothers (L. W. Hoffman, 1974; Huston, 1983).

Young women's vocational attitudes and aspirations are influenced not just by whether a mother is employed but also by the mother's attitudes toward employment. If the mother is satisfied and involved in her work, and if she succeeds at combining the roles of worker, mother, and wife, her daughter often emulates her. A father who supports and accepts his career-oriented wife also contributes to his daughter's vocational attitudes (Baruch, 1972).

In summary, high-achieving women have high-achieving daughters because they provide appropriate role models for combining achievement and family roles, they encourage independence in their daughters, and they have husbands who also encourage independence and female achievement.

Peer group and school influences   Teachers, school counselors, and peer values also affect adolescents' career choices. Boys from lower-class homes have higher educational and vocational aspirations if they attend a largely middle-class school and associate frequently with middle-class boys than if they attend one whose students come primarily from a lower-class background. Increased contact with middle-class peers appears to foster "anticipatory socialization" into middle-class values (Simpson, 1962). Even these school influences may be related to parent values; upwardly mobile lower-class parents often choose their neighborhood for its middle-class schools. In general, parent influence is stronger than that of peers.

Vocational values and social change

The vocational values and attitudes of young people in the 1980s differ in a number of respects from those of their counterparts in the late 1960s and early 1970s. The early 1980s witnessed changing social values, an increasingly uncertain economy, and massive dislocations in the job market. Young people became more concerned with personal material success and financial security and less with philosophical and social issues than the earlier generation (Astin 1983; Bachman & Johnston, 1979; Bachman, Johnston, & O'Malley, 1981; Maggarrell, 1981). For example, between 1969 and 1982, the percentage of first-year college students in the United States who cited "being very well off financially" as an "essential or very important objective" increased from slightly less than half to almost 70 percent. "Developing a philosophy of life" was cited as a very important objective by 86 percent of females and 78.5 percent of males in 1969, but by 1982 these figures had declined to 47.5 percent for females and 46 percent for males. In addition, creative but not necessarily financially rewarding objectives such as becoming a writer or an artist, declined by as much as 50 percent in some instances. Among high school seniors, too, there have been parallel though less dramatic increases in the number rating "the chance to earn a good deal of money" and to have "a predictable, secure future" as very important in a job (Bachman & Johnston, 1979; Bachman et al., 1982).

Reflecting these changing concerns and values, the percentages of college students enrolling in the arts and humanities and the social sciences have steadily declined, while the percentages of those enrolling in such fields as business, engineering, computer science, and preprofessional programs have increased. These changes were particularly evident among women students. For example, while the number of first-year college women aspiring to be teachers declined by more than two-thirds in the past decade (from 38 to 10 percent), the number planning to become businesswomen or executives more than doubled (from less than 4 to nearly 10 percent) (Astin, 1981).

A new "silent generation"?   Do these changes mean, as some observers have suggested, a return to the unquestioning conformity and suppression of individuality that supposedly characterized the "silent generation" of the 1950s? (Conger, 1981). The evidence indicates otherwise. Today's youth are generally more willing to adjust to the demands of the work place and more ready to accept compromise than were their 1960s predecessors. But they are far less willing than pre-1960s youth to suppress their own individuality and needs for self-expression, on or off the job. When American high school seniors in 1980 were asked what things they rated very important in a job, the two most frequent responses were having "interesting things to do" (90 percent) and "using skills or ability" (74 percent), although nearly two-thirds cited "good chances for advancement" and a "predictable, secure future." Furthermore, contemporary young people have much less faith in big business (and other social institutions) than did their 1950s counterparts. For example, 41 percent of college-bound high school seniors in 1980 agreed that there is considerable dishonesty and immorality in the leadership of large corporations, and 29 percent thought that corporations had not been doing a good job for the country. More than half felt that corporations should have less influence on people's lives, and only 9 percent felt they should have more influence (Bachman et al., 1981). In brief, today's young people want to combine challenging work, self-expression, and free time for outside interests with at least a moderately high income, economic security, and the chance to get ahead (Conger & Petersen, 1984; Yankelovich, 1981). How successful they will be in achieving these combined goals is a question for the future.

Vocational prospects in a changing world   What, then, are the future vocational prospects for today's adolescents and young adults? Unemployment rates for young people, women, and minorities have consistently exceeded those for other segments of the population by a significant margin even in the best of times (see Box 14.2 and Figures 14.1 and 14.2). Unemployment among black youth has been rising rapidly since the early 1950s, and by 1983 exceeded 50 percent. In some inner-city areas, the teenage minority unemployment rate reached 70 percent or more.

The problem, of course, is not simply the number of jobs but also the kinds of jobs that will be needed in the 1980s. Automation and rapid technological change (especially in the development and application of computer technology), the consolidation of small businesses and farms into larger ones, and increased urbanization are producing significant shifts in employment patterns. The numbers of jobs available for unskilled industrial workers and farm workers

BOX 14.2
*Women in
the work
force: New
opportunities
and old
realities*

What are the vocational prospects for women now entering the labor market? If one looks only at current statistics for women as a whole, the answer appears to be, not very good. Full-time earnings for women are still only about 60 percent of those for men. Furthermore, the great majority of women still hold jobs in the same fields in which women have been employed since early in the twentieth century.

In some respects, the opportunities for well-educated women are expanding. During the 1970s, the percentage of female lawyers, judges, bank officials, financial managers, scientists, engineers, electricians, and carpenters doubled. During those years, the proportion of women accountants rose from 21.7 percent to 36.2 percent; among sales managers in retail trade, it went from 15.6 percent to 25.7 percent; and among computer specialists it went from 16.8 percent to 25.7 percent (see Table B14.2).

TABLE B14.2

*Changes in selected
employment
patterns for
women and blacks
and other
minorities,
1972–1980*

Occupation	PERCENT FEMALE		PERCENT BLACK AND OTHER MINORITIES	
	1972	1980	1972	1980
Accountants	21.7	36.3	4.3	8.2
Computer specialists	16.8	25.7	5.5	8.0
Engineers	.8	4.0	3.4	5.9
Lawyers and judges	3.8	12.8	3.8	4.2
Life and physical scientists	10.0	20.3	7.8	9.6
Physicians	10.1	13.4	6.2	10.8
Registered nurses	97.6	96.5	8.2	11.4
Social scientists	21.3	36.0	5.7	5.4
Writers, artists, and entertainers	31.7	39.3	4.8	5.9
Managers and administrators (except farm)	17.6	26.1	4.0	5.2
Sales clerks	68.9	71.1	5.0	7.2
Clerical and kindred workers	75.6	80.1	8.7	11.1
Secretaries	99.1	99.1	5.2	6.7
Craft and kindred workers	3.6	6.0	3.6	8.3
Carpenters	.5	1.5	5.9	5.7
Electricians	.6	1.2	3.2	5.7
Telephone installers	1.9	8.7	4.2	7.8
Machine operators	27.0	30.7	14.4	16.1
Bus drivers	34.1	44.9	17.1	19.9
Laborers (except farm)	6.3	11.6	20.2	16.9
Construction laborers	.5	2.8	22.4	16.6
Gardeners	2.2	5.2	20.0	16.3

Source: U.S. Department of Commerce, Bureau of the Census, *Statistical abstract of the United States: 1981*. Washington, D.C.: U.S. Government Printing Office, 1981.

Many of the greatest opportunities for women lie in traditionally masculine fields, partly because these fields are expanding rapidly and partly to redress prior imbalances. These include engineering, mathematics, computer programming, business administration, international banking and government, high-technology jobs, and positions requiring languages such as Russian, Chinese, Japanese, or those of the third world. According to the economist Eli Ginzberg, chair of the National Commission for Employment Policy, academic preparation is critical for entry into such jobs. "It's a question of what you learned or did not learn in college. . . . If you come out with solid training in mathematics, economics, accounting, even biology, you'll have a much easier time" (Bennetts, 1979, p. 58).

Women who succeed in attaining such high-status jobs not only have good training but have career patterns that are like those of high-achieving men. Continuity of job experience is important. Women who leave the labor market during their child-rearing years have difficulty in returning to such positions. Long-term career plans—thinking of a job as a stepping stone in a career rather than as a temporary measure—is also important.

Yet these very demands of high-level careers pose a dilemma for many adolescents. Although 85 percent of today's young women will at some time in their lives have to support themselves, and often a family as well, females are still socialized to put their own careers second to the jobs of their husbands and to the needs of their children. In families with children, society still expects women to assume primary responsibility for the care of those children. Articles abound in the press debating the pros and cons of "working mothers." It would be surprising to see anyone suggest that fathers may be doing harm to their children by working outside the home. And when the children are sick, or the baby sitter cancels, the mother in a two-career family is typically the one who stays home.

There are also many pressures on women to put their husband's career ahead of their own. Women are expected to leave their jobs and follow their husbands if the male receives a promotion or job offer requiring a move. But men rarely expect to disrupt their careers to permit their wives to take a better job. Most men and women also feel uncomfortable about a marriage in which the wife earns more or has a more prestigious position than the husband.

New opportunities for young women exist, but the old realities of job discrimination and stereotypes about women workers have not entirely disappeared. Although the data contradict myths about women workers, many employers still believe that women work for "extra" money, that women are likely to get pregnant and quit, and that women have less career motivation than men.

The adolescent female reaching adulthood today is indeed faced with new opportunities in the job market and a social climate in which pursuit of a career is more readily accepted than it was for her mother's generation. But she also confronts the old realities of societal barriers to good jobs, a socialization history that may not encourage career orientation, and a realistic sense that her responsibility for providing a loving, emotionally healthy environment for her children may conflict with career demands (Bennetts, 1979; Smith, 1979; U.S. Department of Commerce, 1981a).

FIGURE 14.1

*Comparison of teen-
age and adult unem-
ployment rates, 1954–
1982. (From U.S. De-
partment of Labor,
Bureau of Labor
Statistics, 1982.)*

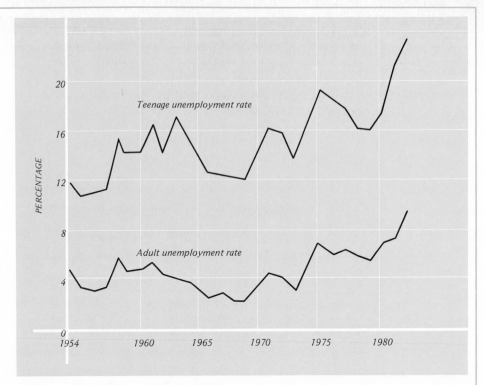

FIGURE 14.2

*Changes in youth
unemployment among
black and white
youth, 1954–1982.
(From U.S. Bureau of
Labor Statistics,
1983.)*

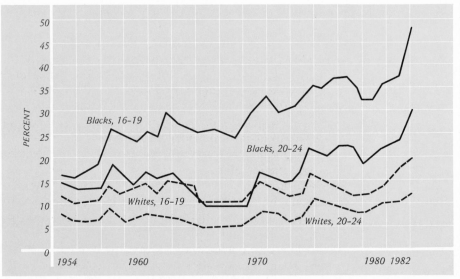

declined between 1972 and 1980; those for professional and technical workers
and for workers engaged in service occupations and clerical and sales positions
rose significantly. These trends are expected to continue through the 1980s
(U.S. Department of Labor, 1980a, 1980b) (see Figure 14.3).

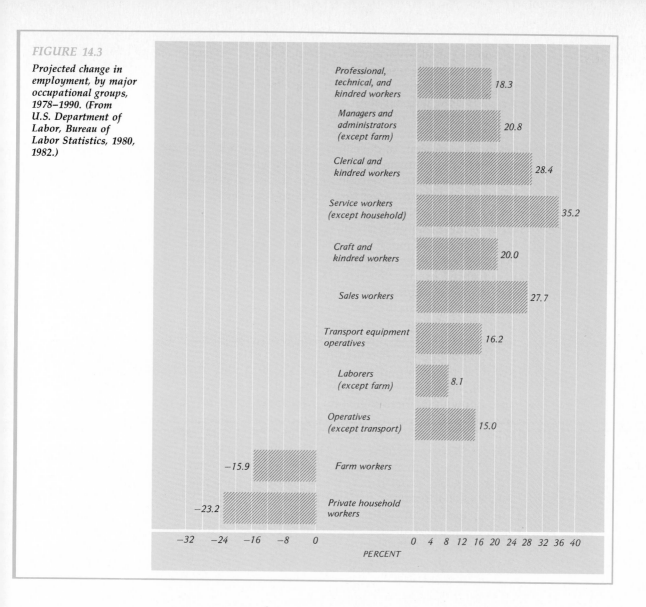

FIGURE 14.3

Projected change in employment, by major occupational groups, 1978–1990. (From U.S. Department of Labor, Bureau of Labor Statistics, 1980, 1982.)

Professional, technical, and kindred workers — 18.3

Managers and administrators (except farm) — 20.8

Clerical and kindred workers — 28.4

Service workers (except household) — 35.2

Craft and kindred workers — 20.0

Sales workers — 27.7

Transport equipment operatives — 16.2

Laborers (except farm) — 8.1

Operatives (except transport) — 15.0

Farm workers — −15.9

Private household workers — −23.2

−32 −24 −16 −8 0   0 4 8 12 16 20 24 28 32 36 40

PERCENT

Poorly educated youth with few skills will find themselves increasingly penalized in the years ahead. Obviously, opportunities will be much greater for youth who have managed to obtain increased skills and education, but even advanced education will not guarantee a high-level job. It is now estimated that between 1978 and 1990, the number of college graduates entering the labor force will exceed by 3.3 million the number of openings in jobs traditionally filled by graduates. College graduates are expected to continue to have a competitive advantage over those with less education, although significant numbers will probably be employed below the level of skill for which they were trained (U.S. Department of Labor, 1980a).

CHAPTER 14 / Adolescence: identity, values, and problems of adjustment

At no time in life are people more concerned about moral values and standards than during adolescence. The increased cognitive capacities of adolescents foster greater awareness of moral questions and values and more sophistication in dealing with them. At the same time, the demands placed upon adolescents by society are changing at an accelerated rate, and this in itself requires a continuing reappraisal of moral values and beliefs—particularly in a society as filled with conflicting pressures and values as our own. Under such circumstances, the problem of developing a strong sense of identity cannot be separated from the problem of values. "If individuals are to be able to maintain some stability in their conception of self and in internal guides to action in a changing world, they must be faithful to some basic values" (Conger, 1977a, p. 516), although they may have to adapt new ways of implementing these values to meet changing circumstances.

Cognitive growth and moral development

The stages of moral judgment postulated by Kohlberg were discussed in Chapter 9. As indicated there, adolescent thinking about moral issues has usually advanced beyond the basic preconventional level. At the level of *conventional morality* (stages 3 and 4 in Kohlberg's system), societal needs and values take primacy over individual interests. Initially, at stage 3, this means a strong emphasis on being "a good person in your own eyes and those of others" (Kohlberg, 1976, p. 34), that is, having socially desirable motives and showing concern about others. The intention behind behavior, not simply the behavior itself, is of major importance; one seeks approval by "being good." In stage 4, this approach is expanded to include a concern with conformity to the social order and with maintaining, supporting, and justifying this order. Adolescents rarely advance beyond this level, to postconventional stages of moral judgment (Colby, Kohlberg, Gibbs, & Lieberman, 1983; Kohlberg, 1976; Kohlberg & Gilligan, 1971; Rest, 1983).

With more advanced cognitive and moral development, adolescents begin to question the social and political beliefs of their parents and other adults. Their personal values and opinions become less absolute and more relative. Political thought also becomes more abstract and less authoritarian. When asked the purpose of laws, a 12-year-old replied, "If we had no laws, people could go around killing people" (Adelson, 1971, p. 1015). In contrast, by 15 or 16 years of age, and certainly by age 18, laws tend to be viewed as codes for guiding human conduct ("something for people to go by," "to set up a standard of behavior") (Adelson, 1982).

Like an adult, an adolescent may be able to conceptualize moral issues with considerable sophistication and to formulate the proper moral course to take but may not always act in accordance with this formulation (M. L. Hoffman, 1970, 1980; Weiss, 1982). In other words, as pointed out in Chapter 9, moral judgments do not relate to moral behavior in a simple way. In one study (Tapp & Levine, 1972), subjects were asked, "Why should people follow rules?" They were then asked, "Why do you follow rules?" Most middle-school children and adolescents showed more "primitive" moral levels in answering the second question than in answering the first. For example, only 3 percent of older adolescents said that people *should* follow rules "to avoid negative consequences," but 25 percent said they personally *would* do so. One study demonstrated that having to wrestle with real-life moral choices (such as whether or not to terminate an adolescent pregnancy) fosters development of a higher level of moral reasoning in some individuals but apparently leads to regression to a lower level in others. Young women who reached a higher level of moral reasoning when they made a decision about abortion showed better subsequent adjustment than those who regressed (Gilligan & Belenky, 1980).

Some adolescents show a reasonable degree of adherence to moral principles, even under duress. Others yield rather quickly to temptation or to group pressure to engage in thoughtless or antisocial behavior. Still others appear to be guided in their behavior solely by the threat of external punishment rather than by internalized standards. Whether moral standards will be internalized and serve as strong guides to behavior depends to a considerable extent on the nature of parent-child relationships. Parents who are warm and whose disciplinary practices are based primarily on *induction* (reasoning and explanations for parental rules or standards) are most likely to have children with mature moral development, as evidenced by internalized moral standards (M. L. Hoffman, 1970, 1980). Inductive techniques are particularly important for adolescents. They "help foster the image of the parent as a rational, nonarbitrary authority. They provide the child with cognitive resources needed to control his own behavior" (Hoffman, 1970, p. 331).

Moral values and personal conflicts

Adolescents' values do not always represent rational decisions logically arrived at. Values are often "chosen" by adolescents for reasons having to do with personal conflicts and motives, many of which are unconscious (Conger & Petersen, 1984; Douvan & Adelson, 1966). Preoccupation with the moral issues of war and peace, for example, may stem from perfectly rational concerns with these important matters, or it may reflect uncertainty about being able to handle the strong aggressive impulses that are likely to accompany adolescence, particularly in boys. Conflicts with parents about morality or politics may reflect efforts to establish an independent identity or to express a deep resentment toward hostile or indifferent parents. Intimate, frequently unconscious motivations and conflicts have much to do with the increased preoccupation with moral values and beliefs that characterizes many adolescents.

Current trends in adolescent values

The greatest danger in discussing trends in adolescent values and behavior and their relationship to social change is that of overgeneralization. In the middle and late 1960s, much was made of a so-called revolution in the values of young people, who were said to be developing a "counterculture." There is no question that the troubled decade of the 1960s brought major changes in the values and behavior of many American adolescents. Significant minorities of young people became increasingly disillusioned by a society that they viewed as unjust, cruel, hypocritical, overly competitive, or, in the broadest sense of the term, immoral (Conger, 1981). In response, some, like the hippies, became social dropouts, while others initiated vigorous efforts to institute social change—efforts that ran the gamut from conventional political activity "within the system" to extreme "revolutionary" tactics.

By no means all adolescents joined the "counterculture" of the 1960s and early 1970s. Its values were most strongly held and expressed by a conspicuous, often highly articulate minority of young people on high school and college campuses, in the streets, and in films and the arts. Although the values of the *average* adolescent of that period did change in important respects, they changed less than popular stereotypes suggested (Harris, 1971; Yankelovich, 1974).

As America entered the 1980s, the risk of overgeneralization again became great. Some critics interpreted the marked decline in political and social activism that occurred during the 1970s as the beginning of an across-the-board return to more conservative and conformist pre-1960s attitudes and values.

As explained in discussing vocational choice, it is true that the social and economic values of adolescents have become somewhat more conservative. There is an increased concern among adolescents and young adults for personal well-being and financial success. In addition, there is a diminished concern for the welfare of others—particularly the disadvantaged—and of society itself (Astin, 1980, 1982, 1983; Bachman, & Johnston, 1979; Bachman et al., 1981, 1982; Conger, 1981). Less than one-fifth of contemporary high school seniors and first-year college students consider "making a contribution to society" or "participating in community action" a very important value (Bachman et al., 1981, 1982). And among entering college students in 1981, "keeping up with political affairs" was cited as very important by 32 percent fewer young women and by 14 percent fewer men than a decade earlier (Astin, 1980, 1982). At a more personal level, the number of college students who considered "helping others in difficulty" an important objective declined slightly in the past decade, from 58 percent to 54 percent among males and from 75 percent to 71 percent among females.

This shift in emphasis from social to personal concerns has been accompanied by a decline in political liberalism. A decade ago, one-third of entering students described themselves as liberals; in 1981, less than 1 in 5 did so (Astin, 1980, 1982). Although the number considering themselves conservative remained constant, the middle-of-the-road group rose sharply, from 45 percent in 1970 to 60 percent in 1981. One reason may be a general skepticism about ideologies and social institutions. Today's young people have reservations about the infallibility, or even at times the morality, of major institutions and their values, including big business, big labor, Congress, the executive branch of government, the courts, the schools, and law enforcement agencies.

Personal and moral values The so-called sexual revolution among middle- and upper-class adolescents and youth in the late 1960s has endured. Not only has there been no return to a more traditional sexual morality, but previous trends are still continuing as indicated by data presented in Chapter 13.

More broadly, the desires for fulfilling oneself as a person and having an opportunity for self-expression also have remained strong. Freedom, self-determination, and equality for women received increasingly broad support in the 1970s and early 1980s. Discrimination on the basis of age is also currently under siege.

In accordance with the continuing emphasis over the past decade on the "freedom to be me," many young people showed a heightened interest in their own physical well-being, as evidenced in jogging, conditioning programs, and concern for nutrition. Others became involved in self-improvement programs and a variety of psychological "therapies," from est and "looking out for number one" to meditation and relaxation programs. Self-realization—physical, psychological, spiritual, or material—appeared to be the predominant message (Conger, 1981).

The appropriate question, in our view, is not whether 1980s adolescents and young adults are engaged in a general retreat from the values of the 1960s and early 1970s. Rather, it is whether the extension and expansion of such personal, moral, and sexual values of the 1960s and 1970s as self-fulfillment and self-expression into the 1980s is psychologically growth-enhancing without a corresponding sense of commitment to the welfare of others and of society itself.

Changing religious beliefs The young person's religious beliefs are likely to become more abstract and less literal between the ages of 12 and 18. For example, God comes to be seen more frequently as an abstract power and less frequently as a fatherly human being. Religious views also become more tolerant and less dogmatic (Conger & Peterson, 1984).

Cultural as well as age changes in religious values appear to be at work (Caplow & Bahr, 1979; Yankelovich, 1974). While most young people still express a general belief in God or a universal spirit, there was a steady erosion during the 1960s and 1970s in the percentage of young people who viewed religion as "a very important personal value" (Yankelovich, 1974). At least part of this decline of interest in religion seems clearly related to changing values among young people and a perception on the part of many of them that religion—at least formal, institutionalized religion—is failing to reflect these changes. For example, rightly or wrongly, approximately half of all adolescents believe churches are not doing their best to understand young people's ideas about sex. Many more contemporary adolescents attribute understanding attitudes about sex to God than to institutionalized religion (Sorensen, 1973). A number of young people, particularly in the women's movement, also feel that the Catholic church and some Protestant denominations are not according full status and recognition to women, and a majority of Catholic youth disagree with the church's position on birth control, annulment and divorce, and the right of priests to marry.

At the same time there has been increased interest in more fundamental religious traditions among a significant number of youth. Nearly half of all Protestant teenagers, and 22 percent of their Catholic peers, report a "born-again" experience—a turning point in their lives achieved by making a personal commitment to Christ (Gallup, 1978). These figures are similar to those obtained among adults.

Another development among young people in the past decade has been the emergence of a number of new religious sects, such as the Jesus Movement, Hare Krishna, Children of God, Sun Myung Moon's Unification Church, and others (Galanter, 1980). Some of these groups are informal and loosely structured. They are held together principally by a concern for others, disillusionment with materialistic values (or the apparent absence of any strong personal values) in contemporary society, and a belief—often simple, direct, and sometimes fundamentalist—in personal salvation. Other groups tend to be highly authoritarian in structure. They may require the surrender of all individual autonomy and complete conformity, both in behavior and belief, to the dictates of leaders. Some young people enlist in such groups as a result of sudden and total conversion experiences following a period of rootlessness and identity confusion. There is often a prior history of difficulties in parent-child relationships, extensive drug use, sexual exploration, and life "on the road." Other young people, particularly in less authoritarian movements, seem to be expressing a satisfying and, for them, workable set of simple, straightforward values in an otherwise chaotic society.

The blue-collar revolution One of the more remarkable aspects of the changes in the values of youth since the late 1960s has been the extent to which the values of noncollege, working-class youth have become more like those of their more economically favored, college-student peers. In 1969, the attitudes and beliefs of noncollege youth were markedly more conservative than those of college youth. This generalization held for a wide range of issues, from sexual freedom, drug use, and conformity in dress to views on the Vietnam war, minority rights, and attitudes toward business and government. Clearly, in the late 1960s, young people, like adults, had their own "silent majority" (Yankelovich, 1969).

In the intervening years, however, there appears to have been a rapid transmission of values from a minority of college youth to youth generally (Conger, 1981; Yankelovich, 1974, 1981). By the early 1980s, differences between college or college-bound young people and their noncollege peers were considerably smaller than in the late 1960s. For example, both groups currently share generally similar views with respect to sexual morality, religion, the work ethic, race relations, the role of women in the work force, and the importance of marriage and family life (Bachman et al., 1981; Yankelovich, 1974, 1981).

THE ROOTS OF ALIENATION

In their attitudes toward their own lives, most young people are reasonably optimistic. Although fewer noncollege youth than college youth feel they are in control of their future (largely for economic reasons), nearly two-thirds do. And among both groups, three-quarters feel that, all in all, "my own life is going well," nearly two-thirds say they are "pretty happy," an additional 20 percent say they are "very happy," and 6 out of 10 state that they anticipate "no difficulty in accepting the kind of life society has to offer" (Bachman et al., 1981). When asked recently if they thought their lives would be better in 5 years, about 8 out of 10 American high school seniors said yes—although 3 out of 5 expected things to get worse for this country and the world during this period (Bachman et al., 1981).

Although young people generally feel reasonably happy, positive about themselves, and optimistic about their own future, there remain significant minorities who do not share these feelings. At least 10 percent feel that their lives are not very useful, that they have few friends they can get together with or turn to for help, and that there is little sense in planning for the future because plans hardly ever work out anyway. Over 16 percent of college-bound high school seniors (and nearly one-third of those not planning 4 years of college) agree or mostly agree that "every time I try to get ahead, something or somebody stops me'' (Bachman et al., 1981, p. 187). Small but significant minorities (10 to 20 percent) express strong disenchantment with government, business, labor, the military, the courts, the police, and the justice system generally, and feel that these social institutions have too much influence in our society (Bachman et al., 1981).

Alienation is a profound rejection of the values of society and an isolation from other people that goes well beyond the skepticism of the average adolescent. Lower-class minority and poor white youth who have suffered economic deprivation and ethnic discrimination clearly have reason to feel alienated from society. However, another kind of alienation became increasingly apparent in the turbulent decade of the 1960s and early 1970s—alienation among privileged middle- and upper-class youth. There were significant variations in the sources of these privileged youths' alienation and the ways in which it was manifested. For some, alienation derived from particular kinds of developmental experiences, such as disturbed parent-child relationships, that would be likely to result in alienation in most societies (Keniston, 1968; Seeman, 1975). For others, specific social concerns played a dominant role: racial oppression, economic discrimination, violations of personal freedom, the bitterly opposed war in Indochina, and the dangers of nuclear war. In still other instances, alienation was both deep and pervasive, amounting to a rejection of society as a whole, a society viewed as inimical to these young people's most deeply held values: intimacy, individuality, autonomy, and honesty (Conger, 1976, 1981; Yankelovich, 1969, 1974).

Political and social alienation have declined markedly since the early 1970s. What appears to have taken place among the current generation of adolescents and youth is an increasing pragmatism and a greater substitution of private for public concerns. Though not enchanted by the state of society and its institutions, these young people currently appear less inclined to view issues as one-sided, less likely to believe that social changes can occur quickly, and more skeptical of the ability of the individual to contribute significantly to them.

Although it is too early to tell whether it will expand, or even to define it with precision, a newer form of alienation has been noted in a minority of adolescents (Conger, 1981; Yankelovich, 1981). This newer alienation is more subtle, elusive, and private than the highly public, multifaceted, intense, and strongly articulated alienation and dissent of the 1960s. It appears to be characterized by increased feelings of loneliness, a desire for—but difficulty in achieving—intimacy, feelings of rootlessness, a decreased sense of purpose and direction in life, and a diffuse sense of self (Conger, 1981; Lasch, 1979; Yankelovich, 1981).

Achieving the capacity for intimacy is the developmental task that follows attainment of identity, according to Erikson's theory (1968). Intimacy is a true sharing of oneself with another that involves caring, trust, and sustained commitment. This is especially true in love, but it is also true in friendship: A "fair weather" friend is just that. The alternative to intimacy is isolation. A recent survey found that 70 percent of Americans—older as well as younger— "now recognize that while they have many acquaintances they have few close friends—and they experience this as a serious void in their lives" (Yankelovich, 1981, p. 25). Furthermore, 2 out of 5 state that they have fewer close friends now than they did in the past. Whether these trends will be reversed, and whether current efforts to develop a greater sense of community (e.g., mutual support groups, neighborhood coalitions) will succeed, is still unclear.

ADOLESCENTS AND DRUGS

In the past two decades, drug use by adolescents increased markedly (Abelson et al., 1977; Johnston, Bachman, & O'Malley, 1979). Although many adults think this increase is unique to young people and almost exclusively a legacy of the drug culture of the late 1960s, such a view is misleading. Widespread drug use is not restricted to adolescents and youth, nor did it begin with the 1960s drug culture. Although there have been, and to some extent still are, significant differences between generations in their patterns of drug use, the fact is that the broader society has been developing increasingly into a "drug culture" for many years. For example, prescriptions for antianxiety medications such as Valium and Librium have more than doubled since 1964. Valium is now the most widely prescribed drug in the nation: An estimated 10 to 15 percent of all Americans took this drug in 1982, and many adults are addicted to it. In the words of one 13-year-old, "We're not supposed to take drugs but TV is full of commercials showing people running for a pill because something is bugging them."

Research has shown that young people whose parents make significant use of such drugs as alcohol, tranquilizers, tobacco, sedatives, and amphetamines are more likely than other adolescents to use marijuana, alcohol, and other drugs themselves (Brook, Lukoff, & Whiteman, 1980; Jessor & Jessor, 1977; Kandel, 1980). As one 15-year-old boy expressed it, "In my house, you can't sneeze without getting a pill. My mother is always taking something for headaches and my father is always taking something to keep awake to get work done at night. They're not drunks but they sure drink a lot. So, now I'm a criminal for smoking pot?" (Conger, 1979, p. 76).

Incidence of drug use

While too many adolescents are becoming serious, high-risk drug users, the majority are not. Many young people use marijuana, alcohol, and tobacco, but relatively few use such "counterculture" drugs as LSD, inhalants (such as glue), "uppers" (amphetamines), "downers" (barbiturates), heroine, cocaine, PCP ("angel dust"), and Quaaludes (see Figure 14.4). In addition, many former occasional users have quit.

By 1982, overall adolescent drug use appeared to have declined (Johnston et al., 1979, 1981, 1982). Regular use of marijuana, which had been rising steadily among high school students for 15 years, showed a steady decline between 1978 and 1982 (from 10.7 to 6.3 percent, in the case of daily use). Decreases also occurred in the annual, monthly, and daily use of inhalants, barbiturates, and tranquilizers; in contrast, use of stimulants (amphetamines) showed a steady increase until 1982, when use declined moderately. In large measure, however, stimulants were used primarily as stay awake pills, rather than to get high (see Table 14.3).

The situation with respect to tobacco use is more complex. While the incidence of smoking among adolescent males declined significantly during the

FIGURE 14.4

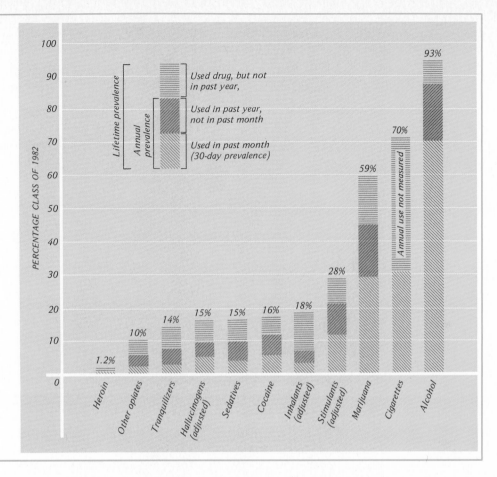

Prevalence and re-
cency of use of 11
types of drugs among
high school gradu-
ates, class of 1982.
(From L. D. Johnston,
J. G. Bachman, &
P. M. O'Malley. Stu-
dent drug use, atti-
tudes, and beliefs,
1975–1982. U.S. De-
partment of Health
and Human Services.
Washington, D.C.:
National Institute on
Drug Abuse, 1982.
DHHS Publication
No. ADM 82–1260.)

1970s, the incidence for females rose dramatically, so that by 1979 female smok-
ers outnumbered males for the first time. In subsequent years, however,
smoking declined significantly among both sexes, although in 1982 this decline
ended, at least temporarily. In 1982, 14.7 percent of adolescent females and 13.1
percent of males reported smoking more than half a pack a day (Johnston et al.,
1981, 1982; *Smoking and Health,* 1979)

The use of cocaine among high school seniors declined in 1982, following
7 years of rapid increase. Heroin use, never large, remained steady, as did the
use of hallucinogens and PCP. The use of other narcotics declined slightly in
1982.

Nevertheless, there is little room for complacency. Almost 10 percent of
14-year-olds are already heavy drinkers. And although regular use of alcohol
among adolescents appears to be decreasing slightly, it is also beginning at
somewhat younger age levels. The fact that over 6 percent of high school seniors
are still using marijuana daily and that a small but significant minority, according to teachers, are arriving at school "stoned" and smoking again during the
school day is hardly reassuring (Johnston et al., 1981, 1982).

CHAPTER 14 / Adolescence: identity, values, and problems of adjustment

TABLE 14.3

Trends in 30-day prevalence of 16 types of drugs

PERCENT WHO USED IN LAST 30 DAYS

	Class of 1975	Class of 1976	Class of 1977	Class of 1978	Class of 1979	Class of 1980	Class of 1981	Class of 1982	1981–1982 change
Approx. N =	(9400)	(15400)	(17100)	(17800)	(15500)	(15900)	(17500)	(17700)	
Marijuana/Hashish	27.1	32.2	35.4	37.1	36.5	33.7	31.6	28.5	−3.1ss
Inhalants[a]	NA	0.9	1.3	1.5	1.7	1.4	1.5	1.5	0.0
Inhalants adjusted[b]	NA	NA	NA	NA	3.1	2.7	2.3	2.5	+0.2
Amyl & Butyl Nitrites[c]	NA	NA	NA	NA	2.4	1.8	1.4	1.1	−0.3
Hallucinogens	4.7	3.4	4.1	3.9	4.0	3.7	3.7	3.4	−0.3
Hallucinogens adjusted[d]	NA	NA	NA	NA	5.5	4.4	4.4	4.3	−0.1
LSD	2.3	1.9	2.1	2.1	2.4	2.3	2.5	2.4	−0.1
PCP[c]	NA	NA	NA	NA	2.4	1.4	1.4	1.0	−0.4
Cocaine	1.9	2.0	2.9	3.9	5.7	5.2	5.8	5.0	−0.8s
Heroin	0.4	0.2	0.3	0.3	0.2	0.2	0.2	0.2	0.0
Other opiates[e]	2.1	2.0	2.8	2.1	2.4	2.4	2.1	1.8	−0.3
Stimulants[e]	8.5	7.7	8.8	8.7	9.9	12.1	15.8	13.7	−2.1sss
Stimulants adjusted[e,f]	NA	NA	NA	NA	NA	NA	NA	10.7	—
Sedatives[e]	5.4	4.5	5.1	4.2	4.4	4.8	4.6	3.4	−1.2sss
Barbiturates[e]	4.7	3.9	4.3	3.2	3.2	2.9	2.6	2.0	−0.6s
Methaqualone[e]	2.1	1.6	2.3	1.9	2.3	3.3	3.1	2.4	−0.7ss
Tranquilizers[e]	4.1	4.0	4.6	3.4	3.7	3.1	2.7	2.4	−0.3
Alcohol	68.2	68.3	71.2	72.1	71.8	72.0	70.7	69.7	−1.0
Cigarettes	36.7	38.8	38.4	36.7	34.4	30.5	29.4	30.0	+0.6

Notes: Level of significance of difference between the two most recent classes: s = .05, ss = .01, sss = .001. NA indicates data not available.

[a] Data based on four questionnaire forms. N is four-fifths of N indicated.

[b] Adjusted for underreporting of amyl and butyl nitrites.

[c] Data based on a single questionnaire form. N is one-fifth of N indicated.

[d] Adjusted for underreporting of PCP.

[e] Only drug use which was not under a doctor's orders is included here.

[f] Adjusted for overreporting of the nonprescription stimulants. Data based on three questionnaire forms. N is three-fifths of N indicated.

Source: L. D. Johnston, J. G. Bachman, & P. M. O'Malley. *Student drug use, attitudes, and beliefs, 1975–1982.* (DHHS Publication No. ADM 82-1260). U.S. Department of Health and Human Services. Washington, D.C.: National Institute on Drug Abuse, 1982.

The greatest danger in the minds of most people who work with adolescents is not the young person who occasionally has a few drinks or smokes a marijuana "joint" at a party with friends "for fun." It is the adolescent who turns repeatedly to drugs in order to cope with insecurity, stress, psychological tension, low self-esteem, feelings of rejection or alienation, conflicts with parents, or problems of daily living. Too many vulnerable adolescents think that they are trying drugs for fun or to experiment only to find that drug use has become a psychological crutch that is increasingly difficult to renounce.

Why do adolescents take drugs?

The reasons adolescents take drugs vary widely. So does the seriousness of their drug use. There is a world of difference between the curious young adolescent who tries marijuana at a party with friends and the lonely despairing young person in an urban ghetto who has become hooked on heroin as "an escape to nowhere," in the words of one 14-year-old ex-addict.

One reason adolescents may try a drug is simply because it is there. Between 75 and 98 percent of adolescent users of most drugs (except LSD, heroin, or other opiates) say they can obtain them fairly easily (Johnston et al., 1981). Adolescents characteristically are curious about their expanding world and are far more inclined than most adults to take risks. They probably do so partly to prove their boldness ("not being chicken") and sense of adventure and partly because they do not really believe, at least initially, that anything disastrous can really happen to *them* (Conger, 1979).

Peer pressure   Peers also play an important part in adolescent drug use (Brook et al., 1980; Brunswick & Boyle, 1979). Indeed, one of the best predictors of whether an adolescent will use a drug is use of that drug by his friends, especially the young person's best friend (Jessor & Jessor, 1977; Kandel, 1978, 1980). A 15-year-old said, "People my age sometimes follow the group so they won't be outcasts. They try to enjoy themselves, but then things get out of hand" (Gallup, 1977).

Rebellion against parents   Whether an adolescent becomes involved in *serious* drug use appears to depend a good deal on the relationship with parents. For the child of democratic, authoritative, accepting parents (especially those with relatively traditional values) who allow the gradual development of independence, the risk of serious drug involvement is generally low. For the child whose parents have not been loving and who are either neglectful (overly permissive) or authoritarian and hostile, the risk of significant drug use is much greater. One 17-year-old young woman said, "I got involved because I was trying to rebel against my father because he never let me do anything that I wanted. You know, I couldn't talk to boys until this year. It was really upsetting, and I just turned to drugs for an escape" (Konopka, 1976, p. 106).

Escape from the pressures of life   Another reason adolescents frequently give for drug use is escape from tension and the pressures of life or from boredom (Conger & Petersen, 1984; Gallup, 1977). If drugs are used to escape the developmental tasks of adolescence—learning to cope with stress and acquiring cognitive, social, and vocational skills—they may interfere with the young person's preparation to meet the additional demands of responsible adulthood.

Emotional disturbance   For other young people, particularly heavy multiple-drug users, reliance on drugs may reflect emotional disturbance. In some such cases, we need to look to significant disturbances in family relationships during the course of development for clues to the young person's difficulties (Brook et al., 1990; Kandel, 1980). Among adolescents in residential treatment centers and halfway houses for alcohol and drug users, common themes acknowledged by both the staff and recovering users are feelings of parental rejection or indifference; lack of acceptance by peers; emotional isolation; and low self-esteem, which the young person feels a need to conceal behind a defense of "appearing cool" (Conger, 1979).

Some young people who have been using alcohol or drugs steadily since preadolescence acknowledge that they had never known any other way to cope with anxiety, boredom, depression, fear of failure, or lack of purpose. Poignantly, an important aim of one treatment program, in addition to helping young people learn to deal with their personal problems and establish genuine friendships with peers, was simply to teach them something many did not know: how to have fun without drugs (Conger & Petersen, 1984).

Alienation or societal rejection   In some instances, adolescent drug use may reflect alienation and a turning inward to the self-preoccupied world of mind-altering drugs (Brown, 1967; Pittel & Miller, 1976). In other instances, an indifferent society does the rejecting. Too many young people face the future without hope. Confronted with economic, social, or racial discrimination, with impossible living conditions, often with untreated physical ills, and with a breakdown in their social environment and in their own families, they may give up the search for meaning and a sense of ego identity entirely and seek escape in the oblivion of hard narcotics, or what one adolescent addict called "death without permanence, life without pain" (Luce, 1970, p. 10).

In summary, there are many reasons adolescents may take drugs, with varying outcomes. Drugs may produce oblivion, temporary escape, or even (in more positive instances) a feeling of greater appreciation for simple beauty in the world. But there is little evidence that they produce a long-term sense of well-being, true creativity, or the ability to cope successfully with the demands of living, and there is considerable evidence that they may impair them (DeLuca, 1981; Petersen, 1979).

DELINQUENCY

In our society, the term *juvenile delinquent* refers to a young person, generally under 16 to 18 years of age, who engages in behavior that is punishable by law. Some delinquent acts, such as robbery, aggravated assault, rape, homicide, or illegal drug use, would also be considered crimes if committed by adults. Others, are "status offenses"—acts such as curfew violations, truancy, "incorrigibility," running away, and underage drinking—that apply only to young people. Furthermore, delinquency itself is a legal rather than a psychological term; what is considered delinquent at one time and place may be lawful at another time or in another place.

After rising rapidly between 1960 and 1976, the delinquency *rate* in this country reached a plateau between 1976 and 1979 (see Figure 14.5). Whether this relatively steady rate will persist (albeit at a distressingly high level), only time will tell. Even at current levels, recent estimates are that at least 12 percent of all young people (and 22 percent of males) are likely to turn up in juvenile court records before the end of adolescence.

Furthermore, since 1960 the incidence of serious offenses among young people has been rising at a faster rate than delinquency in general and twice as fast as comparable adult crimes (U.S. Department of Commerce, 1981b). Although in 1980 persons under age 18 comprised only 28 percent of the total population, they accounted for a far higher percentage of many offenses (see Figure 14.6).

There are clear sex differences in the incidence of recorded delinquency. For many years the ratio of male to female offenses was 4 or 5 to 1 (Conger & Miller, 1966; U.S. Department of Commerce, 1981b). In 1980, total offenses by

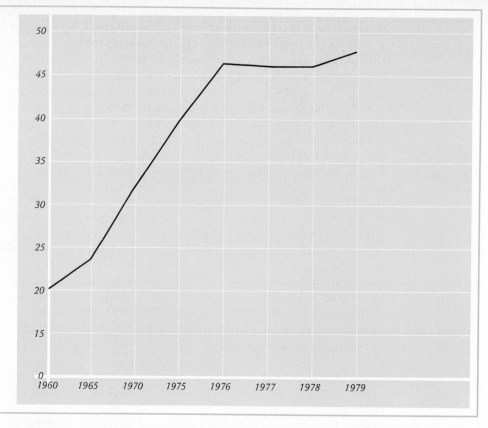

FIGURE 14.5

Rate of delinquency cases disposed of by juvenile courts involving children and adolescents 10 through 17 years of age from 1960 to 1979. (From U.S. Department of Commerce, Bureau of the Census. Statistical abstract of the United States, 1982–1983. Washington, D.C.: U.S. Government Printing Office, 1982.)

males outnumbered those by females by nearly 3.9 to 1 (U.S. Department of Commerce, 1981b). The most frequent complaints against males charge them with active or aggressive behaviors such as joyriding, burglary, malicious mischief, larceny, auto theft, and illegal drug use. Females are more likely to be reported to police for running away from home, "incorrigibility" (parental inability to control them), and illicit sexual behavior. In recent years, there has been a significant increase among females in drug use, often necessitating other crime-related activities, such as shoplifting, robbery, and prostitution (Conger, 1977a; Rutter & Giller, in press).

Both social conditions and individual experiences contribute to juvenile delinquency. Poverty and its associated living conditions are one set of factors. Parent-child relationships and individual personality characteristics also influence a young person's involvement in delinquent behavior.

Social change and poverty

Current high rates of delinquency appear to be related at least in part to changes in the structure of society in the United States and other highly industrialized countries. Our increased mobility as a people has disrupted well-established cultural patterns and family ties, as have social disorganization and population shifts in large metropolitan areas. In addition, widespread unemployment and recent reductions in social programs for the poor have intensified the frustration and financial need of those at or below the poverty line.

Recent research has indicated that economic deprivation is most likely to lead to crime and delinquency when it is associated with marked inequality in the distribution of society's resources. In one study, a number of indices of inequality were used to predict average crime rates in 193 cities over a 6-year period. "The income gap between the poor and the average income earner was shown to be a significant predictor of crime rates" (Braithwaite, 1981, p. 48).

Increases in delinquency, as well as in other adolescent difficulties, appear most likely to occur where a sense of community solidarity and the integrity of the extended family have been most seriously disrupted (for instance, in urban ghettos and in some of the more affluent suburban communities). They are least likely to occur where these ties have been preserved, as in some small, stable, relatively isolated towns and cities (Conger, 1977a). In the past decade, the greatest increase in the juvenile crime rate has occurred in the suburbs. Within the suburbs, increases appear to be greatest in communities and among families characterized by a high degree of social and geographic mobility and a lack of stable ties to other persons and social institutions (National Center for Juvenile Justice, 1975–1979; U.S. Office of Human Development, 1960–1970).

Nevertheless, the absolute rates of delinquency are still highest in deteriorated neighborhoods near the centers of large cities (Braithwaite, 1981; Conger & Miller, 1966; Rutter & Giller, in press). In such areas, which are

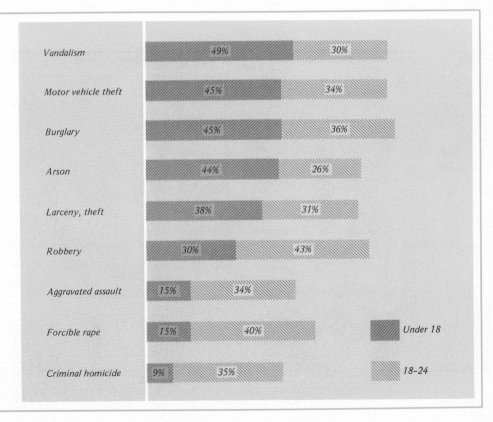

FIGURE 14.6

Arrests of persons under 18 years of age and between 18 and 24 years of age as a percentage of all arrests. (From U.S. Federal Bureau of Investigation, **Crime in the United States, 1981,** *and U.S. Department of Commerce, Bureau of the Census.* **Statistical abstract of the United States, 1981.** *Washington, D.C.: U.S. Government Printing Office, 1981.)*

	Under 18	18-24
Vandalism	49%	30%
Motor vehicle theft	45%	34%
Burglary	45%	36%
Arson	44%	26%
Larceny, theft	38%	31%
Robbery	30%	43%
Aggravated assault	15%	34%
Forcible rape	15%	40%
Criminal homicide	9%	35%

characterized by poverty, rapid population turnover, and general disorganization, there are many opportunities for learning antisocial behavior from delinquent peers, individually or in gangs (Jensen, 1973). Immigrant families and families that have only recently moved to crowded cities are more likely to encounter problems with delinquency than families already long established in urban areas. Parents in such families may lack the knowledge and skills needed to deal successfully with their difficult environment and hence may serve as inadequate role models for their children. They may also be too preoccupied or defeated by their own problems to give their children adequate attention and guidance (Conger & Miller, 1966; Reese, 1982; U.S. Department of Commerce, 1981a).

Lower-class youth in urban ghettos are more likely than middle-class youth to join delinquent gangs. Although many of these groups encourage delinquency, in the past the better organized and less violent also helped meet needs common to all young people—a sense of personal warmth, a meaningful social life and peer group acceptance, and self-preservation (Klein & Crawford, 1967). Unfortunately, inner-city gangs have become increasingly disorganized and violent since the mid-1970s. Gang members in major cities have terrorized, killed, or wounded scores of teachers, elderly citizens, and nongang youth. On top of that, 60 percent of the victims of gang violence are other gang members (Conger & Petersen, 1984; Miller, 1976). One 16-year-old said, "Man, I've been

on the outlaw trail most all my life. Can't help it. What else you got for me? . . . The only real world is what I got in my hand. Everything else is makeup." A 14-year-old summed up, "The human race stinks, man. I'm glad I ain't in it" (Stevens, 1971, p. 91).

Personality factors and parent-child relationships

Even in high-poverty neighborhoods, many adolescents do not become delinquent. Why does one child from a particular neighborhood, school, social class, and ethnic background become delinquent whereas another, apparently subject to the same general environmental influences, does not? In approaching this problem, investigators have typically used a research design in which delinquents and nondelinquents from the same general background are compared with respect to personality characteristics and parent-child relationships at various ages.

As a group, delinquents, particularly recidivists (those with repeated convictions), score somewhat lower (8 to 12 points) than average on IQ tests and have a slightly higher-than-average incidence of mental retardation (Conger & Miller, 1966; Rutter & Giller, in press). However, most delinquents are at least average in IQ, and low intelligence itself does not appear to be a primary factor in delinquency. Among children adopted shortly after birth, delinquency and adult criminality are more closely related to similar behavior of the adoptees' biological parents than of their adoptive parents, suggesting that genetic factors may play some indirect role (possibly through greater impulsiveness or distractibility) in increasing an individual's predisposition to develop delinquent behavior (Hutchings & Kednick, 1974; Robins, 1978). However, family and peer relationships, together with other psychological and social influences, appear to play a far more critical role.

Personality characteristics   Delinquents have generally been found to be more likely than matched groups of nondelinquents to be socially assertive, defiant, ambivalent toward authority, lacking in achievement motivation, resentful, hostile, suspicious, destructive, impulsive, and lacking in self-control (Farrington, Biron, & LeBlanc, 1982; West & Farrington, 1973). Many of these traits appear defensive in nature, reflecting impaired self-concepts and feelings of inadequacy, emotional rejection, and frustration of needs for self-expression (Gold & Mann, 1972). Delinquents, more often than nondelinquents, perceive themselves as "lazy," "bad," "sad," and "ignorant." According to their own self-concepts, delinquents are "undesirable people; they tend not to like, value, or respect themselves. In addition, their self-concepts are confused, conflictual, uncertain, and variable" (Fitts & Hammer, 1969, p. 81).

Differences between nondelinquents and delinquents in social behavior and personality characteristics show up early in development, even though clearly defined delinquent behavior may not begin until later. Several studies have found future delinquents, and especially boys, to differ significantly from nondelinquents by age 10 in peer ratings of honesty, troublesomeness, daring, and unpopularity, in teacher ratings of "aggressive maladjustment," in behavioral problems, and in attentional problems and school difficulties (Farrington et al., 1982; Gold & Petronio, 1979; Rutter & Giller, in press). In one extensive longitudinal study, future adolescent delinquents were already viewed by their teachers as more poorly adapted than their classmates by the end of the third grade. This was true regardless of the child's social class, intelligence, parents' occupations, and residential neighborhood (Conger, 1977a; Conger & Miller, 1966). Future delinquents of both sexes were rated less considerate and fair in dealing with others, less friendly, less responsible, more impulsive, more distractible and less persistent in their school work, and more antagonistic to authority. They were also less well liked and less accepted by their peers. These social and academic problems appeared to reflect underlying emotional problems, and, in the opinion of their teachers, future delinquents more often came from a disturbed home environment.

Family relationships   Within social-class groups, family relationships are the best single predictor of delinquency. The early disciplinary techniques to which delinquents have been subjected are likely to be lax, erratic, or overly strict and to involve physical punishment rather than reasoning with the child about misconduct (Ahlstrom & Havighurst, 1971). Recent research indicates that a particularly critical factor may be lack of parental supervision. In one study in England, the family variable most strongly associated with delinquency was weak parental supervision, as indicated by such items as not requiring children to say where they are going and when they will return home when they go out or not knowing where a child is much of the time (Rutter, 1980; Wilson, 1980). Families of aggressive and delinquent children and adolescents seem to have few if any "house rules." The parents do not monitor the young person's activities, they respond inconsistently to unacceptable behavior, and they lack effective ways of dealing with family conflict (Patterson, 1981a, 1981b). Delinquents' relationships with their parents often lack intimate communication, mutual understanding, and affection. Instead, there is mutual hostility, lack of family cohesiveness, and parental rejection, indifference, dissension, or apathy (Hirschi, 1969; Rutter & Giller, in press). Parents of delinquents are more likely to have minimal aspirations for their children, to avoid engaging as a family in leisure activities, to be hostile or indifferent toward school, to have personal and emotional problems of their own, and to have police records (Cressey & Ward, 1969; Robins, 1966, 1978). For example, in one longitudinal study, it was found that 39 percent of boys with criminal fathers became delinquent, compared to 16 percent of those whose fathers had no criminal record; other studies have yielded similar results (Farrington et al., 1982).

Finally, broken homes are associated with a high incidence of delinquent behavior (Ahlstrom & Havighurst, 1971). However, it has also been shown that the likelihood of adolescent delinquency is far higher in *nonbroken* homes characterized by mutual hostility, indifference or apathy, and a lack of cohesiveness than in *broken* (usually mother-only) homes in which there is cohesiveness and mutual affection and support.

Prevention and treatment of delinquency

A wide variety of approaches have been employed in efforts to prevent or treat delinquency, ranging from psychotherapy and family casework to "street-corner" youth workers, "therapeutic communities," and intensive community-based services. In most cases, the results have not been particularly encouraging (Braithwaite, 1981; Wright & Dixon, 1977). However, most programs have concentrated largely on young people with already serious problems, and they may have offered too little help too late (Sechrest, White, & Brown, 1979).

Correctional institutions   There is considerable evidence that imprisonment in typical correctional institutions generally makes matters worse. It subjects the young person to psychologically traumatic and embittering experiences, frequently including sexual and physical abuse by other inmates and by adults. Such institutions provide little or no psychological, educational, or vocational help; rather, they serve as "finishing schools" for future criminal behavior (Prescott, 1981; Winslow, 1976). Reconviction rates among those previously institutionalized generally run between 60 and 70 percent (Rutter & Giller, in press). In view of these facts, it seems unfortunate that juvenile courts in many states are permitted to institutionalize adolescents who have committed only status offenses (actions that are illegal for minors but not for adults, as explained earlier). In one national survey in the mid-1970s, two-thirds of the females and one-third of the males in correctional institutions were confined solely because of status offenses; many of the females were committed only for sexual activity (Wooden, 1976). In the view of Irving R. Kaufman, Chief Judge of the U.S. Court of Appeals in New York, "Children whose actions do not amount to adult crimes should be dealt with outside the judicial system" (Kaufman, 1979, p. 58).

Ironically, the judicial system sometimes fails to institutionalize adolescents who repeatedly commit serious crimes. Because of the organizational chaos, underfunding, and understaffing of the juvenile court systems in large metropolitan areas like New York City (and in some instances because of peculiarities in the laws regarding juveniles), many adolescents and youth who have repeatedly committed violent offenses—including homicide—serve little or no time in correctional institutions (Kaufman, 1979). The treatment received by one such youth is summarized in Box 14.3.

Behavioral methods   Currently, behavioral methods appear to show the greatest promise for treatment of delinquency (Rutter & Giller, in press). In this approach, appropriate behavior is systematically rewarded, perhaps with tokens that can be exchanged for special privileges. Inappropriate behavior earns the person no reward and may have unpleasant consequences, such as a temporary loss of privileges. Behavioral methods may be applied in an institutional setting, such as a residential treatment center or correctional institution, in school or community programs, or in the family (Burchard & Harig, 1976; Patterson, 1981b; Rutter & Giller, in person; Sarason, 1978).

One of the more promising approaches to the treatment of delinquents places small groups in community-based homes under skilled direction. The warm, intimate homelike atmosphere stands in marked contrast to the cold sterility of the typical training school and permits close individual attention and supervision. In one such program, Achievement Place, developed at the University of Kansas, six to eight boys at a time live with two professional teaching parents and their children, if they have any (Fixsen, Phillips, & Wolf, 1973). Personal interaction and parental warmth are combined with a token economy in which progress in personal and social responsibility is reinforced with tokens and increasing privileges. Compared with similar adolescents placed on probation or in a traditional training school, Achievement Place boys show markedly lower rates of recidivism, higher school attendance, and better

BOX 14.3
*The violent world
of Peewee Brown*[1]

Harold (Peewee) Brown was born on September 24, 1961, the son of an unemployed alcoholic who left his wife when Peewee was 7 months old and who died when the boy was 14. Peewee's mother, Louise, an articulate woman with a high school education, always worked to support herself and her three sons. She had to be at her job by 8 a.m., so she left them alone at home at 7 a.m. and did not return until 5 p.m. Often, she conceded, she did not know what they were doing while she was gone.

"I told them at school, 'When he gets bad, get your stick,'" Mrs. Brown recalled. "I'd tell them, 'You're the kid's mother and father when you're in school. I can't be there. Whomp his behind. . . .'"

There were many at school who tried to help Peewee. He saw psychologists, was assigned to dedicated teachers, and eventually was sent to a special public school. But his violence only increased. He said it was not uncommon for him to stab someone who had inadvertently hurt his feelings and that he once negotiated the price of a sandwich with one of his many guns. In the very beginning, there was a tug of war between the world of school and that of the streets.

"We knew when he was here he was going to kill somebody and that there was nothing we could do to help him," said Coy Cox, the principal of Public School 369, the special school to which Peewee was sent in the sixth grade.

A murderer at 13

Over a 4-year period, from the age of 11 to 15, Peewee was arrested fifteen times on charges ranging from sodomy to assault, although the school system—for reasons of confidentiality—was never informed.

He now admits that those arrests were for only a small number of his crimes. For example, he said, when he was 13 he shot and killed a man on a deserted street corner in Brooklyn, but was never caught. He added that he seriously wounded at least six others and committed countless other robberies.

But even those few times he was caught, Peewee went free. Each time he was arrested, Family Court routinely dismissed the charge or put him on probation, releasing him back into his mother's custody in an absurd cycle of crime, capture, and release that continued until, at the age of 15, Peewee shot and killed a Brooklyn grocer.

Just 3 weeks before, according to court and school records, Peewee had been arrested for having taken a loaded revolver to school. Because Family Court records are sealed, it is impossible to know the court's rationale in disposing of the gun case or any of the others.

"All they would do is send him back," said Mrs. Brown, a 41-year-old framemaker who to this day remains confused by the leniency with which her son was repeatedly treated. "They didn't punish him. I told them: 'He keeps getting into trouble. There should be somewhere he can go.' All they did was send him back to me."

The last time, however, Peewee didn't come back home. Now 20, he has been in prison 5 years for the murder of the Brooklyn grocer.

[1] From D. Kleiman. The violent world of Peewee Brown. *New York Times*, February 28, 1982, p. 22. © 1982 by The New York Times Company. By permission.

grades, at least in the short run. How effective this program will prove over the longer term remains to be seen as "alumni" of Achievement Place homes are followed over several years (Kirigin, Wolf, Braukman, Fixsen, & Phillips, 1979). This experiment also demonstrates the importance of an elusive variable: the quality of the caregivers. Unfortunately, when the program was repeated with the same structure but with colder, less understanding "parents," the success rate dropped.

Several implications emerge rather clearly from current research. One is that in the long run, prevention or intervention efforts have little prospect of significant success unless they include a major emphasis on changing the child's or adolescent's home environment and existing patterns of parent-child relationships. Another is that in most instances, efforts to help the delinquent directly need "to be concerned with improving his social problem-solving skills and social competence generally, rather than just seeking to suppress deviant behavior" (Rutter & Giller, in press). Furthermore, such efforts have their best chance of success if they begin early in life and are part of a larger program of comprehensive psychological and physical care, education, and training directed toward optimal development—a commitment our society currently appears unwilling to make.

PSYCHOLOGICAL AND PSYCHO-PHYSIOLOGICAL DISTURBANCES

People often develop psychological and psychophysiological disturbances during periods of physical, cognitive, or social change that temporarily disrupt their equilibrium. Early adolescence is a time of rapid change, and psychological and psychophysiological disturbances of varying degrees of severity do occur in a significant minority of young people. For some adolescents, the disturbance may be relatively minor and transient; for others, it may be severe and resistant to treatment. It is not possible to review here the full range of adolescent disturbances, with their causes and specialized treatment requirements, but we will consider a few of the most significant ones.

Anxiety reactions

The adolescent with an acute anxiety reaction feels a sudden fearfulness, as if something bad were about to happen. He or she may become agitated and restless, startle easily, and experience physical symptoms such as dizziness, headache, nausea, or vomiting. Attention span may be limited, and the young person may appear distracted. Sleep disturbances are common; there may be difficulty in falling asleep, and sleep itself may be limited and restless, with much tossing and turning, perhaps accompanied by nightmares or sleepwalking (Nemiah, 1980). If there is no obvious external reason for acute anxiety reaction, the adolescent may be puzzled about its apparently mysterious source or may attribute it to relatively trivial external circumstances or incidents. Upon more careful examination, however, it usually becomes clear that far more extensive and fundamental factors are involved—factors of which the adolescent may not be consciously aware, such as disturbed parent-child relationships, concerns about the demands of growing up, or fears and guilt regarding sexual or aggressive impulses.

Therapeutic intervention should begin early, while the relevance of these causative factors is still apparent. Then the anxiety can be dealt with before it becomes chronic and before the individual's responses to it (psychological withdrawal, impairment of school work, continuing physical symptoms such as pains, diarrhea, shortness of breath, fatigue) become a way of life.

Until recently, many clinicians denied that genuine depression can occur among children and younger adolescents (Klerman, 1978; Nicholi, 1978). In early adolescence, young people are unlikely to express their feelings openly, and they tend to deny negative and self-critical attitudes. They do not generally exhibit the gloom, hopelessness, and self-deprecation that adult depressives do. Many adolescents mask depressive feelings with disguises ranging from boredom and restlessness to hypochondriacal complaints or acting-out behavior, such as sexual, aggressive, or delinquent activity (Achenbach & Edelbrock, 1981; Carlson, 1980). Yet depressive feelings are fairly common among adolescents. Recent investigations indicate that up to 40 percent of adolescents have had significant, though usually temporary, feelings of sadness, worthlessness, and pessimism about the future. As many as 8 to 10 percent report having experienced suicidal feelings (Nicholi, 1978; Rutter, 1980).

Adolescent depression is most likely to take one of two forms. The first is expressed as a lack of feeling and a sense of emptiness. It is as though the childhood self had been abandoned and no growing adult self has replaced it; this vacuum engenders a high level of anxiety. This kind of depression resembles a state of mourning, in which the lost loved one is experienced as a part of the self; it is likely to be the least persistent and most resolvable form of depression.

A second type of adolescent depression is often more difficult to resolve. It has its basis in repeated experiences of defeat over a long period of time. The adolescent may actually have tried hard to solve problems and achieve personally meaningful goals, but without success. Perhaps other people fail to accept or understand what the adolescent is trying to do, or perhaps personal inadequacies make the goals impossible to achieve. Many—probably a majority—of adolescent suicide attempts are the result not of a momentary impulse but of a long series of unsuccessful attempts to find alternative solutions to difficulties. Frequently, the final straw in this type of depression is the loss of a meaningful relationship, whether with a parent, friend, or someone with whom the adolescent was in love (Easson, 1977, Inamdar, Siomopoulos, Osborn, & Bianchi, 1979).

Suicide is rare in children and almost as infrequent among young adolescents. Beginning at about age 15, however, the reported suicide rate increases rapidly. It reaches a level of over 20 per 100,000 for ages 15 through 24 among white males, although rates for blacks and females are significantly lower (see Figure 14.7). The overall suicide rate among older adolescents tripled in the three decades from 1950 to 1980 (Holinger, 1978; U.S. Department of Commerce, 1981b).

Females are more likely than males to use passive methods of suicide, such as ingestion of drugs or poisons, and less apt to use active methods, such as shooting or hanging. Among both sexes, firearms or explosives account for the greatest number of *completed* suicides, whereas drugs or poisons account for the greatest number of *attempted* suicides (Holinger, 1978). Although male adolescents outnumber females in completed suicides, attempted suicides are far more common among females.

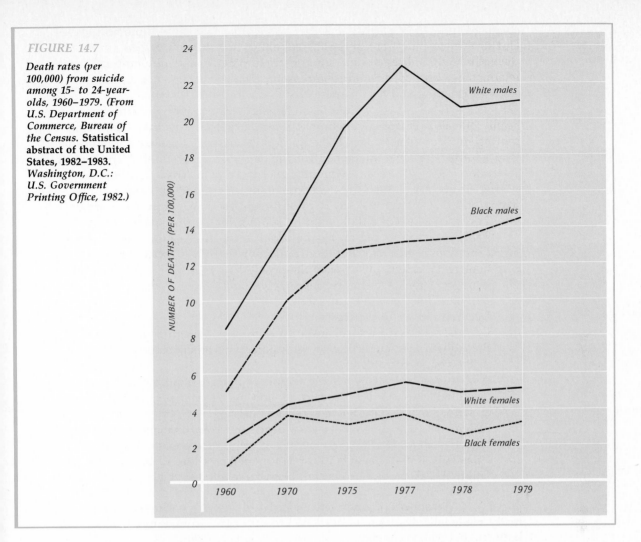

FIGURE 14.7

Death rates (per 100,000) from suicide among 15- to 24-year-olds, 1960–1979. (From U.S. Department of Commerce, Bureau of the Census. Statistical abstract of the United States, 1982–1983. Washington, D.C.: U.S. Government Printing Office, 1982.)

Reasons for adolescent suicide attempts In considering adolescent attempts at suicide, it is important to distinguish between immediate precipitating factors and longer-term predisposing factors. Precipitating events may include the break-up or threatened break-up of a romance, pregnancy (real or imagined), school failure, conflicts with parents, rejection by a friend, being apprehended in a forbidden or delinquent act, loss of a parent or other loved person, and fear of serious illness or imminent mental breakdown (Jacobs, 1971; Miller, Chiles, & Barnes, 1982). On closer examination, however, it becomes clear that the adolescent's reaction to such events is generally the culmination of a series of mounting difficulties. One study of 154 adolescent suicide attempters found that hopelessness, rather than depression resulting from immediate life situations, was most often the critical factor in the suicide attempt (Wetzel, 1976).

Adolescents who attempt suicide frequently have a long history of escalating family instability and discord. They have reached a point of feeling so alienated from their parents that they are unable to communicate with them and to turn to them for support. Frequently, they have struggled to achieve closeness with, and emotional support from, other people only to have these relationships also collapse for one reason or another, leading to a progressive sense of isolation and helplessness.

Prediction of suicide risk   There is a dangerous myth, not only among the lay public but also among some clinicians, that a person who talks about committing suicide will not do so. The tragic fact, however, is that many adolescents (and adults) who have threatened suicide and been ignored — or dismissed as "attention seekers" — *do* subsequently take their own lives. Furthermore, in talking of suicide, adolescents are conveying a message that something is wrong and that they require help, even though they may not yet be seriously intent on suicide as the only remaining solution to their problems.

Talk of suicide should always be taken seriously (Resnick, 1980). Predicting suicide risk is not easy, but there are a number of warning signals that can help to alert the careful observer to the possibility.

1. A persistently depressed or despairing mood.
2. Eating and sleeping disturbances.
3. Declining school performance.
4. Gradual social withdrawal and increasing isolation from others.
5. Breakdown in communication with parents or other important persons in the young person's life.
6. A history of previous suicide attempts or involvement in accidents.
7. Seemingly reckless, self-destructive, and uncharacteristic behavior, such as serious drug or alcohol use, reckless driving.
8. Statements such as "I wish I were dead" or "What is there to live for?"
9. Inquiries about the lethal properties of drugs, poisons, or weapons.
10. Unusually stressful events in the young person's life, such as school failure, break-up of a love affair, loss of a loved one.

Treatment   Treatment of potentially suicidal adolescents or those who have already made suicide attempts must be prompt. Many communities now have hotlines that people considering suicide or feeling desperate can call for immediate help. More extended treatment should deal both with the immediate events and life circumstances that are troubling the young person or precipitated the suicide attempts and with long-standing problems and conflicts.

Eating disorders   Many adolescents go through brief periods in which their weight deviates upward or downward from generally accepted norms. However, once growth has stabilized, most adolescents will correct their weight through regulation of diet; a minority, however, will not. In some cases, sustained overeating may lead to serious *obesity*. In other cases, pathologically prolonged and extreme dieting may lead to serious, sometimes life-threatening degrees of weight loss. This latter condition, known as *anorexia nervosa,* is most likely to occur during adolescence and is far more common among females than males (Bruch, 1973; Hood, Moore, & Garner, 1982; Stunkard, 1980).

Both obese and anorexic young people often lack a clear sense of their own identity as separate and distinct individuals capable of determining and accomplishing their own goals. Anorexia is a particularly puzzling condition because the adolescent has such a distorted perception of her own body. Many anorexic females who appear to neutral observers as little more than an emaciated bundle of skin and bones continue to express worries about putting on too much weight. There is much we still do not know about this condition, which, while relatively rare, seems to be increasing, especially among affluent (rather than disadvantaged) youth. Biological factors (possibly an impairment of the functioning of the anterior pituitary gland at the base of the brain) may play some role, but psychological factors appear to be of primary importance. Parents are often surprised by the onset of anorexia because their child has always seemed so "normal." As children, anorexic adolescents typically seemed almost "too good"—quiet, obedient, always dependable, eager to please. Most have been good students.

When one looks more closely, however, the picture is not as bright. At least unconsciously, most anorexic young people feel that they have been exploited and prevented from leading their own lives and that they have not been able to form a strong identity of their own. Perhaps in reaction, they are likely to display an obsessional need to be in control of every aspect of life, particularly the functions of their bodies. They may also feel incapable of meeting the demands of sexual maturity. Severe undereating, which may interrupt menstruation and make secondary sex characteristics less prominent, may be at least unconsciously, a way of avoiding growing up. Studies of the parents of female anorexic adolescents indicate that the parents have frequently exerted such firm control and regulation during childhood that the girl had difficulty in establishing a sense of identity and confidence in her ability to make decisions for herself. These parents are also likely to have encouraged their children to become perfectionistic overachievers (Minuchin et al., 1978).

Still another eating disorder that appears to be increasing dramatically among female adolescents and young women is *bulimia.* In this disorder, which combines elements of both anorexia and obesity, binge eating (gorging) alternates with forced purging through self-induced vomiting or laxative abuse. Although health is likely to be impaired, often seriously, normal weight may be maintained, making the disorder more difficult to detect. Bulimic individuals characteristically fear not being able to stop this eating pattern (which they recognize as abnormal). They typically report a depressed mood and self-deprecating thoughts following the eating binges. Nearly three-fourths acknowledge adverse effects on their physical health (Johnson, in press).

Obviously, because severe overweight or underweight, as well as bulimic practices, can cause serious, sometimes life-threatening physiological problems, specialized medical care is essential. Over the long term, however, skilled and experienced psychological treatment is also important. And, because disturbed parent-child relations (including problems relating to the development of independence and sexual maturation) typically play an important part in eating disorders, a well-designed therapeutic program for adolescents almost always requires active parental involvement (Minuchin et al., 1978).

Adolescents, of course, may suffer a variety of other kinds of psychological disturbances, such as fears and phobias, as well as more severe disorders, including adolescent schizophrenia, severe (unipolar) depression, and manic-depressive (bipolar) disorder (defined in Chapter 2) (Feinstein & Miller, 1979; Klerman, 1978).

Psychological treatment of adolescents

To work successfully with adolescents, whether individually or in groups, a therapist needs to have specialized training. Regardless of the therapist's particular theoretical orientation, certain personal qualities contribute to success or failure. Adolescents, even more than children, have a particular talent for spotting phoniness—and exploiting it. If therapists are straightforward, neither minimizing their qualifications nor retreating into professional pomposity, the adolescent will usually develop a feeling of trust and respect, though outwardly the young person may still need to make it very clear that he or she isn't awed by "shrinks." The effective adolescent psychotherapist is flexible and can move from listening to questioning to reassurance to clarification of reality to interpretation—even to arguing—and, when necessary, to setting limits (Conger, 1977b; Holmes, 1964). Emotionally disturbed adolescents "need externally imposed limits because, as a result of their confused state, they are not able to set their own limits. They seek a fence beyond which they cannot go, within which they can experiment and by trial and error and accidental success

find a self-concept with which they can feel satisfied" (Josselyn, 1971, p. 146). At the same time, the therapist must keep in mind that the establishment of independence is a critical developmental task of adolescence. Like the wise parent, the psychotherapist must be on guard against the seductive tendency to try to substitute his or her own identity for that of the young person or to prolong therapy unduly (Conger, 1977a). Although their roles inevitably differ in important respects, the effective parent and the effective therapist share some essential characteristics. Neither job is an easy one, but both are less difficult for adults who genuinely like adolescents, which probably means adults who have come to terms with their own adolescence.

SUMMARY

A central task of adolescence is to form a stable sense of identity. According to Erik Erikson's theory, individuals with a strong ego identity see themselves as distinct and separate individuals with an integrity of needs, motives, and behavior Their self-perceptions are reciprocated in the sense that others perceive them as they perceive themselves. Identity formation in modern industrial societies is complicated because of the rapidly changing conditions and the wide variety of potential roles the young person may enter. Problems in identity formation include premature foreclosure and identity confusion, or failure to form a solid identity. Mature identities are often formed after a period of searching and uncertainty.

Gender identity is one major component of identity formation. Different individuals may define different characteristics as part of their gender identity. One female may consider a career central to her feminine identity, while another may think motherhood is a major component. Androgyny is a combination of culturally defined masculine and feminine traits. Adolescents who are androgynous have high self-esteem and high levels of academic achievement, particularly in fields that are stereotyped for the other gender.

Vocational identity is central for many adults and young people in American society. Adolescents who work during adolescence appear slightly better prepared for adult employment, particularly if their jobs are relevant to future vocational interests. Socioeconomic status is one important influence on adolescents' vocational goals, probably because middle-class youth have more opportunities, financial support for higher education, and family encouragement for seeking high-status occupations than lower-class youth do.

Although women have entered the labor market in increasing numbers in recent years, females continue to work primarily in clerical positions, teaching, and other traditionally female jobs. Their average salaries have remained at about 60 percent of the average for males over several decades. Nevertheless, more young women are entering traditionally male professions such as medicine and law. Adolescent females with strong career orientations are independent and assertive; they also plan to marry relatively late and have few children. Although strong career values can improve a young woman's chances for a high-status occupation, she is still faced with societal hurdles because of her sex. Adolescent females appear to be aware that they may experience discrimination in the marketplace and conflicts between their family responsibilities and their work that are difficult to resolve.

Parents are a major influence on vocational choice. For males, the father's occupation is an important predictor of occupational choice, particularly when the father has a high-status job and the father-son relationship is close. Females' career orientation is likely when their mothers are employed, particularly if the mother enjoys her job and the father feels positive about his wife's work.

What values about careers do young people hold? Members of the generation of the late 1970s and early 1980s are more concerned with personal success and financial security and less concerned with philosophical and social issues than their counterparts 10 or 15 years earlier. They have not, however, returned to the unquestioning conformity that supposedly characterized the 1950s. Youth today are more skeptical about the political and economic institutions of our society. The prospects for employment among adolescents are not as good as they were some years ago. In particular, the poorly educated and racial minorities suffer high rates of unemployment.

Moral issues are an important topic for many adolescents, and cognitive advances in moral judgment permit them to think about such issues in new ways. Many adolescents enter the stage of moral thinking that Kohlberg defines as conventional morality. They also begin to question the social and political values of the adults around them.

Like vocational values, adolescent life values in the 1980s are centered on personal fulfillment and achievement. They are relatively unconcerned with the welfare of others, and they are less likely to have strong political leanings, either liberal or conservative. The sexual revolution, begun in the 1960s, has continued. A number of adolescents have become interested in religious issues and in fundamentalist religious groups. In recent years, the values of youth from blue-collar and white-collar families have become more similar than they were 20 years ago.

Although most adolescents are basically optimistic about the future, a minority feel alienated from their society. They feel little involvement with people or with social institutions, often viewing them all with distaste. Some youth are alienated because they live in urban ghettos with little opportunity to escape. Others come from affluent circumstances but appear to lack the capacity for intimacy and deep interpersonal relationships.

Use of drugs such as alcohol, marijuana, tranquilizers, amphetamines, and other illegal drugs increased during the 1960s and 1970s, leveling off near the end of the 1970s. Although most adolescents who have tried drugs use them only occasionally, there is a disturbingly large minority who are heavy and habitual users. Almost 10 percent of 14-year-olds are heavy drinkers. The reasons why adolescents use drugs include peer pressure, rebellion against parents, escape from pressures, emotional disturbance, social alienation, and the desire to try new things.

Delinquency, defined as engaging in behavior that is illegal, also reached a plateau in the late 1970s. Males are more often involved in legal offenses than females, and they more often participate in crimes involving violence.

Both social conditions, such as poverty, and individual experiences contribute to an adolescent's tendency to become delinquent. Delinquency is espe-

cially high in deteriorated urban neighborhoods and areas with little community solidarity. The personality characteristics that distinguish delinquents include impulsivity, lack of self-control, defiance, and lack of achievement motivation. Future delinquents differ from others of their peer group by age 10; they are rated as dishonest, troublesome, and unpopular. Parents of delinquents are often excessively lax, providing little supervision of their children, and hostile or neglectful.

Incarcerating delinquents has little therapeutic benefit; in fact, it often provides training in criminal behavior. Many young people who are placed in correctional institutions have committed only status offenses (behavior that would not be criminal for an adult), such as running away, engaging in sexual activity, or being "incorrigible." Behavioral methods, including direct reinforcement of approved behavior in group-living situations, have been employed with some success.

Although most adolescents do not go through a period of severe "storm and stress," some experience significant psychological problems, including acute anxiety reactions, psychosomatic disorders, depression, and sometimes suicide. Suicide may be precipitated by an immediate unhappy event, but it is usually rooted in long-standing difficulties in coping that lead to feelings of hopelessness. Such adolescents often feel isolated from their families and feel that they have no friends. Often individuals who attempt suicide have talked about it or threatened it, so such threats should not be discounted.

Eating disorders, including obesity, anorexia nervosa, and bulimia sometimes occur during adolescence. In anorexia nervosa, found mainly among females, extreme dieting leads to severe, often life-threatening weight loss; in bulimia, food binges alternate with purging to avoid weight gain. Both obese and anorexic young people often lack a clear sense of being in control of their own lives. Anorexics may also fear sexual and social maturity, partly because they have been excessively protected and controlled by their parents. Like wise parents, those treating adolescents need to be authoritative, rather than either authoritarian or laissez-faire, and they need to genuinely like, and have respect for, young people.

REFERENCES

Abelson, H. I., et al. *National survey on drug abuse, 1977: A nationwide study—youth, young adults, and older people* (DHEW Publication No. ADM 78-618). Rockville, Md.: National Institute on Drug Abuse, 1977.

Achenbach, T. M., & Edelbrock, C. S. Behavioral problems and competencies reported by parents of normal and disturbed children aged four through sixteen. *Monographs of the Society for Research in Child Development*, 1981, 46 (Serial No. 188).

Adelson, J. The political imagination of the young adolescent. *Daedalus*, 1971, *100*, 1013–1050.

Adelson, J. Rites of passage: How children learn the principles of community. *American Educator*, Summer, 1982, 6ff.

Ahlstrom, W. M., & Havighurst, R. J. *400 losers*. San Francisco: Jossey-Bass, 1971.

Areshansel, C. S., & Rosen, B. C. Domestic roles and sex differences in occupational expectations. *Journal of Marriage and the Family*, 1980, *42*, 121–131.

Astin, A. W. Characteristics and attitudes of first-year college students, 1969–1979. *Chronicle of Higher Education*, January 28, 1980, *19*, 4–5.

Astin, A. W. *The American freshman national norms for fall 1980*. Los Angeles: American Council on Education and Graduate School of Education, University of California at Los Angeles, 1981.

Astin, A. W. Freshman characteristics and attitudes. *Chronicle of Higher Education,* February 17, 1982, *21,* 11–12.

Astin, A. W. Characteristics and attitudes of first-year college students. *Chronicles of Higher Education,* January 26, 1983, *25,* 10–12.

Bachman, J. G., & Johnston, L. D. *Fewer rebels, fewer causes: A profile of today's college freshmen.* Ann Arbor, Mich.: Survey Research Center, Institute for Social Research, University of Michigan, 1979.

Bachman, J. G., Johnston, L. D., & O'Malley, P. M. *Monitoring the future: Questionnaire responses from the nation's high school seniors, 1980.* Ann Arbor, Mich.: Survey Research Center, Institute for Social Research, University of Michigan, 1981.

Bachman, J. G., Johnston, L. D., & O'Malley, P. M. *Monitoring the future: Questionnaire responses from the nation's high school seniors, 1981.* Ann Arbor, Mich.: Survey Research Center, Institute for Social Research, University of Michigan, 1982.

Baruch, G. K. Maternal influences upon college women's attitudes toward women and work. *Developmental Psychology,* 1972, *6,* 32–37.

Bem, S. L. Androgyny vs. the tight little lives of fluffy women and chesty men. *Psychology Today,* September 1975, pp. 58–62.

Bem, S. L. Gender schema theory: A cognitive account of sex-typing. *Psychological Review,* 1981, *88,* 354–364.

Bennetts, L. Women: New opportunity, old reality. *New York Times,* National Recruitment Survey, October 14, 1979, p. 58.

Block, J. H. Conceptions of sex role: Some cross-cultural and longitudinal perspectives. *American Psychologist,* 1973, *28,* 515–526.

Borow, H. Career development. In J. F. Adams (Ed.), *Understanding adolescence.* Boston: Allyn & Bacon, 1976.

Bourne, E. The state of research on ego identity: A review and appraisal (Part 1). *Journal of Youth and Adolescence,* 1978, *7,* 223–251. (a)

Bourne, E. The state of research on ego identity: A review and appraisal (Part 2). *Journal of Youth and Adolescence,* 1978, *7,* 371–392. (b)

Braithwaite, J. The myth of social class and criminality reconsidered. *American Sociological Review,* 1981, *46,* 36–57.

Brook, J. S., Lukoff, J. F., & Whiteman, M. Initiation into adolescent marihuana use. *Journal of Genetic Psychology,* 1980, *137,* 133–142.

Brown, J. D. (Ed.). *The hippies.* New York: Time-Life Books, 1967.

Bruch, H. *Eating disorders.* New York: Basic Books, 1973.

Brunswick, A. F., & Boyle, J. M. Patterns of drug involvement: Developmental and secular influences on age of initiation. *Youth and Society,* 1979, *11,* 139–162.

Burchard, J. D., & Harig, P. T. Behavior modification and juvenile delinquency. In H. Leiternberg (Ed.), *Handbook of behavior modification and behavior therapy.* Englewood Cliffs, N.J.: Prentice-Hall, 1976.

Caplow, T., & Bahr, H. M. Half a century of change in adolescent attitudes: Replication of a Middletown survey by the Lynds. *Public Opinion Quarterly,* 1979, *43,* 1–17.

Carlson, G. A. Unmasking masked depression in children and adolescents. *American Journal of Psychiatry,* 1980, *137,* 445–449.

Caro, F. G. Social class and attitudes of youth relevant for the realization of adult goals. *Social Forces,* 1966, *44,* 492–498.

Colby, A., Kohlberg, L., Gibbs, J., & Lieberman, M. A longitudinal study of moral judgment. *Monographs of the Society for Research in Child Development,* 1983, *48* (Serial No. 200).

Conger, J. J. Roots of alienation. In B. Wolman (Ed.), *International encyclopedia of neurology, psychiatry, psychoanalysis, and psychology.* New York: McGraw-Hill, 1976.

Conger, J. J. *Adolescence and youth: Psychological development in a changing world* (2nd ed.). New York: Harper & Row, 1977. (a)

Conger, J. J. Parent-child relationships, social change, and adolescent vulnerability. *Journal of Pediatric Psychology,* 1977, *2,* 93–97. (b)

Conger, J. J. *Adolescence: Generation under pressure.* New York: Harper & Row, 1979.

Conger, J. J. Freedom and commitment: Families, youth, and social change. *American Psychologist,* 1981, *36,* 1475–1484.

Conger, J. J., & Miller, W. C. *Personality, social class, and delinquency.* New York: Wiley, 1966.

Conger, J. J., & Petersen, A. C. *Adolescence and youth: Psychological development in a changing world* (3rd ed.). New York: Harper & Row, 1984.

Cressey, D. R., & Ward, D. A. *Delinquency, crime, and social process.* New York: Harper & Row, 1969.

DeLuca, J. R. (Ed.). Alcohol and health: Fourth special report to the U.S. Congress. Rockville, Md.: National Institute on Alcohol and Alcohol Abuse, 1981.

Donovan, J. M. Ego identity status and interpersonal style. *Journal of Youth and Adolescence,* 1975, *4,* 37–56.

Douvan, E., & Adelson, J. *The adolescent experience.* New York: Wiley, 1966.

Easson, W. M. Depression in adolescents. In S. Feinstein & P. Giovacchini (Eds.), *Adolescent psychiatry* (Vol. 5). New York: Aronson, 1977.

Erikson, E. H. The problem of ego identity. *Journal of the American Psychoanalytic Association,* 1956, *4,* 56–121.

Erikson, E. H. *Childhood and society* (2nd ed.). New York: Norton, 1963.

Erikson, E. H. *Identity: Youth and crisis.* New York: Norton, 1968.

Farrington, D. P., Biron, L., & LeBlanc, M. Personality and delinquency in London and Montreal. In J. C. Gunn & D. P. Farrington (Eds.), *Abnormal offenders: Delinquency and the criminal justice system.* New York: Wiley, 1982.

Feinstein, S. C., & Miller, D. Psychoses of adolescence. In J. D. Noshpitz (Ed.), *Basic handbook of child psychiatry* (Vol. 2): *Disturbances in development.* New York: Basic Books, 1979.

Fitts, W. H., & Hammer, W. T. *The self-concept and delinquency.* Nashville: Mental Health Center (Research Monograph No. 1), 1969.

Fixsen, D. L., Phillips, E. L., & Wolf, M. M. Achievement Place: Experiments in self-government with predelinquents. *Journal of Applied Behavioral Analysis,* 1973, *6,* 31–49.

Galanter, M. Psychological induction into the large group: Findings from a contemporary religious sect. *American Journal of Psychiatry,* 1980, *137,* 1574–1579.

Gallup, G. Gallup youth survey. *Denver Post,* May 29, 1977, p. 48.

Gallup, G. Gallup youth survey. *Denver Post,* January 15, 1978, p. 50.

Gilligan, C., & Belenky, M. F. A naturalistic study of abortion decisions. In R. Selman & R. Yando (Eds.), *Clinical-developmental psychology.* San Francisco: Jossey-Bass, 1980.

Gold, M., & Mann, D. Delinquency as defense. *American Journal of Orthopsychiatry,* 1972, *42,* 463–479.

Gold, M., & Petronio, R. J. Delinquent behavior in adolescence. In J. Adelson (Ed.), *Handbook of adolescent psychology.* New York: Wiley, 1979.

Green, R. *Sexual identity conflict in children and adults.* New York: Basic Books, 1974.

Greenberger, E., & Steinberg, L. D. The workplace as a context for the socialization of youth. *Journal of Youth and Adolescence,* 1981, *10,* 185–211.

Hamilton, S. F., & Crouter, A. C. Work and growth: A review of research on the impact of work experience on adolescent development. *Journal of Youth and Adolescence,* 1980, *9,* 323–338.

Harris, L. Change, yes—upheaval, no. *Life,* January 8, 1971, pp. 22–27.

Hirschi, T. *Causes of delinquency.* Berkeley, Calif.: University of California, 1969.

Hodgson, J. W., & Fischer, J. L. Sex differences in identity and intimacy development in college youth. *Journal of Youth and Adolescence,* 1978, *7,* 333–352.

Hoffman, L. W. Effects of maternal employment on the child—A review of the research. *Developmental Psychology,* 1974, *10,* 204–228.

Hoffman, L. W. Maternal employment: 1979. *American Psychologist,* 1979, *34,* 859–865.

Hoffman, L. W. Work, family, and socialization of the child. In R. D. Parke, et al. (Eds.), *The review of child development research* (Vol. 7): *The family and interdisciplinary perspective.* Chicago: University of Chicago Press, in press.

Hoffman, M. L. Moral development. In P. H. Mussen (Ed.), *Carmichael's manual of child psychology* (Vol. 2). New York: Wiley, 1970.

Hoffman, M. L. Moral development in adolescence. In J. Adelson (Ed.), *Handbook of adolescent psychology*. New York: Wiley, 1980.

Holinger, P. C. Adolescent suicide: An epidemiological study of recent trends. *American Journal of Psychiatry,* 1978, *135,* 754–756.

Hood, J., Moore, T. E., & Garner, D. Locus of control as a measure of ineffectiveness in anorexia nervosa. *Journal of Consulting and Clinical Psychology,* 1982, *50,* 3–13.

Huston, A. C. Sex-typing. In P. H. Mussen & E. M. Hetherington (Eds.), *Handbook of Child Psychology.* (Vol. 4): *Socialization, personality, and social development* (4th ed.). New York: Wiley, 1983.

Hutchings, B., & Mednick, S. A. Registered criminality in the adoptive and biological parents of registered male adoptees. In S. A. Mednick, F. Schulsinger, J. Higgens, & B. Bell (Eds.), *Genetics, environment and psychopathology.* Amsterdam: Elsevier North-Holland, 1974.

Inamdar, S. C., Siomopoulos, G., Osborn, M., & Bianchi, E. C. Phenomenology associated with depressed moods in adolescents. *American Journal of Social Psychiatry,* 1979, *136,* 156–159.

Jacobs, J. *Adolescent suicide.* New York: Wiley, 1971.

Jensen, G. F. Parents, peers, and delinquent action: A test of the differential association perspective. *American Journal of Sociology,* 1973, *78,* 562–575.

Jessor, R., & Jessor, S. L. *Problem behavior and psychosocial development: A longitudinal study of youth.* New York: Academic Press, 1977.

Johnson, C. Anorexia nervosa and bulimia. In J. J. Coates, A. C. Petersen, & C. Perry (Eds.), *Adolescent health: Crossing the barriers.* New York: Academic Press, in press.

Johnston, L. D., Bachman, J. G., & O'Malley, P. M. *1979 highlights: Drugs and the nation's high school students: Five-year national trends* (DHEW Publication No. ADM 80-930). Rockville, Md.: National Institute on Drug Abuse, 1979.

Johnston, L. D., Bachman, J. G., & O'Malley, P. M. *Student drug use in America, 1975–1981* (DHHS Publication No. ADM 82-1208). U.S. Department of Health and Human Services. Washington, D.C.: National Institute on Drug Abuse, 1981.

Josselyn, I. M. *Adolescence.* New York: Harper & Row, 1971.

Kandel, D. B. (Ed.). *Longitudinal research on drug use: Empirical findings and methodological issues.* Washington, D.C.: Hemisphere, 1978.

Kandel, D. B. Drug and drinking behavior among youth. *Annual Review of Sociology,* 1980, *6,* 235–285.

Kaufman, I. R. Juvenile justice: A plea for reform. *New York Times Magazine,* October 14, 1979, pp. 42–60.

Keniston, K. *The uncommitted: Alienated youth in American society.* New York: Harcourt Brace Jovanovich, 1968.

Kirigin, K. A., Wolf, M. M., Braukman, C. J., Fixsen, D. L., & Phillips, E. L. Achievement Place: A preliminary outcome evaluation. In J. S. Stumphauzer (Ed.), *Progress in behavior therapy with delinquents.* Springfield, Ill.: Thomas, 1979.

Klein, M. W., & Crawford, L. Y. Groups, gangs, and cohesiveness. *Journal of Research in Crime and Delinquency,* January 1967, p. 63.

Klerman, G. L. Affective disorders. In A. M. Nicholi, Jr. (Ed.), *The Harvard guide to modern psychiatry.* Cambridge, Mass.: Harvard University Press, 1978.

Kohlberg, L. Moral stages and moralization: The cognitive-developmental approach. In T. Lickona (Ed.), *Moral development and behavior.* New York: Holt, Rinehart and Winston, 1976.

Kohlberg, L., & Gilligan, C. The adolescent as a philosopher: The discovery of the self in a postconventional world. *Daedalus,* Fall 1971, 1051–1086.

Konopka, G. *Young girls: A portrait of adolescence.* Englewood Cliffs, N.J.: Prentice-Hall, 1976.

Lasch, C. *The culture of narcissism: American life in an age of diminishing expectations.* New York: Norton, 1979.

Little, J. K. The occupations of non-college youth. *American Educational Research Journal,* 1967, *4,* 147–153.

Luce, J. End of the road. *San Francisco Sunday Examiner and Chronicle,* November 8, 1970, pp. 8–10.

Maggarrell, J. Today's students, especially women, more materialistic. *Chronicle of Higher Education,* January 28, 1980, *19,* 3.

Maggarrell, J. Fewer liberals, more moderates among this year's freshmen. *Chronicle of Higher Education,* February 9, 1981, *20,* 5.

Marcia, J. E. Identity in adolescence. In J. Adelson (Ed.), *Handbook of adolescent psychology.* New York: Wiley, 1980.

Marini, M. M. Sex differences in the determination of adolescent aspirations: A review. *Sex Roles,* 1978, *4,* 723–753.

Miller, M. L., Chiles, J. A., & Barnes, V. E. Suicide attempters within a delinquent population. *Journal of Consulting and Clinical Psychology,* 1982, *50,* 490–498.

Miller, W. B. Report to the Law Enforcement Assistance Administration, Department of Justice, May 1, 1976.

Minuchin, S., Rosman, B. L., & Baker, L. *Psychosomatic families: Anorexia nervosa in context.* Cambridge, Mass.: Harvard University Press, 1978.

Mortimer, J. T. Social class, work, and the family: Some implications of the father's occupation for familial relationships and sons' career decisions. *Journal of Marriage and the Family,* 1976, *38*(2), 241–256.

Nash, S. C. Sex role as a mediator of intellectual functioning. In M. A. Wittig & A. C. Petersen (Eds.), *Sex-related differences in cognitive functioning.* New York: Academic Press, 1979.

National Center for Juvenile Justice, Pittsburgh, Pa. Unpublished data, 1975–1979.

Nemiah, J. C. Anxiety state. In H. I. Kaplan, A. M. Freedman, & B. J. Sadock (Eds.), *Comprehensive textbook of psychiatry* (Vol. 2) (3rd ed.). Baltimore: Williams & Wilkins, 1980.

Nicholi, A. M., Jr. The adolescent. In A. M. Nicholi, Jr. (Ed.), *The Harvard guide to modern psychiatry.* Cambridge, Mass.: Harvard University Press, 1978.

Orlofsky, J. L. Identity formation, achievement, and fear of success in college men and women. *Journal of Youth and Adolescence,* 1978, *7,* 49–62.

Orlofsky, J. L., Marcia, J. E., & Lesser, I. M. Ego identity status and the intimacy vs. isolation crisis of young adulthood. *Journal of Personality and Social Psychology,* 1973, *27,* 211–219.

Patterson, G. R. *Coercive family processes.* Eugene, Ore.: Castala Publishing Co., 1981. (a)

Patterson, G. R. Some speculations and data relating to children who steal. In T. Hirschi & M. Gottfredson (Eds.), *Theory and fact in contemporary criminology.* Beverly Hills, Calif.: Sage, 1981. (b)

Peterson, R. C. *Marihuana and health: Seventh annual report to the U.S. Congress from the Secretary of Health, Education, and Welfare.* Rockville, Md.: National Institute on Drug Abuse, 1979.

Pittel, S. M., Calef, V., Gryler, R. B., Hilles, L., Hofer, R., & Kempner, P. Developmental factors in adolescent drug use: A study of psychedelic drug users. *Journal of the American Academy of Child Psychiatry,* 1971, *10,* 640–660.

Pittel, S. M., & Miller, H. *Dropping down: The hippie then and now.* Berkeley, Calif.: Haight Ashbury Research Project, Wright Institute, 1976.

Prescott, P. S. *The child savers.* New York: Knopf, 1981.

Reese, M. Life below the poverty line. *Newsweek,* April 5, 1982, pp. 20–28.

Resnick, H. L. P. Suicide. In H. I. Kaplan, A. M. Freedman, & B. J. Sadock (Eds.), *Comprehensive textbook of psychiatry* (Vol. 2) (3rd ed.). Baltimore: Williams & Wilkins, 1980.

Rest, J. R. Morality. In P. H. Mussen, J. Flavell, & E. Markman (Eds.), *Handbook of child psychology* (Vol. 3): *Cognitive development* (4th ed.). New York: Wiley, 1983.

Robins, L. *Deviant children grow up: A sociological and psychiatric study of sociopathic personality.* Baltimore: Williams & Wilkins, 1966.

Robins, L. Sturdy childhood predictors of adult antisocial behavior: Replications from longitudinal studies. *Psychological Medicine,* 1978, *8,* 611–622.

Rohlen, T. P. The promise of adulthood in Japanese spiritualism. *Daedalus,* 1976, *105,* 125–144.

Rutter, M. *Changing youth in a changing society: Patterns of adolescent development and disorder.* Cambridge, Mass.: Harvard University Press, 1980.

Rutter, M., & Giller, H. *Juvenile delinquency: Trends and prospects.* Baltimore: Penguin Books, in press.

Sarason, I. G. A cognitive social learning approach to juvenile delinquency. In R. Hare & D. Schilling (Eds.), *Psychopathic behavior: Approaches to research.* New York: Wiley, 1978.

Sechrest, L., White, S. O., & Brown, E. D. (Eds.). *The rehabilitation of criminal offenders: Problems and prospects.* National Research Council Report. Washington, D.C.: National Academy of Sciences, 1979.

Seeman, M. Alienation studies. In A. Inkeles, J. Coleman, & N. Smelser (Eds.), *Annual review of sociology* (Vol. 1). Palo Alto, Calif.: Annual Reviews, Inc., 1975.

Simpson, R. L. Parental influence, anticipatory socialization, and social mobility. *American Sociological Review,* 1962, *27,* 517–522.

Smith, R. E. (Ed.). *The subtle revolution: Women at work.* Washington, D.C.: Urban Institute, 1979.

Smoking and health: A report of the Surgeon General. (DHEW Publication No. PHS 79-50066). U.S. Government Printing Office, 1979.

Sorenson, R. C. *Adolescent sexuality in contemporary America: Personal values and sexual behavior ages 13–19.* New York: Abrams, 1973.

Spence, J. T., & Helmreich, R. L. *Masculinity and femininity: Their psychological dimensions, correlates, and antecedents.* Austin, Texas: University of Texas Press, 1978.

Spence, J. T., Helmreich, R. L., & Holahan, C. K. Negative and positive components of psychological masculinity and femininity and their relationships to self-reports of neurotic and acting-out behaviors. *Journal of Personality and Social Psychology,* 1979, *37,* 1673–1682.

St. Clair, S., & Day, H. D. Ego identity status and values among high school females. *Journal of Youth and Adolescence,* 1979, *8,* 317–326.

Steinberg, L. D., Greenberger, E., Garduque, L., Ruggiero, M., & Vaux, A. Effects of working on adolescent development. *Developmental Psychology,* 1982, *18,* 385–395.

Stephenson, S. P. From school to work: A transition with job search implications. *Youth and Society,* 1979, *11,* 114–133.

Stephenson, S. R., Jr. Young women and labor: In-school labor force status and early postschool labor market outcomes. *Youth and Society,* 1981, *13,* 123–155.

Stevens, S. The "rat packs" of New York. *New York Times,* November 28, 1971, pp. 29 ff.

Stoller, R. J. Gender identity disorders. In H. I. Kaplan, A. M. Freedman, & B. J. Sadock (Eds.), *Comprehensive textbook of psychiatry* (Vol. 2) (3rd ed.). Baltimore: Williams & Wilkins, 1980.

Stunkard, A. J. Obesity. In H. I. Kaplan, A. M. Freedman, & B. J. Sadock (Eds.), *Comprehensive textbook of psychiatry* (Vol. 3) (3rd ed.). Baltimore: Williams & Wilkins, 1980.

Tapp, J. L., & Levine, F. J. Compliance from kindergarten to college: A speculative research note. *Journal of Adolescence and Youth,* 1972, *1,* 233–249.

Tittle, C. K. *Careers and family: Sex roles and adolescent life plans.* Beverly Hills, Calif.: Sage, 1981.

Toder, N. L., & Marcia, J. E. Ego identity status and response to conformity pressure in college women. *Journal of Personality and Social Psychology,* 1973, *26,* 287–294.

U.S. Department of Commerce, Bureau of the Census. *Population profile of the United States: 1980.* Washington, D.C.: U.S. Government Printing Office, 1981. (a)

U.S. Department of Commerce, Bureau of the Census. *Statistical abstract of the United States: 1981.* Washington, D.C.: U.S. Government Printing Office, 1981. (b)

U.S. Department of Labor, Bureau of Labor Statistics. *Occupational outlook for college graduates, 1980–81 edition* (Bulletin 2076). Washington, D.C.: U.S. Government Printing Office, 1980. (a)

U.S. Department of Labor, Bureau of Labor Statistics. *Occupational projections and training data, 1980 edition* (Bulletin 2052). Washington, D.C.: U.S. Government Printing Office, 1980. (b)

U.S. Office of Human Development and Services & U.S. Office of Youth Development, Washington, D.C. Unpublished data, 1960–1970.

Waterman, A. S. Identity development from adolescence to adulthood: An extension of theory and a review of research. *Developmental Psychology,* 1982, *18,* 341–358.

Waterman, A. S., & Waterman, C. K. A longitudinal study of changes in ego identity status during the freshman to the senior year in college. *Developmental Psychology,* 1974, *10,* 387–392.

Weiss, R. J. Understanding moral thought: Effects on moral reasoning and decision-making. *Developmental Psychology,* 1982, *18,* 852–861.

West, D. J., & Farrington, D. P. *Who becomes delinquent?* London: Heinemann Educational, 1973.

Wetzel, R. Hopelessness, depression, and suicide intent. *Archives of General Psychiatry*, 1976, *33*, 1069–1073.

Wilson, H. Parental supervision: A neglected aspect of delinquency. *British Journal of Criminology*, 1980, *20*, 203–235.

Winslow, R. W. (Ed.). *Juvenile delinquency in a free society*. Encino, Calif.: Dickenson Publishing Co., 1976.

Wooden, K. *Weeping in the playtime of others*. New York: McGraw-Hill, 1976.

Wright, W. E., & Dixon, M. C. Community prevention and treatment of juvenile delinquency: A review of evaluation studies. *Journal of Research on Crime and Delinquency*, 1977, *14*, 35–67.

Yankelovich, D. *Generations apart*. New York: CBS News, 1969.

Yankelovich, D. *The new morality: A profile of American youth in the 1970s*. New York: McGraw-Hill, 1974.

Yankelovich, D. *New rules: Searching for self-fulfillment in a world turned upside down*. New York: Random House, 1981.

Indexes

Index of names

Kil, R. V., 263
King, K. C., 64, 66, 77
King, P., 237, 263
King, R. A., 145, 149
Kingsbury, G. G., 358, 376
Kinsey, A., 485, 489, 505
Kipnis, D. M., 448, 455
Kippax, S., 450, 456
Kirigin, K. A., 547, 559
Kitamura, S., 291, 303
Klaus, R. A., 296, 301
Kleiman, D., 546n
Klein, J. R., 472, 505
Klein, M. W., 542, 559
Klein, R. E., 61, 78, 220, 263, 267, 301
Klemer, R. H., 500, 505
Klerman, G. L., 49, 77, 548, 552, 559
Kliegman, R. M., 64, 66, 77
Klinnert, M. D., 128, 148
Kluovie, R. M., 263
Knoblock, H., 61, 77
Knox, D. H., 500
Koewler, J. H., III, 454
Kohlberg, L., 223, 263, 306, 325–326, 327,
    330, 336, 337, 349, 375, 528, 557, 559
Kohn, M. L., 381, 415
Kojima, H., 252, 264
Kolb, S., 90, 116
Konopka, G., 483, 494, 497, 505, 538, 559
Kopp, C. B., 46, 61, 66, 71, 72, 77
Kosslyn, S. N., 263
Kotelchuck, M., 63, 77
Krauss, R. M., 212, 215, 216
Kraut, R. E., 358, 376
Krawitz, A., 105, 115
Kreutzer, M. A., 145, 148, 248, 263, 308, 338
Kringlen, E., 50, 79
Kron, R. E., 66, 78, 377, 416
Kurdek, A., 407, 415
Kutz, S. L., 454

L

LaBarba, R. C., 61, 77
Labov, W., 199, 207, 216
LaGaipa, J. J., 438, 453
Lahey, L., 191, 214
Lamarck, J., 34
Lamb, M. E., 128, 136, 148, 149, 214, 394,
    413–416, 453, 456, 502
Lambert, W. W., 505
Landy, F., 398, 416
Langer, A., 105, 115
Langer, J., 394, 414
Langlois, J. H., 441, 456
Lapsley, D., 477, 503

Larson, L. E., 496, 505
Lasater, T. M., 402, 413
Lasch, C., 533, 559
Lass, N., 214
Lave, C., 257, 264, 298, 302
Lavine, L. O., 394, 415
LaVoie, J. C., 390, 415
Lazar, I., 294, 295, 300–301
Lazar, J., 29, 377, 454, 456–457
LeBlanc, M., 543, 544, 558
Lebovici, S., 505
Lechtig, A., 61, 78
Lee, S., 291, 303
Lefkowitz, M. M., 23, 29
Lehrman, D. S., 455
Leibowitz, H. W., 263
Leiternberg, H., 557
Lempers, J. C., 209, 237, 263
Lempers, J. D., 217
Lenke, R. R., 78
Leonard, C., 248, 263
Leonard, H. S., 252, 263
Leonard, L. B., 161, 176, 186, 203, 215, 216
Lepper, M. R., 292, 293, 301, 364, 375, 376,
    390, 415
Lerner, J. V., 437, 456
Lerner, R. M., 437, 456
Lesser, I. M., 513, 516, 560
Levin, H., 120, 149, 384, 416
Levine, F. J., 528, 561
Levine, J. A., 381, 415
Levinstein, Phyllis, 157
Levy, H. L., 78
Levy-Shiff, R., 406, 415
Lewis, C. C., 388, 415
Lewis, C. S., 481, 482, 505
Lewis, M., 176, 263
Leyens, J. P., 22, 29
Liberman, D., 398, 416
Lickona, T., 559
Lieberman, M. A., 326, 337, 528, 557
Liebert, R. M., 20, 29
Lifter, K., 191, 214
Lightbown, P., 197, 214
Likona, T., 339
Lindbergh, C., 407, 416
Linn, S., 95, 116
Linton, T., 444, 456
Lipsitt, L., 216
Liss, M. B., 454
Litt, I. F., 472, 505
Litt, M., 66, 78
Little, J. K., 518, 559
Littman, R. A., 441, 456
Liublinskaya, A. A., 204, 216
Livesley, W. J., 319, 338

Livingston, K. R., 247, 263
Lloyd, L. L., 215
Locke, J., 11, 173–174, 236
Loebl, J. H., 286, 302
Loehlin, J. C., 45, 78
Londerville, S., 130, 136, 148
Longfellow, C., 286, 301
Lopez, D., 357, 375
Lorch, E. P., 451, 453
Lorenz, K., 97, 121
Lubchenko, L. O., 54, 55, 58, 61, 67, 68, 71, 72, 78
Luce, J., 539, 559
Lucker, G., 291, 303
Lukoff, J. F., 534, 557
Lynn, D. B., 412, 415
Lytton, H., 45, 78

M

McCall, R. B., 156, 160, 176, 269, 270, 277, 302
McCarthy, D., 16, 29
McCartney, K., 302
McCartney, P. E., 206, 216
McClearn, G. E., 78
Maccoby, E. E., 120, 149, 159, 176, 276, 302, 370, 375, 384, 391, 415, 416, 424, 456
McCombs, M., 454
McConaghy, M. J., 344, 376
McDonald, F. J., 394, 414
McDougall, D., 406, 414
Macfarlane, J. W., 269, 270, 301
McGhee, P. E., 196, 216, 410, 416
McGraw, K. O., 375
McGraw, M. B., 34, 78
McGuire, C. V., 355, 376
McGuire, W. J., 355, 376
Machida, S., 220, 264
MacKinnon, C. W., 263
McLanahan, A. G., 264
McNew, S., 186, 214
McReynolds, L., 214
Madsen, M. C., 376
Maes, P. C. J. M., 290, 301
Maggarrell, J., 559
Maher, B. A., 77, 337, 375
Maher, W. B., 375
Main, M., 130, 136, 148
Majeed, M. A., 64, 75
Maller, J. B., 365, 375
Malone, P. E., 402, 413
Mandler, J. M., 242, 263
Mann, D., 543, 558
Mansfield, A. F., 346, 376
Marantz, S. A., 346, 376

Marcia, J. E., 512, 513, 516, 560, 561
Marcus, R. F., 381, 415
Margolis, H., 252, 263
Marini, M. M., 519, 560
Markman, E. M., 220, 262, 263, 264, 329, 338, 339, 560
Markowitz, A., 357, 375
Marshall, W. A., 463, 464, 468, 505
Martin, B., 384, 385, 415
Martin, C. E., 485, 505
Martin, C. L., 350, 376
Martin, E., 263
Martin, R. J., 77
Martorell, R., 61, 78
Maruyama, G., 358, 376, 396, 415, 455
Marvey, D., 457
Mash, E. J., 376, 381, 415
Mason, W. A., 106, 116
Massad, C. M., 212, 216
Mast, V. K., 100, 116
Masters, J. C., 312, 338
Masters, W. H., 485, 505
Mata, L., 61, 77
Matarazzo, R. G., 71, 77
Matchell-Kernan, C., 376
Matheny, A. P., 50, 78
Matthysse, S., 48, 77, 78
May, M. A., 365, 375
Meacham, I. A., 318, 338
Mead, M., 480, 505
Meadows, L., 407, 416
Mednick, S. A., 543, 559
Medrich, E. A., 436, 456
Meece, J. L., 276, 286, 302, 423, 456
Meltzoff, A. N., 96, 116, 159, 176
Menlove, F. L., 444, 453
Merkatz, J. R., 77
Merrill, M. A., 272, 303
Mervis, C. B., 189, 216, 264
Metcoff, J., 61, 78
Meyer, B., 346, 376
Meyer, K. K., 134, 149
Miller, D., 552, 558
Miller, G. A., 214
Miller, H., 539, 560
Miller, H. C., 174, 176
Miller, M. L., 549, 560
Miller, N., 396, 415
Miller, P. Y., 484, 485, 486, 505
Miller, W. B., 542, 560
Miller, W. C., 499, 503, 539, 541–544, 558
Millie, M. P. W., 280, 302
Minified, F. D., 215
Minton, C., 381, 415
Minturn, L., 505
Minuchin, P. P., 419, 420, 421, 427, 431, 456

*I*ndex of subjects

Nicotine, 65
Nocturnal emission, 473
Nonconformist parents, 387
Number conservation, 231, 238
Nutrition, maternal, 61, 63

O

Obesity, 550–551
Objectivity, 18–19
Object permanence, 111–112
Objects
  distinguishing people from, 308
  symbolic play with, 154–159
Observation, language acquisition and, 197–198
Observational learning, 342–343, 353
Occupational achievement, 276, 277
Open education, 426–427
Operant conditioning, 108–109, 342
Operations
  as dimension of intellectual ability, 267, 268
  in Piaget's theory of cognitive development, 224
Oral stage, 84, 119
Organization, detecting patterns of, 248
Overextensions, 187–189
Overregularization, 191, 201
Ovum, 34, 37–40, 50, 51
  period of, 51–52

P

Parent-child relations
  in adolescence: abusing parents, 480–481; delinquency and, 544; drug use and, 538; parental control, 481–483; vocational choice and, 520–521
  in childhood years. See Socialization
  in infancy: attachment. See Attachment; bidirectionality, 143–144; cultural ideals and, 123–125; theories of, 118–123
  in transition years (second and third year), 171–175
Parents. See also Fathers; Mothers; Parent-child relations
  abusing, 398–402, 480–481
  accepting, 383–384
  age of, quality of parenting and, 405
  authoritarian, 386, 387–388, 481, 482
  authoritative, 386, 387–388, 481, 482
  autocratic, 481, 482
  education in parenting skills for, 402
  equalitarian, 481, 483
  harmonious, 387
  identification with, 391–394
  influence of, versus influence of peers, 440
  laissez-faire, 481, 483
  nonconformist, 387
  permissive, 383, 384, 386, 481, 483
  rejecting, 383, 384
  restrictive, 383, 384, 385
  single, 404, 406–408
Passive versus active nature of child, 12
Peabody Picture Vocabulary Test, 252
Peers
  in adolescence, 493–500; acceptance, neglect, and rejection, 498–499; crowds and cliques, 496–497; drug abuse and, 538; individual friendships, 497–498; love, 499–500; vocational choice and, 521
  in socialization, 434–444; acceptance and rejection, 436–437; developmental patterns, 434–436; friendships, 320–321, 438–439; influence of, 439–444
People
  conceptions about, 315, 317–323
  distinguishing objects from, 308
Perceived Competence Scale, 357
Perception
  defined, 91
  in infants, 91, 93–96, 98
  information-processing approach and, 241–244
Performance, competence and, 220–222
Perinatal stress, 70
Permissive parents, 383, 384, 386, 481, 483
Personality
  delinquency and, 543–544
  genetic influences on, 49–50
Perspective taking, 228–230, 308–314
Phenylketonuria (PKU), 41, 46
Phonemes, 184
Physical features, genetic influence on, 42
Physical growth
  in adolescence, 464–466
  in infancy, 85
Physical milieu of school, 425–426
Pituitary gland, 463
Placenta, 53–54
Play
  in childhood years, 335–336, 434–435
  in transition years (second and third year), 153–159
Point of view of others, understanding, 228–230, 308–314
Polar body, 39
Possession, sense of, 167, 169
Potential competence, 221
Poverty, delinquency and, 540–543
Power assertion, 385
Pragmatics, 183
Praise, teacher, 421–423